GENERAL MOTORS CAVALIER/SUNFIRE 1995-00 REPAIR MANUAL

Covers all U.S. and Canadian models of Chevrolet Cavalier and Pontiac Sunfire

by **Eric Michael Mihalyi**, A.S.E., S.A.E., S.T.S.

PUBLISHED BY **HAYNES NORTH AMERICA**, Inc.

Manufactured in USA
© 1999 Haynes North America, Inc.
ISBN 0-8019-9114-5
Library of Congress Catalog Card No. 99-072299
2345678901 9876543210

Haynes Publishing Group
Sparkford Nr Yeovil
Somerset BA22 7JJ England

Haynes North America, Inc
861 Lawrence Drive
Newbury Park
California 91320 USA

ABCDE
FGHIJ
KL

2H1

W9-BXW-178

Contents

1   GENERAL INFORMATION AND MAINTENANCE

1-2   HOW TO USE THIS BOOK
1-2   TOOLS AND EQUIPMENT
1-6   SERVICING YOUR VEHICLE SAFELY
1-7   FASTENERS, MEASUREMENTS AND CONVERSIONS
1-10   SERIAL NUMBER IDENTIFICATION
1-13   ROUTINE MAINTENANCE AND TUNE-UP
1-32   FLUIDS AND LUBRICANTS
1-45   TOWING THE VEHICLE
1-45   TRAILER TOWING
1-46   JUMP STARTING A DEAD BATTERY
1-47   JACKING
1-48   MAINTENANCE INTERVALS

2   ENGINE ELECTRICAL

2-2   DISTRIBUTORLESS IGNITION SYSTEM (DIS)
2-6   FIRING ORDERS
2-6   CHARGING SYSTEM
2-9   STARTING SYSTEM
2-11   SENDING UNITS AND SENSORS

3   ENGINE AND ENGINE OVERHAUL

3-2   ENGINE MECHANICAL
3-37   EXHAUST SYSTEM
3-39   ENGINE RECONDITIONING

4   DRIVEABILITY AND EMISSIONS CONTROLS

4-2   AIR POLLUTION
4-3   AUTOMOTIVE EMISSIONS
4-5   EMISSION CONTROLS
4-14   ELECTRONIC ENGINE CONTROLS
4-28   TROUBLE CODES
4-31   VACUUM DIAGRAMS

5   FUEL SYSTEM

5-2   BASIC FUEL SYSTEM DIAGNOSIS
5-2   FUEL LINE FITTINGS
5-3   BOTTOM FEED PORT (BFP) INJECTION SYSTEM
5-9   MULTI-PORT (MFI) & SEQUENTIAL (SFI) FUEL INJECTION SYSTEMS
5-19   FUEL TANK

6   CHASSIS ELECTRICAL

6-2   UNDERSTANDING AND TROUBLESHOOTING ELECTRICAL SYSTEMS
6-7   BATTERY CABLES
6-7   AIR BAG (SUPPLEMENTAL RESTRAINT SYSTEM)
6-10   HEATING AND AIR CONDITIONING
6-12   CRUISE CONTROL
6-14   ENTERTAINMENT SYSTEMS
6-16   WINDSHIELD WIPERS AND WASHERS
6-20   INSTRUMENTS AND SWITCHES
6-20   LIGHTING
6-27   TRAILER WIRING
6-27   CIRCUIT PROTECTION
6-33   WIRING DIAGRAMS

Contents

7-2 MANUAL TRANSAXLE   **7-9** AUTOMATIC TRANSAXLE
7-6 CLUTCH

DRIVE TRAIN 7

8-2 WHEELS   **8-13** REAR SUSPENSION
8-4 FRONT SUSPENSION   **8-17** STEERING

SUSPENSION AND STEERING 8

9-2 BRAKE OPERATING SYSTEM   **9-19** PARKING BRAKE
9-7 DISC BRAKES   **9-20** ANTI-LOCK BRAKE SYSTEM
9-13 DRUM BRAKES

BRAKES 9

10-2 EXTERIOR   **10-9** INTERIOR

BODY AND TRIM 10

10-19 GLOSSARY

GLOSSARY

10-23 MASTER INDEX

MASTER INDEX

SAFETY NOTICE

Proper service and repair procedures are vital to the safe, reliable operation of all motor vehicles, as well as the personal safety of those performing repairs. This manual outlines procedures for servicing and repairing vehicles using safe, effective methods. The procedures contain many NOTES, CAUTIONS and WARNINGS which should be followed, along with standard procedures to eliminate the possibility of personal injury or improper service which could damage the vehicle or compromise its safety.

It is important to note that repair procedures and techniques, tools and parts for servicing motor vehicles, as well as the skill and experience of the individual performing the work vary widely. It is not possible to anticipate all of the conceivable ways or conditions under which vehicles may be serviced, or to provide cautions as to all possible hazards that may result. Standard and accepted safety precautions and equipment should be used when handling toxic or flammable fluids, and safety goggles or other protection should be used during cutting, grinding, chiseling, prying, or any other process that can cause material removal or projectiles.

Some procedures require the use of tools specially designed for a specific purpose. Before substituting another tool or procedure, you must be completely satisfied that neither your personal safety, nor the performance of the vehicle will be endangered.

Although information in this manual is based on industry sources and is complete as possible at the time of publication, the possibility exists that some car manufacturers made later changes which could not be included here. While striving for total accuracy, the authors or publishers cannot assume responsibility for any errors, changes or omissions that may occur in the compilation of this data.

PART NUMBERS

Part numbers listed in this reference are not recommendations by Haynes North America, Inc. for any product brand name. They are references that can be used with interchange manuals and aftermarket supplier catalogs to locate each brand supplier's discrete part number.

SPECIAL TOOLS

Special tools are recommended by the vehicle manufacturer to perform their specific job. Use has been kept to a minimum, but where absolutely necessary, they are referred to in the text by the part number of the tool manufacturer. These tools can be purchased, under the appropriate part number, from your local dealer or regional distributor, or an equivalent tool can be purchased locally from a tool supplier or parts outlet. Before substituting any tool for the one recommended, read the SAFETY NOTICE at the top of this page.

ACKNOWLEDGMENTS

Portions of materials contained herein have been reprinted with the permission of General Motors Corporation, Service Technology Group.

HOW TO USE THIS BOOK 1-2
WHERE TO BEGIN 1-2
AVOIDING TROUBLE 1-2
MAINTENANCE OR REPAIR? 1-2
AVOIDING THE MOST COMMON MISTAKES 1-2
TOOLS AND EQUIPMENT 1-2
SPECIAL TOOLS 1-4
SERVICING YOUR VEHICLE SAFELY 1-6
DO'S 1-6
DON'TS 1-6
FASTENERS, MEASUREMENTS AND CONVERSIONS 1-7
BOLTS, NUTS AND OTHER THREADED RETAINERS 1-7
TORQUE 1-7
TORQUE WRENCHES 1-8
TORQUE ANGLE METERS 1-9
STANDARD AND METRIC MEASUREMENTS 1-10
SERIAL NUMBER IDENTIFICATION 1-10
VEHICLE 1-10
BODY 1-11
ENGINE 1-11
TRANSAXLE 1-12
VEHICLE EMISSION CONTROL INFORMATION (VECI) LABEL 1-12
ROUTINE MAINTENANCE AND TUNE-UP 1-13
AIR CLEANER (ELEMENT) 1-15
REMOVAL & INSTALLATION 1-15
FUEL FILTER 1-15
REMOVAL & INSTALLATION 1-15
PCV VALVE 1-16
REMOVAL & INSTALLATION 1-16
EVAPORATIVE CANISTER 1-17
SERVICING 1-17
BATTERY 1-17
PRECAUTIONS 1-17
GENERAL MAINTENANCE 1-17
BATTERY FLUID 1-18
CABLES 1-18
CHARGING 1-18
REPLACEMENT 1-19
BELTS 1-19
INSPECTION 1-19
ADJUSTMENT 1-20
REMOVAL & INSTALLATION 1-20
HOSES 1-21
INSPECTION 1-21
REMOVAL & INSTALLATION 1-21
CV-BOOTS 1-22
INSPECTION 1-22
SPARK PLUGS 1-22
SPARK PLUG HEAT RANGE 1-22
REMOVAL & INSTALLATION 1-22
INSPECTION & GAPPING 1-24
SPARK PLUG WIRES 1-25
TESTING 1-25
REMOVAL & INSTALLATION 1-25
IGNITION TIMING 1-26
GENERAL INFORMATION 1-26
VALVE LASH 1-26
IDLE SPEED ADJUSTMENT 1-26
AIR CONDITIONING SYSTEM 1-27
SYSTEM SERVICE & REPAIR 1-27
PREVENTIVE MAINTENANCE 1-27
SYSTEM INSPECTION 1-27
WINDSHIELD WIPERS 1-28
ELEMENT (REFILL) CARE & REPLACEMENT 1-28
TIRES AND WHEELS 1-29
TIRE ROTATION 1-29
TIRE DESIGN 1-29
TIRE STORAGE 1-30

INFLATION & INSPECTION 1-30
CARE OF SPECIAL WHEELS 1-31
FLUIDS AND LUBRICANTS 1-32
FLUID DISPOSAL 1-32
FUEL AND ENGINE OIL RECOMMENDATIONS 1-32
ENGINE OIL 1-32
FUEL 1-33
OPERATION IN FOREIGN COUNTRIES 1-33
ENGINE 1-33
OIL LEVEL CHECK 1-33
OIL & FILTER CHANGE 1-33
MANUAL TRANSAXLE 1-35
FLUID RECOMMENDATIONS 1-35
LEVEL CHECK 1-35
DRAIN & REFILL 1-35
AUTOMATIC TRANSAXLE 1-35
FLUID RECOMMENDATIONS 1-35
LEVEL CHECK 1-35
PAN & FILTER SERVICE 1-36
COOLING SYSTEM 1-38
FLUID RECOMMENDATIONS 1-38
LEVEL CHECK 1-38
TESTING FOR LEAKS 1-38
DRAIN & REFILL 1-39
FLUSHING & CLEANING THE SYSTEM 1-40
BRAKE MASTER CYLINDER 1-40
FLUID RECOMMENDATIONS 1-40
LEVEL CHECK 1-41
CLUTCH MASTER CYLINDER 1-42
FLUID RECOMMENDATIONS 1-42
LEVEL CHECK 1-42
POWER STEERING PUMP 1-42
FLUID RECOMMENDATIONS 1-42
LEVEL CHECK 1-42
CHASSIS GREASING 1-43
BODY LUBRICATION AND MAINTENANCE 1-43
BODY LUBRICATION 1-43
CAR WASHING 1-43
WAXING 1-44
INTERIOR CLEANING 1-44
WHEEL BEARINGS 1-44
REPACKING 1-44
TOWING THE VEHICLE 1-45
PREFERRED TOWING METHOD— FLATBED 1-45
ALTERNATE TOWING METHOD—WHEEL LIFT 1-45
LAST CHANCE TOWING METHOD— DOLLY 1-45
TOWING YOUR VEHICLE BEHIND ANOTHER VEHICLE 1-45
TRAILER TOWING 1-45
GENERAL RECOMMENDATIONS 1-45
TRAILER WEIGHT 1-45
HITCH (TONGUE) WEIGHT 1-46
ENGINE 1-46
TRANSAXLE 1-46
HANDLING A TRAILER 1-46
JUMP STARTING A DEAD BATTERY 1-46
JUMP STARTING PRECAUTIONS 1-47
JUMP STARTING PROCEDURE 1-47
JACKING 1-47
JACKING PRECAUTIONS 1-48
MAINTENANCE INTERVALS 1-48
SPECIFICATIONS CHARTS
VEHICLE IDENTIFICATION CHART 1-4
ENGINE IDENTIFICATION AND SPECIFICATIONS 1-12
GASOLINE ENGINE TUNE-UP SPECIFICATIONS 1-26
MANUFACTURER RECOMMENDED NORMAL MAINTENANCE INTERVALS 1-48
CAPACITIES 1-49

1

GENERAL INFORMATION AND MAINTENANCE

HOW TO USE THIS BOOK 1-2
TOOLS AND EQUIPMENT 1-2
SERVICING YOUR VEHICLE SAFELY 1-6
FASTENERS, MEASUREMENTS AND CONVERSIONS 1-7
SERIAL NUMBER IDENTIFICATION 1-10
ROUTINE MAINTENANCE AND TUNE-UP 1-13
FLUIDS AND LUBRICANTS 1-32
TOWING THE VEHICLE 1-45
TRAILER TOWING 1-45
JUMP STARTING A DEAD BATTERY 1-46
JACKING 1-47
MAINTENANCE INTERVALS 1-48

HOW TO USE THIS BOOK

Chilton's Total Car Care manual for the 1995–2000 Chevrolet Cavalier and Pontiac Sunfire, also referred to as General Motors J-body vehicles, is intended to help you learn more about the inner workings of your vehicle while saving you money on its upkeep and operation.

The beginning of the book will likely be referred to the most, since that is where you will find information for maintenance and tune-up. The other sections deal with the more complex systems of your vehicle. Operating systems from engine through brakes are covered to the extent that the average do-it-yourselfer becomes mechanically involved. This book will not explain such things as rebuilding a differential for the simple reason that the expertise required and the investment in special tools make this task uneconomical. It will, however, give you detailed instructions to help you change your own brake pads and shoes, replace spark plugs, and perform many more jobs that can save you money, give you personal satisfaction and help you avoid expensive problems.

A secondary purpose of this book is a reference for owners who want to understand their vehicle and/or their mechanics better. In this case, no tools at all are required.

Where to Begin

Before removing any bolts, read through the entire procedure. This will give you the overall view of what tools and supplies will be required. There is nothing more frustrating than having to walk to the bus stop on Monday morning because you were short one bolt on Sunday afternoon. So read ahead and plan ahead. Each operation should be approached logically and all procedures thoroughly understood before attempting any work.

All sections contain adjustments, maintenance, removal and installation procedures, and in some cases, repair or overhaul procedures. When repair is not considered practical, we tell you how to remove the part and then how to install the new or rebuilt replacement. In this way, you at least save labor costs. "Backyard" repair of some components is just not practical.

Avoiding Trouble

Many procedures in this book require you to "label and disconnect . . ." a group of lines, hoses or wires. Don't be lulled into thinking you can remember where everything goes—you won't. If you hook up vacuum or fuel lines incorrectly, the vehicle may run poorly, if at all. If you hook up electrical wiring incorrectly, you may instantly learn a very expensive lesson.

You don't need to know the official or engineering name for each hose or line. A piece of masking tape on the hose and a piece on its fitting will allow you to assign your own label such as the letter A or a short name. As long as you remember your own code, the lines can be reconnected by matching similar letters or names. Do remember that tape will dissolve in gasoline or other fluids; if a component is to be washed or cleaned, use another method of identification. A permanent felt-tipped marker or a metal scribe can be very handy for marking metal parts. Remove any tape or paper labels after assembly.

Maintenance or Repair?

It's necessary to mention the difference between maintenance and repair. Maintenance includes routine inspections, adjustments, and replacement of parts which show signs of normal wear. Maintenance compensates for wear or deterioration. Repair implies that something has broken or is not working. A need for repair is often caused by lack of maintenance. Example: draining and refilling the automatic transmission fluid is maintenance recommended by the manufacturer at specific mileage intervals. Failure to do this can shorten the life of the transmission/transaxle, requiring very expensive repairs. While no maintenance program can prevent items from breaking or wearing out, a general rule can be stated: MAINTENANCE IS CHEAPER THAN REPAIR.

Two basic mechanic's rules should be mentioned here. First, whenever the left side of the vehicle or engine is referred to, it is meant to specify the driver's side. Conversely, the right side of the vehicle means the passenger's side. Second, screws and bolts are removed by turning counterclockwise, and tightened by turning clockwise unless specifically noted.

Safety is always the most important rule. Constantly be aware of the dangers involved in working on an automobile and take the proper precautions. See the information in this section regarding SERVICING YOUR VEHICLE SAFELY and the SAFETY NOTICE on the acknowledgment page.

Avoiding the Most Common Mistakes

Pay attention to the instructions provided. There are 3 common mistakes in mechanical work:

1. Incorrect order of assembly, disassembly or adjustment. When taking something apart or putting it together, performing steps in the wrong order usually just costs you extra time; however, it CAN break something. Read the entire procedure before beginning disassembly. Perform everything in the order in which the instructions say you should, even if you can't immediately see a reason for it. When you're taking apart something that is very intricate, you might want to draw a picture of how it looks when assembled at one point in order to make sure you get everything back in its proper position. We will supply exploded views whenever possible. When making adjustments, perform them in the proper order. One adjustment possibly will affect another.

2. Overtorquing (or undertorquing). While it is more common for overtorquing to cause damage, undertorquing may allow a fastener to vibrate loose causing serious damage. Especially when dealing with aluminum parts, pay attention to torque specifications and utilize a torque wrench in assembly. If a torque figure is not available, remember that if you are using the right tool to perform the job, you will probably not have to strain yourself to get a fastener tight enough. The pitch of most threads is so slight that the tension you put on the wrench will be multiplied many times in actual force on what you are tightening. A good example of how critical torque is can be seen in the case of spark plug installation, especially where you are putting the plug into an aluminum cylinder head. Too little torque can fail to crush the gasket, causing leakage of combustion gases and consequent overheating of the plug and engine parts. Too much torque can damage the threads or distort the plug, changing the spark gap.

There are many commercial products available for ensuring that fasteners won't come loose, even if they are not torqued just right (a very common brand is Loctite. If you're worried about getting something together tight enough to hold, but loose enough to avoid mechanical damage during assembly, one of these products might offer substantial insurance. Before choosing a threadlocking compound, read the label on the package and make sure the product is compatible with the materials, fluids, etc. involved.

3. Crossthreading. This occurs when a part such as a bolt is screwed into a nut or casting at the wrong angle and forced. Crossthreading is more likely to occur if access is difficult. It helps to clean and lubricate fasteners, then to start threading the bolt, spark plug, etc. with your fingers. If you encounter resistance, unscrew the part and start over again at a different angle until it can be inserted and turned several times without much effort. Keep in mind that many parts, especially spark plugs, have tapered threads, so that gentle turning will automatically bring the part you're threading to the proper angle. Don't put a wrench on the part until it's been tightened a couple of turns by hand. If you suddenly encounter resistance, and the part has not seated fully, don't force it. Pull it back out to make sure it's clean and threading properly.

Be sure to take your time and be patient, and always plan ahead. Allow yourself ample time to perform repairs and maintenance. You may find maintaining your car a satisfying and enjoyable experience.

TOOLS AND EQUIPMENT

▶ **See Figures 1 thru 15**

Naturally, without the proper tools and equipment it is impossible to properly service your vehicle. It would also be virtually impossible to catalog every tool that you would need to perform all of the operations in this book. Of course, it would be unwise for the amateur to rush out and buy an expensive set of tools on the theory that he/she may need one or more of them at some time.

The best approach is to proceed slowly, gathering a good quality set of those tools that are used most frequently. Don't be misled by the low cost of bargain tools. It is far better to spend a little more for better quality. Forged wrenches, 6

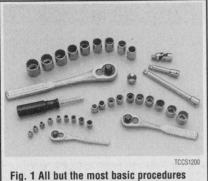
TCCS1200

Fig. 1 All but the most basic procedures will require an assortment of ratchets and sockets

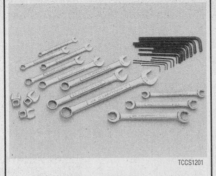
TCCS1201

Fig. 2 In addition to ratchets, a good set of wrenches and hex keys will be necessary

TCCS1202

Fig. 3 A hydraulic floor jack and a set of jackstands are essential for lifting and supporting the vehicle

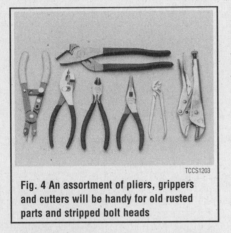
TCCS1203

Fig. 4 An assortment of pliers, grippers and cutters will be handy for old rusted parts and stripped bolt heads

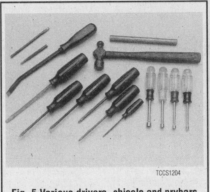
TCCS1204

Fig. 5 Various drivers, chisels and prybars are great tools to have in your toolbox

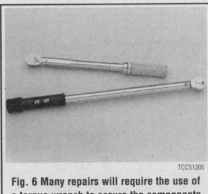
TCCS1205

Fig. 6 Many repairs will require the use of a torque wrench to assure the components are properly fastened

TCCS1209

Fig. 7 Although not always necessary, using specialized brake tools will save time

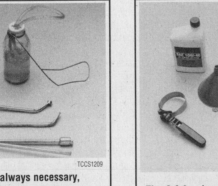
TCCS1210

Fig. 8 A few inexpensive lubrication tools will make maintenance easier

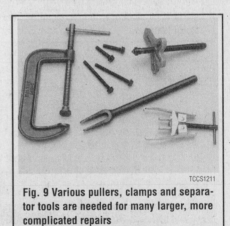
TCCS1211

Fig. 9 Various pullers, clamps and separator tools are needed for many larger, more complicated repairs

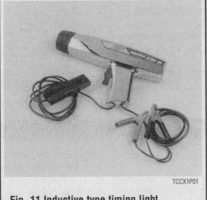
TCCS1212

Fig. 10 A variety of tools and gauges should be used for spark plug gapping and installation

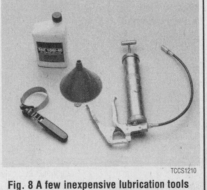
TCCX1P01

Fig. 11 Inductive type timing light

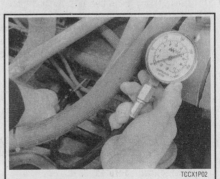
TCCX1P02

Fig. 12 A screw-in type compression gauge is recommended for compression testing

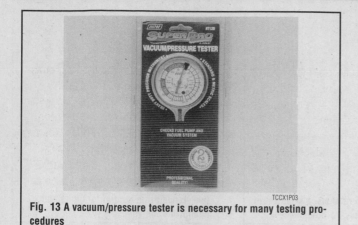

Fig. 13 A vacuum/pressure tester is necessary for many testing procedures

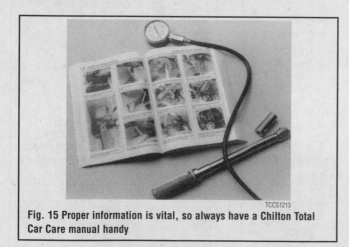

Fig. 14 Most modern automotive multimeters incorporate many helpful features

Fig. 15 Proper information is vital, so always have a Chilton Total Car Care manual handy

or 12-point sockets and fine tooth ratchets are by far preferable to their less expensive counterparts. As any good mechanic can tell you, there are few worse experiences than trying to work on a vehicle with bad tools. Your monetary savings will be far outweighed by frustration and mangled knuckles.

Begin accumulating those tools that are used most frequently: those associated with routine maintenance and tune-up. In addition to the normal assortment of screwdrivers and pliers, you should have the following tools:

• Wrenches/sockets and combination open end/box end wrenches in sizes from 1/8 –3/4 in. or 3–19mm, as well as a 13/16 in. or 5/8 in. spark plug socket (depending on plug type).

➡If possible, buy various length socket drive extensions. Universal-joint and wobble extensions can be extremely useful, but be careful

when using them, as they can change the amount of torque applied to the socket.

• Jackstands for support.
• Oil filter wrench.
• Spout or funnel for pouring fluids.
• Grease gun for chassis lubrication (unless your vehicle is not equipped with any grease fittings—for details, please refer to information on Fluids and Lubricants, later in this section).
• Hydrometer for checking the battery (unless equipped with a sealed, maintenance-free battery).
• A container for draining oil and other fluids.
• Rags for wiping up the inevitable mess.

In addition to the above items there are several others that are not absolutely necessary, but handy to have around. These include Oil Dry((or an equivalent oil absorbent gravel—such as cat litter) and the usual supply of lubricants, antifreeze and fluids, although these can be purchased as needed. This is a basic list for routine maintenance, but only your personal needs and desire can accurately determine your list of tools.

After performing a few projects on the vehicle, you'll be amazed at the other tools and non-tools on your workbench. Some useful household items are: a large turkey baster or siphon, empty coffee cans and ice trays (to store parts), ball of twine, electrical tape for wiring, small rolls of colored tape for tagging lines or hoses, markers and pens, a note pad, golf tees (for plugging vacuum lines), metal coat hangers or a roll of mechanic's wire (to hold things out of the way), dental pick or similar long, pointed probe, a strong magnet, and a small mirror (to see into recesses and under manifolds).

A more advanced set of tools, suitable for tune-up work, can be drawn up easily. While the tools are slightly more sophisticated, they need not be outrageously expensive. There are several inexpensive tach/dwell meters on the market that are every bit as good for the average mechanic as a professional model. Just be sure that it goes to a least 1200–1500 rpm on the tach scale and that it works on 4, 6 and 8-cylinder engines. The key to these purchases is to make them with an eye towards adaptability and wide range. A basic list of tune-up tools could include:

• Tach/dwell meter.
• Spark plug wrench and gapping tool.
• Feeler gauges for valve adjustment.
• Timing light.

The choice of a timing light should be made carefully. A light which works on the DC current supplied by the vehicle's battery is the best choice; it should have a xenon tube for brightness. On any vehicle with an electronic ignition system, a timing light with an inductive pickup that clamps around the No. 1 spark plug cable is preferred.

In addition to these basic tools, there are several other tools and gauges you may find useful. These include:

• Compression gauge. The screw-in type is slower to use, but eliminates the possibility of a faulty reading due to escaping pressure.
• Manifold vacuum gauge.
• 12V test light.
• A combination volt/ohmmeter
• Induction Ammeter. This is used for determining whether or not there is current in a wire. These are handy for use if a wire is broken somewhere in a wiring harness.

As a final note, you will probably find a torque wrench necessary for all but the most basic work. The beam type models are perfectly adequate, although the newer click types (breakaway) are easier to use. The click type torque wrenches tend to be more expensive. Also keep in mind that all types of torque wrenches should be periodically checked and/or recalibrated. You will have to decide for yourself which better fits your pocketbook, and purpose.

Special Tools

Normally, the use of special factory tools is avoided for repair procedures, since these are not readily available for the do-it-yourself mechanic. When it is possible to perform the job with more commonly available tools, it will be pointed out, but occasionally, a special tool was designed to perform a specific function and should be used. Before substituting another tool, you should be convinced that neither your safety nor the performance of the vehicle will be compromised.

Special tools can usually be purchased from an automotive parts store or from your dealer. In some cases special tools may be available directly from the tool manufacturer.

Modern vehicles equipped with computer-controlled fuel, emission and ignition systems require modern electronic tools to diagnose problems. Many of these tools are designed solely for the professional mechanic and are too costly and difficult to use for the average do-it-yourselfer. However, various automotive aftermarket companies have introduced products that address the needs of the average home mechanic, providing sophisticated information at affordable cost. Consult your local auto parts store to determine what is available for your vehicle.

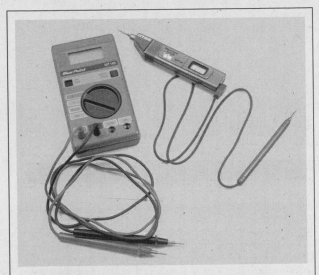

Digital multimeters come in a variety of styles and are a "must-have" for any serious home mechanic. Digital multimeters measure voltage (volts), resistance (ohms) and sometimes current (amperes). These versatile tools are used for checking all types of electrical or electronic components

Trouble code tools allow the home mechanic to extract the "fault code" number from an on-board computer that has sensed a problem (usually indicated by a Check Engine light). Armed with this code, the home mechanic can focus attention on a suspect system or component

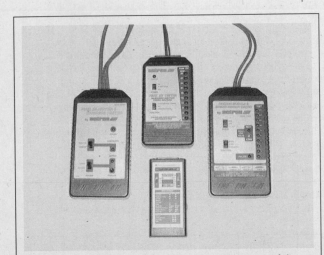

Sensor testers perform specific checks on many of the sensors and actuators used on today's computer-controlled vehicles. These testers can check sensors both on or off the vehicle, as well as test the accompanying electrical circuits

Hand-held scanners represent the most sophisticated of all do-it-yourself diagnostic tools. These tools do more than just access computer codes like the code readers above; they provide the user with an actual interface into the vehicle's computer. Comprehensive

SERVICING YOUR VEHICLE SAFELY

▶ **See Figures 16, 17, 18 and 19**

It is virtually impossible to anticipate all of the hazards involved with automotive maintenance and service, but care and common sense will prevent most accidents.

The rules of safety for mechanics range from "don't smoke around gasoline," to "use the proper tool(s) for the job." The trick to avoiding injuries is to develop safe work habits and to take every possible precaution.

Do's

• Do keep a fire extinguisher and first aid kit handy.

• Do wear safety glasses or goggles when cutting, drilling, grinding or prying, even if you have 20–20 vision. If you wear glasses for the sake of vision, wear safety goggles over your regular glasses.

• Do shield your eyes whenever you work around the battery. Batteries contain sulfuric acid. In case of contact with the eyes or skin, flush the area with water or a mixture of water and baking soda, then seek immediate medical attention.

• Do use safety stands (jackstands) for any undervehicle service. Jacks are for raising vehicles; jackstands are for making sure the vehicle stays raised until you want it to come down. Whenever the vehicle is raised, block the wheels remaining on the ground and set the parking brake.

• Do use adequate ventilation when working with any chemicals or hazardous materials. Like carbon monoxide, the asbestos dust resulting from some brake lining wear can be hazardous in sufficient quantities.

• Do disconnect the negative battery cable when working on the electrical system. The secondary ignition system contains EXTREMELY HIGH VOLTAGE. In some cases it can even exceed 50,000 volts.

• Do follow manufacturer's directions whenever working with potentially hazardous materials. Most chemicals and fluids are poisonous if taken internally.

• Do properly maintain your tools. Loose hammerheads, mushroomed punches and chisels, frayed or poorly grounded electrical cords, excessively worn screwdrivers, spread wrenches (open end), cracked sockets, slipping ratchets, or faulty droplight sockets can cause accidents.

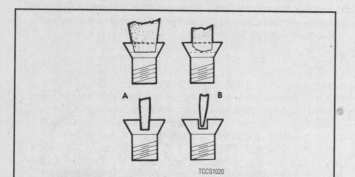

Fig. 16 Screwdrivers should be kept in good condition to prevent injury or damage which could result if the blade slips from the screw

• Likewise, keep your tools clean; a greasy wrench can slip off a bolt head, ruining the bolt and often harming your knuckles in the process.

• Do use the proper size and type of tool for the job at hand. Do select a wrench or socket that fits the nut or bolt. The wrench or socket should sit straight, not cocked.

• Do, when possible, pull on a wrench handle rather than push on it, and adjust your stance to prevent a fall.

• Do be sure that adjustable wrenches are tightly closed on the nut or bolt and pulled so that the force is on the side of the fixed jaw.

• Do strike squarely with a hammer; avoid glancing blows.

• Do set the parking brake and block the drive wheels if the work requires a running engine.

Don'ts

• Don't run the engine in a garage or anywhere else without proper ventilation—EVER! Carbon monoxide is poisonous; it takes a long time to leave the human body and you can build up a deadly supply of it in your system by simply breathing in a little every day. You may not realize you are slowly poisoning yourself. Always use power vents, windows, fans and/or open the garage door.

• Don't work around moving parts while wearing loose clothing. Short sleeves are much safer than long, loose sleeves. Hard-toed shoes with neoprene soles protect your toes and give a better grip on slippery surfaces. Jewelry such as watches, fancy belt buckles, beads or body adornment of any kind is not safe working around a vehicle. Long hair should be tied back under a hat or cap.

• Don't use pockets for toolboxes. A fall or bump can drive a screwdriver deep into your body. Even a rag hanging from your back pocket can wrap around a spinning shaft or fan.

• Don't smoke when working around gasoline, cleaning solvent or other flammable material.

• Don't smoke when working around the battery. When the battery is being charged, it gives off explosive hydrogen gas.

• Don't use gasoline to wash your hands; there are excellent soaps available. Gasoline contains dangerous additives which can enter the body through a cut or through your pores. Gasoline also removes all the natural oils from the skin so that bone dry hands will suck up oil and grease.

• Don't service the air conditioning system unless you are equipped with the necessary tools and training. When liquid or compressed gas refrigerant is released to atmospheric pressure it will absorb heat from whatever it contacts. This will chill or freeze anything it touches.

• Don't use screwdrivers for anything other than driving screws! A screwdriver used as an prying tool can snap when you least expect it, causing injuries. At the very least, you'll ruin a good screwdriver.

• Don't use an emergency jack (that little ratchet, scissors, or pantograph jack supplied with the vehicle) for anything other than changing a flat! These jacks are only intended for emergency use out on the road; they are NOT designed as a maintenance tool. If you are serious about maintaining your vehicle yourself, invest in a hydraulic floor jack of at least a 1½ ton capacity, and at least two sturdy jackstands.

Fig. 17 Power tools should always be properly grounded

Fig. 18 Using the correct size wrench will help prevent the possibility of rounding off a nut

Fig. 19 NEVER work under a vehicle unless it is supported using safety stands (jackstands)

FASTENERS, MEASUREMENTS AND CONVERSIONS

Bolts, Nuts and Other Threaded Retainers

▶ **See Figures 20, 21, 22 and 23**

Although there are a great variety of fasteners found in the modern car or truck, the most commonly used retainer is the threaded fastener (nuts, bolts, screws, studs, etc.). Most threaded retainers may be reused, provided that they are not damaged in use or during the repair. Some retainers (such as stretch bolts or torque prevailing nuts) are designed to deform when tightened or in use and should not be reinstalled.

Whenever possible, we will note any special retainers which should be

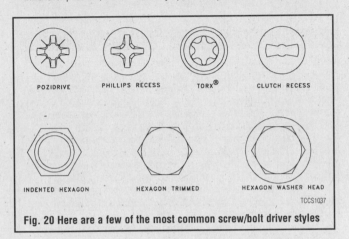

Fig. 20 Here are a few of the most common screw/bolt driver styles

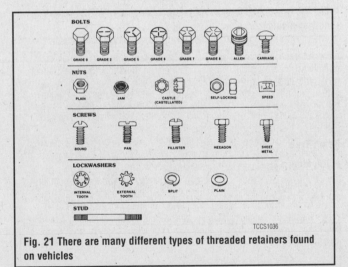

Fig. 21 There are many different types of threaded retainers found on vehicles

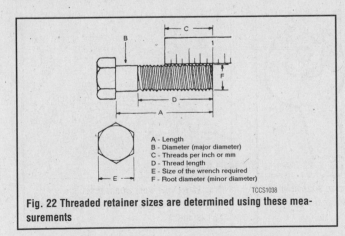

Fig. 22 Threaded retainer sizes are determined using these measurements

A - Length
B - Diameter (major diameter)
C - Threads per inch or mm
D - Thread length
E - Size of the wrench required
F - Root diameter (minor diameter)

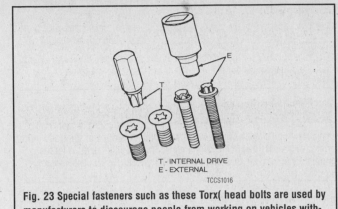

Fig. 23 Special fasteners such as these Torx(head bolts are used by manufacturers to discourage people from working on vehicles without the proper tools

replaced during a procedure. But you should always inspect the condition of a retainer when it is removed and replace any that show signs of damage. Check all threads for rust or corrosion which can increase the torque necessary to achieve the desired clamp load for which that fastener was originally selected. Additionally, be sure that the driver surface of the fastener has not been compromised by rounding or other damage. In some cases a driver surface may become only partially rounded, allowing the driver to catch in only one direction. In many of these occurrences, a fastener may be installed and tightened, but the driver would not be able to grip and loosen the fastener again. (This could lead to frustration down the line should that component ever need to be disassembled again).

If you must replace a fastener, whether due to design or damage, you must ALWAYS be sure to use the proper replacement. In all cases, a retainer of the same design, material and strength should be used. Markings on the heads of most bolts will help determine the proper strength of the fastener. The same material, thread and pitch must be selected to assure proper installation and safe operation of the vehicle afterwards.

Thread gauges are available to help measure a bolt or stud's thread. Most automotive and hardware stores keep gauges available to help you select the proper size. In a pinch, you can use another nut or bolt for a thread gauge. If the bolt you are replacing is not too badly damaged, you can select a match by finding another bolt which will thread in its place. If you find a nut which threads properly onto the damaged bolt, then use that nut to help select the replacement bolt. If however, the bolt you are replacing is so badly damaged (broken or drilled out) that its threads cannot be used as a gauge, you might start by looking for another bolt (from the same assembly or a similar location on your vehicle) which will thread into the damaged bolt's mounting. If so, the other bolt can be used to select a nut; the nut can then be used to select the replacement bolt.

In all cases, be absolutely sure you have selected the proper replacement. Don't be shy, you can always ask the store clerk for help.

✳✳ WARNING

Be aware that when you find a bolt with damaged threads, you may also find the nut or drilled hole it was threaded into has also been damaged. If this is the case, you may have to drill and tap the hole, replace the nut or otherwise repair the threads. NEVER try to force a replacement bolt to fit into the damaged threads.

Torque

Torque is defined as the measurement of resistance to turning or rotating. It tends to twist a body about an axis of rotation. A common example of this would be tightening a threaded retainer such as a nut, bolt or screw. Measuring torque is one of the most common ways to help assure that a threaded retainer has been properly fastened.

When tightening a threaded fastener, torque is applied in three distinct areas, the head, the bearing surface and the clamp load. About 50 percent of the measured torque is used in overcoming bearing friction. This is the friction between the bearing surface of the bolt head, screw head or nut face and the base material or washer (the surface on which the fastener is rotating). Approximately 40 percent of the applied torque is used in overcoming thread friction. This leaves only about 10 percent of the applied torque to develop a useful clamp load (the force which holds a joint together). This means that friction can account for as much as 90 percent of the applied torque on a fastener.

TORQUE WRENCHES

♦ See Figures 24, 25 and 26

In most applications, a torque wrench can be used to assure proper installation of a fastener. Torque wrenches come in various designs and most automotive supply stores will carry a variety to suit your needs. A torque wrench should be used any time we supply a specific torque value for a fas-

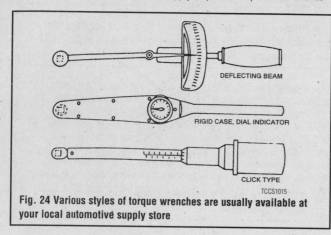

Fig. 24 Various styles of torque wrenches are usually available at your local automotive supply store

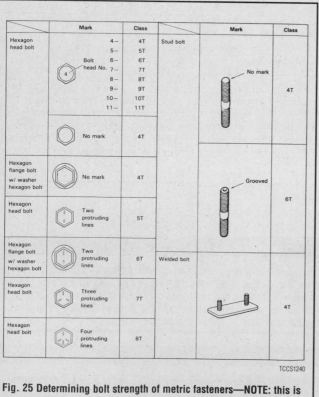

Fig. 25 Determining bolt strength of metric fasteners—NOTE: this is a typical bolt marking system, but there is not a worldwide standard

Class	Diameter mm	Pitch mm	Specified torque					
			Hexagon head bolt			Hexagon flange bolt		
			N·m	kgf·cm	ft·lbf	N·m	kgf·cm	ft·lbf
4T	6	1	5	55	48 in.·lbf	6	60	52 in.·lbf
	8	1.25	12.5	130	9	14	145	10
	10	1.25	26	260	19	29	290	21
	12	1.25	47	480	35	53	540	39
	14	1.5	74	760	55	84	850	61
	16	1.5	115	1,150	83	—	—	—
5T	6	1	6.5	65	56 in.·lbf	7.5	75	65 in.·lbf
	8	1.25	15.5	160	12	17.5	175	13
	10	1.25	32	330	24	36	360	26
	12	1.25	59	600	43	65	670	48
	14	1.5	91	930	67	100	1,050	76
	16	1.5	140	1,400	101	—	—	—
6T	6	1	8	80	69 in.·lbf	9	90	78 in.·lbf
	8	1.25	19	195	14	21	210	15
	10	1.25	39	400	29	44	440	32
	12	1.25	71	730	53	80	810	59
	14	1.5	110	1,100	80	125	1,250	90
	16	1.5	170	1,750	127	—	—	—
7T	6	1	10.5	110	8	12	120	9
	8	1.25	25	260	19	28	290	21
	10	1.25	52	530	38	58	590	43
	12	1.25	95	970	70	105	1,050	76
	14	1.5	145	1,500	108	165	1,700	123
	16	1.5	230	2,300	166	—	—	—
8T	8	1.25	29	300	22	33	330	24
	10	1.25	61	620	45	68	690	50
	12	1.25	110	1,100	80	120	1,250	90
9T	8	1.25	34	340	25	37	380	27
	10	1.25	70	710	51	78	790	57
	12	1.25	125	1,300	94	140	1,450	105
10T	8	1.25	38	390	28	42	430	31
	10	1.25	78	800	58	88	890	64
	12	1.25	140	1,450	105	155	1,600	116
11T	8	1.25	42	430	31	47	480	35
	10	1.25	87	890	64	97	990	72
	12	1.25	155	1,600	116	175	1,800	130

Fig. 26 Typical bolt torques for metric fasteners—WARNING: use only as a guide

tener. A torque wrench can also be used if you are following the general guidelines in the accompanying charts. Keep in mind that because there is no worldwide standardization of fasteners, the charts are a general guideline and should be used with caution. Again, the general rule of "if you are using the right tool for the job, you should not have to strain to tighten a fastener" applies here.

Beam Type

♦ See Figure 27

The beam type torque wrench is one of the most popular types. It consists of a pointer attached to the head that runs the length of the flexible beam (shaft) to

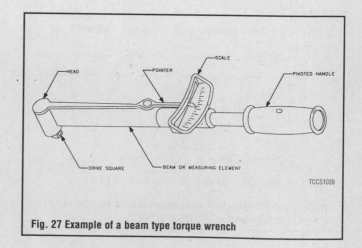

Fig. 27 Example of a beam type torque wrench

a scale located near the handle. As the wrench is pulled, the beam bends and the pointer indicates the torque using the scale.

Click (Breakaway) Type

▶ See Figure 28

Another popular design of torque wrench is the click type. To use the click type wrench you pre-adjust it to a torque setting. Once the torque is reached, the wrench has a reflex signaling feature that causes a momentary breakaway of the torque wrench body, sending an impulse to the operator's hand.

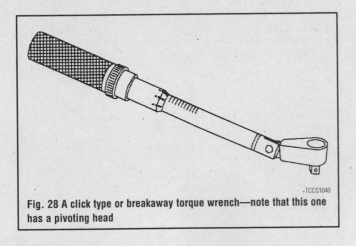

Fig. 28 A click type or breakaway torque wrench—note that this one has a pivoting head

Pivot Head Type

▶ See Figures 28 and 29

Some torque wrenches (usually of the click type) may be equipped with a pivot head which can allow it to be used in areas of limited access. BUT, it must be used properly. To hold a pivot head wrench, grasp the handle lightly, and as you pull on the handle, it should be floated on the pivot point. If the handle comes in contact with the yoke extension during the process of pulling, there is a very good chance the torque readings will be inaccurate because this could alter the wrench loading point. The design of the handle is usually such as to make it inconvenient to deliberately misuse the wrench.

➡ It should be mentioned that the use of any U-joint, wobble or extension will have an effect on the torque readings, no matter what type of wrench you are using. For the most accurate readings, install the socket

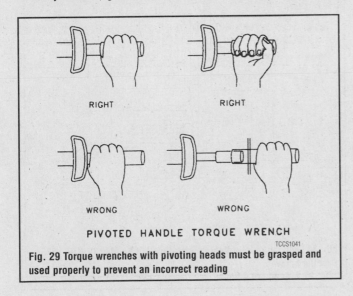

Fig. 29 Torque wrenches with pivoting heads must be grasped and used properly to prevent an incorrect reading

directly on the wrench driver. If necessary, straight extensions (which hold a socket directly under the wrench driver) will have the least effect on the torque reading. Avoid any extension that alters the length of the wrench from the handle to the head/driving point (such as a crow's foot). U-joint or wobble extensions can greatly affect the readings; avoid their use at all times.

Rigid Case (Direct Reading)

▶ See Figure 30

A rigid case or direct reading torque wrench is equipped with a dial indicator to show torque values. One advantage of these wrenches is that they can be held at any position on the wrench without affecting accuracy. These wrenches are often preferred because they tend to be compact, easy to read and have a great degree of accuracy.

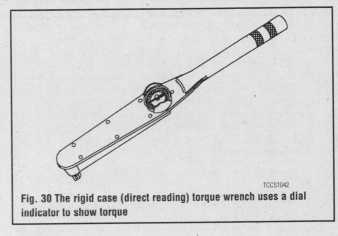

Fig. 30 The rigid case (direct reading) torque wrench uses a dial indicator to show torque

TORQUE ANGLE METERS

▶ See Figure 31

Because the frictional characteristics of each fastener or threaded hole will vary, clamp loads which are based strictly on torque will vary as well. In most applications, this variance is not significant enough to cause worry. But, in certain applications, a manufacturer's engineers may determine that more precise clamp loads are necessary (such is the case with many aluminum cylinder heads). In these cases, a torque angle method of installation would be specified. When installing fasteners which are torque angle tightened, a predetermined seating torque and standard torque wrench are usually used first to remove any compliance from the joint. The fastener is then tightened the specified additional

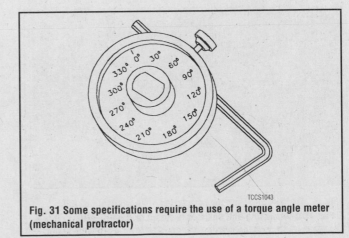

Fig. 31 Some specifications require the use of a torque angle meter (mechanical protractor)

portion of a turn measured in degrees. A torque angle gauge (mechanical protractor) is used for these applications.

Standard and Metric Measurements

▶ See Figure 32

Throughout this manual, specifications are given to help you determine the condition of various components on your vehicle, or to assist you in their installation. Some of the most common measurements include length (in. or cm/mm), torque (ft. lbs., inch lbs. or Nm) and pressure (psi, in. Hg, kPa or mm Hg). In most cases, we strive to provide the proper measurement as determined by the manufacturer's engineers.

Though, in some cases, that value may not be conveniently measured with what is available in your toolbox. Luckily, many of the measuring devices which are available today will have two scales so the Standard or Metric measurements may easily be taken. If any of the various measuring tools which are available to you do not contain the same scale as listed in the specifications, use the accompanying conversion factors to determine the proper value.

The conversion factor chart is used by taking the given specification and multiplying it by the necessary conversion factor. For instance, looking at the first line, if you have a measurement in inches such as "free-play should be 2 in." but your ruler reads only in millimeters, multiply 2 in. by the conversion factor of 25.4 to get the metric equivalent of 50.8mm. Likewise, if the specification was given only in a Metric measurement, for example in Newton Meters (Nm), then look at the center column first. If the measurement is 100 Nm, multiply it by the conversion factor of 0.738 to get 73.8 ft. lbs.

CONVERSION FACTORS

LENGTH–DISTANCE

Inches (in.)	x 25.4	= Millimeters (mm)	x .0394	= Inches
Feet (ft.)	x .305	= Meters (m)	x 3.281	= Feet
Miles	x 1.609	= Kilometers (km)	x .0621	= Miles

VOLUME

Cubic Inches (in3)	x 16.387	= Cubic Centimeters	x .061	= in3
IMP Pints (IMP pt.)	x .568	= Liters (L)	x 1.76	= IMP pt.
IMP Quarts (IMP qt.)	x 1.137	= Liters (L)	x .88	= IMP qt.
IMP Gallons (IMP gal.)	x 4.546	= Liters (L)	x .22	= IMP gal.
IMP Quarts (IMP qt.)	x 1.201	= US Quarts (US qt.)	x .833	= IMP qt.
IMP Gallons (IMP gal.)	x 1.201	= US Gallons (US gal.)	x .833	= IMP gal.
Fl. Ounces	x 29.573	= Milliliters	x .034	= Ounces
US Pints (US pt.)	x .473	= Liters (L)	x 2.113	= Pints
US Quarts (US qt.)	x .946	= Liters (L)	x 1.057	= Quarts
US Gallons (US gal.)	x 3.785	= Liters (L)	x .264	= Gallons

MASS–WEIGHT

Ounces (oz.)	x 28.35	= Grams (g)	x .035	= Ounces
Pounds (lb.)	x .454	= Kilograms (kg)	x 2.205	= Pounds

PRESSURE

Pounds Per Sq. In. (psi)	x 6.895	= Kilopascals (kPa)	x .145	= psi
Inches of Mercury (Hg)	x .4912	= psi	x 2.036	= Hg
Inches of Mercury (Hg)	x 3.377	= Kilopascals (kPa)	x .2961	= Hg
Inches of Water (H₂O)	x .07355	= Inches of Mercury	x 13.783	= H₂O
Inches of Water (H₂O)	x .03613	= psi	x 27.684	= H₂O
Inches of Water (H₂O)	x .248	= Kilopascals (kPa)	x 4.026	= H₂O

TORQUE

Pounds-Force Inches (in-lb)	x .113	= Newton Meters (N·m)	x 8.85	= in-lb
Pounds-Force Feet (ft-lb)	x 1.356	= Newton Meters (N·m)	x .738	= ft-lb

VELOCITY

Miles Per Hour (MPH)	x 1.609	= Kilometers Per Hour (KPH)	x .621	= MPH

POWER

Horsepower (Hp)	x .745	= Kilowatts	x 1.34	= Horsepower

FUEL CONSUMPTION*

Miles Per Gallon IMP (MPG)	x .354	= Kilometers Per Liter (Km/L)	
Kilometers Per Liter (Km/L)	x 2.352	= IMP MPG	
Miles Per Gallon US (MPG)	x .425	= Kilometers Per Liter (Km/L)	
Kilometers Per Liter (Km/L)	x 2.352	= US MPG	

*It is common to covert from miles per gallon (mpg) to liters/100 kilometers (1/100 km), where mpg (IMP) x 1/100 km = 282 and mpg (US) x 1/100 km = 235.

TEMPERATURE

Degree Fahrenheit (°F)	= (°C x 1.8) + 32
Degree Celsius (°C)	= (°F – 32) x .56

TCCS1044

Fig. 32 Standard and metric conversion factors chart

SERIAL NUMBER IDENTIFICATION

Vehicle

▶ See Figures 33 and 34

The Vehicle Identification Number (VIN) is a seventeen digit sequence stamped on a plate attached to the left front of the instrument panel, visible through the windshield.

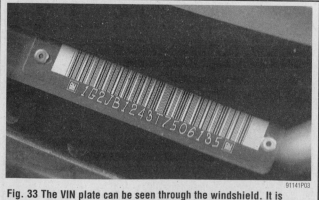

91141P03

Fig. 33 The VIN plate can be seen through the windshield. It is located at the base of the dashboard on the driver's side

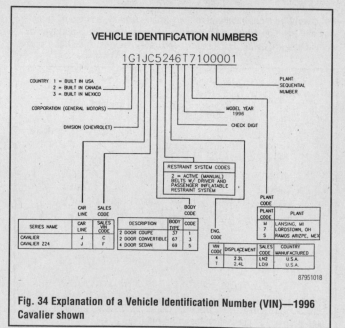

87951018

Fig. 34 Explanation of a Vehicle Identification Number (VIN)—1996 Cavalier shown

VEHICLE IDENTIFICATION CHART

Engine Code							Model Year	
Code	Liters	Cu. In. (cc)	Cyl.	Fuel Sys.	Eng. Mfg.		Code	Year
4	2.2	133 (2180)	4	MFI	CUS		S	1995
D	2.3	138 (2262)	4	MFI	CUS		T	1996
T	2.4	146 (2392)	4	MFI	CUS		V	1997
							W	1998
							X	1999
							Y	2000

CUS - Chevrolet/United States

MFI - Multi-point Fuel Injection

91141C01

Body

The body style identification plate is located on the radiator support, just behind the passenger side headlamp.

Engine

▶ **See Figures 35, 36 and 37**

Engine identification can take place using various methods. The VIN, described earlier in this section, contains a code identifying the engine which was originally installed in the vehicle. In most cases, this should be sufficient for determining the engine with which your car is currently equipped. But, some older vehicles may have had the engine replaced or changed by a previous owner. If this is the case, the first step in identification is to locate an engine serial number and code which is stamped on the block or located on adhesive labels that may be present on valve covers or other engine components.

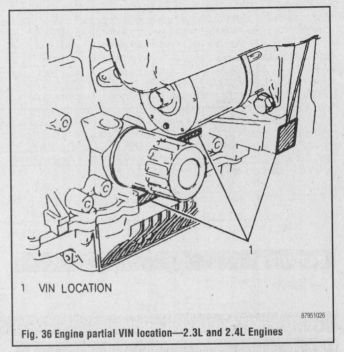

1   VIN LOCATION

87951026

Fig. 36 Engine partial VIN location—2.3L and 2.4L Engines

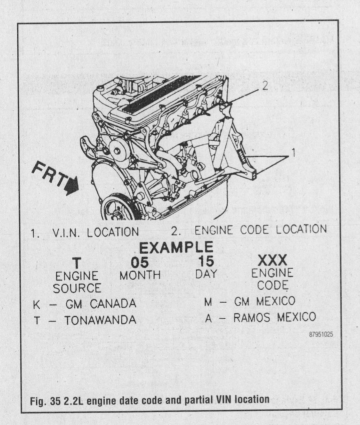

1. V.I.N. LOCATION   2. ENGINE CODE LOCATION

EXAMPLE

T	05	15	XXX
ENGINE SOURCE	MONTH	DAY	ENGINE CODE

K – GM CANADA   M – GM MEXICO

T – TONAWANDA   A – RAMOS MEXICO

87951025

Fig. 35 2.2L engine date code and partial VIN location

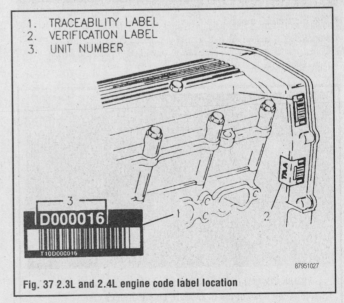

1. TRACEABILITY LABEL
2. VERIFICATION LABEL
3. UNIT NUMBER

D000016

T10D000016

87951027

Fig. 37 2.3L and 2.4L engine code label location

ENGINE IDENTIFICATION AND SPECIFICATIONS

Year	Model	Engine ID/VIN	Engine Displacement Liters (cc)	No. of Cyl.	Engine Type	Fuel System Type	Net Horsepower @ rpm	Net Torque @ rpm (ft. lbs.)	Bore x Stroke (in.)	Compression Ratio	Oil Pressure @ rpm
1995	Cavalier	4	2.2 (2180)	4	OHV	MFI	120@5200	130@3200	3.50x3.46	9.0:1	56@3000
	Cavalier	D	2.3 (2262)	4	DOHC	MFI	150@6100	145@4800	3.62x3.35	9.5:1	30@2000
	Sunfire	4	2.2 (2180)	4	OHV	MFI	120@5200	130@3200	3.50x3.46	9.0:1	56@3000
	Sunfire	D	2.3 (2262)	4	DOHC	MFI	150@6100	145@4800	3.62x3.35	9.5:1	30@2000
1996	Cavalier	4	2.2 (2180)	4	OHV	MFI	120@5200	130@3200	3.50x3.46	9.0:1	56@3000
	Cavalier	T	2.4 (2392)	4	DOHC	MFI	150@6000	155@4400	3.54x3.70	9.5:1	30@3000
	Sunfire	4	2.2 (2180)	4	OHV	MFI	120@5200	130@3200	3.50x3.46	9.0:1	56@3000
	Sunfire	T	2.4 (2392)	4	DOHC	MFI	150@6000	155@4400	3.54x3.70	9.5:1	30@3000
1997	Cavalier	4	2.2 (2180)	4	OHV	MFI	120@5200	130@3200	3.50x3.46	9.0:1	56@3000
	Cavalier	T	2.4 (2392)	4	DOHC	MFI	150@6000	155@4400	3.54x3.70	9.5:1	30@3000
	Sunfire	4	2.2 (2180)	4	OHV	MFI	120@5200	130@3200	3.50x3.46	9.0:1	56@3000
	Sunfire	T	2.4 (2392)	4	DOHC	MFI	150@6000	155@4400	3.54x3.70	9.5:1	30@3000
1998	Cavalier	4	2.2 (2180)	4	OHV	MFI	120@5200	130@3200	3.50x3.46	9.0:1	56@3000
	Cavalier	T	2.4 (2392)	4	DOHC	MFI	150@6000	155@4400	3.54x3.70	9.5:1	30@3000
	Sunfire	4	2.2 (2180)	4	OHV	MFI	120@5200	130@3200	3.50x3.46	9.0:1	56@3000
	Sunfire	T	2.4 (2392)	4	DOHC	MFI	150@6000	155@4400	3.54x3.70	9.5:1	30@3000
1999	Cavalier	4	2.2 (2180)	4	OHV	MFI	120@5200	130@3200	3.50x3.46	9.0:1	56@3000
	Cavalier	T	2.4 (2392)	4	DOHC	MFI	150@6000	155@4400	3.54x3.70	9.5:1	30@3000
	Sunfire	4	2.2 (2180)	4	OHV	MFI	120@5200	130@3200	3.50x3.46	9.0:1	56@3000
	Sunfire	T	2.4 (2392)	4	DOHC	MFI	150@6000	155@4400	3.54x3.70	9.5:1	30@3000
2000	Cavalier	4	2.2 (2180)	4	OHV	MFI	120@5200	130@3200	3.50x3.46	9.0:1	56@3000
	Cavalier	T	2.4 (2392)	4	DOHC	MFI	150@6000	155@4400	3.54x3.70	9.5:1	30@3000
	Sunfire	4	2.2 (2180)	4	OHV	MFI	120@5200	130@3200	3.50x3.46	9.0:1	56@3000
	Sunfire	T	2.4 (2392)	4	DOHC	MFI	150@6000	155@4400	3.54x3.70	9.5:1	30@3000

91141C02

Transaxle

♦ See Figures 38, 39 and 40

The transaxle identification number is on a paper label applied to the transaxle case. Refer to the graphics for identification label locations.

Vehicle Emission Control Information (VECI) Label

The Vehicle Emission Control Information Label is located in the engine compartment, (fan shroud, radiator support, hood underside, etc.) of every vehicle produced by General Motors. The label contains important emission specifications and setting procedures, as well as a vacuum hose schematic with various emissions components identified.

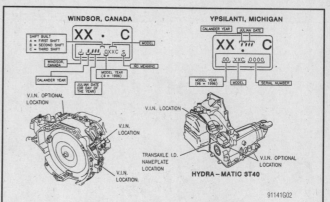

Fig. 39 3T40 automatic transaxle identification number locations

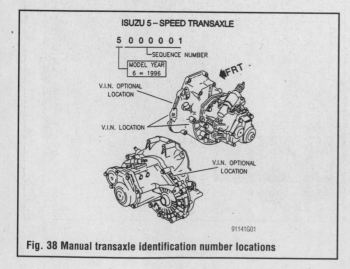

Fig. 38 Manual transaxle identification number locations

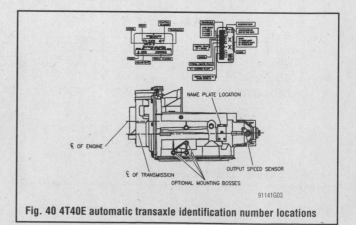

Fig. 40 4T40E automatic transaxle identification number locations

2.2L ENGINE MAINTENANCE COMPONENT LOCATIONS

1. Coolant recovery tank
2. Power steering reservoir
3. Transaxle fluid dipstick
4. Brake master cylinder
5. Air cleaner
6. PCV valve
7. Washer solvent bottle
8. Belt
9. Spark plug
10. Engine oil fill cap/dipstick
11. Battery

2.3L/2.4L ENGINE MAINTENANCE COMPONENT LOCATIONS

1. Coolant recovery tank
2. Engine oil fill cap
3. Engine oil dipstick
4. Brake master cylinder
5. Air cleaner
6. Power steering fluid reservoir
7. Washer solvent reservoir
8. Battery

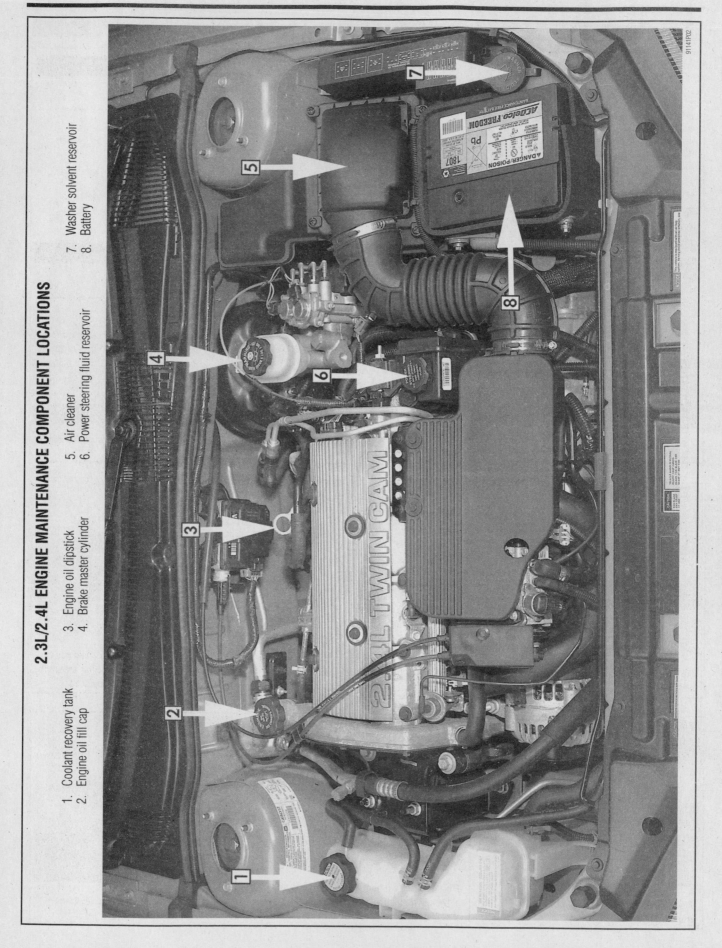

Proper maintenance and tune-up is the key to long and trouble-free vehicle life, and the work can yield its own rewards. Studies have shown that a properly tuned and maintained vehicle can achieve better gas mileage than an out-of-tune vehicle. As a conscientious owner and driver, set aside a Saturday morning, say once a month, to check or replace items which could cause major problems later. Keep your own personal log to jot down which services you performed, how much the parts cost you, the date, and the exact odometer reading at the time. Keep all receipts for such items as engine oil and filters, so that they may be referred to in case of related problems or to determine operating expenses. As a do-it-yourselfer, these receipts are the only proof you have that the required maintenance was performed. In the event of a warranty problem, these receipts will be invaluable.

The literature provided with your vehicle when it was originally delivered includes the factory recommended maintenance schedule. If you no longer have this literature, replacement copies are usually available from the dealer. A maintenance schedule is provided later in this section, in case you do not have the factory literature.

Air Cleaner (Element)

REMOVAL & INSTALLATION

◆ **See Figures 41, 42, 43 and 44**

1. Disconnect the negative battery cable.
2. Remove the retaining screws for the air cleaner lid.
3. Lift the lid up and remove the filter element from the air cleaner box.

To install:

4. Lift the lid up and install a new filter element into the air cleaner box.
5. Tighten the screws for the air cleaner lid.
6. Connect the negative battery cable.

Fuel Filter

REMOVAL & INSTALLATION

◆ **See Figures 45, 46, 47 and 48**

➡ **The vehicles covered in this manual are equipped with "Quick Connect" fuel fittings. For more information regarding these fittings, please refer to Section 5 of this manual.**

An inline filter can be found in the fuel feed line attached to the rear crossmember of the vehicle.

✳ CAUTION

Before disconnecting any component of the fuel system, refer to the fuel pressure release procedures found in Section 5.

Fig. 41 The air cleaner lid is held by four retaining screws

Fig. 42 Remove the retaining screws and . . .

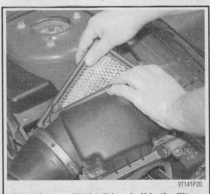

Fig. 43 . . . lift the lid and slide the filter element out

Fig. 44 Bending the filter will allow you to examine the condition of the filter element to determine if it should be replaced

Fig. 45 Remove the quick connect fitting from the filter

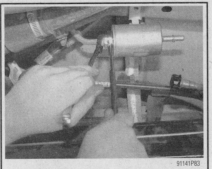

Fig. 46 Using a 21mm back-up wrench and a 16mm wrench on the line, loosen the feed line from the filter

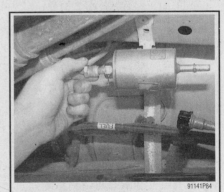

Fig. 47 Carefully unthread the feed line from the filter and . . .

Fig. 48 . . . remove the filter from the retaining bracket by pulling the filter outward

1. Properly relieve the fuel system pressure as outlined in Section 5.
2. Raise and safely support the vehicle with jackstands.
3. Grasp the filter and nylon fuel line fitting on the tank-to-filter line. Twist the "quick-connect" fitting ¼ or a turn in each direction to loosen any dirt within the fitting. Use compressed air to blow out the dirt from the fittings at the end of the fuel filter.
4. Detach the quick-connect fitting by pushing inward toward the filter and grasping the plastic tab around the connector and pull apart. If additional assistance is required to disconnect the fitting, tool J 38778 or equivalent can be placed between the filter and the fitting release mechanism to carefully force the two apart. Be careful not to bend the special tool.

➡**Always use a back-up wrench anytime the fuel filter is removed or installed.**

5. Using a backup wrench (where possible) to prevent overtorquing the lines or fittings, loosen and disconnect the feed line from the filter. Be sure to position a rag in order to catch any remaining fuel which may escape when the fittings are loosened.
6. Remove the fuel filter from the retaining bracket.

To install:

7. Before installing a new filter, apply a few drops of clean engine oil to the male tube end of the filter. This will ensure proper attachment and prevent a fuel leak.
8. Position the filter into the retaining bracket with the directional arrow facing away from the fuel tank, towards the throttle body.

➡**The filter has an arrow (fuel flow direction) on the side of the case, be sure to install it correctly in the system, the with arrow facing away from the fuel tank.**

9. Push the connectors on the quick-connect fitting together to cause the retaining tabs/fingers to snap into place. Pull on both ends of the connection to be sure they are secure.
10. Connect the fuel feed line to the filter, then tighten, using a backup wrench to prevent damage, to 20–22 ft. lbs. (27–30 Nm).
11. Carefully lower the vehicle.

12. Connect the negative battery cable and tighten the fuel filler cap, then start the engine and check for leaks.

PCV Valve

All of the vehicles covered by this manual with the 2.2L engine utilize a Positive Crankcase Ventilation (PCV) or Crankcase Ventilation (CV) valve, which regulates crankcase ventilation during various engine running conditions. At high vacuum (idle speed and partial load range) it will open slightly and at low vacuum (full throttle) it will open fully. This causes vapors to be drawn from the crankcase by engine vacuum and then sucked into the combustion chamber where they are dissipated.

The PCV system must be operating properly in order to allow evaporation of fuel vapors and water from the crankcase. This system should be serviced and the PCV valve replaced every 30,000 miles (48,000 km). Normal service entails cleaning the passages of the system hoses with solvent, inspecting them for cracks and breaks, then replacing them as necessary. The PCV valve contains a check valve and, when working properly, this valve will make a rattling sound when the outside case is tapped. If it fails to rattle, then it is probably stuck in a closed position and needs to be replaced.

The PCV system is designed to prevent the emission of gases from the crankcase into the atmosphere. It does this by connecting a outlet (the valve cover) to the intake with a hose. The crankcase gases travel through the hose to the intake where they are returned to the combustion chamber to be burned. If maintained properly, this system reduces condensation in the crankcase and the resultant formation of harmful acids and oil dilution. A clogged PCV valve will often cause a slow or rough idle due to a richer fuel mixture. A vehicle equipped with a PCV system has air going through a hose to the intake manifold from an outlet at the valve cover. If the PCV valve or hose is clogged, this air doesn't go to the intake manifold and the fuel mixture is too rich. A rough, slow idle results. Clamp the hose shut. If the engine speed decreases less than 50 rpm, the valve is clogged and should be replaced. If the engine speed decreases much more than 50 rpm, then the valve good. The PCV valve is an inexpensive item and it is suggested that is be replaced, if suspect. If the new valve doesn't noticeably improve engine idle, the problem might be a restriction in the PCV hose.

For the 2.3L and 2.4L engines, blow-by gases are passed through a Crankcase Ventilation (CV) oil/air separator hose into the intake manifold. Incorporated in the CV system is a crankcase ventilation heater assembly, a positive temperature coefficient device, which serves to prevent icing in the CV system.

More information regarding the PCV/CV system, including system tests, is located in Section 4 of this manual.

REMOVAL & INSTALLATION

Valve

▶ **See Figures 49, 50, 51, 52 and 53**

The valve is located in a rubber grommet in the valve cover. The valve has a plastic threaded retainer securing it. The valve is connected to the air cleaner housing by a large diameter rubber hose. To replace the valve:

1. Pull the valve (with the hose attached) or the hose from the rubber grommet in the valve cover.

Fig. 49 The PCV valve is attached to the intake by a hose and is located in the valve cover and held by a plastic retainer

Fig. 50 Use a pair of pliers to loosen the PCV valve retainer

Fig. 51 Unthread the retainer from the valve cover to expose the PCV valve

Fig. 52 Pull the PCV valve from the valve cover grommet and . . .

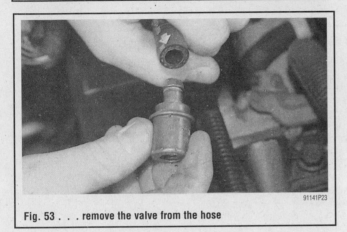

Fig. 53 . . . remove the valve from the hose

2. Remove the valve from the hose.
3. Install a new valve into the hose.
4. Press the valve or hose back into the rubber grommet in the valve cover.
5. Install the retainer and tighten it with a pair of pliers.

Evaporative Canister

SERVICING

▶ See Figure 54

The evaporative canister requires no periodic servicing. However, a careful inspection of the canister and hoses should be made frequently. Replace damaged components as required.

The canister is located behind the front fender on the passenger side of the vehicle.

Fig. 54 The EVAP canister is located behind the front fender, remove the splash shield to access it

Battery

PRECAUTIONS

Always use caution when working on or near the battery. Never allow a tool to bridge the gap between the negative and positive battery terminals. Also, be careful not to allow a tool to provide a ground between the positive cable/terminal and any metal component on the vehicle. Either of these conditions will cause a short circuit, leading to sparks and possible personal injury.

Do not smoke, have an open flame or create sparks near a battery; the gases contained in the battery are very explosive and, if ignited, could cause severe injury or death.

All batteries, regardless of type, should be carefully secured by a battery hold-down device. If this is not done, the battery terminals or casing may crack from stress applied to the battery during vehicle operation. A battery which is not secured may allow acid to leak out, making it discharge faster; such leaking corrosive acid can also eat away at components under the hood.

Always visually inspect the battery case for cracks, leakage and corrosion. A white corrosive substance on the battery case or on nearby components would indicate a leaking or cracked battery. If the battery is cracked, it should be replaced immediately.

GENERAL MAINTENANCE

▶ See Figure 55

A battery that is not sealed must be checked periodically for electrolyte level. You cannot add water to a sealed maintenance-free battery (though not all maintenance-free batteries are sealed); however, a sealed battery must also be checked for proper electrolyte level, as indicated by the color of the built-in hydrometer "eye."

Always keep the battery cables and terminals free of corrosion. Check these components about once a year. Refer to the removal, installation and cleaning procedures outlined in this section.

Keep the top of the battery clean, as a film of dirt can help completely discharge a battery that is not used for long periods. A solution of baking soda and water may be used for cleaning, but be careful to flush this off with clear water. DO NOT let any of the solution into the filler holes. Baking soda neutralizes battery acid and will de-activate a battery cell.

Batteries in vehicles which are not operated on a regular basis can fall victim to parasitic loads (small current drains which are constantly drawing current from the battery). Normal parasitic loads may drain a battery on a vehicle that is in storage and not used for 6–8 weeks. Vehicles that have additional accessories such as a cellular phone, an alarm system or other devices that increase parasitic load may discharge a battery sooner. If the vehicle is to be stored for 6–8 weeks in a secure area and the alarm system, if present, is not necessary, the negative battery cable should be disconnected at the onset of storage to protect the battery charge.

Remember that constantly discharging and recharging will shorten battery life. Take care not to allow a battery to be needlessly discharged.

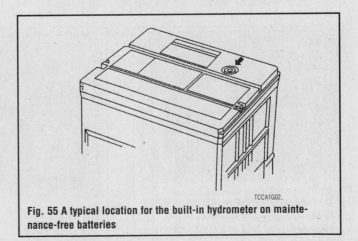

Fig. 55 A typical location for the built-in hydrometer on maintenance-free batteries

BATTERY FLUID

Check the battery electrolyte level at least once a month, or more often in hot weather or during periods of extended vehicle operation. On non-sealed batteries, the level can be checked either through the case on translucent batteries or by removing the cell caps on opaque-cased types. The electrolyte level in each cell should be kept filled to the split ring inside each cell, or the line marked on the outside of the case.

If the level is low, add only distilled water through the opening until the level is correct. Each cell is separate from the others, so each must be checked and filled individually. Distilled water should be used, because the chemicals and minerals found in most drinking water are harmful to the battery and could significantly shorten its life.

If water is added in freezing weather, the vehicle should be driven several miles to allow the water to mix with the electrolyte. Otherwise, the battery could freeze.

Although some maintenance-free batteries have removable cell caps for access to the electrolyte, the electrolyte condition and level on all sealed maintenance-free batteries must be checked using the built-in hydrometer "eye." The exact type of eye varies between battery manufacturers, but most apply a sticker to the battery itself explaining the possible readings. When in doubt, refer to the battery manufacturer's instructions to interpret battery condition using the built-in hydrometer.

➥ **Although the readings from built-in hydrometers found in sealed batteries may vary, a green eye usually indicates a properly charged battery with sufficient fluid level. A dark eye is normally an indicator of a battery with sufficient fluid, but one which may be low in charge. And a light or yellow eye is usually an indication that electrolyte supply has dropped below the necessary level for battery (and hydrometer) operation. In this last case, sealed batteries with an insufficient electrolyte level must usually be discarded.**

Checking the Specific Gravity

▶ **See Figures 56, 57 and 58**

A hydrometer is required to check the specific gravity on all batteries that are not maintenance-free. On batteries that are maintenance-free, the specific gravity is checked by observing the built-in hydrometer "eye" on the top of the battery case. Check with your battery's manufacturer for proper interpretation of its built-in hydrometer readings.

✳✳ CAUTION

Battery electrolyte contains sulfuric acid. If you should splash any on your skin or in your eyes, flush the affected area with plenty of clear water. If it lands in your eyes, get medical help immediately.

The fluid (sulfuric acid solution) contained in the battery cells will tell you many things about the condition of the battery. Because the cell plates must be kept submerged below the fluid level in order to operate, maintaining the fluid level is extremely important. And, because the specific gravity of the acid is an indication of electrical charge, testing the fluid can be an aid in determining if the battery must be replaced. A battery in a vehicle with a properly operating charging system should require little maintenance, but careful, periodic inspection should reveal problems before they leave you stranded.

As stated earlier, the specific gravity of a battery's electrolyte level can be used as an indication of battery charge. At least once a year, check the specific gravity of the battery. It should be between 1.20 and 1.26 on the gravity scale. Most auto supply stores carry a variety of inexpensive battery testing hydrometers. These can be used on any non-sealed battery to test the specific gravity in each cell.

The battery testing hydrometer has a squeeze bulb at one end and a nozzle at the other. Battery electrolyte is sucked into the hydrometer until the float is lifted from its seat. The specific gravity is then read by noting the position of the float. If gravity is low in one or more cells, the battery should be slowly charged and checked again to see if the gravity has come up. Generally, if after charging, the specific gravity between any two cells varies more than 50 points (0.50), the battery should be replaced, as it can no longer produce sufficient voltage to guarantee proper operation.

CABLES

▶ **See Figures 59 thru 64**

Once a year (or as necessary), the battery terminals and the cable clamps should be cleaned. Loosen the clamps and remove the cables, negative cable first. On batteries with posts on top, the use of a puller specially made for this purpose is recommended. These are inexpensive and available in most auto parts stores. Side terminal battery cables are secured with a small bolt.

Clean the cable clamps and the battery terminal with a wire brush, until all corrosion, grease, etc., is removed and the metal is shiny. It is especially important to clean the inside of the clamp thoroughly (an old knife is useful here), since a small deposit of foreign material or oxidation there will prevent a sound electrical connection and inhibit either starting or charging. Special tools are available for cleaning these parts, one type for conventional top post batteries and another type for side terminal batteries. It is also a good idea to apply some dielectric grease to the terminal, as this will aid in the prevention of corrosion.

After the clamps and terminals are clean, reinstall the cables, negative cable last; DO NOT hammer the clamps onto battery posts. Tighten the clamps securely, but do not distort them. Give the clamps and terminals a thin external coating of grease after installation, to retard corrosion.

Check the cables at the same time that the terminals are cleaned. If the cable insulation is cracked or broken, or if the ends are frayed, the cable should be replaced with a new cable of the same length and gauge.

CHARGING

✳✳ CAUTION

The chemical reaction which takes place in all batteries generates explosive hydrogen gas. A spark can cause the battery to explode and splash acid. To avoid serious personal injury, be sure there is proper ventilation and take appropriate fire safety precautions when connecting, disconnecting, or charging a battery and when using jumper cables.

TCCA1P07

Fig. 56 On non-maintenance-free batteries, the fluid level can be checked through the case on translucent models; the cell caps must be removed on other models

TCCA1P08

Fig. 57 If the fluid level is low, add only distilled water through the opening until the level is correct

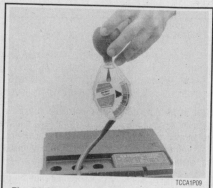

TCCA1P09

Fig. 58 Check the specific gravity of the battery's electrolyte with a hydrometer

Fig. 59 Loosen the battery cable retaining nut . . .

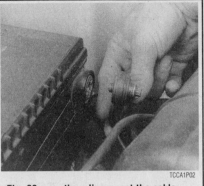

Fig. 60 . . . then disconnect the cable from the battery

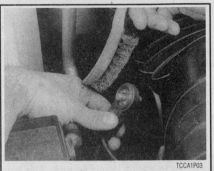

Fig. 61 A wire brush may be used to clean any corrosion or foreign material from the cable

Fig. 62 The wire brush can also be used to remove any corrosion or dirt from the battery terminal

Fig. 63 The battery terminal can also be cleaned using a solution of baking soda and water

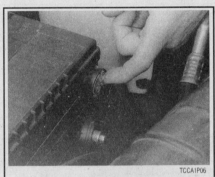

Fig. 64 Before connecting the cables, it's a good idea to coat the terminals with a small amount of dielectric grease

A battery should be charged at a slow rate to keep the plates inside from getting too hot. However, if some maintenance-free batteries are allowed to discharge until they are almost "dead," they may have to be charged at a high rate to bring them back to "life." Always follow the charger manufacturer's instructions on charging the battery.

REPLACEMENT

When it becomes necessary to replace the battery, select one with an amperage rating equal to or greater than the battery originally installed. Deterioration and just plain aging of the battery cables, starter motor, and associated wires makes the battery's job harder in successive years. The slow increase in electrical resistance over time makes it prudent to install a new battery with a greater capacity than the old.

Belts

INSPECTION

▶ **See Figures 65 and 66**

Inspect the belts for signs of glazing or cracking. A glazed belt will be perfectly smooth from slippage, while a good belt will have a slight texture of fabric visible. Cracks will usually start at the inner edge of the belt and run outward. All worn or damaged drive belts should be replaced immediately.

➡️Routine inspection of the belt may reveal cracks in the belt ribs. These cracks will not impair belt performance and therefore should not be considered a problem requiring belt replacement. However, the belt should be replaced if belt slip occurs or if sections of the belt ribs are missing, sometimes referred to as "chunking".

Inspect the marks on the tensioner for the wear limits. If a whining is heard around the tensioner or idler assemblies, check for possible bearing failure.

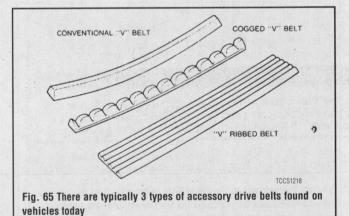

Fig. 65 There are typically 3 types of accessory drive belts found on vehicles today

Fig. 66 Installing too wide a belt can result in serious belt wear and/or breakage

ADJUSTMENT

All engines use an automatic drive belt tensioner. No adjustment is necessary. If the tensioner is at Maximum travel, the belt is most likely stretched or the incorrect belt was installed.

REMOVAL & INSTALLATION

▶ **See Figures 67 thru 72**

1. Disconnect the negative battery cable.

➡ **The proper belt routing is included in this section, however, it is a good idea to make a simple drawing of the belt routing of your engine for installation reference before removing the belt.**

2. Rotate the drive belt tensioner to relieve the belt tension. The procedure is as follows:

Fig. 67 The belt tensioner is released by rotating the tensioner pulley bolt in a CLOCKWISE direction—2.2L engine

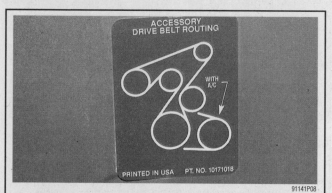

Fig. 68 The belt routing for the vehicle you are working on can usually be found on a label attached to the underside of the hood

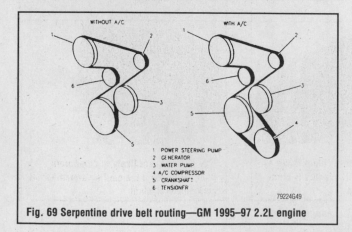

Fig. 69 Serpentine drive belt routing—GM 1995–97 2.2L engine

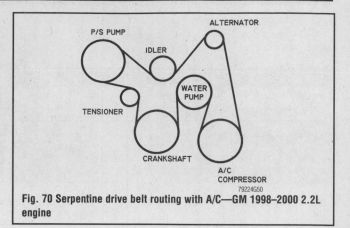

Fig. 70 Serpentine drive belt routing with A/C—GM 1998–2000 2.2L engine

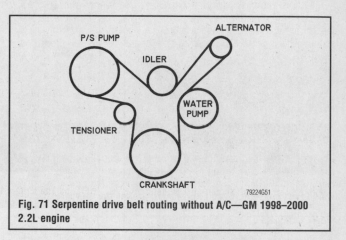

Fig. 71 Serpentine drive belt routing without A/C—GM 1998–2000 2.2L engine

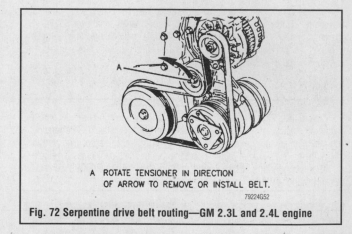

A ROTATE TENSIONER IN DIRECTION OF ARROW TO REMOVE OR INSTALL BELT.

Fig. 72 Serpentine drive belt routing—GM 2.3L and 2.4L engine

   a. On the 2.2L engine, use a 15 mm drive tool or a special belt removal tool to rotate the tensioner clockwise.

   b. On the 2.3L and 2.4L engines, use a 13mm drive tool or a special belt removal tool to rotate the tensioner clockwise.

   c. While holding the tensioner back, remove the belt from around one pulley.

3. Remove the belt from around the remaining pulleys.

To install:

4. Position the belt around the pulleys in the proper routing with the exception of one pulley. It is easiest to keep the belt off of the easiest pulley to access. Hold the belt tight with your hands and using the proper tool for your engine, rotate the tensioner clockwise and place the belt around the final pulley.

5. Release the tensioner slowly until it sits firmly against the belt.

➡ **If the tensioner does not touch the belt or the wear indicator marks are not within specification, the belt is routed incorrectly or the wrong belt has been installed.**

6. Connect the negative battery cable.

7. Start the engine and ensure that the belt runs smoothly and no abnormal noises exist.

Hoses

INSPECTION

▶ See Figures 73, 74, 75 and 76

Upper and lower radiator hoses, along with the heater hoses, should be checked for deterioration, leaks and loose hose clamps at least every 15,000 miles (24,000 km). It is also wise to check the hoses periodically in early spring and at the beginning of the fall or winter when you are performing other maintenance. A quick visual inspection could discover a weakened hose which might have left you stranded if it had remained unrepaired.

Whenever you are checking the hoses, make sure the engine and cooling system are cold. Visually inspect for cracking, rotting or collapsed hoses, and replace as necessary. Run your hand along the length of the hose. If a weak or swollen spot is noted when squeezing the hose wall, the hose should be replaced.

REMOVAL & INSTALLATION

1. Remove the recovery tank pressure cap.

✼✼ CAUTION

Never remove the pressure cap while the engine is running, or personal injury from scalding hot coolant or steam may result. If possible, wait until the engine has cooled to remove the pressure cap. If this is not possible, wrap a thick cloth around the pressure cap and

Fig. 73 The cracks developing along this hose are a result of age-related hardening

turn it slowly to the stop. Step back while the pressure is released from the cooling system. When you are sure all the pressure has been released, use the cloth to turn and remove the cap.

2. Position a clean container under the radiator and/or engine draincock or plug, then open the drain and allow the cooling system to drain to an appropriate level. For some upper hoses, only a little coolant must be drained. To remove hoses positioned lower on the engine, such as a lower radiator hose, the entire cooling system must be emptied.

✼✼ CAUTION

When draining coolant, keep in mind that cats and dogs are attracted by ethylene glycol antifreeze, and are quite likely to drink any that is left in an uncovered container or in puddles on the ground. This will prove fatal in sufficient quantity. Always drain coolant into a sealable container. Coolant may be reused unless it is contaminated or several years old.

3. Loosen the hose clamps at each end of the hose requiring replacement. Clamps are usually either of the spring tension type (which require pliers to squeeze the tabs and loosen) or of the screw tension type (which require screw or hex drivers to loosen). Pull the clamps back on the hose away from the connection.

4. Twist, pull and slide the hose off the fitting, taking care not to damage the neck of the component from which the hose is being removed.

➡If the hose is stuck at the connection, do not try to insert a screwdriver or other sharp tool under the hose end in an effort to free it, as the connection and/or hose may become damaged. Heater connections especially may be easily damaged by such a procedure. If the hose is to be replaced, use a single-edged razor blade to make a slice along the portion of the hose which is stuck on the connection, perpendicular to the end of the hose. Do not cut deep so as to prevent damaging the connection. The hose can then be peeled from the connection and discarded.

5. Clean both hose mounting connections. Inspect the condition of the hose clamps and replace them, if necessary.

To install:

6. Dip the ends of the new hose into clean engine coolant to ease installation.

7. Slide the clamps over the replacement hose, then slide the hose ends over the connections into position.

8. Position and secure the clamps at least ¼ in. (6.35mm) from the ends of the hose. Make sure they are located beyond the raised bead of the connector.

9. Close the radiator or engine drains and properly refill the cooling system with the clean drained engine coolant or a suitable mixture of ethylene glycol coolant and water.

10. If available, install a pressure tester and check for leaks. If a pressure tester is not available, run the engine until normal operating temperature is reached (allowing the system to naturally pressurize), then check for leaks.

Fig. 74 A hose clamp that is too tight can cause older hoses to separate and tear on either side of the clamp

Fig. 75 A soft spongy hose (identifiable by the swollen section) will eventually burst and should be replaced

Fig. 76 Hoses are likely to deteriorate from the inside if the cooling system is not periodically flushed

✳✳ CAUTION

If you are checking for leaks with the system at normal operating temperature, BE EXTREMELY CAREFUL not to touch any moving or hot engine parts. Once temperature has been reached, shut the engine OFF, and check for leaks around the hose fittings and connections which were removed earlier.

CV-Boots

INSPECTION

▶ **See Figures 77 and 78**

The CV (Constant Velocity) boots should be checked for damage each time the oil is changed and any other time the vehicle is raised for service. These boots keep water, grime, dirt and other damaging matter from entering the CV-joints. Any of these could cause early CV-joint failure which can be expensive to repair. Heavy grease thrown around the inside of the front wheel(s) and on the brake caliper/drum can be an indication of a torn boot. Thoroughly check the boots for missing clamps and tears. If the boot is damaged, it should be replaced immediately. Please refer to Section 7 for procedures.

Spark Plugs

▶ **See Figure 79**

A typical spark plug consists of a metal shell surrounding a ceramic insulator. A metal electrode extends downward through the center of the insulator and protrudes a small distance. Located at the end of the plug and attached to the side of the outer metal shell is the side electrode. The side electrode bends in at a 90(angle so that its tip is just past and parallel to the tip of the center electrode. The distance between these two electrodes (measured in thousandths of an inch or hundredths of a millimeter) is called the spark plug gap.

Fig. 77 CV-boots must be inspected periodically for damage

TCCS1011

The spark plug does not produce a spark, but instead provides a gap across which the current can arc. The coil produces anywhere from 20,000 to 50,000 volts (depending on the type and application) which travels through the wires to the spark plugs. The current passes along the center electrode and jumps the gap to the side electrode, and in doing so, ignites the air/fuel mixture in the combustion chamber.

SPARK PLUG HEAT RANGE

▶ **See Figure 80**

Spark plug heat range is the ability of the plug to dissipate heat. The longer the insulator (or the farther it extends into the engine), the hotter the plug will operate; the shorter the insulator (the closer the electrode is to the block's cooling passages) the cooler it will operate. A plug that absorbs little heat and remains too cool will quickly accumulate deposits of oil and carbon since it is not hot enough to burn them off. This leads to plug fouling and consequently to misfiring. A plug that absorbs too much heat will have no deposits but, due to the excessive heat, the electrodes will burn away quickly and might possibly lead to preignition or other ignition problems. Preignition takes place when plug tips get so hot that they glow sufficiently to ignite the air/fuel mixture before the actual spark occurs. This early ignition will usually cause a pinging during low speeds and heavy loads.

The general rule of thumb for choosing the correct heat range when picking a spark plug is: if most of your driving is long distance, high speed travel, use a colder plug; if most of your driving is stop and go, use a hotter plug. Original equipment plugs are generally a good compromise between the 2 styles and most people never have the need to change their plugs from the factory-recommended heat range.

REMOVAL & INSTALLATION

▶ **See Figures 81 thru 86**

A set of spark plugs usually requires replacement after about 20,000–30,000 miles (32,000–48,000 km), depending on your style of driving. In normal operation plug gap increases about 0.001 in. (0.025mm) for every 2500 miles (4000 km). As the gap increases, the plug's voltage requirement also increases. It requires a greater voltage to jump the wider gap and about two to three times as much voltage to fire the plug at high speeds than at idle. The improved air/fuel ratio control of modern fuel injection combined with the higher voltage output of modern ignition systems will often allow an engine to run significantly longer on a set of standard spark plugs, but keep in mind that efficiency will drop as the gap widens (along with fuel economy and power).

When you're removing spark plugs, work on one at a time. Don't start by removing the plug wires all at once, because, unless you number them, they may become mixed up. Take a minute before you begin and number the wires with tape.

1. Disconnect the negative battery cable, and if the vehicle has been run recently, allow the engine to thoroughly cool.

2. On the 2.2L engine:

   a. Carefully twist the spark plug wire boot to loosen it, then pull upward and remove the boot from the plug. Be sure to pull on the boot and not on

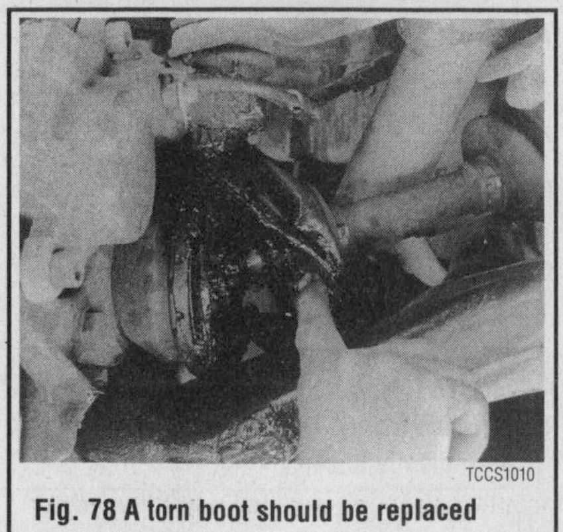

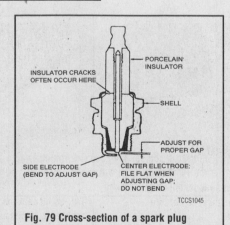

Fig. 78 A torn boot should be replaced immediately

TCCS1010

Fig. 79 Cross-section of a spark plug

- PORCELAIN INSULATOR
- INSULATOR CRACKS OFTEN OCCUR HERE
- SHELL
- ADJUST FOR PROPER GAP
- SIDE ELECTRODE (BEND TO ADJUST GAP)
- CENTER ELECTRODE: FILE FLAT WHEN ADJUSTING GAP; DO NOT BEND

TCCS1045

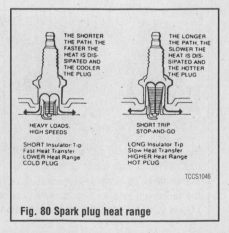

Fig. 80 Spark plug heat range

- THE SHORTER THE PATH, THE FASTER THE HEAT IS DISSIPATED AND THE COOLER THE PLUG
- THE LONGER THE PATH, THE SLOWER THE HEAT IS DISSIPATED AND THE HOTTER THE PLUG
- HEAVY LOADS, HIGH SPEEDS
- SHORT TRIP STOP-AND-GO
- SHORT Insulator Tip Fast Heat Transfer LOWER Heat Range COLD PLUG
- LONG Insulator Tip Slow Heat Transfer HIGHER Heat Range HOT PLUG

TCCS1046

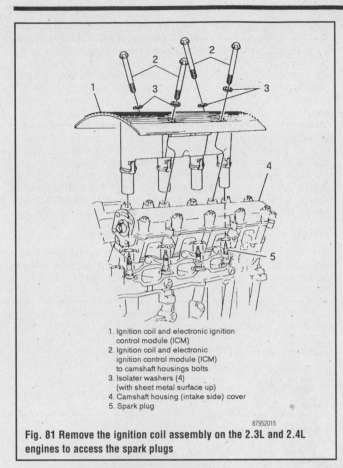

1. Ignition coil and electronic ignition
   control module (ICM)
2. Ignition coil and electronic
   ignition control module (ICM)
   to camshaft housings bolts
3. Isolater washers (4)
   (with sheet metal surface up)
4. Camshaft housing (intake side) cover
5. Spark plug

Fig. 81 Remove the ignition coil assembly on the 2.3L and 2.4L engines to access the spark plugs

the wire, otherwise the connector located inside the boot may become separated.

3. On the 2.3L and 2.4L engines:

   a. Unplug the coil connector and the four retaining bolts and remove the ignition coil assembly. If the connectors stay stuck to the spark plugs, carefully twist them free.

4. Using compressed air, blow any water or debris from the spark plug well to assure that no harmful contaminants are allowed to enter the combustion chamber when the spark plug is removed. If compressed air is not available, use a rag or a brush to clean the area.

➡ Remove the spark plugs when the engine is cold, if possible, to prevent damage to the threads. If removal of the plugs is difficult, apply a few drops of penetrating oil or silicone spray to the area around the base of the plug, and allow it a few minutes to work.

5. Using a spark plug socket that is equipped with a rubber insert to properly hold the plug, turn the spark plug counterclockwise to loosen and remove the spark plug from the bore.

✳✳ WARNING

Be sure not to use a flexible extension on the socket. Use of a flexible extension may allow a shear force to be applied to the plug. A shear force could break the plug off in the cylinder head, leading to costly and frustrating repairs.

To install:

6. Inspect the spark plug boot for tears or damage. If a damaged boot is found, the spark plug wire must be replaced.

7. Using a wire feeler gauge, check and adjust the spark plug gap. When using a gauge, the proper size should pass between the electrodes with a slight drag. The next larger size should not be able to pass while the next smaller size should pass freely.

8. Carefully thread the plug into the bore by hand. If resistance is felt before the plug is almost completely threaded, back the plug out and begin

Fig. 82 Twist and pull the spark plug wire from the spark plug

Fig. 83 Always use a special spark plug socket with a rubber insert to remove the spark plugs. A ⅝ in. socket is required on most of the vehicles covered by this manual

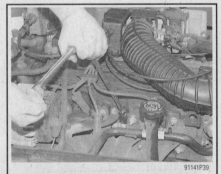

Fig. 84 Use a ratchet and an appropriate extension if necessary to loosen the spark plugs

Fig. 85 When the plug is loosened all the way, the rubber insert in the socket will hold the plug, however, use your finger to hold the plug in until it is out of the engine compartment

Fig. 86 Inspect the spark plugs upon removal and adjust the gap or replace as necessary

threading again. In small, hard to reach areas, an old spark plug wire and boot could be used as a threading tool. The boot will hold the plug while you twist the end of the wire and the wire is supple enough to twist before it would allow the plug to crossthread.

❋❋ WARNING

Do not use the spark plug socket to thread the plugs. Always carefully thread the plug by hand or using an old plug wire to prevent the possibility of crossthreading and damaging the cylinder head bore.

9. Carefully tighten the spark plug. If the plug you are installing is equipped with a crush washer, seat the plug, then tighten about ¼ turn to crush the washer. If you are installing a tapered seat plug, tighten the plug to specifications provided by the vehicle or plug manufacturer.

10. Apply a small amount of silicone dielectric compound to the end of the spark plug lead or inside the spark plug boot to prevent sticking, then install the boot to the spark plug and push until it clicks into place. The click may be felt or heard, then gently pull back on the boot to assure proper contact.

11. On the 2.3L and 2.4L engine, install the coil assembly.

INSPECTION & GAPPING

▶ **See Figures 87, 88, 89, 90 and 91**

Check the plugs for deposits and wear. If they are not going to be replaced, clean the plugs thoroughly. Remember that any kind of deposit will decrease the efficiency of the plug. Plugs can be cleaned on a spark plug cleaning machine, which can sometimes be found in service stations, or you can do an acceptable job of cleaning with a stiff brush. If the plugs are cleaned, the electrodes must be filed flat. Use an ignition points file, not an emery board or the like, which will leave deposits. The electrodes must be filed perfectly flat with sharp edges; rounded edges reduce the spark plug voltage by as much as 50%.

Check spark plug gap before installation. The ground electrode (the L-shaped one connected to the body of the plug) must be parallel to the center electrode and the specified size wire gauge (please refer to the Tune-Up Specifications chart for details) must pass between the electrodes with a slight drag.

➡ **NEVER adjust the gap on a used platinum type spark plug.**

Always check the gap on new plugs as they are not always set correctly at the factory. Do not use a flat feeler gauge when measuring the gap on a used plug, because the reading may be inaccurate. A round-wire type gapping tool is the

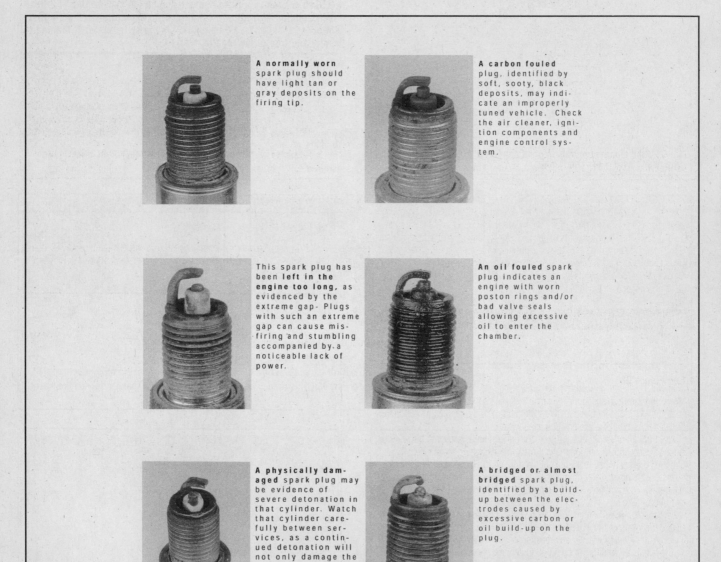

A normally worn spark plug should have light tan or gray deposits on the firing tip.

A carbon fouled plug, identified by soft, sooty, black deposits, may indicate an improperly tuned vehicle. Check the air cleaner, ignition components and engine control system.

This spark plug has been left in the engine too long, as evidenced by the extreme gap. Plugs with such an extreme gap can cause misfiring and stumbling accompanied by a noticeable lack of power.

An oil fouled spark plug indicates an engine with worn poston rings and/or bad valve seals allowing excessive oil to enter the chamber.

A physically damaged spark plug may be evidence of severe detonation in that cylinder. Watch that cylinder carefully between services, as a continued detonation will not only damage the plug, but could also damage the engine.

A bridged or almost bridged spark plug, identified by a build-up between the electrodes caused by excessive carbon or oil build-up on the plug.

TCCA1P40

Fig. 87 Inspect the spark plug to determine engine running conditions

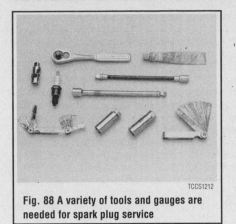

Fig. 88 A variety of tools and gauges are needed for spark plug service

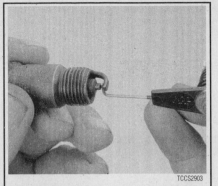

Fig. 89 Checking the spark plug gap with a feeler gauge

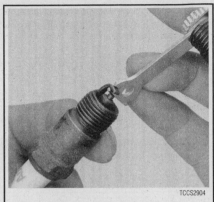

Fig. 90 Adjusting the spark plug gap

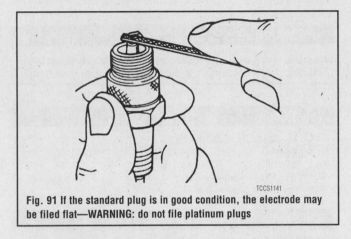

Fig. 91 If the standard plug is in good condition, the electrode may be filed flat—WARNING: do not file platinum plugs

Fig. 92 Checking individual plug wire resistance with a digital ohmmeter

best way to check the gap. The correct gauge should pass through the electrode gap with a slight drag. If you're in doubt, try one size smaller and one larger. The smaller gauge should go through easily, while the larger one shouldn't go through at all. Wire gapping tools usually have a bending tool attached. Use that to adjust the side electrode until the proper distance is obtained. Absolutely never attempt to bend the center electrode. Also, be careful not to bend the side electrode too far or too often as it may weaken and break off within the engine, requiring removal of the cylinder head to retrieve it.

Spark Plug Wires

TESTING

♦ See Figure 92

At every tune-up/inspection, visually check the spark plug cables for burns cuts, or breaks in the insulation. Check the boots and the nipples on the distributor cap and/or coil. Replace any damaged wiring.

Every 50,000 miles (80,000 km) or 60 months, the resistance of the wires should be checked with an ohmmeter. Wires with excessive resistance will cause misfiring, and may make the engine difficult to start in damp weather.

To check resistance, an ohmmeter should be used on each wire to test resistance between the end connectors. Remove and install/replace the wires in order, one-by-one.

Resistance on these wires should be 4,000–6,000 ohms per foot. To properly measure this, remove the wires from the plugs, coil, or the distributor cap. Do not pierce any ignition wire for any reason. Measure only from the two ends. Take the length and multiply it by 6,000 to achieve the maximum resistance allowable in each wire, resistance should not exceed this value. If resistance does exceed this value, replace the wire.

➡ Whenever the high tension wires are removed from the plugs, coil, or distributor, silicone grease must be applied to the boot before reconnection. Coat the entire interior surface with Ford silicone grease D7AZ-19A331-A or its equivalent.

REMOVAL & INSTALLATION

♦ See Figure 93

The 2.2L engine is the only engine covered in this manual that utilizes spark plug wires. the 2.3L and 2.4L engines have an integrated coil assembly that sits over the spark plugs.

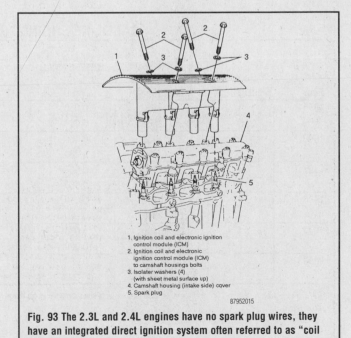

1. Ignition coil and electronic ignition control module (ICM)
2. Ignition coil and electronic ignition control module (ICM) to camshaft housings bolts
3. Isolater washers (4) (with sheet metal surface up)
4. Camshaft housing (intake side) cover
5. Spark plug

Fig. 93 The 2.3L and 2.4L engines have no spark plug wires, they have an integrated direct ignition system often referred to as "coil over plug"

➡If all of the wires must be disconnected from the spark plugs or from the distributor at the same time, be sure to tag the wires to assure proper reconnection.

When installing a new set of spark plug wires, replace the wires one at a time so there will be no mix-up. Start by replacing the longest cable first. Install the boot firmly over the spark plug. Route the wire exactly the same as the original. Insert the nipple firmly onto the tower on the ignition coil, and attach the wire separators to secure the wires. Be sure to apply silicone dielectric compound to the spark plug wire boots and tower connectors prior to installation.

Ignition Timing

GENERAL INFORMATION

The engines covered by this manual are equipped with distributorless ignitions, ignition timing is controlled by the Powertrain Control Module (PCM), as applicable. No adjustments are possible. If ignition timing is not within specification, there is a fault in the engine control system. Diagnose and repair the problem as necessary.

Ignition timing is the measurement, in degrees of crankshaft rotation, of the point at which the spark plugs fire in each of the cylinders. It is measured in degrees before or after Top Dead Center (TDC) of the compression stroke.

Ideally, the air/fuel mixture in the cylinder will be ignited by the spark plug just as the piston passes TDC of the compression stroke. If this happens, the piston will be at the beginning of the power stroke just as the compressed and ignited air/fuel mixture forces the piston down and turns the crankshaft. Because it takes a fraction of a second for the spark plug to ignite the mixture in the cylinder, the spark plug must fire a little before the piston reaches TDC. Otherwise, the mixture will not be completely ignited as the piston passes TDC and the full power of the explosion will not be used by the engine.

The timing measurement is given in degrees of crankshaft rotation before the piston reaches TDC (BTDC). If the setting for the ignition timing is 10 BTDC, each spark plug must fire 10 degrees before each piston reaches TDC. This only holds true, however, when the engine is at idle speed. The combustion process must be complete by 23° ATDC to maintain proper engine performance, fuel mileage, and low emissions.

As the engine speed increases, the pistons go faster. The spark plugs have to ignite the fuel even sooner if it is to be completely ignited when the piston reaches TDC. On all engines covered in this manual, spark timing changes are accomplished electronically by the Powertrain Control Module (PCM), based on input from engine sensors.

If the ignition is set too far advanced (BTDC), the ignition and expansion of the fuel in the cylinder will occur too soon and tend to force the piston down while it is still traveling up. This causes pre ignition or "knocking and pinging". If the ignition spark is set too far retarded, or after TDC (ATDC), the piston will have already started on its way down when the fuel is ignited. The piston will be forced down for only a portion of its travel, resulting in poor engine performance and lack of power.

Timing marks or scales can be found on the rim of the crankshaft pulley and the timing cover. The marks on the pulley correspond to the position of the piston in the No. 1 cylinder. A stroboscopic (dynamic) timing light is hooked onto the No. 1 cylinder spark plug wire (2.2L engine only, on the 2.3L/2.4L engines, special adapters are needed) . Every time the spark plug fires, the timing light flashes. By aiming the light at the timing marks while the engine is running, the exact position of the piston within the cylinder can be easily read (the flash of light makes the mark on the pulley appear to be standing still). Proper timing is indicated when the mark and scale are in specified alignment.

✳✳ WARNING

When checking timing with the engine running, take care not to get the timing light wires tangled in the fan blades and/or drive belts.

Valve Lash

All of the engines are equipped with hydraulic valve lifters that do not require periodic valve lash adjustment. Adjustment to zero lash is maintained automatically by hydraulic pressure in the lifters. Also, the rocker arm retaining nuts are tightened to a specific torque value (refer to the rocker arm procedure) to provide proper rocker arm placement.

Idle Speed Adjustment

The engines covered by this manual utilize sophisticated fuel injection systems in which the PCM utilizes information from various sensors to control idle speed and air/fuel mixtures. No periodic adjustments are either necessary or possible on these systems. If a problem is suspected, please refer to Sections 4 of this manual for more information on electronic engine controls and fuel injection.

GASOLINE ENGINE TUNE-UP SPECIFICATIONS

Year	Engine ID/VIN	Engine Displacement Liters (cc)	Spark Plugs Gap (in.)	Ignition Timing (deg.) MT	Ignition Timing (deg.) AT	Fuel Pump (psi)	Idle Speed (rpm) MT	Idle Speed (rpm) AT	Valve Clearance In.	Valve Clearance Ex.
1995	4	2.2 (2180)	0.060	①	①	41-47	①	①	HYD	HYD
	D	2.3 (2262)	0.060	①	①	41-47	①	①	HYD	HYD
1996	4	2.2 (2180)	0.060	①	①	41-47	①	①	HYD	HYD
	T	2.4 (2392)	0.060	①	①	41-47	①	①	HYD	HYD
1997	4	2.2 (2180)	0.060	①	①	41-47	①	①	HYD	HYD
	T	2.4 (2392)	0.060	①	①	41-47	①	①	HYD	HYD
1998	4	2.2 (2180)	0.060	①	①	41-47	①	①	HYD	HYD
	T	2.4 (2392)	0.060	①	①	41-47	①	①	HYD	HYD
1999	4	2.2 (2180)	0.060	①	①	41-47	①	①	HYD	HYD
	T	2.4 (2392)	0.060	①	①	41-47	①	①	HYD	HYD
2000	4	2.2 (2180)	0.060	①	①	41-47	①	①	HYD	HYD
	T	2.4 (2392)	0.060	①	①	41-47	①	①	HYD	HYD

NOTE: The Vehicle Emission Control Information label often reflects specification changes made during production. The label figures must be used if they differ from those in this chart.

HYD - Hydraulic

① Refer to Vehicle Emission Control Information label

91141C03

Air Conditioning System

SYSTEM SERVICE & REPAIR

▶ **See Figure 94**

➡**It is recommended that the A/C system be serviced by an EPA Section 609 certified automotive technician utilizing a refrigerant recovery/recycling machine.**

The do-it-yourselfer should not service his/her own vehicle's A/C system for many reasons, including legal concerns, personal injury, environmental damage and cost. The following are some of the reasons why you may decide not to service your own vehicle's A/C system.

According to the U.S. Clean Air Act, it is a federal crime to service or repair (involving the refrigerant) a Motor Vehicle Air Conditioning (MVAC) system for money without being EPA certified. It is also illegal to vent R-134a refrigerant into the atmosphere.

State and/or local laws may be more strict than the federal regulations, so be sure to check with your state and/or local authorities for further information. For further federal information on the legality of servicing your A/C system, call the EPA Stratospheric Ozone Hotline.

➡**Federal law dictates that a fine of up to $25,000 may be levied on people convicted of venting refrigerant into the atmosphere. Additionally, the EPA may pay up to $10,000 for information or services leading to a criminal conviction of the violation of these laws.**

When servicing an A/C system you run the risk of handling or coming in contact with refrigerant, which may result in skin or eye irritation or frostbite. Although low in toxicity (due to chemical stability), inhalation of concentrated refrigerant fumes is dangerous and can result in death; cases of fatal cardiac arrhythmia have been reported in people accidentally subjected to high levels of refrigerant. Some early symptoms include loss of concentration and drowsiness.

Also, refrigerants can decompose at high temperatures (near gas heaters or open flame), which may result in hydrofluoric acid, hydrochloric acid and phosgene (a fatal nerve gas).

R-134a refrigerant is a greenhouse gas which, if allowed to vent into the atmosphere, will contribute to global warming (the Greenhouse Effect).

It is usually more economically feasible to have a certified MVAC automotive technician perform A/C system service to your vehicle. While it is illegal to service an A/C system without the proper equipment, the home mechanic would have to purchase an expensive refrigerant recovery/recycling machine to service his/her own vehicle.

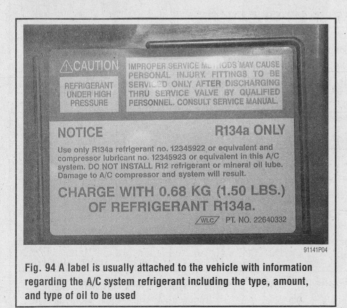

Fig. 94 A label is usually attached to the vehicle with information regarding the A/C system refrigerant including the type, amount, and type of oil to be used

PREVENTIVE MAINTENANCE

Although the A/C system should not be serviced by the do-it-yourselfer, preventive maintenance can be practiced and A/C system inspections can be performed to help maintain the efficiency of the vehicle's A/C system. For preventive maintenance, perform the following:

• The easiest and most important preventive maintenance for your A/C system is to be sure that it is used on a regular basis. Running the system for five minutes each month (no matter what the season) will help ensure that the seals and all internal components remain lubricated.

➡**Some newer vehicles automatically operate the A/C system compressor whenever the windshield defroster is activated. When running, the compressor lubricates the A/C system components; therefore, the A/C system would not need to be operated each month.**

• In order to prevent heater core freeze-up during A/C operation, it is necessary to maintain a proper antifreeze protection. Use a hand-held coolant tester (hydrometer) to periodically check the condition of the antifreeze in your engine's cooling system.

➡**Antifreeze should not be used longer than the manufacturer specifies.**

• For efficient operation of an air conditioned vehicle's cooling system, the radiator cap should have a holding pressure which meets manufacturer's specifications. A cap which fails to hold these pressures should be replaced.

• Any obstruction of or damage to the condenser configuration will restrict air flow which is essential to its efficient operation. It is, therefore, a good rule to keep this unit clean and in proper physical shape.

➡**Bug screens which are mounted in front of the condenser (unless they are original equipment) are regarded as obstructions.**

• The condensation drain tube expels any water, which accumulates on the bottom of the evaporator housing, into the engine compartment. If this tube is obstructed, the air conditioning performance can be restricted and condensation buildup can spill over onto the vehicle's floor.

SYSTEM INSPECTION

Although the A/C system should not be serviced by the do-it-yourselfer, preventive maintenance can be practiced and A/C system inspections can be performed to help maintain the efficiency of the vehicle's A/C system. For A/C system inspection, perform the following:

The easiest and often most important check for the air conditioning system consists of a visual inspection of the system components. Visually inspect the air conditioning system for refrigerant leaks, damaged compressor clutch, abnormal compressor drive belt tension and/or condition, plugged evaporator drain tube, blocked condenser fins, disconnected or broken wires, blown fuses, corroded connections and poor insulation.

A refrigerant leak will usually appear as an oily residue at the leakage point in the system. The oily residue soon picks up dust or dirt particles from the surrounding air and appears greasy. Through time, this will build up and appear to be a heavy dirt impregnated grease.

For a thorough visual and operational inspection, check the following:

• Check the surface of the radiator and condenser for dirt, leaves or other material which might block air flow.

• Check for kinks in hoses and lines. Check the system for leaks.

• Make sure the drive belt is properly tensioned. When the air conditioning is operating, make sure the drive belt is free of noise or slippage.

• Make sure the blower motor operates at all appropriate positions, then check for distribution of the air from all outlets with the blower on **HIGH** or **MAX**.

➡**Keep in mind that under conditions of high humidity, air discharged from the A/C vents may not feel as cold as expected, even if the system is working properly. This is because vaporized moisture in humid air retains heat more effectively than dry air, thereby making humid air more difficult to cool.**

• Make sure the air passage selection lever is operating correctly. Start the engine and warm it to normal operating temperature, then make sure the temperature selection lever is operating correctly.

Windshield Wipers

ELEMENT (REFILL) CARE & REPLACEMENT

▶ **See Figures 95 thru 104**

For maximum effectiveness and longest element life, the windshield and wiper blades should be kept clean. Dirt, tree sap, road tar and so on will cause streaking, smearing and blade deterioration if left on the glass. It is advisable to wash the windshield carefully with a commercial glass cleaner at least once a month. Wipe off the rubber blades with the wet rag afterwards. Do not attempt to move wipers across the windshield by hand; damage to the motor and drive mechanism will result.

To inspect and/or replace the wiper blade elements, place the wiper switch in the **LOW** speed position and the ignition switch in the **ACC** position. When the wiper blades are approximately vertical on the windshield, turn the ignition switch to **OFF**.

Examine the wiper blade elements. If they are found to be cracked, broken or torn, they should be replaced immediately. Replacement intervals will vary with usage, although ozone deterioration usually limits element life to about one year. If the wiper pattern is smeared or streaked, or if the blade chatters across the glass, the elements should be replaced. It is easiest and most sensible to replace the elements in pairs.

If your vehicle is equipped with aftermarket blades, there are several different types of refills and your vehicle might have any kind. Aftermarket blades and arms rarely use the exact same type blade or refill as the original equipment. Here are some typical aftermarket blades; not all may be available for your vehicle:

The Anco(type uses a release button that is pushed down to allow the refill

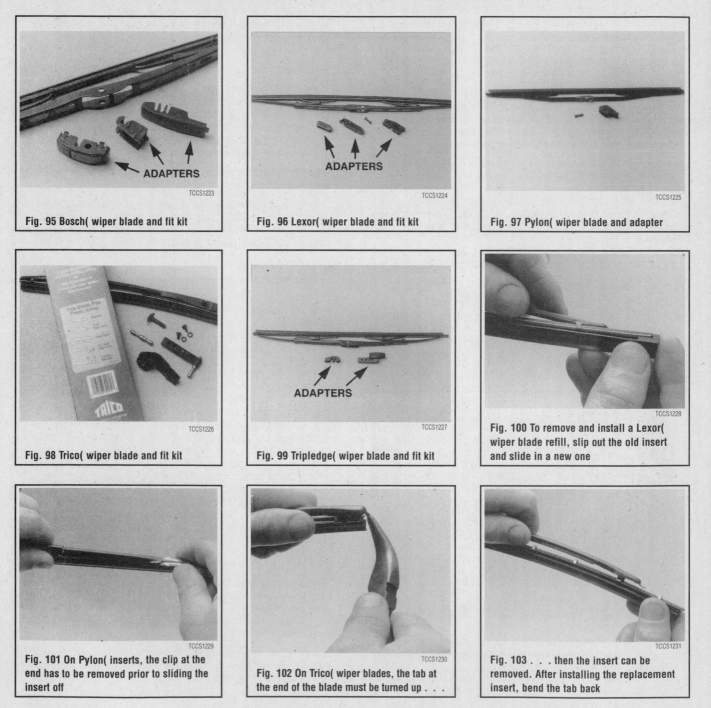

Fig. 95 Bosch(wiper blade and fit kit — TCCS1223

Fig. 96 Lexor(wiper blade and fit kit — TCCS1224

Fig. 97 Pylon(wiper blade and adapter — TCCS1225

Fig. 98 Trico(wiper blade and fit kit — TCCS1226

Fig. 99 Tripledge(wiper blade and fit kit — TCCS1227

Fig. 100 To remove and install a Lexor(wiper blade refill, slip out the old insert and slide in a new one — TCCS1228

Fig. 101 On Pylon(inserts, the clip at the end has to be removed prior to sliding the insert off — TCCS1229

Fig. 102 On Trico(wiper blades, the tab at the end of the blade must be turned up . . . — TCCS1230

Fig. 103 . . . then the insert can be removed. After installing the replacement insert, bend the tab back — TCCS1231

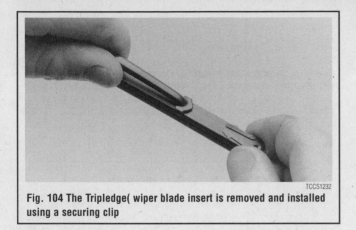

Fig. 104 The Tripledge(wiper blade insert is removed and installed using a securing clip

to slide out of the yoke jaws. The new refill slides back into the frame and locks in place.

Some Trico(refills are removed by locating where the metal backing strip or the refill is wider. Insert a small screwdriver blade between the frame and metal backing strip. Press down to release the refill from the retaining tab.

Other types of Trico(refills have two metal tabs which are unlocked by squeezing them together. The rubber filler can then be withdrawn from the frame jaws. A new refill is installed by inserting the refill into the front frame jaws and sliding it rearward to engage the remaining frame jaws. There are usually four jaws; be certain when installing that the refill is engaged in all of them. At the end of its travel, the tabs will lock into place on the front jaws of the wiper blade frame.

Another type of refill is made from polycarbonate. The refill has a simple locking device at one end which flexes downward out of the groove into which the jaws of the holder fit, allowing easy release. By sliding the new refill through all the jaws and pushing through the slight resistance when it reaches the end of its travel, the refill will lock into position.

To replace the Tridon(refill, it is necessary to remove the wiper blade. This refill has a plastic backing strip with a notch about 1 in. (25mm) from the end. Hold the blade (frame) on a hard surface so that the frame is tightly bowed. Grip the tip of the backing strip and pull up while twisting counterclockwise. The backing strip will snap out of the retaining tab. Do this for the remaining tabs until the refill is free of the blade. The length of these refills is molded into the end and they should be replaced with identical types.

Regardless of the type of refill used, be sure to follow the part manufacturer's instructions closely. Make sure that all of the frame jaws are engaged as the refill is pushed into place and locked. If the metal blade holder and frame are allowed to touch the glass during wiper operation, the glass will be scratched.

Tires and Wheels

Common sense and good driving habits will afford maximum tire life. Fast starts, sudden stops and hard cornering are hard on tires and will shorten their useful life span. Make sure that you don't overload the vehicle or run with incorrect pressure in the tires. Both of these practices will increase tread wear.

➡ **For optimum tire life, keep the tires properly inflated, rotate them often and have the wheel alignment checked periodically.**

Inspect your tires frequently. Be especially careful to watch for bubbles in the tread or sidewall, deep cuts or underinflation. Replace any tires with bubbles in the sidewall. If cuts are so deep that they penetrate to the cords, discard the tire. Any cut in the sidewall of a radial tire renders it unsafe. Also look for uneven tread wear patterns that may indicate the front end is out of alignment or that the tires are out of balance.

TIRE ROTATION

▶ **See Figures 105 and 106**

Tires must be rotated periodically to equalize wear patterns that vary with a tire's position on the vehicle. Tires will also wear in an uneven way as the front steering/suspension system wears to the point where the alignment should be reset.

Rotating the tires will ensure maximum life for the tires as a set, so you will not have to discard a tire early due to wear on only part of the tread. Regular rotation is required to equalize wear.

When rotating "unidirectional tires," make sure that they always roll in the same direction. This means that a tire used on the left side of the vehicle must not be switched to the right side and vice-versa. Such tires should only be rotated front-to-rear or rear-to-front, while always remaining on the same side of the vehicle. These tires are marked on the sidewall as to the direction of rotation; observe the marks when reinstalling the tire(s).

Some styled or "mag" wheels may have different offsets front to rear. In these cases, the rear wheels must not be used up front and vice-versa. Furthermore, if these wheels are equipped with unidirectional tires, they cannot be rotated unless the tire is remounted for the proper direction of rotation.

➡ **The compact or space-saver spare is strictly for emergency use. It must never be included in the tire rotation or placed on the vehicle for everyday use.**

TIRE DESIGN

▶ **See Figures 107 and 108**

For maximum satisfaction, tires should be used in sets of four. Mixing of different types (radial, bias-belted, fiberglass belted) must be avoided. In most cases, the vehicle manufacturer has designated a type of tire on which the vehicle will perform best. Your first choice when replacing tires should be to use the same type of tire that the manufacturer recommends.

When radial tires are used, tire sizes and wheel diameters should be selected to maintain ground clearance and tire load capacity equivalent to the original specified tire. Radial tires should always be used in sets of four.

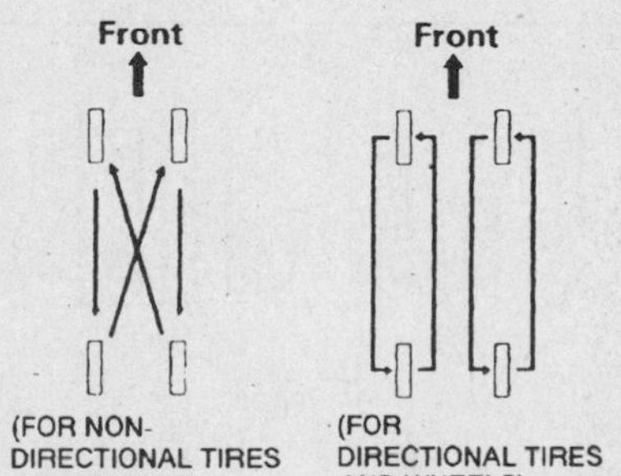

Front   **Front**

(FOR NON-DIRECTIONAL TIRES AND WHEELS)   (FOR DIRECTIONAL TIRES AND WHEELS)

TCCS1260

Fig. 105 Compact spare tires must NEVER be used in the rotation pattern

* TCCS1234

Fig. 106 Unidirectional tires are identifiable by sidewall arrows and/or the word "rotation"

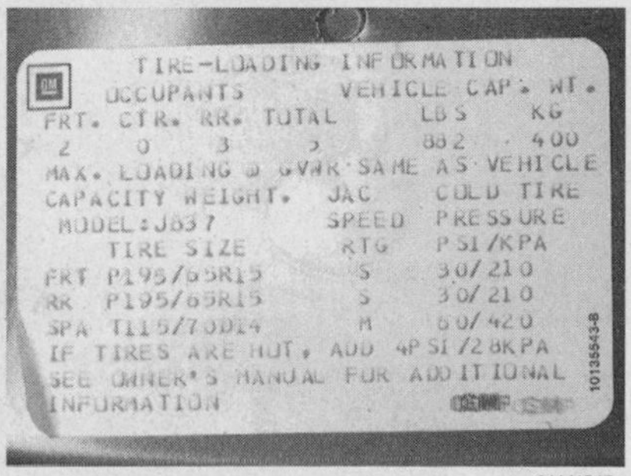

TIRE-LOADING INFORMATION

91141P17

Fig. 107 The tire certification label can be found in the door jamb, usually on the passenger side of the vehicle and contains information regarding the tires including factory recommended pressures

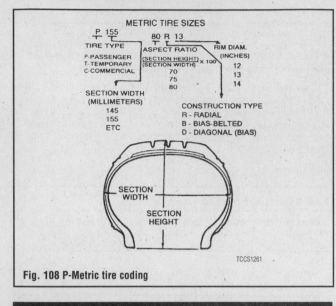

Fig. 108 P-Metric tire coding

✳✳ CAUTION

Radial tires should never be used on only the front axle.

When selecting tires, pay attention to the original size as marked on the tire. Most tires are described using an industry size code sometimes referred to as P-Metric. This allows the exact identification of the tire specifications, regardless of the manufacturer. If selecting a different tire size or brand, remember to check the installed tire for any sign of interference with the body or suspension while the vehicle is stopping, turning sharply or heavily loaded.

Snow Tires

Good radial tires can produce a big advantage in slippery weather, but in snow, a street radial tire does not have sufficient tread to provide traction and control. The small grooves of a street tire quickly pack with snow and the tire behaves like a billiard ball on a marble floor. The more open, chunky tread of a snow tire will self-clean as the tire turns, providing much better grip on snowy surfaces.

To satisfy municipalities requiring snow tires during weather emergencies, most snow tires carry either an M + S designation after the tire size stamped on the sidewall, or the designation "all-season." In general, no change in tire size is necessary when buying snow tires.

Most manufacturers strongly recommend the use of 4 snow tires on their vehicles for reasons of stability. If snow tires are fitted only to the drive wheels, the opposite end of the vehicle may become very unstable when braking or turning on slippery surfaces. This instability can lead to unpleasant endings if the driver can't counteract the slide in time.

Note that snow tires, whether 2 or 4, will affect vehicle handling in all non-snow situations. The stiffer, heavier snow tires will noticeably change the turn-ing and braking characteristics of the vehicle. Once the snow tires are installed, you must re-learn the behavior of the vehicle and drive accordingly.

➡**Consider buying extra wheels on which to mount the snow tires. Once done, the "snow wheels" can be installed and removed as needed. This eliminates the potential damage to tires or wheels from seasonal removal and installation. Even if your vehicle has styled wheels, see if inexpensive steel wheels are available. Although the look of the vehicle will change, the expensive wheels will be protected from salt, curb hits and pothole damage.**

TIRE STORAGE

If they are mounted on wheels, store the tires at proper inflation pressure. All tires should be kept in a cool, dry place. If they are stored in the garage or basement, do not let them stand on a concrete floor; set them on strips of wood, a mat or a large stack of newspaper. Keeping them away from direct moisture is of paramount importance. Tires should not be stored upright, but in a flat position.

INFLATION & INSPECTION

▶ **See Figures 109 thru 116**

The importance of proper tire inflation cannot be overemphasized. A tire employs air as part of its structure. It is designed around the supporting strength of the air at a specified pressure. For this reason, improper inflation drastically reduces the tire's ability to perform as intended. A tire will lose some air in day-to-day use; having to add a few pounds of air periodically is not necessarily a sign of a leaking tire.

Two items should be a permanent fixture in every glove compartment: an accurate tire pressure gauge and a tread depth gauge. Check the tire pressure (including the spare) regularly with a pocket type gauge. Too often, the gauge on the end of the air hose at your corner garage is not accurate because it suffers too much abuse. Always check tire pressure when the tires are cold, as pressure increases with temperature. If you must move the vehicle to check the

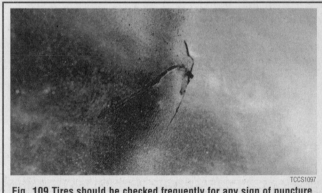

Fig. 109 Tires should be checked frequently for any sign of puncture or damage

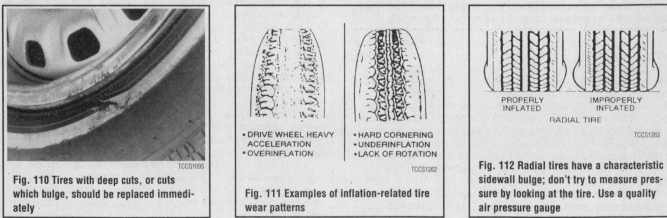

Fig. 110 Tires with deep cuts, or cuts which bulge, should be replaced immediately

- DRIVE WHEEL HEAVY ACCELERATION
- OVERINFLATION

- HARD CORNERING
- UNDERINFLATION
- LACK OF ROTATION

Fig. 111 Examples of inflation-related tire wear patterns

PROPERLY INFLATED IMPROPERLY INFLATED

RADIAL TIRE

Fig. 112 Radial tires have a characteristic sidewall bulge; don't try to measure pressure by looking at the tire. Use a quality air pressure gauge

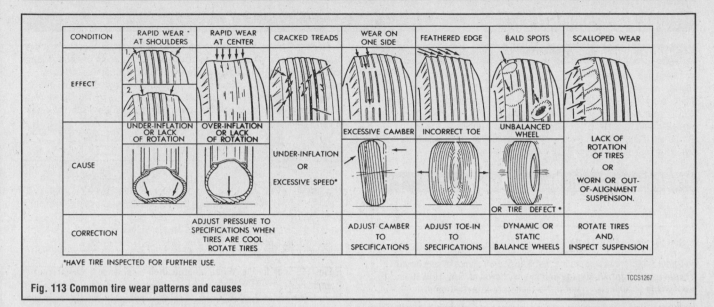

CONDITION	RAPID WEAR AT SHOULDERS	RAPID WEAR AT CENTER	CRACKED TREADS	WEAR ON ONE SIDE	FEATHERED EDGE	BALD SPOTS	SCALLOPED WEAR
EFFECT							
CAUSE	UNDER-INFLATION OR LACK OF ROTATION	OVER-INFLATION OR LACK OF ROTATION	UNDER-INFLATION OR EXCESSIVE SPEED*	EXCESSIVE CAMBER	INCORRECT TOE	UNBALANCED WHEEL OR TIRE DEFECT *	LACK OF ROTATION OF TIRES OR WORN OR OUT-OF-ALIGNMENT SUSPENSION.
CORRECTION		ADJUST PRESSURE TO SPECIFICATIONS WHEN TIRES ARE COOL ROTATE TIRES		ADJUST CAMBER TO SPECIFICATIONS	ADJUST TOE-IN TO SPECIFICATIONS	DYNAMIC OR STATIC BALANCE WHEELS	ROTATE TIRES AND INSPECT SUSPENSION

*HAVE TIRE INSPECTED FOR FURTHER USE.

TCCS1267

Fig. 113 Common tire wear patterns and causes

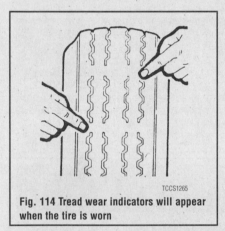

Fig. 114 Tread wear indicators will appear when the tire is worn

TCCS1265

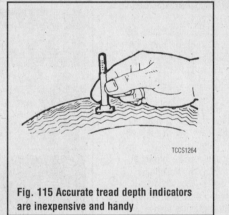

TCCS1264

Fig. 115 Accurate tread depth indicators are inexpensive and handy

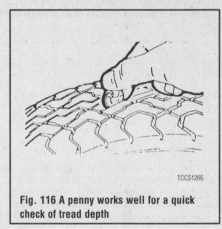

TCCS1266

Fig. 116 A penny works well for a quick check of tread depth

tire inflation, do not drive more than a mile before checking. A cold tire is generally one that has not been driven for more than three hours.

A plate or sticker is normally provided somewhere in the vehicle (door post, hood, tailgate or trunk lid) which shows the proper pressure for the tires. Never counteract excessive pressure build-up by bleeding off air pressure (letting some air out). This will cause the tire to run hotter and wear quicker.

> ✳✳ **CAUTION**
>
> **Never exceed the maximum tire pressure embossed on the tire! This is the pressure to be used when the tire is at maximum loading, but it is rarely the correct pressure for everyday driving. Consult the owner's manual or the tire pressure sticker for the correct tire pressure.**

Once you've maintained the correct tire pressures for several weeks, you'll be familiar with the vehicle's braking and handling personality. Slight adjustments in tire pressures can fine-tune these characteristics, but never change the cold pressure specification by more than 2 psi. A slightly softer tire pressure will give a softer ride but also yield lower fuel mileage. A slightly harder tire will give crisper dry road handling but can cause skidding on wet surfaces. Unless you're fully attuned to the vehicle, stick to the recommended inflation pressures.

All tires made since 1968 have built-in tread wear indicator bars that show up as ½ in. (13mm) wide smooth bands across the tire when 1/16 in. (1.5mm) of tread remains. The appearance of tread wear indicators means that the tires should be replaced. In fact, many states have laws prohibiting the use of tires with less than this amount of tread.

You can check your own tread depth with an inexpensive gauge or by using a Lincoln head penny. Slip the Lincoln penny (with Lincoln's head upside-down)

into several tread grooves. If you can see the top of Lincoln's head in 2 adjacent grooves, the tire has less than 1/16 in. (1.5mm) tread left and should be replaced. You can measure snow tires in the same manner by using the "tails" side of the Lincoln penny. If you can see the top of the Lincoln memorial, it's time to replace the snow tire(s).

CARE OF SPECIAL WHEELS

If you have invested money in magnesium, aluminum alloy or sport wheels, special precautions should be taken to make sure your investment is not wasted and that your special wheels look good for the life of the vehicle.

Special wheels are easily damaged and/or scratched. Occasionally check the rims for cracking, impact damage or air leaks. If any of these are found, replace the wheel. But in order to prevent this type of damage and the costly replacement of a special wheel, observe the following precautions:

• Use extra care not to damage the wheels during removal, installation, balancing, etc. After removal of the wheels from the vehicle, place them on a mat or other protective surface. If they are to be stored for any length of time, support them on strips of wood. Never store tires and wheels upright; the tread may develop flat spots.

• When driving, watch for hazards; it doesn't take much to crack a wheel.

• When washing, use a mild soap or non-abrasive dish detergent (keeping in mind that detergent tends to remove wax). Avoid cleansers with abrasives or the use of hard brushes. There are many cleaners and polishes for special wheels.

• If possible, remove the wheels during the winter. Salt and sand used for snow removal can severely damage the finish of a wheel.

• Make certain the recommended lug nut torque is never exceeded or the wheel may crack. Never use snow chains on special wheels; severe scratching will occur.

FLUIDS AND LUBRICANTS

Fluid Disposal

Used fluids such as engine oil, transmission fluid, antifreeze and brake fluid are hazardous wastes and must be disposed of properly. Before draining any fluids, consult with your local authorities; in many areas, waste oil, antifreeze, etc. is being accepted as a part of recycling programs. A number of service stations and auto parts stores are also accepting waste fluids for recycling.

Be sure of the recycling center's policies before draining any fluids, as many will not accept different fluids that have been mixed together.

Fuel and Engine Oil Recommendations

ENGINE OIL

▶ See Figures 117, 118 and 119

➡General Motors recommends that SAE 5W-30 viscosity engine oil should be used for all climate conditions, however, SAE 10W-30 is acceptable for vehicles operated in moderate-to-hot climates.

When adding oil to the crankcase or changing the oil or filter, it is important that oil of an equal quality to original equipment be used in your car. The use of inferior oils may void the warranty, damage your engine, or both.

The SAE (Society of Automotive Engineers) grade number of oil indicates the viscosity of the oil (its ability to lubricate at a given temperature). The lower the SAE number, the lighter the oil; the lower the viscosity, the easier it is to crank the engine in cold weather but the less the oil will lubricate and protect the engine in high temperatures. This number is marked on every oil container.

Oil viscosity's should be chosen from those oils recommended for the lowest anticipated temperatures during the oil change interval. Due to the need for an oil that embodies both good lubrication at high temperatures and easy cranking in cold weather, multigrade oils have been developed. Basically, a multigrade oil is thinner at low temperatures and thicker at high temperatures. For example, a 10W-40 oil (the W stands for winter) exhibits the characteristics of a 10 weight (SAE 10) oil when the car is first started and the oil is cold. Its lighter weight allows it to travel to the lubricating surfaces quicker and offer less resistance to starter motor cranking than, say, a straight 30 weight (SAE 30) oil. But after the engine reaches operating temperature, the 10W-40 oil begins acting like straight 40 weight (SAE 40) oil, its heavier weight providing greater lubrication with less chance of foaming than a straight 30 weight oil.

Fig. 118 Look for the API oil identification label when choosing your engine oil

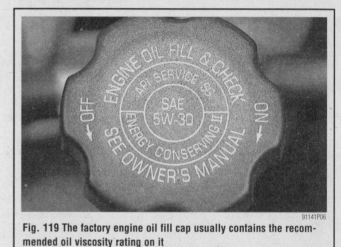

Fig. 119 The factory engine oil fill cap usually contains the recommended oil viscosity rating on it

The API (American Petroleum Institute) designations, also found on the oil container, indicates the classification of engine oil used under certain given operating conditions. Only oils designated for use Service SG heavy duty detergent should be used in your car. Oils of the SG type perform many functions inside the engine besides their basic lubrication. Through a balanced system of metallic detergents and polymeric dispersants, the oil prevents high and low temperature deposits and also keeps sludge and dirt particles in suspension. Acids, particularly sulfuric acid, as well as other by-products of engine combustion are neutralized by the oil. If these acids are allowed to concentrate, they can cause corrosion and rapid wear of the internal engine parts.

✵✵ CAUTION

Non-detergent motor oils or straight mineral oils should not be used in your General Motors gasoline engine.

Synthetic Oil

There are many excellent synthetic and fuel-efficient oils currently available that can provide better gas mileage, longer service life and, in some cases, better engine protection. These benefits do not come without a few hitches, however; the main one being the price of synthetic oil, which is significantly more expensive than conventional oil.

Synthetic oil is not for every car and every type of driving, so you should consider your engine's condition and your type of driving. Also, check your car's warranty conditions regarding the use of synthetic oils.

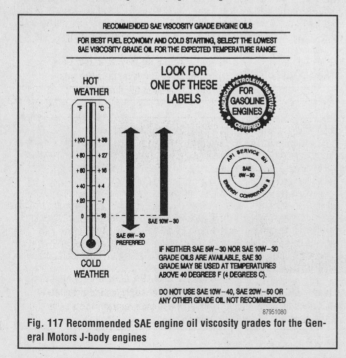

Fig. 117 Recommended SAE engine oil viscosity grades for the General Motors J-body engines

FUEL

Your vehicle is designed to operate using regular unleaded fuel with a minimum of 87 octane. General Motors warns that using gasoline with an octane rating lower than 87 can cause persistent and heavy knocking, and may cause internal engine damage.

If your vehicle is having problems with rough idle or hesitation when the engine is cold, it may be caused by low volatility fuel. If this occurs, try a different grade or brand of fuel.

OPERATION IN FOREIGN COUNTRIES

If you plan to drive your car outside the United States or Canada, there is a possibility that fuels will be too low in anti-knock quality and could produce engine damage. It is wise to consult with local authorities upon arrival in a foreign country to determine the best fuels available. Some gasoline in foreign countries contains lead. **DO NOT** use leaded gasoline or serious damage may occur which would not be covered by your factory warranty.

Engine

OIL LEVEL CHECK

▶ **See Figures 120, 121, 122 and 123**

✳✳ CAUTION

The EPA warns that prolonged contact with used engine oil may cause a number of skin disorders, including cancer! You should make every effort to minimize your exposure to used engine oil.

Protective gloves should be worn when changing the oil. Wash your hands and any other exposed skin areas as soon as possible after exposure to used engine oil. Soap and water, or waterless hand cleaner should be used.

The engine oil dipstick is also the fill cap on the 2.2L engine and is located in front of the engine between the engine and the radiator.

The engine oil dipstick on the 2.3L and 2.4L engines is located in the rear of the engine between the engine and the firewall.

Engine oil level should be checked every time you put fuel in the vehicle or are under the hood performing other maintenance.

1. Park the vehicle on a level surface.
2. The engine may be either hot or cold when checking oil level. However, if it is hot, wait a few minutes after the engine has been turned **OFF** to allow the oil to drain back into the crankcase. If the engine is cold, do not start it before checking the oil level.
3. Open the hood and locate the engine oil dipstick. Pull the dipstick from its tube, wipe it clean, and reinsert it into the tube. Make sure the dipstick is fully inserted.
4. Pull the dipstick from its tube again. Holding it horizontally, read the oil level. The oil should be between the MIN and MAX mark. If the oil is below the MIN mark, add oil of the proper viscosity through the oil fill hole.
5. Replace the dipstick, and check the level again after adding any oil. Be careful not to overfill the crankcase. Approximately one quart of oil will raise the level from the low mark to the high mark. Excess oil will generally be consumed at an accelerated rate even if no damage to the engine seals occurs.

OIL & FILTER CHANGE

▶ **See Figures 124 thru 131**

The oil and filter should be changed every 7,500 miles (12,500 km) under normal service and every 3,000 miles (5,000 km) under severe service.

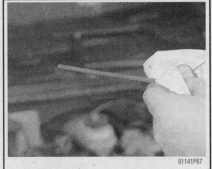

Fig. 120 Turn the oil fill cap and remove it, the dipstick is attached to the cap—2.2L engine only

Fig. 121 Wipe the dipstick off with a rag, reinsert the dipstick and check the level on the dipstick

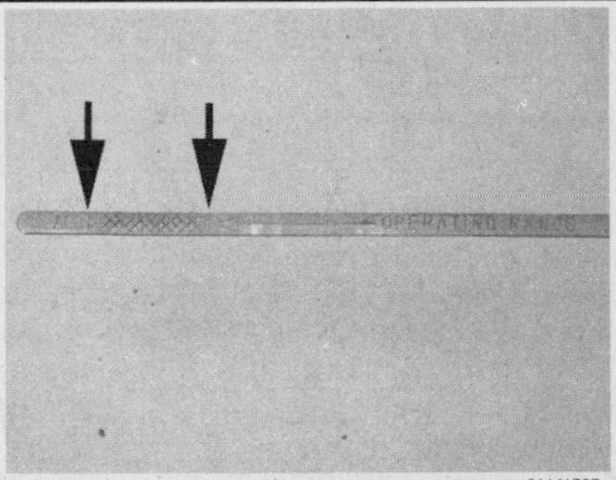

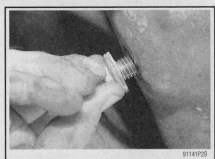

Fig. 122 The oil level is in the "safe" range when the level is in the cross-hatched area of the dipstick

Fig. 123 Use a funnel to avoid spillage and add the oil into the filler/dipstick tube

Fig. 124 Use a wrench to loosen the drain plug located on the oil pan, typically the drain plug requires a 13mm wrench

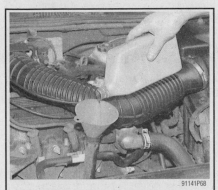

Fig. 125 When the drain plug is almost all the way loose, apply inward pressure to the plug and then remove it in a swift motion . . .

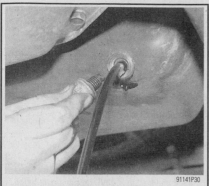

Fig. 126 . . . allowing the oil to flow out into a suitable container

Fig. 127 Inspect the threads on the drain plug and also the gasket and replace as necessary

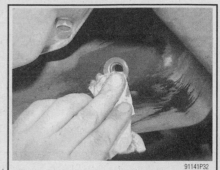

Fig. 128 Wipe the oil pan clean after the oil has completely drained out and inspect the threads for the drain plug

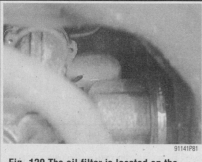

Fig. 129 The oil filter is located on the side of the block, in the rear of the engine compartment and is accessible from beneath the vehicle—2.2L engine

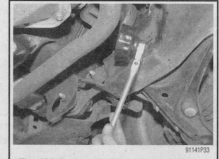

Fig. 130 A cup style filter wrench is best suited to loosen the filter, break the filter loose, continue turning it by hand until it is free and . . .

Fig. 131 . . . remove the filter from the engine

✳✳ CAUTION

The EPA warns that prolonged contact with used engine oil may cause a number of skin disorders, including cancer! You should make every effort to minimize your exposure to used engine oil. Protective gloves should be worn when changing the oil. Wash your hands and any other exposed skin areas as soon as possible after exposure to used engine oil. Soap and water, or waterless hand cleaner should be used.

➡ The engine oil and oil filter should be changed at the recommended intervals on the Maintenance Chart. Though some manufacturer's have at times recommended changing the filter only at every other oil change, Chilton recommends that you always change the filter with the oil. The benefit of fresh oil is quickly lost if the old filter is clogged and unable to do its job. Also, leaving the old filter in place leaves a significant amount of dirty oil in the system.

The oil should be changed more frequently if the vehicle is being operated in a very dusty area. Before draining the oil, make sure that the engine is at operating temperature. Hot oil will hold more impurities in suspension and will flow better, allowing the removal of more oil and dirt.

It is a good idea to warm the engine oil first so it will flow better. This can be accomplished by 15–20 (24–32 km) miles of highway driving. Fluid which is warmed to normal operating temperature will flow faster, drain more completely and remove more contaminants from the engine.

1. Raise and support the vehicle safely on jackstands. Make sure the oil drain plug is at the lowest point on the oil pan. If not, you may have to raise the vehicle slightly higher on one jackstand (side) than the other.

2. Before you crawl under the vehicle, take a look at where you will be working and gather all the necessary tools, such as a few wrenches or a ratchet and strip of sockets, the drain pan, some clean rags and, if the oil filter is more accessible from underneath the vehicle, you will also want to grab a bottle of oil, the new filter and a filter wrench at this time.

3. Position the drain pan beneath the oil pan drain plug. Keep in mind that the fast flowing oil, which will spill out as you pull the plug from the pan, will flow with enough force that it could miss the pan. Position the drain pan accordingly and be ready to move the pan more directly beneath the plug as the oil flow lessens to a trickle.

4. Loosen the drain plug with a wrench (or socket and driver), then carefully unscrew the plug with your fingers. Use a rag to shield your fingers from the heat. Push in on the plug as you unscrew it so you can feel when all of the screw threads are out of the hole (and so you will keep the oil from seeping past the threads until you are ready to remove the plug). You can then remove the plug quickly to avoid having hot oil run down your arm. This will also help assure that have the plug in your hand, not in the bottom of a pan of hot oil.

✳✳ CAUTION

Be careful of the oil; when at operating temperature, it is hot enough to cause a severe burn.

5. Allow the oil to drain until nothing but a few drops come out of the drain hole. Check the drain plug to make sure the threads and sealing surface are not damaged. Carefully thread the plug into position and tighten it with a torque wrench to 35 ft. lbs. (45 Nm) on the 2.2L Engine and 19 ft. lbs. (26 Nm) on the 2.3/2.4L engines. If a torque wrench is not available, snug the drain plug and give a slight additional turn. You don't want the plug to fall out (as you would quickly become stranded), but the pan threads are EASILY stripped from overtightening (and this can be time consuming and/or costly to fix).

6. To remove the filter, you may need an oil filter wrench since the filter may have been fitted too tightly and/or the heat from the engine may have made it even tighter. A filter wrench can be obtained at any auto parts store and is well-worth the investment. Loosen the filter with the filter wrench. With a rag wrapped around the filter, unscrew the filter from the boss on the side of the engine. Be careful of hot oil that will run down the side of the filter. Make sure that your drain pan is under the filter before you start to remove it from the engine; should some of the hot oil happen to get on you, there will be a place to

dump the filter in a hurry and the filter will usually spill a good bit of dirty oil as it is removed.

7. Wipe the base of the mounting boss with a clean, dry cloth. When you install the new filter, smear a small amount of fresh oil on the gasket with your finger, just enough to coat the entire contact surface. When you tighten the filter, rotate it about a quarter-turn after it contacts the mounting boss (or follow any instructions which are provided on the filter or parts box).

❋❋ WARNING

Operating the engine without the proper amount and type of engine oil will result in severe engine damage.

8. Remove the jackstands and carefully lower the vehicle, then IMMEDIATELY refill the engine crankcase with the proper amount of oil. DO NOT WAIT TO DO THIS because if you forget and someone tries to start the vehicle, severe engine damage will occur.

9. Refill the engine crankcase slowly, checking the level often. You may notice that it usually takes less than the amount of oil listed in the capacity chart to refill the crankcase. But, that is only until the engine is run and the oil filter is filled with oil. To make sure the proper level is obtained, run the engine to normal operating temperature, shut the engine **OFF**, allow the oil to drain back into the oil pan, and recheck the level. Top off the oil at this time to the fill mark.

➡If the vehicle is not resting on level ground, the oil level reading on the dipstick may be slightly off. Be sure to check the level only when the vehicle is sitting level.

10. Drain your used oil in a suitable container for recycling.

Manual Transaxle

FLUID RECOMMENDATIONS

The manual transaxle require Synchromesh® transmission fluid, GM part no. 12345349.

❋❋ WARNING

Using the incorrect lubricant in your transaxle can lead to significant transaxle damage and a costly overhaul.

LEVEL CHECK

◆ **See Figure 132**

The fluid level in the manual transaxle should be checked every 12 months or 7,500 miles (12,000 km), whichever comes first. The dipstick is located on the transaxle at the differential near the driver's side axle shaft.

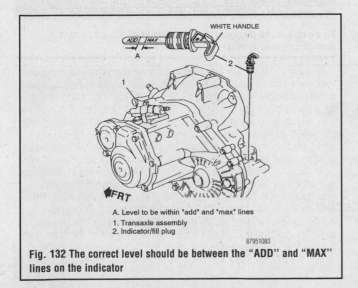

A. Level to be within "add" and "max" lines
1. Transaxle assembly
2. Indicator/fill plug

87951083

Fig. 132 The correct level should be between the "ADD" and "MAX" lines on the indicator

1. Park the car on a level surface. The transaxle should be cool to the touch. If it is hot, check the level later, when it has cooled.
2. Flip the dipstick handle up and remove the dipstick from the transaxle.
3. Clean the dipstick with a rag and reinsert it into the transaxle.
4. Remove the dipstick and check the level with the marks located on the dipstick.
5. If lubricant is needed, add it through the dipstick hole until the level is correct. When the level is correct, reinstall the dipstick firmly.

➡**The dipstick must be fully seated in the filler tube during vehicle operation or leakage will occur at the vent plug.**

DRAIN & REFILL

Under normal conditions, the manual transaxle fluid does not need to be changed. However, if the car is driven in deep water (as high as the transaxle case) it is a good idea to replace the fluid. Little harm can come from a fluid change when you have just purchased a used vehicle, especially since the condition of the transaxle is usually not known.

If the fluid is to be drained, it is a good idea to warm the fluid first so it will flow better. This can be accomplished by 15–20 miles (24–32 km) of highway driving. Fluid which is warmed to normal operating temperature will flow faster, drain more completely and remove more contaminants from the housing.

1. Remove the filler plug (dipstick) from the left side of the transaxle to provide a vent.
2. Raise and support the vehicle safely using jackstands.
3. The drain plug is located on the bottom of the transaxle case. Place a pan under the drain plug and remove it.

❋❋ CAUTION

The fluid will be HOT. Push up against the threads as you unscrew the plug to prevent leakage.

4. Allow the fluid to drain completely. Check the condition of the plug gasket and replace it if necessary. Clean off the plug and replace, tightening it until snug.
5. Fill the transaxle with fluid through the fill or dipstick tube. You will need the aid of a long neck funnel or a funnel and a hose to pour through.
6. Use the dipstick to gauge the level of the fluid.
7. Replace the filler plug (dipstick) and dispose of the old fluid in the same manner as you would old engine oil.
Take a drive in the car, stop on a level surface, and check the oil level.

Automatic Transaxle

FLUID RECOMMENDATIONS

General Motors recommends the use of DEXRON®-III automatic transmission fluid.

LEVEL CHECK

3T40 Automatic Transaxle

◆ **See Figures 133, 134, 135 and 136**

The transmission dipstick is located to the left (if facing the engine) of the brake master cylinder. The dipstick handle is usually **RED**.

1. Park the vehicle on a level surface.
2. The transaxle should be at normal operating temperature when checking fluid level. To ensure the fluid is at normal operating temperature, drive the vehicle at least 10 miles.
3. With the selector lever in **P** and the parking brake applied, start the engine.
4. Open the hood and locate the transaxle fluid dipstick. Pull the dipstick from its tube, wipe it clean, and reinsert it. Make sure the dipstick is fully inserted.
5. Pull the dipstick from its tube again. Holding it horizontally, read the fluid level. The fluid should be between the MIN and MAX mark. If the fluid is below

Fig. 133 Grasp the handle on the dipstick and remove it from the dipstick tube

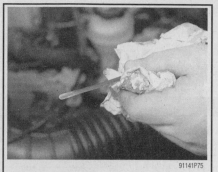

Fig. 134 Wipe the dipstick off with a rag, reinsert the dipstick and check the level on the dipstick

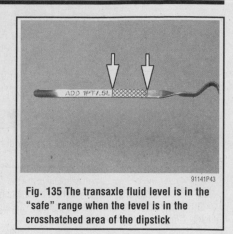

Fig. 135 The transaxle fluid level is in the "safe" range when the level is in the crosshatched area of the dipstick

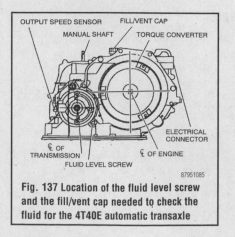

Fig. 136 Use a funnel and add fluid directly into the dipstick tube

the MIN mark, add fluid through the dipstick tube.

6. Insert the dipstick, and check the level again after adding any fluid. Be careful not to overfill the transaxle.

4T40E Automatic Transaxle

♦ See Figure 137

⁕⁕ CAUTION

Removal of the fluid level screw when the transaxle fluid is hot may cause injury. Use care to avoid contact of the transaxle fluid to exhaust pipe.

The fluid level screw is intended to be used for diagnosing a transaxle fluid leak or resetting the transaxle fluid level after service that involves a loss of fluid.

1. The fluid level should be checked when the transaxle is near room temperature or at 104°F (40°C). To acquire this, left the car idle for 3–5 minutes with all of the accessories off.

2. Apply the brake, then move the gear shift selector through all gear ranges, pausing three seconds in each range. Shift the lever into **P**.

3. Raise and safely support the vehicle.

4. Place a suitable drain pan under the check plug to catch any fluid that may drip out.

5. Remove the oil check plug. The oil level should be at the bottom of the oil check hole. Because the transaxle operates correctly over a range of fluid levels, fluid may or may not drain out of the screw hole when the screw is removed.

6. If fluid drains through the screw hole, the transaxle may have been over-filled. When fluid stops draining, then fluid level is correct and the check plug may be installed. If fluid does not drain through the screw hole, the transaxle fluid may have been low. Add fluid at the vent cap location in 1 pint increments until the oil level is at the bottom of the oil check hole.

7. Install the oil check plug/fluid level screw and tighten to 10 ft. lbs. (14 Nm).

8. Carefully lower the vehicle.

PAN & FILTER SERVICE

♦ See Figures 138 thru 149

The fluid should be changed according to the schedule in the Maintenance Intervals chart. If the car is normally used in severe service, such as stop and start driving, trailer towing, or the like, the interval should be halved. If the car is driven under especially nasty conditions, such as in heavy city traffic where the temperature normally reaches 90°F (32°C), or in very hilly or mountainous areas, or in police, taxi, or delivery service, the fluid should be changed every 15,000 miles (24,000 km.).

The fluid must be hot before it is drained; a 20 minute drive should accomplish this.

1. To drain the automatic transaxle fluid, the fluid pan must be removed.

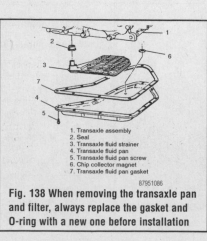

OUTPUT SPEED SENSOR FILL/VENT CAP
MANUAL SHAFT   TORQUE CONVERTER
ELECTRICAL CONNECTOR
₵ OF TRANSMISSION   ₵ OF ENGINE
FLUID LEVEL SCREW

Fig. 137 Location of the fluid level screw and the fill/vent cap needed to check the fluid for the 4T40E automatic transaxle

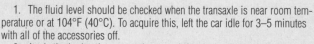

1. Transaxle assembly
2. Seal
3. Transaxle fluid strainer
4. Transaxle fluid pan
5. Transaxle fluid pan screw
6. Chip collector magnet
7. Transaxle fluid pan gasket

Fig. 138 When removing the transaxle pan and filter, always replace the gasket and O-ring with a new one before installation

Fig. 139 The transaxle fluid pan is retained by sixteen bolts

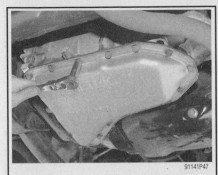

Fig. 140 Remove the bolts, usually requiring a 13mm socket or wrench, except for . . .

Fig. 141 . . . one bolt on each of the four corners of the pan

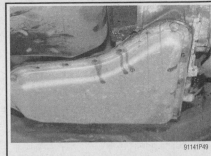

Fig. 142 Loosen the four bolts, but DO NOT remove them. Carefully break one corner of the pan loose until fluid begins to flow out

Fig. 143 When the fluid stops flowing out of the one corner, break the others loose until the fluid is flowing from the entire pan

Fig. 144 Slowly lower the bolts when the fluid stops flowing, then carefully remove one corner's bolt and try to drain any remaining fluid out, then remove the remaining three bolts and remove the pan

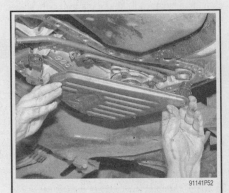

Fig. 145 Remove the filter by pulling down gently to unseat it from the transaxle

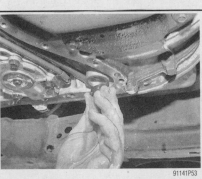

Fig. 146 Be sure to remove the seal on the filter fluid port, it most likely will stay in the transaxle

Fig. 147 Remove the gasket from the pan and discard it

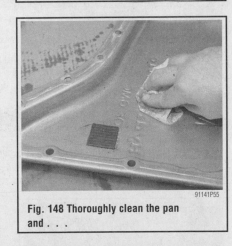

Fig. 148 Thoroughly clean the pan and . . .

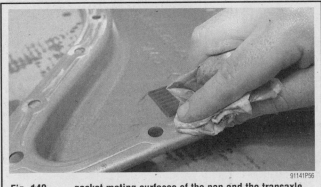

Fig. 149 . . . gasket mating surfaces of the pan and the transaxle before reinstalling the pan

Raise and safely support the vehicle. Place a drain pan underneath the transaxle pan, then remove the pan attaching bolts except on the four corners of the pan.

2. Loosen the four attaching bolts on the corners approximately four turns each, but do not remove them.

3. Very carefully pry the pan loose on one corner. You can use a small pry-bar for this if you work CAREFULLY. Do not distort the pan flange, or score the mating surface of the transaxle case. You'll be very sorry later if you do. As the pan is pried loose, all of the fluid is going to come pouring out.

4. Carefully break the other corners loose until fluid is flowing steadily from the entire pan.

5. After the fluid is down flowing, remove one corner bolt and attempt to drain any remaining fluid. Remove the remaining bolts and remove the pan and gasket. Throw away the gasket.

6. Clean the pan with solvent and allow it to air dry. If you use a rag to wipe out the pan, you risk leaving bits of lint behind, which will clog the dinky hydraulic passages in the transaxle.

7. Remove and discard the filter and the O-ring seal.

To install:

8. Install a new filter and O-ring, locating the filter against the dipstick stop.

9. Position a new gasket on the pan, then install the pan. Tighten the bolts evenly and in rotation to 8 ft. lbs. (11 Nm.). Do not overtighten.

10. Add approximately 4 qts. (3.8 L) of DEXRON®III or IIE automatic transmission fluid to the transaxle through the dipstick tube. You will need a long necked funnel, or a funnel and tube to do this.

11. With the transaxle in **P**, put on the parking brake, block the front wheels, start the engine and let it idle. DO NOT RACE THE ENGINE. DO NOT MOVE THE LEVER THROUGH ITS RANGES.

12. With the lever in Park, check the fluid level. If it's OK, take the car out for a short drive, park on a level surface, and check the level again, as outlined earlier in this section. Add more fluid if necessary. Be careful not to overfill, which will cause foaming and fluid loss.

➡**If the drained fluid is discolored (brown or black), thick, or smells burnt, serious transmission troubles, probably due to overheating, should be suspected. Your car's transaxle should be inspected by a reliable transmission specialist to determine the problem.**

Cooling System

FLUID RECOMMENDATIONS

▶ **See Figure 150**

Whenever adding or changing fluid, use a good quality ethylene glycol antifreeze meeting General Motors specification 6277M (DEX-COOL) or equivalent. Mix it with distilled water until a ⁵⁰⁄₅₀ antifreeze solution is attained.

Fig. 150 A label in the engine compartment usually is present stating the requirements of the cooling system fluid

LEVEL CHECK

▶ **See Figures 151, 152 and 153**

The coolant recovery tank is located on the passenger side of the engine compartment, over the front wheel well.

The proper coolant level is slightly above the FULL COLD marking on the recovery tank when the engine is cold. Top off the cooling system using the recovery tank and its marking as a guideline.

➡**Never overfill the recovery tank.**

A coolant level that consistently drops is usually a sign of a small, hard to detect leak, although in the worst case it could be a sign of an internal engine leak. In most cases, you will be able to trace the leak to a loose fitting or damaged hose.

Evaporating ethylene glycol antifreeze will have a sweet smell and leave small, white (salt-like) deposits, which can be helpful in tracing a leak.

❊❊ CAUTION

Never open, service or drain the radiator or cooling system when hot; serious burns can occur from the steam and hot coolant. Also, when draining engine coolant, keep in mind that cats and dogs are attracted to ethylene glycol antifreeze and could drink any that is left in an uncovered container or in puddles on the ground. This will prove fatal in sufficient quantities. Always drain coolant into a sealable container. Coolant should be reused unless it is contaminated or is several years old.

TESTING FOR LEAKS

▶ **See Figures 154, 155, 156, 157 and 158**

If a the fluid level of your cooling system is constantly low, the chances of a leak are probable. There are several ways to go about finding the source of your leak.

The first way should be a visual inspection. During the visual inspection, look around the entire engine area including the radiator and the heater hoses. The interior of the car should be inspected behind the glove box and passenger side floorboard area, and check the carpet for any signs of moisture. The smartest way to go about finding a leak visually is to first inspect any and all joints in the system such as where the radiator hoses connect to the radiator and the engine. Another thing to look for is white crusty stains that are signs of a leak where the coolant has already dried.

If a visual inspection cannot find the cause of your leak, a pressure test is a logical and extremely helpful way to find a leak. A pressure tester will be needed to perform this and if one is not available they can be purchased or even rented at many auto parts stores. The pressure tester usually has a standard size radiator cap adapter on the pressure port; however, other adapters are available

Fig. 151 Remove the cap for the coolant recovery tank

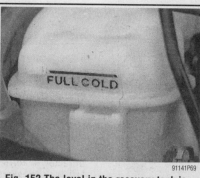

Fig. 152 The level in the recovery tank is ok if the fluid is at the FULL COLD mark when the engine is cold

Fig. 153 Add fluid directly into the recovery tank. It is advisable to use a funnel or to hold the bottle on it's side as shown here to avoid spillage

Fig. 154 Remove the recovery tank cap to allow the pressure tester to be connected to the system

Fig. 155 Use the proper adapter for the cooling system to allow the pressure tester to be connected

Fig. 156 Thread the adapter onto the recovery tank

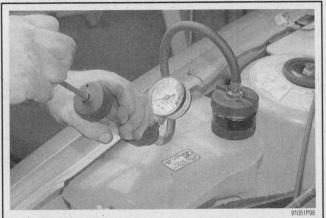

Fig. 157 Pump the cooling system with pressure, making sure not to overpressurize the system or damage can occur

Fig. 158 Watch the gauge on the system and observe the pressure reading

based on the size of the vehicle's radiator neck or recovery tank depending on where the pressure tester connects. when pressurizing the cooling system, make sure you do not exceed the pressure rating of the system, which can be found on the top of the radiator cap, however, if you have and aftermarket or replacement cap that does not have the rating on it, 16psi is a standard to use but some cars are higher. Overpressurizing the system can cause a rupture in a hose or worse in the radiator or heater core and possibly cause an injury or a burn if the coolant is hot. Overpressurizing is normally controlled by the radiator cap which has a vent valve in it which is opened when the system reaches it's maximum pressure rating. To pressure test the system:

➡ The pressure test should be performed with the engine OFF.

1. Remove the radiator or recovery tank cap.
2. Using the proper adapter, insert it onto the opening and connect the pressure tester.
3. Begin pressurizing the system by pumping the pressure tester and watching the gauge, when the maximum pressure is reached, stop.
4. Watch the gauge slowly and see if the pressure on the gauge drops, if it does, a leak is definitely present.
5. If the pressure stayed somewhat stable, visually inspect the system for leaks. If the pressure dropped, repressurize the system and then visually inspect the system.
6. If no signs of a leak are noticed visually, pressurize the system to the maximum pressure rating of the system and leave the pressure tester connected for about 30 minutes. Return after 30 minutes and verify the pressure on the gauge, if the pressure dropped more than 20%, a leak definitely exists, if the pressure drop is less than 20%, the system is most likely okay.

Another way coolant is lost is by a internal engine leak, causing the oil to be contaminated or the coolant to be burned in the process of combustion and sent out the exhaust. To check for oil contamination, remove the dipstick and check the condition of the oil in the oil pan. If the oil is murky and has a white or beige "milkshake" look to it, the coolant is contaminating the oil through an internal leak and the engine must be torn down to find the leak. If the oil appears okay, the coolant can be burned and going out the tailpipe. A quick test for this is a cloud of white smoke appearing from the tailpipe, especially on start-up. On cold days, the white smoke will appear, this is due to condensation and the outside temperature, not a coolant leak. If the "smoke test" does not verify the situation, removing the spark plugs one at a time and checking the electrodes for a green or white tint can verify an internal coolant leak and identify which cylinder(s) is the culprit and aiding your search for the cause of the leak. If the spark plugs appear okay, another method is to use a gas analyzer or emissions tester, or one of several hand-held tools that most professional shops possess. This tools are used to check the cooling system for the presence of Hydrocarbons (HC's) in the coolant.

DRAIN & REFILL

◆ See Figures 151, 152, 153, 159, 160, 161 and 162

Ensure that the engine is completely cool prior to starting this service.

✺✺ CAUTION

Never open, service or drain the radiator or cooling system when hot; serious burns can occur from the steam and hot coolant. Also, when draining engine coolant, keep in mind that cats and dogs are attracted to ethylene glycol antifreeze and could drink any that is left in an uncovered container or in puddles on the ground. This will prove fatal in sufficient quantities. Always drain coolant into a sealable container. Coolant should be reused unless it is contaminated or is several years old.

1. Remove the recovery tank cap.
2. Raise and support the vehicle.

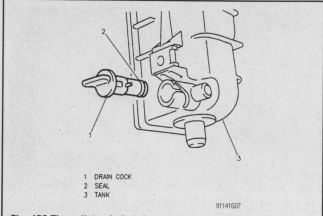

Fig. 159 The radiator drain is located on the radiator and faces the front of the vehicle (adjacent to the condenser-to-radiator bolt), it can be accessed after the lower splash shield is removed

1 DRAIN COCK
2 SEAL
3 TANK

91141G07

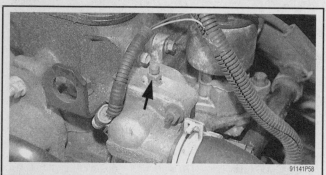

Fig. 160 Remove the bleed valve on the top of the water outlet housing to vent the system, as soon as coolant begins to flow out, install it

91141P58

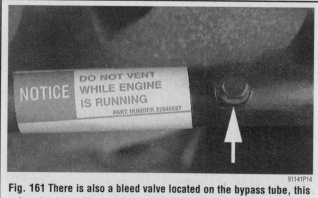

NOTICE DO NOT VENT WHILE ENGINE IS RUNNING PART NUMBER 22645627

91141P14

Fig. 161 There is also a bleed valve located on the bypass tube, this valve should not be used to vent the system when refilling it

3. Remove the splash shield.
4. Place a drain pan of sufficient capacity under the radiator. Open the petcock (drain) on the radiator and begin draining the coolant into the drain pan..

➡ Plastic petcocks easily bind. Before opening a plastic radiator petcock, spray it with some penetrating lubricant.

5. Drain the cooling system completely.
6. Close the petcock.
7. Remove the drain pan.
8. Install the splash shield.

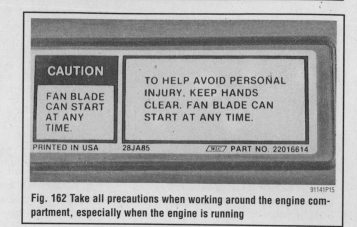

CAUTION
FAN BLADE CAN START AT ANY TIME.

TO HELP AVOID PERSONAL INJURY, KEEP HANDS CLEAR. FAN BLADE CAN START AT ANY TIME.

PRINTED IN USA   28JA85   /WIC/ PART NO. 22016614

91141P15

Fig. 162 Take all precautions when working around the engine compartment, especially when the engine is running

9. Lower the vehicle.
10. Determine the capacity of the cooling system, then properly refill the system at the recovery tank with a 50/50 mixture of fresh coolant and water until it reaches the **MAX** line.
11. Remove the bleedscrew on the water outlet housing and reinstall when new coolant begins to flow out.

✳✳ CAUTION

Install the bleed valve before the engine is started or air could enter the system.

12. Start the engine and allow it to idle until the thermostat opens (the upper radiator hose will become hot). The coolant level should go down, this is normal as the system bleeds the air pockets out of the system.
13. Refill the recovery tank until the coolant level is at the **MAX** line.
14. Turn the engine **OFF** and check for leaks.

FLUSHING & CLEANING THE SYSTEM

1. Drain the cooling system completely as described earlier.
2. Close the petcock and fill the system with a cooling system flush (clean water may also be used, but is not as efficient).
3. Idle the engine until the upper radiator hose gets hot.
4. Allow the engine to cool completely and drain the system again.
5. Repeat this process until the drained water is clear and free of scale.
6. Flush the recovery tank with water and leave empty.

✳✳ CAUTION

Never open, service or drain the radiator or cooling system when hot; serious burns can occur from the steam and hot coolant. Also, when draining engine coolant, keep in mind that cats and dogs are attracted to ethylene glycol antifreeze and could drink any that is left in an uncovered container or in puddles on the ground. This will prove fatal in sufficient quantities. Always drain coolant into a sealable container. Coolant should be reused unless it is contaminated or is several years old.

7. Fill and bleed the cooling system as described earlier.

Brake Master Cylinder

FLUID RECOMMENDATIONS

◆ See Figure 163

When adding fluid to the brake master cylinder, always use Delco Supreme fluid part no. 1052535 or equivalent DOT-3 brake fluid from a clean, sealed container.

Fig. 163 The cap on the master cylinder usually will specify the brake fluid requirements

✳✳ CAUTION

Brake fluid contains polyglycol ethers and polyglycols. Avoid contact with the eyes and wash your hands thoroughly after handling brake fluid. If you do get brake fluid in your eyes, flush your eyes with clean, running water for 15 minutes. If eye irritation persists, or if you have taken brake fluid internally, IMMEDIATELY seek medical assistance.

When adding fluid to the system, ONLY use fresh DOT 3 brake fluid from a sealed container. DOT 3 brake fluid will absorb moisture when it is exposed to the atmosphere, which will lower its boiling point. A container that has been opened once, closed and placed on a shelf will allow enough moisture to enter over time to contaminate the fluid within. If your brake fluid is contaminated with water, you could boil the brake fluid under hard braking conditions and lose all or some braking ability. Don't take the risk, buy fresh brake fluid whenever you must add to the system.

LEVEL CHECK

♦ See Figures 164, 165, 166 and 167

✳✳ CAUTION

Brake fluid contains polyglycol ethers and polyglycols. Avoid contact with the eyes and wash your hands thoroughly after handling brake fluid. If you do get brake fluid in your eyes, flush your eyes with clean, running water for 15 minutes. If eye irritation persists, or if you have taken brake fluid internally, IMMEDIATELY seek medical assistance.

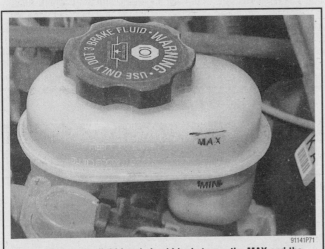

Fig. 164 The brake fluid level should be between the MAX and the MIN lines on the reservoir

Fig. 165 Wipe the outside of the master cylinder off before you remove the cap to prevent contamination

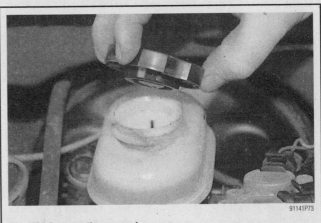

Fig. 166 Remove the cap and . . .

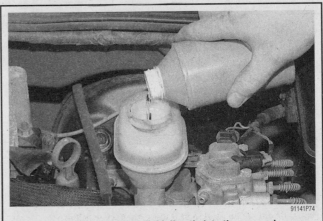

Fig. 167 . . . pour the proper fluid directly into the reservoir

The brake fluid master cylinder is located under the hood, attached to the brake booster and firewall on the driver's side of the engine compartment.

Observe the fluid level indicators on the master cylinder; the fluid level should be between the MIN and MAX lines.

Before removing the master cylinder reservoir cap, make sure the vehicle is resting on level ground and clean all dirt away from the top of the master cylinder. Unscrew the cap and fill the master cylinder until the level is between the MIN and MAX lines.

If the level of the brake fluid is less than half the volume of the reservoir, it is advised that you check the brake system for leaks. Leaks in a hydraulic brake system most commonly occur at the wheel cylinder and brake line junction points.

Clutch Master Cylinder

FLUID RECOMMENDATIONS

♦ **See Figure 168**

Use only hydraulic clutch fluid part No. 12345347 or equivalent DOT-3 brake fluid.

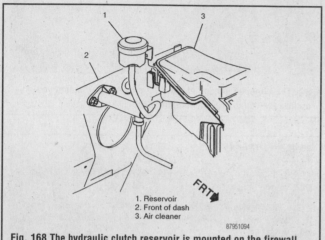

1. Reservoir
2. Front of dash
3. Air cleaner

87951094

Fig. 168 The hydraulic clutch reservoir is mounted on the firewall, next to the brake master cylinder

LEVEL CHECK

The hydraulic clutch fluid does not need to be checked unless you suspect a clutch problem. To check the fluid, remove the clutch hydraulic fluid reservoir cap and if the fluid reaches the step inside the reservoir, the fluid level is correct.

Power Steering Pump

FLUID RECOMMENDATIONS

Use GM Power Steering Fluid no. 1050017 or equivalent. In cold climates use GM Power Steering Fluid no. 12345867/12345866 or equivalent. If you plan to use GM Power Steering Fluid no. 12345867/12345866 or equivalent, you must flush and bleed the system prior to use.

LEVEL CHECK

♦ **See Figures 169 thru 174**

The power steering fluid reservoir is located on the power steering pump assembly. The power steering fluid should be checked at least every 6 months. Power steering fluid level is indicated by marks on a fluid level indicator on the underside of the reservoir cap or by "see-through" marks on the reservoir itself. There is a **COLD** and a **HOT** mark on the dipstick. To prevent possible overfilling, check the fluid level only when the fluid has warmed to operating temperatures and the engine is shut **OFF**. If necessary, add fluid to the power steering pump reservoir.

91141P09

Fig. 169 The power steering fluid reservoir is located on the passenger side of the engine compartment in the rear—2.2L engine

91141P76

Fig. 170 Remove the cap from the reservoir

91141P77

Fig. 171 The power steering fluid reservoir cap contains the dipstick

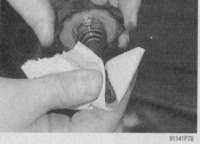

91141P78

Fig. 172 Wipe the dipstick off with a rag and reinsert the dipstick into the reservoir, remove the dipstick and check the level on the dipstick

91141P26

Fig. 173 The power steering fluid dipstick has a H mark which stands for full Hot, a C mark which stands for full Cold, and a ADD line which means Add fluid

91141P79

Fig. 174 Add the proper fluid directly into the power steering fluid reservoir

Chassis Greasing

♦ **See Figures 175, 176, 177 and 178**

There are only two areas which require regular chassis greasing: the front ball joint and the outer tie rod end. These parts should be greased every 12 months or 7,500 miles (12,000 km) with an EP grease meeting G.M. specification 6031M.

If you choose to do this job yourself, you will need to purchase a hand operated grease gun, if you do not own one already, and a long flexible extension hose to reach the various grease fittings. You will also need a cartridge of the appropriate grease.

Press the fitting on the grease gun hose onto the grease fitting on the ball joint or tie rod end. Pump a few shots of grease into the fitting, until the rubber boot on the joint begins to expand, indicating that the joint is full. Remove the gun from the fitting. Be careful not to overfill the joints, which will rupture the rubber boots, allowing the entry of dirt. You can keep the grease fittings clean by covering them with a small square of tin foil.

➡ **This is a good opportunity, while under the vehicle, to check for any tears or holes in the axle CV-joint boots, which may cause loss of or contamination of the axle grease. Damaged boots must be replaced as soon as possible or joint failure could result.**

Body Lubrication and Maintenance

Body lubrication

Every 12 months or 7,500 miles (12,000 km), the various linkages and hinges on the chassis and body should be lubricated, as follows:

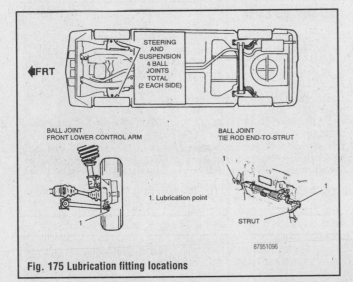

Fig. 175 Lubrication fitting locations

Transaxle Shift Linkage

Lubricate the manual transaxle shift linkage contact points with the EP grease used for chassis greasing, which should meet G.M. specification 6031M. The automatic transaxle linkage should be lubricated with clean engine oil.

Hood Latch And Hinges

Clean the latch surfaces and apply clean engine oil to the latch pilot bolts and the spring anchor. Use the engine oil to lubricate the hood hinges as well. Use a chassis grease to lubricate all the pivot points in the latch release mechanism.

Door Hinges

The gas tank filler door, car door, and rear hatch or trunk lid hinges should be wiped clean and lubricated with clean engine oil. Silicone spray also works well on these parts, but must be applied more often. Use engine oil to lubricate the trunk or hatch lock mechanism and the lock bolt and striker. The door lock cylinders can be lubricated easily with a shot of silicone spray or one of the many dry penetrating lubricants commercially available.

Parking Brake Linkage

➡ **Do NOT lubricate the parking brake cables. Lubrication destroys the plastic coating on the cables.**

Use chassis grease on the parking brake cable guides where they contact the links, levers, and pulleys. The grease should be a water resistant one for durability under the car.

Accelerator Linkage

Lubricate the accelerator pedal lever at the support inside the car with many dry penetrating lubricants commercially available.

CAR WASHING

The car should be washed at regular intervals to remove dirt, dust, insects, and tar and other possibly damaging stains that can adhere to the paint and may cause damage. Proper exterior maintenance also helps in the resale value of the vehicle by maintaining its like-new appearance.

➡ **It is particularly important to frequently wash the car in the wintertime to prevent corrosion, when salt has been used on the roads.**

There are many precautions and tips on washing, including the following:
- When washing the car, do not expose it do direct sunlight.
- Use lukewarm water to soften the dirt before you wash with a sponge, and plenty of water, to avoid scratching.
- A detergent can be used to facilitate the softening of dirt and oil.
- A water-soluble grease solvent may be used in cases of sticky dirt. However, use a washplace with a drainage separator.
- Dry the car with a clean chamois and remember to clean the drain holes in the doors and rocker panels.
- If equipped with a power radio antenna, it must be dried after washing.

Fig. 176 Clean the grease fittings off before you grease the chassis

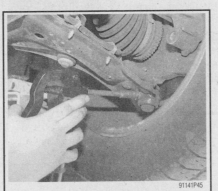

Fig. 177 The lower ball joint fitting is easily accessible

Fig. 178 The tie rod end joint fitting either requires an angle fitting on the grease gun or the wheel removed to access it

❊❊ CAUTION

Never clean the bumpers with gasoline or paint thinner, always use the same agent as used on the painted surfaces of the vehicle.

- Tar spots can be removed with tar remover or kerosene after the car has been washed.
- A stiff-bristle brush and lukewarm soapy water can be used to clean the wiper blades. Frequent cleaning improves visibility when using the wipers considerably.
- Wash off the dirt from the underside (wheel housings, fenders, etc.).
- In areas of high industrial fallout, more frequent washing is recommended.

❊❊ CAUTION

During high pressure washing the spray nozzle must never be closer to the vehicle than 13 inches (30 cm). Do not spray into the locks.

- When washing or steam cleaning the engine, avoid spraying water or steam directly on the electrical components or near the distributor or ignition components. After cleaning the engine, the spark plug wells should be inspected for water and blown dry if necessary.
- Special car washing detergent is the best to use. Liquid dishwashing detergent can remove wax and leave the car's paint unprotected and in addition some liquid detergents contains abrasives which can scratch the paint.
- Bird droppings should be removed from the paintwork as soon as possible, otherwise the finish may be permanently stained.

❊❊ WARNING

When the car is driven immediately after being washed, apply the brakes several times in order to remove any moisture from the braking surfaces.

❊❊ WARNING

Engine cleaning agents should not be used when the engine is warm, a fire risk is present as most engine cleaning agents are highly flammable.

Automatic car washing is a simple and quick way to clean your car, but it is worth remembering that it is not as thorough as when you yourself clean the car. Keeping the underbody clean is vitally important, and some automatic washers do not contain equipment for washing the underside of the car.

When driving into an automatic was, make sure the following precautions have been taken:

- Make sure all windows are up, and no objects that you do not want to get wet are exposed.
- In some cases, rotating the side view mirrors in can help to avoid possible damage.
- If your car is equipped with a power antenna, lower it. If your vehicle has a solid mounted, non-power antenna, it is best to remove it, but this is not always practical. Inspect the surroundings to reduce the risk of possible damage, and check to see if the antenna can be manually lowered.

❊❊ WARNING

Most manufacturers do not recommend automatic car washing in the first six months due to the possibility of insufficient paint curing; a safe bet is to wait until after six months of ownership (when purchased new) to use an automatic car wash.

WAXING

➡ **Before applying wax, the vehicle must be washed and thoroughly dried.**

Waxing a vehicle can help to preserve the appearance of your vehicle. A wide range of polymer-based car waxes are available today. These waxes are easy to use and produce a long-lasting, high gloss finish that protects the body and paint against oxidation, road dirt, and fading.

Sometimes, waxing a neglected vehicle, or one that has sustained chemical or natural element damage (such as acid rain) require more than waxing, and a light-duty compound can be applied. For severely damaged surfaces, it is best to consult a professional to see what would be required to repair the damage.

Waxing procedures differ according to manufacturer, type, and ingredients, so it is best to consult the directions on the wax and/or polish purchased.

INTERIOR CLEANING

Upholstery

Fabric can usually be cleaned with soapy water or a proper detergent. For more difficult spots caused by oil, ice cream, soda, etc., use a fabric cleaner available at most parts stores. Be sure when purchasing the cleaner to read the label to ensure it is safe to use on your type of fabric. A safe method of testing the cleaner is to apply a small amount to an area usually unseen, such as under a seat, or other areas. Wait a while, perhaps even a day to check the spot for fading, discoloring, etc., as some cleaners will only cause these problems after they have dried.

Leather upholstery requires special care, it can be cleaned with a mild soap and a soft cloth. It is recommended that a special leather cleaner be used to clean but also treat the leather surfaces in your vehicle. Leather surfaces can age quickly and can crack if not properly taken care of, so it is vital that the leather surfaces be maintained.

Floor Mats and Carpet

The floor mats and carpet should be vacuumed or brushed regularly. They can be cleaned with a mild soap and water. Special cleaners are available to clean the carpeted surfaces of your vehicle, but take care in choosing them, and again it is best to test them in a usually unseen spot.

Dashboard, Console, Door Panels, Etc.

The dashboard, console, door panels, and other plastic, vinyl, or wood surfaces can be cleaned using a mild soap and water. Caution must be taken to keep water out of electronic accessories and controls to avoid shorts or ruining the components. Again special cleaners are available to clean these surfaces, as with other cleaners care must taken in purchasing and using such cleaners.

There are protectants available which can treat the various surfaces in your car giving them a "shiny new look", however some of these protectants can cause more harm than good in the long run. The shine that is placed on your dashboard attracts sunlight accelerating the aging, fading and possibly even cracking the surfaces. These protectants also attract more dust to stick to the surfaces they treat, increasing the cleaning you must do to maintain the appearance of your vehicle. Personal discretion is advised here.

Wheel Bearings

REPACKING

The J-body models are equipped with sealed hub and bearing assemblies. The hub and bearing assemblies are non-serviceable. If the assembly is damaged, the complete unit must be replaced. Refer to Section 8 for the hub and bearing removal and installation procedure.

TOWING THE VEHICLE

Preferred Towing Method—Flatbed

For maximum safety to the components of your drive train and chassis, it is most desirable to have your vehicle towed by on a flatbed or whole vehicle trailer. The only way to properly place the vehicle on a flatbed is to have it pulled on from the front.

Alternate Towing Method—Wheel Lift

If a flatbed is unavailable, your vehicle can be towed using a wheel lift wrecker. In this case, the front wheels must be off the ground, as this will prevent wear and tear on the drive train. Tow vehicle speed should not exceed 35 mph (56 km/h) when using this method.

Last Chance Towing Method—Dolly

If absolutely necessary, you can tow your vehicle on a wheel lift wrecker from the rear. The front wheels must be placed on a olly. Tow vehicle speed should not exceed 35 mph (56 km/h) when using this method.

Towing Your Vehicle Behind Another Vehicle

◆ **See Figures 179, 180 and 181**

At times, you may want to tow your vehicle behind another vehicle such as a recreational vehicle (RV), a truck, or another car. Before the vehicle is towed a few steps must be taken:
If the vehicle is equipped with an automatic transaxle:
• The front wheels must be placed on a dolly
• Set the parking brake
• Turn the ignition key to **OFF** to unlock the steering wheel
• Clamp the steering wheel in a straight ahead position with a suitable device

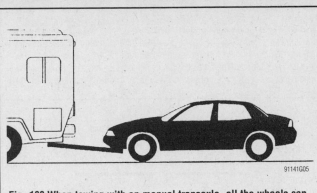

Fig. 180 When towing with an manual transaxle, all the wheels can be on the ground

Fig. 181 NEVER tow the vehicle with the rear wheels first

• Release the parking brake
If the vehicle is equipped with an manual transaxle:
• The vehicle MUST BE TOWED with the FRONT WHEELS FIRST
• Set the parking brake
• Turn the ignition key to **OFF** to unlock the steering wheel
• Clamp the steering wheel in a straight ahead position with a suitable device
• Shift the transaxle into Neutral
• Release the parking brake
When towing your vehicle behind another vehicle a few precautions must be taken:
• Do not tow your vehicle at a speed faster than 55 mph (90 km/h) or the vehicle can be damaged
• Do not tow your vehicle at a speed faster than 55 mph (90 km/h) if you have a manual transaxle

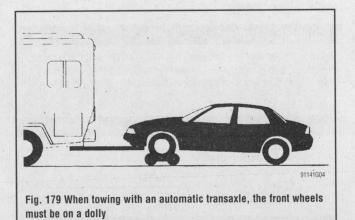

Fig. 179 When towing with an automatic transaxle, the front wheels must be on a dolly

TRAILER TOWING

General Recommendations

Your vehicle was primarily designed to carry passengers and cargo. It is important to remember that towing a trailer will place additional loads on your vehicles engine, drive train, steering, braking and other systems. However, if you decide to tow a trailer, using the prior equipment is a must.

Local laws may require specific equipment such as trailer brakes or fender mounted mirrors. Check your local laws.

Trailer Weight

The weight of the trailer is the most important factor. A good weight-to-horsepower ratio is about 35:1, 35 lbs. of Gross Combined Weight (GCW) for every horsepower your engine develops. Multiply the engine's rated horsepower by 35 and subtract the weight of the vehicle passengers and luggage. The number remaining is the approximate ideal maximum weight you should tow, although a numerically higher axle ratio can help compensate for heavier weight.

Hitch (Tongue) Weight

▶ **See Figure 182**

Calculate the hitch weight in order to select a proper hitch. The weight of the hitch is usually 9–11% of the trailer gross weight and should be measured with the trailer loaded. Hitches fall into various categories: those that mount on the frame and rear bumper, the bolt-on type, or the weld-on distribution type used for larger trailers. Axle mounted or clamp-on bumper hitches should never be used.

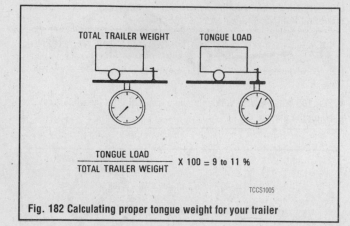

Fig. 182 Calculating proper tongue weight for your trailer

Check the gross weight rating of your trailer. Tongue weight is usually figured as 10% of gross trailer weight. Therefore, a trailer with a maximum gross weight of 2000 lbs. will have a maximum tongue weight of 200 lbs. Class I trailers fall into this category. Class II trailers are those with a gross weight rating of 2000–3000 lbs., while Class III trailers fall into the 3500–6000 lbs. category. Class IV trailers are those over 6000 lbs. and are for use with fifth wheel trucks, only.

When you've determined the hitch that you'll need, follow the manufacturer's installation instructions, exactly, especially when it comes to fastener torques. The hitch will subjected to a lot of stress and good hitches come with hardened bolts. Never substitute an inferior bolt for a hardened bolt.

Engine

One of the most common, if not THE most common, problems associated with trailer towing is engine overheating. If you have a cooling system without an expansion tank, you'll definitely need to get an aftermarket expansion tank kit, preferably one with at least a 2 quart capacity. These kits are easily installed on the radiator's overflow hose, and come with a pressure cap designed for expansion tanks.

Aftermarket engine oil coolers are helpful for prolonging engine oil life and reducing overall engine temperatures. Both of these factors increase engine life. While not absolutely necessary in towing Class I and some Class II trailers, they are recommended for heavier Class II and all Class III towing. Engine oil cooler systems usually consist of an adapter, screwed on in place of the oil filter, a remote filter mounting and a multi-tube, finned heat exchanger, which is mounted in front of the radiator or air conditioning condenser.

Transaxle

An automatic transaxle is usually recommended for trailer towing. Modern automatics have proven reliable and, of course, easy to operate, in trailer towing. The increased load of a trailer, however, causes an increase in the temperature of the automatic transaxle fluid. Heat is the worst enemy of an automatic transaxle. As the temperature of the fluid increases, the life of the fluid decreases.

It is essential, therefore, that you install an automatic transaxle cooler. The cooler, which consists of a multi-tube, finned heat exchanger, is usually installed in front of the radiator or air conditioning compressor, and hooked in-line with the transaxle cooler tank inlet line. Follow the cooler manufacturer's installation instructions.

Select a cooler of at least adequate capacity, based upon the combined gross weights of the vehicle and trailer.

Cooler manufacturers recommend that you use an aftermarket cooler in addition to, and not instead of, the present cooling tank in your radiator. If you do want to use it in place of the radiator cooling tank, get a cooler at least two sizes larger than normally necessary.

➡**A transaxle cooler can, sometimes, cause slow or harsh shifting in the transaxle during cold weather, until the fluid has a chance to come up to normal operating temperature. Some coolers can be purchased with or retrofitted with a temperature bypass valve which will allow fluid flow through the cooler only when the fluid has reached above a certain operating temperature.**

Handling a Trailer

Towing a trailer with ease and safety requires a certain amount of experience. It's a good idea to learn the feel of a trailer by practicing turning, stopping and backing in an open area such as an empty parking lot.

JUMP STARTING A DEAD BATTERY

▶ **See Figure 183**

Whenever a vehicle is jump started, precautions must be followed in order to prevent the possibility of personal injury. Remember that batteries contain a small amount of explosive hydrogen gas which is a by-product of battery charging. Sparks should always be avoided when working around batteries, especially when attaching jumper cables. To minimize the possibility of accidental sparks, follow the procedure carefully.

❋❋ CAUTION

NEVER hook the batteries up in a series circuit or the entire electrical system will go up in smoke, including the starter!

Vehicles equipped with a diesel engine may utilize two 12 volt batteries. If so, the batteries are connected in a parallel circuit (positive terminal to positive terminal, negative terminal to negative terminal). Hooking the batteries up in parallel circuit increases battery cranking power without increasing total battery voltage output. Output remains at 12 volts. On the other hand, hooking two 12 volt batteries up in a series circuit (positive terminal to negative terminal, positive terminal to negative terminal) increases total battery output to 24 volts (12 volts plus 12 volts).

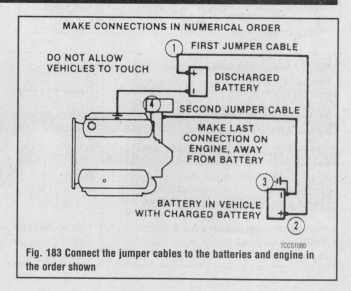

Fig. 183 Connect the jumper cables to the batteries and engine in the order shown

Jump Starting Precautions

- Be sure that both batteries are of the same voltage. Vehicles covered by this manual and most vehicles on the road today utilize a 12 volt charging system.
- Be sure that both batteries are of the same polarity (have the same terminal, in most cases NEGATIVE grounded).
- Be sure that the vehicles are not touching or a short could occur.
- On serviceable batteries, be sure the vent cap holes are not obstructed.
- Do not smoke or allow sparks anywhere near the batteries.
- In cold weather, make sure the battery electrolyte is not frozen. This can occur more readily in a battery that has been in a state of discharge.
- Do not allow electrolyte to contact your skin or clothing.

Jump Starting Procedure

1. Make sure that the voltages of the 2 batteries are the same. Most batteries and charging systems are of the 12 volt variety.
2. Pull the jumping vehicle (with the good battery) into a position so the jumper cables can reach the dead battery and that vehicle's engine. Make sure that the vehicles do NOT touch.
3. Place the transmissions/transaxles of both vehicles in **Neutral** (MT) or **P** (AT), as applicable, then firmly set their parking brakes.

➡**If necessary for safety reasons, the hazard lights on both vehicles may be operated throughout the entire procedure without significantly increasing the difficulty of jumping the dead battery.**

4. Turn all lights and accessories OFF on both vehicles. Make sure the ignition switches on both vehicles are turned to the **OFF** position.
5. Cover the battery cell caps with a rag, but do not cover the terminals.
6. Make sure the terminals on both batteries are clean and free of corrosion or proper electrical connection will be impeded. If necessary, clean the battery terminals before proceeding.
7. Identify the positive (+) and negative terminals on both batteries.
8. Connect the first jumper cable to the positive (+) terminal of the dead battery, then connect the other end of that cable to the positive (+) terminal of the booster (good) battery.

9. Connect one end of the other jumper cable to the negative terminal on the booster battery and the final cable clamp to an engine bolt head, alternator bracket or other solid, metallic point on the engine with the dead battery. Try to pick a ground on the engine that is positioned away from the battery in order to minimize the possibility of the 2 clamps touching should one loosen during the procedure. DO NOT connect this clamp to the negative (–) terminal of the bad battery.

✸✸ CAUTION

Be very careful to keep the jumper cables away from moving parts (cooling fan, belts, etc.) on both engines.

10. Check to make sure that the cables are routed away from any moving parts, then start the donor vehicle's engine. Run the engine at moderate speed for several minutes to allow the dead battery a chance to receive some initial charge.
11. With the donor vehicle's engine still running slightly above idle, try to start the vehicle with the dead battery. Crank the engine for no more than 10 seconds at a time and let the starter cool for at least 20 seconds between tries. If the vehicle does not start in 3 tries, it is likely that something else is also wrong or that the battery needs additional time to charge.
12. Once the vehicle is started, allow it to run at idle for a few seconds to make sure that it is operating properly.
13. Turn ON the headlights, heater blower and, if equipped, the rear defroster of both vehicles in order to reduce the severity of voltage spikes and subsequent risk of damage to the vehicles' electrical systems when the cables are disconnected. This step is especially important to any vehicle equipped with computer control modules.
14. Carefully disconnect the cables in the reverse order of connection. Start with the negative cable that is attached to the engine ground, then the negative cable on the donor battery. Disconnect the positive cable from the donor battery and finally, disconnect the positive cable from the formerly dead battery. Be careful when disconnecting the cables from the positive terminals not to allow the alligator clips to touch any metal on either vehicle or a short and sparks will occur.

JACKING

▶ **See Figures 184, 185, 186, 187 and 188**

Your vehicle was supplied with a jack for emergency road repairs. This jack is fine for changing a flat tire or other short term procedures not requiring you to go beneath the vehicle. If it is used in an emergency situation, carefully follow the instructions provided either with the jack or in your owner's manual. Do not attempt to use the jack on any portions of the vehicle other than specified by the vehicle manufacturer. Always block the diagonally opposite wheel when using a jack.

A more convenient way of jacking is the use of a garage or floor jack. You may use the floor jack on the body just behind the front wheels or the cross-member of the front sub-frame to raise the front of the vehicle, and on the center of the rear torque arm to raise the rear of the vehicle.

Never place the jack under the radiator, engine or transmission components. Severe and expensive damage will result when the jack is raised. Additionally, never jack under the floorpan or bodywork; the metal will deform.

Whenever you plan to work under the vehicle, you must support it on jackstands or ramps. Never use cinder blocks or stacks of wood to support the vehicle, even if you're only going to be under it for a few minutes. Never crawl

Fig. 184 The manufacturer advises against lifting the vehicle by placing a jack under the oil pan

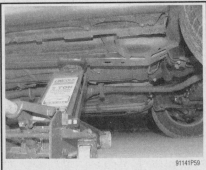
Fig. 185 Raise the vehicle in the front by placing a floor jack under the frame rails in the front

Fig. 186 Place jackstands under the frame rails to support the front of the vehicle

Fig. 187 Raise the vehicle in the rear by placing a floor jack under the rear crossmember

Fig. 188 Place jackstands under the body seams to support the rear of the vehicle

under the vehicle when it is supported only by the tire-changing jack or other floor jack.

➡**Always position a block of wood or small rubber pad on top of the jack or jackstand to protect the lifting point's finish when lifting or supporting the vehicle.**

Small hydraulic, screw, or scissors jacks are satisfactory for raising the vehicle. Drive-on trestles or ramps are also a handy and safe way to both raise and support the vehicle. Be careful though, some ramps may be too steep to drive your vehicle onto without scraping the front bottom panels. Never support the vehicle on any suspension member (unless specifically instructed to do so by a repair manual) or by an underbody panel.

Jacking Precautions

The following safety points cannot be overemphasized:
- Always block the opposite wheel or wheels to keep the vehicle from rolling off the jack.
- When raising the front of the vehicle, firmly apply the parking brake.
- When the drive wheels are to remain on the ground, leave the vehicle in gear to help prevent it from rolling.
- Always use jackstands to support the vehicle when you are working underneath. Place the stands beneath the vehicle's jacking brackets. Before climbing underneath, rock the vehicle a bit to make sure it is firmly supported.

MAINTENANCE INTERVALS

If a vehicle is operated under any of the following conditions it is considered severe service:
- Towing a trailer or using a camper or car-top carrier.
- Repeated short trips of less than 5 miles in temperatures below freezing, or trips of less than 10 miles in any temperature.

- Extensive idling or low-speed driving for long distances as in heavy commercial use, such as delivery, taxi or police cars.
- Operating on rough, muddy or salt-covered roads.
- Operating on unpaved roads or dusty roads.
- Driving in extremely hot (over 90°) conditions.

MANUFACTURER RECOMMENDED NORMAL MAINTENANCE INTERVALS

Component	Type of Service	7.5	15	22.5	30	37.5	45	52.5	60	67.5	75	82.5	90	97.5	105	112.5	120
		12.5	25	37.5	50	62.5	75	87.5	100	112.5	125	137.5	150	162.5	175	187.5	200
Engine oil and filter	Replace	✓	✓	✓	✓	✓	✓	✓	✓	✓	✓	✓	✓	✓	✓	✓	✓
Chassis	Lubricate	✓	✓	✓	✓	✓	✓	✓	✓	✓	✓	✓	✓	✓	✓	✓	✓
Tires	Rotate	✓		✓		✓		✓		✓		✓		✓		✓	
Air cleaner	Replace				✓				✓				✓				✓
Spark plugs ①	Replace																
Drive belts	Inspect				✓				✓				✓				✓
Cooling system	Inspect				✓				✓				✓				✓
Coolant	Replace					✓							✓				
PCV valve	Replace				✓				✓				✓				✓
Automatic transaxle fluid	Replace								✓								✓
EGR system	Inspect				✓				✓				✓				✓
Brake linings and drums	Inspect	✓		✓		✓		✓		✓		✓		✓		✓	
Brake pads and rotors	Inspect	✓		✓		✓		✓		✓		✓		✓		✓	
Spark plug wires	Inspect				✓				✓				✓				✓
CV joint boots	Inspect	✓	✓	✓	✓	✓	✓	✓	✓	✓	✓	✓	✓	✓	✓	✓	✓
Brake line hoses and connections	Inspect	✓		✓		✓		✓		✓		✓		✓		✓*	
Front ball joints	Inspect	✓	✓	✓	✓	✓	✓	✓	✓	✓	✓	✓	✓	✓	✓	✓	✓
Fuel tank, cap, and lines	Inspect				✓				✓				✓				✓
Steering linkage operation	Inspect	✓	✓	✓	✓	✓	✓	✓	✓	✓	✓	✓	✓	✓	✓	✓	✓

Perform maintenace at the same intervals for mileage beyond that on this chart
① Spark plug replacement is at 100,000 miles (160,900 km)

91141C05

MANUFACTURER RECOMMENDED SEVERE MAINTENANCE INTERVALS

VEHICLE MAINTENANCE INTERVAL

Component	Type of Service	Miles (x1000) 3 / km 5	6 / 10	9 / 15	12 / 20	15 / 25	18 / 30	21 / 35	24 / 40	27 / 45	30 / 50	33 / 55	36 / 60	39 / 65	42 / 70	45 / 75	48 / 80	51 / 85	54 / 90	57 / 95	60 / 100
Engine oil and filter	Replace	✓	✓	✓	✓	✓	✓	✓	✓	✓	✓	✓	✓	✓	✓	✓	✓	✓	✓	✓	✓
Chassis	Lubricate		✓		✓		✓		✓		✓		✓		✓		✓		✓		✓
Tires	Rotate		✓				✓				✓				✓				✓		
Air cleaner	Replace										✓										✓
Spark plugs ①	Replace																				
Drive belts	Inspect										✓										✓
Cooling system	Inspect										✓										✓
Coolant	Replace										✓										✓
PCV valve	Replace										✓										✓
Automatic transaxle fluid	Replace										✓										✓
EGR system	Inspect										✓										✓
Brake linings and drums	Inspect		✓				✓				✓				✓				✓		
Brake pads and rotors	Inspect		✓				✓				✓				✓				✓		
Spark plug wires	Inspect										✓										✓
CV joint boots	Inspect		✓		✓		✓		✓		✓		✓		✓		✓		✓		✓
Brake line hoses and connections	Inspect		✓				✓				✓				✓				✓		
Front ball joints	Inspect		✓		✓		✓		✓		✓		✓		✓		✓		✓		✓
Fuel tank, cap, and lines	Inspect										✓										✓
Steering linkage operation	Inspect		✓		✓		✓		✓		✓		✓		✓		✓		✓		✓

Perform maintenace at the same intervals for mileage beyond that on this chart
① Spark plug replacement is at 100,000 miles (160,900 km)

91141C06

CAPACITIES

Year	Model	Engine ID/VIN	Engine Displacement Liters (cc)	Engine Oil with Filter (qts.)	Transmission (qts.)			Transfer Case (pts.)	Drive Axle		Fuel Tank (gal.)	Cooling System (qts.)
					4-Spd	5-Spd	Auto.		Front (pts.)	Rear (pts.)		
1995	Cavalier	4	2.2 (2180)	4.5	—	2.0	7.0 ①	—	—	—	15.2	10.7
	Cavalier	D	2.3 (2262)	4.5	—	2.0	7.0 ①	—	—	—	15.2	10.4
	Sunfire	4	2.2 (2180)	4.5	—	2.0	7.0 ①	—	—	—	15.2	10.7
	Sunfire	D	2.3 (2262)	4.5	—	2.0	7.0 ①	—	—	—	15.2	10.4
1996	Cavalier	4	2.2 (2180)	4.5	—	2.0	7.0 ①	—	—	—	15.2	10.7
	Cavalier	T	2.4 (2392)	4.5	—	2.0	7.0 ①	—	—	—	15.2	10.4
	Sunfire	4	2.2 (2180)	4.5	—	2.0	7.0 ①	—	—	—	15.2	10.7
	Sunfire	T	2.4 (2392)	4.5	—	2.0	7.0 ①	—	—	—	15.2	10.4
1997	Cavalier	4	2.2 (2180)	4.5	—	2.0	7.0 ①	—	—	—	15.2	10.5
	Cavalier	T	2.4 (2392)	4.5	—	2.0	7.0 ①	—	—	—	15.2	10.5
	Sunfire	4	2.2 (2180)	4.5	—	2.0	7.0 ①	—	—	—	15.2	10.5
	Sunfire	T	2.4 (2392)	4.5	—	2.0	7.0 ①	—	—	—	15.2	10.5
1998	Cavalier	4	2.2 (2180)	4.5	—	2.0	7.0 ①	—	—	—	15.2	10.5
	Cavalier	T	2.4 (2392)	4.5	—	2.0	7.0 ①	—	—	—	15.2	10.5
	Sunfire	4	2.2 (2180)	4.5	—	2.0	7.0 ①	—	—	—	15.2	10.5
	Sunfire	T	2.4 (2392)	4.5	—	2.0	7.0 ①	—	—	—	15.2	10.5
1999	Cavalier	4	2.2 (2180)	4.5	—	2.0	7.0 ①	—	—	—	15.2	10.5
	Cavalier	T	2.4 (2392)	4.5	—	2.0	7.0 ①	—	—	—	15.2	10.5
	Sunfire	4	2.2 (2180)	4.5	—	2.0	7.0 ①	—	—	—	15.2	10.5
	Sunfire	T	2.4 (2392)	4.5	—	2.0	7.0 ①	—	—	—	15.2	10.5
2000	Cavalier	4	2.2 (2180)	4.5	—	2.0	7.0 ①	—	—	—	15.2	10.5
	Cavalier	T	2.4 (2392)	4.5	—	2.0	7.0 ①	—	—	—	15.2	10.5
	Sunfire	4	2.2 (2180)	4.5	—	2.0	7.0 ①	—	—	—	15.2	10.5
	Sunfire	T	2.4 (2392)	4.5	—	2.0	7.0 ①	—	—	—	15.2	10.5

NOTE: All capacities are approximate. Add fluid gradually and ensure a proper fluid level is obtained.

① 10.6 pts. if equipped with OVERDRIVE

91141C04

ENGLISH TO METRIC CONVERSION: MASS (WEIGHT)

Current **mass** measurement is expressed in pounds and ounces (lbs. & ozs.). The metric unit of mass (or weight) is the kilogram (kg). Even although this table does not show conversion of masses (weights) larger than 15 lbs, it is easy to calculate larger units by following the data immediately below.

To convert ounces (oz.) to grams (g): multiply th number of ozs. by 28
To convert grams (g) to ounces (oz.): multiply the number of grams by .035

To convert pounds (lbs.) to kilograms (kg): multiply the number of lbs. by .45
To convert kilograms (kg) to pounds (lbs.): multiply the number of kilograms by 2.2

lbs	kg	lbs	kg	oz	kg	oz	kg
0.1	0.04	0.9	0.41	0.1	0.003	0.9	0.024
0.2	0.09	1	0.4	0.2	0.005	1	0.03
0.3	0.14	2	0.9	0.3	0.008	2	0.06
0.4	0.18	3	1.4	0.4	0.011	3	0.08
0.5	0.23	4	1.8	0.5	0.014	4	0.11
0.6	0.27	5	2.3	0.6	0.017	5	0.14
0.7	0.32	10	4.5	0.7	0.020	10	0.28
0.8	0.36	15	6.8	0.8	0.023	15	0.42

ENGLISH TO METRIC CONVERSION: TEMPERATURE

To convert Fahrenheit (F) to Celsius (°C): take number of °F and subtract 32; multiply result by 5; divide result by 9

To convert Celsius (°C) to Fahrenheit (°F): take number of °C and multiply by 9; divide result by 5; add 32 to total

Fahrenheit (F)	Celsius (C)	Celsius (C)	Fahrenheit (F)	Fahrenheit (F)	Celsius (C)	Celsius (C)	Fahrenheit (F)	Fahrenheit (F)	Celsius (C)	Celsius (C)	Fahrenheit (F)
°F	°C	°C	°F	°F	°C	°C	°F	°F	°C	°C	°F
−40	−40	−38	−36.4	80	26.7	18	64.4	215	101.7	80	176
−35	−37.2	−36	−32.8	85	29.4	20	68	220	104.4	85	185
−30	−34.4	−34	−29.2	90	32.2	22	71.6	225	107.2	90	194
−25	−31.7	−32	−25.6	95	35.0	24	75.2	230	110.0	95	202
−20	−28.9	−30	−22	100	37.8	26	78.8	235	112.8	100	212
−15	−26.1	−28	−18.4	105	40.6	28	82.4	240	115.6	105	221
−10	−23.3	−26	−14.8	110	43.3	30	86	245	118.3	110	230
−5	−20.6	−24	−11.2	115	46.1	32	89.6	250	121.1	115	239
0	−17.8	−22	−7.6	120	48.9	34	93.2	255	123.9	120	248
1	−17.2	−20	−4	125	51.7	36	96.8	260	126.6	125	257
2	−16.7	−18	−0.4	130	54.4	38	100.4	265	129.4	130	266
3	−16.1	−16	3.2	135	57.2	40	104	270	132.2	135	275
4	−15.6	−14	6.8	140	60.0	42	107.6	275	135.0	140	284
5	−15.0	−12	10.4	145	62.8	44	112.2	280	137.8	145	293
10	−12.2	−10	14	150	65.6	46	114.8	285	140.6	150	302
15	−9.4	−8	17.6	155	68.3	48	118.4	290	143.3	155	311
20	−6.7	−6	21.2	160	71.1	50	122	295	146.1	160	320
25	−3.9	−4	24.8	165	73.9	52	125.6	300	148.9	165	329
30	−1.1	−2	28.4	170	76.7	54	129.2	305	151.7	170	338
35	1.7	0	32	175	79.4	56	132.8	310	154.4	175	347
40	4.4	2	35.6	180	82.2	58	136.4	315	157.2	180	356
45	7.2	4	39.2	185	85.0	60	140	320	160.0	185	365
50	10.0	6	42.8	190	87.8	62	143.6	325	162.8	190	374
55	12.8	8	46.4	195	90.6	64	147.2	330	165.6	195	383
60	15.6	10	50	200	93.3	66	150.8	335	168.3	200	392
65	18.3	12	53.6	205	96.1	68	154.4	340	171.1	205	401
70	21.1	14	57.2	210	98.9	70	158	345	173.9	210	410
75	23.9	16	60.8	212	100.0	75	167	350	176.7	215	414

TCCS1C01

ENGLISH TO METRIC CONVERSION: LENGTH

To convert inches (ins.) to millimeters (mm): multiply number of inches by 25.4

To convert millimeters (mm) to inches (ins.): multiply number of millimeters by .04

Inches	Decimals	Milli-meters	Inches to millimeters inches	mm	Inches	Decimals	Milli-meters	Inches to millimeters inches	mm
1/64	0.051625	0.3969	0.0001	0.00254	33/64	0.515625	13.0969	0.6	15.24
1/32	0.03125	0.7937	0.0002	0.00508	17/32	0.53125	13.4937	0.7	17.78
3/64	0.046875	1.1906	0.0003	0.00762	35/64	0.546875	13.8906	0.8	20.32
1/16	0.0625	1.5875	0.0004	0.01016	9/16	0.5625	14.2875	0.9	22.86
5/64	0.078125	1.9844	0.0005	0.01270	37/64	0.578125	14.6844	1	25.4
3/32	0.09375	2.3812	0.0006	0.01524	19/32	0.59375	15.0812	2	50.8
7/64	0.109375	2.7781	0.0007	0.01778	39/64	0.609375	15.4781	3	76.2
1/8	0.125	3.1750	0.0008	0.02032	5/8	0.625	15.8750	4	101.6
9/64	0.140625	3.5719	0.0009	0.02286	41/64	0.640625	16.2719	5	127.0
5/32	0.15625	3.9687	0.001	0.0254	21/32	0.65625	16.6687	6	152.4
11/64	0.171875	4.3656	0.002	0.0508	43/64	0.671875	17.0656	7	177.8
3/16	0.1875	4.7625	0.003	0.0762	11/16	0.6875	17.4625	8	203.2
13/64	0.203125	5.1594	0.004	0.1016	45/64	0.703125	17.8594	9	228.6
7/32	0.21875	5.5562	0.005	0.1270	23/32	0.71875	18.2562	10	254.0
15/64	0.234375	5.9531	0.006	0.1524	47/64	0.734375	18.6531	11	279.4
1/4	0.25	6.3500	0.007	0.1778	3/4	0.75	19.0500	12	304.8
17/64	0.265625	6.7469	0.008	0.2032	49/64	0.765625	19.4469	13	330.2
9/32	0.28125	7.1437	0.009	0.2286	25/32	0.78125	19.8437	14	355.6
19/64	0.296875	7.5406	0.01	0.254	51/64	0.796875	20.2406	15	381.0
5/16	0.3125	7.9375	0.02	0.508	13/16	0.8125	20.6375	16	406.4
21/64	0.328125	8.3344	0.03	0.762	53/64	0.828125	21.0344	17	431.8
11/32	0.34375	8.7312	0.04	1.016	27/32	0.84375	21.4312	18	457.2
23/64	0.359375	9.1281	0.05	1.270	55/64	0.859375	21.8281	19	482.6
3/8	0.375	9.5250	0.06	1.524	7/8	0.875	22.2250	20	508.0
25/64	0.390625	9.9219	0.07	1.778	57/64	0.890625	22.6219	21	533.4
13/32	0.40625	10.3187	0.08	2.032	29/32	0.90625	23.0187	22	558.8
27/64	0.421875	10.7156	0.09	2.286	59/64	0.921875	23.4156	23	584.2
7/16	0.4375	11.1125	0.1	2.54	15/16	0.9375	23.8125	24	609.6
29/64	0.453125	11.5094	0.2	5.08	61/64	0.953125	24.2094	25	635.0
15/32	0.46875	11.9062	0.3	7.62	31/32	0.96875	24.6062	26	660.4
31/64	0.484375	12.3031	0.4	10.16	63/64	0.984375	25.0031	27	690.6
1/2	0.5	12.7000	0.5	12.70					

ENGLISH TO METRIC CONVERSION: TORQUE

To convert foot-pounds (ft. lbs.) to Newton-meters: multiply the number of ft. lbs. by 1.3

To convert inch-pounds (in. lbs.) to Newton-meters: multiply the number of in. lbs. by .11

in lbs	N-m	in lbs	N-m	in lbs	N-m	in lbs	N-m	in lbs	N-m
0.1	0.01	1	0.11	10	1.13	19	2.15	28	3.16
0.2	0.02	2	0.23	11	1.24	20	2.26	29	3.28
0.3	0.03	3	0.34	12	1.36	21	2.37	30	3.39
0.4	0.04	4	0.45	13	1.47	22	2.49	31	3.50
0.5	0.06	5	0.56	14	1.58	23	2.60	32	3.62
0.6	0.07	6	0.68	15	1.70	24	2.71	33	3.73
0.7	0.08	7	0.78	16	1.81	25	2.82	34	3.84
0.8	0.09	8	0.90	17	1.92	26	2.94	35	3.95
0.9	0.10	9	1.02	18	2.03	27	3.05	36	4.0

TCCS1C02

ENGLISH TO METRIC CONVERSION: TORQUE

Torque is now expressed as either foot-pounds (ft./lbs.) or inch-pounds (in./lbs.). The metric measurement unit for torque is the Newton-meter (Nm). This unit—the Nm—will be used for all SI metric torque references, both the present ft./lbs. and in./lbs.

ft lbs	N-m	ft lbs	N-m	ft lbs	N-m	ft lbs	N-m
0.1	0.1	33	44.7	74	100.3	115	155.9
0.2	0.3	34	46.1	75	101.7	116	157.3
0.3	0.4	35	47.4	76	103.0	117	158.6
0.4	0.5	36	48.8	77	104.4	118	160.0
0.5	0.7	37	50.7	78	105.8	119	161.3
0.6	0.8	38	51.5	79	107.1	120	162.7
0.7	1.0	39	52.9	80	108.5	121	164.0
0.8	1.1	40	54.2	81	109.8	122	165.4
0.9	1.2	41	55.6	82	111.2	123	166.8
1	1.3	42	56.9	83	112.5	124	168.1
2	2.7	43	58.3	84	113.9	125	169.5
3	4.1	44	59.7	85	115.2	126	170.8
4	5.4	45	61.0	86	116.6	127	172.2
5	6.8	46	62.4	87	118.0	128	173.5
6	8.1	47	63.7	88	119.3	129	174.9
7	9.5	48	65.1	89	120.7	130	176.2
8	10.8	49	66.4	90	122.0	131	177.6
9	12.2	50	67.8	91	123.4	132	179.0
10	13.6	51	69.2	92	124.7	133	180.3
11	14.9	52	70.5	93	126.1	134	181.7
12	16.3	53	71.9	94	127.4	135	183.0
13	17.6	54	73.2	95	128.8	136	184.4
14	18.9	55	74.6	96	130.2	137	185.7
15	20.3	56	75.9	97	131.5	138	187.1
16	21.7	57	77.3	98	132.9	139	188.5
17	23.0	58	78.6	99	134.2	140	189.8
18	24.4	59	80.0	100	135.6	141	191.2
19	25.8	60	81.4	101	136.9	142	192.5
20	27.1	61	82.7	102	138.3	143	193.9
21	28.5	62	84.1	103	139.6	144	195.2
22	29.8	63	85.4	104	141.0	145	196.6
23	31.2	64	86.8	105	142.4	146	198.0
24	32.5	65	88.1	106	143.7	147	199.3
25	33.9	66	89.5	107	145.1	148	200.7
26	35.2	67	90.8	108	146.4	149	202.0
27	36.6	68	92.2	109	147.8	150	203.4
28	38.0	69	93.6	110	149.1	151	204.7
29	39.3	70	94.9	111	150.5	152	206.1
30	40.7	71	96.3	112	151.8	153	207.4
31	42.0	72	97.6	113	153.2	154	208.8
32	43.4	73	99.0	114	154.6	155	210.2

TCCS1C03

ENGLISH TO METRIC CONVERSION: FORCE

Force is presently measured in pounds (lbs.). This type of measurement is used to measure spring pressure, specifically how many pounds it takes to compress a spring. Our present force unit (the pound) will be replaced in SI metric measurements by the Newton (N). This term will eventually see use in specifications for electric motor brush spring pressures, valve spring pressures, etc.

To convert pounds (lbs.) to Newton (N): multiply the number of lbs. by 4.45

lbs	N	lbs	N	lbs	N	oz	N
0.01	0.04	21	93.4	59	262.4	1	0.3
0.02	0.09	22	97.9	60	266.9	2	0.6
0.03	0.13	23	102.3	61	271.3	3	0.8
0.04	0.18	24	106.8	62	275.8	4	1.1
0.05	0.22	25	111.2	63	280.2	5	1.4
0.06	0.27	26	115.6	64	284.6	6	1.7
0.07	0.31	27	120.1	65	289.1	7	2.0
0.08	0.36	28	124.6	66	293.6	8	2.2
0.09	0.40	29	129.0	67	298.0	9	2.5
0.1	0.4	30	133.4	68	302.5	10	2.8
0.2	0.9	31	137.9	69	306.9	11	3.1
0.3	1.3	32	142.3	70	311.4	12	3.3
0.4	1.8	33	146.8	71	315.8	13	3.6
0.5	2.2	34	151.2	72	320.3	14	3.9
0.6	2.7	35	155.7	73	324.7	15	4.2
0.7	3.1	36	160.1	74	329.2	16	4.4
0.8	3.6	37	164.6	75	333.6	17	4.7
0.9	4.0	38	169.0	76	338.1	18	5.0
1	4.4	39	173.5	77	342.5	19	5.3
2	8.9	40	177.9	78	347.0	20	5.6
3	13.4	41	182.4	79	351.4	21	5.8
4	17.8	42	186.8	80	355.9	22	6.1
5	22.2	43	191.3	81	360.3	23	6.4
6	26.7	44	195.7	82	364.8	24	6.7
7	31.1	45	200.2	83	369.2	25	7.0
8	35.6	46	204.6	84	373.6	26	7.2
9	40.0	47	209.1	85	378.1	27	7.5
10	44.5	48	213.5	86	382.6	28	7.8
11	48.9	49	218.0	87	387.0	29	8.1
12	53.4	50	224.4	88	391.4	30	8.3
13	57.8	51	226.9	89	395.9	31	8.6
14	62.3	52	231.3	90	400.3	32	8.9
15	66.7	53	235.8	91	404.8	33	9.2
16	71.2	54	240.2	92	409.2	34	9.4
17	75.6	55	244.6	93	413.7	35	9.7
18	80.1	56	249.1	94	418.1	36	10.0
19	84.5	57	253.6	95	422.6	37	10.3
20	89.0	58	258.0	96	427.0	38	10.6

TCCS1C04

**DISTRIBUTORLESS IGNITION
SYSTEM (DIS) 2-2**
GENERAL INFORMATION 2-2
  SYSTEM COMPONENTS 2-2
DIAGNOSIS AND TESTING 2-3
  SECONDARY SPARK TEST 2-3
  CYLINDER DROP TEST 2-3
ADJUSTMENTS 2-4
IGNITION COIL PACK 2-4
  TESTING 2-4
  REMOVAL & INSTALLATION 2-4
IGNITION MODULE 2-5
  REMOVAL & INSTALLATION 2-5
CRANKSHAFT AND CAMSHAFT
  POSITION SENSORS 2-6
FIRING ORDERS 2-6
CHARGING SYSTEM 2-6
GENERAL INFORMATION 2-6
ALTERNATOR PRECAUTIONS 2-7
ALTERNATOR 2-7
  TESTING 2-7
  REMOVAL & INSTALLATION 2-7
REGULATOR 2-8
STARTING SYSTEM 2-9
GENERAL INFORMATION 2-9
STARTER 2-9
  TESTING 2-9
  REMOVAL & INSTALLATION 2-9
  SOLENOID REPLACEMENT 2-10
**SENDING UNITS AND
SENSORS 2-11**
COOLANT TEMPERATURE SENDER 2-11
  OPERATION 2-11
  TESTING 2-11
  REMOVAL & INSTALLATION 2-11
COOLANT LEVEL SWITCH 2-11
  OPERATION 2-11
  TESTING 2-11
  REMOVAL & INSTALLATION 2-11
OIL LEVEL SWITCH 2-11
  OPERATION 2-11
  REMOVAL & INSTALLATION 2-11
OIL PRESSURE SWITCH 2-12
  OPERATION 2-12
  TESTING 2-12
  REMOVAL & INSTALLATION 2-12

2

ENGINE ELECTRICAL

DISTRIBUTORLESS IGNITION
SYSTEM (DIS) 2-2
FIRING ORDERS 2-6
CHARGING SYSTEM 2-6
STARTING SYSTEM 2-9
SENDING UNITS AND SENSORS 2-11

DISTRIBUTORLESS IGNITION SYSTEM (DIS)

➡For information on understanding electricity and troubleshooting electrical circuits, please refer to Section 6 of this manual.

General Information

The Distributorless Ignition System or Electronic Ignition (EI) system does not use the conventional distributor and ignition coil. The system consists of 2 separate ignition coils, an Ignition Control Module (ICM), crankshaft sensor, Camshaft Position (CMP) sensor, along with the related connecting wires and the Ignition Control (IC) portion of the powertrain control module (PCM).

The distributorless system uses a "waste spark" method of spark distribution. Companion cylinders are paired and the spark occurs simultaneously in the cylinder with the piston coming up on the compression stroke and in the companion cylinder with the piston coming up on the exhaust stroke.

The cylinder on the exhaust stroke requires very little of the available voltage to arc, so the remaining high voltage is used by the cylinder in the firing position (TDC compression). This same process is repeated when the companion cylinders reverse roles.

It is possible in an engine no-load condition, for one plug to fire, even though the spark plug lead from the same coil is disconnected from the other spark plug. The disconnected spark plug lead acts as one plate of a capacitor, with the engine being the other plate. These two capacitor plates are charged as a current surge (spark) jumps across the gap of the connected spark plug.

These plates are then discharged as the secondary energy is dissipated in an oscillating current across the gap of the spark plug still connected. Because of the direction of current flow in the primary windings and thus in the secondary windings, one spark plug will fire from the center electrode to the side electrode, while the other will fire from the side electrode to the center electrode.

These systems utilize the IC signal from the PCM, as do some convention distributor type ignition systems.

In the Direct Ignition or Electronic Ignition system while under 400 rpm, the ICM controls the spark timing through a module timing mode. Over 400 rpm, the PCM controls the spark timing through the IC mode. To properly control the ignition timing, the PCM relies on information from the various sensors including the following:

- Manifold Absolute Pressure (MAP) sensor
- Engine Coolant Temperature (ECT) sensor
- Intake Air Temperature (IAT) sensor
- Crankshaft position
- Knock sensor (KS)
- Throttle Position (TP) sensor

SYSTEM COMPONENTS

Crankshaft Position (CKP) Sensor

▶ See Figure 1

A magnetic crankshaft sensor (Hall Effect switch) is used to provide the ICM and PCM with engine speed data. The sensor protrudes in to the engine block, within about 0.050 in. (1.27mm) of the crankshaft reluctor.

The sensor is a fixed mount magnetic sensor that has voltage induced by a rotating reluctor wheel. The reluctor is a special wheel cast into the crankshaft with seven slots machined into it, six of which are equally spaced 60° apart. A seventh slot is spaced 10° from one of the other slots and serves as a generator of a "sync-pulse". As the reluctor rotates as part of the crankshaft, the slots change the magnetic field of the sensor, creating an induced voltage pulse.

The CKP sensor sends a signal to the ICM which sends a reference signals to the PCM, based on the Crankshaft Position (CKP) sensor pulses, which are used to determine crankshaft position and engine speed. Reference pulses to the PCM occur at a rate of 7 per 360° of crankshaft rotation. This signal is called the 7X reference because it occurs 7 times per crankshaft revolution.

The 7X reference signal is necessary for the PCM to determine when to activate the fuel injectors.

The PCM activates the fuel injectors, based on the recognition of every other reference pulse, beginning at a crankshaft position 120° after piston Top Dead Center (TDC). By comparing the time between the pulses, the Ignition Control Module (ICM) can recognize the pulse representing the seventh slot (sync-pulse) which starts the calculation of ignition coil sequencing.

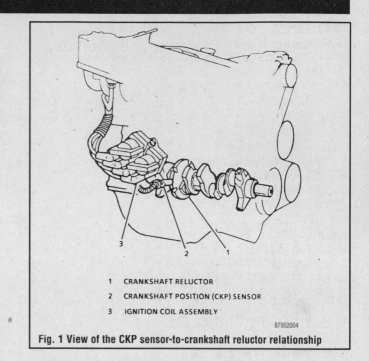

1	CRANKSHAFT RELUCTOR
2	CRANKSHAFT POSITION (CKP) SENSOR
3	IGNITION COIL ASSEMBLY

87952004

Fig. 1 View of the CKP sensor-to-crankshaft reluctor relationship

Ignition Coils

There are two separate coils for the 2.2L and 2.3L/2.4L engines mounted to the coil/module assembly. Spark distribution is synchronized by a signal from the crankshaft sensor which the ignition module uses to trigger each coil at the proper time. Each coil provides the spark for two spark plugs simultaneously (waste spark distribution).

The coils are mounted to the ICM. Each coil can be replaced separately. A fused low current source to the module terminal **M**, provides power for the sensors, ignition coils and internal module circuitry.

Ignition Control Module (ICM)

The DIS module or ICM, as it's called in later years, monitors the crankshaft sensor signal, then, based on these signals, sends a reference signal to the powertrain control module (PCM) so that correct spark and fuel injector control can be maintained during all driving conditions. During cranking, the module monitors the sync-pulse to begin the ignition firing sequence. Below 400 rpm, the module controls the spark advance by triggering each of the ignition coils at a predetermined interval, based on engine speed only. Above 400 rpm, the PCM controls the electronic spark timing (EST) and compensates for all driving conditions. The module must receive a sync-pulse and then a crank signal, in that order, to enable the engine to start.

The DIS module or Ignition Control Module (ICM) is not repairable. When a module is replaced, the remaining DIS/ICM components must be transferred to the new module.

Ignition Control (IC)

The IC system is a series of circuits between the ICM and the PCM that are used to send information about the ignition system. This system includes the following circuits:

- 7X Reference —The CKP sensor generates a signal to the ICM, resulting in a reference pulse which is sent to the PCM. The PCM uses this signal to determine crankshaft position, engine speed and injector pulse width. The engine will not start or run if this circuit is open or grounded.
- Reference low—This wire is grounded through the module and insures that the ground circuit has no voltage drop between the ICM and the PCM which may affect engine performance.
- Ignition control 1 & 2 —The PCM sends the Ignition Control (IC) pulses to the ICM on these circuits. These signals are similar to the 7X reference pulse except that the PCM uses sensor inputs to determine the pulse timing to control

spark advance. When the PCM receives the 7X signal, it will determine which pair of cylinders will be fired. (1-4 or 2-3). It will tell the ICM which cylinder pair will be fired.

Diagnosis and Testing

Before beginning any diagnosis and testing procedures, visually inspect the components of the ignition system and engine control systems. Check for the following:

- Discharged battery
- Damaged or loose connections
- Damaged electrical insulation
- Poor coil and spark plug connections
- Ignition module connections
- Blown fuses
- Damaged vacuum hoses
- Damaged spark plugs

Check the spark plug wires and boots for signs of poor insulation that could cause crossfiring. Make sure the battery is fully charged and that all accessories are off during diagnosis and testing. Make sure the idle speed is within specification.

If an open or ground in the Ignition Control (IC) circuit occurs during engine operation, then engine will continue to run, but using a back-up timing mode (controlled by the ICM) based on preset timing values. The Malfunction Indicator Lamp (MIL) or SERVICE ENGINE SOON light will not illuminate at the first appearance of a break in the circuit. However, if the IC fault is still present once the engine is restarted, a Code 42 will set on OBD 1 systems in the PCM and the MIL will illuminate. Poor performance and fuel economy may be noticed while the engine is running under back-up timing.

When attempting to search for ignition troubles, keep in mind the various sensor inputs which the PCM uses to calculate timing may affect engine performance. The PCM will alter timing based on sensor inputs as follows:

- Low MAP output voltage = More spark advance
- Cold engine = More spark advance
- High MAP output voltage = Less spark advance
- Hot engine = Less spark advance

With this in mind, DETONATION could be caused by low MAP output or high resistance in the coolant sensor circuit. POOR PERFORMANCE could be caused by a high MAP output or low resistance in the coolant sensor circuit.

SECONDARY SPARK TEST

▶ **See Figures 2, 3, 4 and 5**

The best way to perform this procedure is to use a spark tester (available at most automotive parts stores). Three types of spark testers are commonly available. The Neon Bulb type is connected to the spark plug wire and flashes with each ignition pulse. The Air Gap type must be adjusted to the individual spark plug gap specified for the engine. The last type of spark plug tester looks like a spark plug with a grounding clip on the side, but there is no side electrode for the spark to jump to. The last two types of testers allows the user to not only detect the presence of spark, but also the intensity (orange/yellow is weak, blue is strong).

1. Disconnect a spark plug wire at the spark plug end.
2. Connect the plug wire to the spark tester and ground the tester to an appropriate location on the engine.
3. Crank the engine and check for spark at the tester.
4. If spark exists at the tester, the ignition system is functioning properly.
5. If spark does not exist at the spark plug wire, perform diagnosis of the ignition system using individual component diagnosis procedures.

CYLINDER DROP TEST

▶ **See Figures 6, 7 and 8**

The cylinder drop test is performed when an engine misfire is evident. This test helps determine which cylinder is not contributing the proper power. The easiest way to perform this test is to remove the plug wires one at a time from the cylinders with the engine running.

Fig. 2 This spark tester looks just like a spark plug, attach the clip to ground and crank the engine to check for spark

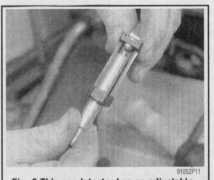

Fig. 3 This spark tester has an adjustable air-gap for measuring spark strength and testing different voltage ignition systems

Fig. 4 Attach the clip to ground and crank the engine to check for spark

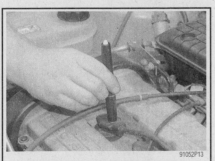

Fig. 5 This spark tester is the easiest to use just place it on a plug wire and the spark voltage is detected and the bulb on the top will flash with each pulse

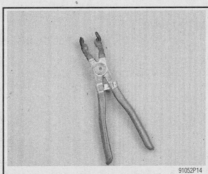

Fig. 6 These pliers are insulated and help protect the user from shock as well as the plug wires from being damaged

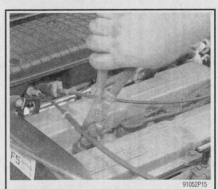

Fig. 7 To perform the cylinder drop test, remove one wire at a time and . . .

Fig. 8 . . . note the idle speed and idle characteristics of the engine. the cylinder(s) with the least drop is the non-contributing cylinder(s)

1. Place the transaxle in **P**, engage the emergency brake, and start the engine and let it idle.
2. Using a spark plug wire removing tool, preferably, the plier type, carefully remove the boot from one of the cylinders.

※※ WARNING

Make sure your body is free from touching any part of the car which is metal. The secondary voltage in the ignition system is high and although it cannot kill you, it will shock you and it does hurt.

3. The engine will sputter, run worse, and possibly nearly stall. If this happens reinstall the plug wire and move to the next cylinder. If the engine runs no differently, or the difference is minimal, shut the engine off and inspect the spark plug wire, spark plug, and if necessary, perform component diagnostics as covered in this section. Perform the test on all cylinders to verify the which cylinders are suspect.

Adjustments

All adjustments in the ignition system are controlled by the Powertrain Control Module (PCM) and Ignition Control Module (ICM) for optimum performance. No adjustments are possible.

Ignition Coil Pack

TESTING

2.2L (VIN 4) Engine

1. Remove the ignition coil(s).
2. Using an ohmmeter, check the resistance between the primary terminals on the underside of the coil. The resistance should be 0.50–0.90 ohms.
3. Check the resistance between the secondary terminals. It should be 5000–10,000 ohms.
4. If the coil failed either test, replace the coil.

2.3L (VIN D) and 2.4L (VIN T) Engines

1. Remove the ignition coil(s).
2. Using an ohmmeter, check the resistance between the secondary terminals. Resistance should be 10,000 ohms.
3. If the coil secondary resistance is out of specification, replace the coil.

REMOVAL & INSTALLATION

2.2L (VIN 4) Engine

▶ See Figures 9, 10 and 11

1. Disconnect the negative battery cable.
2. Raise and safely support the vehicle.
3. Detach the coil assembly electrical connectors.
4. Tag and disconnect the spark plug wires.
5. Unfasten the three ignition coil assembly-to-block bolts, then remove the assembly from the engine.
   To install:
6. Position the ignition coil assembly to the engine. Install the mounting bolts, then tighten to 15–22 ft. lbs. (20–30 Nm).
7. Connect the spark plug wires to the proper coils, as tagged during removal.
8. Attach the coil electrical connectors.
9. Carefully lower the vehicle, then connect the negative battery cable.

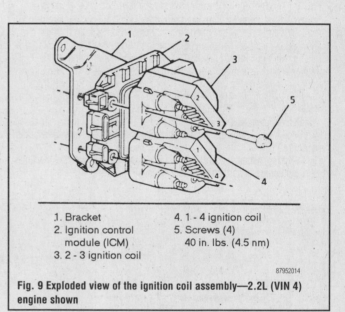

1. Bracket	4. 1 - 4 ignition coil
2. Ignition control module (ICM)	5. Screws (4) 40 in. lbs. (4.5 nm)
3. 2 - 3 ignition coil	

87952014

Fig. 9 Exploded view of the ignition coil assembly—2.2L (VIN 4) engine shown

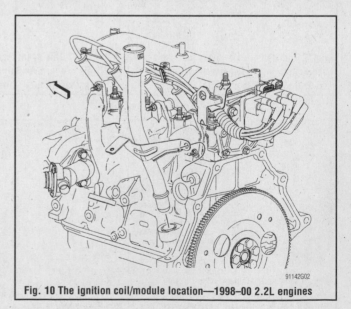

91142G02

Fig. 10 The ignition coil/module location—1998–00 2.2L engines

Fig. 11 The ignition coil assembly is locate on the side of the block towards the firewall and under the intake manifold—2.2L engine

2.3L (VIN D) and 2.4L (VIN T) Engines

▶ See Figure 12

➡On these vehicles, the ignition coils and electronic ignition control module are one assembly.

1. Disconnect the negative battery cable.
2. Detach the electronic Ignition Control Module (ICM) 11-pin harness connector.
3. Unfasten the four ignition coil and ICM assembly-to-camshaft housing bolts, then remove the assembly from the vehicle.

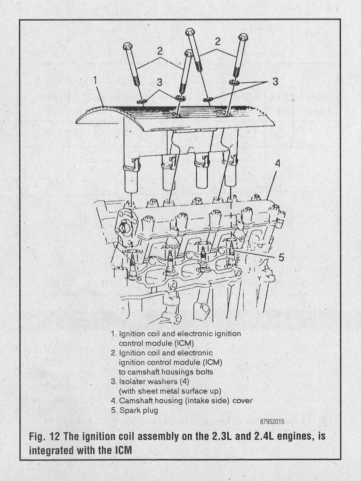

1. Ignition coil and electronic ignition control module (ICM)
2. Ignition coil and electronic ignition control module (ICM) to camshaft housings bolts
3. Isolater washers (4) (with sheet metal surface up)
4. Camshaft housing (intake side) cover
5. Spark plug

Fig. 12 The ignition coil assembly on the 2.3L and 2.4L engines, is integrated with the ICM

➡If the boots stick to the spark plugs, use tool J 36011 or equivalent, to removed by first twisting, then carefully pulling upward on the retainers. Reinstall the boots and retainers on the ignition coil housing secondary terminals. The boots and retainers must be in place on the ignition coil housing prior to installation or damage to the ignition system could result.

To install:
4. Fasten the spark plugs and retainers to the housing.
5. While carefully aligning the boots to the spark plug terminals, position the ignition coil and ICM assembly to the engine.
6. Coat the threads of the retaining bolts with a suitable thread sealant. Install the retaining bolts, then tighten to 16 ft. lbs. (22 Nm).
7. Attach the electronic ICM harness connector.
8. Connect the negative battery cable.

Ignition Module

REMOVAL & INSTALLATION

2.2L Engines

▶ See Figures 13 and 14

1. Disconnect the negative battery cable.
2. On 1995–97 models, raise and safely support the vehicle.
3. Remove the ignition coils from the module.
4. Remove the module from the assembly plate.
5. Installation is the reverse of the removal procedure.

2.3L and 2.4L Engines

▶ See Figure 15

1. Disconnect the negative battery cable.
2. Detach the Electronic Ignition Control Module (ICM) electrical connector.
3. Unfasten the coil and module-to-cam housing bolts, then remove the coil and ignition module assembly from the engine.
4. Unfasten the housing-to-cover screws, then pull the housing from the cover.
5. Detach the coil harness connector from the module.
6. Unfasten the module-to-cover screws, then remove the module.

✳✳ WARNING

Do NOT wipe the grease from the module or coil if the same module is to be replaced. If a new module is to be installed, a package of silicone grease will be included with it. Spread the grease on the metal face of the module and on the cover where the module seats. This grease is necessary for module cooling.

7. Installation is the reverse of the removal procedure.

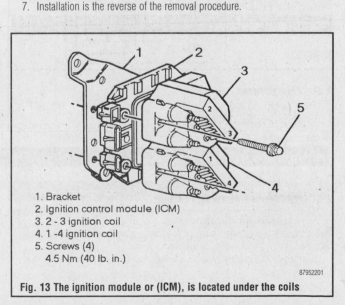

1. Bracket
2. Ignition control module (ICM)
3. 2 - 3 ignition coil
4. 1 -4 ignition coil
5. Screws (4) 4.5 Nm (40 lb. in.)

Fig. 13 The ignition module or (ICM), is located under the coils

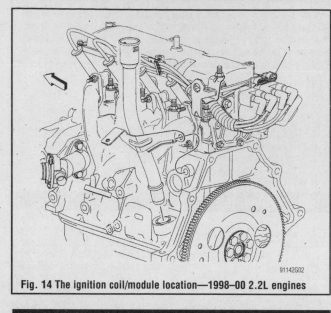

Fig. 14 The ignition coil/module location—1998–00 2.2L engines

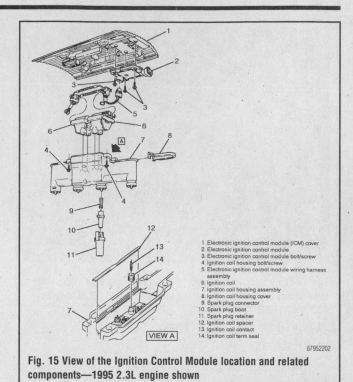

1. Electronic ignition control module (ICM) cover
2. Electronic ignition control module
3. Electronic ignition control module bolt/screw
4. Ignition coil housing bolt/screw
5. Electronic ignition control module wiring harness assembly
6. Ignition coil
7. Ignition coil housing assembly
8. Ignition coil housing cover
9. Spark plug connector
10. Spark plug boot
11. Spark plug retainer
12. Ignition coil spacer
13. Ignition coil contact
14. Ignition coil term seal

Fig. 15 View of the Ignition Control Module location and related components—1995 2.3L engine shown

Crankshaft and Camshaft Position Sensors

For procedures on the position sensors, please refer to Section 4 in this manual.

FIRING ORDERS

▶ **See Figures 16 and 17**

➡ **To avoid confusion, remove and tag the spark plug wires one at a time, for replacement.**

If a distributor is not keyed for installation with only one orientation, it could have been removed previously and rewired. The resultant wiring would hold the correct firing order, but could change the relative placement of the plug towers in relation to the engine. For this reason it is imperative that you label all wires before disconnecting any of them. Also, before removal, compare the current wiring with the accompanying illustrations. If the current wiring does not match, make notes in your book to reflect how your engine is wired.

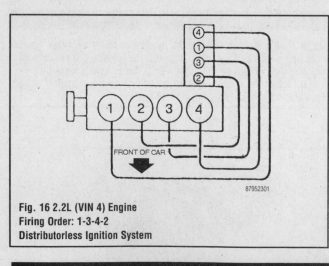

Fig. 16 2.2L (VIN 4) Engine
Firing Order: 1-3-4-2
Distributorless Ignition System

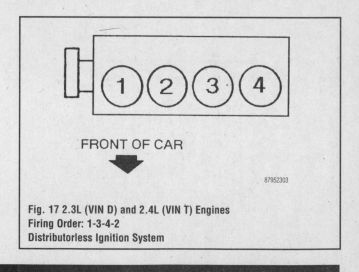

FRONT OF CAR

Fig. 17 2.3L (VIN D) and 2.4L (VIN T) Engines
Firing Order: 1-3-4-2
Distributorless Ignition System

CHARGING SYSTEM

General Information

The automobile charging system provides electrical power for operation of the vehicle's ignition and starting systems and all the electrical accessories. The battery serves as an electrical surge or storage tank, storing (in chemical form) the energy originally produced by the engine driven alternator. The system also provides a means of regulating generator output to protect the battery from being overcharged and to avoid excessive voltage to the accessories.

The storage battery is a chemical device incorporating parallel lead plates in a tank containing a sulfuric acid/water solution. Adjacent plates are slightly dissimilar, and the chemical reaction of the 2 dissimilar plates produces electrical energy when the battery is connected to a load such as the starter motor. The chemical reaction is reversible, so that when the generator is producing a voltage (electrical pressure) greater than that produced by the battery, electricity is forced into the battery, and the battery is returned to its fully charged state.

The vehicle's alternator is driven by a belt that is driven by the engine crankshaft. In an alternator, the field rotates while all the current produced passes only through the stator winding. The brushes bear against continuous slip rings rather than a commutator. This causes the current produced to periodically reverse the direction of its flow creating alternating current (A/C). Diodes (electrical one-way switches) block the flow of current from traveling in the wrong direction. A series of diodes is wired together to permit the alternating flow of the stator to be converted to a pulsating, but unidirectional flow at the alternator output. The alternator's field is wired in series with the voltage regulator.

The regulator consists of several circuits. Each circuit has a core, or magnetic coil of wire, which operates a switch. Each switch is connected to ground through one or more resistors. The coil of wire responds directly to system voltage. When the voltage reaches the required level, the magnetic field created by the winding of wire closes the switch and inserts a resistance into the generator field circuit, thus reducing the output. The contacts of the switch cycle open and close many times each second to precisely control voltage.

Alternator Precautions

Several precautions must be observed when performing work on alternator equipment.
- If the battery is removed for any reason, make sure that it is reconnected with the correct polarity. Reversing the battery connections may result in damage to the one-way rectifiers.
- Never operate the alternator with the main circuit broken. Make sure that the battery, alternator, and regulator leads are not disconnected while the engine is running.
- Never attempt to polarize an alternator.
- When charging a battery that is installed in the vehicle, disconnect the negative battery cable.
- When utilizing a booster battery as a starting aid, always connect it in parallel; negative to negative, and positive to positive.
- When arc (electric) welding is to be performed on any part of the vehicle, disconnect the negative battery cable and alternator leads.
- Never unplug the PCM while the engine is running or with the ignition in the **ON** position. Severe and expensive damage may result within the solid state equipment.

Alternator

TESTING

Voltage Test

1. Make sure the engine is **OFF**, and turn the headlights on for 15–20 seconds to remove any surface charge from the battery.
2. Using a DVOM set to volts DC, probe across the battery terminals.
3. Measure the battery voltage.
4. Write down the voltage reading and proceed to the next test.

No-Load Test

1. Connect a tachometer to the engine.

❊❊ CAUTION

Ensure that the transmission is in PARK and the emergency brake is set. Blocking a wheel is optional and an added safety measure.

2. Turn off all electrical loads (radio, blower motor, wipers, etc.)
3. Start the engine and increase engine speed to approximately 1500 rpm.
4. Measure the voltage reading at the battery with the engine holding a steady 1500 rpm. Voltage should have raised at least 0.5 volts, but no more than 2.5 volts.
5. If the voltage does not go up more than 0.5 volts, the alternator is not charging. If the voltage goes up more than 2.5 volts, the alternator is overcharging.

➡Usually under and overcharging is caused by a defective alternator, or its related parts (regulator), and replacement will fix the problem; however, faulty wiring and other problems can cause the charging system to malfunction. Further testing, which is not covered by this book, will reveal the exact component failure. Many automotive parts stores have

alternator bench testers available for use by customers. An alternator bench test is the most definitive way to determine the condition of your alternator.

6. If the voltage is within specifications, proceed to the next test.

Load Test

1. With the engine running, turn on the blower motor and the high beams (or other electrical accessories to place a load on the charging system).
2. Increase and hold engine speed to 2000 rpm.
3. Measure the voltage reading at the battery.
4. The voltage should increase at least 0.5 volts from the voltage test. If the voltage does not meet specifications, the charging system is malfunctioning.

➡**Usually under and overcharging is caused by a defective alternator, or its related parts (regulator), and replacement will fix the problem; however, faulty wiring and other problems can cause the charging system to malfunction. Further testing, which is not covered by this book, will reveal the exact component failure. Many automotive parts stores have alternator bench testers available for use by customers. An alternator bench test is the most definitive way to determine the condition of your alternator.**

REMOVAL & INSTALLATION

2.2L (VIN 4) Engine

▶ **See Figures 18 thru 25**

1. Disconnect the negative battery cable at the battery.

❊❊ CAUTION

Failure to disconnect the negative cable may result in injury from the positive battery lead at the alternator, and may short the alternator and regulator during the removal process.

2. Rotate the belt tensioner and remove the belt from around the alternator pulley.
3. Disconnect the regulator connector and the B+ cable from the rear of the alternator.
4. Remove the mounting bolts, then remove the alternator from the vehicle.
To install:
5. Place the alternator in its bracket and install the mounting bolts.
6. Attach the regulator connector and B+ cable to the alternator.
7. Rotate the belt tensioner and slip the belt back over the alternator pulley.
8. Connect the negative battery cable.

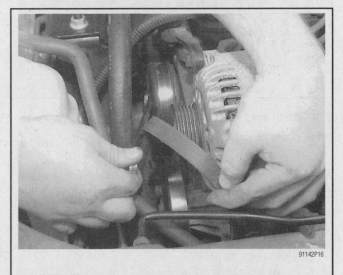

91142P16

Fig. 18 Remove the belt from around the alternator pulley

Fig. 19 Unplug the regulator connector

Fig. 20 Remove the rubber cover over the B+ connection

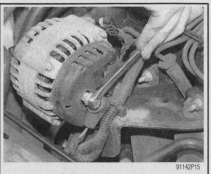

Fig. 21 Remove the nut securing the B+ connection and . . .

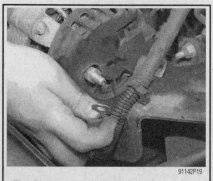

Fig. 22 . . . remove the connection from the alternator

Fig. 23 Remove the front two alternator mounting bolts and . . .

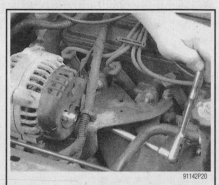

Fig. 24 . . . the rear alternator mounting bolt and . . .

Fig. 25 . . . remove the alternator from the engine

2.3L (VIN D) and 2.4L (VIN T) Engines

▶ See Figure 26

1. Disconnect the negative battery cable.

➡To avoid injuring yourself when rotating the serpentine belt tensioner, use a tight fitting 13mm drive tool that is at least 24 in. (61cm) long. This can be done using tool J 37059 or equivalent.

2. Remove the serpentine belt.
3. Raise and safely support the vehicle.
4. Unfasten and remove the lower alternator mounting bolts.
5. Carefully lower the vehicle.
6. Remove the upper alternator bolt, detach the electrical connectors, then remove the alternator from the vehicle.

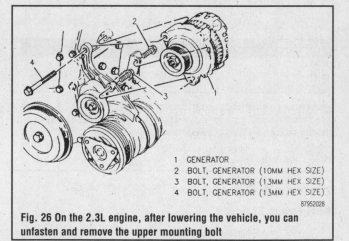

1   GENERATOR
2   BOLT, GENERATOR (10MM HEX SIZE)
3   BOLT, GENERATOR (13MM HEX SIZE)
4   BOLT, GENERATOR (13MM HEX SIZE)

Fig. 26 On the 2.3L engine, after lowering the vehicle, you can unfasten and remove the upper mounting bolt

To install:

7. Position the alternator in the vehicle.
8. Attach the alternator electrical connections. Tighten the "BAT" terminal nut to 65 inch lbs. (7.5 Nm).
9. Install the upper alternator retaining bolt.
10. Raise and safely support the vehicle.
11. Secure the lower alternator mounting bolts, then carefully lower the vehicle.
12. Install the serpentine belt.
13. Connect the negative battery cable.

Regulator

The alternators used in these vehicles have an internal regulator. A solid state regulator is mounted within the alternator. All regulator components are enclosed in a solid mold. The regulator is non-adjustable and requires no maintenance. The alternator is serviced as a complete unit and cannot be overhauled.

STARTING SYSTEM

General Information

The starting system includes the battery, starter motor, solenoid, ignition switch, circuit protection and wiring connecting the components. An inhibitor switch located in the Transmission Range (TR) sensor is included in the starting system to prevent the vehicle from being started with the vehicle in gear.

When the ignition key is turned to the **START** position, current flows and energizes the starter's solenoid coil. The solenoid plunger and clutch shift lever are activated and the clutch pinion engages the ring gear on the flywheel. The switch contacts close and the starter cranks the engine until it starts.

To prevent damage caused by excessive starter armature rotation when the engine starts, the starter incorporates an over-running clutch in the pinion gear.

Starter

TESTING

Voltage Drop Test

➡ **The battery must be in good condition and fully charged prior to performing this test.**

1. Disable the ignition system by unplugging the coil pack. Verify that the vehicle will not start.
2. Connect a voltmeter between the positive terminal of the battery and the starter **B+** circuit.
3. Turn the ignition key to the **START** position and note the voltage on the meter.
4. If voltage reads 0.5 volts or more, there is high resistance in the starter cables or the cable ground, repair as necessary. If the voltage reading is ok proceed to the next step.
5. Connect a voltmeter between the positive terminal of the battery and the starter **M** circuit.
6. Turn the ignition key to the **START** position and note the voltage on the meter.
7. If voltage reads 0.5 volts or more, there is high resistance in the starter. Repair or replace the starter as necessary.

➡ **Many automotive parts stores have starter bench testers available for use by customers. A starter bench test is the most definitive way to determine the condition of your starter.**

REMOVAL & INSTALLATION

2.2L (VIN 4) Engine

▶ **See Figures 27 thru 35**

1. Disconnect the negative battery cable at the battery.
2. Raise and safely support the vehicle.

3. Remove the electrical connections from the back of the starter.
4. Remove the bell-housing cover.
5. Remove the starter support bracket bolt from the engine block.
6. Unfasten the starter motor-to-engine bolts, then carefully lower the starter.
7. Remove the nuts/bolts that hold the starter support bracket to the starter.

To install:

8. Transfer the starter support bracket to the new starter if the starter is being replaced.
9. Raise the starter into position and secure the starter using the starter motor-to-engine bolts. Tighten the bolts to 32 ft. lbs. (43 Nm).
10. Install the starter support bracket-to-engine bolt to 24 ft. lbs. (32 Nm).
11. Install the bell-housing cover.
12. Install the starter electrical connections on the back of the starter. Tighten the "S" terminal to 22 inch lbs. (2.5 Nm) and the battery terminal to 106 inch lbs. (12 Nm).
13. Carefully lower the vehicle, then connect the negative battery cable.

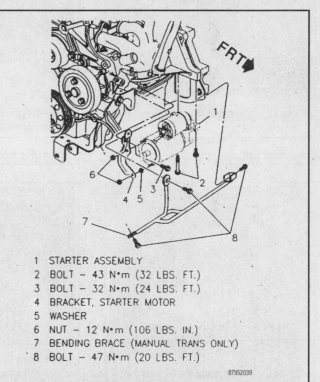

1 STARTER ASSEMBLY
2 BOLT – 43 N•m (32 LBS. FT.)
3 BOLT – 32 N•m (24 LBS. FT.)
4 BRACKET, STARTER MOTOR
5 WASHER
6 NUT – 12 N•m (106 LBS. IN.)
7 BENDING BRACE (MANUAL TRANS ONLY)
8 BOLT – 47 N•m (20 LBS. FT.)

87952039

Fig. 27 Removal and installation of the starter—2.2L engine shown

91142P05

Fig. 28 Remove the starter electrical connections from the back of the starter

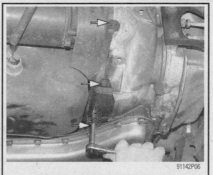

91142P06

Fig. 29 Remove the three bell-housing cover retaining bolts and . . .

91142P07

Fig. 30 . . . remove the bell-housing cover

2.3L (VIN D) and 2.4L (VIN T) Engines

▶ **See Figure 36**

1. Disconnect the negative battery cable at the battery.
2. Detach the air inlet duct from the throttle body.
3. Remove the top starter bolt.
4. Raise and safely support the vehicle.
5. Remove the lower starter retaining bolt.
6. If necessary, position the engine wiring harness aside.
7. Position the starter to enable access to the solenoid wiring, then detach the wiring.
8. Remove the starter from the vehicle.

To install:

9. Raise the starter to the vehicle, then attach the wiring.
10. Position the starter, then secure using the lower starter bolt. Tighten to 66 ft. lbs. (90 Nm)
11. If moved, reposition the engine wiring harness.
12. Carefully lower the vehicle.

13. Install the top starter bolt, then tighten to 66 ft. lbs. (90 Nm).
14. Fasten the air inlet duct to the throttle body.
15. Connect the negative battery cable.

SOLENOID REPLACEMENT

▶ **See Figures 37 and 38**

1. Disconnect the negative battery cable.
2. Remove the starter motor from the vehicle and place on a clean work surface.
3. Disconnect the solenoid-to-starter lead wire.
4. Remove the solenoid mounting bolts and slide out the solenoid. Pull out the solenoid torsion spring, if so equipped. On some models, it may be necessary to remove the starter assembly through bolts from the yoke to remove the solenoid.
5. If equipped with shims between the solenoid and starter, remove and place aside.

Fig. 31 Remove the starter support brace-to-engine bolt

Fig. 32 The starter is retained by two bolts

Fig. 33 Remove the bolts and . . .

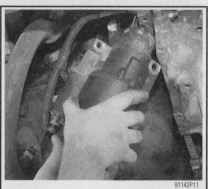

Fig. 34 . . . remove the starter from the engine

Fig. 35 Note that the starter bolts are two different lengths, the longer one goes on the inside

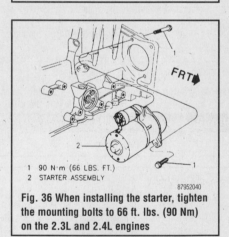

1 90 N·m (66 LBS. FT.)
2 STARTER ASSEMBLY

Fig. 36 When installing the starter, tighten the mounting bolts to 66 ft. lbs. (90 Nm) on the 2.3L and 2.4L engines

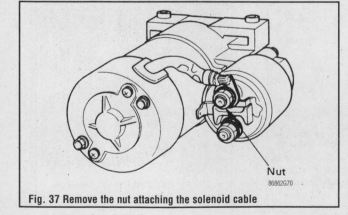

Fig. 37 Remove the nut attaching the solenoid cable

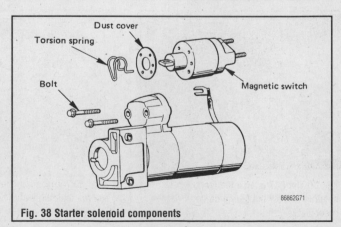

Fig. 38 Starter solenoid components

To install:

6. Install the solenoid with any adjustment shims.
7. Torque the bolts to 15 ft. lbs. (20 Nm).
8. Connect the starter-to-solenoid electrical lead.

9. Install the starter through-bolts if removed.
10. Install the starter motor.
11. Check for proper operation.

SENDING UNITS AND SENSORS

➡This section describes the operating principles of sending units, warning lights and gauges. Sensors which provide information to the Electronic Control Module (PCM) are covered in Section 4 of this manual.

Instrument panels contain a number of indicating devices (gauges and warning lights). These devices are composed of two separate components. One is the sending unit, mounted on the engine or other remote part of the vehicle, and the other is the actual gauge or light in the instrument panel.

Several types of sending units exist, however most can be characterized as being either a pressure type or a resistance type. Pressure type sending units convert liquid pressure into an electrical signal which is sent to the gauge. Resistance type sending units are most often used to measure temperature and use variable resistance to control the current flow back to the indicating device. Both types of sending units are connected in series by a wire to the battery (through the ignition switch). When the ignition is turned **ON**, current flows from the battery through the indicating device and on to the sending unit.

Coolant Temperature Sender

OPERATION

▶ **See Figure 39**

The coolant temperature sensor used by the PCM is used as the temperature sending unit. See Section 4 for more information.

TESTING

See Section 4 for TESTING of the Engine Coolant Temperature (ECT) sensor.

REMOVAL & INSTALLATION

See Section 4 for REMOVAL & INSTALLATION of the Engine Coolant Temperature (ECT) sensor.

Coolant Level Switch

OPERATION

▶ **See Figure 40**

The coolant level switch is located on the bottom side of the coolant recovery tank. The switch contains a reed switch and a magnetic float. When the coolant

level is normal, the float rests away from the reed switch, causing the switch to be "open". When the coolant level decreases in the coolant recovery tank below a specified level, the float rests on the reed switch and the switch "closes", illuminating the LOW COOLANT light.

TESTING

➡**Before testing the coolant level switch, make sure there is a sufficient amount of coolant in the recovery tank. If the coolant level is low, refill the tank with the proper amount of coolant.**

1. Unplug the coolant level switch.
2. With the key **ON**, and the engine **OFF**, use a test light connected to ground and connect the probe end of the test light to the signal circuit.
3. If the wiring, PCM, and Instrument panel are ok, the LOW COOLANT light should light up.
4. If the LOW COOLANT light is illuminated, replace the switch.

REMOVAL & INSTALLATION

The coolant level switch is a part of the coolant recovery tank. If the switch needs to be replaced, the coolant recovery tank must be replaced.

Oil Level Switch

OPERATION

The low oil level switch activates the **OIL** light in the instrument cluster when the oil level in the pan goes below a certain level. The switch is mounted on the oil pan.

REMOVAL & INSTALLATION

▶ **See Figures 41, 42, 43 and 44**

1. Disconnect the negative battery cable.
2. Raise and safely support the vehicle.
3. Position a suitable drain pan under the switch.
4. Detach the switch connector harness.
5. Drain the engine oil into a suitable container.
6. Remove the oil level switch.

To install:

7. Install the oil level switch and tighten it to 89 inch lbs. (10 Nm).
8. Attach the switch harness connector.

Fig. 39 The ECT is also the temperature sending unit for the gauge on the instrument cluster

91142P14

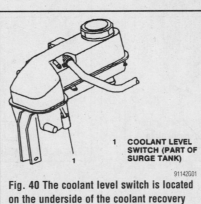

1 COOLANT LEVEL SWITCH (PART OF SURGE TANK)

91142G01

Fig. 40 The coolant level switch is located on the underside of the coolant recovery (surge) tank

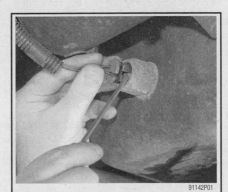

91142P01

Fig. 41 Use a small prytool to disengage the connector tab and . . .

Fig. 42 . . . remove the connector from the switch

Fig. 43 Use a wrench and loosen the switch

Fig. 44 Remove the switch from the oil pan

9. Carefully lower the vehicle.

10. Add the correct type and amount of engine oil to the crankcase, then connect the negative battery cable.

Oil Pressure Switch

OPERATION

▶ **See Figures 45 and 46**

The oil pressure switch relays the oil pressure in the engine to the instrument cluster. The switch will illuminate the **OIL PRESSURE** light if the oil pressure drops below 2psi (13 pa). The switch is usually located on the side of the engine, under the intake manifold on the 2.2L engine and on the side of the intake camshaft housing on the 2.3L/2.4L engine.

TESTING

✷✷ WARNING

This test is for testing the switch only. Verify that the engine has sufficient oil pressure before conducting this test.

1. Unplug the switch electrical connection.

2. Connect one lead of a ohmmeter to the switch terminal and the other lead to the switch body.

3. With the engine off the resistance should be approximately 1 ohm.

4. Start the engine. The resistance should increase as the engine speed increases.

5. If not, replace the switch.

REMOVAL & INSTALLATION

1. Disconnect the negative battery cable

2. Raise and safely support the vehicle.

3. Drain the engine oil.

4. Disconnect the switch electrical lead and unscrew the switch.

To install:

5. Coat the first two or three threads with sealer. Install the switch and tighten until snug.

6. Attach the electrical lead.

7. Lower the vehicle.

8. Connect the battery cable and fill the engine with oil.

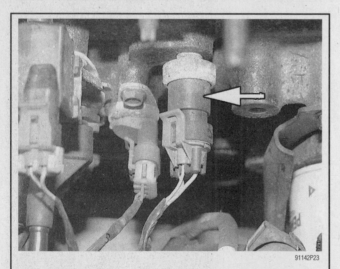

Fig. 45 The oil pressure switch is located on the engine block under the intake manifold and is accessible from underneath the vehicle—2.2L engine

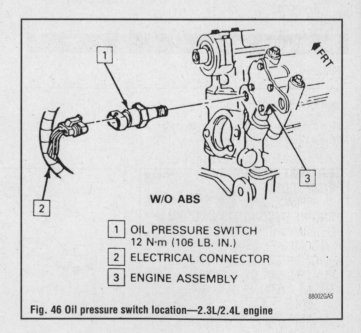

W/O ABS

1	OIL PRESSURE SWITCH 12 N·m (106 LB. IN.)
2	ELECTRICAL CONNECTOR
3	ENGINE ASSEMBLY

Fig. 46 Oil pressure switch location—2.3L/2.4L engine

ENGINE MECHANICAL 3-2
ENGINE 3-2
　REMOVAL & INSTALLATION 3-2
ROCKER ARM (VALVE) COVER 3-4
　REMOVAL & INSTALLATION 3-4
CAMSHAFT CARRIER COVER 3-5
　REMOVAL & INSTALLATION 3-5
ROCKER ARM/SHAFTS 3-7
　REMOVAL & INSTALLATION 3-7
THERMOSTAT 3-8
　REMOVAL & INSTALLATION 3-8
INTAKE MANIFOLD 3-9
　REMOVAL & INSTALLATION 3-9
EXHAUST MANIFOLD 3-13
　REMOVAL & INSTALLATION 3-13
RADIATOR 3-16
　REMOVAL & INSTALLATION 3-16
ENGINE FAN 3-19
　REMOVAL & INSTALLATION 3-19
WATER PUMP 3-19
　REMOVAL & INSTALLATION 3-19
CYLINDER HEAD 3-21
　REMOVAL & INSTALLATION 3-21
OIL PAN 3-24
　REMOVAL & INSTALLATION 3-24
OIL PUMP 3-25
　REMOVAL & INSTALLATION 3-25
CRANKSHAFT PULLEY/DAMPER 3-25
　REMOVAL & INSTALLATION 3-25
TIMING CHAIN COVER AND SEAL 3-26
　REMOVAL & INSTALLATION 3-26
TIMING CHAIN AND GEARS 3-27
　REMOVAL & INSTALLATION 3-27
CAMSHAFT AND BEARINGS 3-30
　REMOVAL & INSTALLATION 3-30
　INSPECTION 3-32
VALVE LIFTERS 3-33
　REMOVAL, INSTALLATION &
　　INSPECTION 3-33
BALANCE SHAFTS 3-33
　REMOVAL & INSTALLATION 3-33
　INSPECTION 3-35
REAR MAIN SEAL 3-36
　REMOVAL & INSTALLATION 3-36
FLYWHEEL/FLEXPLATE 3-37
　REMOVAL & INSTALLATION 3-37
EXHAUST SYSTEM 3-37
INSPECTION 3-37
　REPLACEMENT 3-38
ENGINE RECONDITIONING 3-39
DETERMINING ENGINE CONDITION 3-39
　COMPRESSION TEST 3-39
　OIL PRESSURE TEST 3-40
BUY OR REBUILD? 3-40
ENGINE OVERHAUL TIPS 3-40
　TOOLS 3-40
　OVERHAUL TIPS 3-40
　CLEANING 3-40
　REPAIRING DAMAGED
　　THREADS 3-41

ENGINE PREPARATION 3-42
CYLINDER HEAD 3-42
　DISASSEMBLY 3-42
　INSPECTION 3-45
　REFINISHING & REPAIRING 3-47
　ASSEMBLY 3-48
ENGINE BLOCK 3-49
　GENERAL INFORMATION 3-49
　DISASSEMBLY 3-49
　INSPECTION 3-50
　REFINISHING 3-51
　ASSEMBLY 3-52
ENGINE START-UP AND BREAK-IN 3-54
　STARTING THE ENGINE 3-54
　BREAKING IT IN 3-54
　KEEP IT MAINTAINED 3-54
SPECIFICATIONS CHARTS
　ENGINE MECHANICAL
　　SPECIFICATIONS 3-55
　TORQUE SPECIFICATIONS 3-60

3

ENGINE AND ENGINE OVERHAUL

ENGINE MECHANICAL 3-2
EXHAUST SYSTEM 3-37
ENGINE RECONDITIONING 3-39

ENGINE MECHANICAL

Engine

REMOVAL & INSTALLATION

In the process of removing the engine, you will come across a number of steps which call for the removal of a separate component or system, such as "disconnect the exhaust system" or "remove the radiator." In most instances, a detailed removal procedure can be found elsewhere in this manual.

It is virtually impossible to list each individual wire and hose which must be disconnected, simply because so many different model and engine combinations have been manufactured. Careful observation and common sense are the best possible approaches to any repair procedure.

Removal and installation of the engine can be made easier if you follow these basic points:

• If you have to drain any of the fluids, use a suitable container.
• Always tag any wires or hoses and, if possible, the components they came from before disconnecting them.
• Because there are so many bolts and fasteners involved, store and label the retainers from components separately in muffin pans, jars or coffee cans. This will prevent confusion during installation.
• After unbolting the transaxle, always make sure it is properly supported.
• If it is necessary to disconnect the air conditioning system, have this service performed by a qualified technician using a recovery/recycling station. If the system does not have to be disconnected, unbolt the compressor and set it aside.
• When unbolting the engine mounts, always make sure the engine is properly supported. When removing the engine, make sure that any lifting devices are properly attached to the engine. It is recommended that if your engine is supplied with lifting hooks, your lifting apparatus be attached to them.
• Lift the engine from its compartment slowly, checking that no hoses, wires or other components are still connected.
• After the engine is clear of the compartment, place it on an engine stand or workbench.
• After the engine has been removed, you can perform a partial or full teardown of the engine using the procedures outlined in this manual.

2.2L Engine

1. Properly relieve the fuel system pressure, then disconnect the negative battery cable.
2. Drain the cooling system into a suitable container.
3. Remove the air cleaner outlet duct.
4. Detach the upper radiator hose at the coolant outlet.
5. Disconnect the brake booster vacuum hose.
6. Tag and detach the following electrical connections:
• Idle Air Control (IAC)
• Alternator
• Throttle Position (TP) sensor
• Manifold Absolute Pressure (MAP) sensor
• EVAP emission solenoid
• Fuel injector harness
• Exhaust Gas Recirculation (EGR) valve
• Engine Coolant Temperature (ECT) sensor
• Transaxle Converter Clutch (TCC)
• Oxygen sensor
• Park/Neutral position switch
• Engine grounds
7. Remove the serpentine drive belt.
8. Disconnect the transaxle shift control cable from the range select lever and bracket.
9. Detach the coolant surge tank hose, then remove the tank.
10. Disconnect the vacuum line near the master cylinder.
11. Install a suitable engine support fixture.
12. Disconnect the lower radiator hose from the water pump.
13. Raise and safely support the vehicle.
14. Remove both front wheel and tire assemblies, then remove both splash shields.
15. Disconnect the exhaust pipe at the manifold and catalytic converter.

16. Remove the engine mount strut.
17. Disconnect the wheel speed sensor wire harness from the control arms.
18. Separate the ball joints from the steering knuckles. Using an appropriate tool, separate the tie rod ends from the struts.
19. Detach the brake lines from the suspension supports.
20. If equipped remove the A/C compressor and support with the lines attached.
21. Tag and detach the following electrical connectors:
• Electronic Ignition Module
• Vehicle Speed Sensors (VSS)
• Cooling Fan
• Starter
• A/C compressor
• Oil pressure and level sensors
• Engine grounds
22. Disconnect the power steering lines from the rack and pinion assembly. Detach the flexible coupling joint at the rack and pinion assembly.
23. Disconnect the accelerator control, cruise control (if equipped) and the T.V. cables from the accelerator control bracket.
24. Remove the suspension support assembly.
25. Disconnect the heater hoses at the front of the dash.
26. Remove both drive axles from the transaxle, then position them aside.
27. Disconnect the fuel lines.
28. Detach the cooler lines from the transaxle, then remove the transaxle mount.
29. Remove the engine mount assembly.
30. Place a suitable support under the vehicle. Carefully lower the vehicle so that it rests lightly on the support.
31. Remove the support fixture from the engine, then raise the vehicle, leaving the engine and transaxle assembly on the table.
32. Unfasten the retaining bolts, then separate the engine from the transaxle.
To install:
33. Position the engine to the transaxle, then install the retaining bolts. Refer to Section 7.
34. Lower the vehicle onto the engine and transaxle assembly.
35. Install a suitable engine support fixture onto the engine.
36. Install the engine mount assembly, then install the transaxle mount.
37. Attach the cooler lines to the transaxle.
38. Connect the fuel lines.
39. Install both drive axles into the transaxle.
40. Connect the heater hoses to the front of the cowl.
41. Install the suspension support assembly.
42. Connect the accelerator, cruise control, and T.V. cables to the accelerator control bracket.
43. Attach the flexible coupling joint to the rack and pinion assembly.
44. Connect the power steering lines to the rack and pinion assembly.
45. Attach the following electrical connectors as tagged during removal:
• Electronic Ignition Module
• Vehicle Speed Sensors (VSS)
• Cooling Fan
• Starter
• A/C compressor
• Oil pressure and level sensors
• Engine grounds
46. Install the A/C compressor, if equipped.
47. Connect the brake lines to the suspension support.
48. Fasten the tie rod ends to the struts, then connect the ball joints to the steering knuckles.
49. Connect the wheel speed sensor wire harness to the control arms.
50. Install the engine mount strut.
51. Fasten the exhaust pipe to the exhaust manifold and catalytic converter.
52. Install the splash shields and the wheel and tire assemblies.
53. Carefully lower the vehicle.
54. Connect the lower radiator hose to the water pump.
55. Remove the engine support fixture.
56. Attach the vacuum line, located near the master cylinder.
57. Install the coolant surge tank, then connect the tank's hose.
58. Connect the transaxle shift control cable.
59. Install the serpentine drive belt.

60. Attach the following electrical connectors, as tagged during removal:
- Idle Air Control (IAC)
- Alternator
- Throttle Position (TP) sensor
- Manifold Absolute Pressure (MAP) sensor
- EVAP emission solenoid
- Fuel injector harness
- Exhaust Gas Recirculation (EGR) valve
- Engine Coolant Temperature (ECT) sensor
- Transaxle Converter Clutch (TCC)
- Oxygen sensor
- Park/Neutral position switch
- Engine grounds

61. Connect the brake booster vacuum hose.
62. Attach the upper radiator hose and the air cleaner outlet duct.
63. Fill the cooling system and crankcase with the correct type and amount of fluids.
64. Connect the negative battery cable, then start the engine. Check for proper operation, fluid levels and/or leaks.

2.3L and 2.4L Engines

1. If equipped with A/C, have an MVAC certified technician recover the A/C refrigerant.
2. Disconnect the negative battery.
3. Properly drain the cooling system into an approved container.
4. Relieve the fuel system pressure.
5. Remove the left sound insulator, then disconnect the clutch pushrod form the pedal assembly.
6. Disconnect the heater hose at the thermostat assembly, then detach the radiator inlet (upper) hose.
7. Remove the air cleaner assembly and the coolant fan.
8. If equipped with A/C, disconnect the compressor/condenser hose assembly at the compressor, then discard the O-rings.
9. Disconnect the two vacuum hoses from the front of the engine.
10. Tag and detach the following electrical connectors:
- Alternator
- A/C compressor (if equipped)
- Fuel injector harness
- Idle Air Control (IAC) and TP sensor at the throttle body
- Manifold Absolute Pressure (MAP) sensor
- Intake Air Temperature (IAT) sensor
- EVAP canister purge solenoid
- Starter solenoid
- Ground connections
- Negative battery cable from the transaxle
- Electronic ignition coil and module assembly
- Engine Coolant Temperature (ECT) sensor(s)
- Oil pressure sensor/switch
- Oxygen sensor
- Crankshaft Position (CKP) sensor
- Back-up lamp switch, then position the harness aside

11. Disconnect the power brake vacuum hose from the throttle body. Detach the power brake vacuum tube-to-check valve hose from the tube.
12. Remove the throttle cable and bracket.
13. Unfasten the power steering pump rear bracket, then remove the bracket and vacuum tube as an assembly.
14. Unfasten the power steering pivot bolt, then remove the pump and drive belt. Position the pump aside, with the lines still attached.

✳✳ CAUTION

After relieving the fuel system pressure, a small amount of fuel may be released when servicing the fuel lines or connections. To prevent personal injury, cover the fuel line fittings with a shop towel before disconnecting to catch any fuel that may leak out. Place the towel in an approved container when the disconnection is completed.

15. Carefully disconnect the fuel lines.
16. Disconnect the shift cables. Detach the clutch actuator line.
17. Remove the exhaust manifold and heat shield.
18. Disconnect the radiator outlet (lower) hose from the radiator.

19. Install a suitable engine support fixture.
20. Unfasten the bolt attaching the coolant recovery/surge tank, then position the tank aside with the hoses still connected.
21. Remove the engine mount assembly.
22. Raise and safely support the vehicle, then remove the front wheel and tire assemblies. Remove the right splash shield.
23. Remove the radiator air deflector.
24. Tag and detach the following electrical connections:
- Vehicle Speed Sensor (VSS)
- Knock sensor
- Starter solenoid
- If equipped, both front ABS wheel speed sensors

25. Remove the engine mount strut and the transaxle mount.
26. Separate the ball joints from the steering knuckles.
27. Remove the suspension supports, crossmember, and stabilizer shaft as an assembly.
28. Disconnect the heater outlet hose from the radiator outlet pipe.
29. Remove the axle shaft from the transaxle and intermediate shaft, then position aside.
30. If equipped, disconnect the A/C lines from the oil pan.
31. Remove the flywheel housing cover.
32. Position a suitable support below the engine, then carefully lower the car onto the support.
33. Matchmark the threads on the support fixture hooks so that the setting can be duplicated when reinstalling the engine. Remove the engine support fixture J-hooks.
34. Raise the vehicle slowly off the engine and transaxle assembly. If may be necessary to move the engine/transaxle assembly rearward to clear the intake manifold.
35. Noting the position of the bolts, separate the engine from the transaxle.

To install:

✳✳ WARNING

Be sure the retaining bolts are in their correct locations. If not, engine damage may occur.

36. Assemble the engine to the transaxle. Refer to Section 7.
37. Position the engine and transaxle assembly under the engine compartment, then slowly lower the vehicle over the assembly until the transaxle mount is indexed, then install the retaining bolt.
38. Install the engine support fixture, making sure to adjust it to the previous setting.
39. Install the engine mount assembly and transaxle mount.
40. Carefully raise the vehicle off the support.
41. Attach the axle shafts to the transaxle.
42. Connect the heater outlet hose to the radiator outlet pipe.
43. Install the suspension supports, crossmember and stabilizer shaft assembly.
44. Attach the ball joints to the steering knuckles, then secure with the nuts.
45. Install the engine strut mount.
46. If equipped, connect the A/C line to the oil pan.
47. Attach the following electrical connectors, as tagged during removal:
- Vehicle Speed Sensor (VSS)
- Knock sensor
- Starter solenoid
- If equipped, both front ABS wheel speed sensors

48. Install the flywheel housing cover.
49. Fasten the radiator air deflector.
50. Connect the lower radiator hose.
51. Install the right splash shield, then the front wheel and tire assemblies.
52. Carefully lower the vehicle, then remove the engine support fixture.
53. Install the coolant recovery/surge tank, then secure using the retaining bolt.
54. Attach the following electrical connections, as tagged during removal:
- Alternator
- A/C compressor (if equipped)
- Fuel injector harness
- Idle Air Control (IAC) and TP sensor at the throttle body
- Manifold Absolute Pressure (MAP) sensor

- Intake Air Temperature (IAT) sensor
- EVAP canister purge solenoid
- Starter solenoid
- Ground connections
- Negative battery cable to the transaxle
- Electronic ignition coil and module assembly
- Engine Coolant Temperature (ECT) sensor(s)
- Oil pressure sensor/switch
- Oxygen sensor
- Crankshaft Position (CKP) sensor
- Back-up lamp switch

55. Attach the vacuum hoses.

56. If equipped with A/C, attach the compressor/condenser hose assembly to the compressor.

57. Fasten the clutch actuator line.

58. Install the exhaust manifold and heat shield.

59. Connect the fuel lines.

60. Connect the positive battery cable.

61. Fasten the power steering pump pivot-to-block bolt. Install the power steering pump rear bracket and tension belt.

62. Connect the vacuum hoses to the intake manifold and to the tube from the brake booster.

63. Install the throttle cable and bracket.

64. Install the coolant fan and air cleaner assembly.

65. Attach the radiator outlet (upper) hose. Fill the cooling system with the proper type and quantity of coolant.

66. Connect the clutch pushrod to the pedal assembly, then install the left sound insulator.

67. Attach the heater hose at the thermostat housing.

68. Fill the transaxle with fluid, then fill the crankcase with oil.

69. Connect the negative battery cable.

70. If equipped with A/C, have an MVAC certified technician evacuate, charge and leak test the system.

71. Start the engine and check the fluid levels, proper operation of the engine and/or fluid leakage.

Rocker Arm (Valve) Cover

REMOVAL & INSTALLATION

➡ On the 2.3L and 2.4L engines, there is no valve cover. The engines feature a cover over the cylinder head and camshaft housing. The cover has integrated camshaft bearing caps located on the bottom of the cover.

2.2L Engine

♦ See Figures 1 thru 14

1. Disconnect the negative battery cable.
2. Remove the air cleaner outlet duct.

Fig. 1 Remove the throttle pulley cover

Fig. 2 Disconnect the cruise control (if equipped) . . .

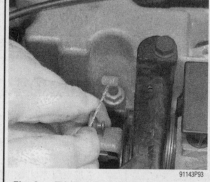

Fig. 3 . . TV (throttle valve or transmission kickdown) and . . .

Fig. 4 . . accelerator cables from the throttle body

Fig. 5 Slide the cables out of the bracket

Fig. 6 Remove the bracket retaining bolts and . . .

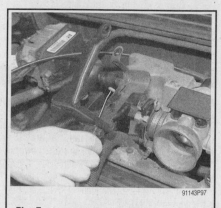

Fig. 7 . . remove the bracket

Fig. 8 Remove the PCV hose from the intake manifold

Fig. 9 The valve cover is retained by six bolts

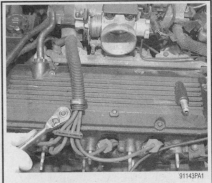

Fig. 10 Remove the valve cover retaining bolts and . . .

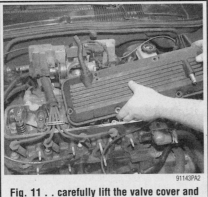

Fig. 11 . . carefully lift the valve cover and remove it from the engine

Fig. 12 Remove the old gasket from the valve cover

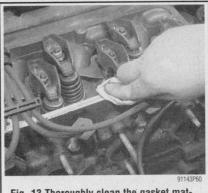

Fig. 13 Thoroughly clean the gasket mating surfaces of the cylinder head and . . .

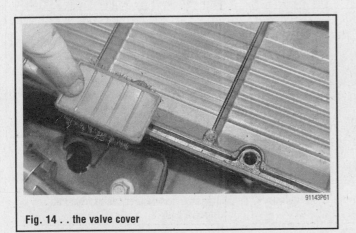

Fig. 14 . . the valve cover

3. Disconnect the accelerator control, cruise control (if equipped), and T.V. cables at the accelerator control bracket.

4. Remove the accelerator control bracket.

5. Disconnect the PCV valve hose.

6. Unfasten the retaining bolts, then remove the rocker arm (valve) cover from the vehicle. Remove and discard the gasket.

7. Clean off the cylinder head and cover sealing surfaces.

To install:

8. Position a new rocker arm gasket, then install the cover. Tighten the retaining bolt to 89 inch lbs. (10 Nm).

9. Connect the PCV valve hose.

10. Install the accelerator control bracket. Tighten the retaining bolts to 18 ft. lbs. (25 Nm).

11. Attach the accelerator control, cruise control (if equipped) and TV cables at the control bracket.

12. Install the air cleaner outlet duct.

13. Connect the negative battery cable, then start the engine and check for leaks.

Camshaft Carrier Cover

REMOVAL & INSTALLATION

➡ On the 2.3L and 2.4L engines, there is no valve cover. The engines feature a cover over the cylinder head and camshaft housing. The cover has integrated camshaft bearing caps located on the bottom of the cover.

2.3L and 2.4L DOHC Engines

INTAKE CAMSHAFT

♦ See Figures 15, 16, 17, 18 and 19

1. Disconnect the negative battery cable.

2. Detach the ignition coil and module assembly electrical connections.

3. Unfasten the ignition coil and module assembly-to-camshaft housing bolts, then remove the assembly by pulling it straight up.

4. Remove the power steering pump.

5. Detach the oil/air separator (crankcase ventilation system). Leave the hoses attached to the separator, disconnect from the oil fill, front cover and intake manifold, then remove as an assembly.

6. Unfasten the vacuum line from the fuel pressure regulator and fuel injector harness connector.

7. Disconnect the fuel line retaining clamp from the bracket on top of the intake cam housing.

8. Unfasten the fuel rail-to-camshaft housing retaining bolts, then remove the fuel rail from the cylinder head. Be sure to cover the injector openings in the cylinder head, cover the injector nozzles and leave the fuel lines attached and position the fuel rail aside (on top of the master cylinder).

9. Disconnect the timing chain housing at the intake camshaft housing but do not remove from the vehicle.

10. Unfasten the cam housing cover-to-housing retaining bolts and the cam housing-to-cylinder head bolts.

11. Use the reverse of the tightening procedure (in the accompanying figure) when loosening the camshaft housing-to-cylinder head bolts.

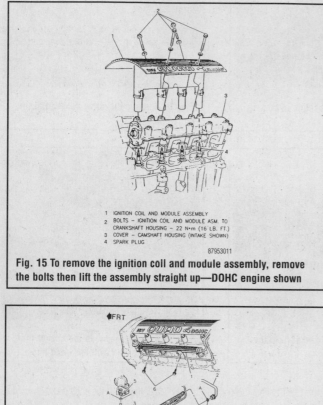

1 IGNITION COIL AND MODULE ASSEMBLY
2 BOLTS – IGNITION COIL AND MODULE ASM. TO CRANKSHAFT HOUSING – 22 N·m (16 LB. FT.)
3 COVER – CAMSHAFT HOUSING (INTAKE SHOWN)
4 SPARK PLUG

87953011

Fig. 15 To remove the ignition coil and module assembly, remove the bolts then lift the assembly straight up—DOHC engine shown

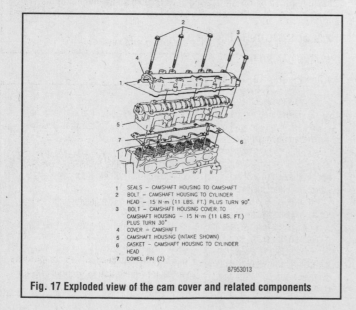

1 FUEL RAIL AND PRESSURE REGULATOR
2 PIPE FUEL FEED 30 N·m (22 LB. FT.)
3 PIPE FUEL RETURN
4 SEAL FUEL LINE
5 BOLT 5 N·m (44 LB. IN.)
6 BOLT 26 N·m (19 LB. FT.)
A LUBRICATE SEAL

87953012

Fig. 16 After removing the fuel rail, cover the injector openings in the cylinder head to prevent any debris from falling in

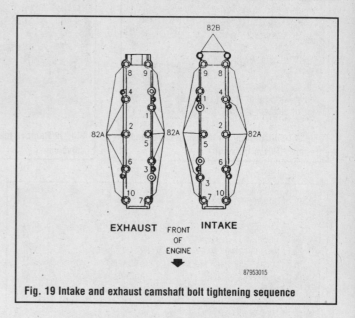

(Fig. 17 — lower left)

1 SEALS – CAMSHAFT HOUSING TO CAMSHAFT
2 BOLT – CAMSHAFT HOUSING TO CYLINDER HEAD – 15 N·m (11 LBS. FT.) PLUS TURN 90°
3 BOLT – CAMSHAFT HOUSING COVER TO CAMSHAFT HOUSING – 15 N·m (11 LBS. FT.) PLUS TURN 30°
4 COVER – CAMSHAFT
5 CAMSHAFT HOUSING (INTAKE SHOWN)
6 GASKET – CAMSHAFT HOUSING TO CYLINDER HEAD
7 DOWEL PIN (2)

87953013

Fig. 17 Exploded view of the cam cover and related components

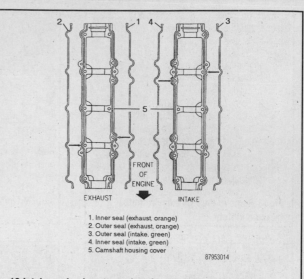

1. Inner seal (exhaust, orange)
2. Outer seal (exhaust, orange)
3. Outer seal (intake, green)
4. Inner seal (intake, green)
5. Camshaft housing cover

87953014

Fig. 18 Intake and exhaust cam housing-to-cover seal locations

87953015

Fig. 19 Intake and exhaust camshaft bolt tightening sequence

12. Push the cover off the housing by threading four of the housing-to-head retaining bolts into the tapped holes in the cover. Make sure to tighten the bolts evenly remove the cover from the vehicle.

13. Remove and discard the cover-to-housing seals and clean the mating surfaces.

To install:

14. Position new seals on the camshaft cover. Refer to the accompanying figure.

15. Apply pipe sealant GM part number 1052080 or equivalent to the camshaft housing and cover retaining bolt threads. Using J 366660, install the bolts, then tighten in sequence to the specifications in the accompanying figure.

16. Fasten the timing chain housing.

17. Uncover fuel injectors, then lubricate new injector O-ring seals with clean engine oil and install on the injectors.

18. Uncover the injector openings in the cylinder head, then install the fuel rail onto the cylinder head. Install the fuel rail-to-cylinder head retaining bolts and tighten to 19 ft. lbs. (26 Nm).

19. Install the fuel line retaining clamp and retainer to the bracket on top of the cam housing.

20. Connect the vacuum line to the fuel pressure regulator. Attach the fuel injector harness connector.

21. Install the oil/air separator assembly. You may want to lubricate the hoses to ease installation.

22. Lubricate the inner surface of the camshaft seal with clean engine oil, then install the seal into the camshaft housing using tool J 36015, or equivalent seal installer.

23. Using tool J 36015 or equivalent pulley installer, install the power steering pump drive pulley onto the intake camshaft.

24. Install the power steering pump assembly and the drive belt. Adjust tension to specification.

25. Fasten any spark plug boot connector assembly that stuck to a spark plug back onto the ignition coil and module assembly.

26. Position the coil and module assembly over the spark plugs, then push the assembly straight down. Make sure it is properly seated.

27. Clean off any loose lubricant from the coil and module assembly-to-camshaft housing bolts. Apply pipe sealant GM part number 1052080 or equivalent, onto the bolts, then tighten the bolts to 16 ft. lbs. (22 Nm).

28. Attach the coil and module electrical connector.

29. Connect the negative battery cable, then start the engine and inspect for oil leaks.

EXHAUST CAMSHAFT

▸ **See Figures 17, 18 and 19**

1. Disconnect the negative battery cable.

2. Detach the ignition coil and module electrical connection. Remove the coil and module assembly-to-camshaft housing bolts, then remove the assembly by lifting it straight up.

3. Disengage the electrical connection from the oil pressure switch.

4. For vehicles equipped with an automatic transaxle, remove the transaxle fluid level indicator tube assembly from the exhaust camshaft cover, then position it aside.

5. Disconnect, but do not remove from the vehicle, the timing chain housing at the exhaust camshaft housing.

6. Remove the exhaust camshaft cover and gasket, then discard the gasket. Clean all old gasket debris from the cover mating surfaces.

To install:

7. Position new camshaft housing-to-cover seals. No sealant is needed.

8. Apply pipe sealant GM part number 1052080 or equivalent to the threads of the camshaft housing and cover retaining bolts.

9. Position the cover onto the housing, then tighten the bolts, in sequence, to specification.

10. Tighten the timing chain housing retainers.

11. Install the transaxle fluid level indicator tube assembly to the exhaust camshaft cover.

12. Attach the oil pressure switch electrical connector.

13. Reinstall any spark plug boot connectors that may have been stuck to a spark plug, back onto the ignition coil and module assembly.

14. Position the coil and module assembly over the spark plugs then push it straight down making sure it is firmly and properly seated.

15. Clean off any lubricant on the coil and module-to-camshaft housing bolts. Apply pipe sealant GM part number 1052080 or equivalent to the bolts, then tighten them to 16 ft. lbs. (22 Nm).

16. Attach the ignition coil and module assembly electrical connector.

17. Connect the negative battery cable, then start the engine and inspect for leaks.

Rocker Arm/Shafts

REMOVAL & INSTALLATION

2.2L Engine

▸ **See Figures 20, 21, 22 and 23**

➡**Place the components in a rack in order to be sure they are installed at the same location and with the same mating surface as when removed.**

1. Disconnect the negative battery cable.

2. Remove the rocker (valve) arm cover.

3. Unfasten the rocker arm nuts.

4. Remove the rocker arm(s) from the cylinder head. Be sure not to lose the pivot ball and washer inside the rocker arm.

5. Remove the pushrods.

To install:

6. Install the pushrods. Be sure to install the pushrods in the correct positions, and be sure they seat properly in the lifters.

7. Coat the bearing surfaces of the rocker arms and pivot balls with a quality assembly lube meeting GM specification 1052365 or equivalent.

8. Install the rocker arm(s).

9. Install the rocker arm nuts, and tighten to 22 ft. lbs. (30 Nm).

10. Install the rocker arm cover.

11. Connect the negative battery cable.

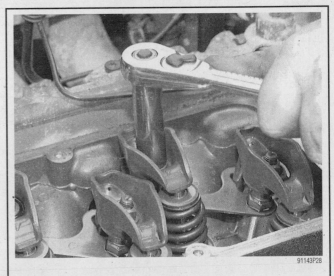

Fig. 20 Loosen and remove the rocker arm nuts

Fig. 21 Remove the rocker ball and washer (which should be inside the rocker arm). Be careful not to loose the ball

Fig. 22 If necessary, remove the pushrod

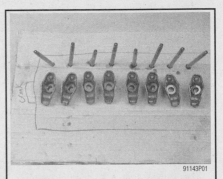

Fig. 23 Be sure to keep all the components in order for reinstallation. A good tool for this is a piece of cardboard as shown

Thermostat

REMOVAL & INSTALLATION

2.2L Engine

▶ See Figures 24 thru 29

➡When adding coolant, it is important that you use GM Goodwrench DEX-COOL® (orange colored, silicate free) coolant meeting GM specifications. On these vehicles, if silicated coolant is added to the system, premature engine, heater core or radiator corrosion may result. In addition, the engine coolant will require change sooner; at 30,000 miles or 24 months.

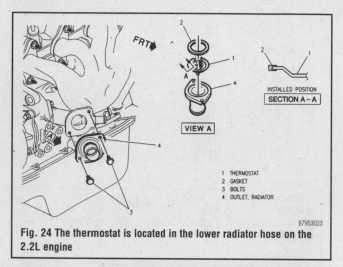

Fig. 24 The thermostat is located in the lower radiator hose on the 2.2L engine

1. Disconnect the negative battery cable.
2. Properly drain and recover the coolant until the level is below the thermostat.
3. Unfasten the coolant outlet-to-inlet manifold attaching bolt and nut, then remove the outlet.
4. Remove the thermostat. Clean the inlet manifold and outlet mating surfaces.

To install:
5. Install a new O-ring onto the thermostat
6. Place the thermostat in the inlet manifold.
7. Attach the coolant outlet to the inlet manifold, using the bolt and nut. Tighten to 89 inch lbs. (10 Nm).
8. Refill the engine cooling system.
9. Connect the negative battery cable, then start the engine and check for coolant leaks.

2.3L and 2.4L Engines

▶ See Figure 30

➡When adding coolant, it is important that you use GM Goodwrench DEX-COOL® (orange colored, silicate free) coolant meeting GM specifications. On these vehicles, if silicated coolant is added to the system, premature engine, heater core or radiator corrosion may result. In addition, the engine coolant will require change sooner; at 30,000 miles or 24 months.

1. Disconnect the negative battery cable.
2. Properly drain and recover the coolant to a level below the thermostat.
3. Unfasten the cover-to-outlet pipe bolt, which is accessible through the exhaust manifold runners.
4. Raise and safely support the vehicle.
5. Disconnect the radiator and heater hoses from the outlet pipe.
6. Unfasten the outlet pipe-to-oil pan bolt and the cover-to-outlet pipe bolts.
7. Remove the thermostat, then clean the old gasket material from the mating surfaces.

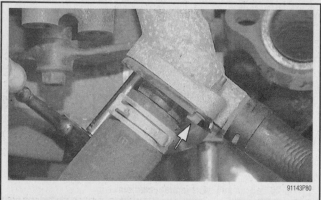

Fig. 25 Remove the two retaining bolts for on the housing

Fig. 26 Separate the housing halves to access the thermostat

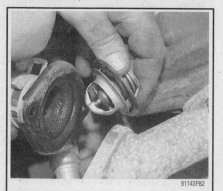

Fig. 27 Pull the thermostat out to remove it from the housing

Fig. 28 The thermostat has an O-ring which goes around the center

Fig. 29 Thoroughly clean the mating surfaces of the thermostat housing

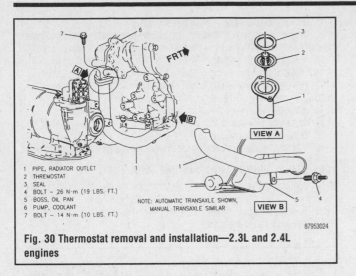

1 PIPE, RADIATOR OUTLET
2 THREMOSTAT
3 SEAL
4 BOLT – 26 N·m (19 LBS. FT.)
5 BOSS, OIL PAN
6 PUMP, COOLANT
7 BOLT – 14 N·m (10 LBS. FT.)

NOTE: AUTOMATIC TRANSAXLE SHOWN, MANUAL TRANSAXLE SIMILAR

VIEW A
VIEW B
FRT

87953024

Fig. 30 Thermostat removal and installation—2.3L and 2.4L engines

To install:

8. Position the thermostat in its correct location, then install the cover-to-outlet pipe bolt. Tighten the bolt to 10 ft. lbs. (14 Nm).

9. Install the outlet pipe-to-oil pan bolt. Tighten the pipe-to-oil pan bolt to 19 ft. lbs. (26 Nm) and the pipe-to-transaxle bolt to 40 ft. lbs. (54 Nm).

10. Connect the radiator and heater hoses to the outlet pipe.

11. Carefully lower the vehicle.

12. Install the cover-to-outlet pipe bolt through the exhaust manifold runner.

13. Properly fill the cooling system, then connect the negative battery cable.

Intake Manifold

REMOVAL & INSTALLATION

2.2L Engine

1995–97 2.2L ENGINE UPPER INTAKE MANIFOLD

♦ See Figures 31 thru 39

These vehicles use a two-piece intake manifold. The upper half, sometimes called a plenum, contains the throttle body and the control cable connections. The lower half has individual port runner to each intake port on the cylinder head. The lower half of the manifold bolts to the cylinder head and houses the fuel injectors. Note that these pieces are cast aluminum. Care should be exercised when working with any light allow component.

1. Properly relieve the fuel system pressure.
2. Disconnect the negative battery cable.
3. Remove the throttle body air intake duct.
4. Drain the cooling system into an approved container.
5. Identify, tag and disconnect all necessary vacuum lines.
6. Disconnect the control cables from the throttle body lever and remove the control cable bracket form the intake manifold.
7. Tag and disconnect the following electrical wires:
- Idle Air Control (IAC) valve
- Throttle Position (TP) sensor
- Manifold Absolute Pressure (MAP) sensor
8. Remove the MAP sensor.
9. Unfasten the upper intake manifold mounting bolts, then remove the upper intake manifold.

To install:

10. Thoroughly clean the upper intake manifold and lower intake manifold sealing surfaces.

91143P62

Fig. 31 Remove the brake booster vacuum hose from the intake manifold

91143P63

Fig. 32 Using a small prying tool, release the clips attaching the vacuum harness to the upper intake and . . .

91143P64

Fig. 33 . . remove the vacuum harness from the manifold

91143P45

Fig. 34 The upper intake manifold is retained by six bolts

91143P65

Fig. 35 Remove the six upper intake retaining bolts

91143P66

Fig. 36 Carefully remove the upper intake from the engine

Fig. 37 Remove the EGR valve injector

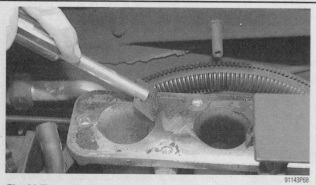

Fig. 38 Thoroughly clean the gasket mating surfaces on the upper and lower intake manifolds

11. Install the EGR valve injector (if removed).
12. Using a new gasket, install the upper intake manifold assembly. Tighten the upper intake manifold nuts in the proper sequence to 22 ft. lbs. (30 Nm).
13. Install the MAP sensor.
14. Attach the electrical connectors to the MAP sensor, Idle Air Control (IAC) valve and the Throttle Position (TP) sensor.
15. Connect the vacuum lines, as tagged during removal.
16. Connect the control cables and cable bracket.
17. Install the air intake duct.
18. Refill the coolant system.
19. Connect the negative battery cable, then start the engine and check for leaks.

1995–97 2.2L ENGINE LOWER INTAKE MANIFOLD

▶ See Figures 40 thru 52

1. Remove the upper intake manifold as described in this Section.
2. Unplug the fuel injectors.

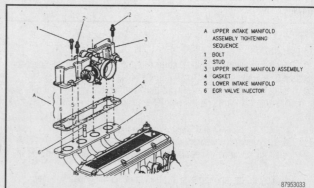

Fig. 39 The upper manifold bolts to the lower one, but be sure to use the correct sequence when tightening

Fig. 40 Unplug the connectors for the fuel injectors and position the harness out of the way

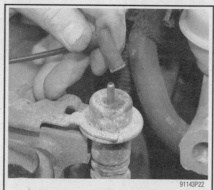

Fig. 41 Remove the vacuum line from the fuel pressure regulator

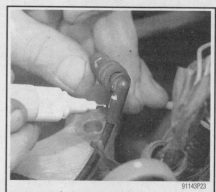

Fig. 42 Mark the vacuum lines to ease reassembly

Fig. 43 The front power steering bracket retaining bolts are accessible through holes in the pulley

Fig. 44 Remove the front bracket bolts. There is also a retaining bolt on the side (toward the firewall) and on the rear of the pump

Fig. 45 Remove the bracket retaining nut for the transaxle dipstick tube and remove the tube from the vehicle

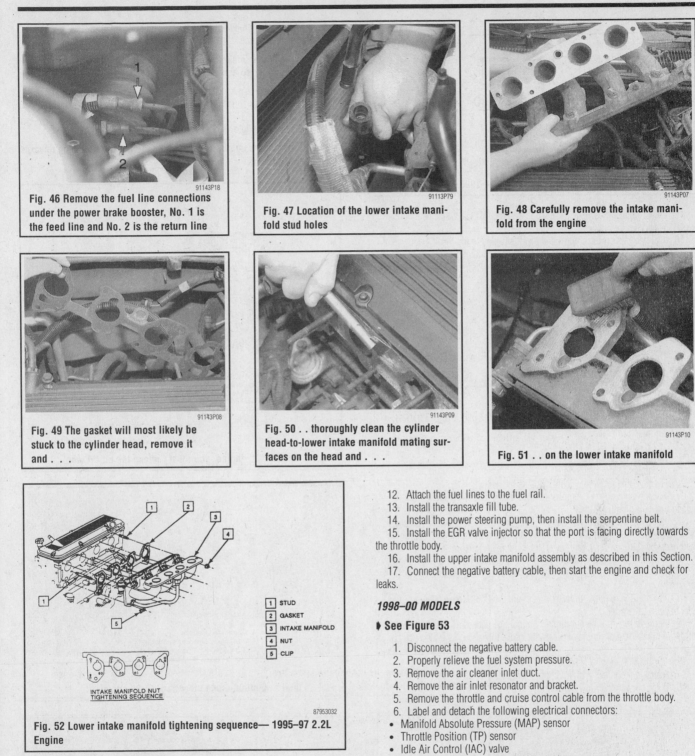

Fig. 46 Remove the fuel line connections under the power brake booster. No. 1 is the feed line and No. 2 is the return line

Fig. 47 Location of the lower intake manifold stud holes

Fig. 48 Carefully remove the intake manifold from the engine

Fig. 49 The gasket will most likely be stuck to the cylinder head, remove it and . . .

Fig. 50 . . thoroughly clean the cylinder head-to-lower intake manifold mating surfaces on the head and . . .

Fig. 51 . . on the lower intake manifold

1	STUD
2	GASKET
3	INTAKE MANIFOLD
4	NUT
5	CLIP

INTAKE MANIFOLD NUT TIGHTENING SEQUENCE

Fig. 52 Lower intake manifold tightening sequence— 1995–97 2.2L Engine

3. Tag and remove the vacuum lines from the fuel pressure regulator and any other necessary vacuum lines.

4. Remove the serpentine belt.

5. Remove the power steering pump and lay it aside with the fluid lines attached.

6. Remove the transaxle fill tube.

7. Disconnect the fuel lines from the fuel rail.

8. If necessary for access, raise and safely support the vehicle.

9. Unfasten the intake manifold nuts, then remove the manifold.

10. Clean the gasket mounting surfaces.

To install:

11. Install a new gasket, then position the lower intake manifold. Tighten the lower intake manifold nuts in the proper sequence to 24 ft. lbs. (33 Nm).

12. Attach the fuel lines to the fuel rail.

13. Install the transaxle fill tube.

14. Install the power steering pump, then install the serpentine belt.

15. Install the EGR valve injector so that the port is facing directly towards the throttle body.

16. Install the upper intake manifold assembly as described in this Section.

17. Connect the negative battery cable, then start the engine and check for leaks.

1998–00 MODELS

▶ See Figure 53

1. Disconnect the negative battery cable.

2. Properly relieve the fuel system pressure.

3. Remove the air cleaner inlet duct.

4. Remove the air inlet resonator and bracket.

5. Remove the throttle and cruise control cable from the throttle body.

6. Label and detach the following electrical connectors:

- Manifold Absolute Pressure (MAP) sensor
- Throttle Position (TP) sensor
- Idle Air Control (IAC) valve

7. Unbolt and remove the throttle body.

8. Disconnect the fuel supply line and the fuel inlet pipe.

9. Remove the intake manifold mounting nuts/bolts, then remove the manifold from the engine.

10. Clean the gasket mating surfaces on the cylinder head, intake manifold and throttle body. Inspect the manifold for cracks, broken flanges, and gasket surface damage.

To install:

11. Install the intake manifold using a new gasket.

12. Tighten the mounting bolts/nuts, in sequence, to 17 ft. lbs. (24 Nm).

13. Install the throttle body and tighten the mounting bolts to 89 inch lbs. (10 Nm).

14. Mount the fuel pipe and connect the fuel supply line.

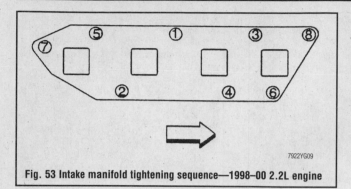

Fig. 53 Intake manifold tightening sequence—1998–00 2.2L engine

15. Attach the MAP sensor, TP sensor, and the IAC valve electrical connectors.
16. Connect the cruise control and throttle cables to the throttle body.
17. Install the air inlet resonator bracket and resonator.
18. Install the air cleaner inlet duct.
19. Connect the negative battery cable.

2.3L and 2.4L Engines

▶ **See Figures 54 thru 59**

1. Properly relieve the fuel system pressure.
2. Disconnect the negative battery cable, then properly drain the cooling system.
3. Tag and detach the following electrical connectors:
- Manifold Absolute Pressure (MAP) sensor
- Intake Air Temperature (IAT) sensor
- EVAP canister purge solenoid
- Fuel injector harness
4. Label and disconnect the vacuum hoses from the fuel regulator and EVAP canister purge solenoid to canister.
5. Unfasten the air cleaner duct.
6. Remove the accelerator control cable bracket.
7. For the 2.4L engine, remove the stud-ended alternator mount bolt, then detach the EGR pipe from the EGR adapter.
8. For the 2.3L engine, remove the oil air separator (crankcase ventilation system) as an assembly. Leave the hoses attached to the separator. Disconnect the hoses from the oil fill, chain cover, intake duct and the intake manifold.
9. For the 2.3L engine, detach the oil/air separator from the oil fill tube.
10. For the 2.3L engine, remove the oil fill cap and oil level indicator assembly.
11. For the 2.3L engine, unfasten the oil fill tube bolt/screw, then pull the tube upward to remove.
12. Remove the fill tube out the top, rotating as necessary to gain clearance for the oil/air separator nipple between the intake tubes and fuel rail electrical harness.
13. For the 2.4L engine, raise and safely support the vehicle.
14. Remove the intake manifold support brace.
15. If raised, carefully lower the vehicle.

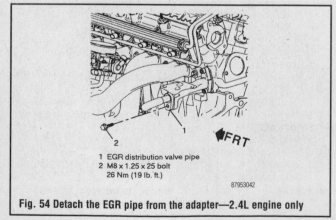

Fig. 54 Detach the EGR pipe from the adapter—2.4L engine only

16. Unfasten the manifold retaining nuts and bolts, then remove the intake manifold from the engine.

➡ **If installing a new intake manifold, transfer all necessary parts from the old manifold to the new one.**

17. Using a suitable scraping tool, clean the old gasket material from the intake manifold mating surfaces. Do NOT let any debris fall into the engine!
To install:
18. Install the manifold with a new gasket.

➡ **Make sure that the numbers stamped on the gasket are facing towards the manifold surface.**

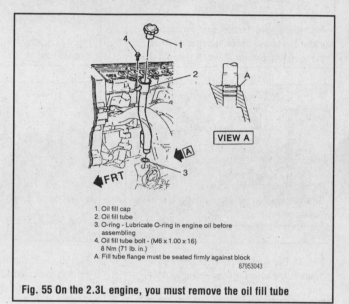

1. Oil fill cap
2. Oil fill tube
3. O-ring - Lubricate O-ring in engine oil before assembling
4. Oil fill tube bolt - (M6 x 1.00 x 16)
   8 Nm (71 lb. in.)
A. Fill tube flange must be seated firmly against block

Fig. 55 On the 2.3L engine, you must remove the oil fill tube

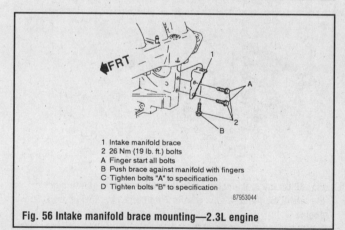

1 Intake manifold brace
2 26 Nm (19 lb. ft.) bolts
A Finger start all bolts
B Push brace against manifold with fingers
C Tighten bolts "A" to specification
D Tighten bolts "B" to specification

Fig. 56 Intake manifold brace mounting—2.3L engine

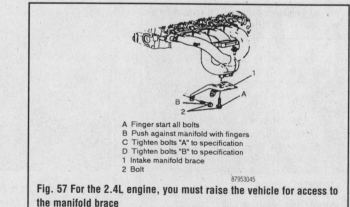

A Finger start all bolts
B Push against manifold with fingers
C Tighten bolts "A" to specification
D Tighten bolts "B" to specification
1 Intake manifold brace
2 Bolt

Fig. 57 For the 2.4L engine, you must raise the vehicle for access to the manifold brace

19. Follow the tightening sequence in the accompanying figure, then tighten the bolts/nuts to 19 ft. lbs. (26 Nm) for 2.3L engines and to 18 ft. lbs. (24 Nm) for 2.4L engines.

20. For the 2.4L engine, raise and safely support the vehicle.

21. Install the intake manifold brace and retainers.

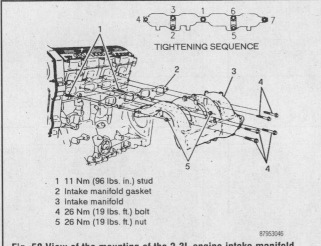

Fig. 58 View of the mounting of the 2.3L engine intake manifold. When tightening the bolts, be sure to follow the proper tightening sequence

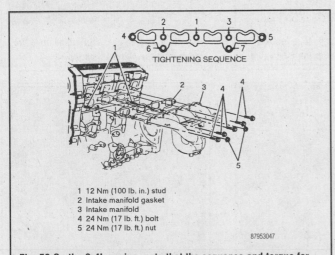

Fig. 59 On the 2.4L engine, note that the sequence and torque for the intake manifold retaining bolts it different from that of the 2.3L engine

22. If raised, carefully lower the vehicle.

23. For the 2.3L engine, install the oil/air separator assembly.

24. For the 2.3L engine, lubricate a new oil fill tube O-ring seal with clean engine oil, then install the tube down between intake manifold. Rotate as needed to gain clearance for the oil/air separator nipple on the fill tube.

25. If removed, position the oil fill tube in its cylinder block opening. Align the fill tube so it is in about its proper position. Place the palm of your hand over the oil fill opening and press straight down to seat the fill tube and O-ring into the cylinder block.

26. If necessary, connect the oil/air separator hose to the oil fill tube. You can lubricate the hose as necessary to ease installation. Install the oil fill tube bolt/screw. Fasten the cap.

27. For the 2.4L engine, attach the EGR pipe to the adapter; tighten the fasteners to 19 ft. lbs. (26 Nm). Install the stud-ended alternator bolt.

28. Install the accelerator control cable bracket.

29. Connect the vacuum hoses to the fuel regulator and EVAP canister purge solenoid.

30. Attach all electrical connectors, as tagged during removal.

31. Install the air cleaner duct.

32. Refill the coolant to it's proper level.

33. Connect the negative battery cable, then start the engine and inspect for leaks.

Exhaust Manifold

REMOVAL & INSTALLATION

2.2L Engine

▶ See Figures 60 thru 77

1. Disconnect the negative battery cable.
2. Raise and support the vehicle safely.
3. Detach the oxygen sensor wire.

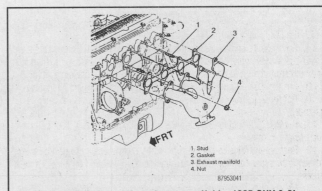

Fig. 60 Exploded view of the exhaust manifold—1995 OHV 2.2L engine

Fig. 61 Remove the two manifold-to-exhaust pipe retaining bolts

Fig. 62 Remove the wire harness clips from the alternator bracket

Fig. 63 Remove the two upper retaining bolts and . . .

Fig. 64 . . the two lower retaining bolts and . . .

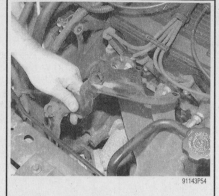

Fig. 65 . . remove the alternator bracket

Fig. 66 Remove the oil dipstick bracket retaining bolt and . . .

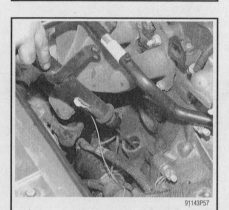

Fig. 67 . . remove the dipstick

Fig. 68 Remove the bypass tube bracket retaining nut located under the EGR valve

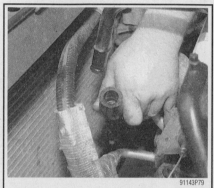

Fig. 69 It may be necessary to remove the hose from the bypass tube to . . .

Fig. 70 . . remove the tube bracket from the exhaust manifold

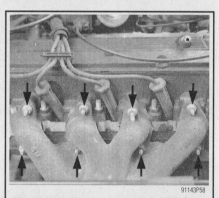

Fig. 71 The exhaust manifold is retained by eight nuts

Fig. 72 Remove the manifold retaining nuts and . . .

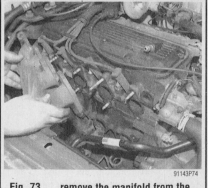

Fig. 73 . . remove the manifold from the engine

Fig. 74 The manifold most likely will have one large gasket and . . .

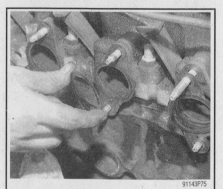

Fig. 75 . . one gasket around each individual exhaust port

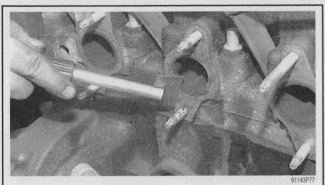

Fig. 76 Thoroughly scrape the old gasket material off of the cylinder head and the manifold (if being reused)

Fig. 77 A wire brush will be of great aid in cleaning the surface and preparing for a new gasket

4. Unfasten the exhaust pipe-to-exhaust manifold bolts, then carefully lower the vehicle.

5. Remove the serpentine belt from around the alternator.

6. Remove the alternator-to-bracket bolts, then support the alternator (with the wires attached) out of the way.

7. Remove the alternator bracket.

8. Remove the oil fill tube and disconnect the heater outlet hose assembly nut from the exhaust manifold.

9. Unfasten the retaining nuts, then remove the exhaust manifold from the vehicle. Remove and discard the gasket(s).

To install:

10. Using a gasket scraper, carefully clean the gasket mounting surfaces.

11. To install, use new gaskets and reverse the removal procedures. Tighten the exhaust manifold-to-cylinder head nuts to 10 ft. lbs. (13 Nm).

12. Start the engine and check for exhaust leaks.

2.3L and 2.4L Engines

▶ **See Figures 78, 79, 80, 81 and 82**

1. Disconnect the negative battery cable.

2. Detach the Oxygen (O_2) sensor connector.

3. Raise and safely support the vehicle.

4. Unfasten the exhaust manifold brace-to-manifold bolt and the oil pan nuts, if necessary.

5. Remove the upper heat shield.

6. For the 2.3L engine, remove the manifold-to-exhaust pipe spring loaded nuts.

➡ **Do NOT bend the exhaust flex decoupler more than necessary to remove it. Excessive movement will damage the flex decoupler.**

7. For the 2.4L engine, remove the manifold-to-exhaust flex decoupler fasteners.

8. Pull down and back on the exhaust pipe to disengage it from the exhaust manifold bolts.

9. Carefully lower the vehicle.

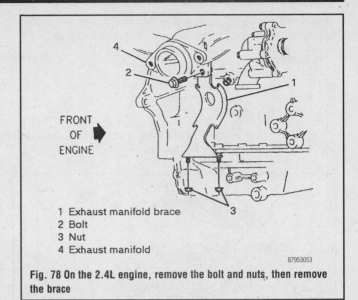

1 Exhaust manifold brace
2 Bolt
3 Nut
4 Exhaust manifold

Fig. 78 On the 2.4L engine, remove the bolt and nuts, then remove the brace

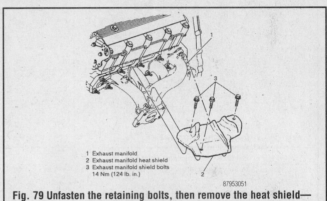

1 Exhaust manifold
2 Exhaust manifold heat shield
3 Exhaust manifold shield bolts
  14 Nm (124 lb. in.)

Fig. 79 Unfasten the retaining bolts, then remove the heat shield— 2.4L engine shown, 2.3L similar

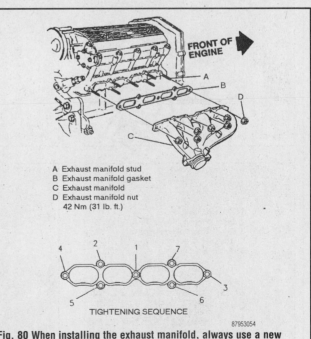

A Exhaust manifold stud
B Exhaust manifold gasket
C Exhaust manifold
D Exhaust manifold nut
  42 Nm (31 lb. ft.)

TIGHTENING SEQUENCE

Fig. 80 When installing the exhaust manifold, always use a new gasket and tighten the retainers in the correct sequence—2.3L engine

10. Unfasten the exhaust manifold-to-cylinder head retaining nuts/bolts, then remove the manifold. Remove and discard the gaskets and/or seals. Clean the mating surfaces.

To install:

11. Use gaskets, then position the exhaust manifold. Tighten the retaining nuts to 31 ft. lbs. (42 Nm) for the 2.3L engine or to 110 inch lbs. (13 Nm) for the 2.4L engine, in the sequence shown in the accompanying figures.

12. Raise and safely support the vehicle.

13. Install the heat shield. Tighten the bolts to 10 ft. lbs. (14 Nm).

14. Fasten the exhaust manifold brace-to-manifold bolt and the oil pan nuts. Tighten the bolts to 41 ft. lbs. (56 Nm) and the nuts to 18 ft. lbs. (24 Nm).

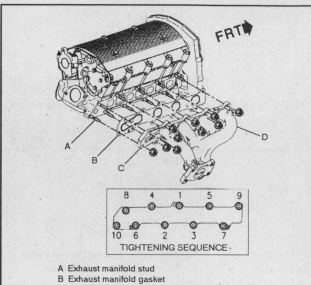

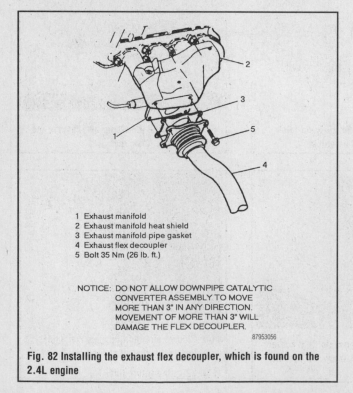

A Exhaust manifold stud
B Exhaust manifold gasket
C Exhaust manifold
D Exhaust manifold nut, must be tightened
   in sequence shown to 12.5 Nm (110 lb. in.)

87953055

Fig. 81 Exhaust manifold installation and fastener tightening sequence—2.4L engine

1 Exhaust manifold
2 Exhaust manifold heat shield
3 Exhaust manifold pipe gasket
4 Exhaust flex decoupler
5 Bolt 35 Nm (26 lb. ft.)

NOTICE: DO NOT ALLOW DOWNPIPE CATALYTIC CONVERTER ASSEMBLY TO MOVE MORE THAN 3" IN ANY DIRECTION. MOVEMENT OF MORE THAN 3" WILL DAMAGE THE FLEX DECOUPLER.

87953056

Fig. 82 Installing the exhaust flex decoupler, which is found on the 2.4L engine

15. For the 2.3L engine, install the manifold-to-exhaust pipe nuts. Be sure to turn both nuts in evenly to avoid cocking the exhaust pipe and binding the nuts.

16. For the 2.4L engine, install the manifold-to-flex decoupler fasteners. Tighten the bolts to 26 ft. lbs. (35 Nm).

17. Carefully lower the vehicle.

18. Attach the O$_2$ connector. Coat the threads of the sensor with a suitable anti-seize compound.

19. Connect the negative battery cable and check for leaks.

Radiator

➡In the process of our vehicle teardown, we checked the factory procedure against our teardown vehicle. We at Chilton determined that an alternative method could be used for vehicles equipped with A/C that would eliminate the need for the A/C system to be recovered. We will cover both methods since the alternative method is slightly more difficult. If your vehicle does not have A/C, use the factory method.

REMOVAL & INSTALLATION

♦ **See Figure 83**

Factory Method

♦ **See Figures 84 thru 94**

➡When adding coolant, it is very important to use GM Goodwrench DEX-COOL®, which is an orange colored, silicate free coolant. If silicated coolant is used on these vehicles, premature engine, heater core and/or radiator corrosion may result. In addition, the engine coolant will require change sooner, at 30,000 miles (50,000km) or 24 months.

1. If equipped with A/C, have a certified repair shop recover the refrigerant.

2. Disconnect the negative battery cable.

3. Disable the Supplemental Inflatable Restraint (SIR) system. For details, please refer to the procedure located in Section 6 of this manual.

4. Properly drain and recover the coolant in an approved container.

5. Unfasten the hood latch from the mounting plate.

6. Remove the right and left headlamp assemblies.

7. Remove the radiator mounts.

8. Raise and safely support the vehicle.

9. Detach the forward SIR sensor harness.

10. Remove the cooling fan assembly. For details, please refer to the procedure located later in this section.

11. Disconnect the lower radiator hose from the radiator.

12. Unfasten the lower transaxle oil cooler line from the radiator.

13. Carefully lower the vehicle.

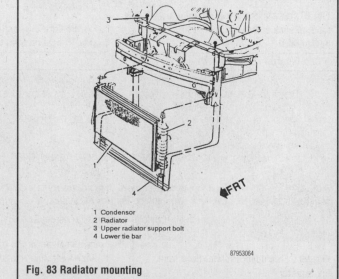

1 Condensor
2 Radiator
3 Upper radiator support bolt
4 Lower tie bar

87953064

Fig. 83 Radiator mounting

14. Remove the hood latch support bracket and the forward SIR sensor with the harness.

15. Disconnect the upper transaxle oil cooler line from the radiator.

16. Detach the upper radiator hose from the radiator.

17. If equipped with A/C, disconnect the compressor and accumulator lines from the condenser. Discard the O-rings.

18. Disconnect the overflow hose from the radiator.

19. Remove the radiator/condenser assembly from the vehicle, then detach the radiator from the condenser, if equipped.

To install:

20. Attach the condenser to the radiator. Position the radiator/condenser assembly into the vehicle.

21. Fasten the overflow hose to the radiator.

22. Install the hood latch bracket, then route the forward sensor harness.

23. Raise and safely support the vehicle.

24. Install the cooling fan assembly, as outlined later in this section.

25. Fasten the lower transaxle oil cooler line to the radiator.

26. Connect the lower radiator hose.

27. Attach the forward SIR sensor connector.

28. Carefully lower the vehicle.

29. Attach the upper radiator hose.

30. Fasten the upper transaxle oil cooler line to the radiator.

31. Install the hood latch support.

32. If equipped, using new O-rings, connect the compressor and accumulator hoses to the condenser.

33. Install the left and right headlamp assemblies.

34. Install the hood latch assembly, then adjust if necessary.

35. Enable the Supplemental Inflatable Restraint (SIR) system. For details, please refer to the procedure in Section 6 of this manual.

36. Connect the negative battery cable.

37. If equipped, have a certified repair shop recharge the A/C system.

38. Fill the cooling system with the proper $^{50}/_{50}$ mix of DEX-COOL coolant and distilled water.

39. Bleed the cooling system.

Fig. 84 Remove the radiator shroud cover from the engine compartment

Fig. 85 Unplug the connector on the crash sensor located on the hood latch support bracket

Fig. 86 Remove the hood latch retaining bolts and remove the latch from the bracket

Fig. 87 Remove the lower retaining bolt (one on each side) for the hood latch support bracket

Fig. 88 Carefully remove the hood latch support bracket from the vehicle

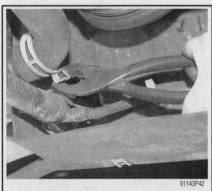

Fig. 89 Release the clamp and remove the lower radiator hose and . . .

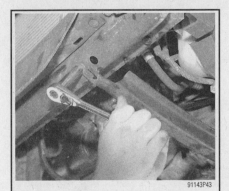

Fig. 90 . . the upper radiator hose from the radiator

Fig. 91 Remove the transaxle fluid cooler lines from the radiator, there are two: the pressure and . . .

Fig. 92 . . the return lines

Fig. 93 It is advisable to plug the openings of the transaxle fluid cooler lines to prevent the system from getting contaminated

Fig. 94 Remove the condenser-to-radiator bolts

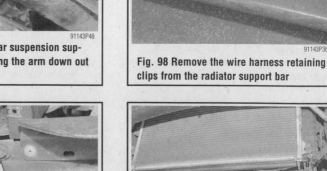

Fig. 95 Use a piece of wire or another suitable device to support the condenser before removal of the radiator

Alternative Method

▶ **See Figures 84 and 89 thru 102**

➡When adding coolant, it is very important to use GM Goodwrench **DEX-COOL®**, which is an orange colored, silicate free coolant. If silicated coolant is used on these vehicles, premature engine, heater core and/or radiator corrosion may result. In addition, the engine coolant will require change sooner, at 30,000 miles (50,000km) or 24 months.

1. Disconnect the negative battery cable.
2. Properly drain and recover the coolant in an approved container.
3. Disconnect the upper transaxle oil cooler line from the radiator and plug the line to avoid contamination.
4. Detach the upper radiator hose from the radiator.
5. Disconnect the overflow hose from the radiator.
6. Support the condenser with some mechanics wire or other suitable device.

7. Raise and safely support the vehicle.
8. Remove the cooling fan assembly. For details, please refer to the procedure located later in this section.
9. Disconnect the lower radiator hose from the radiator.
10. Unfasten the lower transaxle oil cooler line from the radiator.
11. Remove the front bolt from the suspension support arm.
12. Loosen the rear suspension support arm bolt and swing the arm down out of the way.
13. Remove the wire harness retaining clips from the radiator support bar.
14. Remove the retaining clips on the radiator support bar for the splash shield.
15. Remove the four bolts on each side for the radiator support bar and remove the support bar.
16. Have an assistant support the radiator and remove the two radiator-to-condenser bolts, one on each side.
17. Carefully lower the radiator out the bottom of the vehicle.

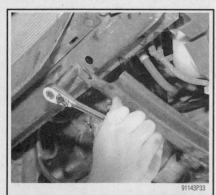

Fig. 96 Remove the front bolt on the suspension support arm

Fig. 97 Loosen the rear suspension support arm bolt and swing the arm down out of the way

Fig. 98 Remove the wire harness retaining clips from the radiator support bar

Fig. 99 Remove the retaining clips on the radiator support bar for the splash shield

Fig. 100 Remove the four bolts on each side (only three shown in the photo) for the radiator support bar and . . .

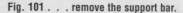

Fig. 101 . . . remove the support bar.

Fig. 102 Carefully lower the radiator out the bottom of the engine compartment

Fig. 103 Remove the retaining bolt for the fan assembly

Fig. 104 Unplug the connector for the cooling fan and . . .

To install:

18.   Position the radiator assembly into the vehicle.

19.   Have an assistant support the radiator and install the two radiator-to-condenser bolts.

20.   Place the radiator support bar into place and finger-tighten the retaining bolts. Tighten the bolts to 18 ft. lbs. (25 Nm).

21.   Raise the suspension support arm and attach the front bolt finger-tight. Tighten the rear bolt and then the front bolt to 18 ft. lbs. (25 Nm).

22.   Attach the wire harness retaining clips onto the radiator support bar.

23.   Install the retaining clips on the radiator support bar for the splash shield.

24.   Fasten the lower transaxle oil cooler line to the radiator.

25.   Connect the lower radiator hose.

26.   Install the cooling fan assembly, as outlined later in this section.

27.   Carefully lower the vehicle.

28.   Remove the condenser support wire or other device.

29.   Fasten the overflow hose to the radiator.

30.   Attach the upper radiator hose.

31.   Fasten the upper transaxle oil cooler line to the radiator.

32.   Connect the negative battery cable.

33.   Fill the cooling system with the proper 50/50 mix of DEX-COOL coolant and distilled water.

34.   Bleed the cooling system.

Engine Fan

REMOVAL & INSTALLATION

▶ **See Figures 103, 104 and 105**

1.   Disconnect the negative battery cable.

2.   Raise and safely support the vehicle.

3.   Unfasten the cooling fan mounting bolt.

4.   Detach the fan electrical connector, then remove the coolant fan assembly out through the bottom of the vehicle.

To install:

5.   Raise the fan assembly into position through the bottom of the vehicle.

6.   Attach the fan electrical connector, then install the mounting bolt. Tighten the bolt to 53 inch lbs. (6 Nm).

7.   Connect the negative battery cable.

Water Pump

REMOVAL & INSTALLATION

✺✺ CAUTION

When draining the coolant, keep in mind that cats and dogs are attracted by ethylene glycol antifreeze, and are quite likely to drink any that is left in an uncovered container or in puddles on the ground. This will prove fatal in sufficient quantity. Always drain the coolant into a sealable container. Coolant should be reused unless it is contaminated or several years old.

2.2L Engine

▶ **See Figures 106 thru 113**

1.   Disconnect the negative battery cable.

2.   Properly drain the cooling system into an approved container.

3.   Remove all accessory drive belts or the serpentine belt.

4.   Remove the alternator and bracket. For details, please refer to Section 2 of this manual.

5.   Unscrew the water pump pulley mounting bolts and then pull off the pulley.

6.   Unfasten the mounting bolts, then remove the water pump.

7.   Using a putty knife, clean the gasket mounting surfaces.

To install:

8.   Place a 1/8 in. (3mm) wide bead of RTV sealant on the water pump seal-

Fig. 105 . . remove the fan assembly out the bottom of the vehicle

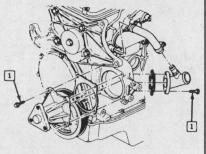

1.   BOLT, – 25 N•m (18 LBS. FT.)

Fig. 106 Location and mounting of the water pump on the 2.2L engine

Fig. 107 If the pulley turns when you try to loosen the bolts, attach sockets and ratchets to two of the bolts, insert a prybar to hold the pulley in place and loosen the bolts—2.2L engine

Fig. 108 Remove the pulley from the water pump

Fig. 109 The water pump is retained by four bolts, remove them and . . .

Fig. 110 . . remove the water pump from the engine

Fig. 111 Thoroughly clean the gasket mating surfaces on the engine block as well as . . .

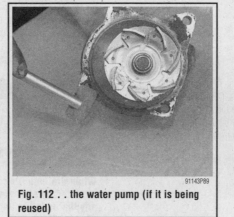

Fig. 112 . . the water pump (if it is being reused)

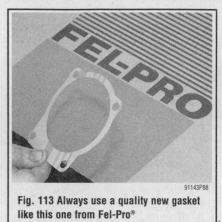

Fig. 113 Always use a quality new gasket like this one from Fel-Pro®

ing surface or install a new gasket, on models so equipped. Install the pump and tighten the retaining bolts to 18 ft. lbs. (25 Nm).

9. Install the water pump pulley, then tighten the mounting bolts to 22 ft. lbs. (30 Nm).

10. As outlined in Section 2, install the alternator and bracket.

11. Install the drive belts or serpentine belt, as applicable.

12. Fill the cooling system to the proper level.

13. Connect the negative battery cable, then start the engine and check for leaks.

2.3L and 2.4L Engines

▶ See Figure 114

1. Disconnect the negative battery cable
2. Detach the oxygen sensor connector.
3. Properly drain the engine coolant into a suitable container. Remove the heater hose from the thermostat housing for more complete coolant drain.
4. Remove upper exhaust manifold heat shield.
5. Remove the bolt that attaches the exhaust manifold brace to the manifold.
6. Remove the lower exhaust manifold heat shield.
7. Break loose the manifold to exhaust pipe spring loaded bolts using a 13mm box wrench.
8. Raise and safely support the vehicle.

➡ It is necessary to relieve the spring pressure from 1 bolt prior to removing the second bolt. If the spring pressure is not relieved, it will cause the exhaust pipe to twist and bind up the bolt as it is removed.

9. Unfasten the two radiator outlet pipe-to-water pump cover bolts.
10. Remove the manifold to exhaust pipe bolts from the exhaust pipe flange as follows:
   a. Unscrew either bolt clockwise 4 turns.
   b. Remove the other bolt.
   c. Remove the first bolt.

➡ On the 2.4L engines, DO NOT rotate the flex coupling more than 4° or damage may occur.

11. Pull down and back on the exhaust pipe to disengage it from the exhaust manifold bolts.

12. Remove the radiator outlet pipe from the oil pan and transaxle. If equipped with a manual transaxle, remove the exhaust manifold brace. Leave the lower radiator hose attached and pull down on the outlet pipe to remove it from the water pump. Leave the radiator outlet pipe hang.

13. Carefully lower the vehicle.

14. Unfasten the exhaust manifold-to-cylinder head retaining nuts, then remove the exhaust manifold, seals and gaskets.

15. For the 2.4L engine, remove the front timing chain cover and the chain tensioner. For details, please refer to the procedure located later in this section.

16. Unfasten the water pump-to-cylinder block bolts. Remove the water pump-to-timing chain housing nuts. Remove the water pump and cover mounting bolts and nuts. Remove the water pump and cover as an assembly, then separate the two pieces.

To install:

17. Thoroughly clean and dry all mounting surfaces, bolts and bolt holes. Using a new gasket, install the water pump to the cover and tighten the bolts finger-tight.

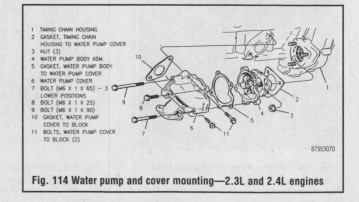

```
1  TIMING CHAIN HOUSING
2  GASKET, TIMING CHAIN
   HOUSING TO WATER PUMP
   COVER
3  NUT (3)
4  WATER PUMP BODY ASM.
5  GASKET, WATER PUMP BODY
   TO WATER PUMP COVER
6  WATER PUMP COVER
7  BOLT (M6 X 1 X 65) – 3
   LOWER POSITIONS
8  BOLT (M6 X 1 X 25)
9  BOLT (M6 X 1 X 90)
10 GASKET, WATER PUMP
   COVER TO BLOCK
11 BOLTS, WATER PUMP COVER
   TO BLOCK (2)
```

Fig. 114 Water pump and cover mounting—2.3L and 2.4L engines

18. Lubricate the splines of the water pump with clean grease and install the assembly to the engine using new gaskets. Install the mounting bolts and nuts finger-tight.

19. Lubricate the radiator outlet pipe O-ring with antifreeze and slid the pipe onto the water pump cover. Install the bolts finger-tight.

20. With all gaps closed, tighten the bolts, in the following sequence, to the proper values:

    a. Pump assembly-to-chain housing nuts—19 ft. lbs. (26 Nm).

    b. Pump cover-to-pump assembly—106 inch lbs. (12 Nm).

    c. Cover-to-block, bottom bolt first—19 ft. lbs. (26 Nm).

    d. Radiator outlet pipe assembly-to-pump cover—125 inch lbs. (14 Nm).

21. Using new gaskets, install the exhaust manifold. Make sure to following the tightening sequence and torque specifications given in the exhaust manifold procedure located in this section.

22. Raise and safely support the vehicle.

23. Index the exhaust manifold bolts into the exhaust pipe flange.

24. Connect the exhaust pipe to the manifold. Install the exhaust pipe flange bolts evenly and gradually to avoid binding. Turn the bolts in until fully seated.

25. Connect the radiator outlet pipe to the transaxle and oil pan. Install the exhaust manifold brace, if removed.

26. On the 2.4L engine, install the timing chain tensioner and front cover.

27. Install the lower heat shield.

28. Carefully lower the vehicle.

29. Fasten the bolt that attaches the exhaust manifold brace to the manifold.

30. Tighten the manifold-to-exhaust pipe nuts to specification.

31. Install the upper heat shield.

32. Attach the oxygen sensor connector.

33. Fill the radiator with coolant until it comes out the heater hose outlet at the thermostat housing. Then connect the heater hose. Leave the radiator cap off.

34. Connect the negative battery cable, then start the engine. Run the vehicle until the thermostat opens, fill the radiator and recovery tank to their proper levels, then turn the engine off.

35. Once the vehicle has cooled, recheck the coolant level.

Cylinder Head

REMOVAL & INSTALLATION

2.2L Engine

▶ See Figures 115 thru 129

> ❋❋ **CAUTION**
>
> **The fuel injection system remains under pressure, even after the engine has been turned OFF. The fuel system pressure must be relieved before disconnecting any fuel lines. Failure to do so may result in fire and/or personal injury.**

1. Relieve fuel system pressure using the recommended procedure.

> ❋❋ **CAUTION**
>
> **After relieving system pressure a small amount of fuel may be released when servicing fuel pipes or connections. In order to reduce the chance of personal injury, cover fuel pipes fittings with a shop towel before disconnecting, to catch any fuel that may leak out. Place the towel in an approved container when disconnect is complete.**

2. Disconnect negative battery cable.

3. Remove air cleaner outlet duct assembly.

4. Label and disconnect vacuum lines.

5. Disconnect and tag for identification the electrical connections on the Engine Coolant Temperature (ECT) sensor, Oxygen Sensor (O2 sensor), IAC, Throttle Position Sensor, MAP sensor, EVAP Canister Purge Solenoid and the fuel injector harness.

6. Remove accelerator control, cruise and TV cables from accelerator control bracket.

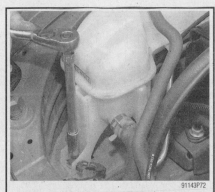

Fig. 115 Remove the overflow tank retaining bolt and . . .

Fig. 116 . . remove the overflow tank

Fig. 117 Remove the motor mount from the vehicle

Fig. 118 Remove the upper radiator hose from the water outlet

Fig. 119 Remove the heater hose from the rear of the cylinder head

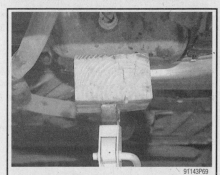

Fig. 120 A jackstand and a block of wood can be used instead of a engine support bar

7. Remove accelerator control cable bracket.
8. Raise and safely support vehicle.
9. Remove exhaust pipe from exhaust manifold.

✳✳ CAUTION

Never open, service or drain the radiator or cooling system when hot; serious burns can occur from the steam and hot coolant.

10. Drain and recover coolant into a suitable container.
11. Lower vehicle.
12. Remove serpentine drive belt.
13. Remove the alternator.
14. Remove the power steering pump and position aside with lines attached.
15. Remove power steering pump bracket.
16. Install engine support fixture J-28467-A or equivalent.
17. Remove the upper motor mount.
18. Remove serpentine drive belt tensioner bracket.
19. Tag and disconnect the spark plug wires.
20. Disconnect EVAP canister purge line, from under manifold.
21. Remove upper hose from coolant outlet.
22. Remove heater hose from coolant outlet.
23. Remove attaching nut holding automatic transaxle filler tube from intake manifold, if equipped.
24. Disconnect fuel lines.
25. Remove valve cover.

➡ **Whenever valvetrain components are removed for service, they should be kept in order. They should be installed in the same locations and with the same mating surfaces as when removed.**

26. Remove rocker arms and pushrods.
27. Remove cylinder head bolts. Two sizes of bolts are used. Note the location of each. These bolts are called "torque-to-yield." This means that, at assembly, after the bolts are tightened to a specific torque, they are tightened another quarter turn. This stretches the bolts slightly. Therefore, new cylinder head bolts are recommended.

28. Remove cylinder head with both manifolds attached.
29. Remove the intake and exhaust manifolds from the cylinder head.

To install:

30. Clean all the gasket surfaces completely. Clean the threads on cylinder head bolts and be sure all bolt holes are clean and free of foreign material. It is good practice to clean all internally threaded openings with the proper size thread cutting tap. This removes rust, dirt and old sealer build-up that can prevent getting a proper torque reading when tightening bolts.
31. Inspect cylinder head and block surface for cracks, nicks, heavy scratches and flatness.
32. Install exhaust and intake manifolds on cylinder head prior to installing cylinder head.
33. Place a new cylinder head gasket in position over the dowel pins on the engine block. Carefully guide the cylinder head into position.
34. Install cylinder head bolts finger-tight. New cylinder head bolts are recommended.
35. Tighten bolts in sequence, tighten the long bolts to 46 ft. lbs. (63 Nm) plus 90 degrees. Tighten the short bolts to 43 ft. lbs. (58 Nm) plus 90 degrees.
36. Install pushrods and rocker arms and rocker arm nuts. Tighten nuts to 22 ft. lbs. (30 Nm).
37. Install valve cover and tighten bolts to 89 inch lbs. (10 Nm).
38. Connect fuel lines.
39. Install transaxle filler tube.
40. Install heater hose to coolant outlet.
41. Install upper radiator hose to coolant.
42. Connect EVAP canister purge line.
43. Attach the ignition wires to spark plugs, as tagged during removal.
44. Install serpentine drive belt tensioner bracket.
45. Remove engine support fixture.
46. Install power steering pump bracket and power steering pump.
47. Install alternator and brace.
48. Install serpentine drive belt.
49. Raise and safely support the vehicle.
50. Connect the exhaust pipe to the exhaust manifold.
51. Lower the vehicle.

Fig. 121 Location of the cylinder head retaining bolt holes

Fig. 122 Use a breaker bar or other suitable tool to loosen the cylinder head bolts

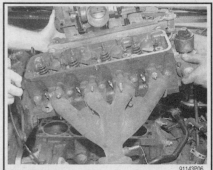

Fig. 123 Have an assistant aid you in lifting the cylinder head and attached manifolds off of the engine block

Fig. 124 Remove and discard the old cylinder head gasket

Fig. 125 Use a scraper to remove the old gasket material from the block and the cylinder head

Fig. 126 A new gasket will marked on one side to tell you which side should be facing up

52. Install the accelerator control cable bracket and bolts. Tighten bolts to 18 inch lbs. (25 Nm).
53. Connect the accelerator control, cruise and TV cables to control bracket.
54. Attach all of the electrical connections for the sensors.
55. Connect the vacuum lines.
56. Install air cleaner outlet duct assembly.
57. Refill the coolant system.
58. Connect negative battery cable.
59. Start vehicle and inspect for leaks.

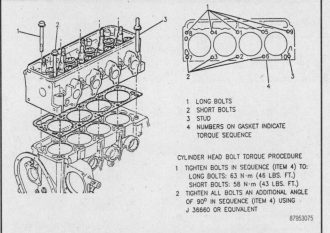

1 LONG BOLTS
2 SHORT BOLTS
3 STUD
4 NUMBERS ON GASKET INDICATE TORQUE SEQUENCE

CYLINDER HEAD BOLT TORQUE PROCEDURE

1 TIGHTEN BOLTS IN SEQUENCE (ITEM 4) TO:
   LONG BOLTS: 63 N·m (46 LBS. FT.)
   SHORT BOLTS: 58 N·m (43 LBS. FT.)
2 TIGHTEN ALL BOLTS AN ADDITIONAL ANGLE OF 90° IN SEQUENCE (ITEM 4) USING J 36660 OR EQUIVALENT

87953075

Fig. 127 Cylinder head bolt torque sequence for 2.2L engines

91143P03

Fig. 128 Make sure you use a torque wrench to tighten the cylinder head bolts or gasket failure is likely

91143P04

Fig. 129 Use a torque angle meter to tighten the bolts an additional 90°

60. Bleed air from coolant system as follows:
   a. Loosen the engine coolant air bleed screw, (located on the top side of the engine coolant outlet) and add coolant until all of the air is evacuated through the air bleed. Tighten the air bleed screw.
   b. When filling the coolant system, use coolant meeting GM specifications.

2.3L and 2.4L Engines

▶ See Figures 130 and 131

> ✳✳ CAUTION
>
> The fuel injection system remains under pressure, even after the engine has been turned OFF. The fuel system pressure must be relieved before disconnecting any fuel lines. Failure to do so may result in fire and/or personal injury.

1. Relieve the fuel system pressure.

> ✳✳ CAUTION
>
> After relieving system pressure, a small amount of fuel may be released when servicing fuel pipes or connections. In order to reduce the chance of personal injury, cover fuel pipe fittings with a shop towel before disconnecting, to catch any fuel that may leak out. Place the towel in an approved container when disconnect is complete.

2. Disconnect the negative battery cable.

> ✳✳ CAUTION
>
> Never open, service or drain the radiator or cooling system when hot; serious burns can occur from the steam and hot coolant.

3. Drain and recover the coolant into a suitable container.
4. Disconnect the heater inlet and throttle body heater hoses from water outlet.
5. Remove the exhaust manifold.
6. Remove the intake camshaft housing and lifters, then remove the exhaust camshaft housing and lifters.
7. Remove the oil fill tube.
8. Remove the throttle body-to-air cleaner duct.
9. Disconnect the power brake vacuum hose from throttle body.
10. Remove the throttle cable bracket.
11. Remove the throttle body from intake manifold, with electrical harness and throttle cable attached. Position it aside.
12. Disconnect the MAP sensor vacuum hose from intake manifold.
13. Remove the intake manifold brace.
14. Disconnect electrical connections from the following sensors: MAP sensor, intake air temperature sensor and EVAP canister purge solenoid.
15. Disconnect the upper radiator hose from water outlet.
16. Detach the coolant temperature sensors connectors.
17. Unfasten the cylinder head bolt, then remove cylinder head and gasket.

To install:
18. This is an aluminum cylinder head and must be treated with care. Do not use abrasive pads to clean the cylinder head or block surfaces. An abrasive pad may damage the cylinder head and block. GM says that abrasive pads should not be used for the following reasons:
   a. Abrasive pads will produce a fine grit that the oil filter will not be able to remove from the oil. This grit is abrasive and has been known to cause internal engine damage.
   b. Abrasive pads can easily remove enough metal to round cylinder head edges. This has been known to affect the gasket's ability to seal, especially in the narrow areas between the combustion chambers and coolant jackets. The cylinder head gasket is likely to leak if these edges are rounded.
   c. Abrasive pads can also remove enough metal to affect cylinder head flatness. It takes only about 15 seconds to remove 0.008 in. (0.20mm) of metal from the cylinder head with an abrasive pad. If the cylinder head flatness is out of specification, the gasket will not be able to seal and the gasket will leak.
19. Use a razor blade gasket scraper to clean the cylinder head and cylinder block gasket surfaces. Be careful not to gouge or scratch the gasket surfaces.

Do not gouge or scrape the combustion chamber surfaces. Use a new razor blade for each cylinder head. Hold the scraper so the razor blade is as parallel to the gasket surface as possible. Do not use any other method or technique to clean these gasket surfaces. In addition, GM warns not to use a tap to clean cylinder head bolt holes.

20. When working on an aluminum head, do not remove spark plugs from an aluminum cylinder head until the cylinder head has cooled. Always clean all dirt and debris from the spark plug recess area. If the spark plug opening threads are damaged and NOT restorable with a Thread Chaser, replace the cylinder head. GM **DOES NOT** approve of the installation of thread inserts into the spark plug openings on this engine. If threads are installed into the spark plug openings, severe engine damage will occur.

21. Clean all the gasket surfaces completely. Clean the threads on cylinder head bolts and be sure all bolt holes are clean and free of debris. New bolts are recommended.

22. Inspect the cylinder head and block surface for cracks, nicks, heavy scratches and flatness.

23. Place a new cylinder head gasket on the block. Do not use any sealing material.

24. Carefully place the cylinder head on dowel pins, being careful not to disturb the gasket.

25. Apply a small amount of clean engine oil to the threads of the cylinder head bolts, and install finger-tight.

26. Tighten head bolts in sequence. Tighten bolts 1 through 8 to 40 ft. lbs. (65 Nm) then, tighten bolts 9 and 10 to 30 ft. lbs. (40 Nm). Turn all 10 bolts an additional 90 degrees (¼ turn) in sequence.

27. Attach the coolant temperature sensor connections.

28. Connect upper radiator hose to coolant outlet.

29. Install manifold brace and tighten to 19 ft. lbs. (26 Nm).

30. Attach all sensor connections.

31. Connect the MAP sensor vacuum hose to intake manifold.

32. Install throttle body to intake manifold, using a new gasket.

33. Install accelerator control cable bracket to the throttle body, and tighten the bolts to 106 inch lbs. (13 Nm). Tighten the nut to 19 ft. lbs. (26 Nm).

34. Install the throttle body-to-air cleaner duct.

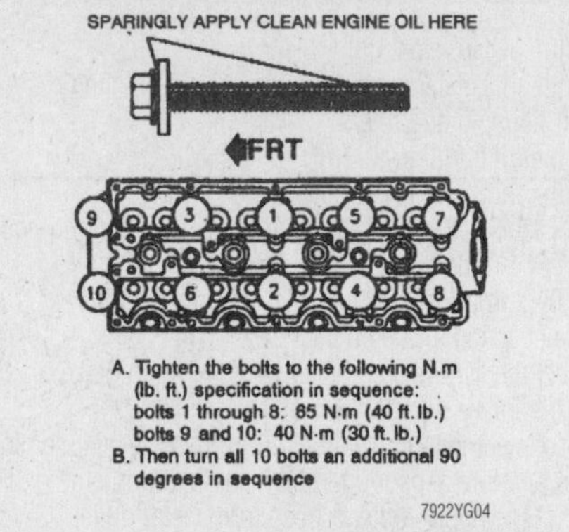

35. Install oil fill tube, tighten attaching bolt to 71 inch lbs. (8 Nm).

36. Install the lifters and camshaft housing.

37. Install the exhaust manifold, then tighten the exhaust nuts to 26 ft. lbs. (35 Nm).

38. Connect negative battery.

39. Fill coolant system and bleed off air from system. An oil and filter change is recommended.

40. Check and verify that vehicle has no coolant or vacuum leaks.

Oil Pan

REMOVAL & INSTALLATION

2.2L Engine

▶ **See Figure 132**

1. Disconnect the negative battery cable.
2. Drain the crankcase. Raise and support the front of the vehicle.
3. Unfasten the exhaust shield and disconnect the exhaust pipe at the manifold.
4. Remove the starter motor and position it out of the way.
5. Remove the flywheel cover.
6. On cars equipped with automatic transaxle, remove the oil filter and extension.
7. Unfasten the oil pan bolts and remove the oil pan.

To install:

8. Prior to oil pan installation, check that the sealing surfaces on the pan, cylinder block and front cover are clean and free of oil. If installing the old pan, be sure that all old RTV has been removed.

9. Apply a ⅛ in. (3mm) bead of RTV sealant to the oil pan sealing surface. Use a new oil pan rear seal and apply a thin coat of RTV sealant to the ends of the gasket down to the ears and install the pan in place.

10. Tighten the oil pan retaining bolts to 89 inch lbs. (10 Nm).

11. On cars equipped with an automatic transaxle, replace the oil filter adapter seal and replace the oil filter adapter.

12. Install the remaining components in the reverse order of removal.

2.3L and 2.4L Engines

▶ **See Figures 133 and 134**

1. Disconnect the negative battery cable. Raise and safely support the vehicle.

2. Properly drain the engine oil and the cooling system into suitable containers.

3. Remove the flywheel housing or transaxle converter cover, as applicable.

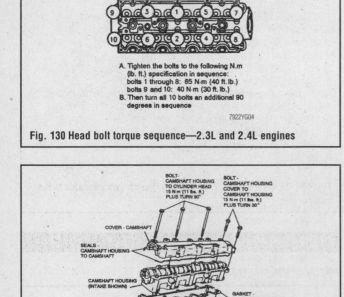

SPARINGLY APPLY CLEAN ENGINE OIL HERE

◀FRT

A. Tighten the bolts to the following N.m (lb. ft.) specification in sequence:
bolts 1 through 8: 65 N·m (40 ft. lb.)
bolts 9 and 10: 40 N·m (30 ft. lb.)
B. Then turn all 10 bolts an additional 90 degrees in sequence

7922YG04

Fig. 130 Head bolt torque sequence—2.3L and 2.4L engines

BOLT-CAMSHAFT HOUSING TO CYLINDER HEAD 15 N·m (11 lbs. ft.) PLUS TURN 90°

BOLT-CAMSHAFT HOUSING COVER TO CAMSHAFT HOUSING 15 N·m (11 lbs. ft.) PLUS TURN 30°

COVER - CAMSHAFT

SEALS - CAMSHAFT HOUSING TO CAMSHAFT

CAMSHAFT HOUSING (INTAKE SHOWN)

DOWEL PIN (2)

GASKET - CAMSHAFT HOUSING TO CYLINDER HEAD

7922YG05

Fig. 131 Exploded view of the camshaft housing cover mounting—2.3L and 2.4L engines

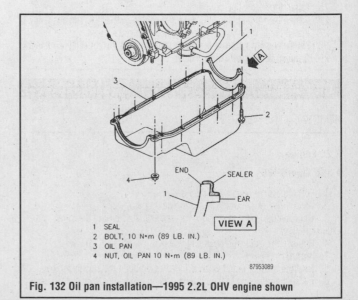

1 SEAL
2 BOLT, 10 N·m (89 LB. IN.)
3 OIL PAN
4 NUT, OIL PAN 10 N·m (89 LB. IN.)

END   SEALER

EAR

VIEW A

87953089

Fig. 132 Oil pan installation—1995 2.2L OHV engine shown

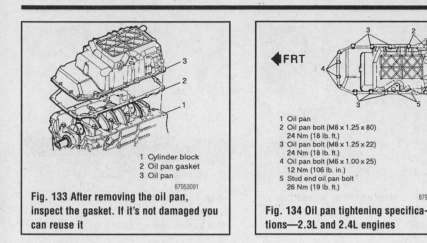

Fig. 133 After removing the oil pan, inspect the gasket. If it's not damaged you can reuse it

1 Cylinder block
2 Oil pan gasket
3 Oil pan

87953091

◀FRT

1 Oil pan
2 Oil pan bolt (M8 x 1.25 x 80)
  24 Nm (18 lb. ft.)
3 Oil pan bolt (M8 x 1.25 x 22)
  24 Nm (18 lb. ft.)
4 Oil pan bolt (M6 x 1.00 x 25)
  12 Nm (106 lb. in.)
5 Stud end oil pan bolt
  26 Nm (19 lb. ft.)

87953092

Fig. 134 Oil pan tightening specifications—2.3L and 2.4L engines

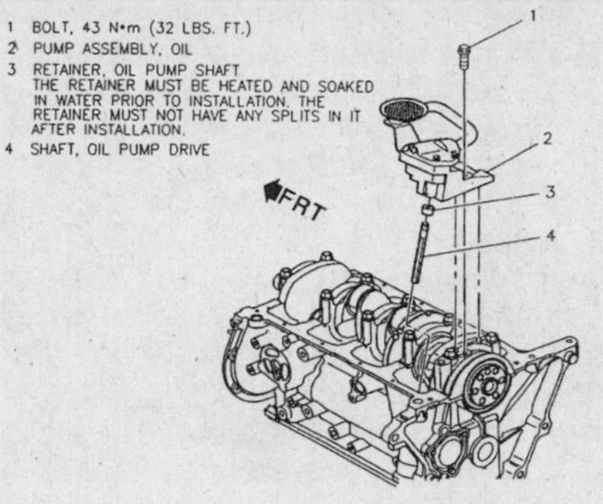

1 BOLT, 43 N•m (32 LBS. FT.)
2 PUMP ASSEMBLY, OIL
3 RETAINER, OIL PUMP SHAFT
  THE RETAINER MUST BE HEATED AND SOAKED
  IN WATER PRIOR TO INSTALLATION. THE
  RETAINER MUST NOT HAVE ANY SPLITS IN IT
  AFTER INSTALLATION.
4 SHAFT, OIL PUMP DRIVE

◀FRT

87953095

Fig. 135 Oil pump mounting—1995 2.2L OHV engine shown

4. Remove the right front wheel and tire assembly, then remove the right splash shield.
5. Remove the serpentine drive belt.
6. Unfasten the A/C compressor lower retaining bolts.
7. Remove the transaxle-to-engine brace.
8. Disconnect the engine mount strut bracket.
9. Unfasten the radiator outlet pipe bolts, then remove the pipes from the oil pan.
10. Remove the exhaust manifold brace.
11. Unfasten the oil pan-to-flywheel cover bolt and nut.
12. Remove the flywheel cover stud for clearance.
13. Disconnect the radiator outlet pipe from the lower radiator hose and oil pan.
14. Detach the oil level sensor connector.
15. Unfasten the oil pan retaining bolts, then remove the pan and gasket. Inspect the gasket for damage. If it's O.K. you can reuse it. No sealer is necessary.

To install:

16. Position the gasket, then install the oil pan. Loosely install the retaining bolts.
17. Place the spacer in its approximate installed location by allow clearance to tighten the pan bolt directly above the spacer. Tighten the oil pan bolts to the specifications given in the accompanying figure.
18. Position the spacer into its proper position, then install the stud.
19. Fasten the oil pan-to-transaxle nut.
20. Attach the oil level sensor connector.
21. Connect the radiator outlet pipe to the oil pan and fasten with the retaining bolts.
22. Install the engine mount strut bracket.
23. Fasten the transaxle-to-engine brace.
24. Secure the A/C compressor bolts.
25. Install the serpentine drive belt.
26. Fasten the right splash shield, then install the wheel and tire assembly.
27. Install the flywheel housing or transaxle converter cover.
28. Fill the cooling system and engine crankcase with the correct type of fluids.
29. Connect the negative battery cable.

Oil Pump

REMOVAL & INSTALLATION

2.2L Engine

▶ See Figure 135

1. Disconnect the negative battery cable.
2. As outlined earlier, remove the engine oil pan.
3. Unfasten the pump to rear bearing cap bolt and remove the pump and extension shaft.
4. Remove the extension shaft and retainer.

To install:

5. Heat the retainer in hot water prior to assembling the extension shaft.
6. Install the extension to the oil pump, being careful not to crack the retainer.

7. Fasten pump to rear bearing cap bolt and torque is 26–38 ft. lbs. (35–51 Nm).
8. Install the oil pan.
9. Connect the negative battery cable.

2.3L and 2.4L Engines

▶ See Figure 136

1. Disconnect the negative battery cable.
2. Remove the oil pan.
3. Remove the balance shaft chain cover and chain guide (tensioner).
4. Unfasten the oil pump bolts, then remove the pump cover.
5. Pull the housing to disconnect the gear from the balance shaft. Remove the oil pump housing assembly from the balance shaft assembly.

To install:

6. Position the oil pump and cover to the balance shaft housing. Tighten the pump-to-block bolts to 40 ft. lbs. (54 Nm).
7. Install the balance shaft chain tensioner. Tighten the bolt to 115 inch lbs. (13 Nm).
8. Install the balance shaft chain cover. Tighten the bolt to 115 inch lbs. (13 Nm).
9. Install the oil pan.
10. Connect the negative battery cable.

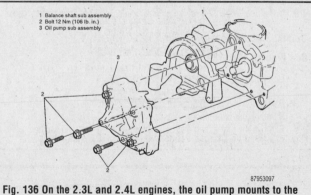

1 Balance shaft sub assembly
2 Bolt 12 Nm (106 lb. in.)
3 Oil pump sub assembly

87953097

Fig. 136 On the 2.3L and 2.4L engines, the oil pump mounts to the balance shaft

Crankshaft Pulley/Damper

REMOVAL & INSTALLATION

2.2L Engines

▶ See Figures 137, 138 and 139

1. Disconnect the negative battery cable.
2. Remove the serpentine drive belt.

Fig. 137 Location of the crankshaft pulley bolts (1) and the hub bolt (2)

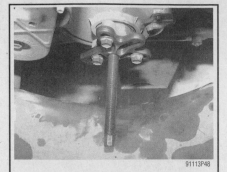

Fig. 138 Unfasten all the pulley and hub bolts, remove the pulley and install a suitable puller on the crankshaft hub

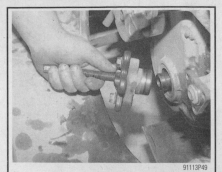

Fig. 139 Use the puller to draw the hub off the crankshaft and remove the hub from the engine compartment

3. Raise the vehicle and support it with jackstands.
4. Remove the inner fender splash shield.
5. Remove the crankshaft pulley bolts.
6. Unfasten the hub bolt and remove the pulley.
7. Attach a suitable puller tool to the crankshaft hub.
8. Turn the center screw of the puller clockwise until it forces the hub from the crankshaft.
9. Inspect the hub for damage and replace it as necessary.
10. Inspect the crankshaft key for damage and replace as necessary.

To install:

11. Coat the front cover seal with clean engine oil.
12. If removed, apply a suitable RTV sealer to the key on the crankshaft and install the key.
13. Place the hub onto the crankshaft making sure to align the key with the notch on the inside diameter of the hub.
14. Install the pulley hub bolt, and tighten the bolt to pull the hub into position taking care and ensuring that the hub goes in straight. Once the hub is fully seated, screw two of the pulley bolts into the hub, use a prybar between the bolts to stop the hub from turning and loosen the hub pulley hub bolt.
15. Remove the two pulley bolts and install the pulley.
16. Install the pulley hub bolts and the center hub bolt. Tighten the pulley bolts to 37 ft. lbs. (50 Nm) and the pulley hub bolt to 77 ft. lbs. (105 Nm).
17. Install the inner fender splash shield.
18. Lower the vehicle.
19. Install the serpentine drive belt and connect the negative battery cable.

2.3L and 2.4L Engines

▶ See Figures 138, 139 and 140

1. Disconnect the negative battery cable.
2. Remove the serpentine drive belt.
3. Raise the vehicle and support it with jackstands.
4. Remove the inner fender splash shield.
5. Remove the crankshaft damper center retaining bolt and washer.
6. Remove the damper assembly using a suitable puller assembly.

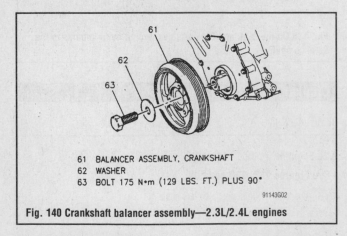

61 BALANCER ASSEMBLY, CRANKSHAFT
62 WASHER
63 BOLT 175 N•m (129 LBS. FT.) PLUS 90°

Fig. 140 Crankshaft balancer assembly—2.3L/2.4L engines

To install:

7. Lubricate the front seal and sealing surface of the damper with chassis grease.
8. Install the damper onto the crankshaft ensuring that the keyway lines up. A rubber or other soft-faced mallet may be needed to lightly tap the damper onto the crankshaft.
9. Install the retaining bolt and washer and tighten the bolt to 129 ft. lbs. (175 Nm), then rotate an additional 90°.
10. Install the inner fender splash shield.
11. Lower the vehicle.
12. Install the serpentine drive belt and connect the negative battery cable.

Timing Chain Cover and Seal

REMOVAL & INSTALLATION

2.2L Engine

▶ See Figures 141 thru 146

➡ The following procedure requires the use of a special tool.

1. Remove the serpentine belt and tensioner.

➡ Although not absolutely necessary, removal of the right front inner fender splash shield will facilitate access to the front cover.

2. Install a suitable engine support fixture.
3. Remove the engine mount assembly.
4. Remove the alternator rear brace, then remove the alternator.
5. Remove the power steering pump, then position it aside with the lines still attached.
6. Raise and safely support the vehicle.
7. Remove the front two oil pan bolts.
8. Remove the crankshaft pulley.
9. Unfasten the front cover-to-block bolts and then remove the front cover. If the front cover is difficult to remove, use a plastic mallet to carefully loosen the cover.

To install:

10. The surfaces of the block and front cover must be clean and free of oil. Install a new gasket and install the front cover using a centering tool (J-23042 or equivalent). Tighten the bolts to 97 inch lbs. (11 Nm).

➡ When applying RTV sealant to the front cover, be sure to keep it out of the bolt holes.

11. Installation of the remaining components is in the reverse order of removal.

2.3L and 2.4L Engines

▶ See Figures 147, 148 and 149

1. Disconnect the negative battery cable.
2. Remove the coolant recovery reservoir.
3. Remove the serpentine drive belt using a 13mm wrench that is at least 24 in. (61cm) long.

Fig. 141 Raise the vehicle, support it jack-stands and remove the front two oil pan nuts

Fig. 142 The front cover is attached to the engine with a number of small bolts

Fig. 143 After unfastening the front cover bolts, remove the cover. You may have to gently pry between the cover and oil pan to break the seal to get the cover off

Fig. 144 Location of the front cover retaining bolt holes and studs

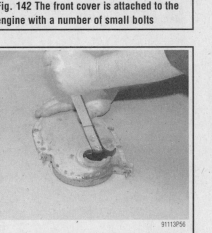

Fig. 145 Use a suitable puller to remove the oil seal

Fig. 146 A sealer driver and a hammer can be used to install a new seal

4. For the 2.3L engine, remove the alternator, then position it aside.

5. For the 2.3L engine, install a suitable engine support. Reinstall the alternator through-bolt, then attach the engine support fixture.

6. For the 2.4L engine, install GM tool K 28467-400 onto the alternator stud-ended bolt, and engine support fixture.

7. Remove upper cover fasteners.

8. Detach the cover vent hose.

9. Remove the right engine mount and the engine mount bracket or bracket adapter. Whenever the engine mounting bracket adapter is removed, the bolts MUST be replaced.

10. Raise and safely support the vehicle.

11. Remove the right front wheel and tire assembly and the splash shield.

12. Remove the crankshaft balancer assembly.

➡Do not install an automatic transaxle-equipped engine balancer on a manual-transaxle equipped engine or vice-versa.

13. Remove lower cover fasteners.

14. Carefully lower the vehicle.

15. Remove the front cover and gasket. Inspect the gasket for damage and replace if necessary.

16. The installation is the reverse of the removal procedure. Tighten the timing chain cover fasteners to 106 inch lbs. (13 Nm). Tighten the balancer attaching bolt to 129 ft. lbs. (175 Nm) plus and additional 90°.

Timing Chain and Gears

REMOVAL & INSTALLATION

2.2L Engine

▶ See Figures 150 thru 156

1. Disconnect the negative battery cable.

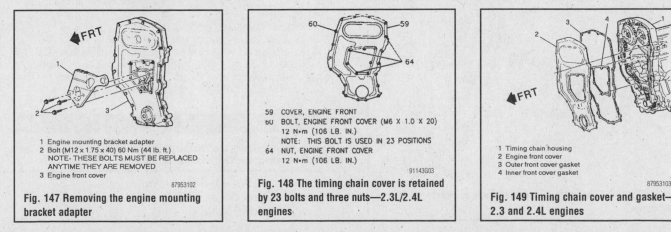

1 Engine mounting bracket adapter
2 Bolt (M12 x 1.75 x 40) 60 Nm (44 lb. ft.)
  NOTE- THESE BOLTS MUST BE REPLACED ANYTIME THEY ARE REMOVED
3 Engine front cover

Fig. 147 Removing the engine mounting bracket adapter

59 COVER, ENGINE FRONT
60 BOLT, ENGINE FRONT COVER (M6 X 1.0 X 20)
   12 N•m (106 LB. IN.)
   NOTE: THIS BOLT IS USED IN 23 POSITIONS
64 NUT, ENGINE FRONT COVER
   12 N•m (106 LB. IN.)

Fig. 148 The timing chain cover is retained by 23 bolts and three nuts—2.3L/2.4L engines

1 Timing chain housing
2 Engine front cover
3 Outer front cover gasket
4 Inner front cover gasket

Fig. 149 Timing chain cover and gasket— 2.3 and 2.4L engines

Fig. 150 The timing marks on the sprockets should be in alignment. If not, turn the crankshaft until the marks are aligned

Fig. 151 The timing chain tensioner is retained by a Torx head bolt (1) and a regular hex head bolt (2)

Fig. 152 Unfasten the camshaft sprocket bolt

Fig. 153 Remove the camshaft sprocket and the timing chain at the same time . . .

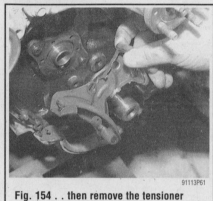

Fig. 154 . . then remove the tensioner assembly

Fig. 155 Compress the tensioner spring and insert a cotter pin or nail in the hole provided to hold the tensioner in position

2. Remove the front cover as previously detailed.

3. Place the No. 1 piston at TDC of the compression stroke so that the marks on the camshaft and crankshaft sprockets are in alignment (see illustration).

4. Loosen the timing chain tensioner nut as far as possible without actually removing it.

5. Remove the camshaft sprocket bolts and remove the sprocket and chain together. If the sprocket does not slide from the camshaft easily, a light blow with a soft mallet at the lower edge of the sprocket will dislodge it.

6. Using a suitable gear puller, remove the crankshaft sprocket.

To install:

7. Press the crankshaft sprocket back onto the crankshaft.

8. Install the timing chain over the camshaft sprocket and then around the crankshaft sprocket. Make sure that the marks on the two sprockets are in alignment (see illustration). Lubricate the thrust surface with Molykote® or its equivalent.

9. Align the dowel in the camshaft with the dowel hole in the sprocket and then install the sprocket onto the camshaft. Use the mounting bolts to draw the sprocket onto the camshaft and then tighten to 66–68 ft. lbs. (91–95 Nm).

10. Lubricate the timing chain with clean engine oil. Tighten the chain tensioner.

11. Installation of the remaining components is in the reverse order of removal.

2.3L and 2.4L Engines

▶ See Figures 157, 158, 159 and 160

Before attempting to remove the timing chain, read the entire procedure.

1. Disconnect the negative battery cable.

2. Remove the timing chain front cover, as outlined earlier in this section.

3. Rotate the crankshaft clockwise, as viewed from the front of engine/normal rotation, until the camshaft sprocket timing dowel pin holes line up with the holes in the timing chain housing. The crankshaft sprocket keyway should point upwards and line up with the centerline of the cylinder bores. This is the "timed" position.

4. Remove the timing chain guides.

5. Raise and safely support the vehicle.

6. Make sure all of the slack in the timing chain is above the tensioner assembly, then remove the tensioner. The timing chain must be disengaged from any wear grooves in the tensioner shoe in order to remove the shoe. Slide a suitable prytool under the timing chain while pulling the shoe outward.

❉❉ WARNING

Do NOT attempt to pry the socket off the camshaft or damage to the sprocket or chain housing could occur.

7. If difficulty is encountered in removing the chain tensioner shoe, remove the intake camshaft sprocket, as follows;

a. Carefully lower the vehicle.

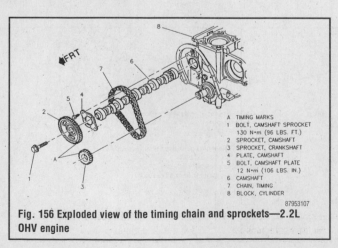

A	TIMING MARKS
1	BOLT, CAMSHAFT SPROCKET 130 N•m (96 LBS. FT.)
2	SPROCKET, CAMSHAFT
3	SPROCKET, CRANKSHAFT
4	PLATE, CAMSHAFT
5	BOLT, CAMSHAFT PLATE 12 N•m (106 LBS. IN.)
6	CAMSHAFT
7	CHAIN, TIMING
8	BLOCK, CYLINDER

Fig. 156 Exploded view of the timing chain and sprockets—2.2L OHV engine

b. Hold the intake camshaft sprocket with a suitable tool and remove the sprocket bolt and washer.

c. Remove the washer from the bolt and rethread the bolt back into the camshaft by hand. The bolt provides a surface to push against.

d. Remove the camshaft sprocket using a three-jaw puller in the three relief holes in the sprocket.

8. Unfasten the tensioner assembly retaining bolts, then remove the tensioner.

➡ **The timing chain and crankshaft sprocket MUST be marked before removal. If the chain or sprocket is installed with the wear pattern in the opposite direction, noise and increased wear may occur.**

9. Mark the crankshaft sprocket and timing chain outer surface for reassembly, then remove the chain.

10. Clean the old sealant off the bolt with a wire brush. Clean the threaded hole in the camshaft with a round nylon brush. Inspect the parts for wear and replace as necessary. Note that some scoring of the chain shoe and guides is normal.

To install:

❉❉ **WARNING**

Failure to follow this procedure may result in severe engine damage.

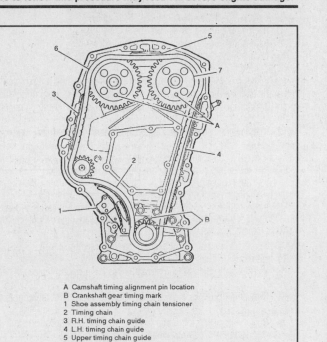

A Camshaft timing alignment pin location
B Crankshaft gear timing mark
1 Shoe assembly timing chain tensioner
2 Timing chain
3 R.H. timing chain guide
4 L.H. timing chain guide
5 Upper timing chain guide
6 Exhaust camshaft sprocket
7 Intake camshaft sprocket

87953108

Fig. 157 The chain must be in the "timed" position—2.3L and 2.4L engines

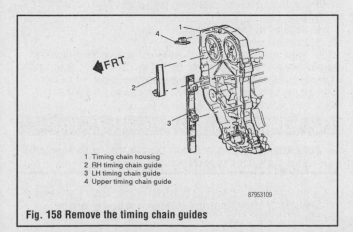

1 Timing chain housing
2 RH timing chain guide
3 LH timing chain guide
4 Upper timing chain guide

87953109

Fig. 158 Remove the timing chain guides

11. Position the intake camshaft sprocket onto the camshaft with the surface marked during removal showing.

12. Install the intake camshaft sprocket retaining bolt and washer, tighten to 52 ft. lbs. (70 Nm) while holding the sprocket with a suitable tool. Use GM sealant 12345493 or equivalent on the camshaft sprocket bolt.

13. Place GM tool J 36008, or equivalent camshaft aligning pins, through the holes in the camshaft sprockets into the holes in the timing chain housing. This positions the cams for correct timing.

14. If the camshafts are out of position and must be rotated more than 1/8 turn in order to install the alignment dowel pins, proceed as follows:

a. The crankshaft MUST be rotate 90° clockwise off of TDC in order to give the valves adequate clearance to open.

b. Once the camshafts are in position and the dowels installed, rotate the crankshaft counter clockwise back to TDC.

❉❉ **WARNING**

Do not rotate the crankshaft clockwise to TDC; valve or piston damage could result.

➡ **The side of the timing chain that was marked during removal must be showing when the chain is installed.**

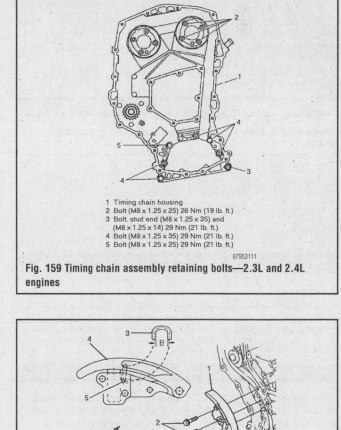

1 Timing chain housing
2 Bolt (M8 x 1.25 x 25) 26 Nm (19 lb. ft.)
3 Bolt, stud end (M8 x 1.25 x 35) and (M8 x 1.25 x 14) 29 Nm (21 lb. ft.)
4 Bolt (M8 x 1.25 x 35) 29 Nm (21 lb. ft.)
5 Bolt (M8 x 1.25 x 25) 29 Nm (21 lb. ft.)

87953111

Fig. 159 Timing chain assembly retaining bolts—2.3L and 2.4L engines

A After installation, remove anti-release from tensioner asm. to release tensioner
B 13 mm (1/2 inch)

1 Timing chain tensioner and shoe assembly
2 10 Nm (89 lbs. in.) bolts
3 Anti-relese keeper - fabricated from heavy gage wire or steel rod
4 Shoe
5 Reset access hole

87953110

Fig. 160 Reloading the tensioner to its "ZERO" position, then install to the chain housing

15. Place the timing chain over the exhaust camshaft sprockets, around the idler sprocket and around the camshaft sprocket.

16. Set the camshafts at the timed position and install the timing chain. Remove the alignment dowel pin from the intake camshaft. Using GM tool J 39579, rotate the intake camshaft sprocket counter clockwise enough to slide the timing chain over the intake camshaft sprocket. Release the camshaft sprocket wrench (J 39579 or equivalent). The length of the chain between the two camshaft sprockets will tighten. If properly timed, the intake camshaft alignment dowel pin should slide in easily. If the dowel pin does not fully index, the camshafts are NOT timed correctly and the procedure must be repeated.

17. Leave the alignment dowel pins installed. Raise and safely support the vehicle.

18. With the slack removed from the chain between the intake camshaft sprocket and the crankshaft sprocket, the timing marks on the crankshaft and cylinder block should be aligned. If the marks are not aligned, move the chain one tooth forward or rearward, remove the slack and recheck the marks.

19. Reload the timing chain tensioner assembly to its "zero" position as follows:

    a. Form a keeper from a piece of heavy gauge wire, as shown in the accompanying figure.

    b. Apply slight force on the tensioner blade to compress the plunger.

    c. Insert a small prytool into the reset access hole, and pry the ratchet pawl away from the ratchet teeth while forcing the plunger completely in the hole.

    d. Install the keeper between the access hole and the blade.

20. Install the tensioner assembly to the timing chain housing. Recheck the plunger assembly installation, it is correctly installed when the long end is toward the crankshaft. Install the tensioner retaining bolts; tighten to 89 inch lbs. (10 Nm).

21. Carefully lower the vehicle enough to reach and remove the alignment dowel pins.

✳✳ WARNING

Severe engine damage could result if the engine is not properly timed.

22. Rotate the crankshaft clockwise (normal rotation) two full rotations. Align the crankshaft keyway with the mark on the cylinder block and reinstall the alignment dowel pins. The pins will slide in easily if the engine is correctly timed.

23. Install the timing chain guides, then install the front (timing chain) cover.

24. Connect the negative battery cable.

Camshaft and Bearings

REMOVAL & INSTALLATION

2.2L Engine

▶ See Figure 161

✳✳ CAUTION

Never open, service or drain the radiator or cooling system when hot; serious burns can occur from the steam and hot coolant. Also, when draining engine coolant, keep in mind that cats and dogs are attracted to ethylene glycol antifreeze and could drink any that is left in an uncovered container or in puddles on the ground. This will prove fatal in sufficient quantities. Always drain coolant into a sealable container. Coolant should be reused unless it is contaminated or is several years old.

1. As outlined earlier, remove the engine and place it on a suitable engine stand.

2. Remove the cylinder head.

3. Unfasten the anti-rotation bracket bolts and brackets, then remove the valve lifters.

4. Unfasten the oil pump drive retaining bolt, then remove the drive by lifting and twisting.

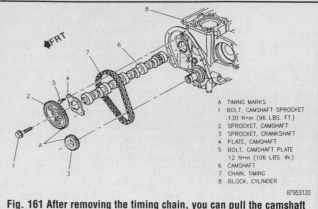

A	TIMING MARKS
1	BOLT, CAMSHAFT SPROCKET -130 N•m (96 LBS. FT.)
2	SPROCKET, CAMSHAFT
3	SPROCKET, CRANKSHAFT
4	PLATE, CAMSHAFT
5	BOLT, CAMSHAFT PLATE 12 N•m (106 LBS. IN.)
6	CAMSHAFT
7	CHAIN, TIMING
8	BLOCK, CYLINDER

87953120

Fig. 161 After removing the timing chain, you can pull the camshaft from the engine. Be sure the camshaft lobes do NOT contact the bearings

5. If equipped, remove the Camshaft Position (CMP) sensor.

6. Remove the crankshaft pulley and hub.

7. Remove the serpentine drive belt idler pulley.

8. Remove the timing cover from the engine.

9. Remove the timing chain and camshaft sprocket.

10. Unfasten the camshaft thrust plate retaining bolts, then remove the plate from the block.

11. Install the sprocket bolts or longer bolts of the same thread into the end of the camshaft as a handle, then pull the camshaft straight out of the engine, turning slightly as it is withdrawn and taking care not to damage the bearings.

12. If removal of camshaft bearings is necessary, use the following procedure:

    a. Install a camshaft bearing removal/installation tool with the shoulder toward the bearing. Ensure that enough threads are engaged.

    b. Using two wrenches, hold the puller screw while turning the nut. When the bearing has been released from the bore, remove the tool.

    c. Assemble the tool on the driver to remove the front and rear bearings.

    d. Install the bearings (outer bearings first) so that the oil holes in the block and the bearing align.

    e. Install a fresh camshaft bearing rear cover using sealant.

To install:

13. Inspect the camshaft, journals and lobes for wear and replace, if necessary.

14. Inspect the bearings for scratches, pits or a loose fit in their bores and replace, if necessary.

15. Coat the camshaft lobes and journals with a high viscosity oil with zinc such as No. 12345501, or equivalent.

16. Carefully insert the camshaft in the engine, turning it slightly from side to side and it is inserted.

17. Install the thrust plate and tighten the retaining bolts to 106 inch lbs. (12 Nm).

18. If equipped, install the CMP sensor.

19. Install the timing chain and camshaft sprocket.

20. Install the timing cover to the engine.

21. Install the serpentine drive belt idler pulley.

22. Install the crankshaft pulley and hub.

23. Install the oil pump drive by inserting while twisting, then install the retaining bolt and tighten to 18 ft. lbs. (25 Nm).

24. Install the valve lifters and the anti-rotation brackets.

25. Install the cylinder head as outlined in this Section.

26. Connect the negative battery cable.

2.3L and 2.4L Engines

INTAKE CAMSHAFT

▶ See Figures 162, 163, 164, 165 and 166

➡Any time the camshaft housing to cylinder head bolts are loosened or removed, the camshaft housing to cylinder head gasket must be replaced.

1. Relieve the fuel system pressure. Disconnect the negative battery cable.

2. Label and detach the ignition coil and module assembly electrical connections.

3. Unfasten the ignition coil and module assembly to camshaft housing bolts, then remove the assembly by pulling straight up. Use a special spark plug boot wire remover tool to remove connector assemblies, if they have stuck to the spark plugs.

4. If equipped, remove the idle speed power steering pressure switch connector.

5. Loosen the three power steering pump pivot bolts and remove drive belt.

6. Disconnect the two rear power steering pump bracket-to-transaxle bolts.

7. Remove the front power steering pump bracket to cylinder block bolt.

8. Disconnect the power steering pump assembly, then position it aside.

9. Using the special tool, remove the power steering pump drive pulley from the intake camshaft.

10. Remove oil/air separator bolts and hoses. Leave the hoses attached to the separator, disconnect from the oil fill, chain housing and intake manifold. Remove as an assembly.

11. Remove vacuum line from fuel pressure regulator and detach the fuel injector harness connector.

12. Disconnect fuel line attaching clamp from bracket on top of intake camshaft housing.

13. Unfasten the fuel rail-to-camshaft housing attaching bolts, then remove the fuel rail from the cylinder head. Cover or plug injector openings in cylinder

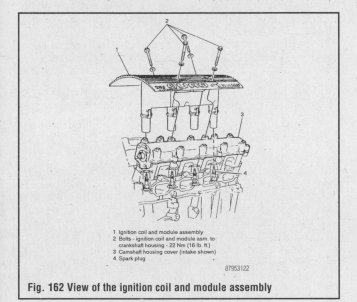

1 Ignition coil and module assembly
2 Bolts - ignition coil and module asm. to crankshaft housing - 22 Nm (16 lb. ft.)
3 Camshaft housing cover (intake shown)
4 Spark plug

87953122

Fig. 162 View of the ignition coil and module assembly

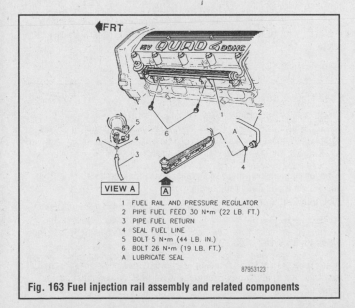

1 FUEL RAIL AND PRESSURE REGULATOR
2 PIPE FUEL FEED 30 N•m (22 LB. FT.)
3 PIPE FUEL RETURN
4 SEAL FUEL LINE
5 BOLT 5 N•m (44 LB. IN.)
6 BOLT 26 N•m (19 LB. FT.)
A LUBRICATE SEAL

87953123

Fig. 163 Fuel injection rail assembly and related components

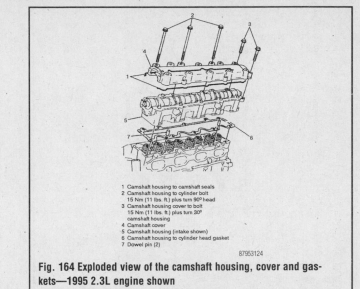

1 Camshaft housing to camshaft seals
2 Camshaft housing to cylinder bolt
  15 Nm (11 lbs. ft.) plus turn 90° head
3 Camshaft housing cover to bolt
  15 Nm (11 lbs. ft.) plus turn 30°
  camshaft housing
4 Camshaft cover
5 Camshaft housing (intake shown)
6 Camshaft housing to cylinder head gasket
7 Dowel pin (2)

87953124

Fig. 164 Exploded view of the camshaft housing, cover and gaskets—1995 2.3L engine shown

head and the injector nozzles. Leave the fuel lines attached, then position fuel rail aside.

14. Disconnect the timing chain and housing, but do NOT remove from the engine.

15. Remove the intake camshaft housing cover-to-camshaft housing attaching bolts.

16. Unfasten the intake camshaft housing-to-cylinder head attaching bolts. Use the reverse of the tightening sequence (shown the accompanying figure) when loosening the bolts. Leave two of the bolts loosely in place to hold the camshaft housing while separating the camshaft cover from housing.

17. Push the cover off the housing by threading four of the housing-to-head attaching bolts into the tapped holes in the cam housing cover. Tighten the bolts evenly so the cover does not bind on the dowel pins.

18. Remove the two loosely installed camshaft housing to head bolts and remove the cover. Discard the gaskets.

19. Note the position of the chain sprocket dowel pin for reassembly.

20. Remove intake camshaft oil seal from camshaft and discard seal. This seal must be replaced any time the housing and cover are separated.

21. Remove the camshaft carrier from the cylinder head and remove the gasket. Discard the gasket.

To install:

22. Thoroughly clean the mating surfaces of the camshaft carrier and the cylinder head, bolts and bolt holes. Install a new gasket and place the housing on the head. Install one bolt loosely to hold it in place.

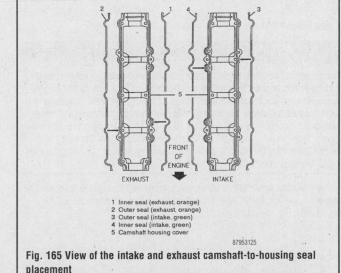

1 Inner seal (exhaust, orange)
2 Outer seal (exhaust, orange)
3 Outer seal (intake, green)
4 Inner seal (intake, green)
5 Camshaft housing cover

87953125

Fig. 165 View of the intake and exhaust camshaft-to-housing seal placement

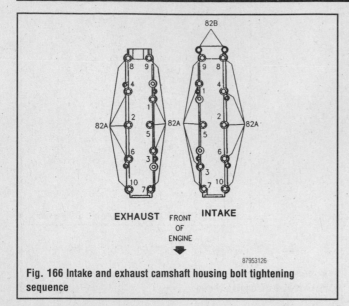

Fig. 166 Intake and exhaust camshaft housing bolt tightening sequence

23. Install the lifters into their bores. If the camshaft is being replaced, the lifters must also be replaced. Lubricate camshaft lobes, journals and lifters with camshaft and lifter prelube. The camshaft lobes and journals must be adequately lubricated or engine damage could occur upon start up.

24. Install the camshaft in the same position as when removed. The timing chain sprocket dowel pin should be straight up and align with the centerline of the lifter bores.

25. Install new camshaft housing to camshaft housing cover seals into cover; do not use sealer. Make sure the correct color seal is placed in each groove. Install the cover to the housing.

26. Apply thread locking compound to the camshaft housing and cover attaching bolt threads.

27. Install the bolts, then tighten to 11 ft. lbs. (15 Nm). Rotate the bolts (except the two rear bolts that hold the fuel pipe to the camshaft housing) an additional 75°, in sequence. Tighten the two rear bolts to 16 ft. lbs. (15 Nm), then rotate an additional 25°.

28. Install the timing chain housing and the timing chain.

29. Uncover fuel injectors, then install new fuel injector O-ring seals lubricated with oil. Install the fuel rail.

30. Fasten the fuel line attaching clamp and retainer to bracket on top of the intake camshaft housing.

31. Connect the vacuum line to the fuel pressure regulator.

32. Attach the fuel injectors harness connector.

33. Install the oil/air separator assembly.

34. Lubricate the inner sealing surface of the intake camshaft seal with oil and install the seal to the housing.

35. Install the power steering pump pulley onto the intake camshaft.

36. Install the power steering pump assembly and drive belt.

37. Connect the idle speed power steering pressure switch connector.

38. Clean any loose lubricant that is present on the ignition coil and module assembly to camshaft housing bolts. Apply an appropriate thread sealing compound onto the ignition coil and module assembly to camshaft housing bolts. Install the bolts and tighten to 13 ft. lbs. (18 Nm).

39. Attach the electrical connectors to ignition coil and module assembly.

40. Connect the negative battery cable, then start the engine and check for leaks.

EXHAUST CAMSHAFT

♦ **See Figures 165 and 166**

➡ **Any time the camshaft housing-to-cylinder head bolts are loosened or removed, the camshaft housing to cylinder head gasket must be replaced.**

1. Relieve the fuel system pressure. Disconnect the negative battery cable.

2. Label and disconnect the ignition coil and module assembly electrical connections.

3. Unfasten the ignition coil and module assembly-to-camshaft housing

bolts, then remove the assembly by pulling straight up. Use a special tool to remove connector assemblies if they have stuck to the spark plugs.

4. If equipped, remove the idle speed power steering pressure switch connector.

5. Remove the transaxle fluid level indicator tube assembly from exhaust camshaft cover and position aside.

6. Remove exhaust camshaft cover and gasket.

7. Disconnect the timing chain and housing but do not remove from the engine.

8. Remove exhaust camshaft housing to cylinder head bolts. Use the reverse of the tightening procedure when loosening camshaft housing while separating camshaft cover from housing.

9. Push the cover off the housing by threading four of the housing to head attaching bolts into the tapped holes in the camshaft cover. When threading the bolt, tighten them evenly so the cover does not bind on the dowel pins.

10. Remove the two loosely installed camshaft housing to cylinder head bolts and remove cover, discard gaskets.

11. Loosely reinstall one camshaft housing to cylinder head bolt to retain the housing during camshaft and lifter removal.

12. Note the position of the chain sprocket dowel pin for reassembly. Remove camshaft being careful not to damage the camshaft or journals.

13. Remove the camshaft carrier from the cylinder head and remove the gasket. Discard the gasket.

To install:

14. Thoroughly clean the mating surfaces of the camshaft carrier and the cylinder head, bolts and bolt holes. Install a new gasket and place the housing on the head. Install 1 bolt loosely to hold in place.

15. Install the lifters into their bores. If the camshaft is being replaced, the lifters must also be replaced. Lubricate camshaft lobes, journals and lifters with camshaft and lifter prelube. The camshaft lobes and journals must be adequately lubricated or engine damage could occur upon start up.

16. Install camshaft in same position as when removed. The timing chain sprocket dowel pin should be straight up and align with the centerline of the lifter bores.

17. Install new camshaft housing-to-camshaft housing cover seals into the cover; do not use sealer. Make sure the correct color seal is placed in each groove. Install the cover to the housing.

18. Apply thread locking compound to the camshaft housing and cover attaching bolt threads.

19. Install bolts, then tighten, in sequence, to 11 ft. lbs. (15 Nm). Then rotate the bolts an additional 75 degrees, in sequence.

20. Install timing chain housing and timing chain.

21. Install the transaxle fluid level indicator tube assembly to the exhaust camshaft cover.

22. Attach the idle speed power steering pressure switch connector.

23. Clean any loose lubricant that is present on the ignition coil and module assembly to camshaft housing bolts. Apply an appropriate thread sealing compound onto the ignition coil and module assembly to camshaft housing bolts. Install the bolts and tighten to 13 ft. lbs. (18 Nm).

24. Attach the electrical connectors to ignition coil and module assembly.

25. Connect the negative battery cable, then start the engine and check for leaks.

INSPECTION

♦ **See Figures 167, 168 and 169**

Using solvent, degrease the camshaft and clean out all of the oil holes. Visually inspect the cam lobes and bearing journals for excessive wear. If a lobe is questionable, check all of the lobes as indicated. If a journal or lobe is worn, the camshaft MUST BE or replaced.

➡ **If a journal is worn, there is a good chance that the bearings or journals are worn and need replacement.**

If the lobes and journals appear intact, place the front and rear journals in V-blocks and rest a dial indicator on the center journal. Rotate the camshaft to check the straightness. If deviation exceeds 0.001 in. (0.0254mm), replace the camshaft.

Check the camshaft lobes with a micrometer, by measuring the lobes from the nose to the base and again at 90° (see illustration). The lobe lift is determined by subtracting the second measurement from the first. If all of the exhaust and intake lobes are not identical, the camshaft must be reground or replace.

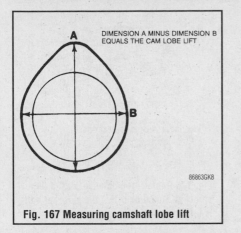

Fig. 167 Measuring camshaft lobe lift

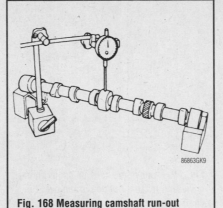

Fig. 168 Measuring camshaft run-out

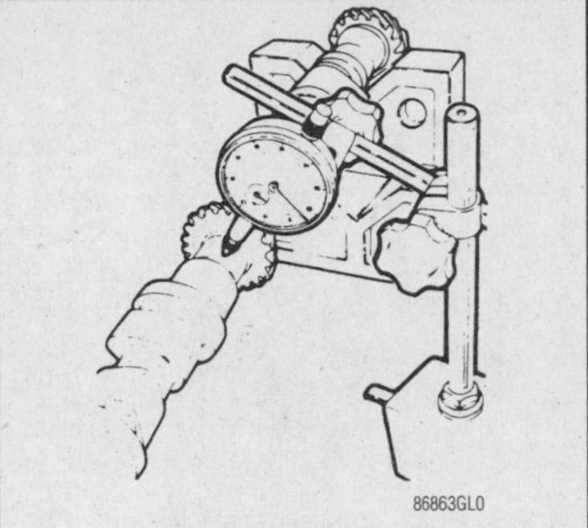

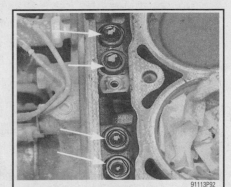

Fig. 169 Measuring camshaft straightness

Valve Lifters

REMOVAL, INSTALLATION & INSPECTION

2.2L Engine

▶ See Figures 170, 171, 172 and 173

When installing new lifters, a pre-lube should always be applied to the lifter body. It is also a good idea to prime hydraulic lifters by submerging them in clean engine oil and depressing the plunger using an old pushrod. This allows the internal components of the hydraulic lifter to coat with oil before initial operation in the engine. All lifters should be replaced when a new camshaft is installed.

➡ If any valve train components (lifters, pushrods, rocker arms) are to be reused, they must be tagged or arranged during removal to assure installation in their original locations.

1. Remove the rocker arm cover.
2. Remove the cylinder head assembly from the engine.
3. Remove the bolts retaining the lifter anti-rotation brackets, then remove the brackets.
4. Remove the hydraulic roller lifters from the bores.
5. Inspect the lifter and lifter bore for wear and scuffing. Examine the roller for freedom of movement and/or flat spots on the roller surface.

To install:

➡ If installing a new lifter, coat the lifter body with a suitable camshaft pre-lube

6. Install each hydraulic lifter to its bore being careful to align the flat sides (top) of the lifters with the flat sides of the anti-rotation brackets. When properly installed the flat sides of each lifter are aligned parallel to the anti-rotation bracket. The roller at the bottom of the lifter is parallel to the camshaft lobe.

➡ Make sure to properly align and install each lifter as improper installation of the lifters or brackets could result in engine damage.

7. Install the anti-rotation bracket retaining bolts and tighten to 97 inch lbs. (11 Nm).
8. Install the cylinder head.
9. Install the rocker arm cover.

Balance Shafts

➡ The balance shafts are only found on the 2.3L and 2.4L engines.

REMOVAL & INSTALLATION

2.3L and 2.4L Engine

▶ See Figures 174 thru 179

1. Disconnect the negative battery cable.
2. Remove the oil pan assembly as outlined in this Section.
3. Remove the balance shaft chain cover.
4. Loosen, but do not remove, the balance shaft chain tensioner.
5. Remove the oil pump cover and the oil pump assembly.
6. Rotate the engine until the number 1 piston is at TDC (Top Dead Center).

✳✳ CAUTION

The balance shaft driven sprocket bolt is left-hand threaded and must be loosened by turning it in a CLOCKWISE direction. If it is not turned in a clockwise direction, it may break.

7. Use tool J41088 to prevent the balance shafts from turning while loosening the driven shaft sprocket bolt.
8. Remove the sprocket bolt, and matchmark the sprocket to the driven balance shaft. Remove the driven sprocket from the balance shaft.
9. Remove the balance shaft housing fasteners and remove the balance shaft housing and shaft assembly.

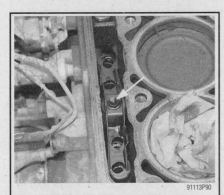

Fig. 170 Remove the bolts retaining the lifter anti-rotation brackets . . .

Fig. 171 . . then remove the anti-rotation brackets

Fig. 172 The lifters are located in bores in the engine block

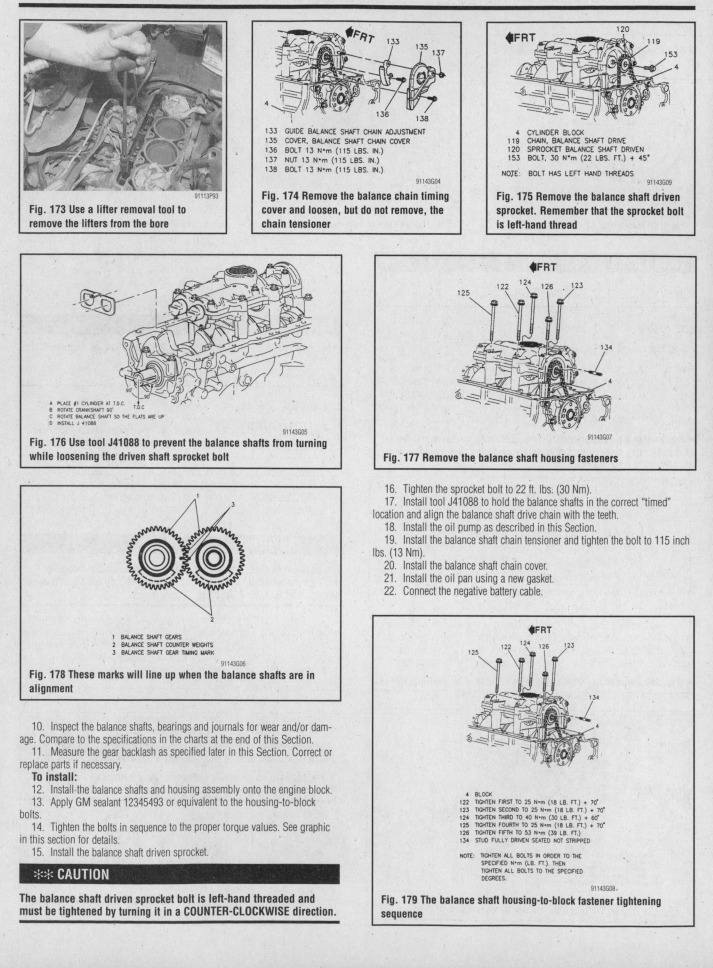

Fig. 173 Use a lifter removal tool to remove the lifters from the bore

Fig. 174 Remove the balance chain timing cover and loosen, but do not remove, the chain tensioner

133 GUIDE BALANCE SHAFT CHAIN ADJUSTMENT
135 COVER, BALANCE SHAFT CHAIN COVER
136 BOLT 13 N•m (115 LBS. IN.)
137 NUT 13 N•m (115 LBS. IN.)
138 BOLT 13 N•m (115 LBS. IN.)

Fig. 175 Remove the balance shaft driven sprocket. Remember that the sprocket bolt is left-hand thread

4 CYLINDER BLOCK
119 CHAIN, BALANCE SHAFT DRIVE
120 SPROCKET BALANCE SHAFT DRIVEN
153 BOLT, 30 N•m (22 LBS. FT.) + 45°

NOTE: BOLT HAS LEFT HAND THREADS

A PLACE #1 CYLINDER AT T.D.C.
B ROTATE CRANKSHAFT 90°
C ROTATE BALANCE SHAFT SO THE FLATS ARE UP
D INSTALL J 41088

Fig. 176 Use tool J41088 to prevent the balance shafts from turning while loosening the driven shaft sprocket bolt

Fig. 177 Remove the balance shaft housing fasteners

1 BALANCE SHAFT GEARS
2 BALANCE SHAFT COUNTER WEIGHTS
3 BALANCE SHAFT GEAR TIMING MARK

Fig. 178 These marks will line up when the balance shafts are in alignment

16. Tighten the sprocket bolt to 22 ft. lbs. (30 Nm).

17. Install tool J41088 to hold the balance shafts in the correct "timed" location and align the balance shaft drive chain with the teeth.

18. Install the oil pump as described in this Section.

19. Install the balance shaft chain tensioner and tighten the bolt to 115 inch lbs. (13 Nm).

20. Install the balance shaft chain cover.

21. Install the oil pan using a new gasket.

22. Connect the negative battery cable.

10. Inspect the balance shafts, bearings and journals for wear and/or damage. Compare to the specifications in the charts at the end of this Section.

11. Measure the gear backlash as specified later in this Section. Correct or replace parts if necessary.

To install:

12. Install the balance shafts and housing assembly onto the engine block.

13. Apply GM sealant 12345493 or equivalent to the housing-to-block bolts.

14. Tighten the bolts in sequence to the proper torque values. See graphic in this section for details.

15. Install the balance shaft driven sprocket.

❖❖ CAUTION

The balance shaft driven sprocket bolt is left-hand threaded and must be tightened by turning it in a COUNTER-CLOCKWISE direction.

4 BLOCK
122 TIGHTEN FIRST TO 25 N•m (18 LB. FT.) + 70°
123 TIGHTEN SECOND TO 25 N•m (18 LB. FT.) + 70°
124 TIGHTEN THIRD TO 40 N•m (30 LB. FT.) + 60°
125 TIGHTEN FOURTH TO 25 N•m (18 LB. FT.) + 70°
126 TIGHTEN FIFTH TO 53 N•m (39 LB. FT.)
134 STUD FULLY DRIVEN SEATED NOT STRIPPED

NOTE: TIGHTEN ALL BOLTS IN ORDER TO THE SPECIFIED N•m (LB. FT.). THEN TIGHTEN ALL BOLTS TO THE SPECIFIED DEGREES.

Fig. 179 The balance shaft housing-to-block fastener tightening sequence

INSPECTION

▶ **See Figures 180, 181, 182, 183 and 184**

1. Remove the balance shaft assembly.
2. Remove the 8 upper-to-lower balance shaft housing bolts.
3. Seperate the housings and remove the balance shafts.
4. Remove the bearings and the thrust plate from the housing.
5. Clean the housing, bearings, shafts, and the thrust plate.
6. Inspect the housing for:
- Cracks
- Scored bearing bores
- Damaged threaded holes

➡ **If the housings contain damage, replace the entire balance shaft assembly.**

7. Inspect the bearings for:
- Gouges
- Scoring
- Discoloration
8. Inspect the balance shafts for:
- Scores or burrs on journals
- Cracks or missing pieces
9. Inspect the thrust plate for:
- Gouges
- Burrs
10. Inspect the sprockets for:
- Bent teeth
- Broken teeth
- Chips
- Ground off teeth
11. Measure the balance shaft journals for following:
- Outside diameter
- Out of round
12. Measure the bearings for bearing clearance.

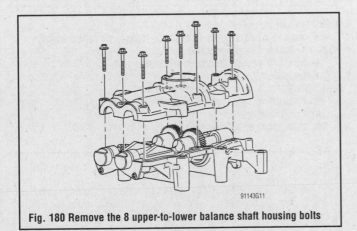

Fig. 180 Remove the 8 upper-to-lower balance shaft housing bolts

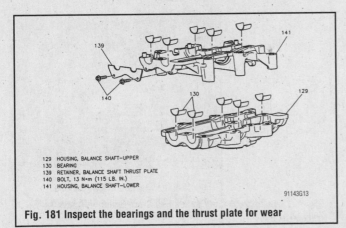

129 HOUSING, BALANCE SHAFT–UPPER
130 BEARING
139 RETAINER, BALANCE SHAFT THRUST PLATE
140 BOLT, 13 N•m (115 LB. IN.)
141 HOUSING, BALANCE SHAFT–LOWER

91143G13

Fig. 181 Inspect the bearings and the thrust plate for wear

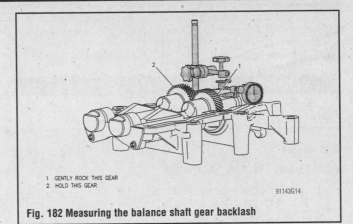

1 GENTLY ROCK THIS GEAR
2 HOLD THIS GEAR

91143G14

Fig. 182 Measuring the balance shaft gear backlash

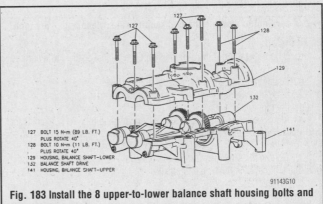

127 BOLT 15 N•m (89 LB. FT.)
     PLUS ROTATE 40°
128 BOLT 10 N•m (11 LB. FT.)
     PLUS ROTATE 40°
129 HOUSING, BALANCE SHAFT–LOWER
132 BALANCE SHAFT DRIVE
141 HOUSING, BALANCE SHAFT–UPPER

91143G10

Fig. 183 Install the 8 upper-to-lower balance shaft housing bolts and tighten them . . .

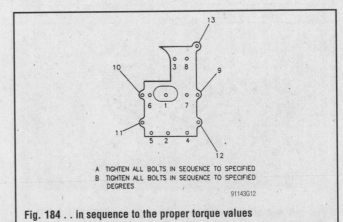

A TIGHTEN ALL BOLTS IN SEQUENCE TO SPECIFIED
B TIGHTEN ALL BOLTS IN SEQUENCE TO SPECIFIED
   DEGREES

91143G12

Fig. 184 . . in sequence to the proper torque values

13. Measure the thrust plate thickness.
14. Measure the gears backlash using a dial indicator.

❋❋ **CAUTION**

If one balance shaft needs replacing, they both must be replaced. Always replace the bearings when replacing the balance shafts.

15. Compare all the measurements to the specifications in the charts at the end of this Section. Replace any component(s) that are out of specification.

To install:

16. Install the bearings into housings and install the balance shafts.
17. Install the thrust plate and tighten the retaining bolts to 115 inch lbs. (13 Nm).
18. Verify the proper gear backlash using a dial indicator.

19. Install the upper and lower housings together and tighten the 8 upper-to-lower balance shaft housing bolts in sequence and to the proper torque values as shown by the graphics in this Section

20. Install the balance shaft housing onto the engine block.

Rear Main Seal

REMOVAL & INSTALLATION

2.2L Engine

◆ **See Figures 185, 186, 187 and 188**

1. Jack up the engine and support it safely.
2. Remove the transaxle as outlined in Section 7.
3. Remove the flywheel.
4. Insert a suitable pry tool in through the dust lip and pry out the seal by moving the tool around the seal until it is removed.

➥ **Use care not to damage the crankshaft seal surface with a pry tool.**

To install:

5. Before installing, lubricate the seal bore to seal surface with engine oil.
6. Install the new seal using a suitable seal driver.
7. Slide the new seal over the mandrel until the dust lip bottoms squarely against the tool collar.
8. Align the dowel pin of the tool with the dowel pin hole in the crankshaft and attach the tool to the crankshaft. Tighten the attaching screws to 2–5 ft. lbs. (2.7–6.8 Nm).
9. Tighten the T-handle of the tool to push the seal into the bore. Continue until the tool collar is flush against the block.

Fig. 185 View of the rear main seal—2.2L engines

10. Loosen the T-handle completely. Remove the attaching screws and the tool.

➥ **Check to see that the seal is squarely seated in the bore.**

11. Install the flywheel and transaxle.
12. Start the engine and check for leaks.

2.3L and 2.4L Engines

◆ **See Figure 189**

1. Disconnect the negative battery cable.
2. Remove the transaxle assembly as outlined in Section 7 of this manual.
3. If equipped with a manual transaxle, remove the pressure plate and clutch disc.
4. Unfasten the flywheel-to-crankshaft bolts, then remove the flywheel.
5. Disconnect the oil pan-to-seal housing bolts
6. Unfasten the seal housing-to-block bolts, then remove the seal housing and gasket.
7. To support the seal housing for seal removal, place two blocks of equal thickness on a flat surface, position the seal housing and blocks so the transaxle side of the seal housing is supported across the dowel pin and center bolt holes on both sides of the seal opening.

➥ **The seal housing could be damaged if not properly supported during seal removal.**

8. Drive the seal evenly out the transaxle side of the seal housing using a small prytool in the relief grooves on the crankshaft side of the seal housing. Discard the seal.

✷✷ WARNING

Be careful not to damage the seal housing sealing surface. If damaged, it may result in an oil leak.

To install:

9. Press a new seal into the housing using tool J 36005 or equivalent seal installation tool.
10. Inspect the oil pan gasket inner silicone bead for damage and repair using a silicone sealant, if necessary.
11. Position a new seal housing-to-block gasket over the alignment. The gasket is reversible.
12. Lubricate the lip of the seal with clean engine oil.
13. Install the housing assembly, then tighten the housing-to-block bolts to 106 inch lbs. (12 Nm).
14. Install the oil pan-to-seal housing bolts, then tighten to 106 inch lbs. (12 Nm).
15. Install the flywheel as outlined later in this section.
16. For vehicles equipped with a manual transaxle, install the clutch, pressure plate and clutch cover assembly.
17. Install the transaxle assembly as outlined in Section 7 of this manual.
18. Connect the negative battery cable, then start the engine and check for leaks.

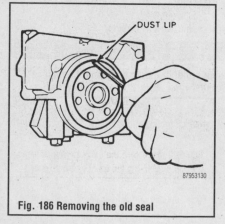

Fig. 186 Removing the old seal

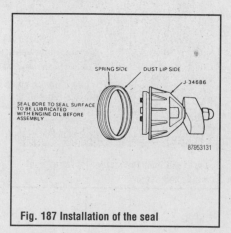

Fig. 187 Installation of the seal

Fig. 188 The rear main seal may be installed using a suitable seal driver tool and a hammer

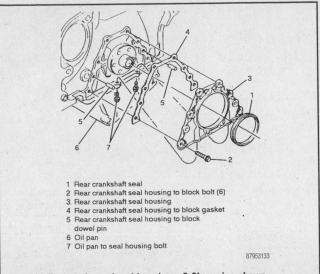

1 Rear crankshaft seal
2 Rear crankshaft seal housing to block bolt (6)
3 Rear crankshaft seal housing
4 Rear crankshaft seal housing to block gasket
5 Rear crankshaft seal housing to block
   dowel pin
6 Oil pan
7 Oil pan to seal housing bolt

87953133

Fig. 189 Rear main seal and housing—2.3L engine shown

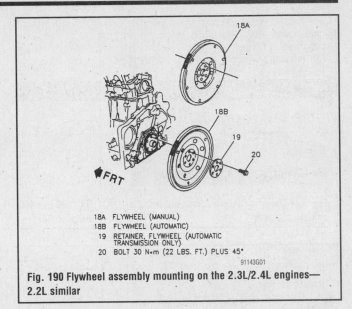

18A FLYWHEEL (MANUAL)
18B FLYWHEEL (AUTOMATIC)
19   RETAINER, FLYWHEEL (AUTOMATIC
     TRANSMISSION ONLY)
20   BOLT 30 N•m (22 LBS. FT.) PLUS 45°

91143G01

Fig. 190 Flywheel assembly mounting on the 2.3L/2.4L engines— 2.2L similar

Flywheel/Flexplate

REMOVAL & INSTALLATION

▶ **See Figure 190**

1. Disconnect the negative battery cable.
2. Remove the transaxle. Refer to Section 7.
3. If equipped with a manual transaxle, mark the clutch disc, pressure plate and flywheel with index marks in relation to each other for installation. Remove the clutch disc and pressure plate. Refer to Section 7.
4. Mark the position of the flywheel on the crankshaft and remove the flywheel retaining bolts.

5. Remove the flywheel and spacer (if equipped).

To install:

6. Coat the threads of the flywheel retaining bolts with thread locking compound.
7. Position the flywheel on the crankshaft flange and install the spacer (if equipped).
8. Install and tighten the bolts in a alternating star pattern to 55 ft. lbs. (75 Nm) on the 2.2L engine, and 22 ft. lbs. (30 Nm) and an additional 45° on the 2.3L and 2.4L engines.
9. If equipped with a manual transaxle, install the clutch and pressure plate.
10. Install the transaxle. Refer to Section 7.
11. Connect the negative battery cable.

EXHAUST SYSTEM

Inspection

▶ **See Figures 191 thru 197**

➡Safety glasses should be worn at all times when working on or near the exhaust system. Older exhaust systems will almost always be covered with loose rust particles which will shower you when disturbed. These particles are more than a nuisance and could injure your eye.

✴✴ CAUTION

DO NOT perform exhaust repairs or inspection with the engine or exhaust hot. Allow the system to cool completely before attempting any work. Exhaust systems are noted for sharp edges, flaking metal and rusted bolts. Gloves and eye protection are required. A healthy supply of penetrating oil and rags is highly recommended.

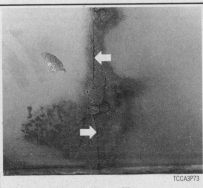

TCCA3P73

Fig. 191 Cracks in the muffler are a guaranteed leak

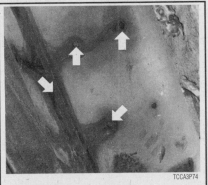

TCCA3P74

Fig. 192 Check the muffler for rotted spot welds and seams

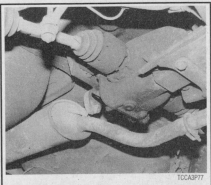

TCCA3P77

Fig. 193 Make sure the exhaust components are not contacting the body or suspension

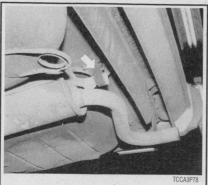

Fig. 194 Check for overstretched or torn exhaust hangers

Fig. 195 Example of a badly deteriorated exhaust pipe

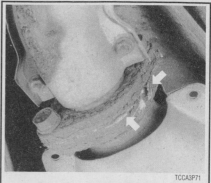

Fig. 196 Inspect flanges for gaskets that have deteriorated and need replacement

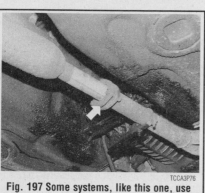

Fig. 197 Some systems, like this one, use large O-rings (doughnuts) in between the flanges

Fig. 198 Nuts and bolts will be extremely difficult to remove when deteriorated with rust

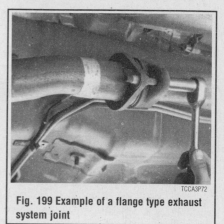

Fig. 199 Example of a flange type exhaust system joint

Your vehicle must be raised and supported safely to inspect the exhaust system properly. By placing 4 safety stands under the vehicle for support should provide enough room for you to slide under the vehicle and inspect the system completely. Start the inspection at the exhaust manifold or turbocharger pipe where the header pipe is attached and work your way to the back of the vehicle. On dual exhaust systems, remember to inspect both sides of the vehicle. Check the complete exhaust system for open seams, holes loose connections, or other deterioration which could permit exhaust fumes to seep into the passenger compartment. Inspect all mounting brackets and hangers for deterioration, some models may have rubber O-rings that can be overstretched and non-supportive. These components will need to be replaced if found. It has always been a practice to use a pointed tool to poke up into the exhaust system where the deterioration spots are to see whether or not they crumble. Some models may have heat shield covering certain parts of the exhaust system , it will be necessary to remove these shields to have the exhaust visible for inspection also.

REPLACEMENT

▶ See Figure 198

There are basically two types of exhaust systems. One is the flange type where the component ends are attached with bolts and a gasket in-between. The other exhaust system is the slip joint type. These components slip into one another using clamps to retain them together.

✳✳ CAUTION

Allow the exhaust system to cool sufficiently before spraying a solvent exhaust fasteners. Some solvents are highly flammable and could ignite when sprayed on hot exhaust components.

Before removing any component of the exhaust system, ALWAYS squirt a liquid rust dissolving agent onto the fasteners for ease of removal. A lot of knuckle skin will be saved by following this rule. It may even be wise to spray the fasteners and allow them to sit overnight.

Flange Type

▶ See Figure 199

✳✳ CAUTION

Do NOT perform exhaust repairs or inspection with the engine or exhaust hot. Allow the system to cool completely before attempting any work. Exhaust systems are noted for sharp edges, flaking metal and rusted bolts. Gloves and eye protection are required. A healthy supply of penetrating oil and rags is highly recommended. Never spray liquid rust dissolving agent onto a hot exhaust component.

Before removing any component on a flange type system, ALWAYS squirt a liquid rust dissolving agent onto the fasteners for ease of removal. Start by unbolting the exhaust piece at both ends (if required). When unbolting the headpipe from the manifold, make sure that the bolts are free before trying to remove them. if you snap a stud in the exhaust manifold, the stud will have to be removed with a bolt extractor, which often means removal of the manifold itself. Next, disconnect the component from the mounting; slight twisting and turning may be required to remove the component completely from the vehicle. You may need to tap on the component with a rubber mallet to loosen the component. If all else fails, use a hacksaw to separate the parts. An oxy-acetylene cutting torch may be faster but the sparks are DANGEROUS near the fuel tank, and at the very least, accidents could happen, resulting in damage to the under-car parts, not to mention yourself.

Slip Joint Type

▶ See Figure 200

Before removing any component on the slip joint type exhaust system, ALWAYS squirt a liquid rust dissolving agent onto the fasteners for ease of removal. Start by unbolting the exhaust piece at both ends (if required). When unbolting the headpipe from the manifold, make sure that the bolts are free before trying to remove them. if you snap a stud in the exhaust manifold, the stud will have to be removed with a bolt extractor, which often means removal of the manifold itself. Next, remove the mounting U-bolts from around the exhaust pipe you are extracting from the vehicle. Don't be surprised if the U-bolts break while removing the nuts. Loosen the exhaust pipe from any mounting brackets retaining it to the floor pan and separate the components.

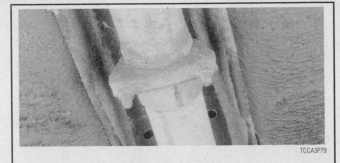

TCCA3P79

Fig. 200 Example of a common slip joint type system

ENGINE RECONDITIONING

Determining Engine Condition

Anything that generates heat and/or friction will eventually burn or wear out (for example, a light bulb generates heat, therefore its life span is limited). With this in mind, a running engine generates tremendous amounts of both; friction is encountered by the moving and rotating parts inside the engine and heat is created by friction and combustion of the fuel. However, the engine has systems designed to help reduce the effects of heat and friction and provide added longevity. The oiling system reduces the amount of friction encountered by the moving parts inside the engine, while the cooling system reduces heat created by friction and combustion. If either system is not maintained, a break-down will be inevitable. Therefore, you can see how regular maintenance can affect the service life of your vehicle. If you do not drain, flush and refill your cooling system at the proper intervals, deposits will begin to accumulate in the radiator, thereby reducing the amount of heat it can extract from the coolant. The same applies to your oil and filter; if it is not changed often enough it becomes laden with contaminates and is unable to properly lubricate the engine. This increases friction and wear.

There are a number of methods for evaluating the condition of your engine. A compression test can reveal the condition of your pistons, piston rings, cylinder bores, head gasket(s), valves and valve seats. An oil pressure test can warn you of possible engine bearing, or oil pump failures. Excessive oil consumption, evidence of oil in the engine air intake area and/or bluish smoke from the tailpipe may indicate worn piston rings, worn valve guides and/or valve seals. As a general rule, an engine that uses no more than one quart of oil every 1000 miles is in good condition. Engines that use one quart of oil or more in less than 1000 miles should first be checked for oil leaks. If any oil leaks are present, have them fixed before determining how much oil is consumed by the engine, especially if blue smoke is not visible at the tailpipe.

COMPRESSION TEST

▶ See Figure 201

A noticeable lack of engine power, excessive oil consumption and/or poor fuel mileage measured over an extended period are all indicators of internal engine wear. Worn piston rings, scored or worn cylinder bores, blown head gaskets, sticking or burnt valves, and worn valve seats are all possible culprits. A check of each cylinder's compression will help locate the problem.

➡A screw-in type compression gauge is more accurate than the type you simply hold against the spark plug hole. Although it takes slightly longer to use, it's worth the effort to obtain a more accurate reading.

1. Make sure that the proper amount and viscosity of engine oil is in the crankcase, then ensure the battery is fully charged.
2. Warm-up the engine to normal operating temperature, then shut the engine OFF.
3. Disable the ignition system.
4. Label and disconnect all of the spark plug wires from the plugs.
5. Thoroughly clean the cylinder head area around the spark plug ports, then remove the spark plugs.
6. Set the throttle plate to the fully open (wide-open throttle) position. You can block the accelerator linkage open for this, or you can have an assistant fully depress the accelerator pedal.
7. Install a screw-in type compression gauge into the No. 1 spark plug hole until the fitting is snug.

✳✳ WARNING

Be careful not to crossthread the spark plug hole.

8. According to the tool manufacturer's instructions, connect a remote starting switch to the starting circuit.
9. With the ignition switch in the OFF position, use the remote starting switch to crank the engine through at least five compression strokes (approximately 5 seconds of cranking) and record the highest reading on the gauge.
10. Repeat the test on each cylinder, cranking the engine approximately the same number of compression strokes and/or time as the first.
11. Compare the highest readings from each cylinder to that of the others. The indicated compression pressures are considered within specifications if the lowest reading cylinder is within 75 percent of the pressure recorded for the highest reading cylinder. For example, if your highest reading cylinder pressure was 150 psi (1034 kPa), then 75 percent of that would be 113 psi (779 kPa). So the lowest reading cylinder should be no less than 113 psi (779 kPa).
12. If a cylinder exhibits an unusually low compression reading, pour a tablespoon of clean engine oil into the cylinder through the spark plug hole and repeat the compression test. If the compression rises after adding oil, it means that the cylinder's piston rings and/or cylinder bore are damaged or worn. If the pressure remains low, the valves may not be seating properly (a valve job is needed), or the head gasket may be blown near that cylinder. If compression in any two adjacent cylinders is low, and if the addition of oil doesn't help raise compression, there is leakage past the head gasket. Oil and coolant in the combustion chamber, combined with blue or constant white smoke from the tailpipe, are symptoms of this problem. However, don't be alarmed by the normal white smoke emitted from the tailpipe during engine warm-up or from cold weather driving. There may be evidence of water droplets on the engine dipstick and/or oil droplets in the cooling system if a head gasket is blown.

TCCS3801

Fig. 201 A screw-in type compression gauge is more accurate and easier to use without an assistant

OIL PRESSURE TEST

Check for proper oil pressure at the sending unit passage with an externally mounted mechanical oil pressure gauge (as opposed to relying on a factory installed dash-mounted gauge). A tachometer may also be needed, as some specifications may require running the engine at a specific rpm.

1. With the engine cold, locate and remove the oil pressure sending unit.

2. Following the manufacturer's instructions, connect a mechanical oil pressure gauge and, if necessary, a tachometer to the engine.

3. Start the engine and allow it to idle.

4. Check the oil pressure reading when cold and record the number. You may need to run the engine at a specified rpm, so check the specifications.

5. Run the engine until normal operating temperature is reached (upper radiator hose will feel warm).

6. Check the oil pressure reading again with the engine hot and record the number. Turn the engine **OFF**.

7. Compare your hot oil pressure reading to that given in the chart. If the reading is low, check the cold pressure reading against the chart. If the cold pressure is well above the specification, and the hot reading was lower than the specification, you may have the wrong viscosity oil in the engine. Change the oil, making sure to use the proper grade and quantity, then repeat the test.

Low oil pressure readings could be attributed to internal component wear, pump related problems, a low oil level, or oil viscosity that is too low. High oil pressure readings could be caused by an overfilled crankcase, too high of an oil viscosity or a faulty pressure relief valve.

Buy or Rebuild?

Now that you have determined that your engine is worn out, you must make some decisions. The question of whether or not an engine is worth rebuilding is largely a subjective matter and one of personal worth. Is the engine a popular one, or is it an obsolete model? Are parts available? Will it get acceptable gas mileage once it is rebuilt? Is the car it's being put into worth keeping? Would it be less expensive to buy a new engine, have your engine rebuilt by a pro, rebuild it yourself or buy a used engine from a salvage yard? Or would it be simpler and less expensive to buy another car? If you have considered all these matters and more, and have still decided to rebuild the engine, then it is time to decide how you will rebuild it.

➡**The editors at Chilton feel that most engine machining should be performed by a professional machine shop. Don't think of it as wasting money, rather, as an assurance that the job has been done right the first time. There are many expensive and specialized tools required to perform such tasks as boring and honing an engine block or having a valve job done on a cylinder head. Even inspecting the parts requires expensive micrometers and gauges to properly measure wear and clearances. Also, a machine shop can deliver to you clean, and ready to assemble parts, saving you time and aggravation. Your maximum savings will come from performing the removal, disassembly, assembly and installation of the engine and purchasing or renting only the tools required to perform the above tasks. Depending on the particular circumstances, you may save 40 to 60 percent of the cost doing these yourself.**

A complete rebuild or overhaul of an engine involves replacing all of the moving parts (pistons, rods, crankshaft, camshaft, etc.) with new ones and machining the non-moving wearing surfaces of the block and heads. Unfortunately, this may not be cost effective. For instance, your crankshaft may have been damaged or worn, but it can be machined undersize for a minimal fee.

So, as you can see, you can replace everything inside the engine, but, it is wiser to replace only those parts which are really needed, and, if possible, repair the more expensive ones. Later in this section, we will break the engine down into its two main components: the cylinder head and the engine block. We will discuss each component, and the recommended parts to replace during a rebuild on each.

Engine Overhaul Tips

Most engine overhaul procedures are fairly standard. In addition to specific parts replacement procedures and specifications for your individual engine, this section is also a guide to acceptable rebuilding procedures. Examples of standard rebuilding practice are given and should be used along with specific details concerning your particular engine.

Competent and accurate machine shop services will ensure maximum perfor-

mance, reliability and engine life. In most instances it is more profitable for the do-it-yourself mechanic to remove, clean and inspect the component, buy the necessary parts and deliver these to a shop for actual machine work.

Much of the assembly work (crankshaft, bearings, piston rods, and other components) is well within the scope of the do-it-yourself mechanic's tools and abilities. You will have to decide for yourself the depth of involvement you desire in an engine repair or rebuild.

TOOLS

The tools required for an engine overhaul or parts replacement will depend on the depth of your involvement. With a few exceptions, they will be the tools found in a mechanic's tool kit (see More in-depth work will require some or all of the following:

- A dial indicator (reading in thousandths) mounted on a universal base
- Micrometers and telescope gauges
- Jaw and screw-type pullers
- Scraper
- Valve spring compressor
- Ring groove cleaner
- Piston ring expander and compressor
- Ridge reamer
- Cylinder hone or glaze breaker
- Plastigage®
- Engine stand

The use of most of these tools is illustrated in this section. Many can be rented for a one-time use from a local parts jobber or tool supply house specializing in automotive work.

Occasionally, the use of special tools is called for. See the information on Special Tools and the Safety Notice in the front of this book before substituting another tool.

OVERHAUL TIPS

Aluminum has become extremely popular for use in engines, due to its low weight. Observe the following precautions when handling aluminum parts:

- Never hot tank aluminum parts (the caustic hot tank solution will eat the aluminum.
- Remove all aluminum parts (identification tag, etc.) from engine parts prior to the tanking.
- Always coat threads lightly with engine oil or anti-seize compounds before installation, to prevent seizure.
- Never overtighten bolts or spark plugs especially in aluminum threads.

When assembling the engine, any parts that will be exposed to frictional contact must be prelubed to provide lubrication at initial start-up. Any product specifically formulated for this purpose can be used, but engine oil is not recommended as a prelube in most cases.

When semi-permanent (locked, but removable) installation of bolts or nuts is desired, threads should be cleaned and coated with Loctite® or another similar, commercial non-hardening sealant.

CLEANING

▶ **See Figures 202, 203, 204 and 205**

Before the engine and its components are inspected, they must be thoroughly cleaned. You will need to remove any engine varnish, oil sludge and/or carbon deposits from all of the components to insure an accurate inspection. A crack in the engine block or cylinder head can easily become overlooked if hidden by a layer of sludge or carbon.

Most of the cleaning process can be carried out with common hand tools and readily available solvents or solutions. Carbon deposits can be chipped away using a hammer and a hard wooden chisel. Old gasket material and varnish or sludge can usually be removed using a scraper and/or cleaning solvent. Extremely stubborn deposits may require the use of a power drill with a wire brush. If using a wire brush, use extreme care around any critical machined surfaces (such as the gasket surfaces, bearing saddles, cylinder bores, etc.). Use of a wire brush is NOT RECOMMENDED on any aluminum components. Always follow any safety recommendations given by the manufacturer of the tool and/or solvent. You should always wear eye protection during any cleaning process involving scraping, chipping or spraying of solvents.

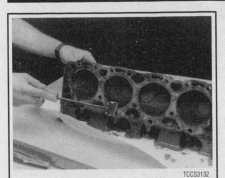

Fig. 202 Use a gasket scraper to remove the old gasket material from the mating surfaces

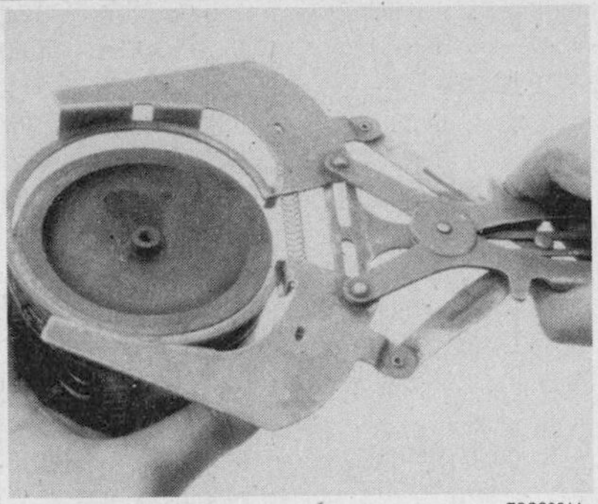

Fig. 203 Use a ring expander tool to remove the piston rings

Fig. 204 Clean the piston ring grooves using a ring groove cleaner tool, or . . .

Fig. 205 . . use a piece of an old ring to clean the grooves. Be careful, the ring can be quite sharp

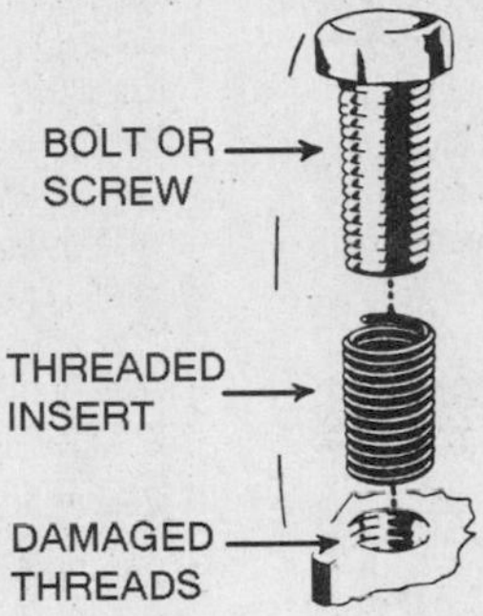

BOLT OR SCREW

THREADED INSERT

DAMAGED THREADS

Fig. 206 Damaged bolt hole threads can be replaced with thread repair inserts

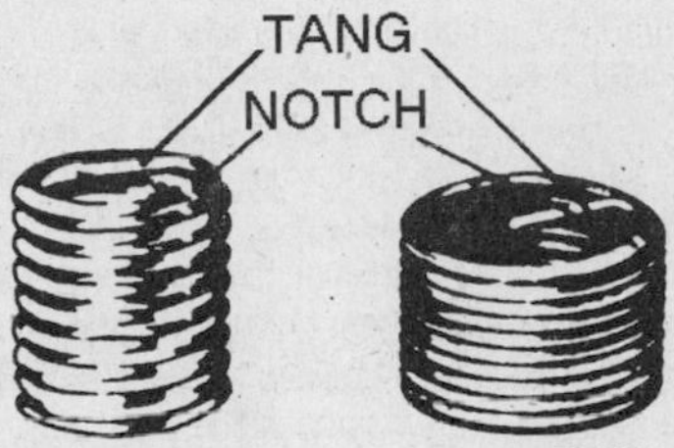

TANG
NOTCH

Fig. 207 Standard thread repair insert (left), and spark plug thread insert

An alternative to the mess and hassle of cleaning the parts yourself is to drop them off at a local garage or machine shop. They will, more than likely, have the necessary equipment to properly clean all of the parts for a nominal fee.

✳✳ CAUTION

Always wear eye protection during any cleaning process involving scraping, chipping or spraying of solvents.

Remove any oil galley plugs, freeze plugs and/or pressed-in bearings and carefully wash and degrease all of the engine components including the fasteners and bolts. Small parts such as the valves, springs, etc., should be placed in a metal basket and allowed to soak. Use pipe cleaner type brushes, and clean all passageways in the components. Use a ring expander and remove the rings from the pistons. Clean the piston ring grooves with a special tool or a piece of broken ring. Scrape the carbon off of the top of the piston. You should never

use a wire brush on the pistons. After preparing all of the piston assemblies in this manner, wash and degrease them again.

✳✳ WARNING

Use extreme care when cleaning around the cylinder head valve seats. A mistake or slip may cost you a new seat.

When cleaning the cylinder head, remove carbon from the combustion chamber with the valves installed. This will avoid damaging the valve seats.

REPAIRING DAMAGED THREADS

▶ **See Figures 206, 207, 208, 209 and 210**

Several methods of repairing damaged threads are available. Heli-Coil® (shown here), Keenserts® and Microdot® are among the most widely used. All involve basically the same principle—drilling out stripped threads, tapping the

Fig. 208 Drill out the damaged threads with the specified size bit. Be sure to drill completely through the hole or to the bottom of a blind hole

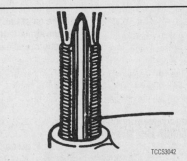

Fig. 209 Using the kit, tap the hole in order to receive the thread insert. Keep the tap well oiled and back it out frequently to avoid clogging the threads

Fig. 210 Screw the insert onto the installer tool until the tang engages the slot. Thread the insert into the hole until it is ¼–½ turn below the top surface, then remove the tool and break off the tang using a punch

hole and installing a prewound insert—making welding, plugging and oversize fasteners unnecessary.

Two types of thread repair inserts are usually supplied: a standard type for most inch coarse, inch fine, metric course and metric fine thread sizes and a spark lug type to fit most spark plug port sizes. Consult the individual tool manufacturer's catalog to determine exact applications. Typical thread repair kits will contain a selection of prewound threaded inserts, a tap (corresponding to the outside diameter threads of the insert) and an installation tool. Spark plug inserts usually differ because they require a tap equipped with pilot threads and a combined reamer/tap section. Most manufacturers also supply blister-packed thread repair inserts separately in addition to a master kit containing a variety of taps and inserts plus installation tools.

Before attempting to repair a threaded hole, remove any snapped, broken or damaged bolts or studs. Penetrating oil can be used to free frozen threads. The offending item can usually be removed with locking pliers or using a screw/stud extractor. After the hole is clear, the thread can be repaired, as shown in the series of accompanying illustrations and in the kit manufacturer's instructions.

Engine Preparation

To properly rebuild an engine, you must first remove it from the vehicle, then disassemble and diagnose it. Ideally you should place your engine on an engine stand. This affords you the best access to the engine components. Follow the manufacturer's directions for using the stand with your particular engine. Remove the flywheel or flexplate before installing the engine to the stand.

Now that you have the engine on a stand, and assuming that you have drained the oil and coolant from the engine, it's time to strip it of all but the necessary components. Before you start disassembling the engine, you may want to take a moment to draw some pictures, or fabricate some labels or containers to mark the locations of various components and the bolts and/or studs which fasten them. Modern day engines use a lot of little brackets and clips which hold wiring harnesses and such, and these holders are often mounted on studs and/or bolts that can be easily mixed up. The manufacturer spent a lot of time and money designing your vehicle, and they wouldn't have wasted any of it by haphazardly placing brackets, clips or fasteners on the vehicle. If it's present when you disassemble it, put it back when you assemble, you will regret not remembering that little bracket which holds a wire harness out of the path of a rotating part.

You should begin by unbolting any accessories still attached to the engine, such as the water pump, power steering pump, alternator, etc. Then, unfasten any manifolds (intake or exhaust) which were not removed during the engine removal procedure. Finally, remove any covers remaining on the engine such as the rocker arm, front or timing cover and oil pan. Some front covers may require the vibration damper and/or crank pulley to be removed beforehand. The idea is to reduce the engine to the bare necessities (cylinder head(s), valve train, engine block, crankshaft, pistons and connecting rods), plus any other 'in block' components such as oil pumps, balance shafts and auxiliary shafts.

Finally, remove the cylinder head(s) from the engine block and carefully place on a bench. Disassembly instructions for each component follow later in this section.

Cylinder Head

There are two basic types of cylinder heads used on today's automobiles: the Overhead Valve (OHV) and the Overhead Camshaft (OHC). The latter can also be broken down into two subgroups: the Single Overhead Camshaft (SOHC) and the Dual Overhead Camshaft (DOHC). Generally, if there is only a single camshaft on a head, it is just referred to as an OHC head. Also, an engine with an OHV cylinder head is also known as a pushrod engine.

Most cylinder heads these days are made of an aluminum alloy due to its light weight, durability and heat transfer qualities. However, cast iron was the material of choice in the past, and is still used on many vehicles today. Whether made from aluminum or iron, all cylinder heads have valves and seats. Some use two valves per cylinder, while the more hi-tech engines will utilize a multi-valve configuration using 3, 4 and even 5 valves per cylinder. When the valve contacts the seat, it does so on precision machined surfaces, which seals the combustion chamber. All cylinder heads have a valve guide for each valve. The guide centers the valve to the seat and allows it to move up and down within it. The clearance between the valve and guide can be critical. Too much clearance and the engine may consume oil, lose vacuum and/or damage the seat. Too little, and the valve can stick in the guide causing the engine to run poorly if at all,

and possibly causing severe damage. The last component all cylinder heads have are valve springs. The spring holds the valve against its seat. It also returns the valve to this position when the valve has been opened by the valve train or camshaft. The spring is fastened to the valve by a retainer and valve locks (sometimes called keepers). Aluminum heads will also have a valve spring shim to keep the spring from wearing away the aluminum.

An ideal method of rebuilding the cylinder head would involve replacing all of the valves, guides, seats, springs, etc. with new ones. However, depending on how the engine was maintained, often this is not necessary. A major cause of valve, guide and seat wear is an improperly tuned engine. An engine that is running too rich, will often wash the lubricating oil out of the guide with gasoline, causing it to wear rapidly. Conversely, an engine which is running too lean will place higher combustion temperatures on the valves and seats allowing them to wear or even burn. Springs fall victim to the driving habits of the individual. A driver who often runs the engine rpm to the redline will wear out or break the springs faster then one that stays well below it. Unfortunately, mileage takes it toll on all of the parts. Generally, the valves, guides, springs and seats in a cylinder head can be machined and re-used, saving you money. However, if a valve is burnt, it may be wise to replace all of the valves, since they were all operating in the same environment. The same goes for any other component on the cylinder head. Think of it as an insurance policy against future problems related to that component.

Unfortunately, the only way to find out which components need replacing, is to disassemble and carefully check each piece. After the cylinder head(s) are disassembled, thoroughly clean all of the components.

DISASSEMBLY

2.2L Engine

▶ **See Figures 211 thru 216**

Before disassembling the cylinder head, you may want to fabricate some containers to hold the various parts, as some of them can be quite small (such as keepers) and easily lost. Also keeping yourself and the components organized will aid in assembly and reduce confusion. Where possible, try to maintain a components original location; this is especially important if there is not going to be any machine work performed on the components.

1. If you haven't already removed the rocker arms and/or shafts, do so now.
2. Position the head so that the springs are easily accessed.
3. Use a valve spring compressor tool, and relieve spring tension from the retainer.

➡**Due to engine varnish, the retainer may stick to the valve locks. A gentle tap with a hammer may help to break it loose.**

4. Remove the valve locks from the valve tip and/or retainer. A small magnet may help in removing the locks.
5. Lift the valve spring, tool and all, off of the valve stem.
6. If equipped, remove the valve seal. If the seal is difficult to remove with the valve in place, try removing the valve first, then the seal. Follow the steps below for valve removal.
7. Position the head to allow access for withdrawing the valve.

➡**Cylinder heads that have seen a lot of miles and/or abuse may have mushroomed the valve lock grove and/or tip, causing difficulty in removal of the valve. If this has happened, use a metal file to carefully remove the high spots around the lock grooves and/or tip. Only file it enough to allow removal.**

8. Remove the valve from the cylinder head.
9. If equipped, remove the valve spring shim. A small magnetic tool or screwdriver will aid in removal.
10. Repeat Steps 3 though 9 until all of the valves have been removed.

2.3L and 2.4L Engines

▶ **See Figures 217 and 218**

Whether it is a single or dual overhead camshaft cylinder head, the disassembly procedure is relatively unchanged. One aspect to pay attention to is careful labeling of the parts on the dual camshaft cylinder head. There will be an intake camshaft and followers as well as an exhaust camshaft and followers and

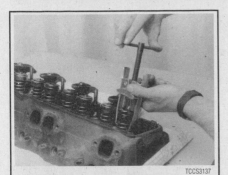

Fig. 211 When removing an OHV valve spring, use a compressor tool to relieve the tension from the retainer

Fig. 212 A small magnet will help in removal of the valve locks

Fig. 213 Be careful not to lose the small valve locks (keepers)

Fig. 214 Remove the valve seal from the valve stem—O-ring type seal shown

Fig. 215 Removing an umbrella/positive type seal

Fig. 216 Invert the cylinder head and withdraw the valve from the valve guide bore

Fig. 217 Exploded view of a valve, seal, spring, retainer and locks from an OHC cylinder head

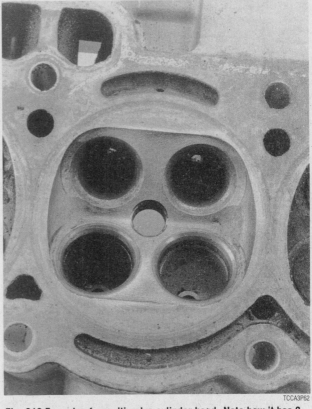

Fig. 218 Example of a multi-valve cylinder head. Note how it has 2 intake and 2 exhaust valve ports

they must be labeled as such. In some cases, the components are identical and could easily be installed incorrectly. DO NOT MIX THEM UP! Determining which is which is very simple; the intake camshaft and components are on the same side of the head as was the intake manifold. Conversely, the exhaust camshaft and components are on the same side of the head as was the exhaust manifold.

CUP TYPE CAMSHAFT FOLLOWERS

▶ **See Figures 219, 220 and 221**

Most cylinder heads with cup type camshaft followers will have the valve spring, retainer and locks recessed within the follower's bore. You will need a C-clamp style valve spring compressor tool, an OHC spring removal tool (or equivalent) and a small magnet to disassemble the head.

1. If not already removed, remove the camshaft(s) and/or followers. Mark their positions for assembly.
2. Position the cylinder head to allow use of a C-clamp style valve spring compressor tool.

➡️**It is preferred to position the cylinder head gasket surface facing you with the valve springs facing the opposite direction and the head laying horizontal.**

3. With the OHC spring removal adapter tool positioned inside of the follower bore, compress the valve spring using the C-clamp style valve spring compressor.
4. Remove the valve locks. A small magnetic tool or screwdriver will aid in removal.
5. Release the compressor tool and remove the spring assembly.
6. Withdraw the valve from the cylinder head.
7. If equipped, remove the valve seal.

➡️**Special valve seal removal tools are available. Regular or needlenose type pliers, if used with care, will work just as well. If using ordinary pliers, be sure not to damage the follower bore. The follower and its bore are machined to close tolerances and any damage to the bore will effect this relationship.**

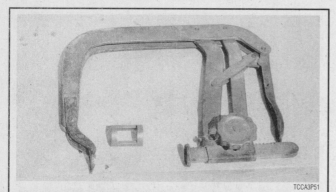

Fig. 219 C-clamp type spring compressor and an OHC spring removal tool (center) for cup type followers

Fig. 220 Most cup type follower cylinder heads retain the camshaft using bolt-on bearing caps

Fig. 221 Position the OHC spring tool in the follower bore, then compress the spring with a C-clamp type tool

8. If equipped, remove the valve spring shim. A small magnetic tool or screwdriver will aid in removal.
9. Repeat Steps 3 through 8 until all of the valves have been removed.

ROCKER ARM TYPE CAMSHAFT FOLLOWERS

▶ **See Figures 222 thru 230**

Most cylinder heads with rocker arm-type camshaft followers are easily disassembled using a standard valve spring compressor. However, certain models may not have enough open space around the spring for the standard tool and may require you to use a C-clamp style compressor tool instead.

1. If not already removed, remove the rocker arms and/or shafts and the camshaft. If applicable, also remove the hydraulic lash adjusters. Mark their positions for assembly.
2. Position the cylinder head to allow access to the valve spring.
3. Use a valve spring compressor tool to relieve the spring tension from the retainer.

➡️**Due to engine varnish, the retainer may stick to the valve locks. A gentle tap with a hammer may help to break it loose.**

4. Remove the valve locks from the valve tip and/or retainer. A small magnet may help in removing the small locks.
5. Lift the valve spring, tool and all, off of the valve stem.
6. If equipped, remove the valve seal. If the seal is difficult to remove with the valve in place, try removing the valve first, then the seal. Follow the steps below for valve removal.
7. Position the head to allow access for withdrawing the valve.

➡️**Cylinder heads that have seen a lot of miles and/or abuse may have mushroomed the valve lock grove and/or tip, causing difficulty in removal of the valve. If this has happened, use a metal file to carefully remove the high spots around the lock grooves and/or tip. Only file it enough to allow removal.**

TCCA3P53

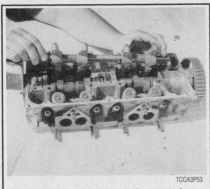

Fig. 222 Example of the shaft mounted rocker arms on some OHC heads

TCCA3P61

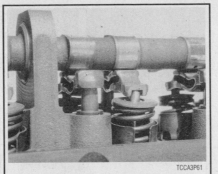

Fig. 223 Another example of the rocker arm type OHC head. This model uses a follower under the camshaft

TCCA3P60

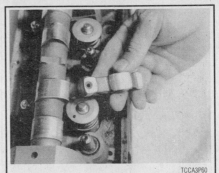

Fig. 224 Before the camshaft can be removed, all of the followers must first be removed . . .

TCCA3P59

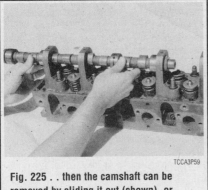

Fig. 225 . . then the camshaft can be removed by sliding it out (shown), or unbolting a bearing cap (not shown)

TCCA3P57

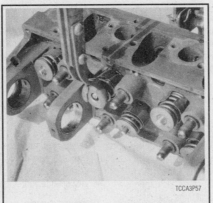

Fig. 226 Compress the valve spring . . .

TCCA3P58

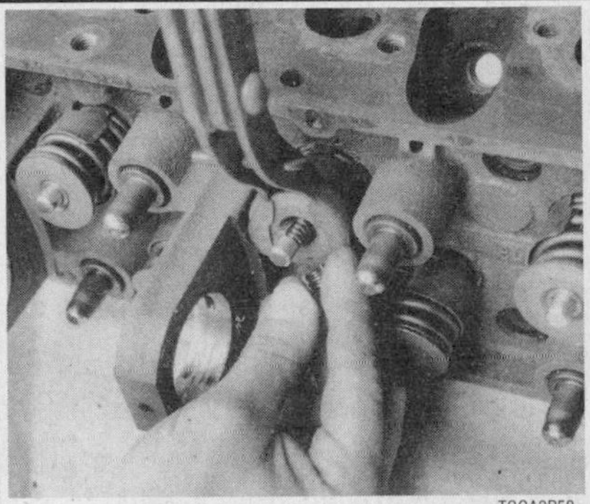

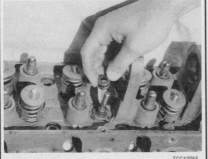

Fig. 227 . . then remove the valve locks from the valve stem and spring retainer

TCCA3P56

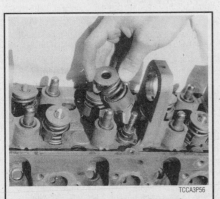

Fig. 228 Remove the valve spring and retainer from the cylinder head

TCCA3P55

Fig. 229 Remove the valve seal from the guide. Some gentle prying or pliers may help to remove stubborn ones

TCCA3P52

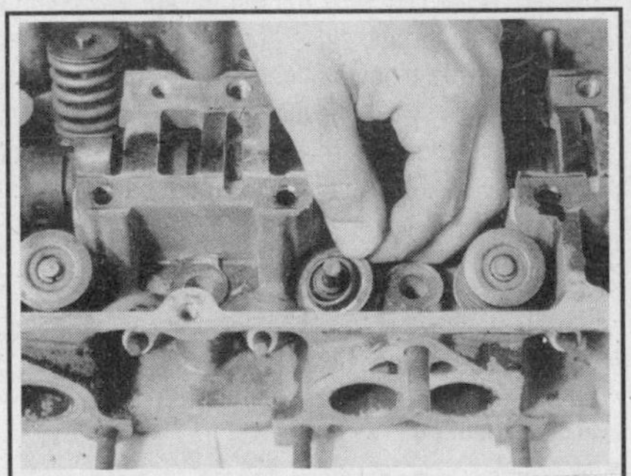

Fig. 230 All aluminum and some cast iron heads will have these valve spring shims. Remove all of them as well

8. Remove the valve from the cylinder head.
9. If equipped, remove the valve spring shim. A small magnetic tool or screwdriver will aid in removal.
10. Repeat Steps 3 though 9 until all of the valves have been removed.

INSPECTION

Now that all of the cylinder head components are clean, it's time to inspect them for wear and/or damage. To accurately inspect them, you will need some specialized tools:

- A 0–1 in. micrometer for the valves
- A dial indicator or inside diameter gauge for the valve guides
- A spring pressure test gauge

If you do not have access to the proper tools, you may want to bring the components to a shop that does.

Valves

See Figures 231 and 232

The first thing to inspect are the valve heads. Look closely at the head, margin and face for any cracks, excessive wear or burning. The margin is the best place to look for burning. It should have a squared edge with an even width all around the diameter. When a valve burns, the margin will look melted and the edges rounded. Also inspect the valve head for any signs of tulipping. This will show as a lifting of the edges or dishing in the center of the head and will usually not occur to all of the valves. All of the heads should look the same, any that seem dished more than others are probably bad. Next, inspect the valve lock grooves and valve tips. Check for any burrs around the lock grooves, especially if you had to file them to remove the valve. Valve tips should appear flat, although slight rounding with high mileage engines is normal. Slightly worn valve tips will need to be machined flat. Last, measure the valve stem diameter with the micrometer.

Fig. 231 Valve stems may be rolled on a flat surface to check for bends

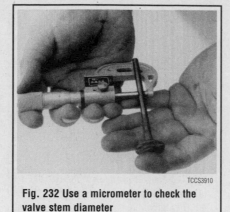

Fig. 232 Use a micrometer to check the valve stem diameter

Fig. 233 Use a caliper to check the valve spring free-length

Measure the area that rides within the guide, especially towards the tip where most of the wear occurs. Take several measurements along its length and compare them to each other. Wear should be even along the length with little to no taper. If no minimum diameter is given in the specifications, then the stem should not read more than 0.001 in. (0.025mm) below the unworn area of the valve stem. Any valves that fail these inspections should be replaced.

Springs, Retainers and Valve Locks

▶ See Figures 233 and 234

The first thing to check is the most obvious, broken springs. Next check the free length and squareness of each spring. If applicable, insure to distinguish between intake and exhaust springs. Use a ruler and/or carpenter's square to measure the length. A carpenter's square should be used to check the springs for squareness. If a spring pressure test gauge is available, check each springs rating and compare to the specifications chart. Check the readings against the specifications given. Any springs that fail these inspections should be replaced.

The spring retainers rarely need replacing, however they should still be checked as a precaution. Inspect the spring mating surface and the valve lock retention area for any signs of excessive wear. Also check for any signs of cracking. Replace any retainers that are questionable.

Valve locks should be inspected for excessive wear on the outside contact area as well as on the inner notched surface. Any locks which appear worn or broken and its respective valve should be replaced.

Cylinder Head

There are several things to check on the cylinder head: valve guides, seats, cylinder head surface flatness, cracks and physical damage.

VALVE GUIDES

▶ See Figure 235

Now that you know the valves are good, you can use them to check the guides, although a new valve, if available, is preferred. Before you measure any-thing, look at the guides carefully and inspect them for any cracks, chips or breakage. Also if the guide is a removable style (as in most aluminum heads), check them for any looseness or evidence of movement. All of the guides should appear to be at the same height from the spring seat. If any seem lower (or higher) from another, the guide has moved. Mount a dial indicator onto the spring side of the cylinder head. Lightly oil the valve stem and insert it into the cylinder head. Position the dial indicator against the valve stem near the tip and zero the gauge. Grasp the valve stem and wiggle towards and away from the dial indicator and observe the readings. Mount the dial indicator 90 degrees from the initial point and zero the gauge and again take a reading. Compare the two readings for a out of round condition. Check the readings against the specifications given. An Inside Diameter (I.D.) gauge designed for valve guides will give you an accurate valve guide bore measurement. If the I.D. gauge is used, compare the readings with the specifications given. Any guides that fail these inspections should be replaced or machined.

VALVE SEATS

A visual inspection of the valve seats should show a slightly worn and pitted surface where the valve face contacts the seat. Inspect the seat carefully for severe pitting or cracks. Also, a seat that is badly worn will be recessed into the cylinder head. A severely worn or recessed seat may need to be replaced. All cracked seats must be replaced. A seat concentricity gauge, if available, should be used to check the seat run-out. If run-out exceeds specifications the seat must be machined (if no specification is given use 0.002 in. or 0.051mm).

CYLINDER HEAD SURFACE FLATNESS

▶ See Figures 236 and 237

After you have cleaned the gasket surface of the cylinder head of any old gasket material, check the head for flatness.

Place a straightedge across the gasket surface. Using feeler gauges, determine the clearance at the center of the straightedge and across the cylinder head at several points. Check along the centerline and diagonally on the head surface. If the warpage exceeds 0.003 in. (0.076mm) within a 6.0 in. (15.2cm) span, or 0.006 in. (0.152mm) over the total length of the head, the cylinder

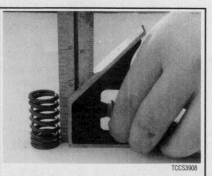

Fig. 234 Check the valve spring for squareness on a flat surface; a carpenter's square can be used

Fig. 235 A dial gauge may be used to check valve stem-to-guide clearance; read the gauge while moving the valve stem

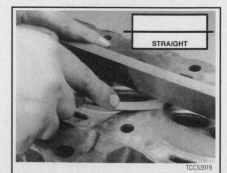

Fig. 236 Check the head for flatness across the center of the head surface using a straightedge and feeler gauge

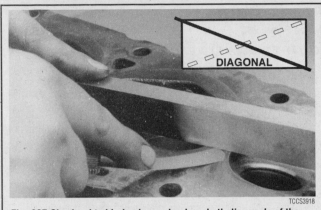

Fig. 237 Checks should also be made along both diagonals of the head surface

head must be resurfaced. After resurfacing the heads of a V-type engine, the intake manifold flange surface should be checked, and if necessary, milled proportionally to allow for the change in its mounting position.

CRACKS AND PHYSICAL DAMAGE

Generally, cracks are limited to the combustion chamber, however, it is not uncommon for the head to crack in a spark plug hole, port, outside of the head or in the valve spring/rocker arm area. The first area to inspect is always the hottest: the exhaust seat/port area.

A visual inspection should be performed, but just because you don't see a crack does not mean it is not there. Some more reliable methods for inspecting for cracks include Magnaflux®, a magnetic process or Zyglo®, a dye penetrant. Magnaflux® is used only on ferrous metal (cast iron) heads. Zyglo® uses a spray on fluorescent mixture along with a black light to reveal the cracks. It is strongly recommended to have your cylinder head checked professionally for cracks, especially if the engine was known to have overheated and/or leaked or consumed coolant. Contact a local shop for availability and pricing of these services.

Physical damage is usually very evident. For example, a broken mounting ear from dropping the head or a bent or broken stud and/or bolt. All of these defects should be fixed or, if unrepairable, the head should be replaced.

Camshaft and Followers

Inspect the camshaft(s) and followers as described earlier in this section.

REFINISHING & REPAIRING

Many of the procedures given for refinishing and repairing the cylinder head components must be performed by a machine shop. Certain steps, if the inspected part is not worn, can be performed yourself inexpensively. However, you spent a lot of time and effort so far, why risk trying to save a couple bucks if you might have to do it all over again?

Valves

Any valves that were not replaced should be refaced and the tips ground flat. Unless you have access to a valve grinding machine, this should be done by a machine shop. If the valves are in extremely good condition, as well as the valve seats and guides, they may be lapped in without performing machine work. It is a recommended practice to lap the valves even after machine work has been performed and/or new valves have been purchased. This insures a positive seal between the valve and seat.

LAPPING THE VALVES

➡Before lapping the valves to the seats, read the rest of the cylinder head section to insure that any related parts are in acceptable enough condition to continue.

➡Before any valve seat machining and/or lapping can be performed, the guides must be within factory recommended specifications.

1. Invert the cylinder head.
2. Lightly lubricate the valve stems and insert them into the cylinder head in their numbered order.
3. Raise the valve from the seat and apply a small amount of fine lapping compound to the seat.
4. Moisten the suction head of a hand-lapping tool and attach it to the head of the valve.
5. Rotate the tool between the palms of both hands, changing the position of the valve on the valve seat and lifting the tool often to prevent grooving.
6. Lap the valve until a smooth, polished circle is evident on the valve and seat.
7. Remove the tool and the valve. Wipe away all traces of the grinding compound and store the valve to maintain its lapped location.

✳✳ WARNING

Do not get the valves out of order after they have been lapped. They must be put back with the same valve seat with which they were lapped.

Springs, Retainers and Valve Locks

There is no repair or refinishing possible with the springs, retainers and valve locks. If they are found to be worn or defective, they must be replaced with new (or known good) parts.

Cylinder Head

Most refinishing procedures dealing with the cylinder head must be performed by a machine shop. Read the sections below and review your inspection data to determine whether or not machining is necessary.

VALVE GUIDE

➡If any machining or replacements are made to the valve guides, the seats must be machined.

Unless the valve guides need machining or replacing, the only service to perform is to thoroughly clean them of any dirt or oil residue.

There are only two types of valve guides used on automobile engines: the replaceable-type (all aluminum heads) and the cast-in integral-type (most cast iron heads). There are four recommended methods for repairing worn guides.
- Knurling
- Inserts
- Reaming oversize
- Replacing

Knurling is a process in which metal is displaced and raised, thereby reducing clearance, giving a true center, and providing oil control. It is the least expensive way of repairing the valve guides. However, it is not necessarily the best, and in some cases, a knurled valve guide will not stand up for more than a short time. It requires a special knurlizer and precision reaming tools to obtain proper clearances. It would not be cost effective to purchase these tools, unless you plan on rebuilding several of the same cylinder head.

Installing a guide insert involves machining the guide to accept a bronze insert. One style is the coil-type which is installed into a threaded guide. Another is the thin-walled insert where the guide is reamed oversize to accept a split-sleeve insert. After the insert is installed, a special tool is then run through the guide to expand the insert, locking it to the guide. The insert is then reamed to the standard size for proper valve clearance.

Reaming for oversize valves restores normal clearances and provides a true valve seat. Most cast-in type guides can be reamed to accept an valve with an oversize stem. The cost factor for this can become quite high as you will need to purchase the reamer and new, oversize stem valves for all guides which were reamed. Oversizes are generally 0.003 to 0.030 in. (0.076 to 0.762mm), with 0.015 in. (0.381mm) being the most common.

To replace cast-in type valve guides, they must be drilled out, then reamed to accept replacement guides. This must be done on a fixture which will allow centering and leveling off of the original valve seat or guide, otherwise a serious guide-to-seat misalignment may occur making it impossible to properly machine the seat.

Replaceable-type guides are pressed into the cylinder head. A hammer and a stepped drift or punch may be used to install and remove the guides. Before removing the guides, measure the protrusion on the spring side of the head and record it for installation. Use the stepped drift to hammer out the old guide from the combustion chamber side of the head. When installing, determine whether or not the guide also seals a water jacket in the head, and if it does, use the recommended sealing agent. If there is no water jacket, grease the valve guide and its bore. Use the stepped drift, and hammer the new guide into the cylinder head from the spring side of the cylinder head. A stack of washers the same thickness as the measured protrusion may help the installation process.

VALVE SEATS

➡️Before any valve seat machining can be performed, the guides must be within factory recommended specifications.

➡️If any machining or replacements were made to the valve guides, the seats must be machined.

If the seats are in good condition, the valves can be lapped to the seats, and the cylinder head assembled. See the valves section for instructions on lapping.

If the valve seats are worn, cracked or damaged, they must be serviced by a machine shop. The valve seat must be perfectly centered to the valve guide, which requires very accurate machining.

CYLINDER HEAD SURFACE

If the cylinder head is warped, it must be machined flat. If the warpage is extremely severe, the head may need to be replaced. In some instances, it may be possible to straighten a warped head enough to allow machining. In either case, contact a professional machine shop for service.

➡️Any OHC cylinder head that shows excessive warpage should have the camshaft bearing journals align bored after the cylinder head has been resurfaced.

❋❋ WARNING

Failure to align bore the camshaft bearing journals could result in severe engine damage including but not limited to: valve and piston damage, connecting rod damage, camshaft and/or crankshaft breakage.

CRACKS AND PHYSICAL DAMAGE

Certain cracks can be repaired in both cast iron and aluminum heads. For cast iron, a tapered threaded insert is installed along the length of the crack. Aluminum can also use the tapered inserts, however welding is the preferred method. Some physical damage can be repaired through brazing or welding. Contact a machine shop to get expert advice for your particular dilemma.

ASSEMBLY

The first step for any assembly job is to have a clean area in which to work. Next, thoroughly clean all of the parts and components that are to be assembled. Finally, place all of the components onto a suitable work space and, if necessary, arrange the parts to their respective positions.

2.2L Engine

1. Lightly lubricate the valve stems and insert all of the valves into the cylinder head. If possible, maintain their original locations.
2. If equipped, install any valve spring shims which were removed.
3. If equipped, install the new valve seals, keeping the following in mind:
• If the valve seal presses over the guide, lightly lubricate the outer guide surfaces.
• If the seal is an O-ring type, it is installed just after compressing the spring but before the valve locks.
4. Place the valve spring and retainer over the stem.
5. Position the spring compressor tool and compress the spring.
6. Assemble the valve locks to the stem.
7. Relieve the spring pressure slowly and insure that neither valve lock becomes dislodged by the retainer.
8. Remove the spring compressor tool.
9. Repeat Steps 2 through 8 until all of the springs have been installed.

2.3L and 2.4L Engines

▶ See Figure 238

CUP TYPE CAMSHAFT FOLLOWERS

To install the springs, retainers and valve locks on heads which have these components recessed into the camshaft follower's bore, you will need a small screwdriver-type tool, some clean white grease and a lot of patience. You will also need the C-clamp style spring compressor and the OHC tool used to disassemble the head.

1. Lightly lubricate the valve stems and insert all of the valves into the cylinder head. If possible, maintain their original locations.
2. If equipped, install any valve spring shims which were removed.
3. If equipped, install the new valve seals, keeping the following in mind:
• If the valve seal presses over the guide, lightly lubricate the outer guide surfaces.
• If the seal is an O-ring type, it is installed just after compressing the spring but before the valve locks.
4. Place the valve spring and retainer over the stem.
5. Position the spring compressor and the OHC tool, then compress the spring.
6. Using a small screwdriver as a spatula, fill the valve stem side of the lock with white grease. Use the excess grease on the screwdriver to fasten the lock to the driver.
7. Carefully install the valve lock, which is stuck to the end of the screwdriver, to the valve stem then press on it with the screwdriver until the grease squeezes out. The valve lock should now be stuck to the stem.
8. Repeat Steps 6 and 7 for the remaining valve lock.
9. Relieve the spring pressure slowly and insure that neither valve lock becomes dislodged by the retainer.
10. Remove the spring compressor tool.
11. Repeat Steps 2 through 10 until all of the springs have been installed.
12. Install the followers, camshaft(s) and any other components that were removed for disassembly.

TCCA3P64

Fig. 238 Once assembled, check the valve clearance and correct as needed

ROCKER ARM TYPE CAMSHAFT FOLLOWERS

1. Lightly lubricate the valve stems and insert all of the valves into the cylinder head. If possible, maintain their original locations.
2. If equipped, install any valve spring shims which were removed.
3. If equipped, install the new valve seals, keeping the following in mind:
• If the valve seal presses over the guide, lightly lubricate the outer guide surfaces.
• If the seal is an O-ring type, it is installed just after compressing the spring but before the valve locks.
4. Place the valve spring and retainer over the stem.
5. Position the spring compressor tool and compress the spring.
6. Assemble the valve locks to the stem.
7. Relieve the spring pressure slowly and insure that neither valve lock becomes dislodged by the retainer.
8. Remove the spring compressor tool.
9. Repeat Steps 2 through 8 until all of the springs have been installed.

10. Install the camshaft(s), rockers, shafts and any other components that were removed for disassembly.

Engine Block

GENERAL INFORMATION

A thorough overhaul or rebuild of an engine block would include replacing the pistons, rings, bearings, timing belt/chain assembly and oil pump. For OHV engines also include a new camshaft and lifters. The block would then have the cylinders bored and honed oversize (or if using removable cylinder sleeves, new sleeves installed) and the crankshaft would be cut undersize to provide new wearing surfaces and perfect clearances. However, your particular engine may not have everything worn out. What if only the piston rings have worn out and the clearances on everything else are still within factory specifications? Well, you could just replace the rings and put it back together, but this would be a very rare example. Chances are, if one component in your engine is worn, other components are sure to follow, and soon. At the very least, you should always replace the rings, bearings and oil pump. This is what is commonly called a "freshen up".

Cylinder Ridge Removal

Because the top piston ring does not travel to the very top of the cylinder, a ridge is built up between the end of the travel and the top of the cylinder bore. Pushing the piston and connecting rod assembly past the ridge can be difficult, and damage to the piston ring lands could occur. If the ridge is not removed before installing a new piston or not removed at all, piston ring breakage and piston damage may occur.

➡ **It is always recommended that you remove any cylinder ridges before removing the piston and connecting rod assemblies. If you know that new pistons are going to be installed and the engine block will be bored oversize, you may be able to forego this step. However, some ridges may actually prevent the assemblies from being removed, necessitating its removal.**

There are several different types of ridge reamers on the market, none of which are inexpensive. Unless a great deal of engine rebuilding is anticipated, borrow or rent a reamer.

1. Turn the crankshaft until the piston is at the bottom of its travel.
2. Cover the head of the piston with a rag.
3. Follow the tool manufacturers instructions and cut away the ridge, exercising extreme care to avoid cutting too deeply.
4. Remove the ridge reamer, the rag and as many of the cuttings as possible. Continue until all of the cylinder ridges have been removed.

DISASSEMBLY

▶ **See Figures 239 and 240**

The engine disassembly instructions following assume that you have the engine mounted on an engine stand. If not, it is easiest to disassemble the engine on a bench or the floor with it resting on the bell housing or transaxle mounting surface. You must be able to access the connecting rod fasteners and turn the crankshaft during disassembly. Also, all engine covers (timing, front, side, oil pan, whatever) should have already been removed. Engines which are seized or locked up may not be able to be completely disassembled, and a core (salvage yard) engine should be purchased.

2.2L Engine

If not done during the cylinder head removal, remove the pushrods and lifters, keeping them in order for assembly. Remove the timing gears and/or timing chain assembly, then remove the oil pump drive assembly and withdraw the camshaft from the engine block. Remove the oil pick-up and pump assembly. If equipped, remove any balance or auxiliary shafts. If necessary, remove the cylinder ridge from the top of the bore. See the cylinder ridge removal procedure earlier in this section.

2.3L and 2.4L Engines

If not done during the cylinder head removal, remove the timing chain/belt and/or gear/sprocket assembly. Remove the oil pick-up and pump assembly and, if necessary, the pump drive. If equipped, remove any balance or auxiliary shafts. If necessary, remove the cylinder ridge from the top of the bore. See the cylinder ridge removal procedure earlier in this section.

All Engines

Rotate the engine over so that the crankshaft is exposed. Use a number punch or scribe and mark each connecting rod with its respective cylinder number. The cylinder closest to the front of the engine is always number 1. However, depending on the engine placement, the front of the engine could either be the flywheel or damper/pulley end. Generally the front of the engine faces the front of the vehicle. Use a number punch or scribe and also mark the main bearing caps from front to rear with the front most cap being number 1 (if there are five caps, mark them 1 through 5, front to rear).

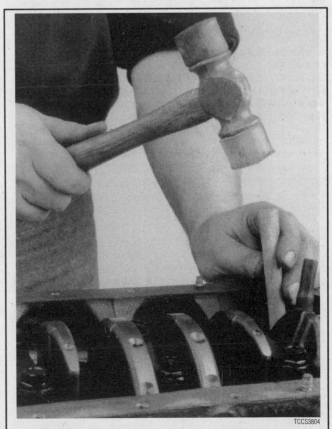

TCCS3804

Fig. 240 Carefully tap the piston out of the bore using a wooden dowel

TCCS3803

Fig. 239 Place rubber hose over the connecting rod studs to protect the crankshaft and cylinder bores from damage

Take special care when pushing the connecting rod up from the crankshaft because the sharp threads of the rod bolts/studs will score the crankshaft journal. Insure that special plastic caps are installed over them, or cut two pieces of rubber hose to do the same.

Again, rotate the engine, this time to position the number one cylinder bore (head surface) up. Turn the crankshaft until the number one piston is at the bottom of its travel, this should allow the maximum access to its connecting rod. Remove the number one connecting rods fasteners and cap and place two lengths of rubber hose over the rod bolts/studs to protect the crankshaft from damage. Using a sturdy wooden dowel and a hammer, push the connecting rod up about 1 in. (25mm) from the crankshaft and remove the upper bearing insert. Continue pushing or tapping the connecting rod up until the piston rings are out of the cylinder bore. Remove the piston and rod by hand, put the upper half of the bearing insert back into the rod, install the cap with its bearing insert installed, and hand-tighten the cap fasteners. If the parts are kept in order in this manner, they will not get lost and you will be able to tell which bearings came form what cylinder if any problems are discovered and diagnosis is necessary. Remove all the other piston assemblies in the same manner. On V-style engines, remove all of the pistons from one bank, then reposition the engine with the other cylinder bank head surface up, and remove that banks piston assemblies.

The only remaining component in the engine block should now be the crankshaft. Loosen the main bearing caps evenly until the fasteners can be turned by hand, then remove them and the caps. Remove the crankshaft from the engine block. Thoroughly clean all of the components.

INSPECTION

Now that the engine block and all of its components are clean, it's time to inspect them for wear and/or damage. To accurately inspect them, you will need some specialized tools:

- Two or three separate micrometers to measure the pistons and crankshaft journals
- A dial indicator
- Telescoping gauges for the cylinder bores
- A rod alignment fixture to check for bent connecting rods

If you do not have access to the proper tools, you may want to bring the components to a shop that does.

Generally, you shouldn't expect cracks in the engine block or its components unless it was known to leak, consume or mix engine fluids, it was severely overheated, or there was evidence of bad bearings and/or crankshaft damage. A visual inspection should be performed on all of the components, but just because you don't see a crack does not mean it is not there. Some more reliable methods for inspecting for cracks include Magnaflux®, a magnetic process or Zyglo®, a dye penetrant. Magnaflux® is used only on ferrous metal (cast iron). Zyglo® uses a spray on fluorescent mixture along with a black light to reveal the cracks. It is strongly recommended to have your engine block checked professionally for cracks, especially if the engine was known to have overheated and/or leaked or consumed coolant. Contact a local shop for availability and pricing of these services.

Engine Block

ENGINE BLOCK BEARING ALIGNMENT

Remove the main bearing caps and, if still installed, the main bearing inserts. Inspect all of the main bearing saddles and caps for damage, burrs or high spots. If damage is found, and it is caused from a spun main bearing, the block will need to be align-bored or, if severe enough, replacement. Any burrs or high spots should be carefully removed with a metal file.

Place a straightedge on the bearing saddles, in the engine block, along the centerline of the crankshaft. If any clearance exists between the straightedge and the saddles, the block must be align-bored.

Align-boring consists of machining the main bearing saddles and caps by means of a flycutter that runs through the bearing saddles.

DECK FLATNESS

The top of the engine block where the cylinder head mounts is called the deck. Insure that the deck surface is clean of dirt, carbon deposits and old gasket material. Place a straightedge across the surface of the deck along its centerline and, using feeler gauges, check the clearance along several points. Repeat the checking procedure with the straightedge placed along both diagonals of the deck surface. If the reading exceeds 0.003 in. (0.076mm) within a 6.0 in. (15.2cm) span, or 0.006 in. (0.152mm) over the total length of the deck, it must be machined.

CYLINDER BORES

▶ See Figure 241

The cylinder bores house the pistons and are slightly larger than the pistons themselves. A common piston-to-bore clearance is 0.0015–0.0025 in. (0.0381mm–0.0635mm). Inspect and measure the cylinder bores. The bore should be checked for out-of-roundness, taper and size. The results of this inspection will determine whether the cylinder can be used in its existing size and condition, or a rebore to the next oversize is required (or in the case of removable sleeves, have replacements installed).

The amount of cylinder wall wear is always greater at the top of the cylinder than at the bottom. This wear is known as taper. Any cylinder that has a taper of 0.0012 in. (0.305mm) or more, must be rebored. Measurements are taken at a number of positions in each cylinder: at the top, middle and bottom and at two points at each position; that is, at a point 90 degrees from the crankshaft centerline, as well as a point parallel to the crankshaft centerline. The measurements are made with either a special dial indicator or a telescopic gauge and micrometer. If the necessary precision tools to check the bore are not available, take the block to a machine shop and have them mike it. Also if you don't have the tools to check the cylinder bores, chances are you will not have the necessary devices to check the pistons, connecting rods and crankshaft. Take these components with you and save yourself an extra trip.

For our procedures, we will use a telescopic gauge and a micrometer. You will need one of each, with a measuring range which covers your cylinder bore size.

1. Position the telescopic gauge in the cylinder bore, loosen the gauges lock and allow it to expand.

➡ **Your first two readings will be at the top of the cylinder bore, then proceed to the middle and finally the bottom, making a total of six measurements.**

2. Hold the gauge square in the bore, 90 degrees from the crankshaft centerline, and gently tighten the lock. Tilt the gauge back to remove it from the bore.

3. Measure the gauge with the micrometer and record the reading.

4. Again, hold the gauge square in the bore, this time parallel to the crankshaft centerline, and gently tighten the lock. Again, you will tilt the gauge back to remove it from the bore.

5. Measure the gauge with the micrometer and record this reading. The difference between these two readings is the out-of-round measurement of the cylinder.

6. Repeat steps 1 through 5, each time going to the next lower position, until you reach the bottom of the cylinder. Then go to the next cylinder, and continue until all of the cylinders have been measured.

The difference between these measurements will tell you all about the wear in your cylinders. The measurements which were taken 90 degrees from the crankshaft centerline will always reflect the most wear. That is because at this position is where the engine power presses the piston against the cylinder bore the hardest. This is known as thrust wear. Take your top, 90 degree measurement and compare it to your bottom, 90 degree measurement. The difference between them is the taper. When you measure your pistons, you will compare these readings to your piston sizes and determine piston-to-wall clearance.

Crankshaft

Inspect the crankshaft for visible signs of wear or damage. All of the journals should be perfectly round and smooth. Slight scores are normal for a used crankshaft, but you should hardly feel them with your fingernail. When measuring the crankshaft with a micrometer, you will take readings at the front and rear of each journal, then turn the micrometer 90 degrees and take two more readings, front and rear. The difference between the front-to-rear readings is the journal taper and the first-to-90 degree reading is the out-of-round measurement. Generally, there should be no taper or out-of-roundness found; however, up to 0.0005 in. (0.0127mm) for either can be overlooked. Also, the readings should fall within the factory specifications for journal diameters.

If the crankshaft journals fall within specifications, it is recommended that it be polished before being returned to service. Polishing the crankshaft insures

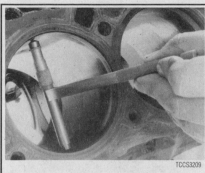

Fig. 241 Use a telescoping gauge to measure the cylinder bore diameter—take several readings within the same bore

Fig. 242 Measure the piston's outer diameter, perpendicular to the wrist pin, with a micrometer

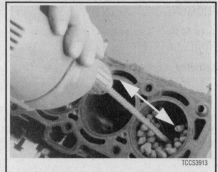

Fig. 243 Use a ball type cylinder hone to remove any glaze and provide a new surface for seating the piston rings

that any minor burrs or high spots are smoothed, thereby reducing the chance of scoring the new bearings.

Pistons and Connecting Rods

PISTONS

▶ See Figure 242

The piston should be visually inspected for any signs of cracking or burning (caused by hot spots or detonation), and scuffing or excessive wear on the skirts. The wrist pin attaches the piston to the connecting rod. The piston should move freely on the wrist pin, both sliding and pivoting. Grasp the connecting rod securely, or mount it in a vise, and try to rock the piston back and forth along the centerline of the wrist pin. There should not be any excessive play evident between the piston and the pin. If there are C-clips retaining the pin in the piston then you have wrist pin bushings in the rods. There should not be any excessive play between the wrist pin and the rod bushing. Normal clearance for the wrist pin is approx. 0.001–0.002 in. (0.025mm–0.051mm).

Use a micrometer and measure the diameter of the piston, perpendicular to the wrist pin, on the skirt. Compare the reading to its original cylinder measurement obtained earlier. The difference between the two readings is the piston-to-wall clearance. If the clearance is within specifications, the piston may be used as is. If the piston is out of specification, but the bore is not, you will need a new piston. If both are out of specification, you will need the cylinder rebored and oversize pistons installed. Generally if two or more pistons/bores are out of specification, it is best to rebore the entire block and purchase a complete set of oversize pistons.

CONNECTING ROD

You should have the connecting rod checked for straightness at a machine shop. If the connecting rod is bent, it will unevenly wear the bearing and piston, as well as place greater stress on these components. Any bent or twisted connecting rods must be replaced. If the rods are straight and the wrist pin clearance is within specifications, then only the bearing end of the rod need be checked. Place the connecting rod into a vice, with the bearing inserts in place, install the cap to the rod and torque the fasteners to specifications. Use a telescoping gauge and carefully measure the inside diameter of the bearings. Compare this reading to the rods original crankshaft journal diameter measurement. The difference is the oil clearance. If the oil clearance is not within specifications, install new bearings in the rod and take another measurement. If the clearance is still out of specifications, and the crankshaft is not, the rod will need to be reconditioned by a machine shop.

➡You can also use Plastigage® to check the bearing clearances. The assembling section has complete instructions on its use.

Camshaft

Inspect the camshaft and lifters/followers as described earlier in this section.

Bearings

All of the engine bearings should be visually inspected for wear and/or damage. The bearing should look evenly worn all around with no deep scores or pits. If the bearing is severely worn, scored, pitted or heat blued, then the bear-

ing, and the components that use it, should be brought to a machine shop for inspection. Full-circle bearings (used on most camshafts, auxiliary shafts, balance shafts, etc.) require specialized tools for removal and installation, and should be brought to a machine shop for service.

Oil Pump

➡The oil pump is responsible for providing constant lubrication to the whole engine and so it is recommended that a new oil pump be installed when rebuilding the engine.

Completely disassemble the oil pump and thoroughly clean all of the components. Inspect the oil pump gears and housing for wear and/or damage. Insure that the pressure relief valve operates properly and there is no binding or sticking due to varnish or debris. If all of the parts are in proper working condition, lubricate the gears and relief valve, and assemble the pump.

REFINISHING

▶ See Figure 243

Almost all engine block refinishing must be performed by a machine shop. If the cylinders are not to be rebored, then the cylinder glaze can be removed with a ball hone. When removing cylinder glaze with a ball hone, use a light or penetrating type oil to lubricate the hone. Do not allow the hone to run dry as this may cause excessive scoring of the cylinder bores and wear on the hone. If new pistons are required, they will need to be installed to the connecting rods. This should be performed by a machine shop as the pistons must be installed in the correct relationship to the rod or engine damage can occur.

Pistons and Connecting Rods

▶ See Figure 244

Only pistons with the wrist pin retained by C-clips are serviceable by the home-mechanic. Press fit pistons require special presses and/or heaters to remove/install the connecting rod and should only be performed by a machine shop.

Fig. 244 Most pistons are marked to indicate positioning in the engine (usually a mark means the side facing the front)

All pistons will have a mark indicating the direction to the front of the engine and the must be installed into the engine in that manner. Usually it is a notch or arrow on the top of the piston, or it may be the letter F cast or stamped into the piston.

C-CLIP TYPE PISTONS

1. Note the location of the forward mark on the piston and mark the connecting rod in relation.
2. Remove the C-clips from the piston and withdraw the wrist pin.

➡ **Varnish build-up or C-clip groove burrs may increase the difficulty of removing the wrist pin. If necessary, use a punch or drift to carefully tap the wrist pin out.**

3. Insure that the wrist pin bushing in the connecting rod is usable, and lubricate it with assembly lube.
4. Remove the wrist pin from the new piston and lubricate the pin bores on the piston.
5. Align the forward marks on the piston and the connecting rod and install the wrist pin.
6. The new C-clips will have a flat and a rounded side to them. Install both C-clips with the flat side facing out.
7. Repeat all of the steps for each piston being replaced.

ASSEMBLY

Before you begin assembling the engine, first give yourself a clean, dirt free work area. Next, clean every engine component again. The key to a good assembly is cleanliness.

Mount the engine block into the engine stand and wash it one last time using water and detergent (dishwashing detergent works well). While washing it, scrub the cylinder bores with a soft bristle brush and thoroughly clean all of the oil passages. Completely dry the engine and spray the entire assembly down with an anti-rust solution such as WD-40® or similar product. Take a clean lint-free rag and wipe up any excess anti-rust solution from the bores, bearing saddles, etc. Repeat the final cleaning process on the crankshaft. Replace any freeze or oil galley plugs which were removed during disassembly.

Crankshaft

▶ **See Figures 245, 246, 247 and 248**

1. Remove the main bearing inserts from the block and bearing caps.
2. If the crankshaft main bearing journals have been refinished to a definite undersize, install the correct undersize bearing. Be sure that the bearing inserts and bearing bores are clean. Foreign material under inserts will distort bearing and cause failure.
3. Place the upper main bearing inserts in bores with tang in slot.

➡ **The oil holes in the bearing inserts must be aligned with the oil holes in the cylinder block.**

4. Install the lower main bearing inserts in bearing caps.
5. Clean the mating surfaces of block and rear main bearing cap.
6. Carefully lower the crankshaft into place. Be careful not to damage bearing surfaces.
7. Check the clearance of each main bearing by using the following procedure:
   a. Place a piece of Plastigage® or its equivalent, on bearing surface across full width of bearing cap and about ¼ in. off center.
   b. Install cap and tighten bolts to specifications. Do not turn crankshaft while Plastigage® is in place.
   c. Remove the cap. Using the supplied Plastigage® scale, check width of Plastigage® at widest point to get maximum clearance. Difference between readings is taper of journal.
   d. If clearance exceeds specified limits, try a 0.001 in. or 0.002 in. undersize bearing in combination with the standard bearing. Bearing clearance must be within specified limits. If standard and 0.002 in. undersize bearing does not bring clearance within desired limits, refinish crankshaft journal, then install undersize bearings.
8. Install the rear main seal.
9. After the bearings have been fitted, apply a light coat of engine oil to the journals and bearings. Install the rear main bearing cap. Install all bearing caps

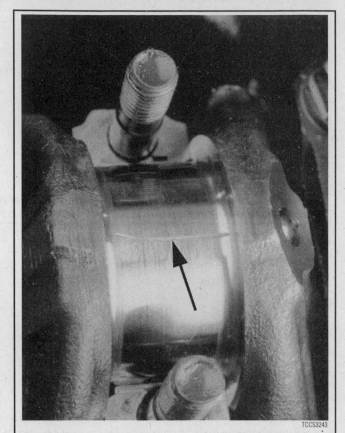

TCCS3243

Fig. 245 Apply a strip of gauging material to the bearing journal, then install and torque the cap

except the thrust bearing cap. Be sure that main bearing caps are installed in original locations. Tighten the bearing cap bolts to specifications.
10. Install the thrust bearing cap with bolts finger-tight.
11. Pry the crankshaft forward against the thrust surface of upper half of bearing.
12. Hold the crankshaft forward and pry the thrust bearing cap to the rear. This aligns the thrust surfaces of both halves of the bearing.
13. Retain the forward pressure on the crankshaft. Tighten the cap bolts to specifications.
14. Measure the crankshaft end-play as follows:
   a. Mount a dial gauge to the engine block and position the tip of the gauge to read from the crankshaft end.
   b. Carefully pry the crankshaft toward the rear of the engine and hold it there while you zero the gauge.
   c. Carefully pry the crankshaft toward the front of the engine and read the gauge.
   d. Confirm that the reading is within specifications. If not, install a new thrust bearing and repeat the procedure. If the reading is still out of specifications with a new bearing, have a machine shop inspect the thrust surfaces of the crankshaft, and if possible, repair it.
15. Rotate the crankshaft so as to position the first rod journal to the bottom of its stroke.

Pistons and Connecting Rods

▶ **See Figures 249, 250, 251 and 252**

1. Before installing the piston/connecting rod assembly, oil the pistons, piston rings and the cylinder walls with light engine oil. Install connecting rod bolt protectors or rubber hose onto the connecting rod bolts/studs. Also perform the following:
   a. Select the proper ring set for the size cylinder bore.
   b. Position the ring in the bore in which it is going to be used.
   c. Push the ring down into the bore area where normal ring wear is not encountered.
   d. Use the head of the piston to position the ring in the bore so that the

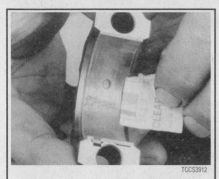

Fig. 246 After the cap is removed again, use the scale supplied with the gauging material to check the clearance

Fig. 247 A dial gauge may be used to check crankshaft end-play

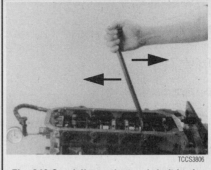

Fig. 248 Carefully pry the crankshaft back and forth while reading the dial gauge for end-play

Fig. 249 Checking the piston ring-to-ring groove side clearance using the ring and a feeler gauge

Fig. 250 The notch on the side of the bearing cap matches the tang on the bearing insert

Fig. 251 Most rings are marked to show which side of the ring should face up when installed to the piston

ring is square with the cylinder wall. Use caution to avoid damage to the ring or cylinder bore.

e. Measure the gap between the ends of the ring with a feeler gauge. Ring gap in a worn cylinder is normally greater than specification. If the ring gap is greater than the specified limits, try an oversize ring set.

f. Check the ring side clearance of the compression rings with a feeler gauge inserted between the ring and its lower land according to specification. The gauge should slide freely around the entire ring circumference without binding. Any wear that occurs will form a step at the inner portion of the lower land. If the lower lands have high steps, the piston should be replaced.

2. Unless new pistons are installed, be sure to install the pistons in the cylinders from which they were removed. The numbers on the connecting rod

Fig. 252 Install the piston and rod assembly into the block using a ring compressor and the handle of a hammer

and bearing cap must be on the same side when installed in the cylinder bore. If a connecting rod is ever transposed from one engine or cylinder to another, new bearings should be fitted and the connecting rod should be numbered to correspond with the new cylinder number. The notch on the piston head goes toward the front of the engine.

3. Install all of the rod bearing inserts into the rods and caps.

4. Install the rings to the pistons. Install the oil control ring first, then the second compression ring and finally the top compression ring. Use a piston ring expander tool to aid in installation and to help reduce the chance of breakage.

5. Make sure the ring gaps are properly spaced around the circumference of the piston. Fit a piston ring compressor around the piston and slide the piston and connecting rod assembly down into the cylinder bore, pushing it in with the wooden hammer handle. Push the piston down until it is only slightly below the top of the cylinder bore. Guide the connecting rod onto the crankshaft bearing journal carefully, to avoid damaging the crankshaft.

6. Check the bearing clearance of all the rod bearings, fitting them to the crankshaft bearing journals. Follow the procedure in the crankshaft installation above.

7. After the bearings have been fitted, apply a light coating of assembly oil to the journals and bearings.

8. Turn the crankshaft until the appropriate bearing journal is at the bottom of its stroke, then push the piston assembly all the way down until the connecting rod bearing seats on the crankshaft journal. Be careful not to allow the bearing cap screws to strike the crankshaft bearing journals and damage them.

9. After the piston and connecting rod assemblies have been installed, check the connecting rod side clearance on each crankshaft journal.

10. Prime and install the oil pump and the oil pump intake tube.

11. On the 2.3L and 2.4L engines, install the auxiliary shaft assembly.

2.2L Engine

CAMSHAFT, LIFTERS AND TIMING ASSEMBLY

1. Install the camshaft.
2. Install the lifters/followers into their bores.
3. Install the timing gears/chain assembly.

CYLINDER HEAD(S)

1. Install the cylinder head(s) using new gaskets.
2. Assemble the rest of the valve train (pushrods and rocker arms and/or shafts).

2.3L and 2.4L Engines

CYLINDER HEAD(S)

1. Install the cylinder head(s) using new gaskets.
2. Install the timing sprockets/gears and the belt/chain assemblies.

Engine Covers and Components

Install the timing cover(s) and oil pan. Refer to your notes and drawings made prior to disassembly and install all of the components that were removed. Install the engine into the vehicle.

Engine Start-up and Break-In

STARTING THE ENGINE

Now that the engine is installed and every wire and hose is properly connected, go back and double check that all coolant and vacuum hoses are connected. Check that your oil drain plug is installed and properly tightened. If not already done, install a new oil filter onto the engine. Fill the crankcase with the proper amount and grade of engine oil. Fill the cooling system with a 50/50 mixture of coolant/water.
1. Connect the vehicle battery.
2. Start the engine. Keep your eye on your oil pressure indicator; if it does not indicate oil pressure within 10 seconds of starting, turn the vehicle off.

✳✳ WARNING

Damage to the engine can result if it is allowed to run with no oil pressure. Check the engine oil level to make sure that it is full. Check for any leaks and if found, repair the leaks before continuing. If there is still no indication of oil pressure, you may need to prime the system.

3. Confirm that there are no fluid leaks (oil or other).
4. Allow the engine to reach normal operating temperature (the upper radiator hose will be hot to the touch).
5. At this point you can perform any necessary checks or adjustments, such as checking the ignition timing.
6. Install any remaining components or body panels which were removed.

BREAKING IT IN

Make the first miles on the new engine, easy ones. Vary the speed but do not accelerate hard. Most importantly, do not lug the engine, and avoid sustained high speeds until at least 100 miles. Check the engine oil and coolant levels frequently. Expect the engine to use a little oil until the rings seat. Change the oil and filter at 500 miles, 1500 miles, then every 3000 miles past that.

KEEP IT MAINTAINED

Now that you have just gone through all of that hard work, keep yourself from doing it all over again by thoroughly maintaining it. Not that you may not have maintained it before, heck you could have had one to two hundred thousand miles on it before doing this. However, you may have bought the vehicle used, and the previous owner did not keep up on maintenance. Which is why you just went through all of that hard work. See?

2.2L ENGINE MECHANICAL SPECIFICATIONS

Description	English Specifications	Metric Specifications
General Information		
Engine type	4 cylinder in-line	
Displacement	134 cubic in.	2.2L
Bore	3.50 in.	89mm
Stroke	3.46 in.	88mm
Compression ratio	8.85:1	
Firing order	1-3-4-2	
Cylinder Head		
Flatness	0.010 in.	0.25mm
Valve seat run-out	0.00196 in.	0.05mm
Valve seat width		
Intake	0.049-0.059 in.	1.25-1.50mm
Exhaust	0.063-0.075 in.	1.60-1.90mm
Valve seat angle	46°	
Cylinder Block		
Bore		
Diameter	3.5036-3.5043 in.	88.991-89.009mm
Out-of-round (max.)	0.0005 in.	0.013mm
Taper (max.)	0.0005 in.	0.013mm
Piston		
Clearance to bore	0.0007-0.0017 in.	0.015-0.045mm
Piston Rings		
End gap		
Compression	0.010-0.020 in.	0.25-0.50mm
Oil	0.010-0.050 in.	0.25-1.27mm
Groove clearance		
Compression	0.0019-0.0027 in.	0.05-0.07mm
Oil	0.0019-0.0082 in.	0.05-0.21mm
Piston Pin		
Diameter	0.8000-0.8002 in.	20.320-20.325mm
Fit in piston	0.0004-0.0009 in.	0.010-0.022mm
Press fit in rod	0.00098-0.0017 in.	0.025-0.045mm
Camshaft		
Lift		
Intake		
1995-97 models	0.288 in.	7.31mm
1998-00 models	0.263 in.	6.685mm
Exhaust		
1995-97 models	0.288 in.	7.31mm
1998-00 models	0.263 in.	6.685mm
Journal diameter	1.867-1.869 in.	47.44-47.49mm
Journal clearance		
1995-97 models	0.001-0.0039 in.	0.026-0.101mm
1998-00 models	0.0005-0.0035 in.	0.013-0.089mm
Crankshaft		
Main journal		
Diameter (all)	2.4945-2.4954 in.	63.360-63.384mm
Taper (max.)	0.00019 in.	0.005mm
Out-of-round (max.)	0.00019 in.	0.005mm
Main bearing		
Clearance (all)	0.0006-0.0019 in.	0.015-0.047mm
Crankshaft end-play	0.002-0.007 in.	0.0511-0.1780mm

91143C01

2.2L ENGINE MECHANICAL SPECIFICATIONS

Description	English Specifications	Metric Specifications
Crankshaft (cont'd)		
Connecting rod		
Diameter	1.9983-1.9994 in.	50.758-50.784mm
Taper (max.)	0.00019 in.	0.005mm
Out-of-round (max.)	0.00019 in.	0.005mm
Rod bearing clearance	0.00098-0.0031 in.	0.025-0.079mm
Rod side clearance	0.0039-0.0149 in.	0.10-0.38mm
Valve System		
Lifter		
Type	Hydraulic	
Leak down rate	12-90 seconds with 50 lb. load	
Body diameter	0.842-0.834 in.	21.38-21.41mm
Bore diameter	0.8435-0.8447 in.	21.42-21.45mm
Clearance in bore	0.008-0.0027 in.	0.203-0.068mm
Rocker arm ratio	1.5:1	
Face angle (all)	45°	
Seat angle (all)	46°	
Seat run-out	0.002 in.	0.05mm
Face run-out (max. all)	0.0012 in.	0.03mm
Seat width		
Intake		
1995-97 models	0.049-0.059 in.	1.25-1.50mm
1998-00 models	0.110 in.	2.80mm
Exhaust		
1995-97 models	0.063-0.075 in.	1.60-1.90mm
1998-00 models	0.138 in.	3.51mm
Valve margin (min.)	0.031 in.	0.08mm
Stem-to-guide		
Clearance		
Intake		
1995-97 models	0.0010-0.002 in.	0.028-0.066mm
1998-00 models	0.0007-0.0020 in.	0.00020mm
Exhaust		
1995-97 models	0.001-0.003 in.	0.035-0.081mm
1998-00 models	0.001-0.002 in.	0.035-0.076mm
Valve spring		
Free length		
1995-97 models	1.89 in.	48mm
1998-00 models	1.94 in.	49mm
Load		
Closed		
1995-97 models	79-85 lbs. @ 1.637 in.	350-380 N @ 41.56mm
1998-00 models	81.2-72.8 lbs. @ 1.600 in.	361-324 N @ 40.64mm
Open		
1995-97 models	225-233 lbs. @ 1.247 in.	956-1036 N @ 31.67mm
1998-00 models	215-201 lbs. @ 1.175 in.	957-883 N @ 29.85mm
Oil Pump		
Pressure @ 3000 rpm 150° F (65° C)	56 psi	348 kPa
Gear lash	0.004-0.008 in.	0.094-0.195mm
Gear pocket		
Depth	1.195-1.198 in.	30.36-30.44mm
Diameter	1.503-1.506 in.	38.18-38.25mm

91143C02

2.2L ENGINE MECHANICAL SPECIFICATIONS

Description	English Specifications	Metric Specifications
Oil Pump Gear		
Length		
Drive gear	1.199-1.20 in.	30.45-30.48mm
Idler	1.199-1.20 in.	30.45-30.48mm
Diameter		
Drive gear	1.498-1.5 in.	38.05-38.10mm
Idler	1.498-1.5 in.	38.05-38.10mm
Side clearance		
Drive gear	0.0015-0.004 in.	0.038-0.102mm
Idler	0.0015-0.004 in.	0.038-0.102mm
End clearance	0.002-0.007 in.	0.05-0.18mm
Valve-to-bore		
Clearance	0.0015-0.0035mm	0.038-0.089mm

9114C03

2.3L ENGINE MECHANICAL SPECIFICATIONS

Description	English Specifications	Metric Specifications
General Information		
Engine type	4 cylinder in-line	
Displacement	138 cubic in.	2.246L
Bore	3.62 in.	92mm
Stroke	3.35 in.	85mm
Compression ratio	9.5:1	
Firing order	1-3-4-2	
Lubrication System		
Oil capacity	4 qts.	3.75L
Oil pressure	30psi @ 3000 RPM	
Oil pump		
Gerotor pocket		
Depth	0.6736-0.6756 in.	17.11-17.16mm
Diameter	2.1273-2.1292 in.	54.033-54.083mm
Inner gerotor tip clearance	0.0059 in.	0.15mm
Outer gerotor diameter clearance	0.0013-0.0052 in.	0.033-0.133mm
Outer gerotor thickness	0.6727-0.6731 in.	17.087-17.099mm
Oil pump-to-driven gear backlash	0.0091-0.0201 in.	0.23-0.51mm
Cylinder Head		
Flatness	0.008 in.	0.203mm
Volume	1.5825-1.6501 oz.	46.8-48.8cc
Run-out	0.00196 in.	0.05mm
Valve seat diameter		
Intake	1.3412 in.	34.066mm
Exhaust	1.1436 in.	29.048mm
Valve guide inside diameter	0.2762-0.2772 in.	7.015-7.041mm
Cylinder Block		
Bore		
Diameter	3.5036-3.5043 in.	91.992-92.008mm
Out-of-round (max.)	0.0004 in.	0.010mm
Taper (max.)	0.0003 in.	0.008mm
Run-out (rear face of block to crank center line- max.)	0.002 in.	0.05mm
Flatness (max.)	0.008 in.	0.203mm
Piston		
Clearance-to-bore	0.0007-0.0020 in.	0.019-0.051mm
Compression height	1.260 in. +/- 0.004 in.	32.0 mm +/- 0.1mm
Piston pin bore inside diameter (at 70 degrees F/21 degrees C)	0.8662-0.8664 in.	22.002-22.006mm
Piston diameter (at 70 degrees F/21 degrees C)	3.6203-3.6210 in.	91.957-91.973mm
Ring groove width-top compression	0.060-0.061 in.	1.53-1.55mm
Ring groove width-second compression	0.0598-0.0606 in.	1.52-1.54mm
Ring groove width-oil control	0.1185-0.1193 in.	3.01-3.03mm
Piston Rings		
Width		
Compression (both)	0.05708-0.05827 in.	1.45-1.48mm
Oil control	0.01957-0.02060 in.	0.497-0.523mm
End gap		
Top compression	0.0138-0.0236 in.	0.35-0.60mm
Second compression	0.0157-0.0256 in.	0.40-0.65mm
Oil control	0.0157-0.0551 in.	0.40-1.40mm
Groove clearance		
Top compression	0.0019-0.0039 in.	0.05-0.1mm
Second compression	0.00157-0.00315 in.	0.04-0.08mm
Oil control		

9114C04

2.3L ENGINE MECHANICAL SPECIFICATIONS

Description	English Specifications	Metric Specifications
Piston Pin		
Diameter	0.8659-0.8661 in.	21.995-22.000mm
Pin-to-piston clearance (at 70 degrees F/21 degrees C)	0.00007-0.00043 in.	0.002-0.011mm
Pin-to-rod clearance	0.00027-0.00122 in.	0.007-0.031mm
End-play on floating pin	0.00-0.0236 in.	0.0-0.06mm
Crankshaft		
Main journal		
Diameter (all)	2.0470-2.0480 in.	51.996-52.C20mm
Taper (max.)	0.0005 in.	0.0127mm
Out-of-round (max.)	0.0005 in.	0.0127mm
Bearing clearance (all)	0.0005-0.0023 in.	0.013-0.058mm
Crankshaft end-play	0.0034-0.0095 in.	0.087-0.243mm
Rod bearing journal		
Diameter (all)	1.8887-1.8897 in.	47.975-48.00mm
Taper (max.)	0.0005 in.	0.0127mm
Out-of-round (max.)	0.0005 in.	0.0127mm
Bearing clearance (all)	0.0005-0.0020 in.	0.013-0.053mm
Side clearance	0.0059-0.0177 in.	0.150-0.450mm
Width	1.0925-1.1024 in.	27.75-28.00mm
Crankshaft run-out at flywheel flange (max.)	0.00098 in.	0.025mm
Run-out of crankshaft (max.)	0.00098 in.	0.025mm
Stoke of crankshaft	3.3366-3.3504 in.	84.9-85.10mm
Timing gear-to-crankshaft snout clearance	1.3004-1.3016 in.	33.03-33.06mm
Connecting Rod		
Inside diameter		
Small end	0.8664-0.8672 in.	22.007-22.027mm
Large end	2.0144-2.0154 in.	51.167-51.193mm
Width		
Small end	0.8622-0.8700 in.	21.9-22.1mm
Large end	1.0846-1.0866 in.	27.55-27.6mm
Rod-to-piston pin clearance	0.00027-0.0122 in.	0.007-0.031mm
Rod length (center-to-center)	5.8051-5.8090 in.	147.45-147.55mm
Camshaft		
Lift		
Intake	0.375 in.	9.525mm
Exhaust	0.375 in.	9.525mm
Journal diameter		
No. 1	1.5720-1.5728 in.	39.95-39.93mm
No. 2-5	1.3751-1.3760 in.	34.93-34.95mm
Journal clearance	0.0019-0.0043 in.	0.05-0.11mm
End-play clearance	0.0009-0.0088 in.	0.025-0.225mm
Camshaft Housing		
Lifter bore inside diameter	1.3775-1.3787 in.	34.989-35.019mm
Lifter outside diameter	1.3763-1.3770 in.	34.959-34.975mm
Lifter-to-bore clearance	0.0006-0.0024 in.	0.014-0.060mm
Lip seal bore inside diameter	1.9675-1.9695 in.	49.975-50.025mm
Lip seal bore outside diameter	1.9740-1.9830 in.	50.140-50.370mm
Cam carrier flatness	0.002 in.	0.05mm
Valve Lifters		
Leak down rate	6-24 seconds @ 50 lbs. (222 N)	
Clearance in bore	0.0006-0.0024 in.	0.014-0.060mm
Valves		
Installed height	0.9840-1.0040 in.	25.0-25.5mm

91143C05

2.3L ENGINE MECHANICAL SPECIFICATIONS

Description	English Specifications	Metric Specifications
Valves (cont'd)		
Valve tip above spring retainer	0.0394-0.0787 in.	1.0-2.0mm
Intake valves		
Face angle	44°	44°
Seat angle	45°	45°
Head diameter	1.4318-1.4421 in.	36.37-36.63mm
Stem diameter	0.27512-0.27445 in.	6.990-6.972mm
Overall length	4.3300 in.	109.984mm
Stem-to-guide clearance	0.0010-0.002 in.	0.025-0.069mm
Seat width	0.0370-0.0748 in.	0.94-1.90mm
Valve seat margin (min.)	0.0098 in.	0.25mm
Valve face run-out	0.0015 in.	0.038mm
Valve tip-to-groove	0.1190-0.1367 in.	3.023-3.473mm
Exhaust valves		
Face angle	44°	44°
Seat angle	45°	45°
Head diameter	1.1764-1.1866 in.	29.88-30.14mm
Stem diameter	0.2740-0.2747 in.	6.959-6.977mm*
Overall length	4.3103 in.	109.482mm
Stem-to-guide clearance	0.0015-0.0032 in.	0.038-0.081mm
Seat width	0.0370-0.0748 in.	0.94-1.90mm
Valve seat margin (min.)	0.0098 in.	0.25mm
Valve face run-out	0.0015 in.	0.038mm
Valve tip-to-groove	0.1190-0.1367 in.	3.023-3.473mm
Valve Springs		
Valve spring pressure		
Load @ 1.4370 in. (36.5mm)-Closed	71-79 ft. lbs.	314-353 Nm
Load @ 1.0433 in. (26.08mm)-Open	193-207 ft. lbs.	857-922 Nm

91143C06

2.4L ENGINE MECHANICAL SPECIFICATIONS

Description	English Specifications	Metric Specifications
General Information		
Engine type	4 cylinder in-line	
Displacement	151 cubic in.	2.4L
Bore	3.54 in.	90mm
Stroke	3.70 in.	94mm
Compression ratio	9.5:1	
Firing order	1-3-4-2	
Lubrication System		
Oil capacity	4 qts.	3.75L
Oil pressure	30psi @ 3000 RPM	
Oil pump		
Gerotor pocket		
Depth	0.6736-0.6756 in.	17.11-17.16mm
Diameter	2.1273-2.1292 in.	54.033-54.083mm
Inner gerotor tip clearance	0.0059 in.	0.15mm
Outer gerotor diameter clearance	0.0013-0.0052 in.	0.033-0.133mm
Outer gerotor thickness	0.6727-0.6731 in.	17.087-17.099mm
Oil pump-to-driven gear backlash	0.0091-0.0201 in.	0.23-0.51mm
Cylinder Head		
Flatness	0.008 in.	0.203mm
Volume	1.5825-1.6501 oz.	46.8-48.8cc
Run-out	0.00196 in.	0.05mm
Valve seat diameter		
Intake	1.3412 in.	34.066mm
Exhaust	1.1436 in.	29.048mm
Valve guide inside diameter		
Intake	0.2331-0.2339 in.	5.921-5.941mm
Exhaust	0.2326-0.2334 in.	5.908-5.928mm
Cylinder Block		
Bore		
Diameter	3.5431-3.5435 in.	89.994-90.006mm
Out-of-round (max.)	0.0004 in.	0.010mm
Taper (max.)	0.0003 in.	0.008mm
Run-out (rear face of block to crank center line- max.)	0.002 in.	0.05mm
Flatness (max.)	0.008 in.	0.203mm
Piston		
Clearance-to-bore	0.0007-0.0020 in.	0.019-0.051mm
Compression height	1.180-1.182 in.	29.27-30.03mm
Piston pin bore inside diameter (at 70 degrees F/21 degrees C)	0.8662-0.8664 in.	22.002-22.006mm
Piston diameter (at 70 degrees F/21 degrees C)	3.6203-3.6210 in.	91.957-91.973mm
Ring groove width-top compression	0.048-0.049 in.	1.23-1.25mm
Ring groove width-second compression	0.0598-0.0606 in.	1.52-1.54mm
Ring groove width-oil control	0.1185-0.1193 in.	3.01-3.03mm
Piston Rings		
Width		
Compression (both)	0.0461-0.0469 in.	1.170-1.190mm
Oil control	0.01957-0.02060 in.	0.497-0.523mm
End gap		
Top compression	0.006-0.012 in.	0.15-0.30mm
Second compression	0.0119-0.0161 in.	0.30-0.41mm
Oil control	0.0157-0.0551 in.	0.40-1.40mm
Groove clearance		
Top compression	0.0016-0.0031 in.	0.04-0.08mm

9143C07

2.4L ENGINE MECHANICAL SPECIFICATIONS

Description	English Specifications	Metric Specifications
Piston Rings (cont'd)		
Groove clearance (cont'd)		
Second compression	0.0012-0.0028 in.	0.03-0.07mm
Oil control		
Piston Pin		
Diameter	0.8659-0.8661 in.	21.995-22.000mm
Pin-to-piston clearance (at 70 degrees F/21 degrees C)	0.00007-0.00043 in.	0.002-0.011mm
Pin-to-rod clearance	0.00027-0.00122 in.	0.007-0.031mm
End-play on floating pin	0.00-0.0236 in.	0.0-0.06mm
Crankshaft		
Main journal		
Diameter (all)	2.3634-2.3626 in.	60.031-60.010mm
Taper (max.)	0.0005 in.	0.0127mm
Out-of-round (max.)	0.0005 in.	0.0127mm
Bearing clearance (all)	0.0005-0.0030 in.	0.013-0.075mm
Crankshaft end-play	0.0034-0.0095 in.	0.087-0.243mm
Rod bearing journal		
Diameter (all)	1.8887-1.8897 in.	47.975-48.00mm
Taper (max.)	0.0005 in.	0.0127mm
Out-of-round (max.)	0.0005-0.0020 in.	0.013-0.053mm
Bearing clearance (all)	0.0059-0.0177 in.	0.150-0.450mm
Side clearance	0.9161-0.0220 in.	23.27-23.42mm
Crankshaft run-out at flywheel flange (max.)	0.00098 in.	0.025mm
Run-out of crankshaft (max.)	0.00098 in.	0.025mm
Stoke of crankshaft	3.70 in.	94mm
Timing gear-to-crankshaft snout clearance	1.3004-1.3016 in.	33.03-33.06mm
Connecting Rod		
Inside diameter		
Small end	0.8664-0.8672 in.	22.007-22.027mm
Large end	2.0144-2.0154 in.	51.167-51.193mm
Width		
Small end	0.9122-0.9142 in.	23.170-23.220mm
Large end	0.9122-0.9142 in.	23.170-23.220mm
Rod-to-piston pin clearance	0.00027-0.0122 in.	0.007-0.031mm
Rod length (center-to-center)	5.6125-5.6164 in.	142.45-144.55mm
Camshaft		
Lift		
Intake	0.354 in.	9.0mm
Exhaust	0.346 in.	8.8mm
Journal diameter		
No. 1	1.5720-1.5728 in.	39.95-39.93mm
No. 2-5	1.3751-1.3760 in.	34.93-34.95mm
Bearing inside diameter		
No. 1	1.5748-1.5764 in.	40.0-40.04mm
No. 2-5	1.3780-1.3795 in.	35.00-35.04mm
Journal clearance	0.0019-0.0043 in.	0.05-0.11mm
End-play clearance	0.0009-0.0088 in.	0.025-0.225mm
Camshaft Housing		
Lifter bore inside diameter	1.3381-1.3393 in.	33.989-34.019mm
Lifter outside diameter	1.3369-1.3375 in.	33.959-33.975mm
Lifter-to-bore clearance	0.0006-0.0024 in.	0.014-0.060mm
Lip seal bore inside diameter	1.9675-1.9695 in.	49.975-50.025mm

9143C08

2.4L ENGINE MECHANICAL SPECIFICATIONS

Description	English Specifications	Metric Specifications
Camshaft Housing (cont'd)		
Lip seal bore outside diameter	1.9740-1.9830 in.	50.140-50.370mm
Cam carrier flatness	0.0028 in.	0.07mm
Valve Lifters		
Clearance in bore	0.0006-0.0024 in.	0.014-0.060mm
Valves		
Installed height	0.9787-1.0024 in.	24.86-25.62mm
Valve tip above spring retainer	0.0237-0.0323 in.	0.602-0.820mm
Intake valves		
Face angle	46°	
Seat angle	45°	
Head diameter	1.3987 in.+/- 0.0011 in.	35.5mm +/- 0.03mm
Stem diameter	0.2331-0.2339 in.	5.921-5.941mm
Overall length	4.2272 in.	107.290mm
Stem-to-guide clearance	0.0010-0.002 in.	0.025-0.069mm
Seat width	0.0370-0.0748 in.	0.94-1.90mm
Valve seat margin (min.)	0.0098 in.	0.25mm
Valve face run-out	0.0015 in.	0.038mm
Valve tip-to-groove	0.1190-0.1367 in.	3.023-3.473mm
Exhaust valves		
Face angle	45.5°	
Seat angle	45°	
Head diameter	1.1366-1.1469 in.	28.870-29.130mm
Stem diameter	0.2326-0.2334 in.	5.908-5.928mm
Overall length	4.2586 in.	108.17mm
Stem-to-guide clearance	0.0015-0.0032 in.	0.038-0.081mm
Seat width	0.0370-0.0748 in.	0.94-1.90mm
Valve seat margin (min.)	0.0098 in.	0.25mm
Valve face run-out	0.0015 in.	0.038mm
Valve tip-to-groove	0.1190-0.1367 in.	3.023-3.473mm
Valve Springs		
Valve spring pressure		
Load @ 1.4370 in. (36.5mm)-Closed	50-55 ft. lbs.	223-247 Nm
Load @ 1.0622 in. (26.98mm)-Open	122-133 ft. lbs.	544-596 Nm
Balance shafts		
Housing flatness (max.)	0.003 in.	0.76mm
Bore roundness	0.0009 in.	0.25mm
Bearing thickness	0.0590-0.0593 in.	1.5-1.508mm
Bearing inside diameter	1.1819-1.1835 in.	30.019-30.061mm
Housing bore	1.3001-1.1801 in.	33.025-33.05mm
Shaft journal outside diameter	1.1791-1.801 in.	29.950-29.975mm
Journal taper (intentional towards counterweight)	0.000-0.0004 in.	0.000-0.010mm
Journal roundness (max.)	0.0002 in.	0.005mm
Bearing clearance	0.0017-0.0044 in.	0.044-0.111mm
Gear diameter over two 2.5mm pins	2.4035-2.4073 in.	61.050-61.145mm
Gear backlash	0.0003-0.0034 in.	0.008-0.0086mm
Chain slack (with 6 lbs. of pressure applied to the guide)	0.04 in.	1.0mm
Shaft groove width	0.127-0.134 in.	3.23-3.40mm
Thrust plate thickness	0.1159-0.1199 in.	2.945-3.045mm
End-play	0.0073-0.0179 in.	0.185-0.455mm

91143C09

2.2L ENGINE TORQUE SPECIFICATIONS

Components	English	Metric
Rocker Arm (Valve) Cover		
Rocker arm cover retainers	89 inch lbs.	10 Nm
Throttle cable bracket	18 ft. lbs.	25 Nm
Bolts		
Rocker Arms and Pushrods		
Rocker arm retaining nuts	22 ft. lbs.	30 Nm
Thermostat		
Thermostat outlet retainers	89 inch lbs.	10 Nm
Intake Manifold		
1995-97 models		
Lower intake manifold retainers	24 ft. lbs. [1]	33 Nm [1]
Upper intake manifold retainers	22 ft. lbs. [1]	30 Nm [1]
Throttle cable bracket bolts	18 ft. lbs.	25 Nm
Alternator rear brace nuts and bolts	18 ft. lbs.	25 Nm
EGR adapter retainers	97 inch lbs.	11 Nm
EGR pipe-to-EGR adapter bolt	18 ft. lbs.	25 Nm
EGR pipe-to-intake manifold bolts	89 inch lbs.	10 Nm
1998-00 models		
Lower intake manifold retainers	17 ft. lbs. [1]	24 Nm [1]
Throttle body retaining bolts	89 inch lbs.	10 Nm
Exhaust Manifold		
Manifold nuts	115 inch lbs.	13 Nm
Engines Cooling Fan		
Fan assembly-to-radia or retainer	53 inch lbs.	6 Nm
Water Pump		
Water pump retainers	18 ft. lbs.	25 Nm
Pulley retaining bolts	22 ft. lbs.	30 Nm
Cylinder Head		
Cylinder head bolts	[1] [2]	[1] [2]
Oil Pan		
Oil pan bolts	89 inch lbs.	10 Nm
Oil Pump		
Oil pump-to-rear bearing cap bolt	37 ft. lbs.	50 Nm
Crankshaft Damper/Pulley		
Pulley bolts	26-38 ft. lbs.	35-51 Nm
Damper bolt	77 ft. lbs.	105 Nm
Timing Chain Cover and Seal		
Timing cover bolts	97 inch lbs.	11 Nm
Timing Chain and Gears		
Tensioner bolts	18 ft. lbs.	25 Nm
Camshaft sprocket bolt	66-68 ft. lbs.	91-95 Nm
Camshaft		
Camshaft sprocket bolt	66-68 ft. lbs.	91-95 Nm
Thrust plate bolts	106 inch lbs.	12 Nm
Oil pump drive bolt	18 ft. lbs.	25 Nm
Valve Lifter		
Anti-rotation bracket bolts	97 inch lbs.	11 Nm
Flywheel		
Flywheel bolts	55 ft. lbs.	75 Nm

91143C10

2.3L/2.4L ENGINE TORQUE SPECIFICATIONS

Components	English	Metric
Camshaft Carrier Cover(s)		
Camshaft carrier cover retaining bolts	①	①
Fuel rail-to-cylinder head	19 ft. lbs.	26 Nm
Ignition coil and module assembly-to-camshaft housing bolts	16 ft. lbs.	22 Nm
Thermostat		
Thermostat outlet retainers	19 ft. lbs.	26 Nm
Pipe-to-transaxle bolt	40 ft. lbs.	54 Nm
Intake Manifold		
1995 2.3L engine		
Intake manifold retaining bolts	19 ft. lbs. ①	26 Nm ①
1996-00 2.4L engine		
Intake manifold retaining bolts	18 ft. lbs. ①	24 Nm ①
EGR pipe-to-EGR adapter bolt	19 ft. lbs.	26 Nm
Exhaust Manifold		
1995 2.3L engine		
Exhaust manifold retaining nuts	31 ft. lbs.	42 Nm
1996-00 2.4L engine		
Exhaust manifold retaining nuts	110 inch lbs.	13 Nm
Heat shield	10 ft. lbs.	14 Nm
Exhaust manifold brace-to-intake manifold	41 ft. lbs.	56 Nm
Engine Cooling Fan		
Fan assembly-to-radiator retainer		
Water Pump		
Water pump-to-chain housing nuts	19 ft. lbs.	26 Nm
Water pump cover-to-pump	106 inch lbs.	13 Nm
Radiator pipe-to-pump cover	19 ft. lbs.	26 Nm
Cylinder Head		
Cylinder head bolts	① ③	① ③
Intake manifold brace	19 ft. lbs.	26 Nm
Accelerator control cable bracket-to-throttle body		
Bolt	106 inch lbs.	13 Nm
Nut	19 ft. lbs.	26 Nm
Oil fill tube attaching bolt	71 inch lbs.	8 Nm
Oil Pan		
Oil pan bolts	①	①
Oil Pump		
Oil pump-to-block bolts	40 ft. lbs.	54 Nm
Crankshaft Damper/Pulley		
Damper bolt	129 ft. lbs. ④	175 Nm ④
Timing Chain Cover and Seal		
Timing cover bolts	106 inch lbs.	13 Nm
Timing Chain and Gears		
Intake camshaft sprocket	52 ft. lbs.	70 Nm
Tensioner bolts	89 inch lbs.	10 Nm
Balance Shaft		
Balance shaft driven gear bolt	22 ft. lbs.	30 Nm
Balance shaft chain tensioner bolt	115 inch lbs.	13 Nm
Rear Main Seal		
Rear main seal housing-to-engine block	106 inch lbs.	13 Nm
Balance shaft driven gear bolt	106 inch lbs.	13 Nm

91143C11

2.3L/2.4L ENGINE TORQUE SPECIFICATIONS

Components	English	Metric
Flywheel		
Flywheel bolts	22 ft. lbs. ⑤	30 Nm ⑤

① Tighten the retainers in the sequence illustrated
② First pass
  Long bolts 46 ft. lbs. (63 Nm)
  Short bolts 43 ft. lbs. (58 Nm)
  Final pass
  Tighten all bolts an additional 90 degree turn
③ Tighten bolts 1-8 to 40 ft. lbs. (65 Nm).
  Tighten bolts 9 and 10 to 30 ft. lbs. (40 Nm).
  Final pass 65 ft. lbs. (90 Nm).
  Tighten all 10 bolts an additional 90°
④ Rotate an additional 90°
⑤ Rotate an additional 45°
⑥ Tighten bolt to 20 ft. lbs. (27 Nm) plus an additional 70°

91143C12

AIR POLLUTION 4-2
NATURAL POLLUTANTS 4-2
INDUSTRIAL POLLUTANTS 4-2
AUTOMOTIVE POLLUTANTS 4-2
   TEMPERATURE INVERSION 4-2
   HEAT TRANSFER 4-2
AUTOMOTIVE EMISSIONS 4-3
EXHAUST GASES 4-3
   HYDROCARBONS 4-3
   CARBON MONOXIDE 4-3
   NITROGEN 4-3
   OXIDES OF SULFUR 4-3
   PARTICULATE MATTER 4-3
CRANKCASE EMISSIONS 4-4
EVAPORATIVE EMISSIONS 4-4
EMISSION CONTROLS 4-5
CRANKCASE VENTILATION SYSTEM 4-7
   OPERATION 4-7
   TESTING 4-7
   REMOVAL & INSTALLATION 4-7
EVAPORATIVE EMISSION CONTROL
  SYSTEM 4-8
   OPERATION 4-8
   TESTING 4-9
   REMOVAL & INSTALLATION 4-9
EXHAUST GAS RECIRCULATION (EGR)
  SYSTEM 4-10
   OPERATION 4-10
   TESTING 4-12
   REMOVAL & INSTALLATION 4-13
CATALYTIC CONVERTER 4-13
   OPERATION 4-13
**ELECTRONIC ENGINE
  CONTROLS 4-14**
POWERTRAIN CONTROL MODULE
  (PCM) 4-14
   OPERATION 4-14
   REMOVAL & INSTALLATION 4-14
OXYGEN SENSOR 4-15
   OPERATION 4-15
   TESTING 4-15
   REMOVAL & INSTALLATION 4-16
IDLE AIR CONTROL (IAC) VALVE 4-17
   OPERATION 4-17
   TESTING 4-17
   REMOVAL & INSTALLATION 4-18
ENGINE COOLANT TEMPERATURE
  SENSOR 4-18
   OPERATION 4-18
   TESTING 4-18
   REMOVAL & INSTALLATION 4-19
INTAKE AIR TEMPERATURE
  SENSOR 4-20
   OPERATION 4-20
   TESTING 4-20
   REMOVAL & INSTALLATION 4-20
MANIFOLD ABSOLUTE PRESSURE (MAP)
  SENSOR 4-21
   OPERATION 4-21

TESTING 4-21
   REMOVAL & INSTALLATION 4-22
THROTTLE POSITION SENSOR 4-23
   OPERATION 4-23
   TESTING 4-23
   REMOVAL & INSTALLATION 4-23
CRANKSHAFT POSITION (CKP)
  SENSOR 4-24
   OPERATION 4-24
   TESTING 4-24
   REMOVAL & INSTALLATION 4-24
CAMSHAFT POSITION (CMP)
  SENSOR 4-25
   OPERATION 4-25
   TESTING 4-25
   REMOVAL & INSTALLATION 4-26
KNOCK SENSOR 4-26
   OPERATION 4-26
   TESTING 4-26
   REMOVAL & INSTALLATION 4-26
VEHICLE SPEED SENSOR 4-26
   OPERATION 4-26
   TESTING 4-26
   REMOVAL & INSTALLATION 4-27
TROUBLE CODES 4-28
GENERAL INFORMATION 4-28
   SCAN TOOLS 4-28
   ELECTRICAL TOOLS 4-28
DIAGNOSIS AND TESTING 4-28
   VISUAL/PHYSICAL
    INSPECTION 4-28
   INTERMITTENTS 4-28
   CIRCUIT/COMPONENT REPAIR 4-28
READING CODES 4-29
   OBD-I SYSTEMS 4-29
   OBD-II SYSTEMS 4-29
CLEARING CODES 4-29
VACUUM DIAGRAMS 4-31
COMPONENT LOCATIONS
  ELECTRONIC ENGINE CONTROL
   COMPONENTS—2.2L ENGINE 4-5
  ELECTRONIC ENGINE CONTROL
   COMPONENTS—2.4L ENGINE 4-6

4

DRIVEABILITY AND EMISSIONS CONTROLS

AIR POLLUTION 4-2
AUTOMOTIVE EMISSIONS 4-3
EMISSION CONTROLS 4-5
ELECTRONIC ENGINE CONTROLS 4-14
TROUBLE CODES 4-28
VACUUM DIAGRAMS 4-31

AIR POLLUTION

The earth's atmosphere, at or near sea level, consists approximately of 78 percent nitrogen, 21 percent oxygen and 1 percent other gases. If it were possible to remain in this state, 100 percent clean air would result. However, many varied sources allow other gases and particulates to mix with the clean air, causing our atmosphere to become unclean or polluted.

Some of these pollutants are visible while others are invisible, with each having the capability of causing distress to the eyes, ears, throat, skin and respiratory system. Should these pollutants become concentrated in a specific area and under certain conditions, death could result due to the displacement or chemical change of the oxygen content in the air. These pollutants can also cause great damage to the environment and to the many man made objects that are exposed to the elements.

To better understand the causes of air pollution, the pollutants can be categorized into 3 separate types, natural, industrial and automotive.

Natural Pollutants

Natural pollution has been present on earth since before man appeared and continues to be a factor when discussing air pollution, although it causes only a small percentage of the overall pollution problem. It is the direct result of decaying organic matter, wind born smoke and particulates from such natural events as plain and forest fires (ignited by heat or lightning), volcanic ash, sand and dust which can spread over a large area of the countryside.

Such a phenomenon of natural pollution has been seen in the form of volcanic eruptions, with the resulting plume of smoke, steam and volcanic ash blotting out the sun's rays as it spreads and rises higher into the atmosphere. As it travels into the atmosphere the upper air currents catch and carry the smoke and ash, while condensing the steam back into water vapor. As the water vapor, smoke and ash travel on their journey, the smoke dissipates into the atmosphere while the ash and moisture settle back to earth in a trail hundreds of miles long. In some cases, lives are lost and millions of dollars of property damage result.

Industrial Pollutants

Industrial pollution is caused primarily by industrial processes, the burning of coal, oil and natural gas, which in turn produce smoke and fumes. Because the burning fuels contain large amounts of sulfur, the principal ingredients of smoke and fumes are sulfur dioxide and particulate matter. This type of pollutant occurs most severely during still, damp and cool weather, such as at night. Even in its less severe form, this pollutant is not confined to just cities. Because of air movements, the pollutants move for miles over the surrounding countryside, leaving in its path a barren and unhealthy environment for all living things.

Working with Federal, State and Local mandated regulations and by carefully monitoring emissions, big business has greatly reduced the amount of pollutant introduced from its industrial sources, striving to obtain an acceptable level. Because of the mandated industrial emission clean up, many land areas and streams in and around the cities that were formerly barren of vegetation and life, have now begun to move back in the direction of nature's intended balance.

Automotive Pollutants

The third major source of air pollution is automotive emissions. The emissions from the internal combustion engines were not an appreciable problem years ago because of the small number of registered vehicles and the nation's small highway system. However, during the early 1950's, the trend of the American people was to move from the cities to the surrounding suburbs. This caused an immediate problem in transportation because the majority of suburbs were not afforded mass transit conveniences. This lack of transportation created an attractive market for the automobile manufacturers, which resulted in a dramatic increase in the number of vehicles produced and sold, along with a marked increase in highway construction between cities and the suburbs. Multi-vehicle families emerged with a growing emphasis placed on an individual vehicle per family member. As the increase in vehicle ownership and usage occurred, so did pollutant levels in and around the cities, as suburbanites drove daily to their businesses and employment, returning at the end of the day to their homes in the suburbs.

It was noted that a smoke and fog type haze was being formed and at times, remained in suspension over the cities, taking time to dissipate. At first this "smog," derived from the words "smoke" and "fog," was thought to result from industrial pollution but it was determined that automobile emissions shared the blame. It was discovered that when normal automobile emissions were exposed to sunlight for a period of time, complex chemical reactions would take place.

It is now known that smog is a photo chemical layer which develops when certain oxides of nitrogen (NOx) and unburned hydrocarbons (HC) from automobile emissions are exposed to sunlight. Pollution was more severe when smog would become stagnant over an area in which a warm layer of air settled over the top of the cooler air mass, trapping and holding the cooler mass at ground level. The trapped cooler air would keep the emissions from being dispersed and diluted through normal air flows. This type of air stagnation was given the name "Temperature Inversion."

TEMPERATURE INVERSION

In normal weather situations, surface air is warmed by heat radiating from the earth's surface and the sun's rays. This causes it to rise upward, into the atmosphere. Upon rising it will cool through a convection type heat exchange with the cooler upper air. As warm air rises, the surface pollutants are carried upward and dissipated into the atmosphere.

When a temperature inversion occurs, we find the higher air is no longer cooler, but is warmer than the surface air, causing the cooler surface air to become trapped. This warm air blanket can extend from above ground level to a few hundred or even a few thousand feet into the air. As the surface air is trapped, so are the pollutants, causing a severe smog condition. Should this stagnant air mass extend to a few thousand feet high, enough air movement with the inversion takes place to allow the smog layer to rise above ground level but the pollutants still cannot dissipate. This inversion can remain for days over an area, with the smog level only rising or lowering from ground level to a few hundred feet high. Meanwhile, the pollutant levels increase, causing eye irritation, respiratory problems, reduced visibility, plant damage and in some cases, even disease.

This inversion phenomenon was first noted in the Los Angeles, California area. The city lies in terrain resembling a basin and with certain weather conditions, a cold air mass is held in the basin while a warmer air mass covers it like a lid.

Because this type of condition was first documented as prevalent in the Los Angeles area, this type of trapped pollution was named Los Angeles Smog, although it occurs in other areas where a large concentration of automobiles are used and the air remains stagnant for any length of time.

HEAT TRANSFER

Consider the internal combustion engine as a machine in which raw materials must be placed so a finished product comes out. As in any machine operation, a certain amount of wasted material is formed. When we relate this to the internal combustion engine, we find that through the input of air and fuel, we obtain power during the combustion process to drive the vehicle. The by-product or waste of this power is, in part, heat and exhaust gases with which we must dispose.

The heat from the combustion process can rise to over 4000°F (2204°C). The dissipation of this heat is controlled by a ram air effect, the use of cooling fans to cause air flow and a liquid coolant solution surrounding the combustion area to transfer the heat of combustion through the cylinder walls and into the coolant. The coolant is then directed to a thin-finned, multi-tubed radiator, from which the excess heat is transferred to the atmosphere by 1 of the 3 heat transfer methods, conduction, convection or radiation.

The cooling of the combustion area is an important part in the control of exhaust emissions. To understand the behavior of the combustion and transfer of its heat, consider the air/fuel charge. It is ignited and the flame front burns progressively across the combustion chamber until the burning charge reaches the cylinder walls. Some of the fuel in contact with the walls is not hot enough to burn, thereby snuffing out or quenching the combustion process. This leaves unburned fuel in the combustion chamber. This unburned fuel is then forced out of the cylinder and into the exhaust system, along with the exhaust gases.

Many attempts have been made to minimize the amount of unburned fuel in the combustion chambers due to quenching, by increasing the coolant temperature and lessening the contact area of the coolant around the combustion area. However, design limitations within the combustion chambers prevent the complete burning of the air/fuel charge, so a certain amount of the unburned fuel is still expelled into the exhaust system, regardless of modifications to the engine.

AUTOMOTIVE EMISSIONS

Before emission controls were mandated on internal combustion engines, other sources of engine pollutants were discovered along with the exhaust emissions. It was determined that engine combustion exhaust produced approximately 60 percent of the total emission pollutants, fuel evaporation from the fuel tank and carburetor vents produced 20 percent, with the final 20 percent being produced through the crankcase as a by-product of the combustion process.

Exhaust Gases

The exhaust gases emitted into the atmosphere are a combination of burned and unburned fuel. To understand the exhaust emission and its composition, we must review some basic chemistry.

When the air/fuel mixture is introduced into the engine, we are mixing air, composed of nitrogen (78 percent), oxygen (21 percent) and other gases (1 percent) with the fuel, which is 100 percent hydrocarbons (HC), in a semi-controlled ratio. As the combustion process is accomplished, power is produced to move the vehicle while the heat of combustion is transferred to the cooling system. The exhaust gases are then composed of nitrogen, a diatomic gas (N_2), the same as was introduced in the engine, carbon dioxide (CO_2), the same gas that is used in beverage carbonation, and water vapor (H_2O). The nitrogen (N_2), for the most part, passes through the engine unchanged, while the oxygen (O_2) reacts (burns) with the hydrocarbons (HC) and produces the carbon dioxide (CO_2) and the water vapors (H_2O). If this chemical process would be the only process to take place, the exhaust emissions would be harmless. However, during the combustion process, other compounds are formed which are considered dangerous. These pollutants are hydrocarbons (HC), carbon monoxide (CO), oxides of nitrogen (NOx) oxides of sulfur (SOx) and engine particulates.

HYDROCARBONS

Hydrocarbons (HC) are essentially fuel which was not burned during the combustion process or which has escaped into the atmosphere through fuel evaporation. The main sources of incomplete combustion are rich air/fuel mixtures, low engine temperatures and improper spark timing. The main sources of hydrocarbon emission through fuel evaporation on most vehicles used to be the vehicle's fuel tank and carburetor float bowl.

To reduce combustion hydrocarbon emission, engine modifications were made to minimize dead space and surface area in the combustion chamber. In addition, the air/fuel mixture was made more lean through the improved control which feedback carburetion and fuel injection offers and by the addition of external controls to aid in further combustion of the hydrocarbons outside the engine. Two such methods were the addition of air injection systems, to inject fresh air into the exhaust manifolds and the installation of catalytic converters, units that are able to burn traces of hydrocarbons without affecting the internal combustion process or fuel economy.

To control hydrocarbon emissions through fuel evaporation, modifications were made to the fuel tank to allow storage of the fuel vapors during periods of engine shut-down. Modifications were also made to the air intake system so that at specific times during engine operation, these vapors may be purged and burned by blending them with the air/fuel mixture.

CARBON MONOXIDE

Carbon monoxide is formed when not enough oxygen is present during the combustion process to convert carbon (C) to carbon dioxide (CO_2). An increase in the carbon monoxide (CO) emission is normally accompanied by an increase in the hydrocarbon (HC) emission because of the lack of oxygen to completely burn all of the fuel mixture.

Carbon monoxide (CO) also increases the rate at which the photo chemical smog is formed by speeding up the conversion of nitric oxide (NO) to nitrogen dioxide (NO_2). To accomplish this, carbon monoxide (CO) combines with oxygen (O_2) and nitric oxide (NO) to produce carbon dioxide (CO_2) and nitrogen dioxide (NO_2). ($CO + O_2 + NO = CO_2 + NO_2$).

The dangers of carbon monoxide, which is an odorless and colorless toxic gas are many. When carbon monoxide is inhaled into the lungs and passed into the blood stream, oxygen is replaced by the carbon monoxide in the red blood cells, causing a reduction in the amount of oxygen supplied to the many parts of the body. This lack of oxygen causes headaches, lack of coordination, reduced mental alertness and, should the carbon monoxide concentration be high enough, death could result.

NITROGEN

Normally, nitrogen is an inert gas. When heated to approximately 2500°F (1371°C) through the combustion process, this gas becomes active and causes an increase in the nitric oxide (NO) emission.

Oxides of nitrogen (NOx) are composed of approximately 97–98 percent nitric oxide (NO). Nitric oxide is a colorless gas but when it is passed into the atmosphere, it combines with oxygen and forms nitrogen dioxide (NO_2). The nitrogen dioxide then combines with chemically active hydrocarbons (HC) and when in the presence of sunlight, causes the formation of photo-chemical smog.

Ozone

To further complicate matters, some of the nitrogen dioxide (NO_2) is broken apart by the sunlight to form nitric oxide and oxygen. (NO_2 + sunlight = NO + O). This single atom of oxygen then combines with diatomic (meaning 2 atoms) oxygen (O_2) to form ozone (O_3). Ozone is one of the smells associated with smog. It has a pungent and offensive odor, irritates the eyes and lung tissues, affects the growth of plant life and causes rapid deterioration of rubber products. Ozone can be formed by sunlight as well as electrical discharge into the air.

The most common discharge area on the automobile engine is the secondary ignition electrical system, especially when inferior quality spark plug cables are used. As the surge of high voltage is routed through the secondary cable, the circuit builds up an electrical field around the wire, which acts upon the oxygen in the surrounding air to form the ozone. The faint glow along the cable with the engine running that may be visible on a dark night, is called the "corona discharge." It is the result of the electrical field passing from a high along the cable, to a low in the surrounding air, which forms the ozone gas. The combination of corona and ozone has been a major cause of cable deterioration. Recently, different and better quality insulating materials have lengthened the life of the electrical cables.

Although ozone at ground level can be harmful, ozone is beneficial to the earth's inhabitants. By having a concentrated ozone layer called the "ozonosphere," between 10 and 20 miles (16–32 km) up in the atmosphere, much of the ultra violet radiation from the sun's rays are absorbed and screened. If this ozone layer were not present, much of the earth's surface would be burned, dried and unfit for human life.

OXIDES OF SULFUR

Oxides of sulfur (SOx) were initially ignored in the exhaust system emissions, since the sulfur content of gasoline as a fuel is less than 1/10 of 1 percent. Because of this small amount, it was felt that it contributed very little to the overall pollution problem. However, because of the difficulty in solving the sulfur emissions in industrial pollution and the introduction of catalytic converters to automobile exhaust systems, a change was mandated. The automobile exhaust system, when equipped with a catalytic converter, changes the sulfur dioxide (SO_2) into sulfur trioxide (SO_3).

When this combines with water vapors (H_2O), a sulfuric acid mist (H_2SO_4) is formed and is a very difficult pollutant to handle since it is extremely corrosive. This sulfuric acid mist that is formed, is the same mist that rises from the vents of an automobile battery when an active chemical reaction takes place within the battery cells.

When a large concentration of vehicles equipped with catalytic converters are operating in an area, this acid mist may rise and be distributed over a large ground area causing land, plant, crop, paint and building damage.

PARTICULATE MATTER

A certain amount of particulate matter is present in the burning of any fuel, with carbon constituting the largest percentage of the particulates. In gasoline, the remaining particulates are the burned remains of the various other compounds used in its manufacture. When a gasoline engine is in good internal condition, the particulate emissions are low but as the engine wears internally, the particulate emissions increase. By visually inspecting the tail pipe emissions, a determination can be made as to where an engine defect may exist. An engine with light gray or blue smoke emitting from the tail pipe normally indicates an increase in the oil consumption through burning due to internal engine wear. Black smoke would indicate a defective fuel delivery system, causing the engine to operate in a rich mode. Regardless of the color of the smoke, the internal part of the engine or the fuel delivery system should be repaired to prevent excess particulate emissions.

Diesel and turbine engines emit a darkened plume of smoke from the exhaust system because of the type of fuel used. Emission control regulations are mandated for this type of emission and more stringent measures are being used to prevent excess emission of the particulate matter. Electronic components are being introduced to control the injection of the fuel at precisely the proper time of piston travel, to achieve the optimum in fuel ignition and fuel usage. Other particulate after-burning components are being tested to achieve a cleaner emission.

Good grades of engine lubricating oils should be used, which meet the manufacturer's specification. Cut-rate oils can contribute to the particulate emission problem because of their low flash or ignition temperature point. Such oils burn prematurely during the combustion process causing emission of particulate matter.

The cooling system is an important factor in the reduction of particulate matter. The optimum combustion will occur, with the cooling system operating at a temperature specified by the manufacturer. The cooling system must be maintained in the same manner as the engine oiling system, as each system is required to perform properly in order for the engine to operate efficiently for a long time.

Crankcase Emissions

Crankcase emissions are made up of water, acids, unburned fuel, oil fumes and particulates. These emissions are classified as hydrocarbons (HC) and are formed by the small amount of unburned, compressed air/fuel mixture entering the crankcase from the combustion area (between the cylinder walls and piston rings) during the compression and power strokes. The head of the compression and combustion help to form the remaining crankcase emissions.

Since the first engines, crankcase emissions were allowed into the atmosphere through a road draft tube, mounted on the lower side of the engine block. Fresh air came in through an open oil filler cap or breather. The air passed through the crankcase mixing with blow-by gases. The motion of the vehicle and the air blowing past the open end of the road draft tube caused a low pressure area (vacuum) at the end of the tube. Crankcase emissions were simply drawn out of the road draft tube into the air.

To control the crankcase emission, the road draft tube was deleted. A hose and/or tubing was routed from the crankcase to the intake manifold so the blow-by emission could be burned with the air/fuel mixture. However, it was found that intake manifold vacuum, used to draw the crankcase emissions into the manifold, would vary in strength at the wrong time and not allow the proper emission flow. A regulating valve was needed to control the flow of air through the crankcase.

Testing, showed the removal of the blow-by gases from the crankcase as quickly as possible, was most important to the longevity of the engine. Should large accumulations of blow-by gases remain and condense, dilution of the engine oil would occur to form water, soots, resins, acids and lead salts, resulting in the formation of sludge and varnishes. This condensation of the blow-by gases occurs more frequently on vehicles used in numerous starting and stopping conditions, excessive idling and when the engine is not allowed to attain normal operating temperature through short runs.

Evaporative Emissions

Gasoline fuel is a major source of pollution, before and after it is burned in the automobile engine. From the time the fuel is refined, stored, pumped and transported, again stored until it is pumped into the fuel tank of the vehicle, the gasoline gives off unburned hydrocarbons (HC) into the atmosphere. Through the redesign of storage areas and venting systems, the pollution factor was diminished, but not eliminated, from the refinery standpoint. However, the automobile still remained the primary source of vaporized, unburned hydrocarbon (HC) emissions.

Fuel pumped from an underground storage tank is cool but when exposed to a warmer ambient temperature, will expand. Before controls were mandated, an owner might fill the fuel tank with fuel from an underground storage tank and park the vehicle for some time in warm area, such as a parking lot. As the fuel would warm, it would expand and should no provisions or area be provided for the expansion, the fuel would spill out of the filler neck and onto the ground, causing hydrocarbon (HC) pollution and creating a severe fire hazard. To correct this condition, the vehicle manufacturers added overflow plumbing and/or gasoline tanks with built in expansion areas or domes.

However, this did not control the fuel vapor emission from the fuel tank. It was determined that most of the fuel evaporation occurred when the vehicle was stationary and the engine not operating. Most vehicles carry 5–25 gallons (19–95 liters) of gasoline. Should a large concentration of vehicles be parked in one area, such as a large parking lot, excessive fuel vapor emissions would take place, increasing as the temperature increases.

To prevent the vapor emission from escaping into the atmosphere, the fuel systems were designed to trap the vapors while the vehicle is stationary, by sealing the system from the atmosphere. A storage system is used to collect and hold the fuel vapors from the carburetor (if equipped) and the fuel tank when the engine is not operating. When the engine is started, the storage system is then purged of the fuel vapors, which are drawn into the engine and burned with the air/fuel mixture.

EMISSION CONTROLS

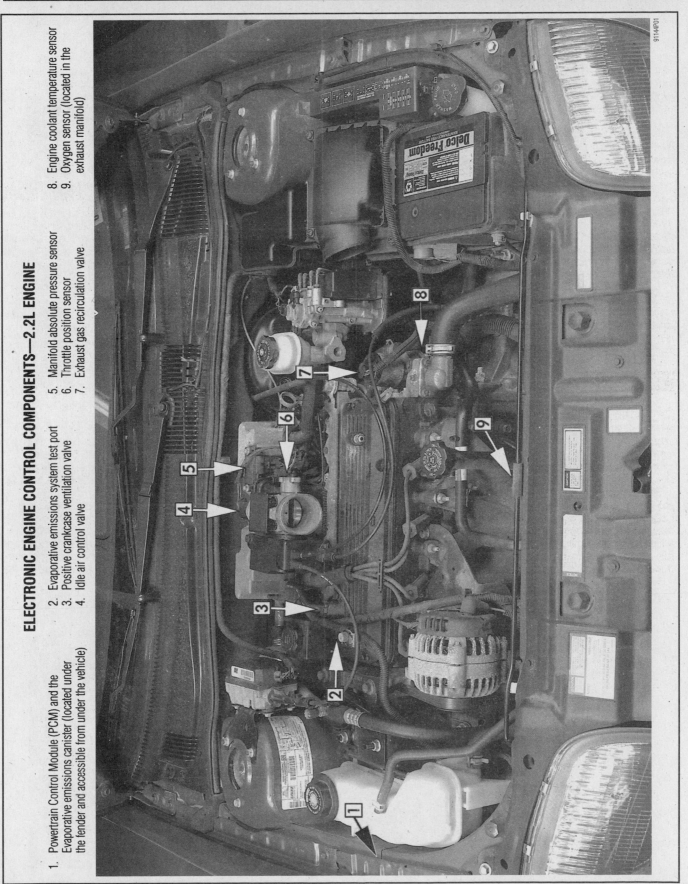

ELECTRONIC ENGINE CONTROL COMPONENTS—2.2L ENGINE

1. Powertrain Control Module (PCM) and the Evaporative emissions canister (located under the fender and accessible from under the vehicle)
2. Evaporative emissions system test port
3. Positive crankcase ventilation valve
4. Idle air control valve
5. Manifold absolute pressure sensor
6. Throttle position sensor
7. Exhaust gas recirculation valve
8. Engine coolant temperature sensor
9. Oxygen sensor (located in the exhaust manifold)

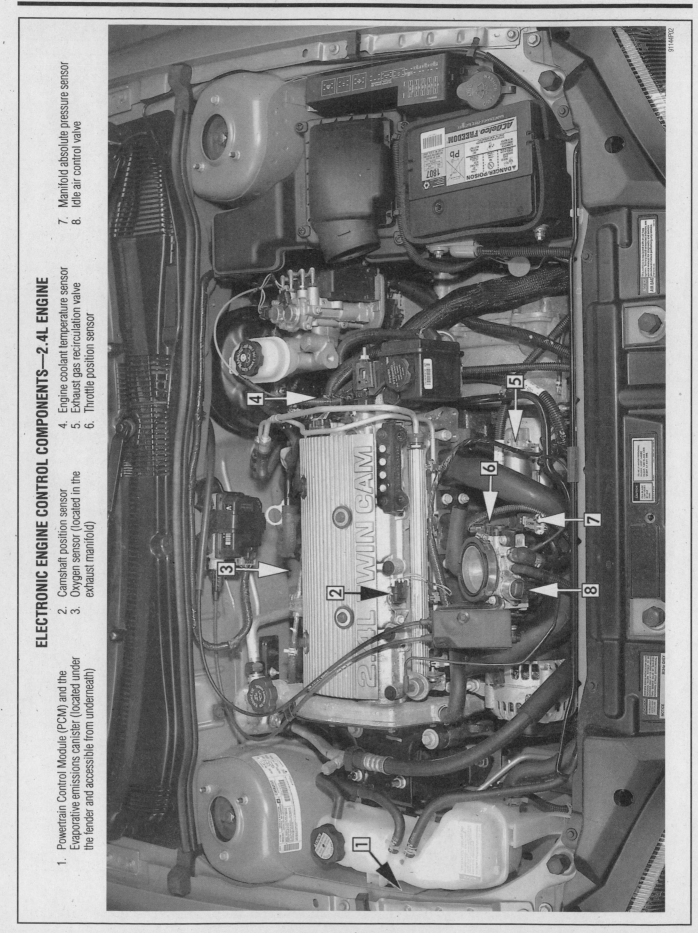

ELECTRONIC ENGINE CONTROL COMPONENTS—2.4L ENGINE

1. Powertrain Control Module (PCM) and the Evaporative emissions canister (located under the fender and accessible from underneath)
2. Camshaft position sensor
3. Oxygen sensor (located in the exhaust manifold)
4. Engine coolant temperature sensor
5. Exhaust gas recirculation valve
6. Throttle position sensor
7. Manifold absolute pressure sensor
8. Idle air control valve

Crankcase Ventilation System

OPERATION

▶ **See Figures 1, 2 and 3**

A crankcase ventilation system is used on all vehicles to evacuate the crankcase vapors. There are 2 types of ventilation systems: Crankcase Ventilation (CV) and Positive Crankcase Ventilation (PCV). Both systems purge crankcase vapors and differ only in the use of fresh air.

The CV system, used on the 2.3L and 2.4L engines, allows crankcase vapors to escape but does not introduce fresh air into the crankcase. The blow-by vapors are drawn into the oil/air separator through a hose from the timing chain housing. Crankcase vapors are passed through the oil/air separator into the air cleaner outlet resonator. The oil/air separator is attached to the engine block and returns any oil suspended in the blow-by vapors to the crankcase. These blow-by gases will then be mixed with the intake air in the air cleaner outlet resonator instead of the manifold. The blow-by vapors are then drawn into the engine by normal engine vacuum and burned by the combustion process.

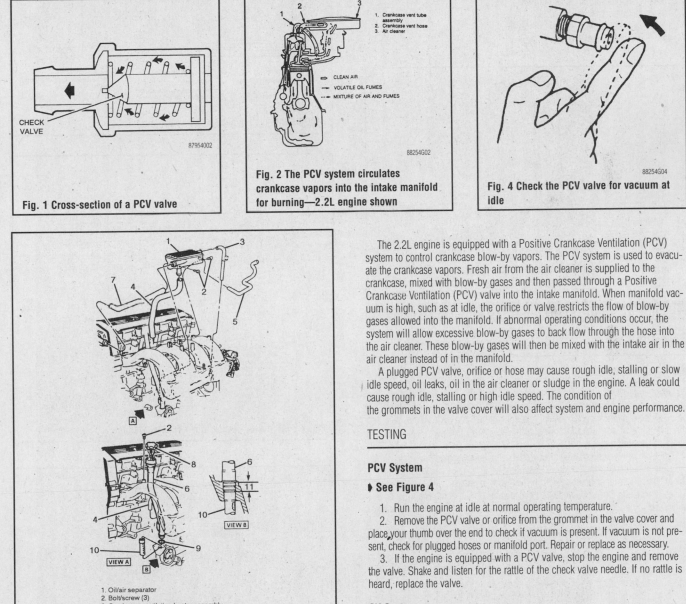

Fig. 1 Cross-section of a PCV valve

Fig. 2 The PCV system circulates crankcase vapors into the intake manifold for burning—2.2L engine shown

Fig. 4 Check the PCV valve for vacuum at idle

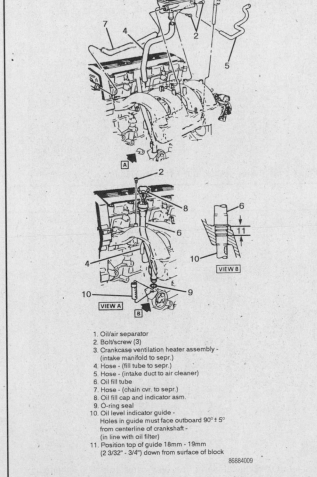

1. Oil/air separator
2. Bolt/screw (3)
3. Crankcase ventilation heater assembly - (intake manifold to sepr.)
4. Hose - (fill tube to sepr.)
5. Hose - (intake duct to air cleaner)
6. Oil fill tube
7. Hose - (chain cvr. to sepr.)
8. Oil fill cap and indicator asm.
9. O-ring seal
10. Oil level indicator guide -
    Holes in guide must face outboard 90° ± 5° from centerline of crankshaft - (in line with oil filter)
11. Position top of guide 18mm - 19mm (2 3/32" - 3/4") down from surface of block

86884009

Fig. 3 The CV system does not use a PCV valve—2.3L engine shown

The 2.2L engine is equipped with a Positive Crankcase Ventilation (PCV) system to control crankcase blow-by vapors. The PCV system is used to evacuate the crankcase vapors. Fresh air from the air cleaner is supplied to the crankcase, mixed with blow-by gases and then passed through a Positive Crankcase Ventilation (PCV) valve into the intake manifold. When manifold vacuum is high, such as at idle, the orifice or valve restricts the flow of blow-by gases allowed into the manifold. If abnormal operating conditions occur, the system will allow excessive blow-by gases to back flow through the hose into the air cleaner. These blow-by gases will then be mixed with the intake air in the air cleaner instead of in the manifold.

A plugged PCV valve, orifice or hose may cause rough idle, stalling or slow idle speed, oil leaks, oil in the air cleaner or sludge in the engine. A leak could cause rough idle, stalling or high idle speed. The condition of the grommets in the valve cover will also affect system and engine performance.

TESTING

PCV System

▶ **See Figure 4**

1. Run the engine at idle at normal operating temperature.
2. Remove the PCV valve or orifice from the grommet in the valve cover and place your thumb over the end to check if vacuum is present. If vacuum is not present, check for plugged hoses or manifold port. Repair or replace as necessary.
3. If the engine is equipped with a PCV valve, stop the engine and remove the valve. Shake and listen for the rattle of the check valve needle. If no rattle is heard, replace the valve.

CV System

1. Check the CV system for proper flow by looking for oil sludging or leaks.
2. If noted, check the smaller nipple of the oil/air separator by blowing through it or inserting a 0.06 in. (1.52mm) plug gauge into the orifice inside the nipple.
3. If the orifice is plugged, replace the CV oil/air separator assembly.

REMOVAL & INSTALLATION

PCV Valve (2.2L Engine Only)

Removal and installation of the PCV valve refer to Section 1 of this manual.

Oil/Air Separator (2.3L/2.4L Engines Only)

▶ See Figures 4 and 5

1. Disconnect the negative battery cable.
2. Remove the air cleaner outlet resonator.
3. Remove the intake manifold. Refer to Section 3.
4. Label and disconnect the oil/air separator hoses.
5. Remove the oil/air separator mounting bolts.
6. Remove the oil/air separator.

To install:

7. Install the oil/air separator.
8. Tighten the oil/air separator mounting bolts to 15–18 ft. lbs. (20–28 Nm).
9. Connect the oil/air separator hoses.
10. Install the intake manifold.
11. Install the air cleaner outlet resonator.
12. Connect the negative battery cable.

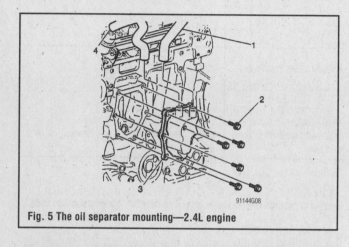

Fig. 5 The oil separator mounting—2.4L engine

Evaporative Emission Control System

OPERATION

▶ See Figures 6, 7 and 8

Changes in atmospheric temperature cause fuel tanks to breathe, that is, the air within the tank expands and contracts with outside temperature changes. If an unsealed system was used, when the temperature rises, air would escape through the tank vent tube or the vent in the tank cap. The air which escapes contains gasoline vapors.

The Evaporative Emission Control System provides a sealed fuel system with the capability to store and condense fuel vapors. When the fuel evaporates in the fuel tank, the vapor passes through the pressure control valve, through vent hoses or tubes to a carbon filled evaporative canister. When the engine is operating, and at normal operating temperature, the vapors are drawn into the intake manifold and burned during combustion..

A sealed, maintenance free evaporative canister is used. The canister is filled with granules of an activated carbon mixture. Fuel vapors entering the canister are absorbed by the charcoal granules. A vent cap is located on the top of the canister to provide fresh air to the canister when it is being purged. The vent cap opens to provide fresh air into the canister, which circulates through the charcoal, releasing trapped vapors and carrying them to the engine to be burned.

Fuel tank pressure vents fuel vapors into the canister. They are held in the canister until they can be drawn into the intake manifold. The canister purge valve allows the canister to be purged at a pre-determined time and engine operating conditions.

Vacuum to the canister is controlled by the canister purge valve. The valve is operated by the PCM. The PCM regulates the valve by switching the ground circuit on and off based on engine operating conditions. When energized, the valve prevents vacuum from reaching the canister. When not energized the valve allows vacuum to purge the vapors from the canister.

During warm up and for a specified time after hot starts, the PCM energizes (grounds) the valve preventing vacuum from reaching the canister.

When the engine temperature reaches the operating level of about 120°F (49°C), the PCM removes the ground from the valve allowing vacuum to flow through the canister and purges vapors through the throttle body. During certain idle conditions, the purge valve may be grounded to control fuel mixture calibrations.

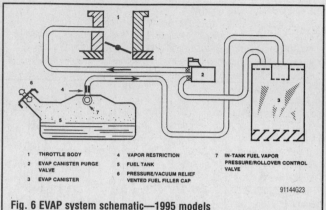

1	THROTTLE BODY	4	VAPOR RESTRICTION	7	IN-TANK FUEL VAPOR
2	EVAP CANISTER PURGE VALVE	5	FUEL TANK		PRESSURE/ROLLOVER CONTROL VALVE
3	EVAP CANISTER	6	PRESSURE/VACUUM RELIEF VENTED FUEL FILLER CAP		

Fig. 6 EVAP system schematic—1995 models

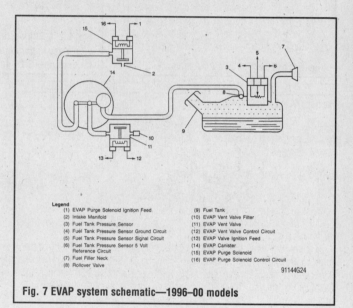

Legend
(1) EVAP Purge Solenoid Ignition Feed
(2) Intake Manifold
(3) Fuel Tank Pressure Sensor
(4) Fuel Tank Pressure Sensor Ground Circuit
(5) Fuel Tank Pressure Sensor Signal Circuit
(6) Fuel Tank Pressure Sensor 5 Volt Reference Circuit
(7) Fuel Filler Neck
(8) Rollover Valve

(9) Fuel Tank
(10) EVAP Vent Valve Filter
(11) EVAP Vent Valve
(12) EVAP Vent Valve Control Circuit
(13) EVAP Valve Ignition Feed
(14) EVAP Canister
(15) EVAP Purge Solenoid
(16) EVAP Purge Solenoid Control Circuit

Fig. 7 EVAP system schematic—1996–00 models

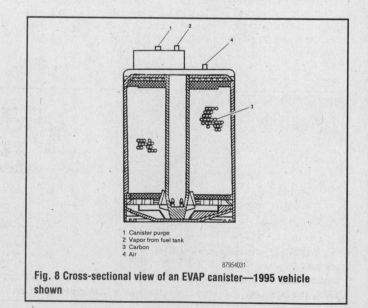

1 Canister purge
2 Vapor from fuel tank
3 Carbon
4 Air

Fig. 8 Cross-sectional view of an EVAP canister—1995 vehicle shown

The fuel tank is sealed with a pressure-vacuum relief filler cap. The relief valve in the cap is a safety feature, preventing excessive pressure or vacuum in the fuel tank. If the cap is malfunctioning, and needs to be replaced, ensure that the replacement is the identical cap to ensure correct system operation.

OBD-II EVAP System Monitor

▶ See Figure 9

1996–00 models have added system components due to the EVAP system monitor incorporated in the OBD-II engine control system. A pressure sensor is mounted on the fuel tank which measures pressure inside the tank, and a purge flow sensor measures the flow of the gases from the canister into the engine. The vent valve for the canister is now controlled by the PCM. It performs the same functions as the purge valve, however it looks slightly different. A canister vent solenoid is mounted on the canister, taking the place of the vent cap, providing a source of fresh air to the canister.

The PCM can store trouble codes for EVAP system performance, a list of the codes is provided later in this section. Normal testing procedure can be used, see EVAP System Component Testing in this Section.

As part of the OBD-II diagnostic system, a test port is installed in the purge line connecting the purge solenoid to the canister. This test port is used to connect a special tester that pressurizes the EVAP system and measure the leakage rate. This tool is very expensive and requires training to operate or you could do damage to the vehicle, however, many professional shops have this device. If you suspect a leak in your EVAP system, you may want to consult a professional shop about performing this test on your car.

TESTING

Evaporative Emissions Canister

Generally, the only testing done to the canister is a visual inspection. Look the canister over and replace it with a new one if there is any evidence of cracks or other damage.

Canister Purge Control Valve

1. Connect a clean length of hose to the fuel tank vapor line connection on the canister and attempt to blow through the purge control valve. It should be difficult or impossible to blow through the purge control valve. If air passes easily, the valve is stuck open and should be replaced.

2. Connect a hand-held vacuum pump to the top vacuum line fitting of the purge control valve. Apply a vacuum of 15 in. Hg (51 kPa) to the purge valve diaphragm. If the diaphragm does not hold vacuum for at least 20 seconds, the diaphragm is leaking. Replace the control valve. If it is impossible to blow through the valve, it is stuck closed and must be replaced.

3. On vehicles with a solenoid activated purge control valve, unplug the connector and use jumper wires to supply 12 volts to the solenoid connections on the valve. With the vacuum still applied to the control vacuum tube, the purge control valve should open and it should be easy to blow through. If not, replace the valve.

Tank Pressure Control Valve

▶ See Figure 10

1. Using a hand-held vacuum pump, apply a vacuum of 15 in. Hg (51 kPa) through the control vacuum signal tube to the purge valve diaphragm. If the diaphragm does not hold vacuum for at least 20 seconds, the diaphragm is leaking. Replace the control valve.

2. With the vacuum still applied to the control vacuum tube, attach a short piece of hose to the valve's tank tube side and blow into the hose. Air should pass through the valve. If it does not, replace the control valve.

Tank Pressure Sensor (1996–00 Models Only)

The fuel tank pressure sensor is tested using the GM Tech-1A® scan tool or equivalent. The sensor must be monitored and compared with pressure values using the EVAP system test port and the pressure tester. Follow the instructions included with the scan tool and/or use the guided diagnostics on the scan tool.

REMOVAL & INSTALLATION

Evaporative Emissions Canister

▶ See Figures 11 thru 16

1. Disconnect the negative battery cable.
2. Raise and safely support the vehicle securely on jackstands.
3. Remove the passenger side wheel well splash shield.
4. Tag and disconnect the hoses from the canister.
5. Remove the retaining bolt from the EVAP canister bracket and slide the canister up and to the right to release the retaining tab.
6. Remove the canister from the vehicle.

➡Always replace any vapor hose(s) that may be showing signs of wear.

7. Installation is the reverse of the removal procedure. Tighten the canister bracket retaining bolt to 6–9 ft. lbs. (8–12 Nm). Refer to the Vehicle Emission Control Information label, located in the engine compartment, for proper routing of the vacuum hoses.

Canister Purge Control Solenoid Valve

1995–97 2.2L ENGINE

▶ See Figure 17

1. Disconnect the negative battery cable.
2. Raise and safely support the vehicle securely on jackstands.

➡The EVAP canister purge solenoid is located under the intake manifold and to the right and slightly above the ignition coils. It is accessible from underneath the vehicle.

3. Tag and detach the electrical connector from the solenoid valve.
4. Remove the hoses from the purge solenoid.
5. Remove the purge solenoid from the mounting bracket.

Fig. 9 1996 and later vehicles with OBD-II are outfitted with a test port to connect a pressure tester to measure leakage in the EVAP system

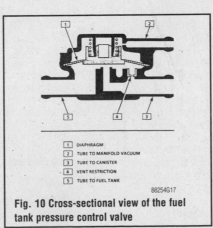

1	DIAPHRAGM
2	TUBE TO MANIFOLD VACUUM
3	TUBE TO CANISTER
4	VENT RESTRICTION
5	TUBE TO FUEL TANK

Fig. 10 Cross-sectional view of the fuel tank pressure control valve

Fig. 11 Remove the retaining bolts for the splash shield and . . .

Fig. 12 . . . remove the splash shield

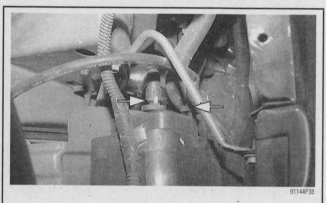

Fig. 13 Remove the EVAP lines from the canister

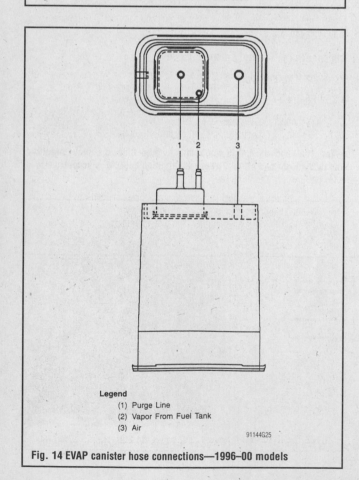

Legend
(1) Purge Line
(2) Vapor From Fuel Tank
(3) Air

91144G25

Fig. 14 EVAP canister hose connections—1996–00 models

6. If the solenoid mounting bracket needs to be removed, remove the retaining nut and remove the bracket.
7. Installation is the reverse of the removal procedure.

1998–00 2.2L ENGINE AND 2.3L/2.4L ENGINE

▶ See Figures 18 and 19

➡The purge solenoid is located on the valve cover on the 1998–00 2.2L engine and on the intake manifold, just above the A/C compressor on the 2.3L/2.4L engines.

1. Disconnect the negative battery cable.
2. Detach the electrical connector from the solenoid valve.
3. Remove the hoses from the purge solenoid.
4. Remove the purge solenoid from the mounting bracket.
5. If the solenoid mounting bracket needs to be removed, remove the retaining nut and remove the bracket.
6. Installation is the reverse of the removal procedure.

Tank Pressure Control Valve

1. Tag and disconnect the hoses from the control valve.
2. Unfasten the mounting hardware.
3. Remove the control valve from the vehicle.
4. Installation is the reverse of the removal procedure. Refer to the Vehicle Emission Control Information label, located in the engine compartment, for proper routing of the vacuum hoses.

Tank Pressure Sensor (1996–00 Models Only)

1. Disconnect the negative battery cable.
2. Raise and safely support the vehicle securely on jackstands.
3. Remove the fuel tank assembly. Refer to Section 5.
4. Release the retaining clip and remove the sensor from the tank.
To install:
5. Install the sensor into the tank and attach the retaining clip.
6. Install the fuel tank assembly.
7. Lower the vehicle.
8. Connect the negative battery cable.

Vacuum Vent Valve (1996–00 Models Only)

1. Disconnect the negative battery cable.
2. Raise and safely support the vehicle securely on jackstands.
3. Remove the passenger side wheel well splash shield.
4. Tag and disconnect the hose from the vent valve.
5. Remove the vent valve from the mounting bracket.
6. Installation is the reverse of removal.

Exhaust Gas Recirculation (EGR) System

OPERATION

▶ See Figure 20

➡The 2.3L engine does not use an EGR valve.

The Exhaust Gas Recirculation (EGR) system is designed to reintroduce exhaust gas into the combustion chambers, thereby lowering combustion temperatures and reducing the formation of Oxides of Nitrogen (NO_x).

The amount of exhaust gas that is reintroduced into the combustion cycle is determined by several factors, such as: engine speed, engine vacuum, exhaust system backpressure, coolant temperature, throttle position. All EGR valves are vacuum operated. There are two types of EGR valves used on the 1995–00 GM J-body vehicles. The EGR vacuum diagram for your particular vehicle is displayed on the Vehicle Emission Control Information (VECI) label.

Negative Backpressure EGR Valve

▶ See Figure 21

The negative backpressure EGR valve, used on the 1995 2.2L engine, varies the amount of exhaust gas flow into the intake manifold depending on manifold

Fig. 15 Remove the retaining bolt from the canister bracket and . . .

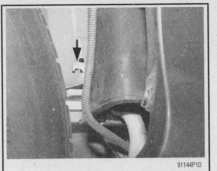

Fig. 16 . . . slide the canister up and to the right to release the retaining tab and remove the canister

Fig. 17 The EVAP canister purge solenoid is located under the intake manifold—2.2L engine

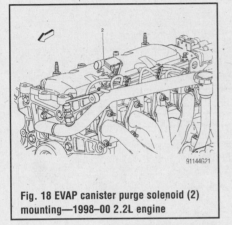

Fig. 18 EVAP canister purge solenoid (2) mounting—1998–00 2.2L engine

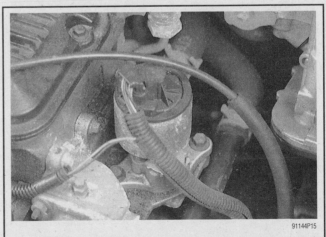

Fig. 19 EVAP canister purge solenoid mounting—2.3L/2.4L engines

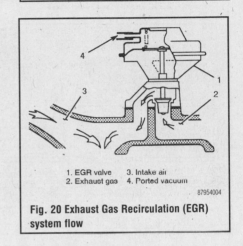

1. EGR valve
2. Exhaust gas
3. Intake air
4. Ported vacuum

Fig. 20 Exhaust Gas Recirculation (EGR) system flow

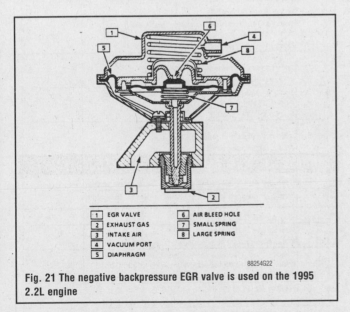

1	EGR VALVE	6	AIR BLEED HOLE
2	EXHAUST GAS	7	SMALL SPRING
3	INTAKE AIR	8	LARGE SPRING
4	VACUUM PORT		
5	DIAPHRAGM		

Fig. 21 The negative backpressure EGR valve is used on the 1995 2.2L engine

Linear EGR Valve (1996–00 2.2L And 2.4L Engines)

♦ See Figure 22

The linear EGR valve, used on the 1996–00 2.2L and 2.4L engines, is designed to accurately apply EGR to an engine, independent of intake manifold vacuum. The valve controls EGR flow from the exhaust to the intake manifold through an orifice with a PCM controlled pintle. During operation, the PCM controls pintle position by monitoring the pintle position feedback signal. The PCM uses information from the Engine Coolant Temperature (ECT) sensor, Throttle Position (TP) sensor and the Mass Air Flow (MAF) sensor to determine the appropriate rate of flow for a particular engine operating condition.

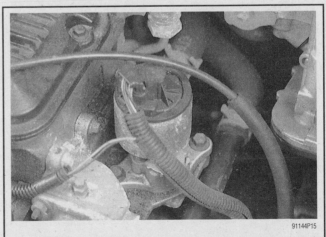

Fig. 22 The linear EGR valve equipped on the 2.2L and 2.4L engines

vacuum and variations in exhaust backpressure. An air bleed valve, located inside the EGR valve assembly acts as a vacuum regulator. The bleed valve controls the amount of vacuum in the vacuum chamber by bleeding vacuum to outside air during the open phase of the cycle. The diaphragm on the valve has an internal air bleed hole which is held closed by a small spring when there is no exhaust backpressure. Engine vacuum opens the EGR valve against the pressure of a spring. When manifold vacuum combines with negative exhaust backpressure, the vacuum bleed hole opens and the EGR valve closes. This valve will open if vacuum is applied with the engine not running.

TESTING

Negative Backpressure EGR Valve (1995 Vehicles With 2.2L Engine Only)

▶ **See Figures 23 and 24**

Refer to the appropriate diagnostic charts.

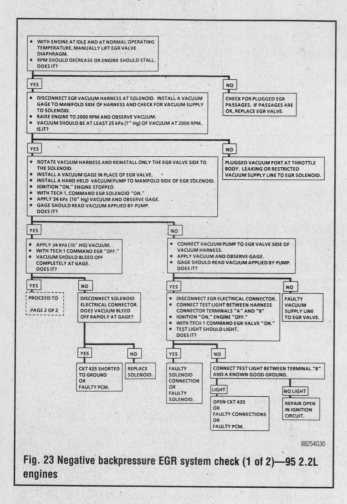

Fig. 23 Negative backpressure EGR system check (1 of 2)—95 2.2L engines

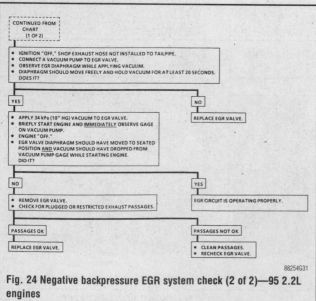

Fig. 24 Negative backpressure EGR system check (2 of 2)—95 2.2L engines

Linear EGR Valve (1996–00 2.2L And 2.4L Engines)

▶ **See Figures 25 and 26**

Refer to the appropriate diagnostic charts.

Step	Action	Value(s)
1	Was the Powertrain On-Board Diagnostic (OBD) System Check performed?	—
2	1. Turn the ignition Switch ON, with the engine OFF. 2. Install a scan tool. 3. Command the EGR valve to the specified values. Does the *Actual EGR Position* follow the *Desired EGR Position*?	25%, 50%, 75%, 100%
3	1. Turn the ignition Switch ON, with the engine OFF. 2. Disconnect the EGR valve electrical connector. 3. With a test light connected to ground, probe the ignition feed circuit to the EGR valve. Does the test light illuminate?	—

91144G06

Fig. 25 Linear EGR valve diagnostic chart (1 of 2)

Step	Action	Value(s)
4	1. Connect the test light to B+. 2. Probe the EGR control circuit to the EGR valve. 3. Command the EGR valve to the specified values. As the commanded percentage is raised, does the test light: • Maintain a steady glow • Flash • Glow dimly and grow brighter?	25%, 50%, 75%, 100%
5	Repair open in the EGR valve ignition feed circuit. Is the action complete?	—
6	Using a DVM connected to ground, probe the 5 volt reference circuit to the EGR valve. Does the DVM read the specified value?	5.0V
7	Check for an open or a short in the EGR control circuit and repair as necessary. Was a repair necessary?	—
8	Using a DVM connected to B+, probe the EGR valve sensor ground circuit. Does the DVM read the specified value?	B+
9	Check for an open or a short in the EGR valve 5 volt reference circuit and repair as necessary. Was a repair necessary?	—
10	Jumper the EGR valve 5 volt reference circuit to the signal circuit. Does the *Actual EGR Position* display the specified value?	90–100%
11	Check for an open in the EGR valve sensor ground circuit and repair as necessary. Was a repair necessary?	—
12	Replace the EGR valve. Is the action complete?	—
13	Check for an open or a short in the EGR valve signal circuit and repair as necessary. Was a repair necessary?	—
14	Replace the PCM. Is the action complete?	—
15	1. Using the scan tool, clear the DTC's. 2. Start the engine and idle at normal operating temperature. 3. Operate the vehicle within the conditions for setting this DTC as specified in the supporting text. Does the scan tool indicate that this diagnostic has ran and passed?	—
16	Check if any additional DTC's are set. Are any DTC's displayed that have not been diagnosed?	—

91144G07

Fig. 26 Linear EGR valve diagnostic chart (2 of 2)

REMOVAL & INSTALLATION

EGR Valve

▶ **See Figures 21 and 27 thru 32**

1. Disconnect the negative battery cable.
2. Remove the air cleaner outlet tube.
3. Detach the EGR valve connector.
4. Remove the two bolts and remove the EGR valve.
5. Thoroughly clean the EGR mounting surface.

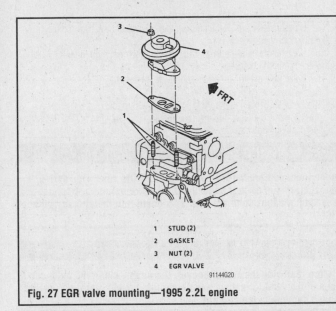

1	STUD (2)
2	GASKET
3	NUT (2)
4	EGR VALVE

91144G20

Fig. 27 EGR valve mounting—1995 2.2L engine

To install:

6. Install a new gasket and position the EGR valve onto the engine.
7. Tighten the two EGR valve retaining bolts to 16–22 ft. lbs. (22–30 Nm).
8. Attach the EGR valve connector.
9. Install the air cleaner outlet tube.
10. Connect the negative battery cable.

EGR Control Solenoid (1995 Vehicles With 2.2L Engine Only)

▶ **See Figure 33**

1. Disconnect the negative battery cable.
2. Remove the MAP sensor, as outlined in this section.
3. Detach the electrical connector from the solenoid.
4. Tag and disconnect the vacuum hoses.
5. Unfasten the retaining screw, then remove the EGR solenoid.

To install:

6. Install the solenoid and bracket and tighten the screw to 17 ft. lbs. (24 Nm) for 1992 vehicles or to 22 ft. lbs. (30 Nm) for 1993–95 vehicles. Do NOT overtighten the retainers.
7. Connect the vacuum hoses, as tagged during removal.
8. Attach the electrical connector to the solenoid.
9. Install the seal on the MAP sensor, then install the MAP sensor and tighten the screws to 27 inch lbs. (3 Nm).
10. Connect the negative battery cable.

Catalytic Converter

OPERATION

All engines covered by this manual are equipped with a catalytic converter in order to reduce tail pipe emissions. The catalytic converter is mounted in the engine exhaust stream ahead of the muffler. Its function is to combine carbon monoxide (CO) and hydrocarbons (HC) with oxygen and break down nitrogen

91144P34

Fig. 28 Detach the connector on the EGR valve

91144P35

Fig. 29 Remove the two EGR valve retaining bolts and . . .

91144P40

Fig. 30 . . . remove the EGR valve from the engine

91144P41

Fig. 31 The EGR valve has a gasket, always replace the gasket even if you are using the old EGR valve

91144P42

Fig. 32 Thoroughly clean the EGR valve mounting surface

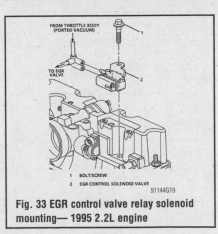

91144G19

Fig. 33 EGR control valve relay solenoid mounting— 1995 2.2L engine

oxide (NOx) compounds. These gasses are converted to mostly CO_2 and water. It heats to operating temperature within about 1–2 minutes, depending on ambient temperature and driving conditions and will operate at temperatures up to about 1500°F (816 °C). Inside the converter housing is a single or dual bed ceramic monolith, coated with various combinations of platinum, palladium and rhodium.

The catalytic converter is not serviceable. If tests and visual inspection show the converter to be damaged, it must be replaced. There are 2 types of failures:

melting or fracturing. The most common failure is melting, resulting from unburned gasoline contacting the monolith, such as when a cylinder does not fire. Usually when the monolith melts, high backpressure results. When it cracks, it begins to break up into small particles that get blown out the tail pipe.

Poor fuel mileage and/or a lack of power can often be traced to a melted or plugged catalytic converter. The damage may be the result of engine malfunction or the use of leaded gasoline in the vehicle. Proper diagnosis for a restricted exhaust system is essential before any components are replaced.

ELECTRONIC ENGINE CONTROLS

Powertrain Control Module (PCM)

OPERATION

The Powertrain Control Module (PCM) performs many functions on your vehicle. The module accepts information from various engine sensors and computes the required fuel flow rate necessary to maintain the correct amount of air/fuel ratio throughout the entire engine operational range.

Based on the information that is received and programmed into the PCM's memory, the PCM generates output signals to control relays, actuators and solenoids. The PCM also sends out a command to the fuel injectors that meters the appropriate quantity of fuel. The module automatically senses and compensates for any changes in altitude when driving your vehicle.

REMOVAL & INSTALLATION

▶ See Figures 34 thru 41

1. Turn the ignition switch **OFF**.
2. Disconnect the negative battery cable.

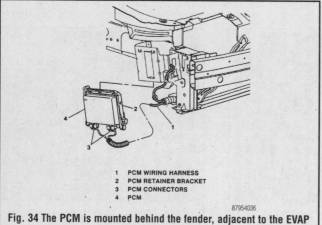

1	PCM WIRING HARNESS
2	PCM RETAINER BRACKET
3	PCM CONNECTORS
4	PCM

87954036

Fig. 34 The PCM is mounted behind the fender, adjacent to the EVAP canister

3. Remove the right hand engine splash shield.
4. Unfasten the horn attaching bolt, then detach the electrical connector and remove the horn.
5. Unfasten the module-to-bracket retaining screws, then slide the PCM out of the mounting bracket.
6. Detach the electrical harness connectors from the PCM.
7. Remove the retainer from the PCM.
8. If you are replacing the PCM on a 1995–96 model:
   a. Remove the Electronic Programmable Read Only Memory (EPROM) module, also known as the KS module, cover.

✳✳ WARNING

If the foam pad around the base of the EPROM cover rips during removal, this is normal and should not be remedied by applying any kind of adhesive to the pad. This could ruin the circuitry of the PCM.

✳✳ WARNING

Before removing the EPROM cover, thoroughly clean the outer surface of the PCM to remove any debris that could enter the PCM and cause damage to the circuitry.

✳✳ WARNING

To prevent a possible discharge of static electricity, which could ruin the PCM, do not touch the connector pins or the soldered components on the circuit board.

   b. Remove the KS module by squeezing both retaining clips together and at the same time, grasp it at both ends and lift it up out of the socket.
   To install:

➡ **Before replacement of a defective computer control module, first check the resistance of each PCM controlled solenoid.**

9. If the PCM is being replaced, open the package on the new PCM and verify that the PCM numbers match or an updated number is given before you attempt installation.
10. If you have a 1995–96 model:

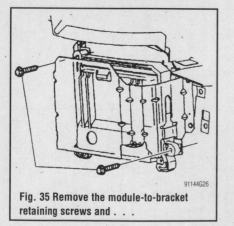

91144G26

Fig. 35 Remove the module-to-bracket retaining screws and . . .

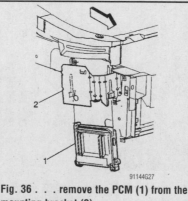

91144G27

Fig. 36 . . . remove the PCM (1) from the mounting bracket (2)

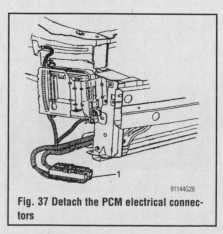

91144G28

Fig. 37 Detach the PCM electrical connectors

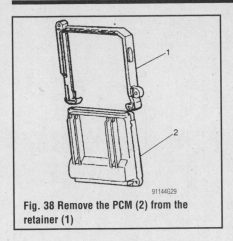

Fig. 38 Remove the PCM (2) from the retainer (1)

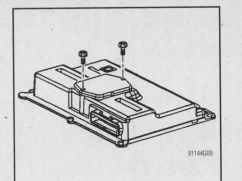

Fig. 39 The EPROM cover is retained by two screws

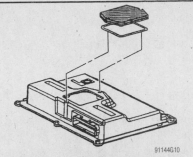

Fig. 40 Remove the EPROM cover, if the seal tears, this is normal, do not apply an adhesive to the pad, the adhesive could drip onto the circuitry and ruin the PCM

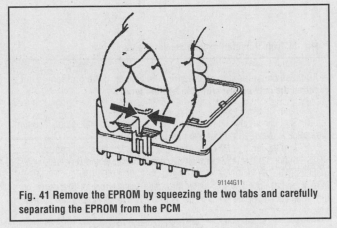

Fig. 41 Remove the EPROM by squeezing the two tabs and carefully separating the EPROM from the PCM

Fig. 42 Front O2 sensor mounting—2.4L engine

a. Install the EPROM into the PCM.

b. Install the EPROM cover and tighten the retaining screws to 25–28 inch lbs. (3 Nm).

11. Install the PCM retainer.

12. Attach the module electrical harness connectors.

13. Position the PCM in the vehicle, then install the module-to-bracket retaining screws.

14. Install the horn, attach the electrical connector, then fasten with the horn attaching bolt. Tighten the bolt to 6–9 ft. lbs. (8–12 Nm).

15. Install the right hand splash shield.

16. Check that the ignition switch is **OFF**, then connect the negative battery cable.

17. Enter the self-diagnostic system and check for trouble codes to be sure the PCM and the KS module are properly installed. For details, refer to the procedure for checking trouble codes.

Oxygen Sensor

OPERATION

▶ See Figure 42

There are two types of oxygen sensor's used in these vehicles. They are the single wire oxygen sensor (02S) and the heated oxygen sensor (H02S). The oxygen sensor (O2) is a device which produces an electrical voltage when exposed to the oxygen present in the exhaust gases. The sensor is mounted in the exhaust system, usually in the manifold or a boss located on the down pipe before the catalyst.. Some of the oxygen sensors used on the GM J-body are electrically heated internally for faster switching when the engine is started cold. The oxygen sensor produces a voltage within 0 and 1 volt. When there is a large amount of oxygen present (lean mixture), the sensor produces a low voltage (less than 0.4v). When there is a lesser amount present (rich mixture) it produces a higher voltage (0.6–1.0v).The stoichiometric or correct fuel to air ratio will read between 0.4 and 0.6v. By monitoring the oxygen content and convert-

ing it to electrical voltage, the sensor acts as a rich-lean switch. The voltage is transmitted to the PCM.

Some models have two sensors, one before the catalyst and one after. This is done for a catalyst efficiency monitor that is a part of the OBD-II engine controls that are on 1996–00 year vehicles. The one before the catalyst measures the exhaust emissions right out of the engine, and sends the signal to the PCM about the state of the mixture as previously talked about. The second sensor reports the difference in the emissions after the exhaust gases have gone through the catalyst. This sensor reports to the PCM the amount of emissions reduction the catalyst is performing.

The oxygen sensor will not work until a predetermined temperature is reached, until this time the PCM is running in what as known as OPEN LOOP operation. OPEN LOOP means that the PCM has not yet begun to correct the air-to-fuel ratio by reading the oxygen sensor. After the engine comes to operating temperature, the PCM will monitor the oxygen sensor and correct the air/fuel ratio from the sensor's readings. This is what is known as CLOSED LOOP operation.

A heated oxygen sensor (H02S) has a heating element that keeps the sensor at proper operating temperature during all operating modes. Maintaining correct sensor temperature at all times allows the system to enter into CLOSED LOOP operation sooner.

In CLOSED LOOP operation the PCM monitors the sensor input (along with other inputs) and adjusts the injector pulse width accordingly. During OPEN LOOP operation the PCM ignores the sensor input and adjusts the injector pulse to a preprogrammed value based on other inputs.

TESTING

Single Wire Sensor

▶ See Figure 43

1. Perform a visual inspection on the sensor as follows:

a. Remove the sensor from the exhaust.

b. If the sensor tip has a black/sooty deposit, this may indicate a rich fuel mixture.

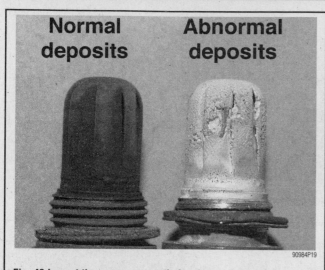

Normal deposits **Abnormal deposits**

90984P19

Fig. 43 Inspect the oxygen sensor tip for abnormal deposits

c. If the sensor tip has a white gritty deposit, this may indicate an internal anti-freeze leak.

d. If the sensor tip has a brown deposit, this could indicate oil consumption.

➡**All these contaminates can destroy the sensor, if the problem is not repaired the new sensor will also be damaged.**

2. Reinstall the sensor.

3. Start the engine and bring it to normal operating temperature, then run the engine above 1200 rpm for two minutes.

4. Backprobe with a high impedance averaging voltmeter (set to the DC voltage scale) between the oxygen sensor (02S) and battery ground.

5. Verify that the 02S voltage fluctuates rapidly between 0.40–0.60 volts.

6. If the 02S voltage is stabilized at the middle of the specified range (approximately 0.45–0.55 volts) or if the 02S voltage fluctuates very slowly between the specified range (02S signal crosses 0.5 volts less than 5 times in ten seconds), the 02S may be faulty.

7. If the 02S voltage stabilizes at either end of the specified range, the PCM is probably not able to compensate for a mechanical problem such as a vacuum leak or a faulty pressure regulator. These types of mechanical problems will cause the 02S to sense a constant lean or constant rich mixture. The mechanical problem will first have to be repaired and then the 02S test repeated.

8. Pull a vacuum hose located after the throttle plate. Voltage should drop to approximately 0.12 volts (while still fluctuating rapidly). This tests the ability of the 02S to detect a lean mixture condition. Reattach the vacuum hose.

9. Richen the mixture using a propane enrichment tool. Voltage should rise to approximately 0.90 volts (while still fluctuating rapidly). This tests the ability of the 02S to detect a rich mixture condition.

10. If the 02S voltage is above or below the specified range, the 02S and/or the 02S wiring may be faulty. Check the wiring for any breaks, repair as necessary and repeat the test.

Heated Oxygen Sensor

▶ **See Figures 44 and 45**

✳ WARNING

Do not pierce the wires when testing this sensor; this can lead to wiring harness damage. Backprobe the connector to properly read the voltage of the HO2S.

1. Perform a visual inspection on the sensor as follows:

a. Remove the sensor from the exhaust.

b. If the sensor tip has a black/sooty deposit, this may indicate a rich fuel mixture.

c. If the sensor tip has a white gritty deposit, this may indicate an internal anti-freeze leak.

d. If the sensor tip has a brown deposit, this could indicate oil consumption.

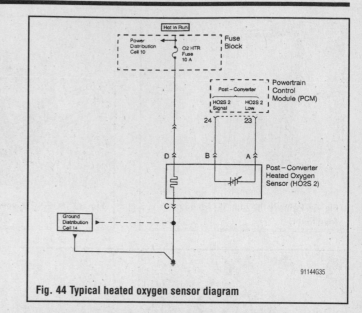

91144G35

Fig. 44 Typical heated oxygen sensor diagram

➡**All these contaminates can destroy the sensor, if the problem is not repaired the new sensor will also be damaged.**

2. Reinstall the sensor.

3. Start the engine and bring it to normal operating temperature, then run the engine above 1200 rpm for two minutes.

4. Turn the ignition **OFF** and disengage the H02S harness connector.

5. Connect a test light between harness terminals **A** and **B** (refer to graphic). With the ignition switch **ON** and the engine off, verify that the test light is lit. If the test light is not lit, either the supply voltage to the H02S heater or the ground circuit of the H02S heater is faulty. Check the H02S wiring and the fuse.

6. Next, connect a high impedance ohmmeter between the H02S terminals **B** and **A** (refer to graphic) and verify that the resistance is 3.5–14.0 ohms.

7. If the H02S heater resistance is not as specified, the H02S may be faulty.

8. Start the engine and bring it to normal operating temperature, then run the engine above 1200 rpm for two minutes.

9. Backprobe with a high impedance averaging voltmeter (set to the DC voltage scale) between the oxygen sensor (02S) and battery ground.

10. Verify that the 02S voltage fluctuates rapidly between 0.40–0.60 volts.

11. If the 02S voltage is stabilized at the middle of the specified range (approximately 0.45–0.55 volts) or if the 02S voltage fluctuates very slowly between the specified range (02S signal crosses 0.5 volts less than 5 times in ten seconds), the 02S may be faulty.

12. If the 02S voltage stabilizes at either end of the specified range, the PCM is probably not able to compensate for a mechanical problem such as a vacuum leak or a faulty fuel pressure regulator. These types of mechanical problems will cause the 02S to sense a constant lean or constant rich mixture. The mechanical problem will first have to be repaired and then the 02S test repeated.

13. Pull a vacuum hose located after the throttle plate. Voltage should drop to approximately 0.12 volts (while still fluctuating rapidly). This tests the ability of the 02S to detect a lean mixture condition. Reattach the vacuum hose.

14. Richen the mixture using a propane enrichment tool. Voltage should rise to approximately 0.90 volts (while still fluctuating rapidly). This tests the ability of the 02S to detect a rich mixture condition.

15. If the 02S voltage is above or below the specified range, the 02S and/or the 02S wiring may be faulty. Check the wiring for any breaks, repair as necessary and repeat the test.

REMOVAL & INSTALLATION

▶ **See Figures 46, 47, 48 and 49**

✳ WARNING

The sensor uses a permanently attached pigtail and connector. This pigtail should not be removed from the sensor. Damage or removal of the pigtail or connector will affect the proper operation of the

Fig. 45 The HO2S can be monitored with an appropriate and Data-stream capable scan tool

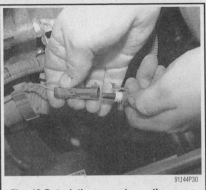

Fig. 46 Detach the connector on the oxygen sensor

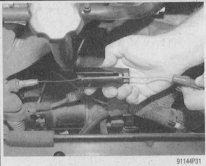

Fig. 47 A special socket is available to remove the oxygen sensor. the socket contains a slot that the wire slides out of

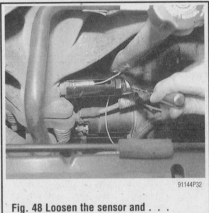

Fig. 48 Loosen the sensor and . . .

Fig. 49 . . . remove it from the exhaust manifold/pipe

Fig. 50 Test the Idle Air Control (IAC) valve resistance between A and B and terminals C and D. The resistance should be 20–80 ohms

sensor. Keep the electrical connector and louvered end of the sensor clean and free of grease. **NEVER use cleaning solvents of any type on the sensor! The oxygen sensor may be difficult to remove when the temperature of the engine is below 120°F (49°C). Excessive force may damage the threads in the exhaust manifold or exhaust pipe.**

1. Disconnect the negative battery cable.
2. Unplug the electrical connector and any attaching hardware.
3. Remove the sensor.

To install:

4. Coat the threads of the sensor with a GM anti-seize compound, part number 5613695, or its equivalent, before installation. New sensors are pre-coated with this compound.

➡**The GM anti-seize compound is NOT a conventional anti-seize paste. The use of a regular paste may electrically insulate the sensor, rendering it useless. The threads MUST be coated with the proper electrically conductive anti-seize compound.**

5. Install the sensor and tighten to 30 ft. lbs. (40 Nm). Use care in making sure the silicone boot is in the correct position to avoid melting it during operation.
6. Attach the electrical connector.
7. Connect the negative battery cable.

Idle Air Control (IAC) Valve

OPERATION

The engine idle speed is controlled by the PCM through the Idle Air Control (IAC) valve mounted on the throttle body. The PCM sends voltage pulses to the IAC motor causing the IAC motor shaft and pintle to move in or out a given distance (number of steps) for each pulse, (called counts).

This movement controls air flow around the throttle plate, which in turn, controls engine idle speed, either cold or hot. IAC valve pintle position counts can be seen using a scan tool. Zero counts corresponds to a fully closed passage, while 140 or more counts (depending on the application) corresponds to full flow.

TESTING

▶ **See Figures 50 and 51**

1. Disengage the IAC electrical connector.
2. Using an ohmmeter, measure the resistance between IAC terminals **A** and **B**. Next measure the resistance between terminals **C** and **D**.
3. Verify that the resistance between both sets of IAC terminals is 20–80 ohms. If the resistance is not as specified, the IAC may be faulty.

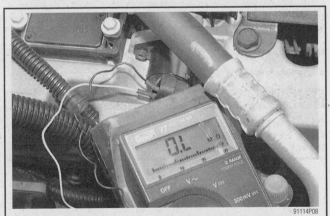

Fig. 51 Test the Idle Air Control (IAC) valve resistance between B and C and terminals A and D. The resistance should be infinite

4. Measure the resistance between IAC terminals **B** and **C**. Next measure the resistance between terminals **A** and **D**.

5. Verify that the resistance between both sets of IAC terminals is infinite. If the resistance is not infinite, the IAC may be faulty.

6. Also, with a small mirror, inspect IAC air inlet passage and pintle for debris. Clean as necessary, as this can cause IAC malfunction.

REMOVAL & INSTALLATION

▶ **See Figures 52 thru 57**

1. Disconnect the negative battery cable.
2. Remove the air cleaner outlet tube.
3. Unplug the electrical connection.
4. Remove the IAC valve. On thread-mounted units, use 1¼ in. (32mm) wrench and on flange-mounted units, remove the screw assemblies.
5. Remove the IAC valve gasket or O-ring and discard it.

To install:

6. Clean the old gasket material from the surface of the throttle body assembly on the thread mounted valve. On the flange-mounted valve clean the surface to ensure proper O-ring sealing

7. If installing a new IAC valve (except for 1998–00 2.2L equipped models and all models with the 2.3L or 2.4L engine, for those models see the last step in this procedure), measure the distance between the tip of the valve pintle and the mounting flange. If the distance is greater than 1.10 inch (28mm), use finger pressure to slowly retract the pintle until the measurement is within specification (refer to the accompanying illustration).

8. Install the valve with a new gasket or O-ring. Tighten the thread mounted assembly 13 ft. lbs. (18 Nm) and tighten the flange mounted attaching screws to 28 inch. lbs. (3 Nm).

9. Engage the electrical connector to the IAC valve.
10. Install the air cleaner outlet tube.
11. Connect the negative battery cable.
12. To set the pintle position on 1998–00 models equipped with the 2.2L engine and all models equipped wit the 2.3L/2.4L engines, turn the ignition key

to the **ON**, engine **OFF** position for five seconds. Turn the ignition key to the **OFF** position for ten seconds, then start the engine and check for proper idle operation.

Engine Coolant Temperature Sensor

OPERATION

▶ **See Figures 58, 59 and 60**

The Engine Coolant Temperature (ECT) sensor resistance changes in response to engine coolant temperature. The sensor resistance decreases as the coolant temperature increases, and increases as the coolant temperature decreases. This provides a reference signal to the PCM, which indicates engine coolant temperature. The signal sent to the PCM by the ECT sensor helps the PCM to determine spark advance, EGR flow rate, air/fuel ratio, and engine temperature. The ECT also is used for temperature gauge operation by sending it's signal to the instrument cluster. The ECT is a two wire sensor, a 5-volt reference signal is sent to the sensor and the signal return is based upon the change in the measured resistance due to temperature.

TESTING

▶ **See Figures 61, 62 and 63**

1. Disconnect the engine wiring harness from the ECT sensor.
2. Connect an ohmmeter between the ECT sensor terminals.
3. With the engine cold and the ignition switch in the **OFF** position, measure and note the ECT sensor resistance.
4. Connect the engine wiring harness to the sensor.
5. Start the engine and allow the engine to reach normal operating temperature.
6. Once the engine has reached normal operating temperature, turn the engine **OFF**.

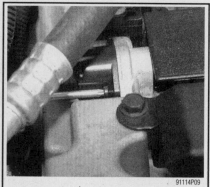

Fig. 52 Unfasten the IAC valve screws and . . .

Fig. 53 . . . remove the IAC valve

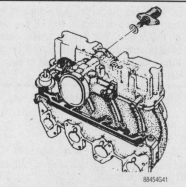

Fig. 54 Location of the IAC valve—1995–97 2.2L engine shown

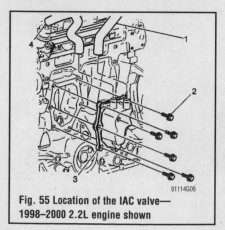

Fig. 55 Location of the IAC valve—1998–2000 2.2L engine shown

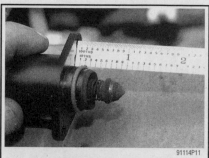

Fig. 56 When installing a new IAC valve, measure the distance between the tip of the valve pintle and the mounting flange. The distance should be 1.10 inch (28mm)

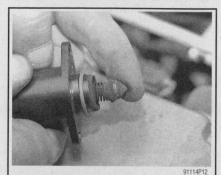

Fig. 57 Use finger pressure to slowly retract the pintle until the measurement is within specification

Fig. 58 The ECT sensor is located in the water outlet housing, adjacent to where the upper radiator hose connects to the engine

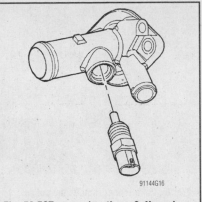

Fig. 59 ECT sensor location—2.4L engine

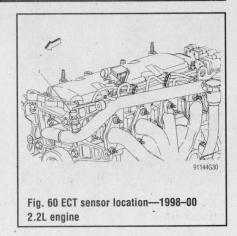

Fig. 60 ECT sensor location—1998–00 2.2L engine

Fig. 61 Detach the connector on the ECT sensor

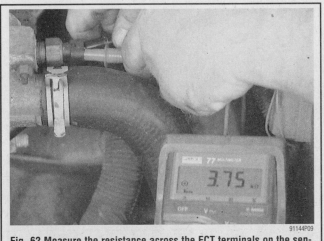

Fig. 62 Measure the resistance across the ECT terminals on the sensor

°C	°F	OHMS
Temperature vs Resistance Values (Approximate)		
100	212	177
90	194	241
80	176	332
70	158	467
60	140	667
50	122	973
45	113	1188
40	104	1459
35	95	1802
30	86	2238
25	77	2796
20	68	3520
15	59	4450
10	50	5670
5	41	7280
0	32	9420
-5	23	12300
-10	14	16180
-15	5	21450
-20	-4	28680
-30	-22	52700
-40	-40	100700

Fig. 63 ECT sensor resistance value chart

7. Once again, disconnect the engine wiring harness from the ECT sensor.
8. Measure and note the ECT sensor resistance with the engine hot.
9. Compare the cold and hot ECT sensor resistance measurements with the accompanying chart.
10. If readings do not approximate those in the chart, the sensor may be faulty.

REMOVAL & INSTALLATION

▶ See Figures 64, 65, 66, 67 and 68

1. Disconnect the negative battery cable.
2. Drain and recycle the engine coolant.
3. Remove the air cleaner outlet tube.
4. Unplug the ECT electrical connection.
5. Using an appropriate tool, loosen the ECT sensor and remove it from the engine.

To install:
6. Use a suitable thread sealant and apply it to the threads of the ECT sensor.
7. Install the ECT sensor and tighten it to 18 ft. lbs. (25 Nm).
8. Attach the ECT connector.
9. Refill and bleed the cooling system.
10. Connect the negative battery cable.

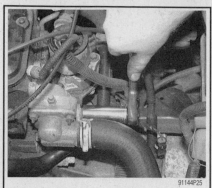

Fig. 64 Use a deep well socket to loosen the ECT sensor

Fig. 65 Once loose, remove the sensor from the water outlet housing

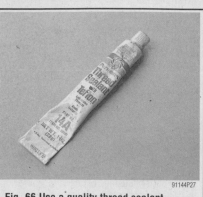

Fig. 66 Use a quality thread sealant and . . .

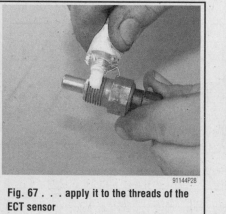

Fig. 67 . . . apply it to the threads of the ECT sensor

Fig. 68 Tighten the sensor using a torque wrench, or the housing may crack if you over-tighten it

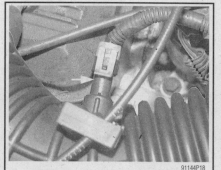

Fig. 69 The IAT sensor is located in the air cleaner outlet tube—2.2L engine and 2.4L engine

Intake Air Temperature Sensor

OPERATION

▶ See Figure 69

The Intake Air Temperature (IAT) sensor determines the air temperature inside the intake manifold. Resistance changes in response to the ambient air temperature. The sensor has a negative temperature coefficient. As the temperature of the sensor rises the resistance across the sensor decreases. This provides a signal to the PCM indicating the temperature of the incoming air charge. This sensor helps the PCM to determine spark timing and air/fuel ratio. Information from this sensor is added to the pressure sensor information to calculate the air mass being sent to the cylinders. The IAT is a two wire sensor, a 5-volt reference signal is sent to the sensor and the signal return is based upon the change in the measured resistance due to temperature.

TESTING

▶ See Figures 70 and 71

1. Turn the ignition switch **OFF**.
2. Disconnect the wiring harness from the IAT sensor.
3. Measure the resistance between the sensor terminals.
4. Compare the resistance reading with the accompanying chart.
5. If the resistance is not within specification, the IAT may be faulty.
6. Connect the wiring harness to the sensor.

REMOVAL & INSTALLATION

2.2L Engine and 2.4L Engine

▶ See Figures 69, 72 and 73

1. Disconnect the negative battery cable.

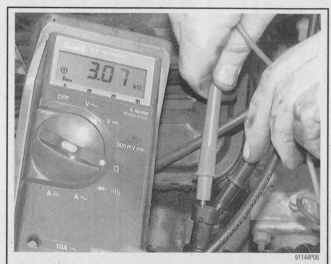

Fig. 70 Measure the resistance across the IAT terminals on the sensor

2. Detach the connector for the IAT sensor.
3. Carefully twist the IAT sensor out of the air cleaner outlet tube.
To install:
4. Carefully twist the IAT sensor into the air cleaner outlet tube.
5. Attach the connector for the IAT sensor.
6. Connect the negative battery cable.

2.3L Engine (1995 Only)

▶ See Figure 74

1. Disconnect the negative battery cable.

°C	°F	OHMS
Temperature vs Resistance Values (Approximate)		
100	212	177
90	194	241
80	176	332
70	158	467
60	140	667
50	122	973
45	113	1188
40	104	1459
35	95	1802
30	86	2238
25	77	2796
20	68	3520
15	59	4450
10	50	5670
5	41	7280
0	32	9420
-5	23	12300
-10	14	16180
-15	5	21450
-20	-4	28680
-30	-22	52700
-40	-40	100700

88254G69

Fig. 71 IAT sensor resistance value chart

2. Detach the connector for the IAT sensor.
3. Loosen the IAT sensor using a deep-well socket.
4. Remove the IAT sensor from the intake manifold.
To install:
5. Use a suitable thread sealant and apply it to the threads of the IAT sensor.
6. Install the IAT sensor and tighten it to 18 ft. lbs. (25 Nm).
7. Attach the IAT connector.
8. Connect the negative battery cable.

Manifold Absolute Pressure (MAP) Sensor

OPERATION

The Manifold Absolute Pressure (MAP) sensor measures the changes in intake manifold pressure, which result from the engine load and speed changes, and converts this to a voltage output.

A closed throttle on engine coastdown will produce a low MAP output, while a wide-open throttle will produce a high output. This high output is produced because the pressure inside the manifold is the same as outside the manifold, so 100 percent of the outside air pressure is measured.

The MAP sensor reading is the opposite of what you would measure on a vacuum gauge. When manifold pressure is high, vacuum is low. The MAP sensor is also used to measure barometric pressure under certain conditions, which allows the PCM to automatically adjust for different altitudes.

The PCM sends a 5 volt reference signal to the MAP sensor. As the manifold pressure changes, the electrical resistance of the sensor also changes. By monitoring the sensor output voltage, the PCM knows the manifold pressure. A higher pressure, low vacuum (high voltage) requires more fuel, while a lower pressure, higher vacuum (low voltage) requires less fuel.

The PCM uses the MAP sensor to control fuel delivery and ignition timing.

TESTING

♦ **See Figures 75 and 76**

1. Backprobe with a high impedance voltmeter at MAP sensor terminals **A** and **C**.
2. With the key **ON** and engine off, the voltmeter reading should be approximately 5.0 volts.
3. If the voltage is not as specified, either the wiring to the MAP sensor or the PCM may be faulty. Correct any wiring or PCM faults before continuing test.
4. Backprobe with the high impedance voltmeter at MAP sensor terminals **B** and **A**.
5. Verify that the sensor voltage is approximately 0.5 volts with the engine not running (at sea level).
6. Record MAP sensor voltage with the key **ON** and engine off.
7. Start the vehicle.
8. Verify that the sensor voltage is greater than 1.5 volts (above the recorded reading) at idle.
9. Verify that the sensor voltage increases to approximately 4.5 volts (above the recorded reading) at Wide Open Throttle (WOT).
10. If the sensor voltage is as specified, the sensor is functioning properly.
11. If the sensor voltage is not as specified, check the sensor and the sensor vacuum source for a leak or a restriction. If no leaks or restrictions are found, the sensor may be defective and should be replaced.

91144P37

Fig. 72 Grasp the IAT sensor and . . .

91144P19

Fig. 73 . . . gently twist it out of the air cleaner outlet tube

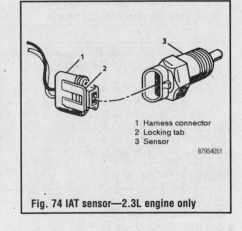

1 Harness connector
2 Locking tab
3 Sensor

87954051

Fig. 74 IAT sensor—2.3L engine only

Fig. 75 Using jumper wires and a high impedance voltmeter test between MAP sensor terminals A and C with the key ON and engine off. The voltage should be approximately 5 volts

Fig. 76 Next test between MAP sensor terminals A and B with the key ON and engine off. The voltage should be approximately 0.5 volts

REMOVAL & INSTALLATION

1995–97 2.2L Engines

▶ See Figures 77, 78, 79 and 80

1. Disconnect the negative battery cable.
2. Tag and disconnect the vacuum harness assembly.
3. Unplug the electrical connector.
4. To remove the sensor, release the locktabs, or unfasten the bolts or simply pull the sensor from the grommet, whichever applies to your vehicle.
5. Installation is the reverse of removal.

1998–00 2.2L Models 2.3L/2.4L Engines

▶ See Figure 81

1. Disconnect the negative battery cable.
2. Remove the throttle body. Refer to Section 5.
3. Unplug the electrical connection.
4. Remove the sensor from the intake manifold.
5. Installation is the reverse of removal.

2.3L/2.4L Engines

▶ See Figure 82

1. Disconnect the negative battery cable.
2. Unplug the electrical connection and vacuum hose.

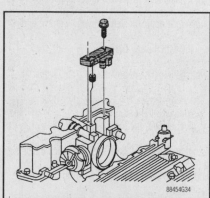

Fig. 77 Manifold Absolute Pressure (MAP) sensor location—1995–97 2.2L engine

Fig. 78 Unplug the Manifold Absolute Pressure (MAP) sensor electrical connection

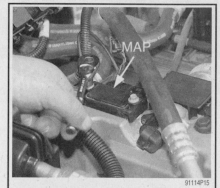

Fig. 79 Unfasten the Manifold Absolute Pressure (MAP) sensor retainers . . .

Fig. 80 . . . then remove the MAP sensor

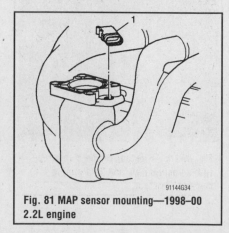

Fig. 81 MAP sensor mounting—1998–00 2.2L engine

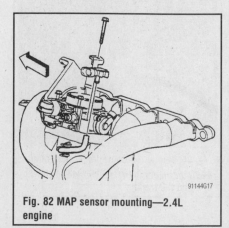

Fig. 82 MAP sensor mounting—2.4L engine

3. Unfasten the bracket retaining screw and remove the bracket.
4. Remove the sensor from the intake manifold.
5. Installation is the reverse of removal.

Throttle Position Sensor

OPERATION

The Throttle Position (TP) sensor is a potentiometer that provides a signal to the PCM that is directly proportional to the throttle plate position. The TP sensor is mounted on the side of the throttle body and is connected to the throttle plate shaft. The TP sensor monitors throttle plate movement and position, and transmits an appropriate electrical signal to the PCM. These signals are used by the PCM to adjust the air/fuel mixture, spark timing and EGR operation according to engine load at idle, part throttle, or full throttle. The TP sensor is not adjustable.

The TP sensor receives a 5 volt reference signal and a ground circuit from the PCM. A return signal circuit is connected to wiper that runs on a resistor internally on the sensor. The further the throttle is opened, the wiper moves along the resistor, at wide open throttle, the wiper essentially creates a loop between the reference signal and the signal return returning the full or nearly full 5 volt signal back to the PCM. At idle the signal return should be approximately 0.9 volts.

TESTING

♦ See Figures 83, 84, 85, 86 and 87

1. With the engine **OFF** and the ignition **ON**, check the voltage at the signal return circuit of the TP sensor by carefully backprobing the connector using a DVOM.
2. Voltage should be between 0.2 and 1.4 volts at idle.
3. Slowly move the throttle pulley to the wide open throttle (WOT) position and watch the voltage on the DVOM. The voltage should slowly rise to slightly less than 4.8v at Wide Open Throttle (WOT).
4. If no voltage is present, check the wiring harness for supply voltage (5.0v) and ground (0.3v or less), by referring to your corresponding wiring guide. If supply voltage and ground are present, but no output voltage from TP, replace the TP sensor. If supply voltage and ground do not meet specifications, make necessary repairs to the harness or PCM.

REMOVAL & INSTALLATION

♦ See Figures 88, 89, 90, 91 and 92

1. Disconnect the negative battery cable.
2. Remove the air cleaner outlet tube.
3. Unplug the electrical connection.
4. Remove the two retaining screws and remove the sensor from the throttle body.

To install:
5. With the throttle plate full closed, carefully slide the rotary tangs on the sensor into position over the throttle shaft, then rotate the sensor counterclockwise to the align the bolt holes..

✳✳ CAUTION

Failure to install the TP sensor in this manner may result in sensor damage or high idle speeds.

➡The TP sensor is not adjustable.

6. Install and tighten the sensor mounting screws to 18–35 inch lbs. (2–4 Nm).
7. Connect the wiring harness to the sensor.
8. Iinstall the air intake resonator.
9. Connect the negative battery cable.

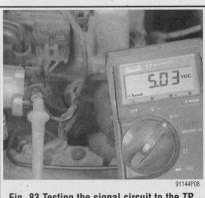

Fig. 83 Testing the signal circuit to the TP sensor

Fig. 84 Testing the signal return circuit of the TP sensor

Fig. 85 Testing the ground circuit of the TP sensor

Fig. 86 Testing the operation of the potentiometer inside the TP sensor while slowly opening the throttle

Fig. 87 The TP sensor can be monitored with an appropriate and Data-stream capable scan tool

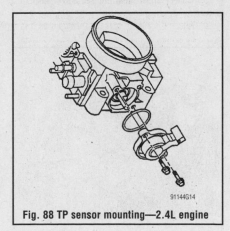

Fig. 88 TP sensor mounting—2.4L engine

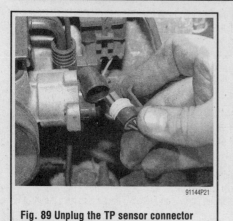

Fig. 89 Unplug the TP sensor connector

Fig. 90 Remove the two retaining bolts and . . .

Fig. 91 . . . remove the sensor from the throttle body

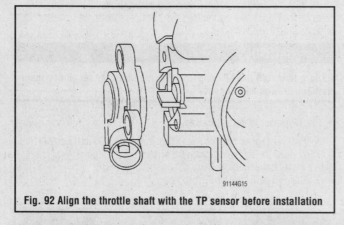

Fig. 92 Align the throttle shaft with the TP sensor before installation

Crankshaft Position (CKP) Sensor

OPERATION

The Crankshaft Position (CKP) sensor provides a signal through the ignition module which the PCM uses as a reference to calculate rpm and crankshaft position.

TESTING

▶ See Figure 93

1. Turn the ignition key **OFF**.
2. Unplug the sensor electrical harness and check the terminals for corrosion and damage.
3. Check the sensor wiring harness wires for continuity and repair as necessary.
4. Attach the sensor harness making sure it is firmly engaged.

Fig. 93 Attach suitable jumper wires between the CKP sensor and CKP sensor harness. A DC volt meter can then be attached to the necessary terminals to test the sensor as the engine is being cranked

5. Using a Digital Volt Ohm Meter (DVOM) set on the DC scale, backprobe the sensor signal terminal (terminal A) with the positive lead of the meter and backprobe the sensor ground terminal (terminal B) with the negative lead of the meter.
6. Have an assistant crank the engine and observe the meter.
7. You should have approximately a 5 volt reference signal pulse. If not the sensor may be defective.

REMOVAL & INSTALLATION

▶ See Figures 94, 95, 96 and 97

1. Disconnect the negative battery cable.
2. Raise the vehicle and support it with jackstands.

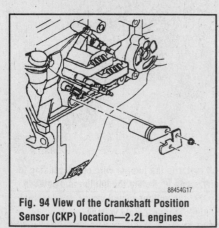

Fig. 94 View of the Crankshaft Position Sensor (CKP) location—2.2L engines

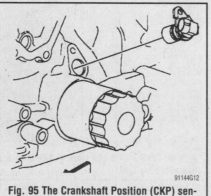

Fig. 95 The Crankshaft Position (CKP) sensor location—2.3L/2.4L engines

Fig. 96 Unfasten the Crankshaft Position (CKP) sensor retaining bolt—2.2L engine shown

Fig. 97 After the Crankshaft Position (CKP) sensor retaining bolt has been removed, grasp the sensor and pull it from its bore in the engine block using a slight twisting motion—2.2L engine shown

Fig. 98 The CMP is located on the side of the block under the intake manifold—2.2L engine

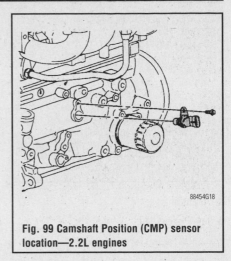

Fig. 99 Camshaft Position (CMP) sensor location—2.2L engines

3. Unplug the sensor harness connector at the sensor.
4. Unfasten the retaining bolt, then remove the sensor from below the coil pack on 2.2L engines, and above the oil filter on the 2.3L/2.4L engines. Inspect the sensor O-ring for wear, cracks or leakage and replace if necessary.

To install:

5. Lubricate the O-ring with clean engine oil, then place it on the sensor.
6. Install the sensor and tighten the retaining bolt to 71 inch lbs. On the 2.2L engine and 88 inch lbs. (10 Nm) on the 2.3L/2.4L engine.
7. Attach the sensor harness connector.
8. If removed, install the steering linkage shield.
9. Lower the vehicle.
10. Connect the negative battery cable.

Camshaft Position (CMP) Sensor

OPERATION

▶ See Figures 98 and 99

The PCM uses the camshaft signal to determine the position of the No. 1 cylinder piston during its power stroke. The signal is used by the PCM to calculate fuel injection mode of operation.

If the cam signal is lost while the engine is running, the fuel injection system will shift to a calculated fuel injected mode based on the last fuel injection pulse, and the engine will continue to run.

TESTING

▶ See Figures 100, 101 and 102

1. Remove the PCM fuse to prevent the engine from starting. Removal of the PCM fuse does not disable the sensor power supply and allows testing of this sensor safely.

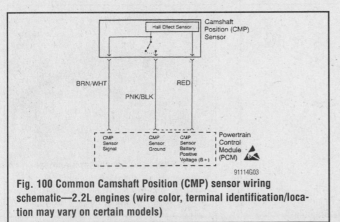

Fig. 100 Common Camshaft Position (CMP) sensor wiring schematic—2.2L engines (wire color, terminal identification/location may vary on certain models)

2. Disconnect the CMP sensor wiring harness and attach suitable jumper wires between the CMP sensor and CMP sensor harness. Connect a DC volt meter to the jumper wires corresponding to CMP IGN or PWR terminal and sensor ground.

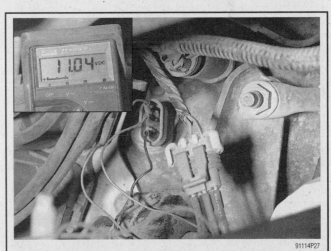

Fig. 101 Attach suitable jumper wires between the CMP sensor and CMP sensor harness. Connect a DC volt meter to the jumper wires corresponding to IGN and sensor ground terminals and note the reading

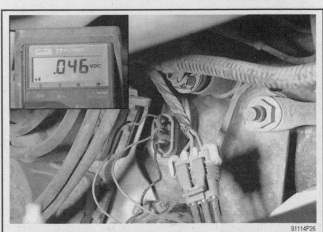

Fig. 102 Connect the volt meter to the jumper wire corresponding to signal and sensor ground terminals, rotate the engine and observe the volt meter and verify that the voltage signal varies from approximately zero volts to slightly less than supply voltage

3. With the ignition **ON** and the engine off, verify that the voltage is approximately battery voltage. The supply voltage should be slightly less than battery voltage.

4. If not as specified, repair or replace the fuse and/or wiring.

5. Connect a DC volt meter to the jumper wires corresponding to CMP signal terminal and sensor ground.

6. Place a socket and breaker bar or the crankshaft pulley bolt and rotate the engine slowly by hand. Observe the volt meter and verify that the voltage signal varies from approximately zero volts to slightly less than supply voltage. The voltage will switch on when the target passes the sensor and will show little or no voltage when the target is past the sensor.

7. If it is not as specified, the CMP sensor may be faulty.

REMOVAL & INSTALLATION

2.2L Engines

▶ **See Figures 103, 104 and 105**

1. Disconnect the negative battery cable.
2. Raise the vehicle and support it with safety stands.
3. Remove the right hand tire assembly.
4. Unplug the sensor harness connector at the sensor.
5. Unfasten the retaining bolt, then remove the sensor from the camshaft housing.

To install:

6. Place the sensor into position.
7. Install the CMP sensor retaining bolt, then tighten to 88 inch lbs. (10 Nm).
8. Attach the sensor harness connector.
9. Install the tire assembly and lower the vehicle.
10. Connect the negative battery cable.

2.3L/2.4L Engines

1. Disconnect the negative battery cable.
2. Unplug the sensor harness connector at the sensor.
3. Unfasten the retaining bolt, then remove the sensor from the camshaft housing.

To install:

4. Place the sensor into position.
5. Install the CMP sensor retaining bolt, then tighten to 88 inch lbs. (10 Nm).
6. Attach the sensor harness connector.
7. Connect the negative battery cable.

Knock Sensor

OPERATION

▶ **See Figure 106**

The operation of the Knock Sensor (KS) is to monitor preignition or "engine knocks" and send the signal to the PCM. The PCM responds by adjusting ignition timing until the "knocks" stop. The sensor works by gener-

ating a signal produced by the frequency of the knock as recorded by the piezoelectric ceramic disc inside the KS. The disc absorbs the shock waves from the knocks and exerts a pressure on the metal diaphragm inside the KS. This compresses the crystals inside the disc and the disc generates an A/C voltage signal proportional to the frequency of the knocks ranging from zero to 1 volt.

TESTING

There is real no test for this sensor, the sensor produces its own signal based on information gathered while the engine is running. The sensors also are usually inaccessible without major component removal. The sensors can be monitored with an appropriate scan tool using a data display or other data stream information. Follow the instructions included with the scan tool for information on accessing the data. The only test available is to test the continuity of the harness from the PCM to the sensor.

REMOVAL & INSTALLATION

▶ **See Figures 107 and 108**

1. Disconnect the negative battery cable.
2. Raise and safely support the vehicle.
3. Detach the wiring harness connector from the Knock Sensor (KS).
4. Remove the knock sensor from the engine block.

To install:

5. Install the knock sensor into the engine block. Tighten to 12–16 ft. lbs. (16–22 Nm).
6. Attach the wiring harness connector to the sensor.
7. Carefully lower the vehicle.
8. Connect the negative battery cable.

Vehicle Speed Sensor

OPERATION

The Vehicle Speed Sensor (VSS) is a magnetic pick-up sensor that sends a signal to the Powertrain Control Module (PCM) and the speedometer. The sensor measures the rotation of the output shaft on the transaxle and sends an AC voltage signal to the PCM which determines the corresponding vehicle speed.

TESTING

1. To test the VSS, backprobe the VSS terminals with a high impedance voltmeter (set at the AC voltage scale).
2. Safely raise and support the entire vehicle using jackstands. Make absolutely sure the vehicle is stable.
3. Start the vehicle and place it in gear.
4. Verify that the VSS voltage increases as the drive shaft speed increases.
5. If the VSS voltage is not as specified the VSS may be faulty.

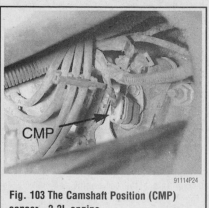

Fig. 103 The Camshaft Position (CMP) sensor—2.2L engine

Fig. 104 The Camshaft Position (CMP) sensor—2.3L/2.4L engines

Fig. 105 Unplug CMP sensor electrical connection and unfasten the sensor retainer, then remove the sensor from its bore in the block—2.2L engine

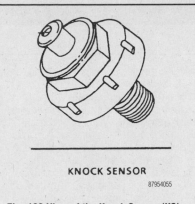

KNOCK SENSOR

87954055

Fig. 106 View of the Knock Sensor (KS)

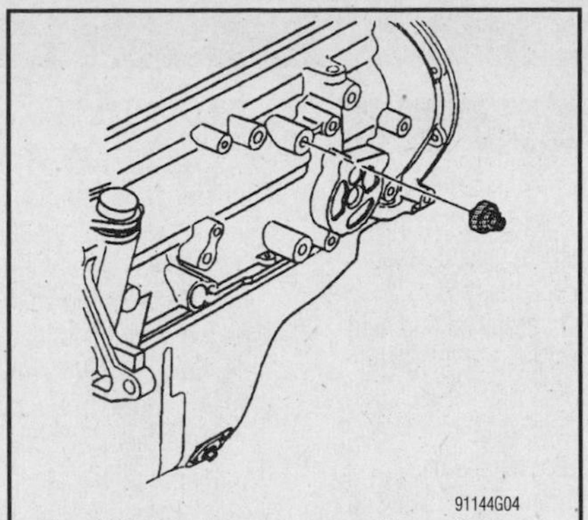

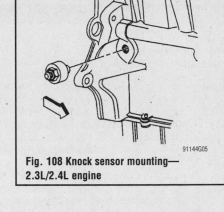

91144G04

Fig. 107 Knock sensor mounting—2.2L engine

Fig. 108 Knock sensor mounting—2.3L/2.4L engine

91144G05

REMOVAL & INSTALLATION

3T40 Automatic Transaxle

▶ **See Figure 109**

1. Raise and safely support the vehicle securely on jackstands.
2. Unplug the electrical connector.
3. Remove the speed sensor housing retaining bolts.
4. Remove the speed sensor from the transaxle case.

To install:

5. Inspect the sensor O-ring for wear, cracks or leakage and replace if necessary.
6. Lubricate the O-ring with some automatic transaxle fluid.
7. Install the O-ring onto the transaxle and place the sensor housing onto the transaxle case.
8. Tighten the retaining bolt to 97 inch lbs. (11 Nm).
9. Attach the electrical connector to the sensor.
10. Lower the vehicle.

4T40E Automatic Transaxle

▶ **See Figure 110**

1. Raise and safely support the vehicle securely on jackstands.
2. Unplug the electrical connector.
3. Remove the speed sensor retaining bolt.
4. Remove the speed sensor from the transaxle case.

To install:

5. Inspect the sensor O-ring for wear, cracks or leakage and replace if necessary.
6. Lubricate the O-ring with some automatic transaxle fluid.
7. Install the O-ring onto the sensor and insert the sensor into the transaxle case.
8. Tighten the retaining bolt to 97 inch lbs. (11 Nm).
9. Attach the electrical connector to the sensor.
10. Lower the vehicle.

Manual Transaxle

▶ **See Figure 111**

1. Raise and safely support the vehicle securely on jackstands.
2. Unplug the electrical connector.
3. Remove the speed sensor retaining bolt.
4. Remove the speed sensor retainer and remove the speed sensor from the transaxle case.

To install:

5. Inspect the sensor O-ring for wear, cracks or leakage and replace if necessary.
6. Lubricate the O-ring with some Syncromesh® transaxle fluid.
7. Install the O-ring onto the sensor and insert the sensor into the transaxle case.
8. Install the retainer and tighten the retaining bolt to 80 inch lbs. (9 Nm).
9. Attach the electrical connector to the sensor.
10. Lower the vehicle.

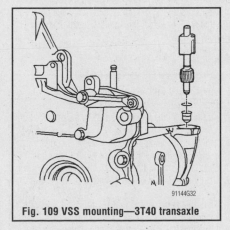

91144G32

Fig. 109 VSS mounting—3T40 transaxle

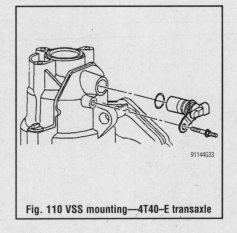

91144G33

Fig. 110 VSS mounting—4T40–E transaxle

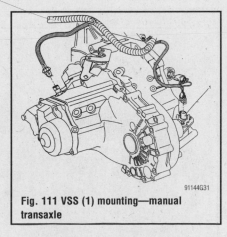

91144G31

Fig. 111 VSS (1) mounting—manual transaxle

TROUBLE CODES

General Information

Since the control module is programmed to recognize the presence and value of electrical inputs, it will also note the lack of a signal or a radical change in values. It will, for example, react to the loss of signal from the vehicle speed sensor or note that engine coolant temperature has risen beyond acceptable (programmed) limits. Once a fault is recognized, a numeric code is assigned and held in memory. The dashboard warning lamp: CHECK ENGINE or SERVICE ENGINE SOON (SES), will illuminate to advise the operator that the system has detected a fault. This lamp is also known as the Malfunction Indicator Lamp (MIL).

More than one code may be stored. Keep in mind not every engine uses every code. Additionally, the same code may carry different meanings relative to each engine or engine family.

In the event of an computer control module failure, the system will default to a pre-programmed set of values. These are compromise values, which allow the engine to operate, although possibly at reduced efficiency. This is variously known as the default, limp-in or back-up mode. Driveability is almost always affected when the PCM enters this mode.

SCAN TOOLS

▶ **See Figure 112**

On 1995 models, the stored codes may be read with only the use of a small jumper wire, however the use of a hand-held scan tool such as GM's TECH-1® or equivalent is recommended. On all 1996–00 models, an OBD-II compliant scan tool must be used. There are many manufacturers of these tools; a purchaser must be certain that the tool is proper for the intended use. If you own a scan type tool, it probably came with comprehensive instructions on proper use. Be sure to follow the instructions that came with your unit if they differ from what is given here; this is a general guide with useful information included.

The scan tool allows any stored codes to be read from the PCM memory. The tool also allows the operator to view the data being sent to the computer control module while the engine is running. This ability has obvious diagnostic advantages; the use of the scan tool is frequently required for component testing. The scan tool makes collecting information easier; an operator familiar with the system must correctly interpret the data.

An example of the usefulness of the scan tool may be seen in the case of a temperature sensor, which has changed its electrical characteristics. The PCM is reacting to an apparently warmer engine (causing a driveability problem), but the sensor's voltage has not changed enough to set a fault code. Connecting the scan tool, the voltage signal being sent to the PCM may be viewed; comparison to normal values or a known good vehicle reveals the problem quickly.

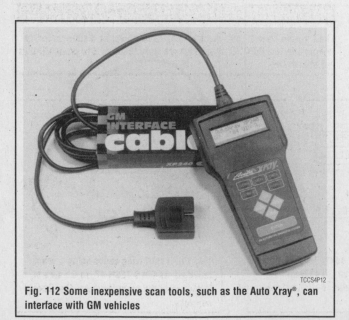

Fig. 112 Some inexpensive scan tools, such as the Auto Xray®, can interface with GM vehicles

TCCS4P12

ELECTRICAL TOOLS

The most commonly required electrical diagnostic tool is the digital multimeter, allowing voltage, ohmage (resistance) and amperage to be read by one instrument. The multimeter must be a high-impedance unit, with 10 megohms of impedance in the voltmeter. This type of meter will not place an additional load on the circuit it is testing; this is extremely important in low voltage circuits. The multimeter must be of high quality in all respects. It should be handled carefully and protected from impact or damage. Replace batteries frequently in the unit.

Other necessary tools include an unpowered test light, a quality tachometer with an inductive (clip-on) pick up, and the proper tools for releasing GM's Metri-Pack, Weather Pack and Micro-Pack terminals as necessary. The Micro-Pack connectors are used at the PCM electrical connector. A vacuum pump/gauge may also be required for checking sensors, solenoids and valves.

Diagnosis and Testing

Diagnosis of a driveablility and/or emissions problems requires attention to detail and following the diagnostic procedures in the correct order. Resist the temptation to perform any repairs before performing the preliminary diagnostic steps. In many cases this will shorten diagnostic time and often cure the problem without electronic testing.

The proper troubleshooting procedure for these vehicles is as follows:

VISUAL/PHYSICAL INSPECTION

This is possibly the most critical step of diagnosis and should be performed immediately after retrieving any codes. A detailed examination of connectors, wiring and vacuum hoses can often lead to a repair without further diagnosis. Performance of this step relies on the skill of the technician performing it; a careful inspector will check the undersides of hoses as well as the integrity of hard-to-reach hoses blocked by the air cleaner or other component. Wiring should be checked carefully for any sign of strain, burning, crimping, or terminal pull-out from a connector. Checking connectors at components or in harnesses is required; usually, pushing them together will reveal a loose fit.

INTERMITTENTS

If a fault occurs intermittently, such as a loose connector pin breaking contact as the vehicle hits a bump, the PCM will note the fault as it occurs and energize the dash warning lamp. If the problem self-corrects, as with the terminal pin again making contact, the dash lamp will extinguish after 10 seconds but a code will remain stored in the computer control module's memory.

When an unexpected code appears during diagnostics, it may have been set during an intermittent failure that self-corrected; the codes are still useful in diagnosis and should not be discounted.

CIRCUIT/COMPONENT REPAIR

The fault codes and the scan tool data will lead to diagnosis and checking of a particular circuit. It is important to note that the fault code indicates a fault or loss of signal in an PCM-controlled system, not necessarily in the specific component.

Refer to the appropriate Diagnostic Code chart to determine the codes meaning. The component may then be tested following the appropriate component test procedures found in this section. If the component is OK, check the wiring for shorts or opens. Further diagnoses should be left to an experienced driveability technician.

If a code indicates the PCM to be faulty and the PCM is replaced, but does not correct the problem, one of the following may be the reason:

- There is a problem with the PCM terminal connections: The terminals may have to be removed from the connector in order to check them properly.
- The PCM or PROM is not correct for the application: The incorrect PCM or PROM may cause a malfunction and may or may not set a code.
- The problem is intermittent: This means that the problem is not present at the time the system is being checked. In this case, make a careful physical inspection of all portions of the system involved.

• Shorted solenoid, relay coils or harness: Solenoids and relays are turned on and off by the PCM using internal electronic switches called drivers. Each driver is part of a group of four called Quad-Drivers. A shorted solenoid, relay coil or harness may cause an PCM to fail, and a replacement PCM to fail when it is installed. Use a short tester, J34696, BT 8405, or equivalent, as a fast, accurate means of checking for a short circuit.

• The Programmable Read Only Memory (PROM) may be faulty: Although the PROM rarely fails, it operates as part of the PCM. Therefore, it could be the cause of the problem. Substitute a known good PROM.

• The replacement PCM may be faulty: After the PCM is replaced, the system should be rechecked for proper operation. If the diagnostic code again indicates the PCM is the problem, substitute a known good PCM. Although this is a very rare condition, it could happen.

Reading Codes

OBD-I SYSTEMS

▶ **See Figure 113, 117, 118, 119 and 120**

Listings of the trouble codes for the various engine control systems covered in this manual are located in this section. Remember that a code only points to the faulty circuit NOT necessarily to a faulty component. Loose, damaged or corroded connections may contribute to a fault code on a circuit when the sensor or component is operating properly. Be sure that the components are faulty before replacing them, especially the expensive ones.

The Assembly Line Diagnostic Link (ALDL) connector or Data Link Connector (DLC) may be located under the dash and sometimes covered with a plastic cover labeled DIAGNOSTIC CONNECTOR.

1. On all 1995 models the diagnostic trouble codes can be read by grounding test terminal **B**. The terminal is most easily grounded by connecting it to terminal **A** (internal ECM ground). This is the terminal to the right of terminal B on the top row of the ALDL connector.

2. Once the terminals have been connected, the ignition switch must be moved to the **ON** position with the engine not running.

3. The Service Engine Soon or Check Engine light should be flashing. If it isn't, turn the ignition **OFF** and remove the jumper wire. Turn the ignition **ON** and confirm that light is now on. If it is not, replace the bulb and try again. If the bulb still will not light, or if it does not flash with the test terminal grounded, the system should be diagnosed by an experienced driveability technician. If the light is OK, proceed as follows.

4. The code(s) stored in memory may be read through counting the flashes of the dashboard warning lamp. The dash warning lamp should begin to flash Code 12. The code will display as one flash, a pause and two flashes. Code 12 is not a fault code. It is used as a system acknowledgment or handshake code; its presence indicates that the PCM can communicate as requested. Code 12 is used to begin every diagnostic sequence. Some vehicles also use Code 12 after all diagnostic codes have been sent.

5. After Code 12 has been transmitted 3 times, the fault codes, if any, will each be transmitted 3 times. The codes are stored and transmitted in numeric order from lowest to highest.

➡**The order of codes in the memory does not indicate the order of occurrence.**

6. If there are no codes stored, but a driveability or emissions problem is evident, the system should be diagnosed by an experienced driveability technician.

7. If one or more codes are stored, record them. Refer to the applicable Diagnostic Code chart in this section.

8. Switch the ignition **OFF** when finished with code retrieval or scan tool readings.

➡**After making repairs, clear the trouble codes and operate the vehicle to see if it will reset, indicating further problems.**

OBD-II SYSTEMS

▶ **See Figures 114, 115 and 116**

All 1996–00 models, an OBD-II compliant scan tool must be used to retrieve the trouble codes. Follow the scan tool manufacturer's instructions on how to connect the scan tool to the vehicle and how to retrieve the codes.

Clearing Codes

Stored fault codes may be erased from memory at any time by removing power from the PCM for at least 30 seconds. It may be necessary to clear stored codes during diagnosis to check for any recurrence during a test drive, but the stored codes must be written down when retrieved. The codes may still be required for subsequent troubleshooting. Whenever a repair is complete, the stored codes must be erased and the vehicle test driven to confirm correct operation and repair.

☀ WARNING

The ignition switch must be OFF any time power is disconnected or restored to the PCM. Severe damage may result if this precaution is not observed.

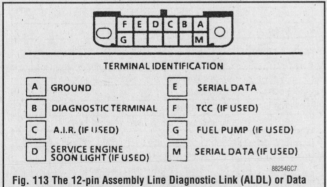

TERMINAL IDENTIFICATION

A	GROUND	E	SERIAL DATA
B	DIAGNOSTIC TERMINAL	F	TCC (IF USED)
C	A.I.R. (IF USED)	G	FUEL PUMP (IF USED)
D	SERVICE ENGINE SOON LIGHT (IF USED)	M	SERIAL DATA (IF USED)

88254GC7

Fig. 113 The 12-pin Assembly Line Diagnostic Link (ALDL) or Data Link Connector (DLC) is located under the dash—1995 vehicles

91144P39

Fig. 114 The OBD-II connector is located under the driver's side of the instrument panel

16 PIN DLC

TERMINAL IDENTIFICATION

2	SERIAL DATA (CLASS 2)	6	OUTPUT/FIELD SERVICE ENABLE
4	GROUND	9	SERIAL DATA
5	GROUND	16	B+

88254GC8

Fig. 115 A Tech 1®, or equivalent scan tool must be used to retrieve codes from 1996–00 models with the 16-pin DLC connector

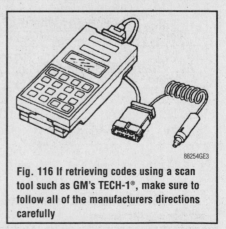

88254GE3

Fig. 116 If retrieving codes using a scan tool such as GM's TECH-1®, make sure to follow all of the manufacturers directions carefully

PCM DIAGNOSTIC TROUBLE CODES

DTC	DESCRIPTION	ILLUMINATE MIL
13	Oxygen Sensor (O2S) Circuit - open circuit	YES
14	Engine Coolant Temperature (ECT) Sensor Circuit - high temperature	YES
15	Engine Coolant Temperature (ECT) Sensor Circuit - low temperature	YES
19	Intermittent 7X Reference Signal	YES
21	Throttle Position (TP) Sensor Circuit - signal voltage high	YES
22	Throttle Position (TP) Sensor Circuit - signal voltage low	YES
23	Intake Air Temperature (IAT) Sensor Circuit - low temperature	YES
24	Vehicle Speed Sensor (VSS) Circuit	YES
25	Intake Air Temperature (IAT) Sensor Circuit - high temperature	YES
27	Quad-Driver Module (QDM1)	YES
28	Quad- Driver Module (QDM2)	NO
31	PRNDL Error	NO
32	Exhaust Gas Recirculation (EGR) Valve	YES
33	Manifold Absolute Pressure (MAP) Sensor Circuit - signal voltage high - low vacuum	YES
34	Manifold Absolute Pressure (MAP) Sensor Circuit - signal voltage low - high vacuum	YES
35	Idle Speed Error	YES
43	Knock Sensor (KS) Circuit	YES
44	Oxygen Sensor (O2S) Circuit - lean exhaust indicated	YES
45	Oxygen Sensor (O2S) Circuit - rich exhaust indicated	YES
51	EPROM Error	YES
53	Battery Voltage Error	YES
55	Fuel Lean Monitor	NO
66	A/C Refrigerant Pressure Sensor Circuit	NO
72	Loss of Serial Data	NO

87954083

Fig. 117 Diagnostic Trouble Codes—1995 Cavalier and Sunfire

DTC	Description
P0106	Manifold Absolute Pressure (MAP) System Performance
P0107	Manifold Absolute Pressure (MAP) Sensor Circuit Low Voltage
P0108	Manifold Absolute Pressure (MAP) Sensor Circuit High Voltage
P0112	Intake Air Temperature (IAT) Sensor Circuit Low Voltage
P0113	Intake Air Temperature (IAT) Sensor Circuit High Voltage
P0117	Engine Coolant Temperature (ECT) Sensor Low Voltage
P0118	Engine Coolant Temperature (ECT) Sensor High Voltage
P0121	Throttle Position (TP) Sensor Performance
P0122	Throttle Position (TP) Sensor Low Voltage
P0123	Throttle Position (TP) Sensor High Voltage
P0125	Engine Coolant Temperature (ECT) Excessive Time To Closed Loop
P0131	Oxygen Sensor (O2S) Circuit Low Voltage Sensor 1
P0132	Oxygen Sensor (O2S) Circuit High Voltage Sensor 1
P0133	Oxygen Sensor (O2S) Slow Response Sensor 1
P0134	Oxygen Sensor (O2S) Circuit Insufficient Activity Sensor 1
P0137	Heated Oxygen Sensor (HO2S) Circuit Low Voltage Sensor 2

91144G01

Fig. 118 OBD-II Diagnostic Trouble Codes—1996–00 Cavalier and Sunfire

DTC	Description
P0138	Heated Oxygen Sensor (HO2S) Circuit High Voltage Sensor 2
P0140	Heated Oxygen Sensor (HO2S) Circuit Insufficient Activity Sensor 2
P0141	Heated Oxygen Sensor (HO2S) Heater Circuit Sensor 2
P0171	Fuel Trim System Lean
P0172	Fuel Trim System Rich
P0200	Injector Control Circuit
P0300	Engine Misfire Detected
P0301	Cylinder 1 Misfire Detected
P0302	Cylinder 2 Misfire Detected
P0303	Cylinder 3 Misfire Detected
P0304	Cylinder 4 Misfire Detected
P0325	Knock Sensor (KS) Module Circuit
P0335	CKP Sensor Circuit
P0341	CMP Circuit Performance
P0342	CMP Sensor Circuit Low Voltage
P0401	EGR System
P0404	EGR Valve Open Pintle Position
P0405	EGR Valve Sensor Signal Low
P0420	TWC System Low Efficiency Bank 1
P0440	EVAP System
P0442	EVAP Control System Small Leak Detected
P0446	EVAP Canister Vent Blocked
P0452	Fuel Tank Pressure Sensor Circuit Low Voltage
P0453	Fuel Tank Pressure Sensor Circuit High Voltage
P0460	Fuel Level Sensor Circuit
P0480	FC Relay Control Circuit
P0502	VSS Circuit Low Input (MT)
P0506	Idle Control System Low RPM
P0507	Idle Control System High RPM
P0530	A/C Refrigerant Pressure Sensor Circuit
P0562	System Voltage Low
P0563	System Voltage High
P0601	PCM Memory
P0602	PCM Not Programmed
P0705	Transmission Range Switch Circuit (A/T)
P1133	Oxygen Sensor (O2S) Insufficient Switching Sensor 1
P1171	Fuel System Lean During Acceleration
P1336	CKP System Variation Not Learned
P1380	EBCM DTC Detected – Rough Road Data Unusable
P1381	Misfire Detected – No EBCM/PCM Serial Data
P1404	EGR Valve Closed Pintle Position

91144G02

Fig. 119 OBD-II Diagnostic Trouble Codes—1996–00 Cavalier and Sunfire, continued

DTC	Description
P1441	Evaporative Emissions (EVAP) System Flow During Non–Purge
P1621	PCM Memory Performance
P1629	Theft Deterrent Crank Signal Malfunction
U1016	Serial Communication Malfunction

91144G03

Fig. 120 OBD-II Diagnostic Trouble Codes—1996–00 Cavalier and Sunfire, continued

Depending on the electrical distribution of the particular vehicle, power to the PCM may be disconnected by removing the PCM fuse in the fusebox, disconnecting the in-line fuse holder near the positive battery terminal or disconnecting the PCM power lead at the battery terminal. Disconnecting the negative battery cable to clear codes is not recommended as this will also clear other memory data in the vehicle such as radio presets.

VACUUM DIAGRAMS

◆ **See Figures 121 thru 126**

Following are vacuum diagrams for most of the engine and emissions package combinations covered by this manual. Because vacuum circuits will vary based on various engine and vehicle options, always refer first to the vehicle emission control information label, if present. Should the label be missing, or should vehicle be equipped with a different engine from the vehicle's original equipment, refer to the diagrams below for the same or similar configuration.

If you wish to obtain a replacement emissions label, most manufacturers make the labels available for purchase. The labels can usually be ordered from a local dealer.

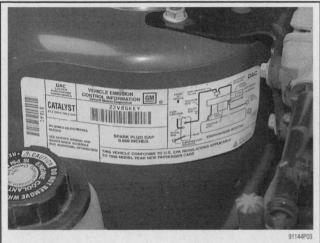

Fig. 121 The Vehicle Emission Control Information or VECI label is usually attached to the passenger side strut tower in the engine compartment

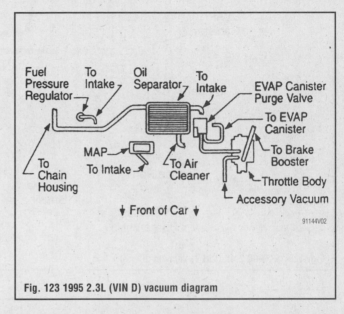

Fig. 123 1995 2.3L (VIN D) vacuum diagram

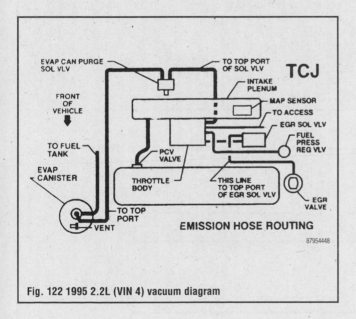

Fig. 122 1995 2.2L (VIN 4) vacuum diagram

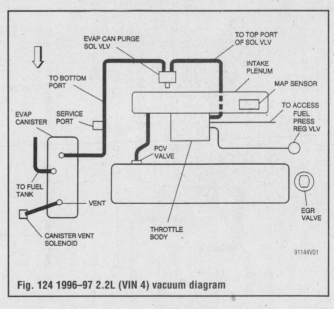

Fig. 124 1996–97 2.2L (VIN 4) vacuum diagram

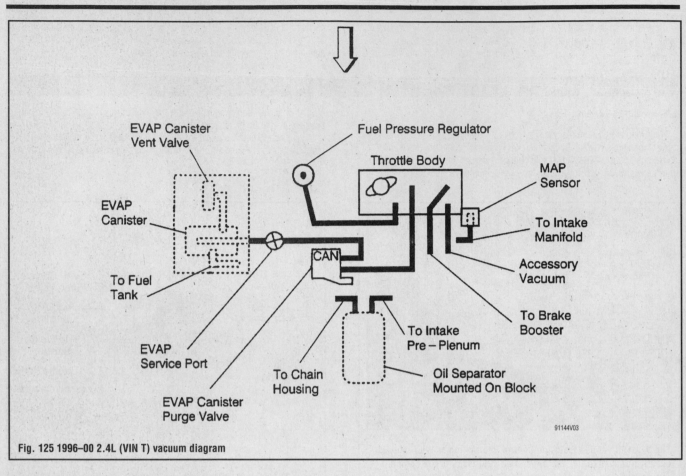

Fig. 125 1996–00 2.4L (VIN T) vacuum diagram

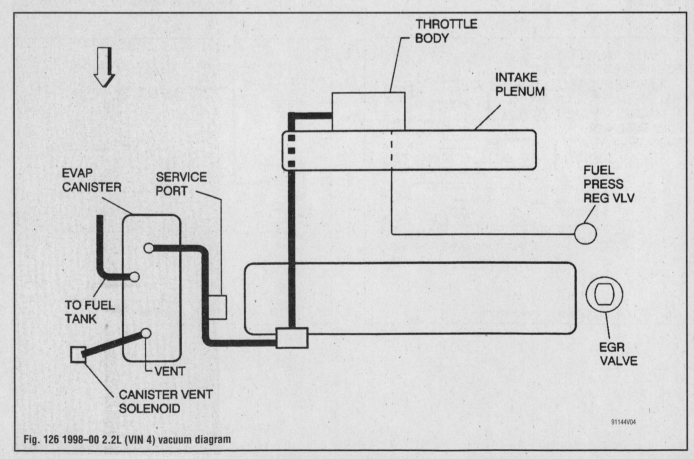

Fig. 126 1998–00 2.2L (VIN 4) vacuum diagram

**BASIC FUEL SYSTEM
  DIAGNOSIS 5-2**
FUEL LINE FITTINGS 5-2
QUICK-CONNECT FITTINGS 5-2
  REMOVAL & INSTALLATION 5-2
**BOTTOM FEED PORT (BFP)
  INJECTION SYSTEM 5-3**
SYSTEM DESCRIPTION 5-3
FUEL SYSTEM PRESSURE RELIEF 5-3
FUEL PUMP 5-3
  TESTING 5-3
  REMOVAL & INSTALLATION 5-4
THROTTLE BODY 5-5
  REMOVAL & INSTALLATION 5-5
BOTTOM FEED PORT FUEL
  INJECTORS 5-5
  TESTING 5-5
  REMOVAL & INSTALLATION 5-6
FUEL PRESSURE REGULATOR 5-8
  REMOVAL & INSTALLATION 5-8
**MULTI-PORT (MFI) & SEQUENTIAL
  (SFI) FUEL INJECTION
  SYSTEMS 5-9**
GENERAL INFORMATION 5-9
RELIEVING FUEL SYSTEM
  PRESSURE 5-9
FUEL PUMP 5-9
  TESTING 5-9
  REMOVAL & INSTALLATION 5-13
THROTTLE BODY 5-13
  REMOVAL & INSTALLATION 5-13
FUEL INJECTORS 5-15
  TESTING 5-15
  REMOVAL & INSTALLATION 5-15
FUEL RAIL ASSEMBLY 5-16
  REMOVAL & INSTALLATION 5-16
FUEL PRESSURE REGULATOR 5-18
  REMOVAL & INSTALLATION 5-18
FUEL TANK 5-19
TANK ASSEMBLY 5-19
  REMOVAL & INSTALLATION 5-19

5

FUEL SYSTEM

BASIC FUEL SYSTEM DIAGNOSIS 5-2
FUEL LINE FITTINGS 5-2
BOTTOM FEED PORT (BFP)
INJECTION SYSTEM 5-3
MULTI-PORT (MFI) & SEQUENTIAL
(SFI) FUEL INJECTION SYSTEMS 5-9
FUEL TANK 5-19

BASIC FUEL SYSTEM DIAGNOSIS

When there is a problem starting or driving a vehicle, two of the most important checks involve the ignition and the fuel systems. The questions most mechanics attempt to answer first, "is there spark?" and "is there fuel?" will often lead to solving most basic problems. For ignition system diagnosis and testing, please refer to the information on engine electrical components and ignition systems found earlier in this manual. If the ignition system checks out (there is spark), then you must determine if the fuel system is operating properly (is there fuel?).

FUEL LINE FITTINGS

Quick-Connect Fittings

REMOVAL & INSTALLATION

▶ See Figures 1, 2 and 3

➥This procedure requires Tool Set J37088–A fuel line quick-connect separator.

1. Grasp both sides of the fitting. Twist the female connector ¼ turn in each direction to loosen any dirt within the fittings. Using compressed air, blow out the dirt from the quick-connect fittings at the end of the fittings.

✳✳ CAUTION

Safety glasses MUST be worn when using compressed air to avoid eye injury due to flying dirt particles!

2. For plastic (hand releasable) fittings, squeeze the plastic retainer release tabs, then pull the connection apart.
3. For metal fittings, choose the correct tool from kit J37088–A for the size of the fitting to be disconnected. Insert the proper tool into the female connector, then push inward to release the locking tabs. Pull the connection apart.

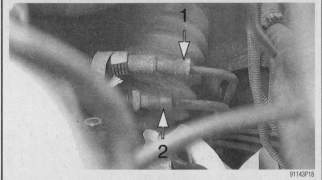

Fig. 2 The fuel line connections under the power brake booster, No. 1 is the feed line and No. 2 is the return line

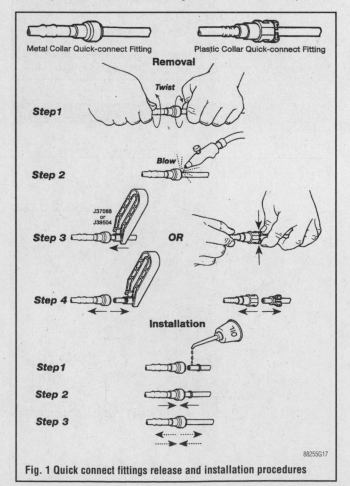

Fig. 1 Quick connect fittings release and installation procedures

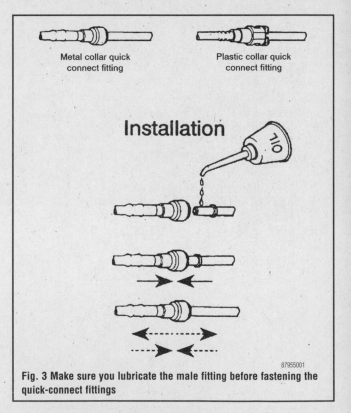

Fig. 3 Make sure you lubricate the male fitting before fastening the quick-connect fittings

4. If it is necessary to remove rust or burrs from the male tube end of a quick-connect fitting, use emery cloth in a radial motion with the tube end to prevent damage to the O-ring sealing surfaces. Using a clean shop towel, wipe off the male tube ends. Inspect all connectors for dirt and burrs. Clean and/or replace if required.

To install:

5. Apply a few drops of clean engine oil to the male tube end of the fitting.
6. Push the connectors together to cause the retaining tabs/fingers to snap into place.
7. Once installed, pull on both ends of each connection to make sure they are secure.

BOTTOM FEED PORT (BFP) INJECTION SYSTEM

System Description

▶ See Figure 4

➡**The Bottom Feed Port (BFP) injection system is used on the 1995–97 2.2L OHV (VIN 4) engines.**

The function of the fuel metering system is to deliver the correct amount of fuel to the engine under all operating conditions. In this system, fuel is delivered to the engine by individual bottom feed type multi-port fuel injectors mounted in the lower intake manifold near each cylinder.

The Powertrain Control Module (PCM) pulses the fuel injectors in pairs. Alternate pairs are pulsed every 180° of crankshaft revolution. This is called Alternating Synchronous Double Fire (ASDF) injection. The PCM uses two injector driver circuits, each controlling a pair of injectors. The current in each circuit is allowed to climb to a peak of 4 amps and then is reduced to 1 amp to hold the injector open. This happens very quickly.

The main control sensor of this system is the Oxygen (O_2) sensor, located in the exhaust manifold. This sensor indicates to the computer control module how much oxygen is in the exhaust gas, and the PCM changes the air/fuel ratio to the engine by controlling the fuel injectors. The best mixture to keep exhaust emissions to a minimum is 14.7:1 which allows the catalytic converter to operate most efficiently. Because of the constant measuring and adjusting of the air/fuel ratio, the fuel injection system is called a "Closed Loop" system.

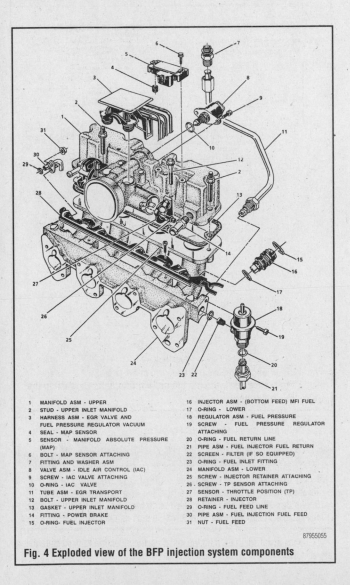

1 MANIFOLD ASM - UPPER	16 INJECTOR ASM - (BOTTOM FEED) MFI FUEL
2 STUD - UPPER INLET MANIFOLD	17 O-RING - LOWER
3 HARNESS ASM - EGR VALVE AND	18 REGULATOR ASM - FUEL PRESSURE
FUEL PRESSURE REGULATOR VACUUM	19 SCREW - FUEL PRESSURE REGULATOR
4 SEAL - MAP SENSOR	ATTACHING
5 SENSOR - MANIFOLD ABSOLUTE PRESSURE	20 O-RING - FUEL RETURN LINE
(MAP)	21 PIPE ASM - FUEL INJECTOR FUEL RETURN
6 BOLT - MAP SENSOR ATTACHING	22 SCREEN - FILTER (IF SO EQUIPPED)
7 FITTING AND WASHER ASM	23 O-RING - FUEL INLET FITTING
8 VALVE ASM - IDLE AIR CONTROL (IAC)	24 MANIFOLD ASM - LOWER
9 SCREW - IAC VALVE ATTACHING	25 SCREW - INJECTOR RETAINER ATTACHING
10 O-RING - IAC VALVE	26 SCREW - TP SENSOR ATTACHING
11 TUBE ASM - EGR TRANSPORT	27 SENSOR - THROTTLE POSITION (TP)
12 BOLT - UPPER INLET MANIFOLD	28 RETAINER - INJECTOR
13 GASKET - UPPER INLET MANIFOLD	29 O-RING - FUEL FEED LINE
14 FITTING - POWER BRAKE	30 PIPE ASM - FUEL INJECTION FUEL FEED
15 O-RING- FUEL INJECTOR	31 NUT - FUEL FEED

87955055

Fig. 4 Exploded view of the BFP injection system components

Fuel System Pressure Relief

▶ See Figure 5

1. Loosen the fuel filler cap to relieve tank pressure (do not tighten at this time).
2. Start the engine and let it idle.
3. Remove the fuel pump relay from the power distribution block in the engine compartment.
4. Let the engine run until the fuel supply remaining in the fuel pipes is consumed. Engage the starter for 3 seconds to assure relief of any remaining pressure.
5. Replace the fuel pump fuse in the fuse block.
6. Disconnect the negative battery cable to avoid possible fuel discharge if an accidental attempt is made to start the engine.

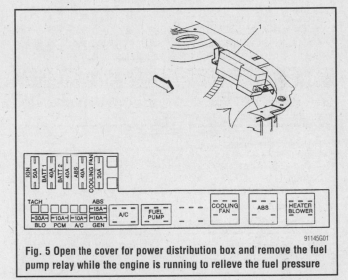

91145G01

Fig. 5 Open the cover for power distribution box and remove the fuel pump relay while the engine is running to relieve the fuel pressure

Fuel Pump

TESTING

▶ See Figures 6 thru 11

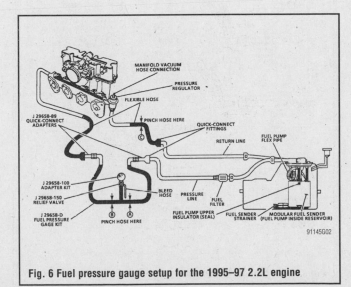

91145G02

Fig. 6 Fuel pressure gauge setup for the 1995–97 2.2L engine

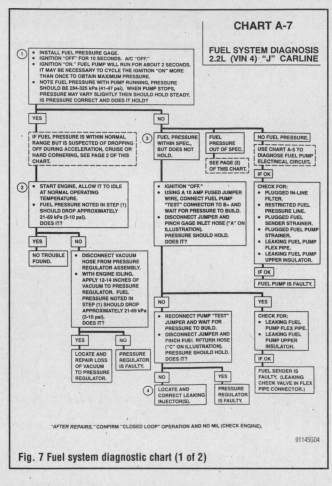

CHART A-7

FUEL SYSTEM DIAGNOSIS
2.2L (VIN 4) "J" CARLINE

① • INSTALL FUEL PRESSURE GAGE.
• IGNITION "OFF" FOR 10 SECONDS. A/C "OFF."
• IGNITION "ON." FUEL PUMP WILL RUN FOR ABOUT 2 SECONDS. IT MAY BE NECESSARY TO CYCLE THE IGNITION "ON" MORE THAN ONCE TO OBTAIN MAXIMUM PRESSURE.
• NOTE FUEL PRESSURE WITH PUMP RUNNING, PRESSURE SHOULD BE 284-325 kPa (41-47 psi). WHEN PUMP STOPS, PRESSURE MAY VARY SLIGHTLY THEN SHOULD HOLD STEADY. IS PRESSURE CORRECT AND DOES IT HOLD?

"AFTER REPAIRS," CONFIRM "CLOSED LOOP" OPERATION AND NO MIL (CHECK ENGINE).

91145G04

Fig. 7 Fuel system diagnostic chart (1 of 2)

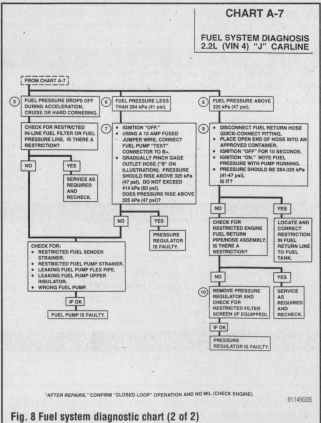

CHART A-7

FUEL SYSTEM DIAGNOSIS
2.2L (VIN 4) "J" CARLINE

"AFTER REPAIRS," CONFIRM "CLOSED LOOP" OPERATION AND NO MIL (CHECK ENGINE).

91145G05

Fig. 8 Fuel system diagnostic chart (2 of 2)

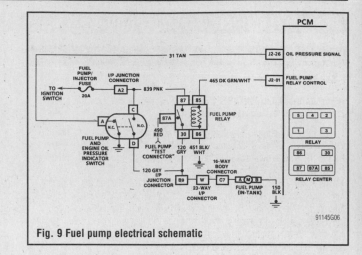

Fig. 9 Fuel pump electrical schematic

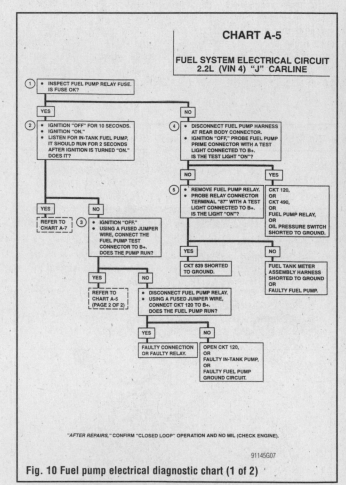

CHART A-5

FUEL SYSTEM ELECTRICAL CIRCUIT
2.2L (VIN 4) "J" CARLINE

"AFTER REPAIRS," CONFIRM "CLOSED LOOP" OPERATION AND NO MIL (CHECK ENGINE).

91145G07

Fig. 10 Fuel pump electrical diagnostic chart (1 of 2)

REMOVAL & INSTALLATION

▶ See Figures 12 and 13

❊❊ CAUTION

The fuel injection system remains under pressure, even after the engine has been turned OFF. The fuel system pressure must be relieved before disconnecting any fuel lines. Failure to do so may result in fire and/or personal injury.

1. Relieve the fuel system pressure using the recommended procedure.
2. Disconnect the negative battery cable.

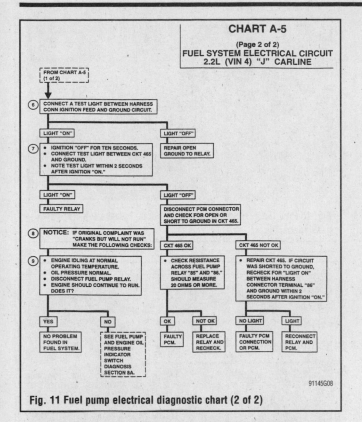

CHART A-5

(Page 2 of 2)
**FUEL SYSTEM ELECTRICAL CIRCUIT
2.2L (VIN 4) "J" CARLINE**

FROM CHART A-5
(1 of 2)

6 CONNECT A TEST LIGHT BETWEEN HARNESS CONN IGNITION FEED AND GROUND CIRCUIT.

LIGHT "ON" → **7** • IGNITION "OFF" FOR TEN SECONDS. • CONNECT TEST LIGHT BETWEEN CKT 465 AND GROUND. • NOTE TEST LIGHT WITHIN 2 SECONDS AFTER IGNITION "ON."

LIGHT "OFF" → REPAIR OPEN GROUND TO RELAY.

LIGHT "ON" → FAULTY RELAY

LIGHT "OFF" → DISCONNECT PCM CONNECTOR AND CHECK FOR OPEN OR SHORT TO GROUND IN CKT 465.

8 NOTICE: IF ORIGINAL COMPLAINT WAS "CRANKS BUT WILL NOT RUN" MAKE THE FOLLOWING CHECKS:

CKT 465 OK → • CHECK RESISTANCE ACROSS FUEL PUMP RELAY "85" AND "86". SHOULD MEASURE 20 OHMS OR MORE.

CKT 465 NOT OK → • REPAIR CKT 465. IF CIRCUIT WAS SHORTED TO GROUND, RECHECK FOR "LIGHT ON" BETWEEN HARNESS CONNECTOR TERMINAL "86" AND GROUND WITHIN 2 SECONDS AFTER IGNITION "ON."

9 • ENGINE IDLING AT NORMAL OPERATING TEMPERATURE. • OIL PRESSURE NORMAL. • DISCONNECT FUEL PUMP RELAY. • ENGINE SHOULD CONTINUE TO RUN. DOES IT?

YES → NO PROBLEM FOUND IN FUEL SYSTEM.

NO → SEE FUEL PUMP AND ENGINE OIL PRESSURE INDICATOR SWITCH DIAGNOSIS SECTION 8A.

OK → FAULTY PCM.

NOT OK → REPLACE RELAY AND RECHECK.

NO LIGHT → FAULTY PCM CONNECTION OR PCM.

LIGHT → RECONNECT RELAY AND PCM.

91145G08

Fig. 11 Fuel pump electrical diagnostic chart (2 of 2)

3. Drain the fuel tank, then remove the fuel tank from the vehicle.
4. While holding the modular fuel sender assembly down, remove the snap-ring from the designated slots located on the retainer.

☀ WARNING

The modular fuel sender assembly may spring up from its position. When removing the modular fuel sender from the tank, be aware that the reservoir bucket is full of fuel. It must be tipped slightly during removal to avoid damage to the float.

5. Remove the external fuel strainer.
6. Detach the Connector Position Assurance (CPA) piece from the electrical connector and detach the fuel pump electrical connector.

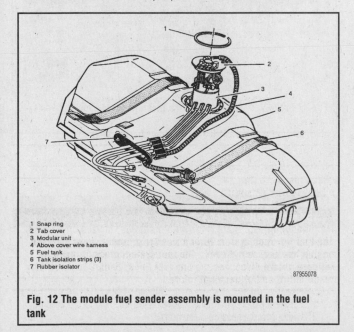

1 Snap ring
2 Tab cover
3 Modular unit
4 Above cover wire harness
5 Fuel tank
6 Tank isolation strips (3)
7 Rubber isolator

87955078

Fig. 12 The module fuel sender assembly is mounted in the fuel tank

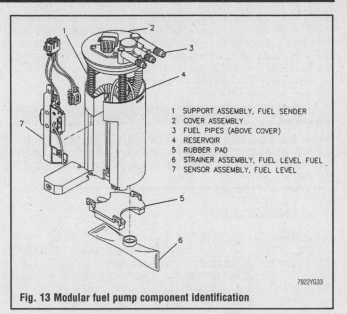

1 SUPPORT ASSEMBLY, FUEL SENDER
2 COVER ASSEMBLY
3 FUEL PIPES (ABOVE COVER)
4 RESERVOIR
5 RUBBER PAD
6 STRAINER ASSEMBLY, FUEL LEVEL FUEL
7 SENSOR ASSEMBLY, FUEL LEVEL

7922YG33

Fig. 13 Modular fuel pump component identification

7. Gently release the tabs on the sides of the fuel sender at the cover assembly. Begin by squeezing the sides of the reservoir and releasing the tab opposite the fuel level sensor. Move clockwise to release the second and third tabs In the same manner.
8. Lift the cover assembly out far enough to detach the fuel pump electrical connection.
9. Rotate the fuel pump baffle counterclockwise and remove the baffle and pump assembly from the retainer.
10. Slide the fuel pump outlet out of slot, then remove the fuel pump outlet seal.

To install:
11. Install the fuel pump outlet seal, then slide the fuel pump outlet in the slots of reservoir cover.
12. Install the fuel pump and baffle assembly onto the reservoir retainer and rotate clockwise until seated.
13. Install the lower retainer assembly partially into the reservoir. Line up all 3 sleeve tabs. Press the retainer onto the reservoir making sure all 3 tabs are firmly seated.

➡**Gently pull on the fuel pump reservoir from retainer to assure a secure fastening. If not secure, replace the entire fuel sender.**

14. Attach the fuel pump connector.
15. Fasten the CPA connector to the fuel sender cover.
16. Install a new external fuel strainer.
17. Install the modular fuel sender.
18. Install the fuel tank in the vehicle.
19. Connect the negative battery cable.
20. Pressurize the fuel system and verify no leaks.

Throttle Body

REMOVAL & INSTALLATION

The throttle body on the 1995–97 2.2L engine is cast part of the upper intake manifold. To replace the throttle body, you must replace the entire upper intake manifold. Refer to Section 3 for the removal and installation of the upper intake manifold.

Bottom Feed Port Fuel Injectors

TESTING

The easiest way to test the operation of the fuel injectors is to listen for a clicking sound coming from the injectors while the engine is running. This is accomplished using a mechanic's stethoscope, or a long screwdriver. Place the end of the stethoscope or the screwdriver (tip end, not handle) onto the body of the injector. Place the ear pieces of the stethoscope in your ears, or if using a screwdriver, place your ear on top of the handle. An audible clicking noise should be heard; this is the solenoid operating. If the injector makes this noise, the injector driver circuit and computer are operating as designed. Continue testing all the injectors this way.

✳✳ CAUTION

Be extremely careful while working on an operating engine, make sure you have no dangling jewelry, extremely loose clothes, power tool cords or other items that might get caught in a moving part of the engine.

All Injectors Clicking

If all the injectors are clicking, but you have determined that the fuel system is the cause of your driveability problem, continue diagnostics. Make sure that you have checked fuel pump pressure as outlined earlier in this section. An easy way to determine a weak or unproductive cylinder is a cylinder drop test. This is accomplished by removing one spark plug wire at a time, and seeing which cylinder causes the least difference in the idle. The one that causes the least change is the weak cylinder.

If the injectors were all clicking and the ignition system is functioning properly, remove the injector of the suspect cylinder and bench test it. This is accomplished by checking for a spray pattern from the injector itself. Install a fuel supply line to the injector (or rail if the injector is left attached to the rail) and momentarily apply 12 volts DC and a ground to the injector itself; a visible fuel spray should appear. If no spray is achieved, replace the injector and check the running condition of the engine.

One or More Injectors Are Not Clicking

▶ See Figures 14, 15, 16 and 17

If one or more injectors are found to be not operating, testing the injector driver circuit and computer can be accomplished using a "noid" light. First, with the engine not running and the ignition key in the **OFF** position, remove the connector from the injector you plan to test, then plug the "noid" light tool into the injector connector. Start the engine and the "noid" light should flash, signaling that the injector driver circuit is working. If the "noid" light flashes, but the injector does not click when plugged in, test the injector's resistance. resistance should be between 11–18 ohms.

If the "noid" light does not flash, the injector driver circuit is faulty. Disconnect the negative battery cable. Unplug the "noid" light from the injector connector and also unplug the PCM. Check the harness between the appropriate pins on the harness side of the PCM connector and the injector connector. Resistance should be less than 5.0 ohms; if not, repair the circuit. If resistance is within specifications, the injector driver inside the PCM is faulty and replacement of the PCM will be necessary.

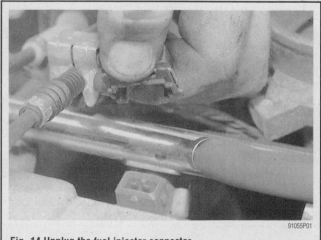
Fig. 14 Unplug the fuel injector connector

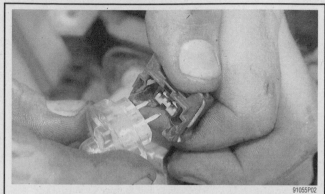
Fig. 15 Plug the correct "noid" light directly into the injector harness connector

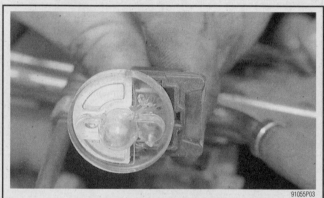
Fig. 16 If the correct "noid" light flashes while the engine is running, the injector driver circuit inside the PCM is working

Fig. 17 Probe the two terminals of a fuel injector to check it's resistance

REMOVAL & INSTALLATION

▶ See Figures 18 thru 24

✳✳ WARNING

Any time the injectors are removed for service, always remove the fuel pressure regulator to drain excess fuel, and prevent fuel from entering the engine cylinders. Flooded cylinders could result in engine damage.

1. Relieve the fuel system pressure as outlined earlier.
2. Disconnect the negative battery cable.
3. Remove the upper manifold assembly.

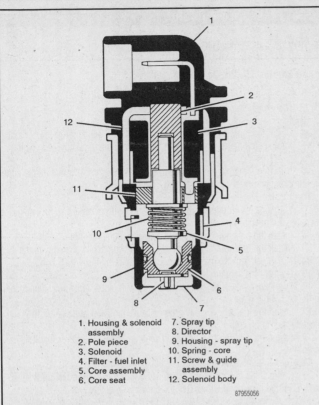

Fig. 18 Cross-section view of a bottom feed fuel injector

1. Housing & solenoid assembly
2. Pole piece
3. Solenoid
4. Filter - fuel inlet
5. Core assembly
6. Core seat
7. Spray tip
8. Director
9. Housing - spray tip
10. Spring - core
11. Screw & guide assembly
12. Solenoid body

87955056

✳✳ CAUTION

To reduce the chance of personal injury, cover the fuel line connections with a shop towel, when disconnecting.

4. Disconnect the fuel return line retaining bracket nut and move the return line away from the regulator.
5. Remove the pressure regulator assembly.

✳✳ WARNING

Do not try to remove the injectors by lifting up on the injector retaining bracket while the injectors are still installed in the in the bracket slots or damage to the bracket and/or injectors could result. Do not attempt to remove the bracket without first removing the pressure regulator.

6. Remove the injector retainer bracket attaching screws and carefully slide the bracket off to clear the injector slots and regulator.
7. Detach the injector electrical connectors.
8. Remove the fuel injector(s), then remove and discard the O-ring seals.

✳✳ CAUTION

To reduce the risk fire and personal injury, make sure that the lower (small) O-ring of each injector does not remain in the lower manifold. If the O-ring is not removed with the injector, the replacement injector, with new O-rings, will not seat properly in the injector socket and could cause a fuel leak.

9. Cover the injector sockets to prevent dirt from entering the opening.

➡Each injector is calibrated with a different flow rate so be sure to replace the injector with the identical part numbers.

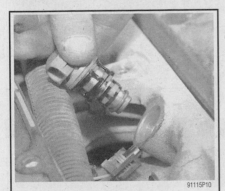

Fig. 19 Remove the fuel injector retainer bracket attaching screws (arrows)

91115P07

Fig. 20 Remove the bracket by carefully sliding it off to clear the injector slots

91115P08

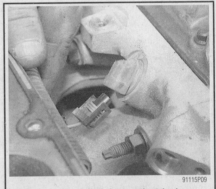

Fig. 21 Unplug the injector electrical connectors

91115P09

Fig. 22 Remove the fuel injectors from the lower intake manifold assembly

91115P10

Fig. 23 Remove the injector O-rings and discard them

91115P11

Fig. 24 You may need to use a pick to remove the O-rings as the are sometimes hard to get a hold of

91115P12

To install:

10. Lubricate the new injector O-ring seals with clean engine oil and install on the injector assembly.

11. Install the injector assembly into the lower manifold injector socket, with the electrical connectors facing inward.

12. Carefully position the injector retainer bracket so that the injector retaining slots and regulator are aligned with the bracket slots.

13. Attach the injector electrical connectors.

14. Install the pressure regulator assembly.

15. Install the injector retainer bracket retaining screws, coated with thread locking material and tighten to 31 inch lbs. (3.5 Nm).

16. Install the accelerator cable bracket with the attaching bolts/nuts finger-tight at this time.

※※ WARNING

The accelerator bracket must be aligned with the accelerator cam to prevent cable wear, which could result in cable breakage.

17. Align the accelerator bracket as follows:

a. Place a steel rule across the bore of the throttle body, with one end in contact with the accelerator bracket.

b. Adjust the accelerator bracket to obtain a $^{25}\!/_{64}$ in. (9–11mm) gap between the bracket and the throttle body.

c. Tighten the top bolt first and tighten all bolts/nuts to 18 ft. lbs. (25 Nm).

18. Tighten the fuel filer cap.

19. Connect the negative battery cable and turn the ignition **ON** for 2 seconds, **OFF** for 10 seconds, then **ON** and check for fuel leaks.

20. Install the air intake duct.

Fuel Pressure Regulator

REMOVAL & INSTALLATION

▶ **See Figures 25, 26, 27, 28 and 29**

1. Relieve the fuel system pressure as outlined earlier.
2. Disconnect the negative battery cable.
3. Remove the vacuum hose from the regulator.
4. Place a rag under the connection and remove the fuel return pipe clamp.
5. Remove the fuel return pipe and O-ring from the regulator. Discard the O-ring.
6. Unfasten the pressure regulator bracket attaching screw, then remove the pressure regulator assembly and O-ring. Discard the O-ring.

To install:

7. Lubricate a new pressure regulator O-ring with clean engine oil, then install on the pressure regulator.
8. Install the pressure regulator assembly onto the manifold.
9. Install the pressure regulator bracket attaching screw coated with the appropriate thread locking material and tighten to 31 inch lbs. (3.5 Nm).
10. Connect the vacuum hose to the regulator.
11. Lubricate a new fuel return pipe O-ring with clean engine oil, then install on the end of the pipe.
12. Install the fuel return pipe to the pressure regulator and tighten the attaching nut to 22 inch lbs. (30 Nm).
13. Fasten the fuel return pipe clamp attaching nut to the lower manifold assembly.
14. Tighten the fuel filler cap.
15. Connect the negative battery cable and turn the ignition **ON** for 2 seconds, **OFF** for 10 seconds, then **ON** and check for fuel leaks.

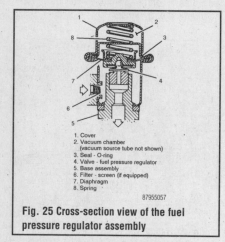

1. Cover
2. Vacuum chamber
   (vacuum source tube not shown)
3. Seal - O-ring
4. Valve - fuel pressure regulator
5. Base assembly
6. Filter - screen (if equipped)
7. Diaphragm
8. Spring

87955057

Fig. 25 Cross-section view of the fuel pressure regulator assembly

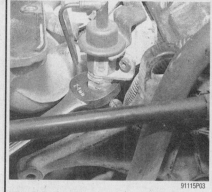

91115P03

Fig. 26 Use a wrench to unfasten the fuel line-to-regulator fitting

91115P04

Fig. 27 Disconnect the vacuum hose from the regulator

91115P05

Fig. 28 Remove the pressure regulator attaching screw

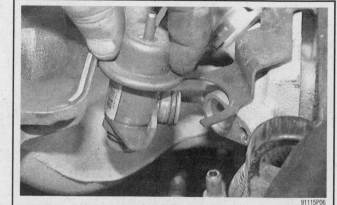

91115P06

Fig. 29 Remove the regulator from the manifold and discard the O-ring

MULTI-PORT (MFI) & SEQUENTIAL (SFI) FUEL INJECTION SYSTEMS

General Information

On the 1995 2.3L engines, the fuel system is a multi-port fuel injection (MFI) system. The MFI system is controlled by a powertrain control module (PCM) which monitors engine operations and generates output signals to provide the correct air/fuel mixture, ignition timing and engine idle speed control. Input to the control unit is provided by an oxygen sensor, coolant temperature sensor, knock sensor, hot film air mass sensor and throttle position sensor. The PCM also receives information concerning engine rpm, road speed, transmission gear position, power steering and air conditioning.

On the 1996 and later 2.4L engines, and 1998 and later 2.2L engines, a sequential port fuel injection system (SFI) is used for more precise fuel control. With SFI, metered fuel is timed and injected sequentially through injectors into individual cylinder ports. Each cylinder receives one injection per working cycle (every two revolutions), just prior to the opening of the intake valve. The main difference between the two types of fuel injection systems is the manner in which fuel is injected. In the multiport system, all injectors work simultaneously, injecting half the fuel charge each engine revolution. The PCMs are different for SFI and MFI systems, but most other components are similar. The MFI system PCM has two injector drivers inside, one for two cylinders each and the SFI system PCM has four injector drive circuits, one for each cylinder.

Both systems use Bosch injectors, one at each intake port. The injectors are mounted on a fuel rail and are activated by a signal from the PCM. The injector is a solenoid-operated valve which remains open depending on the width of the electronic pulses (length of the signal) from the PCM; the longer the open time, the more fuel is injected. In this manner, the air/fuel mixture can be precisely controlled for maximum performance with minimum emissions.

Fuel is pumped from the tank by a high pressure fuel pump, located inside the fuel tank. It is a positive displacement roller vane pump. The impeller serves as a vapor separator and pre-charges the high pressure assembly. A pressure regulator maintains 28–36 psi in the fuel line to the injectors and the excess fuel is fed back to the tank.

Relieving Fuel System Pressure

▶ See Figure 30

1. Loosen the fuel filler cap to relieve tank pressure (do not tighten at this time).
2. Start the engine and let it idle.
3. Remove the fuel pump relay from the power distribution block in the engine compartment.
4. Let the engine run until the fuel supply remaining in the fuel pipes is consumed. Engage the starter for 3 seconds to assure relief of any remaining pressure.
5. Replace the fuel pump fuse in the fuse block.

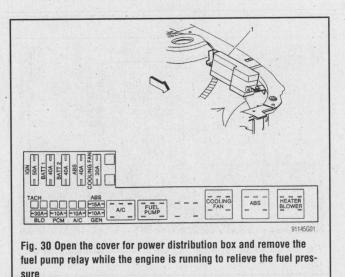

Fig. 30 Open the cover for power distribution box and remove the fuel pump relay while the engine is running to relieve the fuel pressure

6. Disconnect the negative battery cable to avoid possible fuel discharge if an accidental attempt is made to start the engine.

Fuel Pump

TESTING

▶ See Figures 31 thru 51

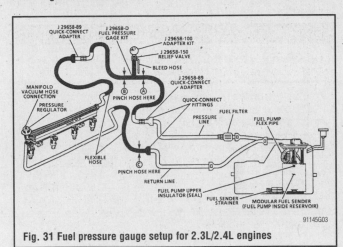

Fig. 31 Fuel pressure gauge setup for 2.3L/2.4L engines

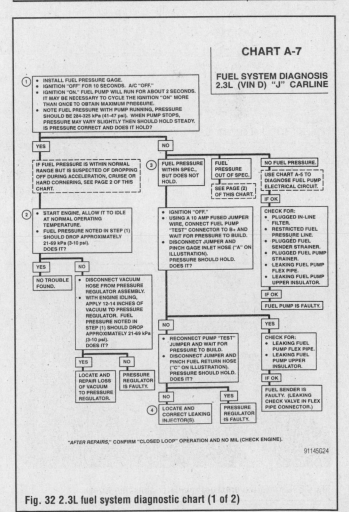

Fig. 32 2.3L fuel system diagnostic chart (1 of 2)

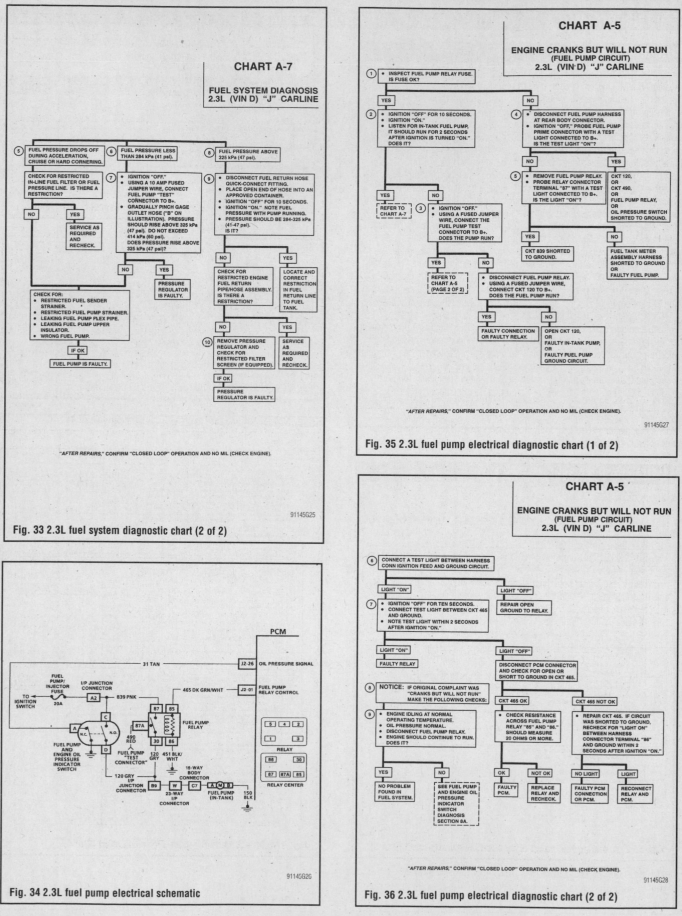

CHART A-7

FUEL SYSTEM DIAGNOSIS
2.3L (VIN D) "J" CARLINE

⑤ FUEL PRESSURE DROPS OFF DURING ACCELERATION, CRUISE OR HARD CORNERING.

CHECK FOR RESTRICTED IN-LINE FUEL FILTER OR FUEL PRESSURE LINE. IS THERE A RESTRICTION?

NO → SERVICE AS REQUIRED AND RECHECK.

⑥ FUEL PRESSURE LESS THAN 284 kPa (41 psi).

⑦ • IGNITION "OFF."
• USING A 10 AMP FUSED JUMPER WIRE, CONNECT FUEL PUMP "TEST" CONNECTOR TO B+.
• GRADUALLY PINCH GAGE OUTLET HOSE ("B" ON ILLUSTRATION). PRESSURE SHOULD RISE ABOVE 325 kPa (47 psi). DO NOT EXCEED 414 kPa (60 psi). DOES PRESSURE RISE ABOVE 325 kPa (47 psi)?

NO

YES → PRESSURE REGULATOR IS FAULTY.

CHECK FOR:
• RESTRICTED FUEL SENDER STRAINER.
• RESTRICTED FUEL PUMP STRAINER.
• LEAKING FUEL PUMP FLEX PIPE.
• LEAKING FUEL PUMP UPPER INSULATOR.
• WRONG FUEL PUMP.

IF OK

FUEL PUMP IS FAULTY.

⑧ FUEL PRESSURE ABOVE 325 kPa (47 psi).

⑨ • DISCONNECT FUEL RETURN HOSE QUICK-CONNECT FITTING.
• PLACE OPEN END OF HOSE INTO AN APPROVED CONTAINER.
• IGNITION "OFF" FOR 10 SECONDS.
• IGNITION "ON." NOTE FUEL PRESSURE WITH PUMP RUNNING.
• PRESSURE SHOULD BE 284-325 kPa (41-47 psi). IS IT?

NO → CHECK FOR RESTRICTED ENGINE FUEL RETURN PIPE/HOSE ASSEMBLY. IS THERE A RESTRICTION?

YES → LOCATE AND CORRECT RESTRICTION IN FUEL RETURN LINE TO FUEL TANK.

NO → ⑩ REMOVE PRESSURE REGULATOR AND CHECK FOR RESTRICTED FILTER SCREEN (IF EQUIPPED).

YES → SERVICE AS REQUIRED AND RECHECK.

IF OK

PRESSURE REGULATOR IS FAULTY.

"AFTER REPAIRS," CONFIRM "CLOSED LOOP" OPERATION AND NO MIL (CHECK ENGINE).

91145G25

Fig. 33 2.3L fuel system diagnostic chart (2 of 2)

CHART A-5

ENGINE CRANKS BUT WILL NOT RUN
(FUEL PUMP CIRCUIT)
2.3L (VIN D) "J" CARLINE

① • INSPECT FUEL PUMP RELAY FUSE. IS FUSE OK?

YES

② • IGNITION "OFF" FOR 10 SECONDS.
• IGNITION "ON."
• LISTEN FOR IN-TANK FUEL PUMP, IT SHOULD RUN FOR 2 SECONDS AFTER IGNITION IS TURNED "ON." DOES IT?

YES → REFER TO CHART A-7

NO → ③ • IGNITION "OFF."
• USING A FUSED JUMPER WIRE, CONNECT THE FUEL PUMP TEST CONNECTOR TO B+. DOES THE PUMP RUN?

YES → REFER TO CHART A-5 (PAGE 2 OF 2)

NO → • DISCONNECT FUEL PUMP RELAY.
• USING A FUSED JUMPER WIRE, CONNECT CKT 120 TO B+. DOES THE FUEL PUMP RUN?

YES → FAULTY CONNECTION OR FAULTY RELAY.

NO → OPEN CKT 120, OR FAULTY IN-TANK PUMP, OR FAULTY FUEL PUMP GROUND CIRCUIT.

NO → ④ • DISCONNECT FUEL PUMP HARNESS AT REAR BODY CONNECTOR.
• IGNITION "OFF," PROBE FUEL PUMP PRIME CONNECTOR WITH A TEST LIGHT CONNECTED TO B+. IS THE TEST LIGHT "ON"?

NO → ⑤ • REMOVE FUEL PUMP RELAY.
• PROBE RELAY CONNECTOR TERMINAL "87" WITH A TEST LIGHT CONNECTED TO B+. IS THE LIGHT "ON"?

YES → CKT 839 SHORTED TO GROUND.

NO → FUEL TANK METER ASSEMBLY HARNESS SHORTED TO GROUND OR FAULTY FUEL PUMP.

YES → CKT 120, OR CKT 490, OR FUEL PUMP RELAY, OR OIL PRESSURE SWITCH SHORTED TO GROUND.

"AFTER REPAIRS," CONFIRM "CLOSED LOOP" OPERATION AND NO MIL (CHECK ENGINE).

91145G27

Fig. 35 2.3L fuel pump electrical diagnostic chart (1 of 2)

Fig. 34 2.3L fuel pump electrical schematic

PCM

31 TAN → J2-26 OIL PRESSURE SIGNAL

465 DK GRN/WHT → J2-01 FUEL PUMP RELAY CONTROL

FUEL PUMP/INJECTOR FUSE
I/P JUNCTION CONNECTOR
A2 839 PNK
20A
TO IGNITION SWITCH

87 85
FUEL PUMP RELAY
87A 30 86
490 RED
FUEL PUMP AND ENGINE OIL PRESSURE INDICATOR SWITCH
FUEL PUMP "TEST" CONNECTOR
120 GRY 451 BLK/WHT
120 GRY I/P JUNCTION CONNECTOR
B9
15-WAY BODY CONNECTOR
W C7
23-WAY I/P CONNECTOR
A M B
FUEL PUMP (IN-TANK)
150 BLK

RELAY
5 4 2
1 3

86 30
87 87A 85
RELAY CENTER

91145G26

CHART A-5

ENGINE CRANKS BUT WILL NOT RUN
(FUEL PUMP CIRCUIT)
2.3L (VIN D) "J" CARLINE

⑥ CONNECT A TEST LIGHT BETWEEN HARNESS CONN IGNITION FEED AND GROUND CIRCUIT.

LIGHT "ON"

⑦ • IGNITION "OFF" FOR TEN SECONDS.
• CONNECT TEST LIGHT BETWEEN CKT 465 AND GROUND.
• NOTE TEST LIGHT WITHIN 2 SECONDS AFTER IGNITION "ON."

LIGHT "ON"

FAULTY RELAY

LIGHT "OFF" → REPAIR OPEN GROUND TO RELAY.

LIGHT "OFF" → DISCONNECT PCM CONNECTOR AND CHECK FOR OPEN OR SHORT TO GROUND IN CKT 465.

CKT 465 OK → ⑧ NOTICE: IF ORIGINAL COMPLAINT WAS "CRANKS BUT WILL NOT RUN" MAKE THE FOLLOWING CHECKS:

⑨ • ENGINE IDLING AT NORMAL OPERATING TEMPERATURE.
• OIL PRESSURE NORMAL.
• DISCONNECT FUEL PUMP RELAY.
• ENGINE SHOULD CONTINUE TO RUN. DOES IT?

YES → NO PROBLEM FOUND IN FUEL SYSTEM.

NO → SEE FUEL PUMP AND ENGINE OIL PRESSURE INDICATOR SWITCH DIAGNOSIS SECTION 8A.

• CHECK RESISTANCE ACROSS FUEL PUMP RELAY "85" AND "86". SHOULD MEASURE 20 OHMS OR MORE.

OK → FAULTY PCM.

NOT OK → REPLACE RELAY AND RECHECK.

CKT 465 NOT OK → REPAIR CKT 465. IF CIRCUIT WAS SHORTED TO GROUND, RECHECK FOR "LIGHT ON" BETWEEN HARNESS CONNECTOR TERMINAL "86" AND GROUND WITHIN 2 SECONDS AFTER IGNITION "ON."

NO LIGHT → FAULTY PCM CONNECTION OR PCM.

LIGHT → RECONNECT RELAY AND PCM.

"AFTER REPAIRS," CONFIRM "CLOSED LOOP" OPERATION AND NO MIL (CHECK ENGINE).

91145G28

Fig. 36 2.3L fuel pump electrical diagnostic chart (2 of 2)

Step	Action	Value(s)	Yes	No
1	Did you perform the Powertrain On-Board Diagnostic (OBD) System Check?	—	Go to Step 2	Go to Powertrain OBD System Check
2	Inspect the fuel pump relay fuse. Is the fuse OK?	—	Go to Step 3	Go to Step 20
3	1. Turn ON the ignition switch leaving the engine OFF. 2. Install a scan tool. 3. Command the fuel pump relay ON with the scan tool. Does the in-tank fuel pump run when the fuel pump relay is commanded ON?	—	Go to Fuel System Diagnosis	Go to Step 4
4	1. Disconnect the fuel pump relay. 2. Using a fused jumper wire, connect the fuel pump feed terminal to the fuel pump relay ignition feed terminal. Does the fuel pump run?	—	Go to Step 5	Go to Step 6
5	1. Connect a test light to ground and probe the fuel pump relay control terminal. 2. Command the fuel pump ON with the scan tool. Does the test light illuminate?	—	Go to Step 7	Go to Step 8
6	Connect a test light to ground and probe the ignition feed terminal to the fuel pump relay. Is the test light ON?	—	Go to Step 9	Go to Step 10
7	Connect a test light to B+ and probe the ground terminal to the fuel pump relay. Is the test light ON?	—	Go to Step 11	Go to Step 12
8	Check for an open or short to ground in the fuel pump control circuit and repair the circuit as necessary. Was a repair necessary?	—	Go to Step 25	Go to Step 13

91145G10

Fig. 37 2.4L engine fuel pump relay circuit diagnosis chart (1 of 3)

Step	Action	Value(s)	Yes	No
21	Repair the short to ground in the fuel pump feed circuit. Is the action complete?	—	Go to Step 25	—
22	Connect a test light to B+ and probe the fuel pump relay ignition feed circuit terminal. Does the test light illuminate?	—	Go to Step 23	Go to Step 24
23	Repair the short to ground in the fuel pump relay ignition feed circuit. Is the action complete?	—	Go to Step 25	—
24	1. Check the fuel pump feed circuit in the fuel pump harness for a short to ground. 2. Repair the fuel pump feed circuit in the fuel pump harness as necessary. Was a repair necessary?	—	Go to Step 25	Go to Step 19
25	1. Using the scan tool, clear the DTCs. 2. Attempt to start the engine. Does the engine start and continue to run?	—	Go to Step 26	Go to Step 2
26	1. Idle the engine until the normal operation temperature is reached. 2. Check to see if any additional DTCs are set. Does the scan tool display any DTCs that you have not diagnosed?	—	Go to applicable DTC table	System OK

91145G12

Fig. 39 2.4L engine fuel pump relay circuit diagnosis chart (3 of 3)

Step	Action	Value(s)	Yes	No
1	Did you perform the Powertrain On-Board Diagnostic (OBD) System Check?	—	Go to Step 2	Go to Powertrain OBD System Check
2	1. Turn OFF the ignition. 2. Turn OFF the air conditioning system. 3. Relieve the fuel pressure. Refer to Fuel Pressure Relief Procedure. 4. Install the fuel pressure gauge. Refer to the illustration on the facing page. 5. Turn ON the ignition. 6. Bleed the air out of the fuel pressure gauge into an approved gasoline container. 7. Turn OFF the ignition for 10 seconds. 8. Turn ON the ignition. Important: The fuel pump will run for approximately 2 seconds. Cycle the ignition switch as necessary in order to achieve the highest possible fuel pressure. 9. Observe the fuel pressure indicated by the fuel pressure gauge with the fuel pump running. Is the fuel pressure within the specified limits?	284–325 kPa (41–47 psi)	Go to Step 3	Go to Step 12

91145G13

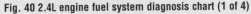

Fig. 40 2.4L engine fuel system diagnosis chart (1 of 4)

Step	Action	Value(s)	Yes	No
9	1. Reinstall the fuel pump relay. 2. Disconnect the fuel pump electrical harness at the rear body connector. 3. Connect a test light to ground and probe the fuel pump feed terminal (body side). 4. Command the fuel pump ON with the scan tool. Does the test light illuminate?	—	Go to Step 14	Go to Step 15
10	Repair the open in the ignition feed circuit for the fuel pump relay. Is the action complete?	—	Go to Step 25	—
11	Replace the fuel pump relay. Is the action complete?	—	Go to Step 25	—
12	Repair the open ground circuit to the fuel pump relay. Is the action complete?	—	Go to Step 25	—
13	Inspect the electrical connections and the terminals at the PCM and repair the electrical connections and the terminals as necessary. Was a repair necessary?	—	Go to Step 25	Go to Step 16
14	Connect a test light to B+ and probe the fuel pump ground circuit (body side). Does the test light illuminate?	—	Go to Step 17	Go to Step 18
15	Repair the open fuel pump feed circuit. Is the action complete?	—	Go to Step 25	—
16	1. Turn OFF the ignition switch. 2. Replace the PCM. Is the action complete?	—	Go to Step 25	—
17	1. Check the fuel pump feed and ground circuits in the fuel pump harness for an open. 2. Repair the fuel pump feed and ground circuits in the fuel pump harness as necessary. Was a repair necessary?	—	Go to Step 25	Go to Step 19
18	Repair the open fuel pump ground circuit. Is the action complete?	—	Go to Step 25	—
19	Replace the fuel pump. Is the action complete?	—	Go to Step 25	—
20	1. Disconnect the fuel pump electrical harness at the rear body harness electrical connector. 2. Disconnect the fuel pump relay. 3. Turn OFF the ignition switch. 4. Connect a test light to B+ and probe the fuel pump feed terminal. Does the test light illuminate?	—	Go to Step 21	Go to Step 22

91145G11

Fig. 38 2.4L engine fuel pump relay circuit diagnosis chart (2 of 3)

Step	Action	Value(s)	Yes	No
3	Important: The fuel pressure may vary slightly when the fuel pump stops running. Then, the fuel pressure should stabilize and then remain constant. Observe the fuel pressure after the fuel pump stops running. Does the fuel pressure drop more than the specified value in 10 minutes?	34 (5 psi)	Go to Step 10	Go to Step 4
4	1. Relieve the fuel pressure to the first specified value. 2. Monitor the fuel pressure. Does the fuel pressure drop more than the second specified value in 10 minutes?	69 kPa (10 psi) 14 kPa (2 psi)	Go to Step 21	Go to Step 5
5	Is the fuel pressure suspected of dropping-off during acceleration, during cruise, or during hard cornering?	—	Go to Step 6	Go to Step 8
6	Visually and physically inspect the following items for a restriction: • The in-line fuel filter • The fuel feed pipe Did you find a restriction?	—	Go to Step 24	Go to Step 7
7	1. Remove the modular sender assembly. Refer to Fuel Sender Assembly Replacement. 2. Visually and physically inspect the following items: • The fuel pump strainer for a restriction. • The fuel pump flex pipe for leaks. • Verify that the fuel pump is the correct fuel pump for this vehicle. • Check the fuel pump electrical wiring for high resistance. Was a problem present in any of these areas?	—	Go to Step 24	Go to Step 21
8	1. Start the engine. 2. Idle the engine at the normal operating temperature. Does the fuel pressure drop by the amount specified?	21–69 kPa (3–10 psi)	Go to Symptoms	Go to Step 9
9	1. Disconnect the vacuum hose from the fuel pressure regulator. 2. With the engine idling, apply 12-14 inches of vacuum to the fuel pressure regulator. Does the fuel pressure indicated by the fuel pressure gauge drop by the amount specified?	21–69 kPa (3–10 psi)	Go to Step 19	Go to Step 20
10	1. Turn OFF the ignition. 2. Place the bleed hose of the fuel pressure gauge into an approved gasoline container. 3. Turn ON the ignition. 4. Bleed the air out of the fuel pressure gauge. 5. Pressurize the fuel system with the scan tool. Important: Repeat pressurizing the fuel system with the scan tool as necessary to achieve the highest possible fuel pressure. 6. Wait for the fuel pressure to build. 7. Pinch the gauge inlet hose (refer to 4 on the illustration). Does the fuel pressure remain constant?	—	Go to Step 21	Go to Step 11

91145G14

Fig. 41 2.4L engine fuel system diagnosis chart (2 of 4)

Step	Action	Value(s)	Yes	No
11	1. Pressurize the fuel system with the scan tool. 2. Wait for the fuel pressure to build. 3. Pinch the fuel return hose (refer to 9 on illustration). Does the fuel pressure indicated by the fuel pressure gauge remain constant?	—	Go to Step 20	Go to Step 22
12	Is the fuel pressure above the specified limit?	325 kPa (47 psi)	Go to Step 13	Go to Step 15
13	1. Relieve the fuel pressure by placing the bleed hose of the fuel pressure gauge into an approved gasoline container and by opening the relief valve. 2. Disconnect the fuel return hose quick-connect fitting. Refer to *Quick Connect Fitting(s) Service (Metal Collar).* 3. Place the open end of the flexible hose into an approved gasoline container. 4. Turn OFF the ignition for approximately 10 seconds. 5. Turn ON the ignition. 6. Observe the fuel pressure gauge with the fuel pump running. Is the fuel pressure within the specified limits?	284–325 kPa (41–47 psi)	Go to Step 23	Go to Step 14
14	Visually and physically inspect the fuel rail outlet passages for a restriction. Was a restriction found?	—	Go to Step 24	Go to Step 20
15	Is the fuel pressure above the specified value?	0 kPa (0 psi)	Go to Step 16	Go to Step 17
16	1. Relieve the fuel pressure by placing the bleed hose of the fuel pressure gauge into an approved gasoline container and by opening the relief valve. 2. Pressurize the fuel system with the scan tool. 3. Bleed the air out of the fuel pressure gauge. **Important:** Repeat pressurizing the fuel system with the scan tool as necessary in order to achieve the highest possible fuel pressure. 4. Wait for the fuel pressure to build. *Notice:* Do not allow the fuel pressure to exceed the specified value because damage to the fuel pressure regulator or the fuel pressure gauge may result. 5. Slowly pinch the gauge outlet hose (refer to 3 on illustration). Does the fuel pressure indicated by the fuel pressure gauge rise above the first specified value?	325 kPa (47 psi) 414 kPa (60 psi)	Go to Step 20	Go to Step 7
17	Use the Engine Cranks But Will Not Run Table in order to diagnose the fuel pump electrical circuit. Was a problem present with the fuel pump electrical circuit?	—	Go to Step 24	Go to Step 18

91145G15

Fig. 42 2.4L engine fuel system diagnosis chart (3 of 4)

Step	Action	Value(s)	Yes	No
18	Visually and physically inspect the following items: • The in-line fuel filter for obstructions • The fuel feed pipe for a restriction • The fuel pump strainer for obstructions • The fuel pump flex pipe for leaks Was a problem present in any of these areas?	—	Go to Step 24	Go to Step 21
19	Locate and repair the loss of vacuum to the fuel pressure regulator. Is the action complete?	—	System OK	—
20	Replace the fuel pressure regulator. Is the action complete?	—	System OK	—
21	Replace the modular fuel sender. Is the action complete?	—	System OK	—
22	Locate and replace any leaking fuel injector(s). Is the action complete?	—	System OK	—
23	Locate and correct the restriction in the fuel return pipe. Is the action complete?	—	System OK	—
24	Repair the problem as necessary. Is the action complete?	—	System OK	—

91145G16

Fig. 43 2.4L engine fuel system diagnosis chart (4 of 4)

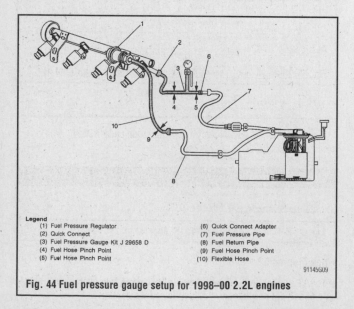

Legend

(1)	Fuel Pressure Regulator	(6)	Quick Connect Adapter
(2)	Quick Connect	(7)	Fuel Pressure Pipe
(3)	Fuel Pressure Gauge Kit J 29658 D	(8)	Fuel Return Pipe
(4)	Fuel Hose Pinch Point	(9)	Fuel Hose Pinch Point
(5)	Fuel Hose Pinch Point	(10)	Flexible Hose

91145G09

Fig. 44 Fuel pressure gauge setup for 1998–00 2.2L engines

Step	Action	Value(s)	Yes	No
1	Did you perform the Powertrain On-Board Diagnostic (OBD) System Check?	—	Go to Step 2	Go to *Powertrain OBD System* / *Powertrain OBD System*
2	Inspect the fuel pump relay fuse. Is the fuse OK?	—	Go to Step 3	Go to Step 20
3	1. Turn ON the ignition switch leaving the engine OFF. 2. Install a scan tool. 3. Command the fuel pump relay ON with the scan tool. Does the in-tank fuel pump run when the fuel pump relay is commanded ON?	—	Go to *Fuel System Diagnosis* / *Fuel System Diagnosis*	Go to Step 4
4	1. Disconnect the fuel pump relay. 2. Using a fused jumper wire, connect the fuel pump feed terminal to the fuel pump relay ignition feed terminal. Does the fuel pump run?	—	Go to Step 5	Go to Step 6
5	1. Connect a test light to ground and probe the fuel pump relay control terminal. 2. Command the fuel pump ON with the scan tool. Does the test light illuminate?	—	Go to Step 7	Go to Step 8
6	Connect a test light to ground and probe the ignition feed terminal to the fuel pump relay. Is the test light ON?	—	Go to Step 9	Go to Step 10

91145G17

Fig. 45 1998–00 2.2L engine fuel pump relay circuit diagnosis chart (1 of 3)

Step	Action	Value(s)	Yes	No
7	Connect a test light to B+ and probe the ground terminal to the fuel pump relay. Is the test light ON?	—	Go to Step 11	Go to Step 12
8	Check for an open or short to ground in the fuel pump control circuit and repair the circuit as necessary. Was a repair necessary?	—	Go to Step 25	Go to Step 13
9	1. Reinstall the fuel pump relay. 2. Disconnect the fuel pump electrical harness at the rear body connector. 3. Connect a test light to ground and probe the fuel pump feed terminal (body side). 4. Command the fuel pump ON with the scan tool. Does the test light illuminate?	—	Go to Step 14	Go to Step 15
10	Repair the open in the ignition feed circuit for the fuel pump relay. Is the action complete?	—	Go to Step 25	—
11	Replace the fuel pump relay. Is the action complete?	—	Go to Step 25	—
12	Repair the open ground circuit to the fuel pump relay. Is the action complete?	—	Go to Step 25	—
13	Inspect the electrical connections and the terminals at the PCM and repair the electrical connections and the terminals as necessary. Was a repair necessary?	—	Go to Step 25	Go to Step 16
14	Connect a test light to B+ and probe the fuel pump ground circuit (body side). Does the test light illuminate?	—	Go to Step 17	Go to Step 18
15	Repair the open fuel pump feed circuit. Is the action complete?	—	Go to Step 25	—
16	1. Turn OFF the ignition switch. 2. Replace the PCM. Is the action complete?	—	Go to Step 25	—
17	1. Check the fuel pump feed and ground circuits in the fuel pump harness for an open. 2. Repair the fuel pump feed and ground circuits in the fuel pump harness as necessary. Was a repair necessary?	—	Go to Step 25	Go to Step 19
18	Repair the open fuel pump ground circuit. Is the action complete?	—	Go to Step 25	—

91145G18

Fig. 46 1998–00 2.2L engine fuel pump relay circuit diagnosis chart (2 of 3)

Step	Action	Value(s)	Yes	No
19	Replace the fuel pump. Is the action complete?	—	Go to Step 25	—
20	1. Disconnect the fuel pump electrical harness at the rear body harness electrical connector. 2. Disconnect the fuel pump relay. 3. Turn OFF the ignition switch. 4. Connect a test light to B+ and probe the fuel pump feed terminal. Does the test light illuminate?	—	Go to Step 21	Go to Step 22
21	Repair the short to ground in the fuel pump feed circuit. Is the action complete?	—	Go to Step 25	—
22	Connect a test light to B+ and probe the fuel pump relay ignition feed circuit terminal. Does the test light illuminate?	—	Go to Step 23	Go to Step 24
23	Repair the short to ground in the fuel pump relay ignition feed circuit. Is the action complete?	—	Go to Step 25	—
24	1. Check the fuel pump feed circuit in the fuel pump harness for a short to ground. 2. Repair the fuel pump feed circuit in the fuel pump harness as necessary. Was a repair necessary?	—	Go to Step 25	Go to Step 19
25	1. Using the scan tool, clear the DTCs. 2. Attempt to start the engine. Does the engine start and continue to run?	—	Go to Step 26	Go to Step 2
26	1. Idle the engine until the normal operation temperature is reached. 2. Check to see if any additional DTCs are set. Does the scan tool display any DTCs that you have not diagnosed?	—	Go to applicable DTC table	System OK

91145G19

Fig. 47 1998–00 2.2L engine fuel pump relay circuit diagnosis chart (3 of 3)

Step	Action	Value(s)	Yes	No
1	Did you perform the Powertrain On-Board Diagnostic (OBD) System Check?	—	Go to Step 2	Go to Powertrain OBD System Check
2	1. Turn OFF the ignition. 2. Turn OFF the air conditioning system. 3. Relieve the fuel pressure. Refer to *Fuel Pressure Relief Procedure.* 4. Install the fuel pressure gauge. Refer to the illustration on the facing page. 5. Turn ON the ignition. 6. Bleed the air out of the fuel pressure gauge into an approved gasoline container. 7. Turn OFF the ignition for 10 seconds. 8. Turn ON the ignition. **Important:** The fuel pump will run for approximately 2 seconds. Cycle the ignition switch as necessary in order to achieve the highest possible fuel pressure. 9. Observe the fuel pressure indicated by the fuel pressure gauge with the fuel pump running. Is the fuel pressure within the specified limits?	284-325 kPa (41-47 psi)	Go to Step 3	Go to Step 12

91145G20

Fig. 48 1998–00 2.2L engine fuel system diagnosis chart (1 of 4)

Step	Action	Value(s)	Yes	No
3	**Important:** The fuel pressure may vary slightly when the fuel pump stops running. Then, the fuel pressure should stabilize and then remain constant. Observe the fuel pressure after the fuel pump stops running. Does the fuel pressure drop more than the specified value in 10 minutes?	34 (5 psi)	Go to Step 10	Go to Step 4
4	1. Relieve the fuel pressure to the first specified value. 2. Monitor the fuel pressure. Does the fuel pressure drop more than the second specified value in 10 minutes?	69 kPa (10 psi) 14 kPa (2 psi)	Go to Step 21	Go to Step 5
5	Is the fuel pressure suspected of dropping-off during acceleration, during cruise, or during hard cornering?	—	Go to Step 6	Go to Step 8
6	Visually and physically inspect the following items for a restriction: • The in-line fuel filter • The fuel feed pipe. Did you find a restriction?	—	Go to Step 24	Go to Step 7
7	1. Remove the modular sender assembly. Refer to *Fuel Sender Assembly Replacement.* 2. Visually and physically inspect the following items: • The fuel pump strainer for a restriction • The fuel pump flex pipe for leaks • Verify that the fuel pump is the correct fuel pump for this vehicle. • Check the fuel pump electrical wiring for high resistance. Was a problem present in any of these areas?	—	Go to Step 24	Go to Step 21
8	1. Start the engine. 2. Idle the engine at the normal operating temperature. Does the fuel pressure drop to the amount specified?	21-69 kPa (3-10 psi)	Go to Symptoms	Go to Step 9
9	1. Disconnect the vacuum hose from the fuel pressure regulator. 2. With the engine idling, apply 12-14 inches of vacuum to the fuel pressure regulator. Does the fuel pressure indicated by the fuel pressure gauge drop by the amount specified?	21-69 kPa (3-10 psi)	Go to Step 19	Go to Step 20

91145G21

Fig. 49 1998–00 2.2L engine fuel system diagnosis chart (2 of 4)

Step	Action	Value(s)	Yes	No
10	1. Turn OFF the ignition. 2. Place the bleed hose of the fuel pressure gauge into an approved gasoline container. 3. Turn ON the ignition. 4. Bleed the air out of the fuel pressure gauge. 5. Pressurize the fuel system with the scan tool. **Important:** Repeat pressurizing the fuel system with the scan tool as necessary to achieve the highest possible fuel pressure. 6. Pinch the gauge inlet hose (refer to 5 on the illustration). Does the fuel pressure remain constant?	—	Go to Step 21	Go to Step 11
11	1. Pressurize the fuel system with the scan tool. 2. Wait for the fuel pressure to build. 3. Pinch the fuel return hose (refer to 9 on illustration). Does the fuel pressure indicated by the fuel pressure gauge remain constant?	—	Go to Step 20	Go to Step 22
12	Is the fuel pressure above the specified limit?	325 kPa (47 psi)	Go to Step 13	Go to Step 15
13	1. Relieve the fuel pressure by placing the bleed hose of the fuel pressure gauge into an approved gasoline container and by opening the relief valve. 2. Disconnect the fuel return hose quick-connect fitting. Refer to *Quick Connect Fitting(s) Service (Metal Collar).* 3. Place the open end of the flexible hose into an approved gasoline container. 4. Turn OFF the ignition for approximately 10 seconds. 5. Turn ON the ignition. 6. Observe the fuel pressure gauge with the fuel pump running. Is the fuel pressure within the specified limits?	284-325 kPa (41-47 psi)	Go to Step 23	Go to Step 14
14	Visually and physically inspect the fuel rail outlet passages for a restriction. Was a restriction found?	—	Go to Step 24	Go to Step 20
15	Is the fuel pressure above the specified value?	0 kPa (0 psi)	Go to Step 16	Go to Step 17

91145G22

Fig. 50 1998–00 2.2L engine fuel system diagnosis chart (3 of 4)

Step	Action	Value(s)	Yes	No
16	1. Relieve the fuel pressure by placing the bleed hose of the fuel pressure gauge into an approved gasoline container and by opening the relief valve. 2. Pressurize the fuel system with the scan tool. **Important:** Repeat pressurizing the fuel system with the scan tool as necessary in order to achieve the highest possible fuel pressure. 3. Wait for the fuel pressure to build. **Notice:** Do not allow the fuel pressure to exceed the specified value because damage to the fuel pressure regulator or the fuel pressure gauge may result. 4. Slowly pinch the gauge outlet hose (refer to 4 on illustration). Does the fuel pressure indicated by the fuel pressure gauge rise above the first specified value?	325 kPa (47 psi) 414 kPa (60 psi)	Go to Step 20	Go to Step 7
17	Use the Engine Cranks But Will Not Run Table in order to diagnose the fuel pump electrical circuit. Was a problem present with the fuel pump electrical circuit?	—	Go to Step 24	Go to Step 18
18	Visually and physically inspect the following items: • The in-line fuel filter for obstructions • The fuel feed pipe for a restriction • The fuel pump strainer for obstructions • The fuel pump flex pipe for leaks. Was a problem present in any of these areas?	—	Go to Step 24	Go to Step 21
19	Locate and repair the loss of vacuum to the fuel pressure regulator. Is the action complete?	—	System OK	—
20	Replace the fuel pressure regulator. Is the action complete?	—	System OK	—
21	Replace the modular fuel sender. Is the action complete?	—	System OK	—
22	Locate and replace any leaking fuel injector(s). Is the action complete?	—	System OK	—
23	Locate and correct the restriction in the fuel return pipe. Is the action complete?	—	System OK	—
24	Repair the problem as necessary. Is the action complete?	—	System OK	—

91145G23

Fig. 51 1998–00 2.2L engine fuel system diagnosis chart (4 of 4)

REMOVAL & INSTALLATION

Please refer to fuel pump removal and installation under Bottom Feed Port Injection System earlier in this Section.

Throttle Body

REMOVAL & INSTALLATION

2.3L Engine

⏵ **See Figures 52 and 53**

➥The TP sensor and IAC valve should **NOT** come into contact with any type of solvent or cleanser, as this may cause damage.

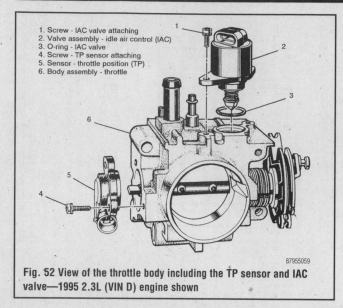

1. Screw - IAC valve attaching
2. Valve assembly - idle air control (IAC)
3. O-ring - IAC valve
4. Screw - TP sensor attaching
5. Sensor - throttle position (TP)
6. Body assembly - throttle

87955059

Fig. 52 View of the throttle body including the TP sensor and IAC valve—1995 2.3L (VIN D) engine shown

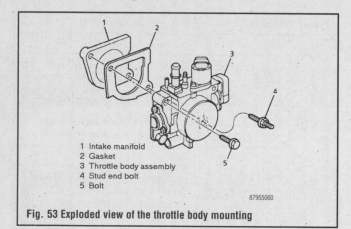

1 Intake manifold
2 Gasket
3 Throttle body assembly
4 Stud end bolt
5 Bolt

87955060

Fig. 53 Exploded view of the throttle body mounting

1. Properly relieve the fuel system pressure.
2. Disconnect the negative battery cable.
3. Remove the air cleaner cover and air duct.
4. Partially drain the coolant to allow the coolant hoses at the throttle body to be removed.
5. Disconnect the vacuum hose from the fuel pressure regulator.
6. Detach the electrical connectors from the TP sensor and IAC valve.
7. Disconnect the throttle, transaxle control and cruise control (if equipped) cables.
8. Unfasten the throttle body attaching bolts, then loosen the throttle body from the intake manifold.
9. Disconnect the coolant hoses from the throttle body.
10. Detach the vacuum hose from the bottom of the throttle body.
11. Remove the throttle body and gasket. Discard the gasket.
To install:
12. Connect the vacuum hose to the bottom of the throttle body.
13. Fasten the coolant hoses to the throttle body.
14. Position the throttle body, with a new gasket, against the manifold, then secure with the attaching bolts. Tighten the bolts to 11 ft. lbs. (15 Nm).
15. Fasten the throttle, cruise control and transaxle cables to the throttle body.
16. Attach the TP sensor and IAC valve electrical connectors.
17. Connect the vacuum hose to the fuel pressure regulator.
18. Refill the cooling system to the proper level.

19. Install the air duct and air cleaner cover.
20. Connect the negative battery cable.

2.4L Engine and 1998–00 2.2L Engine

♦ **See Figures 54 and 55**

1. Disconnect the negative battery cable.
2. Remove the air cleaner resonator and outlet hose from the vehicle.
3. Detach the connectors for the TP sensor and IAC valve.
4. Remove the vacuum hoses from the throttle body.
5. Remove the throttle, cruise (if equipped), and transmission control (automatic transaxles only) cables from the throttle body.
6. On the 2.4L engine, remove the MAP sensor.
7. Remove the accelerator cable bracket.
8. Remove the throttle body attaching bolts.
9. Remove the throttle body from the intake manifold.
To install:
10. Thoroughly clean the throttle body and intake manifold mounting surfaces.
11. Install the throttle body onto the intake manifold.
12. Tighten the throttle body retaining bolts to 89 inch lbs. (10 Nm) on the 2.2L engine and 58 inch lbs. (7 Nm) on the 2.4L engine.
13. Install the accelerator cable bracket.
14. On the 2.4L engine, install the MAP sensor.
15. Install the throttle, cruise (if equipped), and transmission control (automatic transaxles only) cables.
16. Connect the vacuum hoses from the throttle body.
17. Attach the connectors for the TP sensor and IAC valve.
18. Install the air cleaner resonator and outlet hose.
19. Connect the negative battery cable.

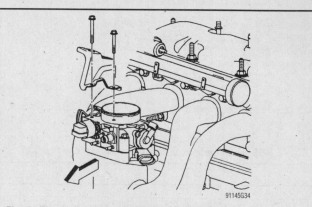

91145G34

Fig. 54 Throttle body assembly mounting—1998–00 2.2L engine

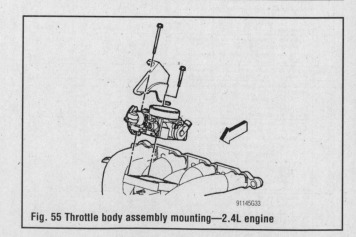

91145G33

Fig. 55 Throttle body assembly mounting—2.4L engine

Fuel Injectors

TESTING

The easiest way to test the operation of the fuel injectors is to listen for a clicking sound coming from the injectors while the engine is running. This is accomplished using a mechanic's stethoscope, or a long screwdriver. Place the end of the stethoscope or the screwdriver (tip end, not handle) onto the body of the injector. Place the ear pieces of the stethoscope in your ears, or if using a screwdriver, place your ear on top of the handle. An audible clicking noise should be heard; this is the solenoid operating. If the injector makes this noise, the injector driver circuit and computer are operating as designed. Continue testing all the injectors this way.

✳✳ CAUTION

Be extremely careful while working on an operating engine, make sure you have no dangling jewelry, extremely loose clothes, power tool cords or other items that might get caught in a moving part of the engine.

All Injectors Clicking

If all the injectors are clicking, but you have determined that the fuel system is the cause of your driveability problem, continue diagnostics. Make sure that you have checked fuel pump pressure as outlined earlier in this section. An easy way to determine a weak or unproductive cylinder is a cylinder drop test. This is accomplished by removing one spark plug wire at a time, and seeing which cylinder causes the least difference in the idle. The one that causes the least change is the weak cylinder.

If the injectors were all clicking and the ignition system is functioning properly, remove the injector of the suspect cylinder and bench test it. This is accomplished by checking for a spray pattern from the injector itself. Install a fuel supply line to the injector (or rail if the injector is left attached to the rail) and momentarily apply 12 volts DC and a ground to the injector itself; a visible fuel spray should appear. If no spray is achieved, replace the injector and check the running condition of the engine.

One or More Injectors Are Not Clicking

▶ **See Figures 56, 57, 58 and 59**

If one or more injectors are found to be not operating, testing the injector driver circuit and computer can be accomplished using a "noid" light. First, with the engine not running and the ignition key in the **OFF** position, remove the connector from the injector you plan to test, then plug the "noid" light tool into the injector connector. Start the engine and the "noid" light should flash, signaling that the injector driver circuit is working. If the "noid" light flashes, but the injector does not click when plugged in, test the injector's resistance. resistance should be between 11–18 ohms.

If the "noid" light does not flash, the injector driver circuit is faulty. Disconnect the negative battery cable. Unplug the "noid" light from the injector connector and also unplug the PCM. Check the harness between the appropriate

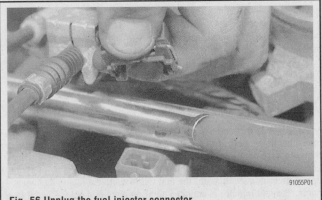

Fig. 56 Unplug the fuel injector connector

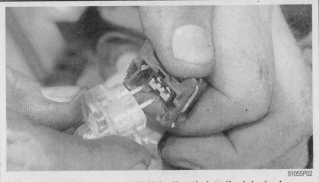

Fig. 57 Plug the correct "noid" light directly into the injector harness connector

Fig. 58 If the correct "noid" light flashes while the engine is running, the injector driver circuit inside the PCM is working

Fig. 59 Probe the two terminals of a fuel injector to check it's resistance

pins on the harness side of the PCM connector and the injector connector. Resistance should be less than 5.0 ohms; if not, repair the circuit. If resistance is within specifications, the injector driver inside the PCM is faulty and replacement of the PCM will be necessary.

REMOVAL & INSTALLATION

2.3L and 2.4L Engines

▶ **See Figures 60 and 61**

✳✳ WARNING

Use care in removing the fuel injectors to prevent damage to the electrical connector pins on the injector and the nozzle. The fuel injector is serviced as a complete assembly only and should not be immersed in any kind of cleaner.

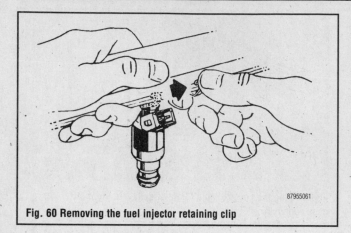

Fig. 60 Removing the fuel injector retaining clip

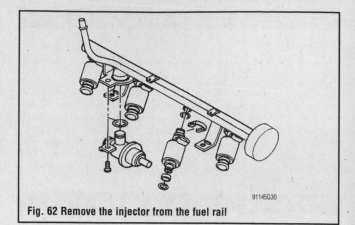

Fig. 62 Remove the injector from the fuel rail

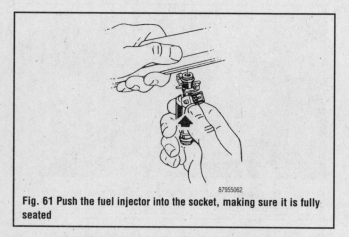

Fig. 61 Push the fuel injector into the socket, making sure it is fully seated

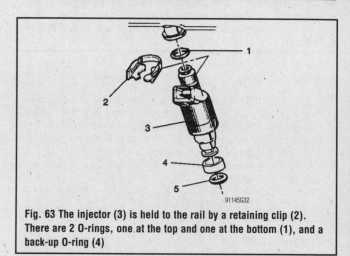

Fig. 63 The injector (3) is held to the rail by a retaining clip (2). There are 2 O-rings, one at the top and one at the bottom (1), and a back-up O-ring (4)

1. Properly relieve fuel system pressure, as outlined earlier in this section.
2. Disconnect the negative battery cable.
3. On the 2.3L engine, remove the throttle body from the intake manifold.
4. As outlined later in this section, remove the fuel rail.
5. Unfasten and discard the injector retaining clip, then remove the injector assembly. Remove and discard the O-rings from each end of the injector.

To install:

6. Lubricate new O-rings with clean engine oil, the install on the injector.
7. Position a new injector retaining clip on the injector.
8. Install the injector assembly into the fuel rail injector socket, with the electrical connector facing inward toward the manifold. Push the socket in far enough to engage the retainer clip with the groove on the rail.
9. Install the fuel rail assembly.
10. On the 2.3L engine install the throttle body as outlined in this Section..
11. Connect the negative battery cable.

1998–00 2.2L Engine

♦ See Figures 62 and 63

1. Properly relieve the fuel system pressure.
2. Disconnect the negative battery cable.
3. Remove the air cleaner outlet resonator.
4. Remove the fuel rail as outlined in this Section.
5. Remove the fuel injector retaining clip and remove the injector from the fuel rail.

To install:

6. Discard the old O-rings on the injectors.
7. Lubricate the new O-rings with clean engine oil and install them on the injectors.
8. Install the fuel injector onto the fuel rail and attach the retaining clip.
9. Install the fuel rail as outlined in this Section.
10. Install the air cleaner outlet resonator.
11. Connect the negative battery cable.
12. Start the vehicle and check for leaks.

Fuel Rail Assembly

REMOVAL & INSTALLATION

2.3L Engine

♦ See Figure 64

1. Properly relieve the fuel system pressure.
2. Disconnect the negative battery cable.
3. Disconnect the hoses at the front and side of the crankcase ventilation oil/air separator. Leave the vacuum hoses attached to the canister purge valve.
4. Unfasten the bolts securing the crankcase ventilation oil/air separator and canister purge valve.
5. Disconnect the hose from the bottom of the separator, then remove the separator. Position the canister purge valve out of the way.
6. Remove the fuel pipe clamp bolt.
7. Disconnect the vacuum hose at the pressure regulator.
8. Unfasten the fuel rail attaching bolts, then remove the fuel rail assembly from the cylinder head.
9. Detach the fuel injector electrical connectors. Push in the wire connector clip, while pulling the connector away from the injector.
10. Remove the fuel rail assembly, making sure to cover all openings with masking tape to prevent dirt entry. Remove discard all O-rings and seals and replace with new ones during installation.

➥If any injectors become separated from the fuel rail and remain in the intake manifold, both O-ring seals and injector retaining clip must be replaced. Use care in removing the fuel rail assembly, to prevent damage to the injector electrical connector terminals and the injector spray tips. When removed, support the fuel rail to avoid damaging its components. The fuel injector is serviced as a complete unit only. Since it is an electrical component, it should not be immersed in any type of cleaner.

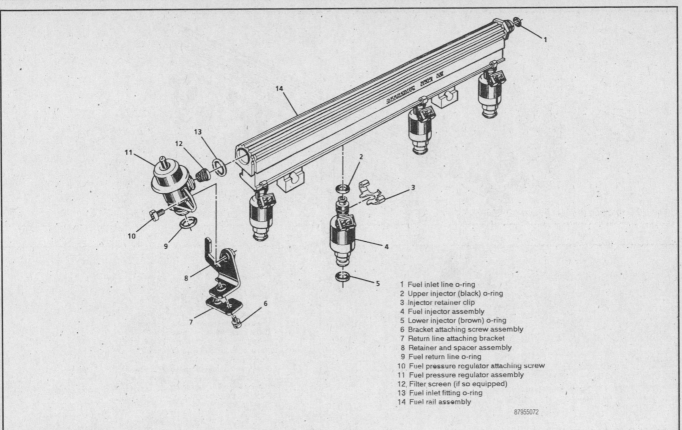

Fig. 64 Exploded view of the fuel rail and related components—2.3L engine shown

1 Fuel inlet line o-ring
2 Upper injector (black) o-ring
3 Injector retainer clip
4 Fuel injector assembly
5 Lower injector (brown) o-ring
6 Bracket attaching screw assembly
7 Return line attaching bracket
8 Retainer and spacer assembly
9 Fuel return line o-ring
10 Fuel pressure regulator attaching screw
11 Fuel pressure regulator assembly
12 Filter screen (if so equipped)
13 Fuel inlet fitting o-ring
14 Fuel rail assembly

87955072

To install:

11. Be sure to lubricate all the new O-rings and seals with clean engine oil. Carefully push the injectors into the cylinder head intake ports until the bolt holes on the fuel rail and manifold are aligned.

12. The remainder of the installation is the reverse order of the removal procedure.

13. Apply a coating of a suitable thread locking compound on the treads of the fittings. Tighten the fuel rail retaining bolts to 19 ft. lbs. (26 Nm), the fuel feed line nut to 22 ft. lbs. (30 Nm) and the fuel pipe fittings to 20 ft. lbs. (26 Nm).

14. Connect the negative battery cable. Turn the ignition to the **ON** position for two seconds, then turn it to the **OFF** position for ten seconds. Turn again to the **ON** position and check for fuel leaks.

2.4L Engine

▶ See Figure 65

1. Properly relieve the fuel system pressure.
2. Disconnect the negative battery cable.
3. Remove the air cleaner outlet resonator.
4. Remove the fuel pressure regulator vacuum hose.
5. Remove the fuel rail attaching bolts.
6. Detach the Camshaft Position (CMP) sensor connector.
7. Detach the fuel injector connectors.
8. Remove the fuel feed line retaining bolt and remove the line from the fuel rail.
9. Lift the fuel rail from the cylinder head.
10. Loosen the fuel return line retaining bracket attaching screw. Rotate the retaining bracket so that the return line can be removed.
11. Remove the return line from the pressure regulator.
12. Detach the fuel feed and fuel return line quick-connect fittings and remove the fuel lines from the vehicle.
13. Remove the fuel rail assembly from the vehicle.

To install:

14. With the fuel rail outside the vehicle, attach the fuel feed and return lines to the rail.

15. Tighten the feed line retaining bolt to 22 ft. lbs. (30 Nm). Tighten the return line bracket bolts to 53 inch lbs. (6 Nm).

16. Place the fuel rail over the cylinder head and attach the fuel injector connectors. Rotate the fuel injectors if necessary to avoid stretching the wire harness.

17. Replace the O-rings on the injectors and lubricate them with clean engine oil before installation.

18. Install the fuel rail into the cylinder head. Ensure that the O-rings are in place and the fuel rail is fully seated.

19. Attach the Camshaft Position (CMP) sensor connector.

20. Tighten the fuel rail attaching bolts to 19 ft. lbs. (26 Nm).

21. Attach the fuel pressure regulator vacuum hose.

22. Attach the fuel feed and return line quick connect fittings.

23. Install the air cleaner outlet resonator.

24. Connect the negative battery cable.

25. Start the vehicle and check for leaks.

1998–00 2.2L Engine

▶ See Figure 66

1. Properly relieve the fuel system pressure.
2. Disconnect the negative battery cable.
3. Remove the air cleaner outlet resonator.
4. Remove the fuel rail bracket.
5. Detach the fuel injector connectors.
6. Detach the fuel feed and fuel return line quick-connect fittings.
7. Remove the fuel rail attaching bolts.
8. Remove the fuel rail from the cylinder head.

To install:

9. Install the fuel rail into the cylinder head. Ensure that the O-rings are in place and the fuel rail is fully seated.

10. Tighten the fuel rail attaching bolts to 18 ft. lbs. (24 Nm).

11. Attach the fuel feed and return line quick connect fittings.

12. Attach the fuel injector connectors.

13. Install the fuel rail bracket bolts and nuts and tighten to:
- Tighten the front nuts to 89 inch lbs. (10 Nm).
- Tighten the remaining bolts and nuts to 18 ft. lbs. (25 Nm).

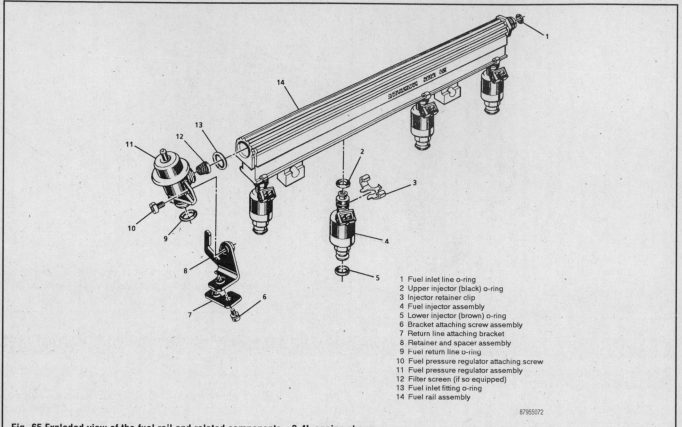

1 Fuel inlet line o-ring
2 Upper injector (black) o-ring
3 Injector retainer clip
4 Fuel injector assembly
5 Lower injector (brown) o-ring
6 Bracket attaching screw assembly
7 Return line attaching bracket
8 Retainer and spacer assembly
9 Fuel return line o-ring
10 Fuel pressure regulator attaching screw
11 Fuel pressure regulator assembly
12 Filter screen (if so equipped)
13 Fuel inlet fitting o-ring
14 Fuel rail assembly

87955072

Fig. 65 Exploded view of the fuel rail and related components—2.4L engine shown

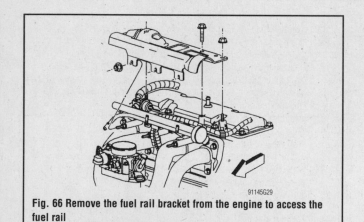

91145G29

Fig. 66 Remove the fuel rail bracket from the engine to access the fuel rail

14. Install the air cleaner outlet resonator.
15. Connect the negative battery cable.
16. Start the vehicle and check for leaks.

Fuel Pressure Regulator

REMOVAL & INSTALLATION

2.3L and 2.4L Engines

▶ See Figure 67

☀☀ CAUTION

To reduce the risk of fire or personal injury, it is necessary to relieve the fuel system pressure before servicing the fuel system.

1. Properly relieve the fuel system pressure.
2. Disconnect the negative battery cable.
3. Remove the fuel rail assembly from the vehicle.
4. Unfasten the pressure regulator attaching screw, then remove the regulator, twisting it back and forth while pulling it apart. Remove and discard O-ring.
5. If the regulator is to reinstalled, inspect the filter screen for contamination and discard if necessary.
To install:
6. Lubricate a new rail-to-regulator inlet fitting O-ring seal with clean engine oil, then install in regulator.
7. Install the regulator assembly. Align with the retainer and spacer assembly mounting hole. Coat the retaining screw with Loctite® 262 or equivalent, then tighten to 102 inch lbs. (15 Nm).
8. Install the fuel rail assembly.
9. Connect the negative battery cable.

1998–00 2.2L Engine

▶ See Figure 68

1. Properly relieve the fuel system pressure.
2. Disconnect the negative battery cable.
3. Remove the air cleaner outlet resonator.
4. Remove the fuel rail bracket.
5. Remove the pressure regulator bracket attaching screw.
6. Remove the pressure regulator from the fuel rail.
To install:
7. Install the pressure regulator using a new O-ring.
8. Tighten the pressure regulator bracket retaining bolt to 31 inch lbs. (4 Nm).
9. Install the fuel rail bracket bolts and nuts and tighten to:
• Tighten the front nuts to 89 inch lbs. (10 Nm).
• Tighten the remaining bolts and nuts to 18 ft. lbs. (25 Nm).
10. Install the air cleaner outlet resonator.
11. Connect the negative battery cable.
12. Start the vehicle and check for leaks.

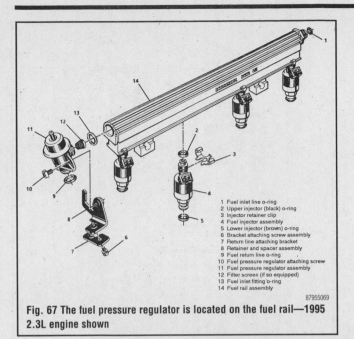

Fig. 67 The fuel pressure regulator is located on the fuel rail—1995 2.3L engine shown

1 Fuel inlet line o-ring
2 Upper injector (black) o-ring
3 Injector retainer clip
4 Fuel injector assembly
5 Lower injector (brown) o-ring
6 Bracket attaching screw assembly
7 Return line attaching bracket
8 Retainer and spacer assembly
9 Fuel return line o-ring
10 Fuel pressure regulator attaching screw
11 Fuel pressure regulator assembly
12 Filter screen (if so equipped)
13 Fuel inlet fitting o-ring
14 Fuel rail assembly

87955069

Fig. 68 The fuel pressure regulator (2) has an O-ring (4) at the top where it enters the fuel rail (1), and is held by a retaining screw (3) on the bracket

FUEL TANK

Tank Assembly

REMOVAL & INSTALLATION

♦ See Figures 69, 70 and 71

1. Disconnect the negative battery cable.
2. Drain the fuel tank by using a hand-operated pump device to drain as much fuel through the filler tube as possible.
3. Raise and safely support the vehicle.
4. Unfasten the muffler hanger bolts.
5. Remove the exhaust rubber hangers, then allow the exhaust system to rest on the rear axle.
6. Disconnect the hoses from the fuel tank sender. Grasp the filter and one nylon fuel connection line fitting. Twist the quick-connect fitting ¼ turn in each direction to loosen any dirt within the fitting. Repeat for the other fitting. Using compressed air, blow out the dirt from the quick-connect fittings at the end of the fuel filter.
7. Detach the quick-connect fittings by pulling the release tabs back on the fuel line quick connector and pulling apart. If difficulty is encountered, tool J 38778 or equivalent can be used to separate the fitting.
8. Disconnect the hoses at the tank from the filler, vent and vapor pipes.
9. With the help of an assistant, support the fuel tank, then disconnect the two tank retaining straps and lower the tank.
10. Detach the fuel sender electrical connector.
11. On 1996–00 vehicles, detach the fuel pressure sensor connector.
12. Remove the tank from the vehicle.
To install:
13. If the tank is being replaced, perform the following:
a. Remove the sound insulators.
b. Remove the modular fuel sender, as outlined earlier in this section.
c. Inspect all connectors for dirt and burrs. Clean or replace, as required. Inspect the fuel line O-rings for cuts, nicks, swelling and/or distortion and replace as necessary.
d. Install the fuel sender assembly to the new tank, as outlined earlier in this section.
e. Install the sound insulators.
14. With the help of an assistant, raise the fuel tank to the vehicle and attach the fuel sender connector and, if equipped, the fuel pressure sensor connector.
15. Raise the fuel tank into position then fasten the retaining straps. Tighten the retaining bolts to 26 ft. lbs. (35 Nm).
16. Connect the hoses to the filler, vent and vapor pipes.

17. Attach the nylon fuel feed and return connecting line quick-connect fittings to the fuel sender, as follows:
a. Apply a few drops of clean engine oil to the male connector tube ends.
b. Push the connectors together to cause the retaining tabs/fingers to snap into place.
c. Once installed, pull on both ends of each connection to be sure they are secure.
18. Install the exhaust rubber hangers.
19. Install the muffler hanger bolts, then tighten to 11 ft. lbs. (15 Nm).
20. Attach the fuel tank sender electrical connector.
21. Carefully lower the vehicle.
22. Refill the fuel tank, then connect the negative battery cable.
23. Turn the ignition to the **ON** position for two seconds, then turn it to the **OFF** position for ten seconds. Turn again to the **ON** position and check for fuel leaks.

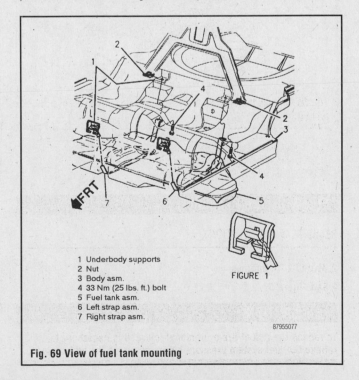

1 Underbody supports
2 Nut
3 Body asm.
4 33 Nm (25 lbs. ft.) bolt
5 Fuel tank asm.
6 Left strap asm.
7 Right strap asm.

87955077

Fig. 69 View of fuel tank mounting

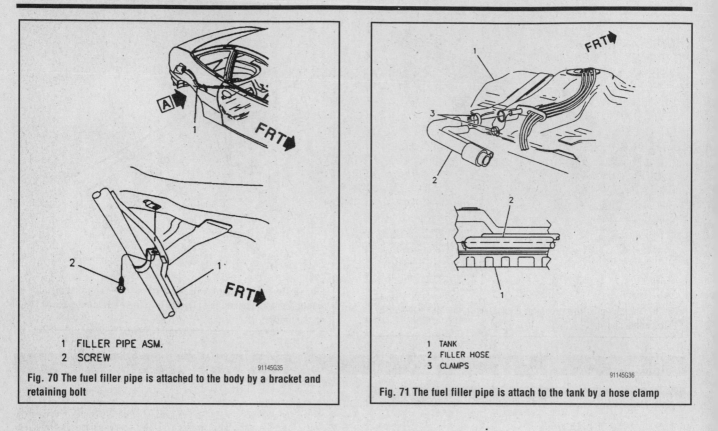

1 FILLER PIPE ASM.
2 SCREW

91145G35

Fig. 70 The fuel filler pipe is attached to the body by a bracket and retaining bolt

1 TANK
2 FILLER HOSE
3 CLAMPS

91145G36

Fig. 71 The fuel filler pipe is attach to the tank by a hose clamp

UNDERSTANDING AND
TROUBLESHOOTING ELECTRICAL
SYSTEMS 6-2
BASIC ELECTRICAL THEORY 6-2
    HOW DOES ELECTRICITY WORK: THE
    WATER ANALOGY 6-2
    OHM'S LAW 6-2
ELECTRICAL COMPONENTS 6-2
    POWER SOURCE 6-2
    GROUND 6-3
    PROTECTIVE DEVICES 6-3
    SWITCHES & RELAYS 6-3
    LOAD 6-3
    WIRING & HARNESSES 6-4
    CONNECTORS 6-4
TEST EQUIPMENT 6-4
    JUMPER WIRES 6-4
    TEST LIGHTS 6-4
    MULTIMETERS 6-5
TROUBLESHOOTING ELECTRICAL
SYSTEMS 6-5
TESTING 6-6
    OPEN CIRCUITS 6-6
    SHORT CIRCUITS 6-6
    VOLTAGE 6-6
    VOLTAGE DROP 6-6
    RESISTANCE 6-6
WIRE AND CONNECTOR REPAIR 6-7
BATTERY CABLES 6-7
DISCONNECTING THE CABLES 6-7
AIR BAG (SUPPLEMENTAL
RESTRAINT SYSTEM) 6-7
GENERAL INFORMATION 6-7
    SYSTEM OPERATION 6-7
    SYSTEM COMPONENTS 6-8
    SERVICE PRECAUTIONS 6-9
    DISABLING THE SYSTEM 6-10
    ENABLING THE SYSTEM 6-10
HEATING AND AIR
CONDITIONING 6-10
BLOWER MOTOR 6-10
    REMOVAL & INSTALLATION 6-10
HEATER CORE 6-10
    REMOVAL & INSTALLATION 6-10
HEATER WATER CONTROL VALVE 6-11
    REMOVAL & INSTALLATION 6-11
AIR CONDITIONING COMPONENTS 6-11
    REMOVAL & INSTALLATION 6-11
TEMPERATURE CONTROL CABLE 6-11
    REMOVAL & INSTALLATION 6-11
    ADJUSTMENT 6-11
CONTROL PANEL 6-11
    REMOVAL & INSTALLATION 6-11
CRUISE CONTROL 6-12
GENERAL INFORMATION 6-12
ENTERTAINMENT SYSTEMS 6-14
RADIO RECEIVER/TAPE PLAYER/CD
PLAYER 6-14
    REMOVAL & INSTALLATION 6-14

SPEAKERS 6-14
    REMOVAL & INSTALLATION 6-14
WINDSHIELD WIPERS AND
WASHERS 6-16
WINDSHIELD WIPER BLADE AND
ARM 6-16
    REMOVAL & INSTALLATION 6-16
    ADJUSTMENT 6-17
WINDSHIELD WIPER MOTOR 6-17
    REMOVAL & INSTALLATION 6-17
WINDSHIELD WASHER FLUID
RESERVOIR AND PUMP 6-19
    REMOVAL & INSTALLATION 6-19
INSTRUMENTS AND
SWITCHES 6-20
INSTRUMENT CLUSTER 6-20
    REMOVAL & INSTALLATION 6-20
GAUGES 6-20
    REMOVAL & INSTALLATION 6-20
LIGHTING 6-20
HEADLIGHTS 6-20
    REMOVAL & INSTALLATION 6-20
    AIMING THE HEADLIGHTS 6-20
SIGNAL AND MARKER LIGHTS 6-22
    REMOVAL & INSTALLATION 6-22
FOG/DRIVING LIGHTS (CHEVROLET
CAVALIER Z-24 ONLY) 6-25
    REMOVAL & INSTALLATION 6-25
    INSTALLING AFTERMARKET
    AUXILIARY LIGHTS 6-26
    AIMING 6-27
TRAILER WIRING 6-27
CIRCUIT PROTECTION 6-27
FUSES 6-27
    GENERAL INFORMATION 6-27
    REPLACEMENT 6-28
CIRCUIT BREAKERS 6-28
    RESETTING AND/OR REPLACEMENT
    6-28
FUSIBLE LINKS 6-29
    REPLACEMENT 6-29
FLASHERS 6-29
    REPLACEMENT 6-29
WIRING DIAGRAMS 6-33
TROUBLESHOOTING CHART
CRUISE CONTROL
    TROUBLESHOOTING 6-14

6

CHASSIS ELECTRICAL

UNDERSTANDING AND
TROUBLESHOOTING ELECTRICAL
SYSTEMS 6-2
BATTERY CABLES 6-7
AIR BAG (SUPPLEMENTAL
RESTRAINT SYSTEM) 6-7
HEATING AND AIR
CONDITIONING 6-10
CRUISE CONTROL 6-12
ENTERTAINMENT SYSTEMS 6-14
WINDSHIELD WIPERS AND
WASHERS 6-16
INSTRUMENTS AND
SWITCHES 6-20
LIGHTING 6-20
TRAILER WIRING 6-27
CIRCUIT PROTECTION 6-27
WIRING DIAGRAMS 6-33

UNDERSTANDING AND TROUBLESHOOTING ELECTRICAL SYSTEMS

Basic Electrical Theory

♦ **See Figure 1**

For any 12 volt, negative ground, electrical system to operate, the electricity must travel in a complete circuit. This simply means that current (power) from the positive (+) terminal of the battery must eventually return to the negative (–) terminal of the battery. Along the way, this current will travel through wires, fuses, switches and components. If, for any reason, the flow of current through the circuit is interrupted, the component fed by that circuit will cease to function properly.

Perhaps the easiest way to visualize a circuit is to think of connecting a light bulb (with two wires attached to it) to the battery—one wire attached to the negative (–) terminal of the battery and the other wire to the positive (+) terminal. With the two wires touching the battery terminals, the circuit would be complete and the light bulb would illuminate. Electricity would follow a path from the battery to the bulb and back to the battery. It's easy to see that with longer wires on our light bulb, it could be mounted anywhere. Further, one wire could be fitted with a switch so that the light could be turned on and off.

The normal automotive circuit differs from this simple example in two ways. First, instead of having a return wire from the bulb to the battery, the current travels through the frame of the vehicle. Since the negative (–) battery cable is attached to the frame (made of electrically conductive metal), the frame of the vehicle can serve as a ground wire to complete the circuit. Secondly, most automotive circuits contain multiple components which receive power from a single circuit. This lessens the amount of wire needed to power components on the vehicle.

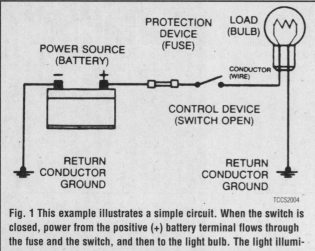

Fig. 1 This example illustrates a simple circuit. When the switch is closed, power from the positive (+) battery terminal flows through the fuse and the switch, and then to the light bulb. The light illuminates and the circuit is completed through the ground wire back to the negative (–) battery terminal. In reality, the two ground points shown in the illustration are attached to the metal frame of the vehicle, which completes the circuit back to the battery

HOW DOES ELECTRICITY WORK: THE WATER ANALOGY

Electricity is the flow of electrons—the subatomic particles that constitute the outer shell of an atom. Electrons spin in an orbit around the center core of an atom. The center core is comprised of protons (positive charge) and neutrons (neutral charge). Electrons have a negative charge and balance out the positive charge of the protons. When an outside force causes the number of electrons to unbalance the charge of the protons, the electrons will split off the atom and look for another atom to balance out. If this imbalance is kept up, electrons will continue to move and an electrical flow will exist.

Many people have been taught electrical theory using an analogy with water. In a comparison with water flowing through a pipe, the electrons would be the water and the wire is the pipe.

The flow of electricity can be measured much like the flow of water through a pipe. The unit of measurement used is amperes, frequently abbreviated as amps (a). You can compare amperage to the volume of water flowing through a pipe.

When connected to a circuit, an ammeter will measure the actual amount of current flowing through the circuit. When relatively few electrons flow through a circuit, the amperage is low. When many electrons flow, the amperage is high.

Water pressure is measured in units such as pounds per square inch (psi); The electrical pressure is measured in units called volts (v). When a voltmeter is connected to a circuit, it is measuring the electrical pressure.

The actual flow of electricity depends not only on voltage and amperage, but also on the resistance of the circuit. The higher the resistance, the higher the force necessary to push the current through the circuit. The standard unit for measuring resistance is an ohm. Resistance in a circuit varies depending on the amount and type of components used in the circuit. The main factors which determine resistance are:

• Material—some materials have more resistance than others. Those with high resistance are said to be insulators. Rubber materials (or rubber-like plastics) are some of the most common insulators used in vehicles as they have a very high resistance to electricity. Very low resistance materials are said to be conductors. Copper wire is among the best conductors. Silver is actually a superior conductor to copper and is used in some relay contacts, but its high cost prohibits its use as common wiring. Most automotive wiring is made of copper.

• Size—the larger the wire size being used, the less resistance the wire will have. This is why components which use large amounts of electricity usually have large wires supplying current to them.

• Length—for a given thickness of wire, the longer the wire, the greater the resistance. The shorter the wire, the less the resistance. When determining the proper wire for a circuit, both size and length must be considered to design a circuit that can handle the current needs of the component.

• Temperature—with many materials, the higher the temperature, the greater the resistance (positive temperature coefficient). Some materials exhibit the opposite trait of lower resistance with higher temperatures (negative temperature coefficient). These principles are used in many of the sensors on the engine.

OHM'S LAW

There is a direct relationship between current, voltage and resistance. The relationship between current, voltage and resistance can be summed up by a statement known as Ohm's law.

Voltage (E) is equal to amperage (I) times resistance (R): $E = I \times R$

Other forms of the formula are $R = E/I$ and $I = E/R$

In each of these formulas, E is the voltage in volts, I is the current in amps and R is the resistance in ohms. The basic point to remember is that as the resistance of a circuit goes up, the amount of current that flows in the circuit will go down, if voltage remains the same.

The amount of work that the electricity can perform is expressed as power. The unit of power is the watt (w). The relationship between power, voltage and current is expressed as:

Power (w) is equal to amperage (I) times voltage (E): $W = I \times E$

This is only true for direct current (DC) circuits; The alternating current formula is a tad different, but since the electrical circuits in most vehicles are DC type, we need not get into AC circuit theory.

Electrical Components

POWER SOURCE

Power is supplied to the vehicle by two devices: The battery and the alternator. The battery supplies electrical power during starting or during periods when the current demand of the vehicle's electrical system exceeds the output capacity of the alternator. The alternator supplies electrical current when the engine is running. Just not does the alternator supply the current needs of the vehicle, but it recharges the battery.

The Battery

In most modern vehicles, the battery is a lead/acid electrochemical device consisting of six 2 volt subsections (cells) connected in series, so that the unit is capable of producing approximately 12 volts of electrical pressure. Each subsection consists of a series of positive and negative plates held a short distance apart in a solution of sulfuric acid and water.

The two types of plates are of dissimilar metals. This sets up a chemical reaction, and it is this reaction which produces current flow from the battery when its positive and negative terminals are connected to an electrical load. The power removed from the battery is replaced by the alternator, restoring the battery to its original chemical state.

The Alternator

On some vehicles there isn't an alternator, but a generator. The difference is that an alternator supplies alternating current which is then changed to direct current for use on the vehicle, while a generator produces direct current. Alternators tend to be more efficient and that is why they are used.

Alternators and generators are devices that consist of coils of wires wound together making big electromagnets. One group of coils spins within another set and the interaction of the magnetic fields causes a current to flow. This current is then drawn off the coils and fed into the vehicles electrical system.

GROUND

Two types of grounds are used in automotive electric circuits. Direct ground components are grounded to the frame through their mounting points. All other components use some sort of ground wire which is attached to the frame or chassis of the vehicle. The electrical current runs through the chassis of the vehicle and returns to the battery through the ground (−) cable; if you look, you'll see that the battery ground cable connects between the battery and the frame or chassis of the vehicle.

➡ It should be noted that a good percentage of electrical problems can be traced to bad grounds.

PROTECTIVE DEVICES

▶ **See Figure 2**

It is possible for large surges of current to pass through the electrical system of your vehicle. If this surge of current were to reach the load in the circuit, the surge could burn it out or severely damage it. It can also overload the wiring, causing the harness to get hot and melt the insulation. To prevent this, fuses, circuit breakers and/or fusible links are connected into the supply wires of the electrical system. These items are nothing more than a built-in weak spot in the system. When an abnormal amount of current flows through the system, these protective devices work as follows to protect the circuit:

- Fuse— when an excessive electrical current passes through a fuse, the fuse "blows" (the conductor melts) and opens the circuit, preventing the passage of current.
- Circuit Breaker—a circuit breaker is basically a self-repairing fuse. It will open the circuit in the same fashion as a fuse, but when the surge subsides, the circuit breaker can be reset and does not need replacement.

- Fusible Link—a fusible link (fuse link or main link) is a short length of special, high temperature insulated wire that acts as a fuse. When an excessive electrical current passes through a fusible link, the thin gauge wire inside the link melts, creating an intentional open to protect the circuit. To repair the circuit, the link must be replaced. Some newer type fusible links are housed in plug-in modules, which are simply replaced like a fuse, while older type fusible links must be cut and spliced if they melt. Since this link is very early in the electrical path, it's the first place to look if nothing on the vehicle works, yet the battery seems to be charged and is properly connected.

✳ CAUTION

Always replace fuses, circuit breakers and fusible links with identically rated components. Under no circumstances should a component of higher or lower amperage rating be substituted.

SWITCHES & RELAYS

▶ **See Figures 3 and 4**

Switches are used in electrical circuits to control the passage of current. The most common use is to open and close circuits between the battery and the various electric devices in the system. Switches are rated according to the amount of amperage they can handle. If a sufficient amperage rated switch is not used in a circuit, the switch could overload and cause damage.

Some electrical components which require a large amount of current to operate use a special switch called a relay. Since these circuits carry a large amount of current, the thickness of the wire in the circuit is also greater. If this large wire were connected from the load to the control switch, the switch would have to carry the high amperage load and the fairing or dash would be twice as large to accommodate the increased size of the wiring harness. To prevent these problems, a relay is used.

Relays are composed of a coil and a set of contacts. When the coil has a current passed though it, a magnetic field is formed and this field causes the contacts to move together, completing the circuit. Most relays are normally open, preventing current from passing through the circuit, but they can take any electrical form depending on the job they are intended to do. Relays can be considered "remote control switches." They allow a smaller current to operate devices that require higher amperages. When a small current operates the coil, a larger current is allowed to pass by the contacts. Some common circuits which may use relays are the horn, headlights, starter, electric fuel pump and other high draw circuits.

LOAD

Every electrical circuit must include a "load" (something to use the electricity coming from the source). Without this load, the battery would attempt to deliver

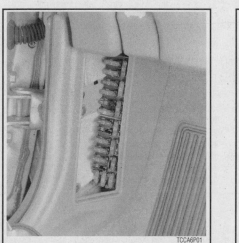

TCCA6P01

Fig. 2 Most vehicles use one or more fuse panels. This one is located on the driver's side kick panel

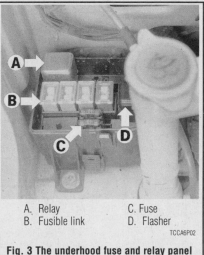

A. Relay
B. Fusible link
C. Fuse
D. Flasher

TCCA6P02

Fig. 3 The underhood fuse and relay panel usually contains fuses, relays, flashers and fusible links

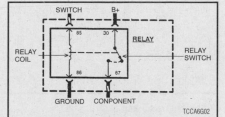

TCCA6G02

Fig. 4 Relays are composed of a coil and a switch. These two components are linked together so that when one operates, the other operates at the same time. The large wires in the circuit are connected from the battery to one side of the relay switch (B+) and from the opposite side of the relay switch to the load (component). Smaller wires are connected from the relay coil to the control switch for the circuit and from the opposite side of the relay coil to ground

its entire power supply from one pole to another. This is called a "short circuit." All this electricity would take a short cut to ground and cause a great amount of damage to other components in the circuit by developing a tremendous amount of heat. This condition could develop sufficient heat to melt the insulation on all the surrounding wires and reduce a multiple wire cable to a lump of plastic and copper.

WIRING & HARNESSES

The average vehicle contains meters and meters of wiring, with hundreds of individual connections. To protect the many wires from damage and to keep them from becoming a confusing tangle, they are organized into bundles, enclosed in plastic or taped together and called wiring harnesses. Different harnesses serve different parts of the vehicle. Individual wires are color coded to help trace them through a harness where sections are hidden from view.

Automotive wiring or circuit conductors can be either single strand wire, multi-strand wire or printed circuitry. Single strand wire has a solid metal core and is usually used inside such components as alternators, motors, relays and other devices. Multi-strand wire has a core made of many small strands of wire twisted together into a single conductor. Most of the wiring in an automotive electrical system is made up of multi-strand wire, either as a single conductor or grouped together in a harness. All wiring is color coded on the insulator, either as a solid color or as a colored wire with an identification stripe. A printed circuit is a thin film of copper or other conductor that is printed on an insulator backing. Occasionally, a printed circuit is sandwiched between two sheets of plastic for more protection and flexibility. A complete printed circuit, consisting of conductors, insulating material and connectors for lamps or other components is called a printed circuit board. Printed circuitry is used in place of individual wires or harnesses in places where space is limited, such as behind instrument panels.

Since automotive electrical systems are very sensitive to changes in resistance, the selection of properly sized wires is critical when systems are repaired. A loose or corroded connection or a replacement wire that is too small for the circuit will add extra resistance and an additional voltage drop to the circuit.

The wire gauge number is an expression of the cross-section area of the conductor. Vehicles from countries that use the metric system will typically describe the wire size as its cross-sectional area in square millimeters. In this method, the larger the wire, the greater the number. Another common system for expressing wire size is the American Wire Gauge (AWG) system. As gauge number increases, area decreases and the wire becomes smaller. An 18 gauge wire is smaller than a 4 gauge wire. A wire with a higher gauge number will carry less current than a wire with a lower gauge number. Gauge wire size refers to the size of the strands of the conductor, not the size of the complete wire with insulator. It is possible, therefore, to have two wires of the same gauge with different diameters because one may have thicker insulation than the other.

It is essential to understand how a circuit works before trying to figure out why it doesn't. An electrical schematic shows the electrical current paths when a circuit is operating properly. Schematics break the entire electrical system down into individual circuits. In a schematic, usually no attempt is made to represent wiring and components as they physically appear on the vehicle; switches and other components are shown as simply as possible. Face views of harness connectors show the cavity or terminal locations in all multi-pin connectors to help locate test points.

CONNECTORS

▶ **See Figures 5 and 6**

Three types of connectors are commonly used in automotive applications—weatherproof, molded and hard shell.

• Weatherproof—these connectors are most commonly used where the connector is exposed to the elements. Terminals are protected against moisture and dirt by sealing rings which provide a weathertight seal. All repairs require the use of a special terminal and the tool required to service it. Unlike standard blade type terminals, these weatherproof terminals cannot be straightened once they are bent. Make certain that the connectors are properly seated and all of the sealing rings are in place when connecting leads.

• Molded—these connectors require complete replacement of the connector if found to be defective. This means splicing a new connector assembly into the harness. All splices should be soldered to insure proper contact. Use care when probing the connections or replacing terminals in them, as it is possible

to create a short circuit between opposite terminals. If this happens to the wrong terminal pair, it is possible to damage certain components. Always use jumper wires between connectors for circuit checking and NEVER probe through weatherproof seals.

• Hard Shell—unlike molded connectors, the terminal contacts in hard-shell connectors can be replaced. Replacement usually involves the use of a special terminal removal tool that depresses the locking tangs (barbs) on the connector terminal and allows the connector to be removed from the rear of the shell. The connector shell should be replaced if it shows any evidence of burning, melting, cracks, or breaks. Replace individual terminals that are burnt, corroded, distorted or loose.

Test Equipment

Pinpointing the exact cause of trouble in an electrical circuit is most times accomplished by the use of special test equipment. The following describes different types of commonly used test equipment and briefly explains how to use them in diagnosis. In addition to the information covered below, the tool manufacturer's instructions booklet (provided with the tester) should be read and clearly understood before attempting any test procedures.

JUMPER WIRES

✳✳ CAUTION

Never use jumper wires made from a thinner gauge wire than the circuit being tested. If the jumper wire is of too small a gauge, it may overheat and possibly melt. Never use jumpers to bypass high resistance loads in a circuit. Bypassing resistances, in effect, creates a short circuit. This may, in turn, cause damage and fire. Jumper wires should only be used to bypass lengths of wire or to simulate switches.

Jumper wires are simple, yet extremely valuable, pieces of test equipment. They are basically test wires which are used to bypass sections of a circuit. Although jumper wires can be purchased, they are usually fabricated from lengths of standard automotive wire and whatever type of connector (alligator clip, spade connector or pin connector) that is required for the particular application being tested. In cramped, hard-to-reach areas, it is advisable to have insulated boots over the jumper wire terminals in order to prevent accidental grounding. It is also advisable to include a standard automotive fuse in any jumper wire. This is commonly referred to as a "fused jumper". By inserting an in-line fuse holder between a set of test leads, a fused jumper wire can be used for bypassing open circuits. Use a 5 amp fuse to provide protection against voltage spikes.

Jumper wires are used primarily to locate open electrical circuits, on either the ground (–) side of the circuit or on the power (+) side. If an electrical component fails to operate, connect the jumper wire between the component and a good ground. If the component operates only with the jumper installed, the ground circuit is open. If the ground circuit is good, but the component does not operate, the circuit between the power feed and component may be open. By moving the jumper wire successively back from the component toward the power source, you can isolate the area of the circuit where the open is located. When the component stops functioning, or the power is cut off, the open is in the segment of wire between the jumper and the point previously tested.

You can sometimes connect the jumper wire directly from the battery to the "hot" terminal of the component, but first make sure the component uses 12 volts in operation. Some electrical components, such as fuel injectors or sensors, are designed to operate on about 4 to 5 volts, and running 12 volts directly to these components will cause damage.

TEST LIGHTS

▶ **See Figure 7**

The test light is used to check circuits and components while electrical current is flowing through them. It is used for voltage and ground tests. To use a 12 volt test light, connect the ground clip to a good ground and probe wherever necessary with the pick. The test light will illuminate when voltage is detected. This does not necessarily mean that 12 volts (or any particular amount of voltage) is present; it only means that some voltage is present. It is advisable before

Fig. 5 Hard shell (left) and weatherproof (right) connectors have replaceable terminals

Fig. 6 Weatherproof connectors are most commonly used in the engine compartment or where the connector is exposed to the elements

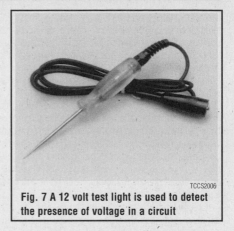

Fig. 7 A 12 volt test light is used to detect the presence of voltage in a circuit

using the test light to touch its ground clip and probe across the battery posts or terminals to make sure the light is operating properly.

✳✳ WARNING

Do not use a test light to probe electronic ignition, spark plug or coil wires. Never use a pick-type test light to probe wiring on computer controlled systems unless specifically instructed to do so. Any wire insulation that is pierced by the test light probe should be taped and sealed with silicone after testing.

Like the jumper wire, the 12 volt test light is used to isolate opens in circuits. But, whereas the jumper wire is used to bypass the open to operate the load, the 12 volt test light is used to locate the presence of voltage in a circuit. If the test light illuminates, there is power up to that point in the circuit; if the test light does not illuminate, there is an open circuit (no power). Move the test light in successive steps back toward the power source until the light in the handle illuminates. The open is between the probe and a point which was previously probed.

The self-powered test light is similar in design to the 12 volt test light, but contains a 1.5 volt penlight battery in the handle. It is most often used in place of a multimeter to check for open or short circuits when power is isolated from the circuit (continuity test).

The battery in a self-powered test light does not provide much current. A weak battery may not provide enough power to illuminate the test light even when a complete circuit is made (especially if there is high resistance in the circuit). Always make sure that the test battery is strong. To check the battery, briefly touch the ground clip to the probe; if the light glows brightly, the battery is strong enough for testing.

➡A self-powered test light should not be used on any computer controlled system or component. The small amount of electricity transmitted by the test light is enough to damage many electronic automotive components.

MULTIMETERS

Multimeters are an extremely useful tool for troubleshooting electrical problems. They can be purchased in either analog or digital form and have a price range to suit any budget. A multimeter is a voltmeter, ammeter and ohmmeter (along with other features) combined into one instrument. It is often used when testing solid state circuits because of its high input impedance (usually 10 megaohms or more). A brief description of the multimeter main test functions follows:

• Voltmeter—the voltmeter is used to measure voltage at any point in a circuit, or to measure the voltage drop across any part of a circuit. Voltmeters usually have various scales and a selector switch to allow the reading of different voltage ranges. The voltmeter has a positive and a negative lead. To avoid damage to the meter, always connect the negative lead to the negative (–) side of the circuit (to ground or nearest the ground side of the circuit) and connect the positive lead to the positive (+) side of the circuit (to the power source or the nearest power source). Note that the negative voltmeter lead will always be black and that the positive voltmeter will always be some color other than black (usually red).

• Ohmmeter—the ohmmeter is designed to read resistance (measured in ohms) in a circuit or component. Most ohmmeters will have a selector switch which permits the measurement of different ranges of resistance (usually the selector switch allows the multiplication of the meter reading by 10, 100, 1,000 and 10,000). Some ohmmeters are "auto-ranging" which means the meter itself will determine which scale to use. Since the meters are powered by an internal battery, the ohmmeter can be used like a self-powered test light. When the ohmmeter is connected, current from the ohmmeter flows through the circuit or component being tested. Since the ohmmeter's internal resistance and voltage are known values, the amount of current flow through the meter depends on the resistance of the circuit or component being tested. The ohmmeter can also be used to perform a continuity test for suspected open circuits. In using the meter for making continuity checks, do not be concerned with the actual resistance readings. Zero resistance, or any ohm reading, indicates continuity in the circuit. Infinite resistance indicates an opening in the circuit. A high resistance reading where there should be none indicates a problem in the circuit. Checks for short circuits are made in the same manner as checks for open circuits, except that the circuit must be isolated from both power and normal ground. Infinite resistance indicates no continuity, while zero resistance indicates a dead short.

✳✳ WARNING

Never use an ohmmeter to check the resistance of a component or wire while there is voltage applied to the circuit.

• Ammeter—an ammeter measures the amount of current flowing through a circuit in units called amperes or amps. At normal operating voltage, most circuits have a characteristic amount of amperes, called "current draw" which can be measured using an ammeter. By referring to a specified current draw rating, then measuring the amperes and comparing the two values, one can determine what is happening within the circuit to aid in diagnosis. An open circuit, for example, will not allow any current to flow, so the ammeter reading will be zero. A damaged component or circuit will have an increased current draw, so the reading will be high. The ammeter is always connected in series with the circuit being tested. All of the current that normally flows through the circuit must also flow through the ammeter; if there is any other path for the current to follow, the ammeter reading will not be accurate. The ammeter itself has very little resistance to current flow and, therefore, will not affect the circuit, but it will measure current draw only when the circuit is closed and electricity is flowing. Excessive current draw can blow fuses and drain the battery, while a reduced current draw can cause motors to run slowly, lights to dim and other components to not operate properly.

Troubleshooting Electrical Systems

When diagnosing a specific problem, organized troubleshooting is a must. The complexity of a modern automotive vehicle demands that you approach any problem in a logical, organized manner. There are certain troubleshooting techniques, however, which are standard:

• Establish when the problem occurs. Does the problem appear only under certain conditions? Were there any noises, odors or other unusual symptoms? Isolate the problem area. To do this, make some simple tests and observations, then eliminate the systems that are working properly. Check for obvious problems, such as broken wires and loose or dirty connections. Always check the obvious before assuming something complicated is the cause.

• Test for problems systematically to determine the cause once the problem area is isolated. Are all the components functioning properly? Is there power going to electrical switches and motors. Performing careful, systematic checks will often turn up most causes on the first inspection, without wasting time checking components that have little or no relationship to the problem.

• Test all repairs after the work is done to make sure that the problem is fixed. Some causes can be traced to more than one component, so a careful verification of repair work is important in order to pick up additional malfunctions that may cause a problem to reappear or a different problem to arise. A blown fuse, for example, is a simple problem that may require more than another fuse to repair. If you don't look for a problem that caused a fuse to blow, a shorted wire (for example) may go undetected.

Experience has shown that most problems tend to be the result of a fairly simple and obvious cause, such as loose or corroded connectors, bad grounds or damaged wire insulation which causes a short. This makes careful visual inspection of components during testing essential to quick and accurate troubleshooting.

Testing

OPEN CIRCUITS

▶ **See Figure 8**

This test already assumes the existence of an open in the circuit and it is used to help locate the open portion.

1. Isolate the circuit from power and ground.
2. Connect the self-powered test light or ohmmeter ground clip to the ground side of the circuit and probe sections of the circuit sequentially.
3. If the light is out or there is infinite resistance, the open is between the probe and the circuit ground.
4. If the light is on or the meter shows continuity, the open is between the probe and the end of the circuit toward the power source.

SHORT CIRCUITS

➡**Never use a self-powered test light to perform checks for opens or shorts when power is applied to the circuit under test. The test light can be damaged by outside power.**

1. Isolate the circuit from power and ground.
2. Connect the self-powered test light or ohmmeter ground clip to a good ground and probe any easy-to-reach point in the circuit.

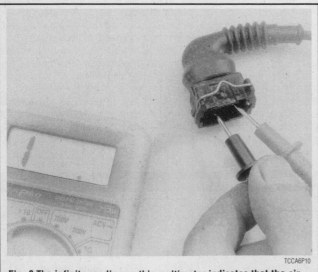

TCCA6P10

Fig. 8 The infinite reading on this multimeter indicates that the circuit is open

3. If the light comes on or there is continuity, there is a short somewhere in the circuit.
4. To isolate the short, probe a test point at either end of the isolated circuit (the light should be on or the meter should indicate continuity).
5. Leave the test light probe engaged and sequentially open connectors or switches, remove parts, etc. until the light goes out or continuity is broken.
6. When the light goes out, the short is between the last two circuit components which were opened.

VOLTAGE

This test determines voltage available from the battery and should be the first step in any electrical troubleshooting procedure after visual inspection. Many electrical problems, especially on computer controlled systems, can be caused by a low state of charge in the battery. Excessive corrosion at the battery cable terminals can cause poor contact that will prevent proper charging and full battery current flow.

1. Set the voltmeter selector switch to the 20V position.
2. Connect the multimeter negative lead to the battery's negative (−) post or terminal and the positive lead to the battery's positive (+) post or terminal.
3. Turn the ignition switch **ON** to provide a load.
4. A well charged battery should register over 12 volts. If the meter reads below 11.5 volts, the battery power may be insufficient to operate the electrical system properly.

VOLTAGE DROP

▶ **See Figure 9**

When current flows through a load, the voltage beyond the load drops. This voltage drop is due to the resistance created by the load and also by small resistances created by corrosion at the connectors and damaged insulation on the wires. The maximum allowable voltage drop under load is critical, especially if there is more than one load in the circuit, since all voltage drops are cumulative.

1. Set the voltmeter selector switch to the 20 volt position.
2. Connect the multimeter negative lead to a good ground.
3. Operate the circuit and check the voltage prior to the first component (load).
4. There should be little or no voltage drop in the circuit prior to the first component. If a voltage drop exists, the wire or connectors in the circuit are suspect.
5. While operating the first component in the circuit, probe the ground side of the component with the positive meter lead and observe the voltage readings. A small voltage drop should be noticed. This voltage drop is caused by the resistance of the component.
6. Repeat the test for each component (load) down the circuit.
7. If a large voltage drop is noticed, the preceding component, wire or connector is suspect.

RESISTANCE

▶ **See Figures 10 and 11**

❊❊ WARNING

Never use an ohmmeter with power applied to the circuit. The ohmmeter is designed to operate on its own power supply. The normal 12 volt electrical system voltage could damage the meter!

1. Isolate the circuit from the vehicle's power source.
2. Ensure that the ignition key is **OFF** when disconnecting any components or the battery.
3. Where necessary, also isolate at least one side of the circuit to be checked, in order to avoid reading parallel resistances. Parallel circuit resistances will always give a lower reading than the actual resistance of either of the branches.
4. Connect the meter leads to both sides of the circuit (wire or component) and read the actual measured ohms on the meter scale. Make sure the selector switch is set to the proper ohm scale for the circuit being tested, to avoid misreading the ohmmeter test value.

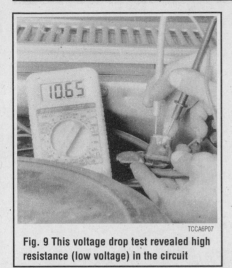

Fig. 9 This voltage drop test revealed high resistance (low voltage) in the circuit

TCCA6P07

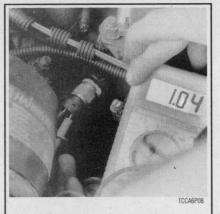

TCCA6P08

Fig. 10 Checking the resistance of a coolant temperature sensor with an ohm-meter. Reading is 1.04 kilohms

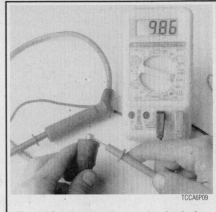

TCCA6P09

Fig. 11 Spark plug wires can be checked for excessive resistance using an ohmmeter

Wire and Connector Repair

Almost anyone can replace damaged wires, as long as the proper tools and parts are available. Wire and terminals are available to fit almost any need. Even the specialized weatherproof, molded and hard shell connectors are now available from aftermarket suppliers.

Be sure the ends of all the wires are fitted with the proper terminal hardware and connectors. Wrapping a wire around a stud is never a permanent solution and will only cause trouble later. Replace wires one at a time to avoid confusion. Always route wires exactly the same as the factory.

➡ If connector repair is necessary, only attempt it if you have the proper tools. Weatherproof and hard shell connectors require special tools to release the pins inside the connector. Attempting to repair these connectors with conventional hand tools will damage them.

BATTERY CABLES

Disconnecting the Cables

When working on any electrical component on the vehicle, it is always a good idea to disconnect the negative (–) battery cable. This will prevent potential damage to many sensitive electrical components such as the Engine Control Module (ECM), radio, alternator, etc.

➡ Any time you disengage the battery cables, it is recommended that you disconnect the negative (–) battery cable first. This will prevent your accidentally grounding the positive (+) terminal to the body of the vehicle when disconnecting it, thereby preventing damage to the above mentioned components.

Before you disconnect the cable(s), first turn the ignition to the **OFF** position. This will prevent a draw on the battery which could cause arcing (electricity trying to ground itself to the body of a vehicle, just like a spark plug jumping the gap) and, of course, damaging some components such as the alternator diodes.

When the battery cable(s) are reconnected (negative cable last), be sure to check that your lights, windshield wipers and other electrically operated safety components are all working correctly. If your vehicle contains an Electronically Tuned Radio (ETR), don't forget to also reset your radio stations. Ditto for the clock.

AIR BAG (SUPPLEMENTAL RESTRAINT SYSTEM)

General Information

▶ See Figure 12

Driver's side and passenger air bags are standard equipment on all models covered by this manual. The Supplemental Inflatable Restraint (SIR) system offers protection in addition to that provided by the seat belt by deploying an air bag from the center of the steering wheel or dash panel. The air bag deploys when the vehicle is involved in a frontal crash of sufficient force up to 30° off the centerline of the vehicle. To further absorb the crash energy, there is also a knee bolster located beneath the instrument panel in the driver's area and the steering wheel is collapsible.

The system has an energy reserve, which can store a large enough electrical charge to deploy the air bag(s) for up to ten minutes after the battery has been disconnected or damaged. The system **MUST** be disabled before any service is performed on or around SIR components or SIR wiring.

SYSTEM OPERATION

The SIR system contains a deployment loop for each air bag and a Diagnostic Energy Reserve Module (DERM). The deployment loop supplies current through the inflator module which will cause air bag deployment in the event of a frontal collision of sufficient force. The DERM supplies the necessary power, even if the battery has been damaged.

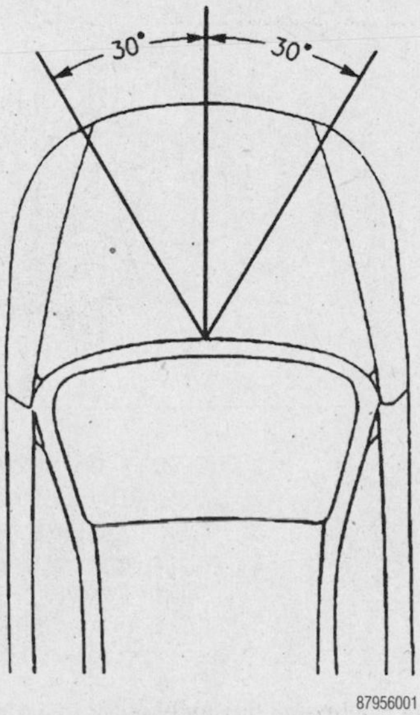

87956001

Fig. 12 SIR system "deployment window"

The deployment loop is made up of the arming sensors, coil assembly, inflator module and the discriminating sensors. The inflator module is only supplied sufficient current when the arming sensor and at least one of the two discriminating sensors close simultaneously. The function of the DERM is to supply the deployment loop a 36 Volt Loop Reserve (36VLR) to assure sufficient voltage to deploy the air bag if ignition voltage is lost in a frontal crash.

The DERM, in conjunction with the sensor resistors, makes it possible to detect circuit and component malfunctions within the deployment loop. If the voltages monitored by the DERM fall outside expected limits, the DERM will indicate a malfunction by storing a diagnostic trouble code and illuminating the AIR BAG lamp.

SYSTEM COMPONENTS

♦ **See Figure 13**

Diagnostic Energy Reserve Module (DERM)

The DERM is designed to perform five main functions: energy reserve, malfunction detection, malfunction recording, driver notification and frontal crash recording.

The DERM maintains a reserve voltage supply to provide deployment energy for a few seconds when the vehicle voltage is low or lost in a frontal crash. The

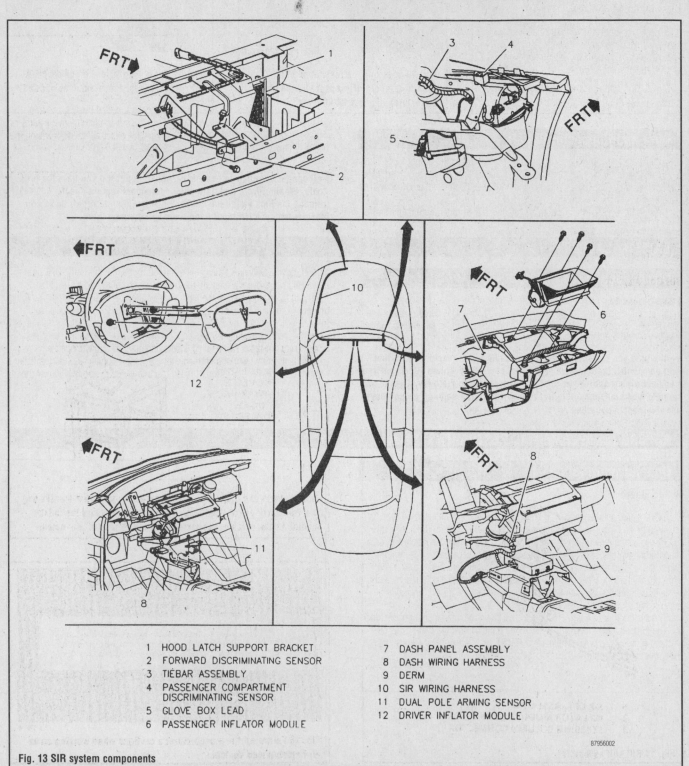

1	HOOD LATCH SUPPORT BRACKET	7	DASH PANEL ASSEMBLY
2	FORWARD DISCRIMINATING SENSOR	8	DASH WIRING HARNESS
3	TIEBAR ASSEMBLY	9	DERM
4	PASSENGER COMPARTMENT DISCRIMINATING SENSOR	10	SIR WIRING HARNESS
5	GLOVE BOX LEAD	11	DUAL POLE ARMING SENSOR
6	PASSENGER INFLATOR MODULE	12	DRIVER INFLATOR MODULE

87956002

Fig. 13 SIR system components

DERM performs diagnostic monitoring of the SIR system and records malfunctions in the form of diagnostic trouble codes, which can be obtained from a hand scan tool and/or on-board diagnostics. The DERM warns the driver of SIR system malfunctions by controlling the AIR BAG warning lamp and records SIR system status during a frontal crash.

AIR BAG Warning Lamp

The AIR BAG warning/indicator lamp is used to verify lamp and DERM operation by flashing 7 times when the ignition is first turned **ON**. It is also used to warn the driver of an SIR system malfunction.

Discriminating Sensors

All vehicles covered by this manual are equipped with two discriminating sensors. The forward discriminating sensor is located in front of the radiator. The passenger compartment discriminating sensor is located behind the right side of the instrument panel.

The discriminating sensor consists of a sensing element, diagnostic resistor and normally open switch contacts. The sensing element closes the switch contact when vehicle velocity changes are severe enough to warrant air bag deployment.

Dual Pole Arming Sensor

The dual pole arming sensor is contained in the same housing as the passenger compartment discriminating sensor and is referred to as the dual sensor.

The arming sensor is a switch located in the power side of the deployment loop. It is calibrated to close at low level velocity changes (lower than the discriminating sensors), assuring that the inflator module is connected directly to the 36VLR output of the DERM or Ignition 1 voltage when any discriminating sensor closes.

SIR Coil Assembly

▶ **See Figure 14**

The SIR coil assembly consists of two current carrying coils. They are attached to the steering column and allow rotation of the steering wheel while maintaining continuous deployment loop contact through the inflator module.

There is a shorting bar on the lower steering column connector that connects the SIR coil to the SIR wiring harness. The shorting bar shorts the circuit when the connector is disengaged. The circuit to the inflator module is shorted in this way to prevent unwanted air bag deployment when servicing the steering column or other SIR components.

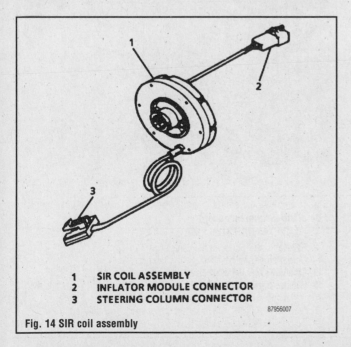

1	SIR COIL ASSEMBLY
2	INFLATOR MODULE CONNECTOR
3	STEERING COLUMN CONNECTOR

87956007

Fig. 14 SIR coil assembly

Inflator Module

The inflator module consists of an inflatable bag and an inflator (a canister of gas-generating material and an initiating device). When the vehicle is in a frontal crash of sufficient force to close the arming sensor and at least one discriminating sensor simultaneously, current flows through the deployment loop. Current passing through the initiator ignites the material in the inflator module, causing a reaction which produces a gas that rapidly inflates the air bag.

All vehicles are equipped with a driver's side inflator module located in the steering wheel and a passenger side inflator module located in the dash panel.

SERVICE PRECAUTIONS

▶ **See Figures 15 and 16**

- When performing service around the SIR system components or wiring, the SIR system MUST be disabled. Failure to do so could result in possible air bag deployment, personal injury or unneeded SIR system repairs.
- When carrying a live inflator module, make sure that the bag and trim cover are pointed away from you. Never carry the inflator module by the wires or connector on the underside of the module. In case of accidental deployment, the bag will then deploy with minimal chance of injury.

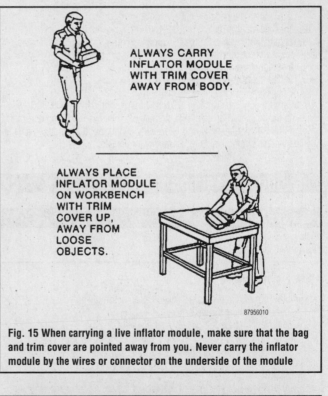

ALWAYS CARRY INFLATOR MODULE WITH TRIM COVER AWAY FROM BODY.

ALWAYS PLACE INFLATOR MODULE ON WORKBENCH WITH TRIM COVER UP, AWAY FROM LOOSE OBJECTS.

87956010

Fig. 15 When carrying a live inflator module, make sure that the bag and trim cover are pointed away from you. Never carry the inflator module by the wires or connector on the underside of the module

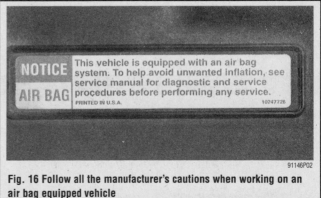

NOTICE AIR BAG — This vehicle is equipped with an air bag system. To help avoid unwanted inflation, see service manual for diagnostic and service procedures before performing any service.
PRINTED IN U.S.A. 10247726

91146P02

Fig. 16 Follow all the manufacturer's cautions when working on an air bag equipped vehicle

• When placing a live inflator module on a bench or other surface, always face the bag and trim cover up, away from the surface.

DISABLING THE SYSTEM

▶ See Figure 17

➡With the "AIR BAG" fuse removed and the ignition switch ON, the "AIR BAG" warning lamp will be on. The is normal and does not indicate any system malfunction.

1. Turn the steering wheel so that the vehicle's wheels are pointing straight ahead.
2. Turn the ignition switch to **LOCK**, remove the key, then disconnect the negative battery cable.
3. Remove the "AIR BAG" fuse from the fuse block.
4. Remove the steering column filler panel.
5. Disengage the Connector Position Assurance (CPA) and both yellow two way connectors and corresponding CPAs located near the base of the steering column.
6. Connect the negative battery cable.

ENABLING THE SYSTEM

▶ See Figure 17

1. Disconnect the negative battery cable.
2. Turn the ignition switch to **LOCK**, then remove the key.
3. Engage both yellow SIR connectors and corresponding CPAs located near the base of the steering column.
4. Install the steering column filler panel.
5. Install the "AIR BAG" fuse to the fuse block.
6. Connect the negative battery cable.
7. Turn the ignition switch to **RUN** and make sure that the "AIR BAG" warning lamp flashes seven times and then shuts off. If the warning lamp does not shut off, make sure that the wiring is properly connected. If the light remains on, take the vehicle to a reputable repair facility for service.

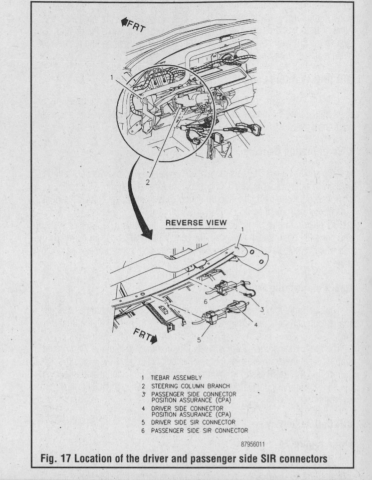

1 TIEBAR ASSEMBLY
2 STEERING COLUMN BRANCH
3 PASSENGER SIDE CONNECTOR POSITION ASSURANCE (CPA)
4 DRIVER SIDE CONNECTOR POSITION ASSURANCE (CPA)
5 DRIVER SIDE SIR CONNECTOR
6 PASSENGER SIDE SIR CONNECTOR

87956011

Fig. 17 Location of the driver and passenger side SIR connectors

HEATING AND AIR CONDITIONING

Blower Motor

REMOVAL & INSTALLATION

▶ See Figures 18 and 19

The blower motor and fan are serviced as an assembly only.
1. Disconnect the negative battery cable.
2. Remove the passenger side sound insulator.
3. Detach the electrical connections from the blower motor.
4. Remove the blower motor retaining screws, then remove blower motor and fan assembly.

To install:
5. Install blower motor and fan assembly, then secure using the retaining screws.
6. If equipped, connect the blower motor cooling tube.
7. Attach the electrical connections to the blower motor.
8. Install the right side sound insulator.
9. Connect the negative battery cable.

Heater Core

REMOVAL & INSTALLATION

▶ See Figure 20

1. Disable the SIR system, as outlined in this section.
2. Disconnect the negative battery cable.
3. Properly drain the cooling system.

91146P69

Fig. 18 Remove the sound insulator from underneath the passenger side of the instrument panel

4. Raise and safely support the vehicle.
5. Detach the heater hoses from the heater core.
6. Carefully lower the vehicle.
7. Remove the instrument panel. For details, please refer to the procedure located in Section 10 of this manual.
8. Remove the DERM with the attaching bracket.
9. Detach the heater core cover.

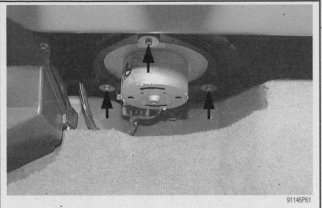

Fig. 19 Remove the retaining bolts for the blower motor assembly

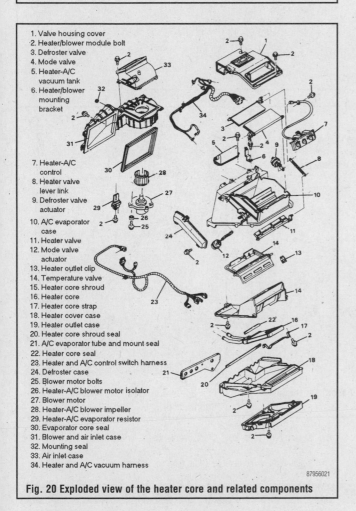

1. Valve housing cover
2. Heater/blower module bolt
3. Defroster valve
4. Mode valve
5. Heater-A/C vacuum tank
6. Heater/blower mounting bracket
7. Heater-A/C control
8. Heater valve lever link
9. Defroster valve actuator
10. A/C evaporator case
11. Heater valve
12. Mode valve actuator
13. Heater outlet clip
14. Temperature valve
15. Heater core shroud
16. Heater core
17. Heater core strap
18. Heater cover case
19. Heater outlet case
20. Heater core shroud seal
21. A/C evaporator tube and mount seal
22. Heater core seal
23. Heater and A/C control switch harness
24. Defroster case
25. Blower motor bolts
26. Heater-A/C blower motor isolator
27. Blower motor
28. Heater-A/C blower impeller
29. Heater-A/C evaporator resistor
30. Evaporator core seal
31. Blower and air inlet case
32. Mounting seal
33. Air inlet case
34. Heater and A/C vacuum harness

Fig. 20 Exploded view of the heater core and related components

10. Unfasten the heater core mounting clamps, then remove the heater core.

To install:

11. Position the heater core, then secure with the mounting clamps.
12. Attach the heater core cover.
13. Install the DERM with the attaching bracket.
14. Install the instrument panel, as outlined in Section 10 of this manual.
15. Raise and safely support the vehicle.
16. Connect the heater hoses to the core.
17. Carefully lower the vehicle.
18. Properly refill the engine cooling system and check for leaks.
19. Enable the SIR system.
20. Connect the negative battery cable, then start the engine and check for proper system operation and/or leaks.

Heater Water Control Valve

REMOVAL & INSTALLATION

The heater water control valve is incorporated into the heater hoses and is replaced only by replacing the entire hose assembly.

Air Conditioning Components

REMOVAL & INSTALLATION

Repair or service of air conditioning components is not covered by this manual, because of the risk of personal injury or death, and because of the legal ramifications of servicing these components without the proper EPA certification and experience. Cost, personal injury or death, environmental damage, and legal considerations (such as the fact that it is a federal crime to vent refrigerant into the atmosphere), dictate that the A/C components on your vehicle should be serviced only by a Motor Vehicle Air Conditioning (MVAC) trained, and EPA certified automotive technician.

➡**If your vehicle's A/C system uses R-12 refrigerant and is in need of recharging, the A/C system can be converted over to R-134a refrigerant (less environmentally harmful and expensive). Refer to Section 1 for additional information on R-12 to R-134a conversions, and for additional considerations dealing with your vehicle's A/C system.**

Temperature Control Cable

REMOVAL & INSTALLATION

▶ **See Figure 21**

1. Disconnect the negative battery cable.
2. Remove the right side sound insulator panel.
3. If necessary for access, remove the instrument panel (I/P) compartment.
4. Disconnect the cable at the module.
5. Remove the control panel trim plate and control panel assembly, as outlined later in this section.
6. Disconnect the cable from the control assembly, then remove the cable.
7. Installation is the reverse of the removal procedure. Adjust temperature control cable, as outlined later in this section.

ADJUSTMENT

▶ **See Figure 22**

If the temperature control lever fails to move to full COLD or HOT, or a large amount of lever spring back is noticed when moving to either of the full positions, the cable clip may need adjustment. Failure to grip clip in the correct manner will damage its ability to hold position on the cable. The temperature control cable must be replaced if clip retention fails.

1. To adjust the clip, grip the clip (refer to the accompanying illustration for the correct manner to grip the cable) at module end of cable while pulling temperature control lever to the correct full position (COLD or HOT) and connect.
2. Verify correct adjustment by observing for little or no spring back of the temperature control lever and listening for temperature door "slam" when the control lever is moved to full positions quickly.

Control Panel

REMOVAL & INSTALLATION

▶ **See Figures 23 and 24**

1. Disconnect the negative battery cable.
2. Remove the instrument panel trim and pad.

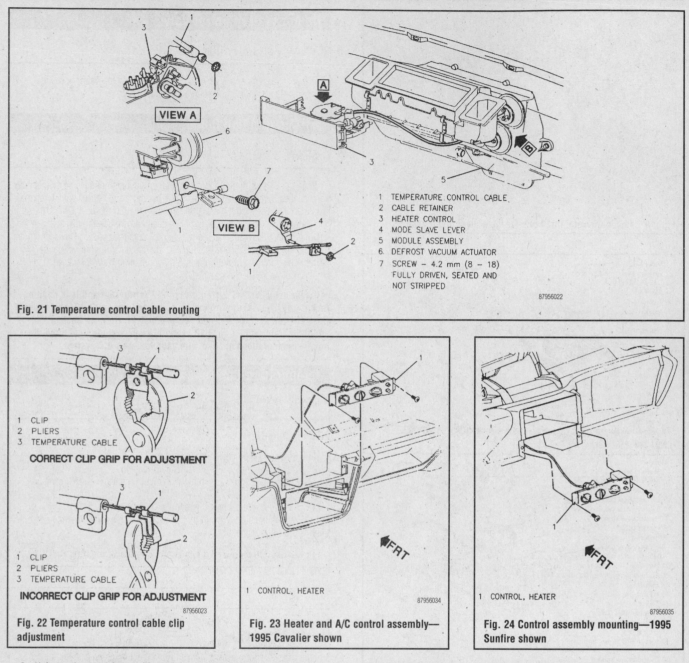

VIEW A

VIEW B

1 TEMPERATURE CONTROL CABLE
2 CABLE RETAINER
3 HEATER CONTROL
4 MODE SLAVE LEVER
5 MODULE ASSEMBLY
6 DEFROST VACUUM ACTUATOR
7 SCREW – 4.2 mm (8 – 18)
   FULLY DRIVEN, SEATED AND
   NOT STRIPPED

87956022

Fig. 21 Temperature control cable routing

1 CLIP
2 PLIERS
3 TEMPERATURE CABLE

CORRECT CLIP GRIP FOR ADJUSTMENT

1 CLIP
2 PLIERS
3 TEMPERATURE CABLE

INCORRECT CLIP GRIP FOR ADJUSTMENT

87956023

Fig. 22 Temperature control cable clip adjustment

◀FRT

1 CONTROL, HEATER

87956034

Fig. 23 Heater and A/C control assembly—1995 Cavalier shown

◀FRT

1 CONTROL, HEATER

87956035

Fig. 24 Control assembly mounting—1995 Sunfire shown

3. Unfasten the control assembly retaining screws, then pull the control assembly away from the instrument panel.

4. Detach the electrical and vacuum connections.

5. Detach the temperature control cable, then remove the assembly from the vehicle.

6. Installation is the reverse of the removal procedure.

CRUISE CONTROL

General Information

▶ **See Figures 25, 26, 27, 28 and 29**

Cruise control is a speed control system that maintains a desired vehicle speed under normal driving conditions. However, steep grades up or down may cause variations in the selected speeds. The electronic cruise control system has the capability to cruise, coast, resume speed, accelerate, "tap-up" and "tap-down".

The main parts of the cruise control system are the functional control switches, cruise control module assembly, vehicle speed sensor and the release switches.

The cruise control system uses the module assembly to obtain the desired operation. Two components in the module help to do this. One is the electronic controller and the second is the electric stepper motor. The controller monitors the vehicle speed and operates the stepper motor. The motor moves a ribbon and throttle linkage in response to the controller. The cruise control module assembly contains a low speed limit which will prevent system engagement below 25 mph (40 km/h). The module is controlled by the functional switches in the turn signal/headlamp switch and windshield wiper lever.

The release switches are mounted on the brake/clutch/accelerator pedal bracket. When the brake or clutch pedal is depressed, the cruise control system is electrically disengaged and the throttle is returned to the idle position.

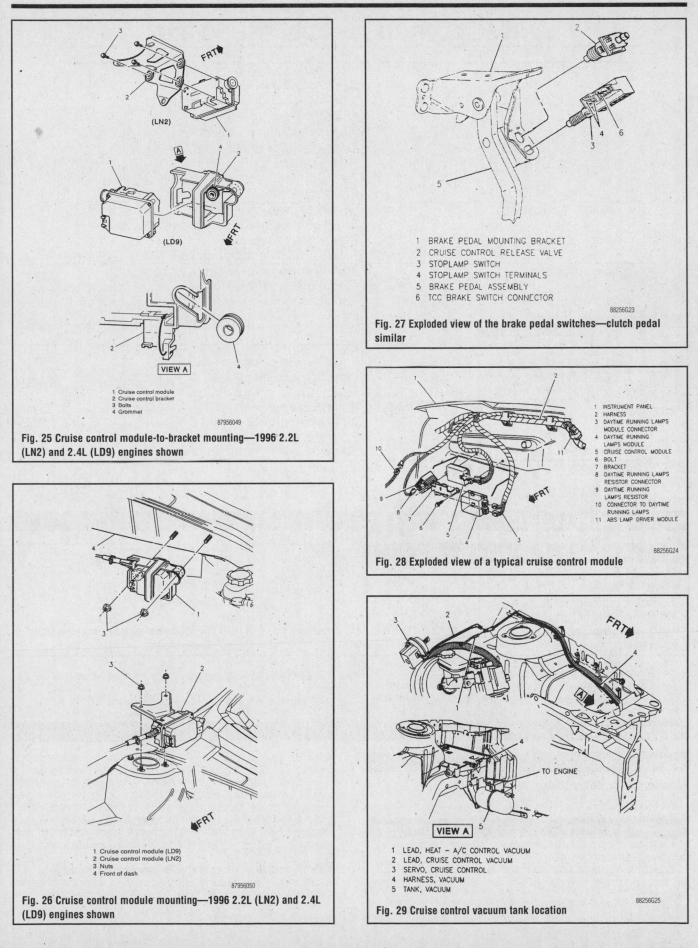

1 Cruise control module
2 Cruise control bracket
3 Bolts
4 Grommet

87956049

Fig. 25 Cruise control module-to-bracket mounting—1996 2.2L (LN2) and 2.4L (LD9) engines shown

1 Cruise control module (LD9)
2 Cruise control module (LN2)
3 Nuts
4 Front of dash

87956050

Fig. 26 Cruise control module mounting—1996 2.2L (LN2) and 2.4L (LD9) engines shown

1 BRAKE PEDAL MOUNTING BRACKET
2 CRUISE CONTROL RELEASE VALVE
3 STOPLAMP SWITCH
4 STOPLAMP SWITCH TERMINALS
5 BRAKE PEDAL ASSEMBLY
6 TCC BRAKE SWITCH CONNECTOR

88256G23

Fig. 27 Exploded view of the brake pedal switches—clutch pedal similar

1 INSTRUMENT PANEL
2 HARNESS
3 DAYTIME RUNNING LAMPS MODULE CONNECTOR
4 DAYTIME RUNNING LAMPS MODULE
5 CRUISE CONTROL MODULE
6 BOLT
7 BRACKET
8 DAYTIME RUNNING LAMPS RESISTOR CONNECTOR
9 DAYTIME RUNNING LAMPS RESISTOR
10 CONNECTOR TO DAYTIME RUNNING LAMPS
11 ABS LAMP DRIVER MODULE

88256G24

Fig. 28 Exploded view of a typical cruise control module

1 LEAD, HEAT – A/C CONTROL VACUUM
2 LEAD, CRUISE CONTROL VACUUM
3 SERVO, CRUISE CONTROL
4 HARNESS, VACUUM
5 TANK, VACUUM

88256G25

Fig. 29 Cruise control vacuum tank location

CRUISE CONTROL TROUBLESHOOTING

Problem	Possible Cause
Will not hold proper speed	Incorrect cable adjustment
	Binding throttle linkage
	Leaking vacuum servo diaphragm
	Leaking vacuum tank
	Faulty vacuum or vent valve
	Faulty stepper motor
	Faulty transducer
	Faulty speed sensor
	Faulty cruise control module
Cruise intermittently cuts out	Clutch or brake switch adjustment too tight
	Short or open in the cruise control circuit
	Faulty transducer
	Faulty cruise control module
Vehicle surges	Kinked speedometer cable or casing
	Binding throttle linkage
	Faulty speed sensor
	Faulty cruise control module
Cruise control inoperative	Blown fuse
	Short or open in the cruise control circuit
	Faulty brake or clutch switch
	Leaking vacuum circuit
	Faulty cruise control switch
	Faulty stepper motor
	Faulty transducer
	Faulty speed sensor
	Faulty cruise control module

Note: Use this chart as a guide. Not all systems will use the components listed.

TCCA6C01

ENTERTAINMENT SYSTEMS

Radio Receiver/Tape Player/CD Player

REMOVAL & INSTALLATION

▶ **See Figures 30 and 31**

1. Disable the SIR system, as outlined earlier in this section.
2. If not done already, disconnect the negative battery cable.
3. For the Cavalier, remove the instrument panel cluster trim plate.
4. For the Sunfire, remove the accessory trim plate.
5. Unfasten the retaining screws, then pull the radio assembly forward.
Detach the electrical and antenna lead connections, then remove the assembly from the vehicle.

To install:
6. Attach the electrical and antenna lead connections to the radio assembly.
7. Position the assembly, then secure with the retaining screws.
8. For the Cavalier, install the instrument panel cluster trim plate.
9. For the Sunfire, install the accessory trim plate.
10. Connect the negative battery cable.
11. Enable the SIR system, as outlined earlier in this section.

Speakers

REMOVAL & INSTALLATION

All J-body vehicles covered by this manual have 4 speakers, two in the front door and two in the rear mounted on the rear package shelf, just under the rear window.

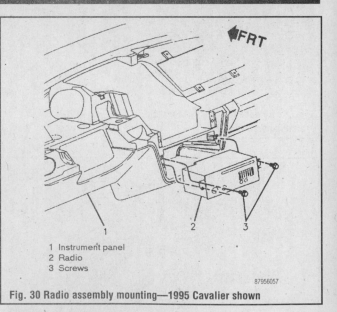

1 Instrument panel
2 Radio
3 Screws

87956057

Fig. 30 Radio assembly mounting—1995 Cavalier shown

Front Door Speaker

▶ **See Figures 32, 33, 34, 35 and 36**

1. Disconnect the negative battery cable.
2. Remove the door trim panel for access to the speaker.
3. Detach the connector for the door speaker.

4. Unfasten the retaining screws, then pull speaker and pod assembly out.

5. Remove the speaker-to-pod retaining screws and remove the speaker from the pod.

To install:

6. Place the speaker into the pod and tighten the retaining screws

7. Position the speaker and pod assembly into the opening in the door.

8. Tighten the speaker retaining screws.

9. Attach the connector for the speaker.

10. Install the door trim panel.

11. Connect the negative battery cable.

Rear Speakers

▶ **See Figures 37, 38 and 39**

1. Disconnect the negative battery cable.

2. Remove the rear window panel trim, as outlined in Section 10 of this manual.

3. Press the tab on the front of the rear speaker spacer and lift the spacer.

4. Pull forward on the rear speaker spacer.

5. Detach the speaker wire harness connector.

6. Remove the speaker spacer and speaker.

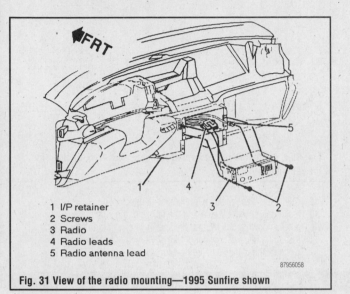

1 I/P retainer
2 Screws
3 Radio
4 Radio leads
5 Radio antenna lead

87956058

Fig. 31 View of the radio mounting—1995 Sunfire shown

91146P46

Fig. 32 Detach the connector for the door speaker

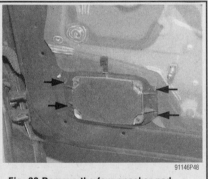

91146P48

Fig. 33 Remove the four speaker pod retaining screws and . . .

91146P47

Fig. 34 . . . remove the speaker and pod assembly from the vehicle

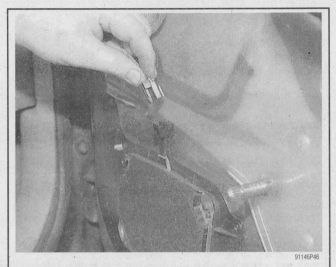

91146P49

Fig. 35 Remove the four speaker-to-pod retaining screws and . . .

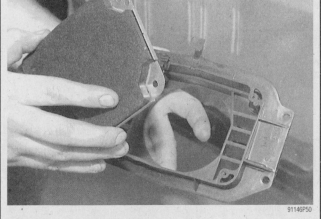

91146P50

Fig. 36 . . . remove the speaker from the pod

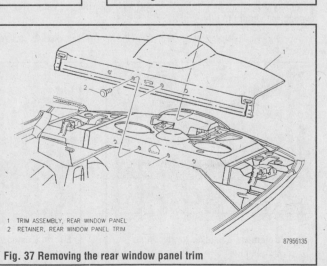

1 TRIM ASSEMBLY, REAR WINDOW PANEL
2 RETAINER, REAR WINDOW PANEL TRIM

87956135

Fig. 37 Removing the rear window panel trim

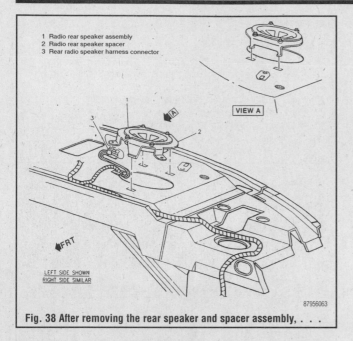

1 Radio rear speaker assembly
2 Radio rear speaker spacer
3 Rear radio speaker harness connector

VIEW A

FRT

LEFT SIDE SHOWN
RIGHT SIDE SIMILAR

87956063

Fig. 38 After removing the rear speaker and spacer assembly, . . .

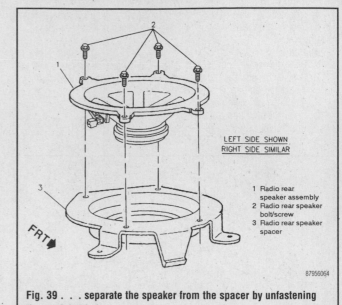

LEFT SIDE SHOWN
RIGHT SIDE SIMILAR

1 Radio rear
  speaker assembly
2 Radio rear speaker
  bolt/screw
3 Radio rear speaker
  spacer

FRT

87956064

Fig. 39 . . . separate the speaker from the spacer by unfastening the retaining bolts

7. Unfasten the retaining bolts, then remove the speaker from the spacer.

To install:

8. Position the speaker to the spacer, and secure using the retaining bolts. Tighten the bolts to 13 inch lbs (1.5 Nm).

9. Attach the rear speaker wire harness connector.
10. Install the spacer by inserting the tabs into the slot at the rear window shelf and press down at the front of the spacer to snap it into place..
11. Install the rear window panel trim.
12. Connect the negative battery cable.

WINDSHIELD WIPERS AND WASHERS

Windshield Wiper Blade and Arm

REMOVAL & INSTALLATION

♦ **See Figures 40 thru 45**

1. Turn the ignition switch to the **ACCY** position, then set the wiper switch to the PULSE position.
2. When the wiper arms are at the inner-wipe position and not moving, turn the ignition switch **OFF**.
3. Disconnect the washer hose from the washer nozzle.
4. Remove the cover from the nut.
5. Unfasten the nut from the wiper arm assembly and the wiper transmission assembly driveshaft.

➡**If the wiper arm assembly cannot be removed from the transmission assembly driveshaft by rocking it, a battery puller may be used with the windshield wipers in mid-wipe.**

6. Remove the wiper arm assembly from the transmission pivot by rocking.

7. If necessary, replace the blade refill as outlined in Section 1 of this manual.

To install:

8. If removed, install the blade refill.
9. Install the wiper arm assembly on the transmission driveshaft.
  a. Put the ignition switch in the **ACCY** position.
  b. Set the wiper switch to the PULSE position. The windshield wiper system should be operating.
  c. Turn the ignition switch **OFF** when wipers are in this innerwipe position and not moving.
  d. Install the wiper arm assembly on the transmission drive shaft while maintaining a distance of 3.46 in. (87.8mm) for the left hand side or 3.83 in. (97.5mm) for the right hand side between the wiper blade assembly and the bottom of the windshield (see accompanying figure for details).
10. Install the retaining nut on the wiper transmission driveshaft and wiper arm assembly. Tighten the nut to 20 ft. lbs. (27 Nm), then install the cover on the nut.

➡**Lubricate the washer hose with windshield washer solvent to ease installation on the nozzle.**

11. Attach the washer hose to the washer nozzle.
12. Operate the wipers and check for proper operation.

91146P03

Fig. 40 Remove the cover for the wiper arm retaining nut

91146P51

Fig. 41 Remove the wiper arm retaining nut

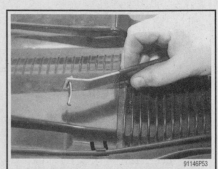

91146P53

Fig. 42 If the wiper arm is stuck to the pivot, a special tool is available to release the arm from the pivot, however, . . .

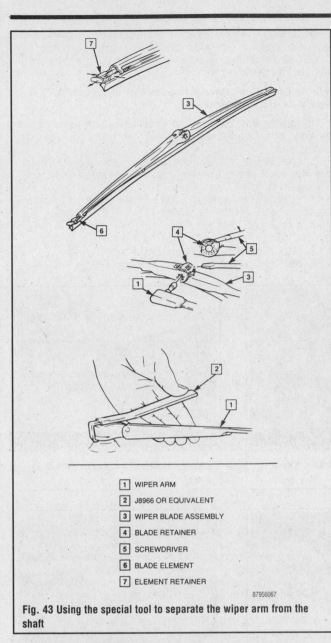

1 WIPER ARM
2 J8966 OR EQUIVALENT
3 WIPER BLADE ASSEMBLY
4 BLADE RETAINER
5 SCREWDRIVER
6 BLADE ELEMENT
7 ELEMENT RETAINER

87956067

Fig. 43 Using the special tool to separate the wiper arm from the shaft

91146P54

Fig. 44 . . . a battery terminal puller also works more than adequately

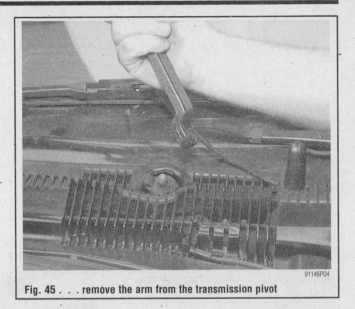

91146P04

Fig. 45 . . . remove the arm from the transmission pivot

ADJUSTMENT

The only adjustment for the wiper arms is to remove an arm from the transmission shaft, rotate the arm the required distance and direction and then install the arm back in position so it is in line with the blackout line on the glass. The wiper motor must be in the park position.

The correct blade-out wipe position on the driver's side is 9/16–1¾ in. (15–45mm) from the tip of the blade to the left windshield pillar molding (driver's side). The correct blade-down wipe position on the passenger side of the car is in line with the blackout line at the bottom of the glass.

Windshield Wiper Motor

REMOVAL & INSTALLATION

▶ **See Figures 46 thru 62**

1. Disconnect the negative battery cable.
2. Remove the wiper arm assemblies.
3. Remove the wiper cowl assembly from the vehicle.
4. Disconnect the electrical connector from the wiper motor.
5. Remove the 3 retaining bolts from the wiper drive module and remove from the vehicle.

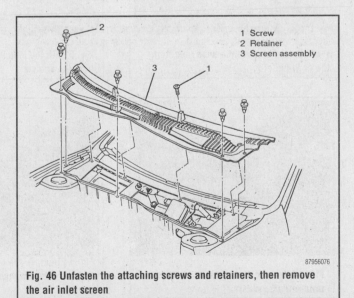

1 Screw
2 Retainer
3 Screen assembly

87956076

Fig. 46 Unfasten the attaching screws and retainers, then remove the air inlet screen

6. Disconnect the wiper transmission assembly from the wiper motor crank arm assembly.

7. Disconnect the wiper crank arm assembly from the wiper motor assembly.

   a. Loosen the wiper motor crank screw.

   b. Tap on the wiper motor crank screw with a plastic mallet while holding up on the wiper motor crank arm assembly, until the crank arm assembly is loose.

   c. Remove the wiper motor screw and wiper motor crank arm assembly.

   d. Remove the 3 mounting screws from the bracket and remove the wiper motor.

To install:

8. Install the wiper motor to the mounting bracket and install the 3 mounting screws. Tighten the screws to 62 inch lbs. (7 Nm).

9. Attach the wiper motor crank arm assembly to the wiper motor assembly.

10. Attach the electrical connector to the wiper motor.

11. Connect the negative battery cable.

12. Turn the ignition switch to the **ACCY** position and set the wiper switch to **PULSE**. Verify wiper motor operation, turn the ignition switch **OFF** while the motor is still operating. Wiper motor assembly will then return to PARK.

13. Disconnect the negative battery cable and then disconnect the electrical connector from the wiper motor.

➡ **Do not rotate the wiper motor assembly shaft during installation of wiper motor crank arm assembly.**

14. Install the wiper motor crank arm assembly onto the wiper motor assembly, while maintaining a 4–8mm gap between the wiper motor crank arm and the bracket tab.

15. Install the wiper motor crank arm screw and tighten to 144 inch lbs. (16 Nm). Make sure the gap between wiper motor crank arm and bracket tab is still 0.16–0.32 in. (4–8mm).

16. Install the wiper transmission assembly onto the wiper motor crank arm assembly using tool J-39529 or equivalent.

17. Install the wiper drive system module and tighten the 3 screws to 88 inch lbs. (10 Nm).

18. Install the electrical connector to the wiper motor assembly.

19. Install the wiper cowl assembly.

Fig. 47 The cowl panel is retained by trim clips on either side of the vehicle

Fig. 48 Remove the clips from the cowl panel

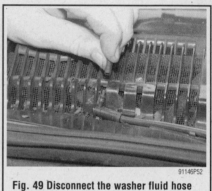

Fig. 49 Disconnect the washer fluid hose and . . .

Fig. 50 . . . remove the hose tube from the cowl panel

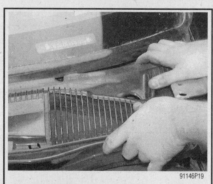

Fig. 51 Lift the panel up and remove it from the vehicle

Fig. 52 Detach the connector for the wiper motor

Fig. 53 The wiper motor assembly is retained by three retaining bolts

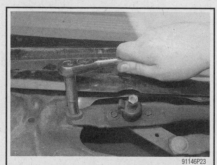

Fig. 54 Remove the three retaining bolts for the wiper motor drive assembly and . . .

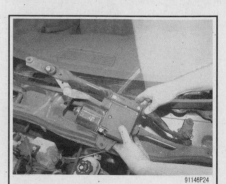

Fig. 55 . . . remove the assembly from the vehicle

20. Install the wiper arm assemblies onto the vehicle.
21. Connect the negative battery cable.
22. Operate the wipers and check for proper operation.

Windshield Washer Fluid Reservoir and Pump

REMOVAL & INSTALLATION

▶ See Figures 63 and 64

1. Disconnect the negative battery cable.
2. Detach the connector and the hose from the washer pump.
3. Unfasten the two lower screws and the upper screw, then remove the reservoir from the vehicle.

4. Remove the air induction assembly and two retainers from the reservoir container.
5. Remove the pump as follows:
   a. Pull the top of the washer pump out from the side of the reservoir.
   b. Pull the washer pump up out of the reservoir.

To install:
6. Install the pump in the reservoir as follows:
   a. Push the pump down into the reservoir completely.
   b. Push the top of the pump into the side of the reservoir container.
7. Fasten the air induction assembly on the reservoir and secure with the two retainers.
8. Install the reservoir into the vehicle and secure with the three screws. Tighten the screws to 88 inch lbs. (10 Nm).
9. Attach the hose and the electrical connector to the washer pump.
10. Attach the negative battery cable.

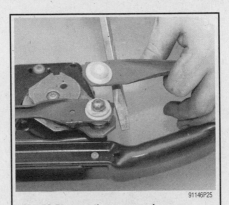

Fig. 56 Remove the upper and . . .

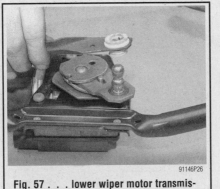

Fig. 57 . . . lower wiper motor transmission driveshaft from the wiper motor crank

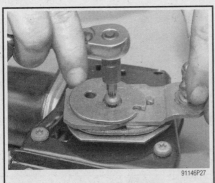

Fig. 58 Loosen the crank retaining screw and . . .

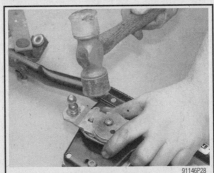

Fig. 59 . . . gently tap the crank bolt until the crank becomes loose and . . .

Fig. 60 . . . remove the crank from the motor

Fig. 61 Remove the three bracket retaining screws . . .

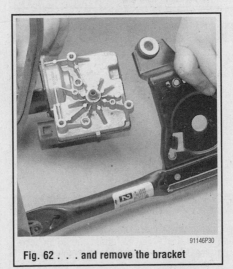

Fig. 62 . . . and remove the bracket

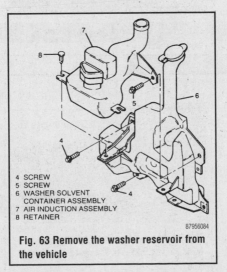

Fig. 63 Remove the washer reservoir from the vehicle

4 SCREW
5 SCREW
6 WASHER SOLVENT CONTAINER ASSEMBLY
7 AIR INDUCTION ASSEMBLY
8 RETAINER

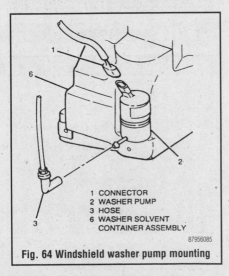

Fig. 64 Windshield washer pump mounting

1 CONNECTOR
2 WASHER PUMP
3 HOSE
6 WASHER SOLVENT CONTAINER ASSEMBLY

INSTRUMENTS AND SWITCHES

Instrument Cluster

REMOVAL & INSTALLATION

Cavalier

▶ See Figure 65

1. Disconnect the negative battery cable.
2. Disable the SIR system, as outlined earlier in this section.
3. Remove the instrument panel cluster trim plate.
4. Unfasten the screws from the top of the cluster, then pull the cluster rearward to remove.

To install:

5. Position the cluster to the instrument panel, then fasten the screws at the top of the cluster.
6. Install the instrument panel trim plate.
7. Connect the negative battery cable.
8. Enable the SIR system.

Sunfire

▶ See Figure 66

1. Disconnect the negative battery cable.
2. Disable the SIR system, as outlined earlier in this section.

3. Remove the instrument panel trim pad.
4. Unfasten the screws from the top of the cluster, then pull the cluster rearward to remove.

To install:

5. Position the cluster to the instrument panel, then fasten the screws at the top of the cluster.
6. Install the instrument panel trim pad.
7. Connect the negative battery cable.
8. Enable the SIR system.

Gauges

REMOVAL & INSTALLATION

The gauges can be removed from the cluster assembly by:
- Removing the lens.
- Removing the printed circuit board from the back of the cluster.
- Removing the gauge attaching screws.
- Installation is the reverse of removal.

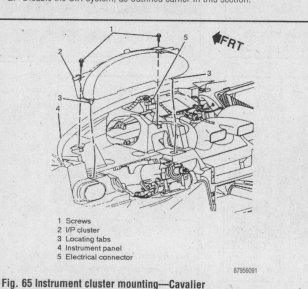

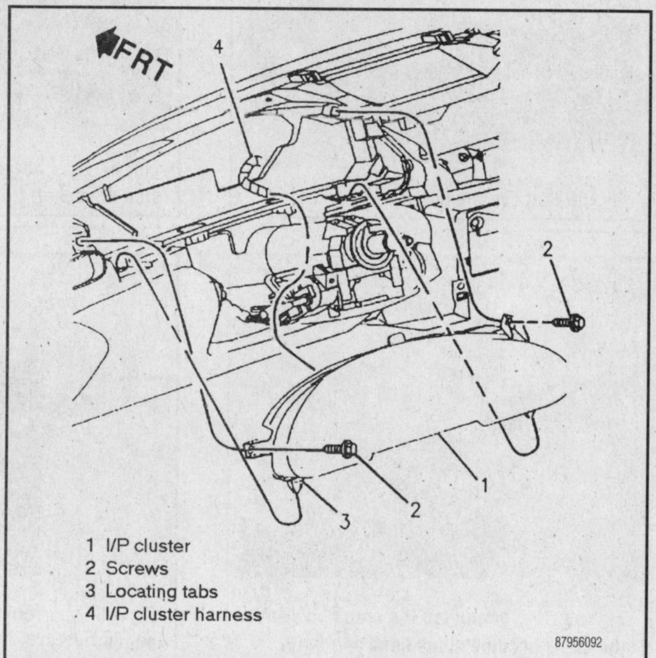

1 Screws
2 I/P cluster
3 Locating tabs
4 Instrument panel
5 Electrical connector

87956091

Fig. 65 Instrument cluster mounting—Cavalier

1 I/P cluster
2 Screws
3 Locating tabs
4 I/P cluster harness

87956092

Fig. 66 Instrument cluster mounting—Sunfire

LIGHTING

Headlights

REMOVAL & INSTALLATION

▶ See Figures 67 thru 74

1. Remove the air intake splash shield from the vehicle.
2. Remove the headlamp retaining bolts.
3. Remove the lamp assembly from the front of the vehicle.
4. Detach the headlamp connector.
5. Remove the headlamp bulb retaining ring.
6. Remove the headlamp bulb from the headlamp.

To install:

7. Insert the headlamp bulb into the headlamp.
8. Install and rotate the retaining ring until the tangs on the ring are engaged.
9. Attach the headlamp connector.

10. Place the headlamp assembly into place and tighten the retaining bolts.
11. Install the air intake splash shield.

AIMING THE HEADLIGHTS

▶ See Figures 75, 76 and 77

The headlights must be properly aimed to provide the best, safest road illumination. The lights should be checked for proper aim and adjusted as necessary. Certain state and local authorities have requirements for headlight aiming; these should be checked before adjustment is made.

✳✦ CAUTION

About once a year, when the headlights are replaced or any time front end work is performed on your vehicle, the headlight should be accurately aimed by a reputable repair shop using the proper equipment.

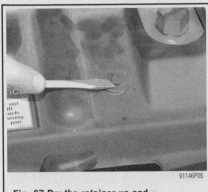

Fig. 67 Pry the retainer up and . . .

Fig. 68 . . . remove the clips from the air intake splash shield

Fig. 69 Remove the air intake splash shield from the vehicle

Fig. 70 Remove the two headlamp retaining bolts and . . .

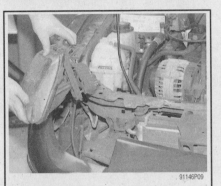

Fig. 71 . . . slide the lamp assembly out to access the bulb

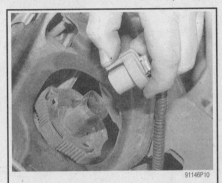

Fig. 72 Detach the connector for the bulb and . . .

Fig. 73 . . . remove the bulb retaining ring

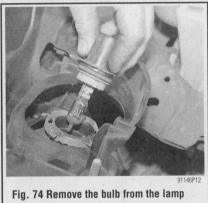

Fig. 74 Remove the bulb from the lamp assembly

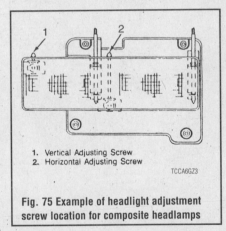

1. Vertical Adjusting Screw
2. Horizontal Adjusting Screw

TCCA6GZ3

Fig. 75 Example of headlight adjustment screw location for composite headlamps

Headlights not properly aimed can make it virtually impossible to see and may blind other drivers on the road, possibly causing an accident. Note that the following procedure is a temporary fix, until you can take your vehicle to a repair shop for a proper adjustment.

Headlight adjustment may be temporarily made using a wall, as described below, or on the rear of another vehicle. When adjusted, the lights should not glare in oncoming car or truck windshields, nor should they illuminate the passenger compartment of vehicles driving in front of you. These adjustments are rough and should always be fine-tuned by a repair shop which is equipped with headlight aiming tools. Improper adjustments may be both dangerous and illegal.

For most of the vehicles covered by this manual, horizontal and vertical aiming of each sealed beam unit is provided by two adjusting screws which move the retaining ring and adjusting plate against the tension of a coil spring. There is no adjustment for focus; this is done during headlight manufacturing.

➡**Because the composite headlight assembly is bolted into position, no adjustment should be necessary or possible. Some applications, however, may be bolted to an adjuster plate or may be retained by adjusting**

screws. If so, follow this procedure when adjusting the lights, BUT always have the adjustment checked by a reputable shop.

Before removing the headlight bulb or disturbing the headlamp in any way, note the current settings in order to ease headlight adjustment upon reassembly. If the high or low beam setting of the old lamp still works, this can be done using the wall of a garage or a building:

1. Park the vehicle on a level surface, with the fuel tank about ½ full and with the vehicle empty of all extra cargo (unless normally carried). The vehicle should be facing a wall which is no less than 6 feet (1.8m) high and 12 feet (3.7m) wide. The front of the vehicle should be about 25 feet from the wall.

2. If aiming is to be performed outdoors, it is advisable to wait until dusk in order to properly see the headlight beams on the wall. If done in a garage, darken the area around the wall as much as possible by closing shades or hanging cloth over the windows.

3. Turn the headlights **ON** and mark the wall at the center of each light's low beam, then switch on the brights and mark the center of each light's high beam. A short length of masking tape which is visible from the front of the vehicle may be used. Although marking all four positions is advisable, marking one position from each light should be sufficient.

4. If neither beam on one side is working, and if another like-sized vehicle is available, park the second one in the exact spot where the vehicle was and mark the beams using the same-side light. Then switch the vehicles so the one to be aimed is back in the original spot. It must be parked no closer to or farther away from the wall than the second vehicle.

5. Perform any necessary repairs, but make sure the vehicle is not moved, or is returned to the exact spot from which the lights were marked. Turn the headlights **ON** and adjust the beams to match the marks on the wall.

6. Have the headlight adjustment checked as soon as possible by a reputable repair shop.

Signal and Marker Lights

REMOVAL & INSTALLATION

Front Turn Signal and Parking Lights

▶ **See Figures 78, 79, 80, 81 and 82**

1. Remove the inner wheel well splash shield.
2. Grasp the bulb socket and rotate it counter-clockwise to remove it from the lamp.
3. Remove the bulb from the socket.
4. Installation is the reverse of removal.

Rear Turn Signal, Brake and Parking Lights

▶ **See Figures 83, 84, 85, 86 and 87**

1. Remove the retaining clips and move the trunk trim to access the taillamp bulbs.
2. Squeeze the retaining tabs on the bulb socket and remove the socket from the lamp.
3. Remove the bulb from the socket.
4. Installation is the reverse of removal.

Back-up Lamps

ALL CAVAILER AND SUNFIRE COUPE

▶ **See Figures 88 and 89**

1. Grasp the bulb socket and rotate it counter-clockwise to remove it from the lamp.
2. Remove the bulb from the socket.
3. Installation is the reverse of removal.

SUNFIRE SEDAN

▶ **See Figure 90**

1. Remove the screws from the back-up lamp lens and remove the lamp from the rear fascia.
2. Detach the connector for the back-up lamp.
3. Grasp the bulb socket and rotate it counter-clockwise to remove it from the lamp.
4. Installation is the reverse of removal.

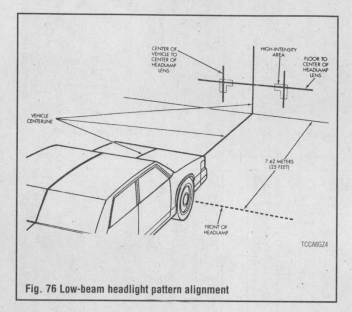

Fig. 76 Low-beam headlight pattern alignment

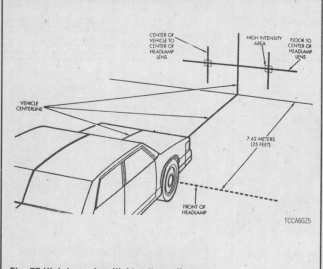

Fig. 77 High-beam headlight pattern alignment

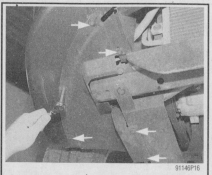

Fig. 78 Remove the retaining bolts for the splash shield and . . .

Fig. 79 . . . remove the splash shield from the vehicle

Fig. 80 Twist the bulb socket to remove it from the lamp and . . .

Fig. 81 . . . lower the socket down to access the bulb

Fig. 82 Pull the bulb straight out to remove it from the socket

Fig. 83 Remove the trunk trim retaining clips and push the trim out of the way

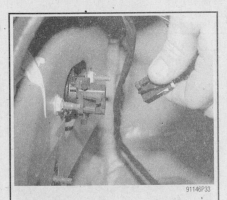

Fig. 84 Detach the connector for the lamp

Fig. 85 Squeeze the retaining tab and . . .

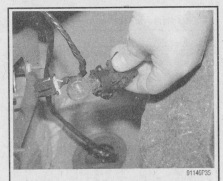

Fig. 86 . . . remove the socket from the lamp

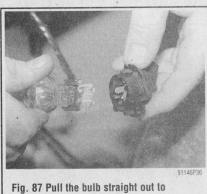

Fig. 87 Pull the bulb straight out to remove it from the socket

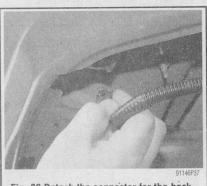

Fig. 88 Detach the connector for the back-up lamp

Fig. 89 Remove the bulb from the lamp assembly

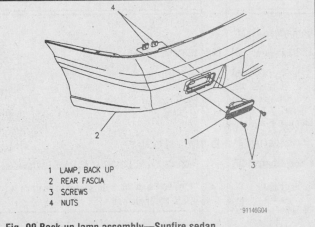

1 LAMP, BACK UP
2 REAR FASCIA
3 SCREWS
4 NUTS

Fig. 90 Back-up lamp assembly—Sunfire sedan

High-mount Brake Light

ALL CAVALIER AND SUNFIRE SEDAN

▶ See Figures 91 and 92

1. Remove the rear window trim panel.
2. From the rear compartment, push up on the high mounted stop lamp ratchet mechanism and slide the lamp assembly forward.
3. Detach the connector for the high mount brake lamp.
4. Grasp the bulb socket and rotate it counter-clockwise to remove it from the lamp.
5. Pull the bulb out to remove it from the socket.
6. Installation is the reverse of removal.

SUNFIRE COUPE

▶ See Figures 93, 94, 95 and 96

1. Remove the two retaining screws from the lens.
2. Remove the lens from the spoiler.

1 TRIM ASSEMBLY, REAR WINDOW PANEL
2 RETAINER, REAR WINDOW PANEL TRIM

87956135

Fig. 91 Removing the rear window panel trim

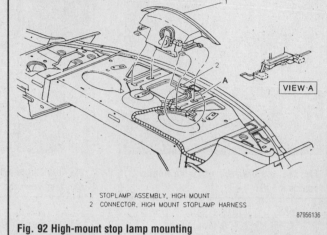

1 STOPLAMP ASSEMBLY, HIGH MOUNT
2 CONNECTOR, HIGH MOUNT STOPLAMP HARNESS

87956136

Fig. 92 High-mount stop lamp mounting

91146P43

Fig. 93 Remove the two retaining screws and . . .

91146P44

Fig. 94 . . . remove the brake lamp assembly

91146P45

Fig. 95 Twist the bulb socket to release it from the lamp assembly

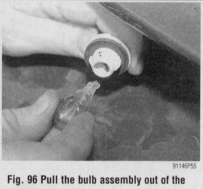

91146P55

Fig. 96 Pull the bulb assembly out of the socket to remove

91146P39

Fig. 97 Remove the retaining screw for the side marker light and . . .

91146P40

Fig. 98 . . . remove the lens from the quarter panel

3. Grasp the bulb socket and rotate it counter-clockwise to remove it from the lamp.
4. Pull the bulb out to remove it from the socket.
5. Installation is the reverse of removal.

Side Marker Light

▶ **See Figures 97, 98, 99 and 100**

1. Remove the two retaining screws from the lens.
2. Remove the lens from the rear fascia.
3. Grasp the bulb socket and rotate it counter-clockwise to remove it from the lamp.
4. Pull the bulb out to remove it from the socket.
5. Installation is the reverse of removal.

Dome/Map Light

▶ **See Figures 101, 102, 103 and 104**

1. Pry the lens of the dome/map lamp off.
2. Grasp the map and/or dome lamp bulbs and remove them.
3. Install new bulbs and snap the lens into place.

License Plate Lights

ALL CAVALIER AND SUNFIRE SEDAN

▶ **See Figure 105**

1. Detach the connector for the license plate lamp.
2. Grasp the bulb socket and rotate it counter-clockwise to remove it from the lamp.
3. Installation is the reverse of removal.

Fig. 99 Twist the bulb socket to release it from the lens

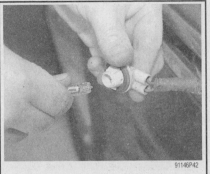

Fig. 100 Pull the bulb assembly out of the socket to remove

Fig. 101 Use a small screwdriver and to pry the lens loose and . . .

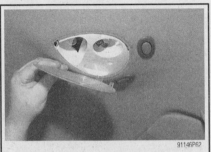

Fig. 102 . . . remove the lens from the lamp assembly

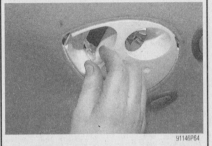

Fig. 103 Grasp the dome light bulb and remove it from the lamp assembly

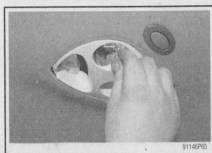

Fig. 104 Grasp the map light bulb(s) and remove it from the lamp assembly

SUNFIRE COUPE

▶ **See Figures 106, 107, 108, 109 and 110**

1. Open the trunklid.
2. Remove the nuts retaining the rear lamp housing to the trunklid.
3. Remove the lamp housing from the trunklid.
4. Detach the connector for the license plate lamp.
5. Grasp the bulb socket and rotate it counter-clockwise to remove it from the lamp.
6. Pull the bulb out to remove it from the socket.
7. Installation is the reverse of removal.

Fog/Driving Lights (Chevrolet Cavalier Z-24 Only)

REMOVAL & INSTALLATION

▶ **See Figure 111**

1. Disconnect the negative battery cable.
2. Detach the connector for the foglamp.

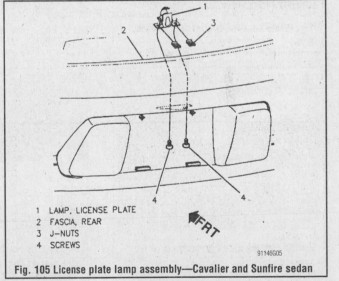

1 LAMP, LICENSE PLATE
2 FASCIA, REAR
3 J-NUTS
4 SCREWS

Fig. 105 License plate lamp assembly—Cavalier and Sunfire sedan

Fig. 106 Remove the nuts that secure the rear lamp assembly

Fig. 107 . . . to the trunklid

Fig. 108 Remove the rear lamp assembly and . . .

Fig. 109 . . . remove the bulb sockets from the lamp

Fig. 110 Pull the bulb out of the sockets

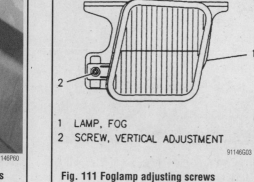

1 LAMP, FOG
2 SCREW, VERTICAL ADJUSTMENT

Fig. 111 Foglamp adjusting screws

3. Twist the foglamp bulb ¼ of a turn and remove the bulb from the foglamp lens.

To install:

4. Twist the bulb until the tangs engage into the foglamp lens.
5. Attach the connector for the foglamp.
6. Connect the negative battery cable.

INSTALLING AFTERMARKET AUXILIARY LIGHTS

➡**Before installing any aftermarket light, make sure it is legal for road use. Most acceptable lights will have a DOT approval number. Also check your local and regional inspection regulations. In certain areas, aftermarket lights must be installed in a particular manner or they may not be legal for inspection.**

1. Disconnect the negative battery cable.
2. Unpack the contents of the light kit purchased. Place the contents in an open space where you can easily retrieve a piece if needed.
3. Choose a location for the lights. If you are installing fog lights, below the bumper and apart from each other is desirable. Most fog lights are mounted below or very close to the headlights. If you are installing driving lights, above the bumper and close together is desirable. Most driving lights are mounted between the headlights.

4. Drill the needed hole(s) to mount the light. Install the light, and secure using the supplied retainer nut and washer. Tighten the light mounting hardware, but not the light adjustment nut or bolt.
5. Install the relay that came with the light kit in the engine compartment, in a rigid area, such as a fender. Always install the relay with the terminals facing down. This will prevent water from entering the relay assembly.
6. Using the wire supplied, locate the ground terminal on the relay, and connect a length of wire from this terminal to a good ground source. You can drill a hole and screw this wire to an inside piece of metal; just scrape the paint away from the hole to ensure a good connection.
7. Locate the light terminal on the relay; and attach a length of wire between this terminal and the fog/driving lamps.
8. Locate the ignition terminal on the relay, and connect a length of wire between this terminal and the light switch.
9. Find a suitable mounting location for the light switch and install. Some examples of mounting areas are a location close to the main light switch, auxiliary light position in the dash panel, if equipped, or in the center of the dash panel.
10. Depending on local and regional regulations, the other end of the switch can be connected to a constant power source such as the battery, an ignition opening in the fuse panel, or a parking or headlight wire.
11. Locate the power terminal on the relay, and connect a wire with an in-line fuse of at least 10 amperes between the terminal and the battery.

Chevrolet

BULB USAGE - CHEVROLET	Trade No.
EXTERIOR	
Backup	3057
Front-Park-Turn (Except Z24)	3357
Front-Park-Turn (Z24)	3357NA
Headlamps-Low Beam	9006
Headlamps-High Beam	9005
License	194
Front Side Marker	194
Tail-Stop-Turn	3057
Center High Mounted Stop	
Package Shelf Mounted	912
Aero Wing Mounted	912
Fog	881X
INTERIOR	
Shift Indicator	LED
I/P Compartment	194
Courtesy Lamps	168
HVAC Controls	561
Rear Compartment Lamp	561
INSTRUMENT CLUSTER	
Panel Illumination	PC195
High Beam	PC74
Turn Signal Indicator	PC74
Seat Belt Warning	LED
Brake Warning	LED
Generator	LED
Check Engine	LED
Check Gages	LED
Low Coolant	LED
Upshift Indicator	LED
Daytime Running Lights	LED

Fig. 112 Bulb application chart—Chevrolet Cavalier

BULB USAGE

Pontiac

BULB USAGE - PONTIAC	Trade No.
EXTERIOR	
Rear Applique	912
Backup	3156
Front-Park-Turn (Except GT)	3357
Front-Park-Turn (GT)	3357NA
Headlamps	9007
License	194
Front Side Marker	194
Rear Side Marker	194
Tail-Stop-Turn	3057
Center High Mounted Stop Lamp	
Package Shelf Mounted	912
Aero Wing Mounted	912
INTERIOR	
Shift Indicator (Man. Trans)	LED
I/P Compartment	194
Courtesy Lamps	194
Reading Lamp	192
Rear Compartment Lamp	561
INSTRUMENT CLUSTER	
Check Oil	LED
Panel Illumination	PC74
High Beam	PC74
Turn Signal Indicator	PC74
Fasten Belts	LED
Brake Warning	LED
Charge (UH7)	LED
Service Engine Soon	LED
Low Coolant	LED
Oil (UH7)	LED
Check Gages	LED

Fig. 113 Bulb application chart—Ponitac Sunfire

12. With all the wires connected and tied up neatly, connect the negative battery cable.

13. Turn the lights ON and adjust the light pattern, if necessary.

AIMING

▶ **See Figure 111**

1. Park the vehicle on level ground, so it is perpendicular to and, facing a flat wall about 25 ft. (7.6m) away.

2. Remove any stone shields, if equipped, and switch ON the lights.

3. Loosen the mounting hardware of the lights so you can aim them as follows:

   a. The horizontal distance between the light beams on the wall should be the same as between the lights themselves.

   b. The vertical height of the light beams above the ground should be 4 in. (10cm) less than the distance between the ground and the center of the lamp lenses for fog lights. For driving lights, the vertical height should be even with the distance between the ground and the center of the lamp.

4. Tighten the mounting hardware.

5. Test to make sure the lights work correctly, and the light pattern is even.

TRAILER WIRING

Wiring the vehicle for towing is fairly easy. There are a number of good wiring kits available and these should be used, rather than trying to design your own.

All trailers will need brake lights and turn signals as well as tail lights and side marker lights. Most areas require extra marker lights for overwide trailers. Also, most areas have recently required back-up lights for trailers, and most trailer manufacturers have been building trailers with back-up lights for several years.

Additionally, some Class I, most Class II and just about all Class III and IV trailers will have electric brakes. Add to this number an accessories wire, to operate trailer internal equipment or to charge the trailer's battery, and you can have as many as seven wires in the harness.

Determine the equipment on your trailer and buy the wiring kit necessary. The kit will contain all the wires needed, plus a plug adapter set which includes the female plug, mounted on the bumper or hitch, and the male plug, wired into, or plugged into the trailer harness.

When installing the kit, follow the manufacturer's instructions. The color coding of the wires is usually standard throughout the industry. One point to note: some domestic vehicles, and most imported vehicles, have separate turn signals. On most domestic vehicles, the brake lights and rear turn signals operate with the same bulb. For those vehicles without separate turn signals, you can purchase an isolation unit so that the brake lights won't blink whenever the turn signals are operated.

One, final point, the best kits are those with a spring loaded cover on the vehicle mounted socket. This cover prevents dirt and moisture from corroding the terminals. Never let the vehicle socket hang loosely; always mount it securely to the bumper or hitch.

CIRCUIT PROTECTION

Fuses

GENERAL INFORMATION

▶ **See Figures 114 thru 120**

Fuses protect all the major electrical systems in the car. In case of an electrical overload, the fuse melts, breaking the circuit and stopping the flow of electricity.

If a fuse blows, the cause should be investigated and corrected before the installation of a new fuse. This, however, is easier to say than to do. Because each fuse protects a limited number of components, your job is narrowed down somewhat. Begin your investigation by looking for obvious fraying, loose connections, breaks in insulation, etc. Use the techniques outlined at the beginning of this section. Electrical problems are almost always a real headache to solve, but if you are patient and persistent, and approach the problem logically (that is, don't start replacing electrical components randomly), you will eventually find the solution.

Each fuse block uses miniature fuses (normally plug-in blade terminal-type

Fig. 114 The power distribution box in the engine compartment contains fuses and relays

Fig. 115 Remove the cover for the interior fuse panel

Fig. 116 A fuse puller tool is located inside the fuse panel to aid in the removal of the fuses

Fig. 117 Grasp the fuses with the puller and pull straight out to remove the fuses

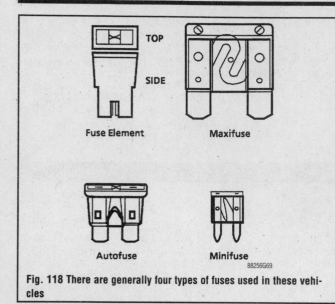

Fuse Element   Maxifuse

Autofuse   Minifuse

88256G69

Fig. 118 There are generally four types of fuses used in these vehicles

AUTOFUSE

CURRENT RATING	COLOR
3	VIOLET
5	TAN
7.5	BROWN
10	RED
15	BLUE
20	YELLOW
25	NATURAL
30	GREEN

MAXIFUSE

CURRENT RATING	COLOR
20	YELLOW
30	GREEN
40	AMBER
50	RED
60	BLUE
70	BROWN
80	NATURAL

MINIFUSE

CURRENT RATING	COLOR
5	TAN
7.5	BROWN
10	RED
15	BLUE
20	YELLOW
25	NATURAL
30	GREEN

PACIFIC FUSE ELEMENT

CURRENT RATING	COLOR
30	PINK
40	GREEN
50	RED
60	YELLOW

88256G70

Fig. 119 Fuse current rating and color code chart

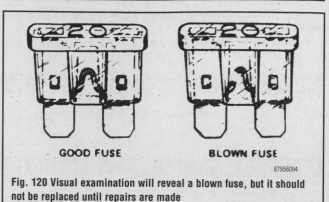

GOOD FUSE   BLOWN FUSE

87956094

Fig. 120 Visual examination will reveal a blown fuse, but it should not be replaced until repairs are made

for these vehicles) which are designed for increased circuit protection and greater reliability. The compact plug-in or blade terminal design allows for fingertip removal and replacement.

Although most fuses are interchangeable in size, the amperage values are not. Should you install a fuse with too high a value, damaging current could be allowed to destroy the component you were attempting to protect by using a fuse in the first place. The plug-in type fuses have a volt number molded on them and are color coded for easy identification. Be sure to only replace a fuse with the proper amperage rated substitute.

A blown fuse can easily be checked by visual inspection or by continuity checking.

The fuse block is located on the lower left side of the instrument panel. To access the fuse panel, open the driver's side door. Pull off the fuse panel cover to get to the fuses. Spare fuses and a fuse puller should always be kept here. Various convenience connectors, which snap-lock into the fuse block, add to the serviceability of this unit.

REPLACEMENT

1. Locate the fuse for the circuit in question.

➡When replacing the fuse, always use a replacement fuse of the same amperage value. NEVER use one with a higher amperage rating.

2. Check the fuse by pulling it from the fuse block and observing the element. If it is broken, install a replacement fuse the same amperage rating. If the fuse blows again, check the circuit for a short to ground or faulty device in the circuit protected by the fuse.

3. Continuity can also be checked with the fuse installed in the fuse block with the use of a test light connected across the 2 test points on the end of the fuse. If the test light lights, replace the fuse. Check the circuit for a short to ground or faulty device in the circuit protected by the fuse.

Circuit Breakers

RESETTING AND/OR REPLACEMENT

Circuit breakers differ from fuses in that they are reusable. Circuit breakers open when the flow of current exceeds specified value and will close after a few seconds when current flow returns to normal. Some of the circuits protected by circuit breakers include electric windows and power accessories. Circuits breakers are used in these applications due to the fact that they must operated at times under prolonged high current flow due to demand even though there is not malfunction in the circuit.

There are 2 types of circuit breakers. The first type opens when high current flow is detected. A few seconds after the excessive current flow has been removed, the circuit breaker will close. If the high current flow is experienced again, the circuit will open again.

The second type is referred to as the Positive Temperature Coefficient (PTC) circuit breaker. When excessive current flow passes through the PTC circuit breaker, the circuit is not opened but its resistance increases. As the device heats ups with the increase in current flow, the resistance increases to the point where the circuit is effectively open. Unlike other circuit breakers, the PTC circuit breaker will not reset until the circuit is opened, removing voltage from the terminals. Once the voltage is removed, the circuit breaker will re-close within a few seconds.

Replace the circuit breaker by unplugging the old one and plugging in the new one. Confirm proper circuit operation.

Fusible Links

A fusible link is a protective device used in an electrical circuit. When the current increases beyond a certain amperage, the fusible metal of the wire link melts, thus breaking the electrical circuit and preventing further damage to other components and wiring. Whenever a fusible link is melted because of a short circuit, correct the cause before installing a new one. There are four different gauge sizes commonly used and they are usually color coded so that they may be easily installed in their original positions.

REPLACEMENT

▶ **See Figures 121 and 122**

1. Disconnect the negative battery cable, followed by the positive cable.
2. Locate the burned out link.
3. If both ends of the link are ring terminal connectors which are easily accessed:
   a. Measure the installed length necessary for the new link.
   b. Unbolt and remove the link and connector pieces.
   c. Obtain a suitable length of link, then strip the insulation off the harness wire back ½ in. (12.7mm) to allow soldering of the new connectors.
   d. Position the new connector around the new link and crimp it securely. Then, solder the connection, using rosin core solder and sufficient heat to guarantee a good connection. Repeat for the remaining connection.

➡ **Whenever splicing a new wire, always bond the splice with rosin core solder, then cover with electrical tape. Use acid core solder may cause corrosion.**

4. If the ends of the connector are not easily access, repair the length in the vehicle:
   a. Strip away the melted insulation and cut the burned link ends from the wire.
   b. Strip the wire back ½ in. (12.7mm) to allow soldering of the new link.
   c. Using a new fusible link of appropriate gauge and length, solder it into the circuit.

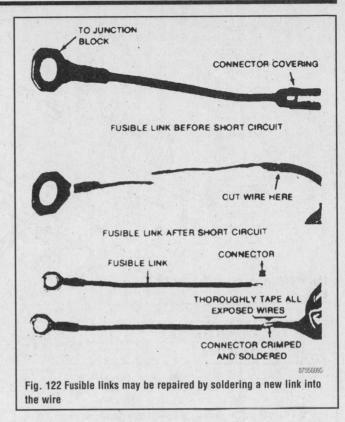

Fig. 122 Fusible links may be repaired by soldering a new link into the wire

5. Tape all exposed wiring with electrical tape and seal with silicone or use a heat shrink tube, if available, to weatherproof the repair.
6. If removed from the vehicle, install the link and secure the connectors.
7. Reconnect the positive, followed by the negative battery cables.

Flashers

REPLACEMENT

1995 Vehicles

▶ **See Figures 123 and 124**

The turn signal flasher is mounted in a clip on the right side of the steering column support bracket. The hazard flasher is located in the component center, under the instrument panel, on the right side. Replace the flasher by unplugging the old one and plugging in the new one.

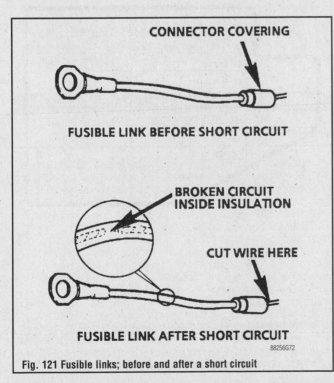

Fig. 121 Fusible links; before and after a short circuit

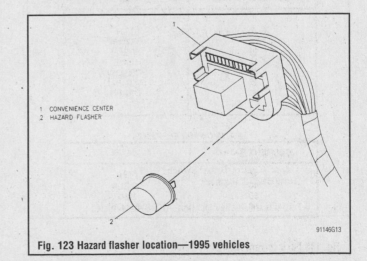

Fig. 123 Hazard flasher location—1995 vehicles

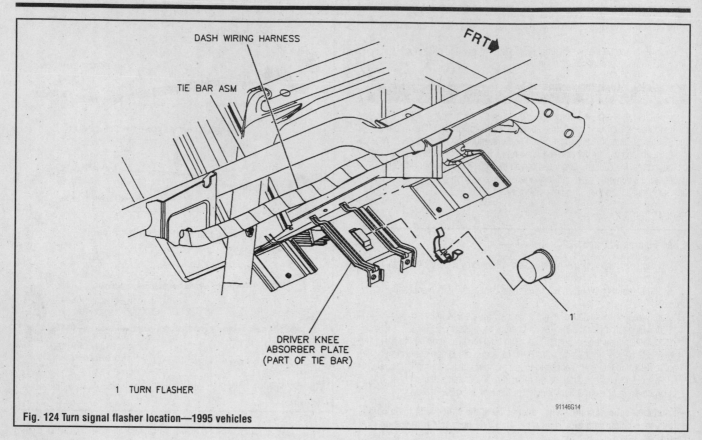

DASH WIRING HARNESS

TIE BAR ASM

FRT

DRIVER KNEE
ABSORBER PLATE
(PART OF TIE BAR)

1 TURN FLASHER

91146G14

Fig. 124 Turn signal flasher location—1995 vehicles

1996–00 Vehicles

▶ See Figure 125

The turn and hazard flashers are integrated into one flasher on these models. The flasher is located on a bracket above the brake pedal. Replace the flasher by unplugging the old one, removing it from the bracket, and plugging in the new one.

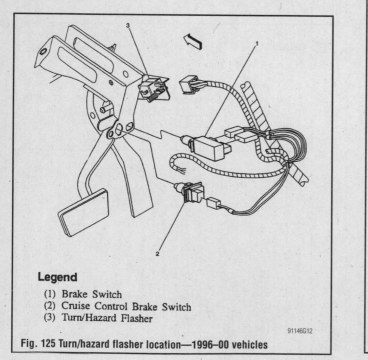

Legend

(1) Brake Switch
(2) Cruise Control Brake Switch
(3) Turn/Hazard Flasher

91146G12

Fig. 125 Turn/hazard flasher location—1996–00 vehicles

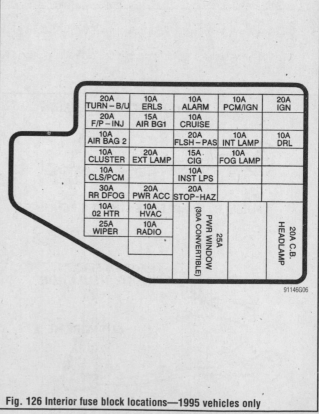

20A TURN – B/U	10A ERLS	10A ALARM	10A PCM/IGN	20A IGN
20A F/P – INJ	15A AIR BG1	10A CRUISE		
10A AIR BAG 2		20A FLSH – PAS	10A INT LAMP	10A DRL
10A CLUSTER	20A EXT LAMP	15A CIG	10A FOG LAMP	
10A CLS/PCM		10A INST LPS		
30A RR DFOG	20A PWR ACC	20A STOP–HAZ		
10A 02 HTR	10A HVAC			
25A WIPER	10A RADIO	30A PWR WINDOW (30A CONVERTIBLE)	25A	20A C.B. HEADLAMP
				20A C.B. HEADLAMP

91146G06

Fig. 126 Interior fuse block locations—1995 vehicles only

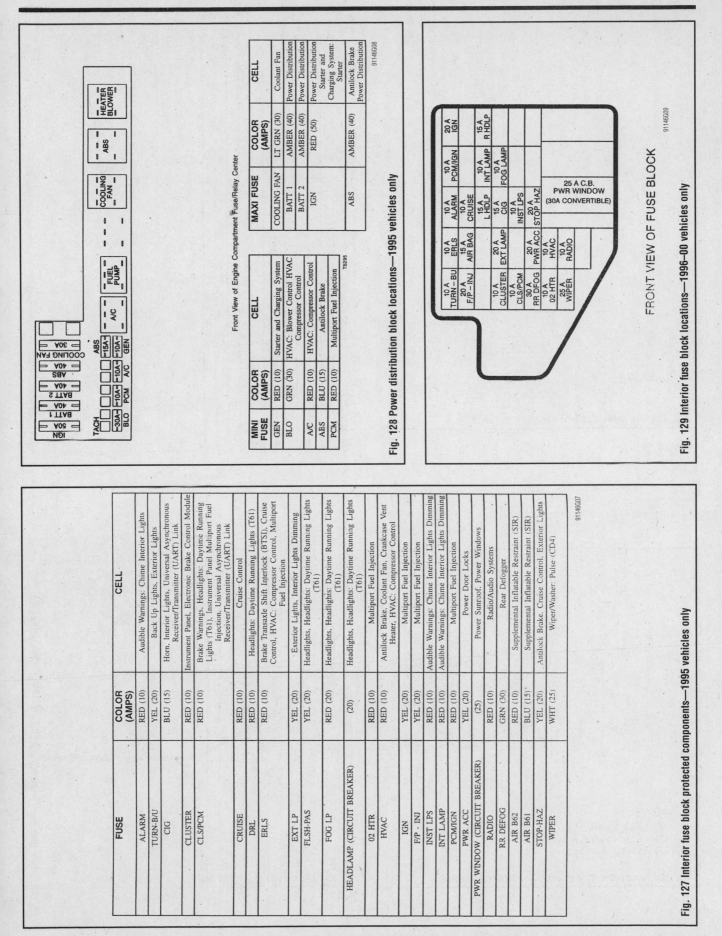

Fig. 127 Interior fuse block protected components—1995 vehicles only

FUSE	COLOR (AMPS)	CELL
ALARM	RED (10)	Audible Warnings: Chime Interior Lights
TURN-B/U	YEL (20)	Back Up Lights, Exterior Lights
CIG	BLU (15)	Horn, Interior Lights, Universal Asynchronous Receiver/Transmitter (UART) Link
CLUSTER	RED (10)	Instrument Panel, Electronic Brake Control Module
CLS/PCM	RED (10)	Brake Warnings, Headlights: Daytime Running Lights (T61), Instrument Panel Multiport Fuel Injection, Universal Asynchronous Receiver/Transmitter (UART) Link
CRUISE	RED (10)	Cruise Control
DRL	RED (10)	Headlights: Daytime Running Lights (T61)
ERLS	RED (10)	Brake Transaxle Shift Interlock (BTSI), Cruise Control, HVAC: Compressor Control, Multiport Fuel Injection
EXT LP	YEL (20)	Exterior Lights, Interior Lights Dimming
FLSH-PAS	YEL (20)	Headlights, Headlights: Daytime Running Lights (T61)
FOG LP	RED (20)	Headlights, Headlights: Daytime Running Lights (T61)
HEADLAMP (CIRCUIT BREAKER)	(20)	Headlights, Headlights: Daytime Running Lights (T61)
02 HTR	RED (10)	Multiport Fuel Injection
HVAC	RED (10)	Antilock Brake, Coolant Fan, Crankcase Vent Heater, HVAC: Compressor Control
IGN	YEL (20)	Multiport Fuel Injection
F/P - INJ	YEL (20)	Multiport Fuel Injection
INST LPS	RED (10)	Audible Warnings: Chime Interior Lights Dimming
INT LAMP	RED (10)	Audible Warnings: Chime Interior Lights Dimming
PCM/IGN	RED (10)	Multiport Fuel Injection
PWR ACC	YEL (20)	Power Door Locks
PWR WINDOW (CIRCUIT BREAKER)	(25)	Power Sunroof, Power Windows
RADIO	RED (10)	Radio/Audio Systems
RR DEFOG	GRN (30)	Rear Defogger
AIR B62	RED (10)	Supplemental Inflatable Restraint (SIR)
AIR B61	BLU (15)	Supplemental Inflatable Restraint (SIR)
STOP-HAZ	YEL (20)	Antilock Brake, Cruise Control, Exterior Lights
WIPER	WHT (25)	Wiper/Washer: Pulse (CD4)

Front View of Engine Compartment Fuse/Relay Center

MINI FUSE	COLOR (AMPS)	CELL
GEN	RED (10)	Starter and Charging System
BLO	GRN (30)	HVAC: Blower Control HVAC Compressor Control
A/C	RED (10)	HVAC: Compressor Control
ABS	BLU (15)	Antilock Brake
PCM	RED (10)	Multiport Fuel Injection

MAXI FUSE	COLOR (AMPS)	CELL
COOLING FAN	LT GRN (30)	Coolant Fan
BATT 1	AMBER (40)	Power Distribution
BATT 2	AMBER (40)	Power Distribution
IGN	RED (50)	Starter and Charging System: Starter
ABS	AMBER (40)	Antilock Brake Power Distribution

Fig. 128 Power distribution block locations—1995 vehicles only

FRONT VIEW OF FUSE BLOCK

Fig. 129 Interior fuse block locations—1996-00 vehicles only

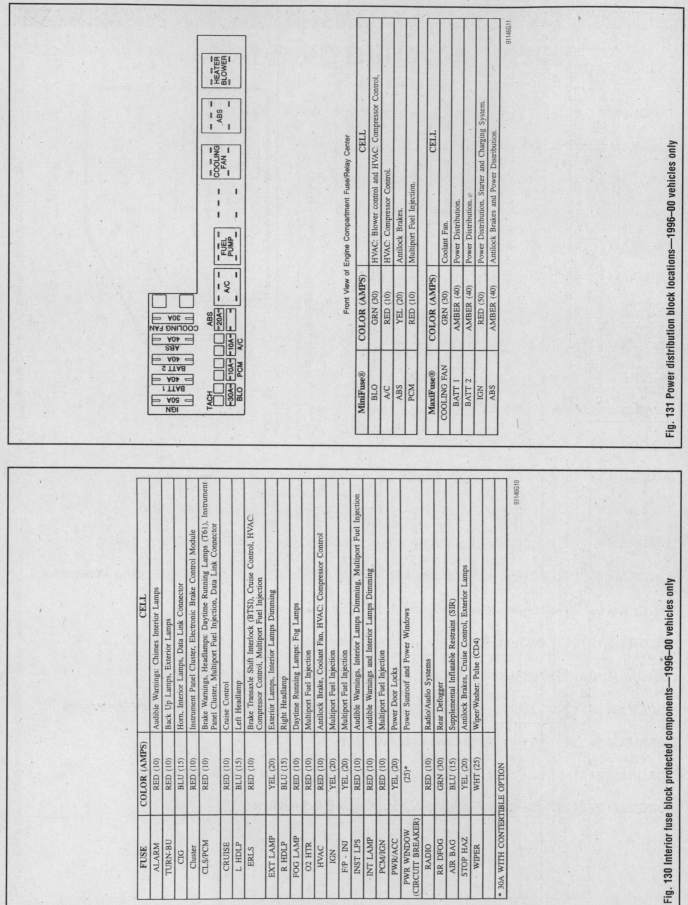

Fig. 130 Interior fuse block protected components—1996–00 vehicles only

FUSE	COLOR (AMPS)	CELL
ALARM	RED (10)	Audible Warnings: Chimes Interior Lamps
TURN-BU	RED (10)	Back Up Lamps, Exterior Lamps
CIG	BLU (15)	Horn, Interior Lamps, Data Link Connector
Cluster	RED (10)	Instrument Panel Cluster, Electronic Brake Control Module
CLS/PCM	RED (10)	Brake Warnings, Headlamps: Daytime Running Lamps (T61), Instrument Panel Cluster, Multiport Fuel Injection, Data Link Connector
CRUISE	RED (10)	Cruise Control
L HDLP	BLU (15)	Left Headlamp
ERLS	RED (10)	Brake Transaxle Shift Interlock (BTSI), Cruise Control, HVAC: Compressor Control, Multiport Fuel Injection
EXT LAMP	YEL (20)	Exterior Lamps, Interior Lamps Dimming
R HDLP	BLU (15)	Right Headlamp
FOG LAMP	RED (10)	Daytime Running Lamps: Fog Lamps
O2 HTR	RED (10)	Multiport Fuel Injection
HVAC	RED (10)	Antilock Brake, Coolant Fan, HVAC: Compressor Control
IGN	YEL (20)	Multiport Fuel Injection
F/P - INJ	YEL (20)	Multiport Fuel Injection
INST LPS	RED (10)	Audible Warnings, Interior Lamps Dimming, Multiport Fuel Injection
INT LAMP	RED (10)	Audible Warnings and Interior Lamps Dimming
PCM/IGN	RED (10)	Multiport Fuel Injection
PWR/ACC	YEL (20)	Power Door Locks
PWR WINDOW (CIRCUIT BREAKER)	(25)*	Power Sunroof and Power Windows
RADIO	RED (10)	Radio/Audio Systems
RR DFOG	GRN (30)	Rear Defogger
AIR BAG	BLU (15)	Supplemental Inflatable Restraint (SIR)
STOP HAZ	YEL (20)	Antilock Brakes, Cruise Control, Exterior Lamps
WIPER	WHT (25)	Wiper/Washer: Pulse (CD4)

* 30A WITH CONVERTIBLE OPTION

Fig. 131 Power distribution block locations—1996–00 vehicles only

Front View of Engine Compartment Fuse/Relay Center

MiniFuse®	COLOR (AMPS)	CELL
BLO	GRN (30)	HVAC: Blower control and HVAC: Compressor Control,
A/C	RED (10)	HVAC: Compressor Control.
ABS	YEL (20)	Antilock Brakes.
PCM	RED (10)	Multiport Fuel Injection.

MaxiFuse®	COLOR (AMPS)	CELL
COOLING FAN	GRN (30)	Coolant Fan.
BATT 1	AMBER (40)	Power Distribution.
BATT 2	AMBER (40)	Power Distribution.
IGN	RED (50)	Power Distribution, Starter and Charging System.
ABS	AMBER (40)	Antilock Brakes and Power Distribution.

INDEX OF WIRING DIAGRAMS

DIAGRAM 1   Sample Diagram: How To Read & Interpret Wiring Diagrams

DIAGRAM 2   Wiring Diagram Symbols

DIAGRAM 3   1995 2.2L (Vin 4) Engine Schematic

DIAGRAM 4   1995 2.3L (Vin D) Engine Schematic

DIAGRAM 5   1996 2.2L (Vin 4) Engine Schematic

DIAGRAM 6   1996 2.4L (Vin T) Engine Schematic

DIAGRAM 7   1997-00 2.2L Engine Schematic

DIAGRAM 8   1997-002.4L Engine Schematic

DIAGRAM 9   1995 J-body Wiring Schematic

DIAGRAM 10 1995 J-Body Wiring Schematic

DIAGRAM 11 1996 J-Body Wiring Schematic

DIAGRAM 12 1996 J-Body Wiring Schematic

DIAGRAM 13 1997-00 Starting, Charging, Fuel Pump, Cooling Fan Chassis Schematics

DIAGRAM 14 1997-00 Windsheild Wiper/Washer, Back-up Lights, Horn Chassis Schematics

DIAGRAM 15 1997-00 Pontiac Headlights w/DRL, 1997 Chevrolet Headlights w/DRL Chassis Schematics

DIAGRAM 16 1998-00 Chevrolet Headlights w/DRL Chassis Schematic

DIAGRAM 17 1997-00 Turn/Hazard Lights Chassis Schematic

DIAGRAM 18 1997-00 Park/Marker Lights (Except 98-00 Z24) Chassis Schematics

DIAGRAM 19 1998 Chevrolet Z24 Parking/Marker Lights, 1997-00 Power Mirrors Chassis Schematics

DIAGRAM 20 1997-00 Fog Lights Chassis Schematics

DIAGRAM 21 1997-00 Power Door Locks, Power Windows (2-Door) Chassis Schematics

DIAGRAM 22 1997-00 Power Windows (4-Door) Chassis Schematics

91146W01

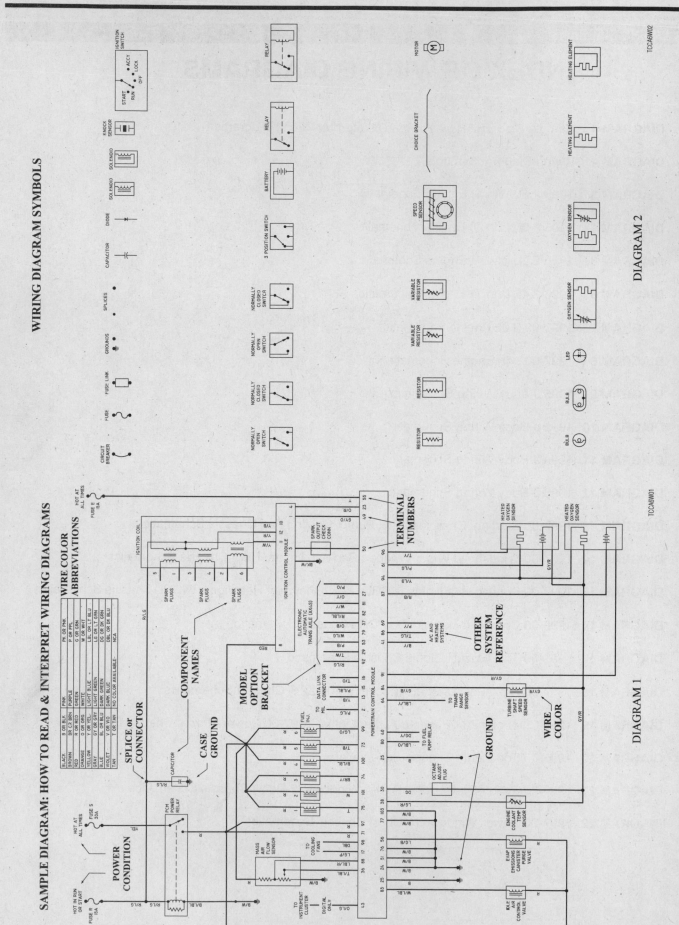

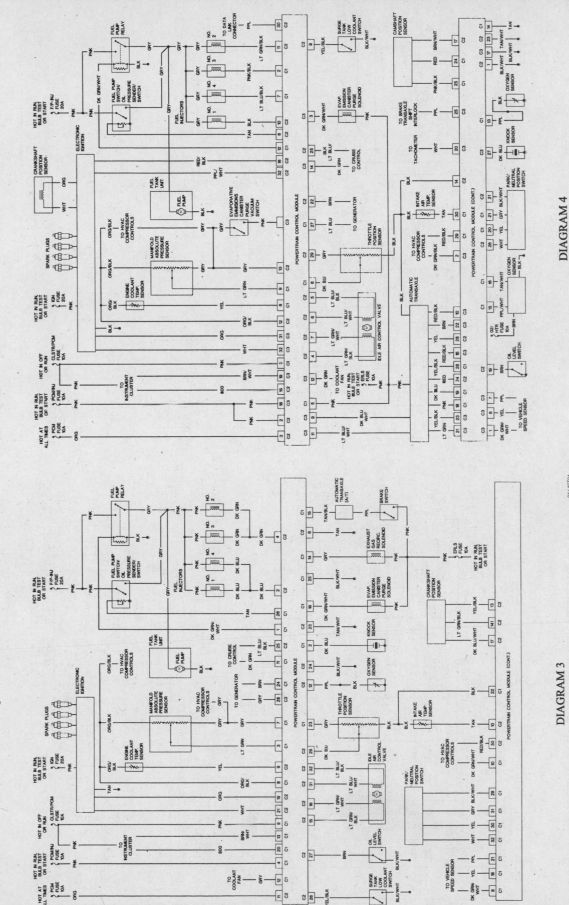

1995 2.3L (VIN D) J-BODY ENGINE SCHEMATIC

1995 2.2L (VIN 4) J-BODY ENGINE SCHEMATIC

DIAGRAM 4

DIAGRAM 3

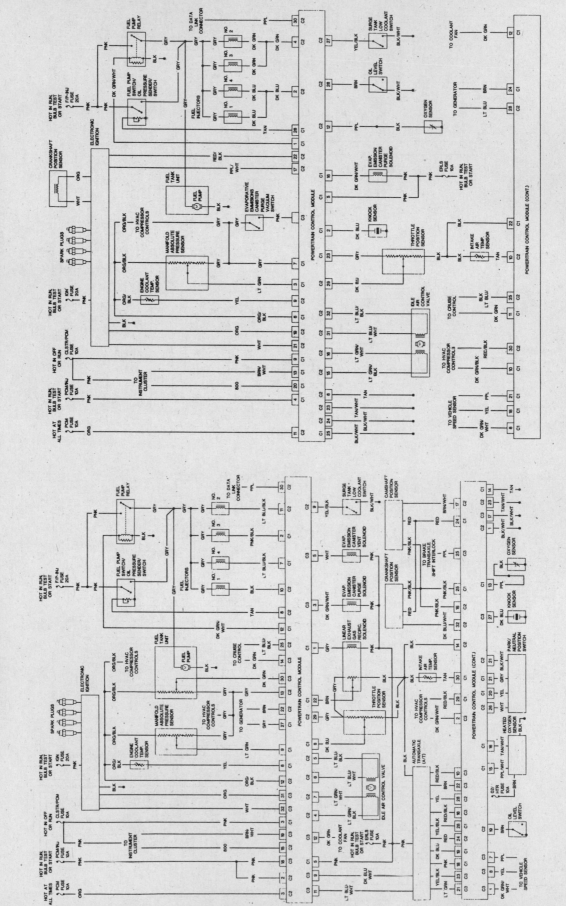

1996 2.4L (VIN T) J-BODY ENGINE SCHEMATIC

DIAGRAM 6

1996 2.2L (VIN 4) J-BODY ENGINE SCHEMATIC

DIAGRAM 5

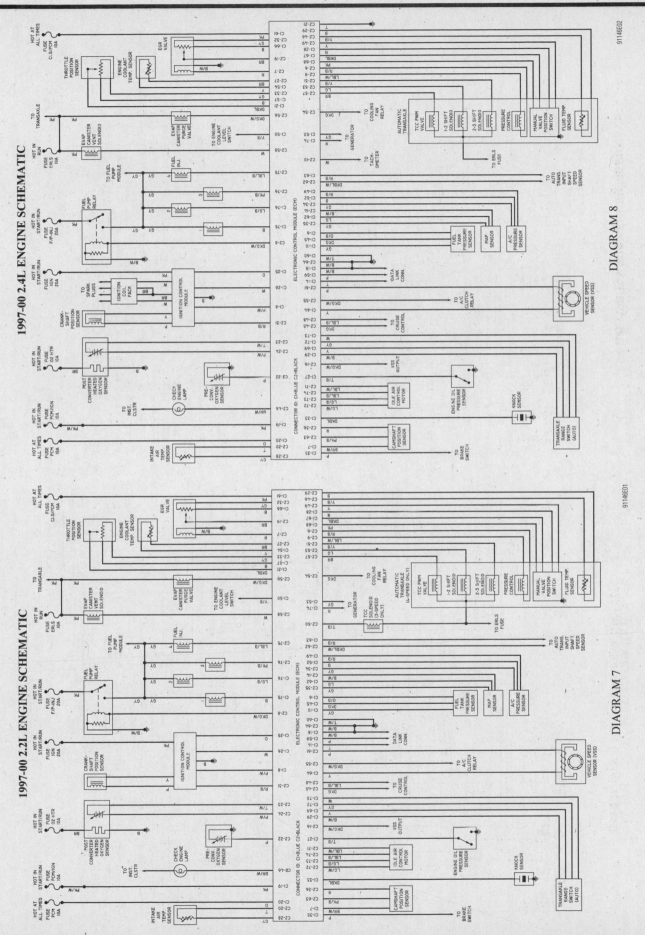

1997-00 2.4L ENGINE SCHEMATIC

1997-00 2.2L ENGINE SCHEMATIC

DIAGRAM 8

DIAGRAM 7

1995 J-BODY WIRING SCHEMATIC

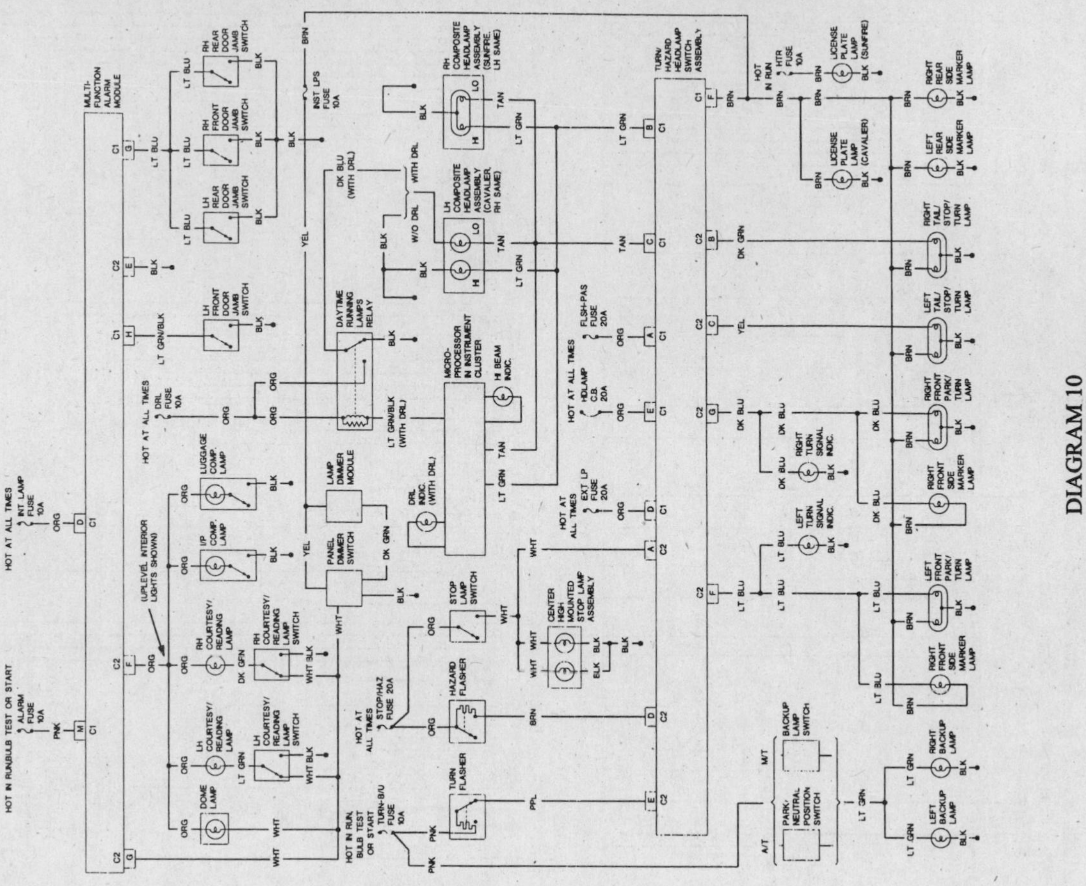

DIAGRAM 10

1995 J-BODY WIRING SCHEMATIC

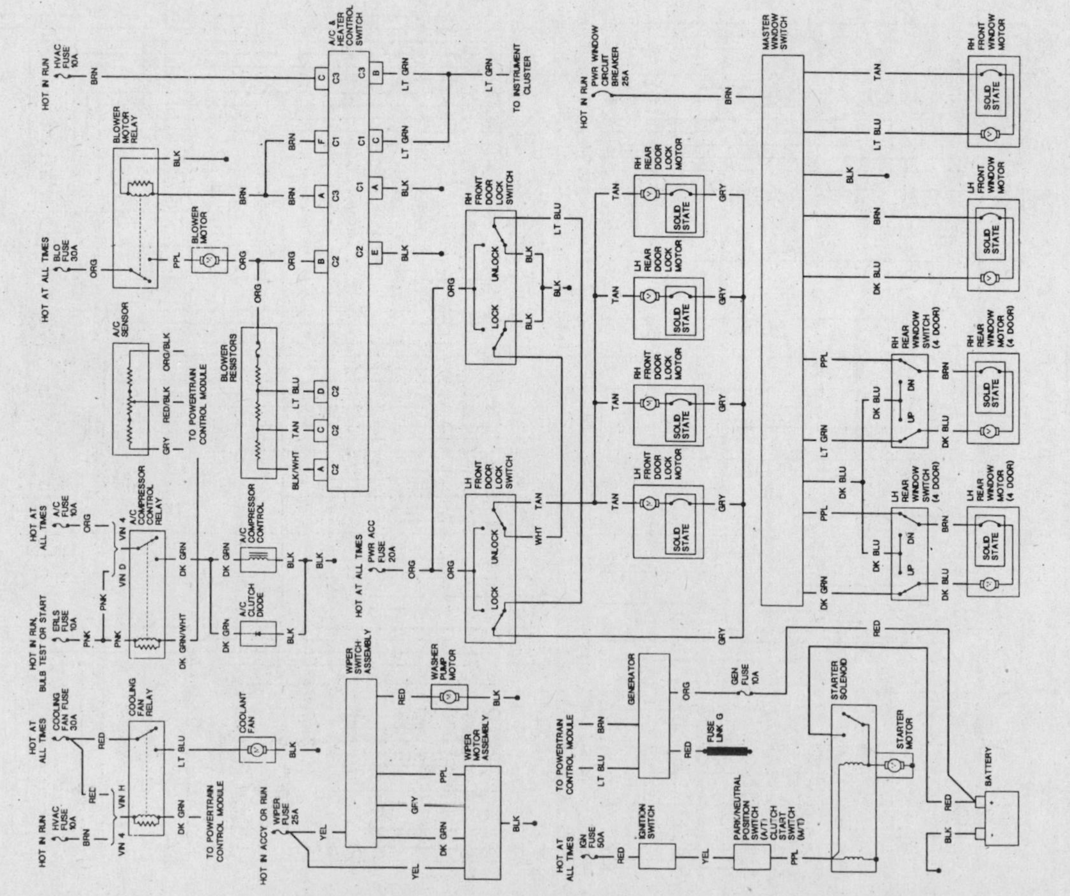

DIAGRAM 9

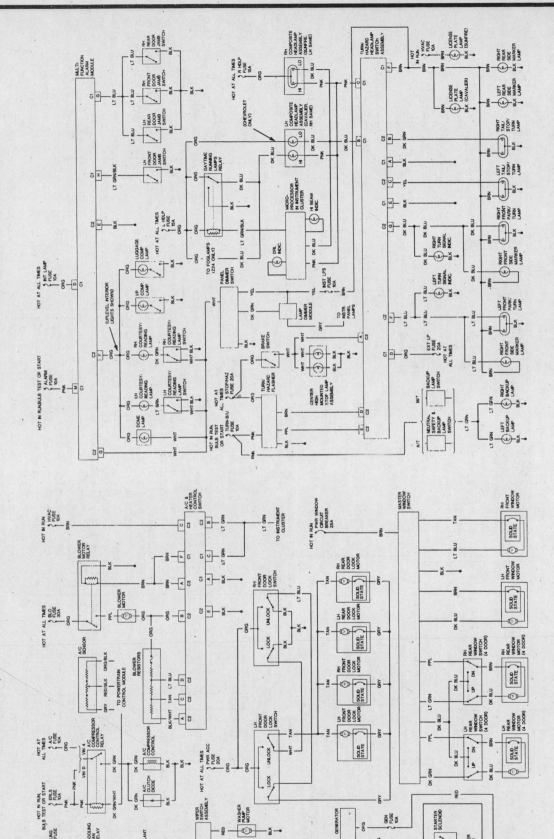

DIAGRAM 12

1996 J-BODY WIRING SCHEMATIC

DIAGRAM 11

1996 J-BODY WIRING SCHEMATIC

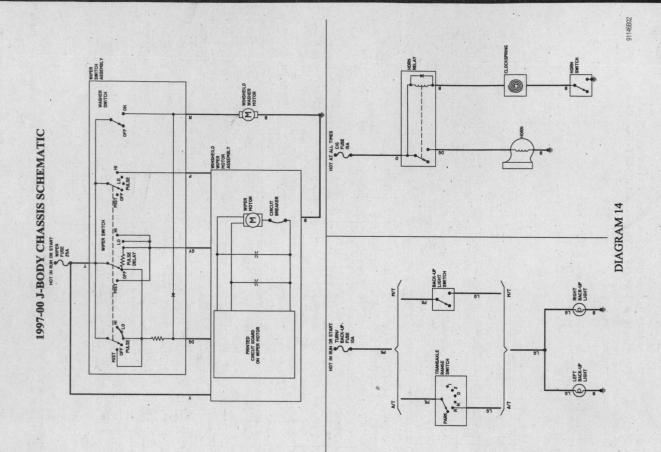

DIAGRAM 14

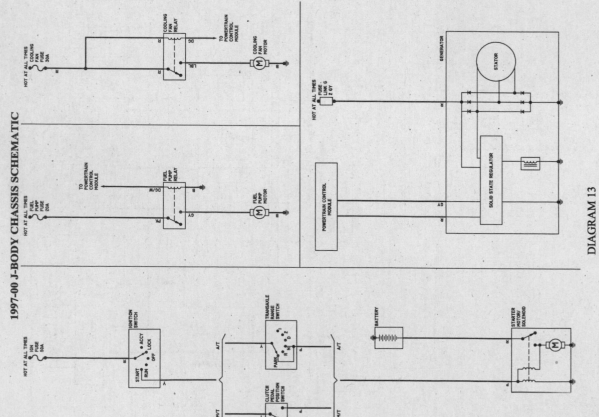

DIAGRAM 13

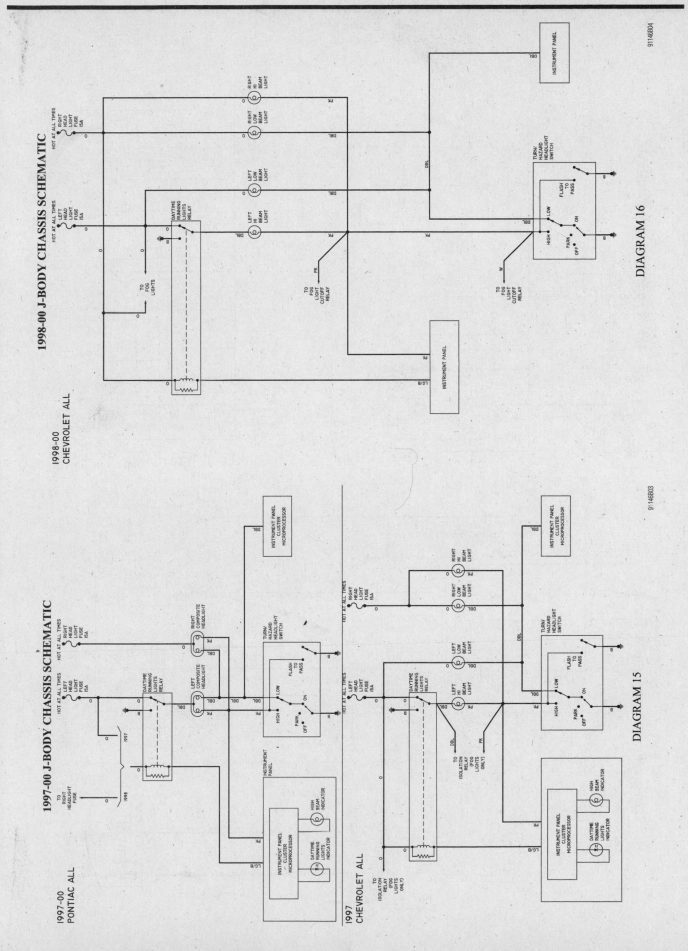

1998-00 J-BODY CHASSIS SCHEMATIC

1998-00
CHEVROLET ALL

DIAGRAM 16

91146B04

1997-00 J-BODY CHASSIS SCHEMATIC

1997-00
PONTIAC ALL

1997
CHEVROLET ALL

DIAGRAM 15

91146B03

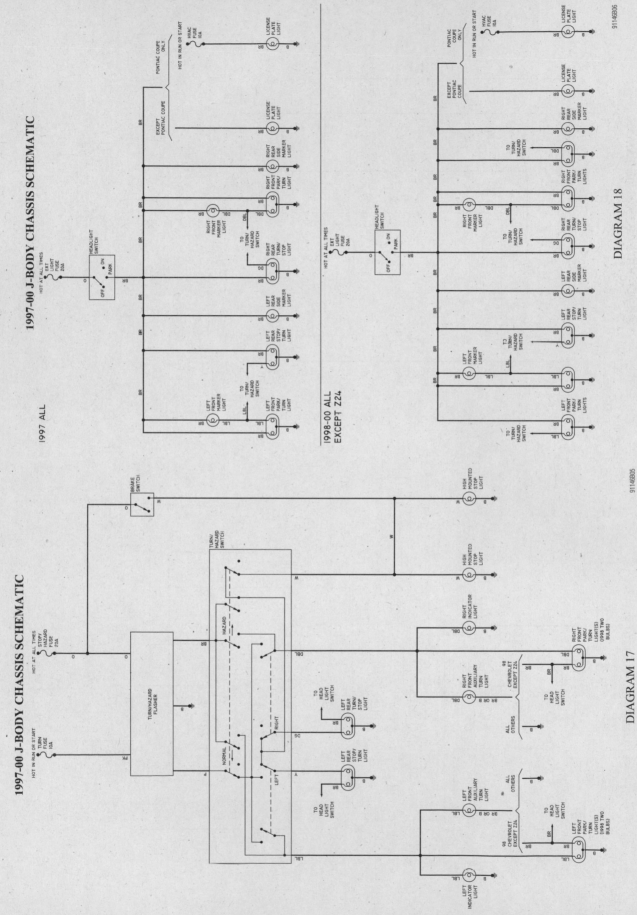

1997-00 J-BODY CHASSIS SCHEMATIC

DIAGRAM 18

1997 ALL

1998-00 ALL EXCEPT Z24

1997-00 J-BODY CHASSIS SCHEMATIC

DIAGRAM 17

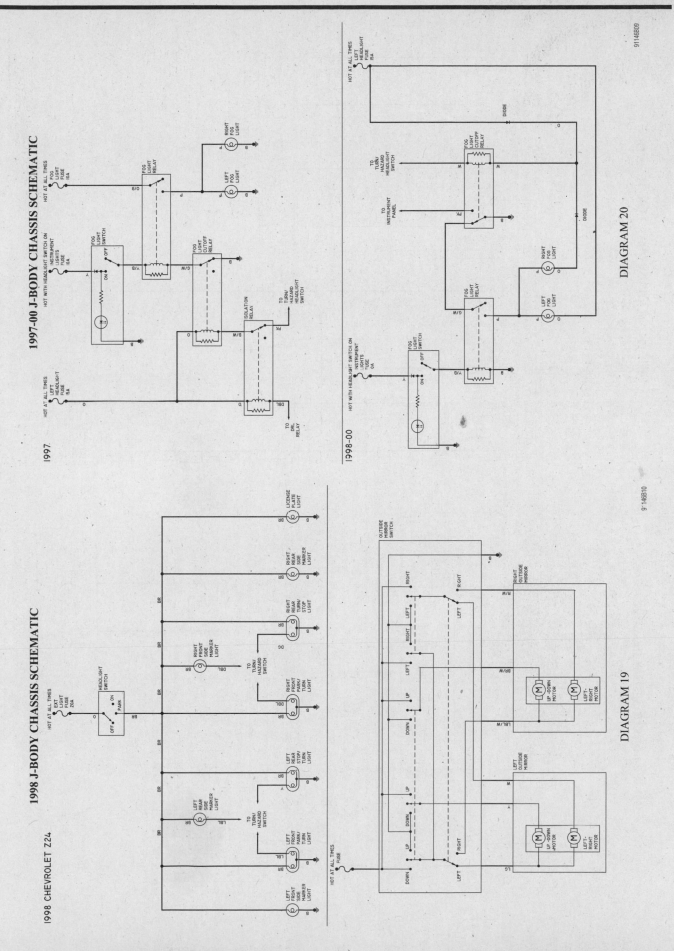

1997-00 J-BODY CHASSIS SCHEMATIC

1997

1998 J-BODY CHASSIS SCHEMATIC

1998 CHEVROLET Z24

1998-00

DIAGRAM 20

DIAGRAM 19

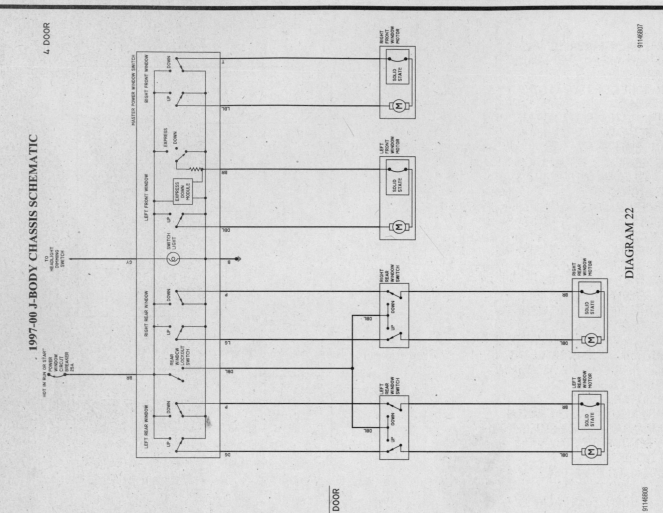

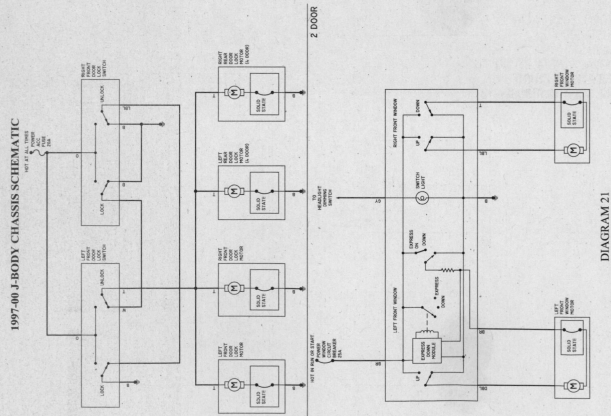

MANUAL TRANSAXLE 7-2
UNDERSTANDING THE MANUAL
  TRANSAXLE 7-2
BACK-UP LIGHT SWITCH 7-2
  REMOVAL & INSTALLATION 7-2
MANUAL TRANSAXLE ASSEMBLY 7-2
  REMOVAL & INSTALLATION 7-2
HALFSHAFTS 7-3
  REMOVAL & INSTALLATION 7-3
  CV-JOINTS OVERHAUL 7-5
CLUTCH 7-6
UNDERSTANDING THE CLUTCH 7-6
DRIVEN DISC AND PRESSURE
  PLATE 7-6
  REMOVAL & INSTALLATION 7-6
  ADJUSTMENTS 7-8
MASTER CYLINDER 7-8
  REMOVAL & INSTALLATION 7-8
ACTUATOR (SLAVE) CYLINDER 7-9
  REMOVAL & INSTALLATION 7-9
  HYDRAULIC SYSTEM BLEEDING 7-9
AUTOMATIC TRANSAXLE 7-9
UNDERSTANDING THE AUTOMATIC
  TRANSAXLE 7-9
FLUID PAN 7-9
PARK/NEUTRAL SAFETY SWITCH
  (TRANSAXLE RANGE SENSOR) 7-9
  REMOVAL & INSTALLATION 7-9
  ADJUSTMENT 7-10
AUTOMATIC TRANSAXLE
  ASSEMBLY 7-10
  REMOVAL & INSTALLATION 7-10
  ADJUSTMENTS 7-11
HALFSHAFTS 7-11
  REMOVAL & INSTALLATION 7-11
SPECIFICATIONS CHART
  TORQUE SPECIFICATIONS 7-12

7

DRIVE TRAIN

MANUAL TRANSAXLE 7-2
CLUTCH 7-6
AUTOMATIC TRANSAXLE 7-9

MANUAL TRANSAXLE

Understanding the Manual Transaxle

Because of the way an internal combustion engine breathes, it can produce torque, or twisting force, only within a narrow speed range. Most modern, overhead valve pushrod engines must turn at about 2500 rpm to produce their peak torque. By 4500 rpm they are producing so little torque that continued increases in engine speed produce no power increases. The torque peak on overhead camshaft engines is generally much higher, but much narrower.

The manual transaxle and clutch are employed to vary the relationship between engine speed and the speed of the wheels so that adequate engine power can be produced under all circumstances. The clutch allows engine torque to be applied to the transaxle input shaft gradually, due to mechanical slippage. Consequently, the vehicle may be started smoothly from a full stop. The transaxle changes the ratio between the rotating speeds of the engine and the wheels by the use of gears. The gear ratios allow full engine power to be applied to the wheels during acceleration at low speeds and at highway/passing speeds.

In a front wheel drive transaxle, power is usually transmitted from the input shaft to a mainshaft or output shaft located slightly beneath and to the side of the input shaft. The gears of the mainshaft mesh with gears on the input shaft, allowing power to be carried from one to the other. All forward gears are in constant mesh and are free from rotating with the shaft unless the synchronizer and clutch is engaged. Shifting from one gear to the next causes one of the gears to be freed from rotating with the shaft and locks another to it. Gears are locked and unlocked by internal dog clutches which slide between the center of the gear and the shaft. The forward gears employ synchronizers; friction members which smoothly bring gear and shaft to the same speed before the toothed dog clutches are engaged.

Back-up Light Switch

REMOVAL & INSTALLATION

▶ **See Figure 1**

1. Disconnect the negative battery cable.
2. Detach the back-up lamp connector.
3. Unscrew then remove the back-up lamp switch assembly.

To install:

4. Coat the threads of the back-up lamp switch with a suitable thread locking compound.
5. Install the switch and tighten to 24 ft. lbs. (33 Nm).
6. Attach the switch electrical connector.
7. Connect the negative battery cable.

Manual Transaxle Assembly

REMOVAL & INSTALLATION

▶ **See Figures 2, 3 and 4**

1. Disconnect the negative battery cable.
2. Install a suitable engine support device, and raise the engine enough to take the pressure off the transaxle mounts.
3. Remove the left side hush panel.
4. Disconnect the clutch master cylinder pushrod from the clutch pedal.
5. Remove the air cleaner and duct assembly from the throttle body.
6. Remove the wiring harness from the mount bracket.
7. Remove the upper transaxle mount-to-transaxle bolts.
8. Remove the clutch master cylinder from the clutch actuator.
9. Disconnect the ground cables from the transaxle mounting studs.
10. Detach the back-up light switch connector.
11. Disconnect the transaxle vent tube.
12. Remove the rear transaxle-to-engine bolts.
13. Lower the engine support fixture enough to ease removal and installation of the transaxle.
14. Raise and safely support the vehicle.

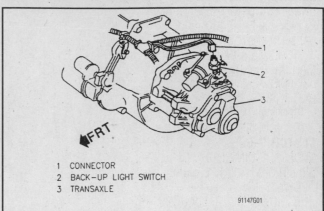

1 CONNECTOR
2 BACK-UP LIGHT SWITCH
3 TRANSAXLE

91147G01

Fig. 1 The back-up lamp switch mounting—manual transaxle

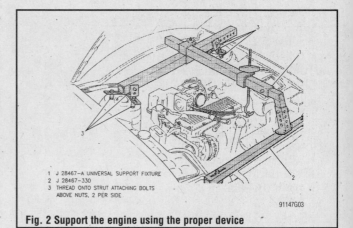

1 J 28467-A UNIVERSAL SUPPORT FIXTURE
2 J 28467-330
3 THREAD ONTO STRUT ATTACHING BOLTS ABOVE NUTS, 2 PER SIDE

91147G03

Fig. 2 Support the engine using the proper device

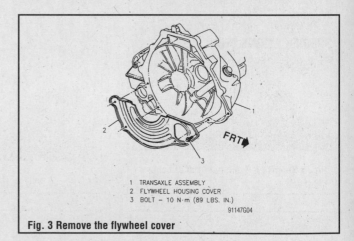

1 TRANSAXLE ASSEMBLY
2 FLYWHEEL HOUSING COVER
3 BOLT – 10 N·m (89 LBS. IN.)

91147G04

Fig. 3 Remove the flywheel cover

15. Drain the transaxle fluid into a suitable container.
16. Remove the tire and wheel assemblies.
17. Remove the left side splash shield.
18. Disconnect both front ABS wheel speed sensor harness and move out of the way.
19. Remove the flywheel cover.
20. Disconnect the vehicle speed sensor at the transaxle.
21. Remove the left and right ball joint nuts and separate them from the steering knuckle.
22. Remove the left stabilizer link pin.
23. Remove the left side U-bolt from the stabilizer bar.
24. Remove the left side suspension support attaching bolts.
25. Remove the drive axles from the transaxle.

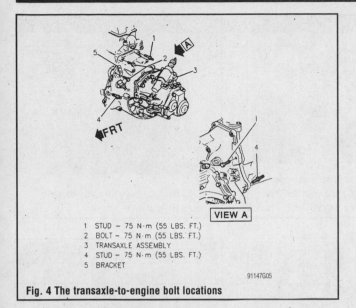

1 STUD — 75 N·m (55 LBS. FT.)
2 BOLT — 75 N·m (55 LBS. FT.)
3 TRANSAXLE ASSEMBLY
4 STUD — 75 N·m (55 LBS. FT.)
5 BRACKET

91147G05

Fig. 4 The transaxle-to-engine bolt locations

26. Remove the front lower transaxle mount.
27. Position a suitable jack under the transaxle.
28. Remove the transaxle-to-engine mounting bolts (noting their location).
29. Remove the transaxle away from the engine by carefully lowering the jack.

To install:
30. Position the transaxle on the jack and move it into place.
31. Install the transaxle-to-engine mounting bolts and tighten them to 55 ft. lbs. (75 Nm).
32. Install the front transaxle mount.
33. Install the flywheel cover.
34. Install the drive axles into the transaxle assembly.
35. Install the left side suspension support and attaching bolts.

36. Install the left side U-bolt to the stabilizer bar.
37. Connect the ball joints to the steering knuckle and install the nuts, tighten to 41 ft. lbs. (55 Nm).
38. Install the left side stabilizer link pin assembly.
39. Route the left side ABS wheel speed sensor wiring harness and connect both front wheel speed sensor connectors.
40. Install the inner splash shield.
41. Connect the vehicle speed sensor to the transaxle.
42. Install both tire and wheel assemblies.
43. Lower the vehicle.
44. Install the ground cables to the transaxle mounting studs.
45. Install the vent tube to the transaxle.
46. Attach the back-up light switch connector.
47. Install the upper transaxle mounting bolts and tighten to 55 ft. lbs. (75 Nm).
48. Install the clutch master cylinder to clutch actuator cylinder.
49. Install the rear transaxle mount. Tighten the bolts to 55 ft. lbs. (75 Nm).
50. Clip the wiring harness to the mount bracket.
51. Remove the engine support fixture.
52. Connect the shift cables clamp and nut. Tighten the nut to 89 inch lbs. (10 Nm).
53. Install the air cleaner and duct assembly to the throttle body.
54. Connect the pushrod to the clutch pedal.
55. Install the left side hush panel.
56. Connect the negative battery cable.
57. Fill the transaxle with Synchromesh® Transaxle Fluid.
58. Road test the vehicle and verify proper operation.

Halfshafts

REMOVAL & INSTALLATION

▶ **See Figures 5 thru 23**

1. Disconnect the negative battery cable.
2. With the weight of the vehicle still on the wheels, loosen, but do not remove the front hub nut. This may require an assistant holding the brakes to

91147P02

Fig. 5 Remove the hub nut from the axle shaft and . . .

91147P01

Fig. 6 . . . the washer behind it

91149P22

Fig. 7 Remove the brake caliper from the hub assembly and support it using mechanic's wire or another suitable device

91149P09

Fig. 8 Remove the rotor from the hub assembly

91148P37

Fig. 9 The tie rod end must be removed from the hub assembly to allow the access needed to remove the halfshaft

91148P04

Fig. 10 Remove the cotter pin from the tie rod end and . . .

Fig. 11 . . . remove the retaining nut from the tie rod end

Fig. 12 A special puller is recommended for removing the tie rod end from the hub assembly without damaging the tie rod end

Fig. 13 Remove the cotter pin from the lower ball joint and . . .

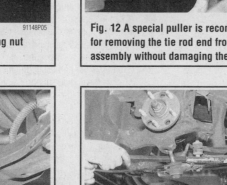

Fig. 14 . . . using a wrench, loosen and remove the ball joint retaining nut

Fig. 15 Use a suitable prytool to remove the lower ball joint/control arm from the hub assembly

Fig. 16 Remove the tie rod end from the hub assembly

Fig. 17 Detach the wheel speed sensor connector

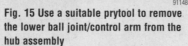

Fig. 18 A large punch can be used to drive the halfshaft out of the hub. Ensure that the punch is placed in the centering hole of the halfshaft and do not hit the threads of the halfshaft

Fig. 19 Remove the halfshaft from the hub

Fig. 20 A large prytool (although not recommended) can be used to release the halfshaft from the transaxle then . . .

Fig. 21 . . . remove the halfshaft from the vehicle

Fig. 22 Inspect the axle retaining ring located on the output shaft of the transaxle differential

keep the front halfshaft from turning. It is good practice to wire-brush the exposed threads on the outer CV-joint stub shaft and apply a generous amount of penetrating oil before attempting to loosen the hub nut.

3. Raise and safely support the vehicle.
4. Remove the tire and wheel assembly.
5. Remove the hub nut and washer.
6. Install the axle boot seal protector J-33162 or the equivalent on the right-hand inner boot, if equipped.
7. Remove and support the brake caliper.
8. Remove the brake rotor.
9. Remove the lower ball joint cotter pin and nut and loosen the joint. If removing the right halfshaft, turn the wheel to the left. If removing the left halfshaft turn the wheel to the right.
10. Disconnect the ABS sensor, if equipped.
11. Separate the lower ball joint from the steering knuckle.
12. Disengage the halfshaft stub end from the front wheel bearing and hub assembly using a suitable press-type tool, pressing until the halfshaft splines are just loose.

➡**A hammer and a suitable punch can be used to drive the axle out of the hub.**

13. Separate the hub and bearing assembly from the halfshaft. Move the strut and knuckle assembly rearward.
14. Separate the inner joint from the transaxle using the proper puller tools such as J-33008 and J-29764 or their equivalents.

➡**A large prytool can be used to disengage the halfshaft from the transaxle. Care must be taken as to what is used to pry on for leverage, prying on the wrong item can cause damage.**

15. Remove the halfshaft from the transaxle. Do not pull the halfshaft by the CV-joint boot or on the joint itself.
To install:
16. Prior to installation, cover all sharp edges in the area of the halfshaft with shop towels so the CV-joint boots will be protected from damage. When a halfshaft is removed for any reason, the transaxle (the halfshaft male and female shank) and knuckle sealing surfaces should be inspected for debris and corrosion. If debris or corrosion are present, clean with 320 grit crocus cloth or equivalent. Transaxle fluid may be used to clean off any remaining debris. The surface should be wiped clean and dry before attempting to install the halfshaft.
17. Install the halfshaft into the transaxle (or intermediate shaft, if equipped) by placing a brass drift pin into the groove on the joint housing and tapping until seated. Be careful not to damage the axle seal or dislodge the seal garter spring when installing the axle.

➡**Be sure the halfshaft is fully engaged in the transaxle. Verify that the halfshaft is seated by grasping the inner joint housing and pulling outward. Do not pull on the shaft or the boot, but on the inner joint housing only.**

18. Install the drive axle into the hub and bearing assembly.
19. Install the lower ball joint to the steering knuckle. Tighten the ball joint-to-steering knuckle nut to 41 ft. lbs. (55 Nm) to install the cotter pin. Do not loosen the nut at any time during installation. Install a new cotter pin.

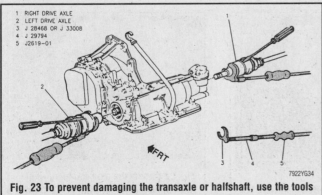

1	RIGHT DRIVE AXLE
2	LEFT DRIVE AXLE
3	J 28468 OR J 33008
4	J 29794
5	J2619-01

7922YG34

Fig. 23 To prevent damaging the transaxle or halfshaft, use the tools as shown to remove the halfshafts

20. Install the washer and a new hub nut. To keep the hub from turning while the hub nut is being torqued, insert a drift pin through the caliper opening into one of the ventilation openings in the brake rotor. This should lock the assembly together. Tighten the hub nut to 185 ft. lbs. (260 Nm).
21. Install the tire and wheel assembly.
22. Lower the vehicle.
23. Test drive vehicle to verify no front drive noise.

CV-JOINTS OVERHAUL

These vehicles use several different types of joints. Engine size, transaxle type, whether the joint is an inboard or outboard joint, even which side of the vehicle is being serviced could make a difference in joint type. Be sure to properly identify the joint before attempting joint or boot replacement. Look for identification numbers at the large end of the boots and/or on the end of the metal retainer bands.

The 3 types of joints used are the Birfield Joint, (B.J.), the Tripod Joint (T.J.) and the Double Offset Joint (D.O.J.).

➡**Do not disassemble a Birfield joint. Service with a new joint or clean and repack using a new boot kit.**

The distance between the large and small boot bands is important and should be checked prior to and after boot service. This is so the boot will not be installed either too loose or too tight, which could cause early wear and cracking, allowing the grease to get out and water and dirt in, leading to early joint failure.

➡**The driveshaft joints use special grease; do not add any grease other than that supplied with the kit.**

Double Offset Joint

The Double Offset Joint (D.O.J.) is bigger than other joints and, in these applications, is normally used as an inboard joint.
1. Remove the halfshaft from the vehicle.
2. Side cutter pliers can be used to cut the metal retaining bands. Remove the boot from the joint outer race.
3. Locate and remove the large circlip at the base of the joint. Remove the outer race (the body of the joint).
4. Remove the small snapring and take off the inner race, cage and balls as an assembly. Clean the inner race, cage and balls without disassembling.
5. If the boot is to be reused, wipe the grease from the splines and wrap the splines in vinyl tape before sliding the boot from the shaft.
6. Remove the inner (D.O.J.) boot from the shaft. If the outer (B.J.) boot is to be replaced, remove the boot retainer rings and slide the boot down and off of the shaft at this time.
To install:
7. Be sure to tape the shaft splines before installing the boots. Fill the inside of the boot with the specified grease. Often the grease supplied in the replacement parts kit is meant to be divided in half, with half being used to lubricate the joint and half being used inside the boot.
8. Install the cage onto the halfshaft so the small diameter side of the cage is installed first. With a brass drift pin, tap lightly and evenly around the inner race to install the race until it comes into contact with the rib of the shaft. Apply the specified grease to the inner race and cage and fit them together. Insert the balls into the cage.
9. Install the outer race (the body of the joint) after filling with the specified grease. The outer race should be filled with this grease.
10. Tighten the boot bands securely. Make sure the distance between the boot bands is correct.
11. Install the halfshaft to the vehicle.

Except Double Offset Joint

1. Disconnect the negative battery cable. Remove the halfshaft.
2. Use side cutter pliers to remove the metal retaining bands from the boot(s) that will be removed. Slide the boot from the T.J. case.
3. Remove the snapring and the tripod joint spider assembly from the halfshaft. Do not disassemble the spider and use care in handling.
4. If the boot is be reused, wrap vinyl tape around the spline part of the shaft so the boot(s) will not be damaged when removed. Remove the dynamic damper, if used, and the boots from the shaft.

To install:

5. Double check that the correct replacement parts are being installed. Wrap vinyl tape around the splines to protect the boot and install the boots and damper, if used, in the correct order.

6. Install the joint spider assembly to the shaft and install the snapring.

7. Fill the inside of the boot with the specified grease. Often the grease sup-plied in the replacement parts kit is meant to be divided in half, with half being used to lubricate the joint and half being used inside the boot. Keep grease off the rubber part of the dynamic damper (if used).

8. Secure the boot bands with the halfshaft in a horizontal position. Make sure distance between boot bands is correct.

9. Install the halfshaft to the vehicle and reconnect the negative battery cable.

CLUTCH

Understanding the Clutch

✳✳ CAUTION

The clutch driven disc may contain asbestos, which has been deter-mined to be a cancer causing agent. Never clean clutch surfaces with compressed air! Avoid inhaling any dust from any clutch sur-face! When cleaning clutch surfaces, use a commercially available brake cleaning fluid.

The purpose of the clutch is to disconnect and connect engine power at the transaxle. A vehicle at rest requires a lot of engine torque to get all that weight moving. An internal combustion engine does not develop a high starting torque (unlike steam engines) so it must be allowed to operate without any load until it builds up enough torque to move the vehicle. Torque increases with engine rpm. The clutch allows the engine to build up torque by physi-cally disconnecting the engine from the transaxle, relieving the engine of any load or resistance.

The transfer of engine power to the transaxle (the load) must be smooth and gradual; if it weren't, drive line components would wear out or break quickly. This gradual power transfer is made possible by gradually releasing the clutch pedal. The clutch disc and pressure plate are the connecting link between the engine and transaxle. When the clutch pedal is released, the disc and plate contact each other (the clutch is engaged) physically joining the engine and transaxle. When the pedal is pushed inward, the disc and plate separate (the clutch is disengaged) disconnecting the engine from the transaxle.

Most clutches utilize a single plate, dry friction disc with a diaphragm-style spring pressure plate. The clutch disc has a splined hub which attaches the disc to the input shaft. The disc has friction material where it contacts the flywheel and pressure plate. Torsion springs on the disc help absorb engine torque pulses. The pressure plate applies pressure to the clutch disc, holding it tight against the surface of the flywheel. The clutch operating mechanism consists of a release bearing, fork and cylinder assembly.

The release fork and actuating linkage transfer pedal motion to the release bearing. In the engaged position (pedal released) the diaphragm spring holds the pressure plate against the clutch disc, so engine torque is transmitted to the input shaft. When the clutch pedal is depressed, the release bearing pushes the diaphragm spring center toward the flywheel. The diaphragm spring pivots the fulcrum, relieving the load on the pressure plate. Steel spring straps riveted to the clutch cover lift the pressure plate from the clutch disc, disengaging the engine drive from the transaxle and enabling the gears to be changed.

The clutch is operating properly if:

- It will stall the engine when released with the vehicle held stationary.
- The shift lever can be moved freely between 1st and reverse gears when the vehicle is stationary and the clutch disengaged.

Driven Disc and Pressure Plate

REMOVAL & INSTALLATION

▶ See Figures 24 thru 38

✳✳ CAUTION

The clutch driven disc may contain asbestos, which has been deter-mined to be a cancer causing agent. Never clean clutch surfaces with compressed air! Avoid inhaling any dust from any clutch sur-face! When cleaning clutch surfaces, use a commercially available brake cleaning fluid.

➡**Prior to any vehicle service that requires the removal of the actuator cylinder, the master cylinder pushrod must be disconnected from the clutch pedal. If not disconnected, permanent damage to the actuator cylinder will occur if the clutch pedal is depressed while the actuator cylinder is disconnected.**

1. Disconnect the negative battery cable.
2. Remove the clutch master cylinder pushrod from the clutch pedal.
3. Remove the transaxle.

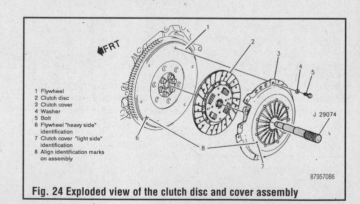

1 Flywheel
2 Clutch disc
3 Clutch cover
4 Washer
5 Bolt
6 Flywheel "heavy side" identification
7 Clutch cover "light side" identification
8 Align identification marks on assembly

Fig. 24 Exploded view of the clutch disc and cover assembly

Fig. 25 Loosen and remove the clutch and pressure plate bolts evenly, a little at a time . . .

Fig. 26 . . . then carefully removing the clutch and pressure plate assembly from the flywheel

Fig. 27 Check across the flywheel surface, it should be flat

Fig. 28 If necessary, lock the flywheel in place and remove the retaining bolts . . .

Fig. 29 . . . then remove the flywheel from the crankshaft in order replace it or have it machined

Fig. 30 Upon installation, it is usually a good idea to apply a threadlocking compound to the flywheel bolts

Fig. 31 Check the pressure plate for excessive wear

Fig. 32 Be sure that the flywheel surface is clean, before installing the clutch

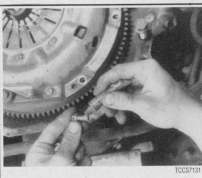

Fig. 33 Typical clutch alignment tool, note how the splines match the Transaxle's input shaft

Fig. 34 Use the clutch alignment tool to align the clutch disc during assembly

Fig. 35 Pressure plate-to-flywheel bolt holes should align

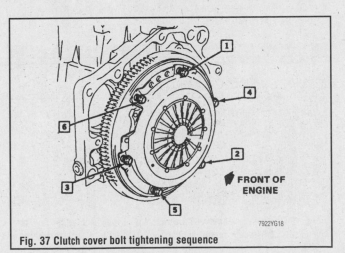

Fig. 36 You may want to use a threadlocking compound on the clutch assembly bolts

4. If any of the parts are to be reused, mark the pressure plate assembly and the flywheel so they can be assembled in the same position. They were balanced as an assembly at the factory.

5. Loosen the attaching bolts one turn at a time until spring tension is relieved.

6. Support the pressure plate and remove the bolts. Remove the pressure plate and clutch disc. Do not disassemble the pressure plate assembly. Replace it if defective.

7. Inspect the flywheel, clutch disc, pressure plate, throwout bearing and the clutch fork and pivot shaft assembly for wear. Replace the parts as required. If the flywheel shows any signs of overheating or if it is badly grooved or scored, it should be resurfaced or replaced.

8. Clean the pressure plate and flywheel mating surfaces thoroughly.

To install:

9. Clean all parts well. Apply a small amount of high temperature grease to the pilot bearing inside the end of the crankshaft.

10. Position the clutch disc and pressure plate into the installed position, and support with clutch aligning tool J-29074 or equivalent. The clutch plate is assembled with the damper springs offset toward the transaxle. One side of the factory supplied clutch disc should be stamped "Flywheel Side."

Fig. 37 Clutch cover bolt tightening sequence

Fig. 38 Be sure to use a torque wrench to tighten all bolts

11. Install the pressure plate-to-flywheel bolts. Tighten them gradually in a cross pattern as follows:
    a. Install lightly seat all bolts.
    b. Tighten bolts 1, 2, 3, then 4, 5, and 6 to 12 ft. lbs. (16 Nm).
    c. Final torque bolts 1, 2, 3, then 4, 5, 6 to 15 ft. lbs. (20 Nm).
12. Lubricate the outside groove and the inside recess of the release bearing with high temperature grease. Wipe off any excess. Install the release bearing.
13. Pack the inside recess of the release bearing completely full of chassis grease.

➡ **Be sure the bearing pads are located on the fork ends and both spring ends are in the fork holes with the spring completely seated in bearing groove.**

14. Install the transaxle.
15. Install clutch master cylinder pushrod to the clutch pedal and install the retaining clip.
16. If equipped with cruise control, check switch adjustment at clutch pedal bracket.

➡ **When adjusting the cruise control switch, do not exert an upward force on the clutch pedal pad of more than 20 ft. lbs. (27 Nm) or damage to the master cylinder pushrod retaining ring can result.**

17. Connect the negative battery cable.
18. Bleed clutch system as necessary and road test vehicle.

ADJUSTMENTS

The clutch system in the General Motors J-Body vehicles is a hydraulic system and requires no adjustments. If the system is malfunctioning, use normal clutch diagnosis to determine the problem.

Master Cylinder

REMOVAL & INSTALLATION

▶ **See Figures 39, 40 and 41**

Service this vehicle with Hydraulic Clutch Fluid GM P/N 12345347 or equivalent.
1. Disconnect the negative battery cable.
2. Remove the sound insulator from inside the vehicle.
3. Disconnect the clutch master cylinder pushrod from the clutch pedal.
4. Unfasten the clutch master cylinder retaining nuts at the front of the cowl, then remove the remote reservoir.
5. Detach the master cylinder assembly from the actuator cylinder by disconnecting the hydraulic line, then remove the master cylinder from the vehicle.

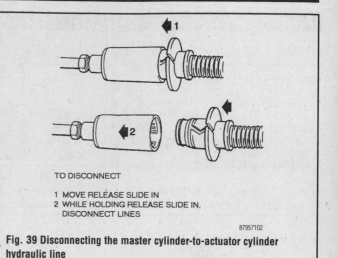

TO DISCONNECT

1 MOVE RELEASE SLIDE IN
2 WHILE HOLDING RELEASE SLIDE IN, DISCONNECT LINES

87957102

Fig. 39 Disconnecting the master cylinder-to-actuator cylinder hydraulic line

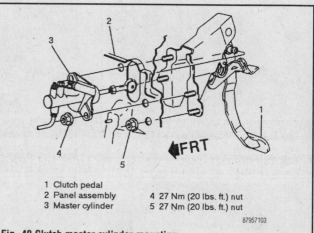

1 Clutch pedal
2 Panel assembly
3 Master cylinder
4 27 Nm (20 lbs. ft.) nut
5 27 Nm (20 lbs. ft.) nut

87957103

Fig. 40 Clutch master cylinder mounting

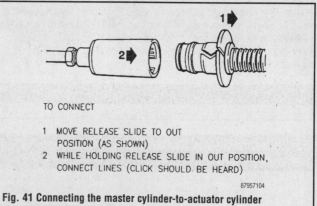

TO CONNECT

1 MOVE RELEASE SLIDE TO OUT POSITION (AS SHOWN)
2 WHILE HOLDING RELEASE SLIDE IN OUT POSITION, CONNECT LINES (CLICK SHOULD BE HEARD)

87957104

Fig. 41 Connecting the master cylinder-to-actuator cylinder hydraulic line

To install:
6. Attach the master cylinder to the actuator cylinder by fastening the hydraulic line.
7. Install the remote fluid reservoir, then secure with the retaining nuts. Tighten the nuts evenly to 18 ft. lbs. (25 Nm).
8. Connect the pushrod to the clutch pedal. If equipped, adjust the cruise control switch, as outlined in Section 6 of this manual.
9. Install the sound insulator.
10. Bleed the hydraulic system, as outlined later in this section.
11. Connect the negative battery cable.
12. Road test the vehicle and verify proper operation.

Actuator (Slave) Cylinder

REMOVAL & INSTALLATION

▶ **See Figures 39, 41 and 42**

1. Disconnect the negative battery cable.
2. Detach the master cylinder assembly from the actuator cylinder by disconnecting the hydraulic line.
3. Remove the transaxle assembly, as outlined earlier in this section.

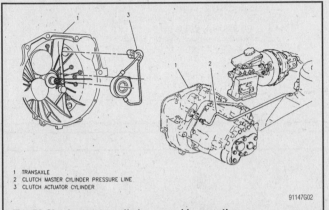

1 TRANSAXLE
2 CLUTCH MASTER CYLINDER PRESSURE LINE
3 CLUTCH ACTUATOR CYLINDER

91147G02

Fig. 42 Clutch actuator cylinder assembly mounting

4. Remove the clutch actuator cylinder from the transaxle.

To install:

5. Lubricate the inside diameter of the bearing with clutch bearing lubricant GM part no. 12345777 or equivalent.
6. Install the actuator cylinder in the transaxle, then install the transaxle assembly.
7. Connect the master cylinder-to-actuator hydraulic line.
8. Bleed the hydraulic system, as outlined later in this section.
9. If removed, install the air intake duct.
10. Connect the negative battery cable.

HYDRAULIC SYSTEM BLEEDING

Do not use fluid which has been bled from a system to fill the reservoir as it may be aerated, have too much moisture content or possibly be contaminated. Clean the dirt and grease from the cap to ensure that no foreign substances enter the system. It is also important to maintain the fluid level in the clutch reservoir to the top step with hydraulic clutch fluid Hydraulic Clutch Fluid GM P/N 12345347 or equivalent.

1. Attach a hose to the bleeder screw on the clutch actuator assembly and submerge the other end of the hose in a container of hydraulic clutch fluid.
2. Depress the clutch pedal slowly and hold.
3. Loosen the bleeder screw to purge air.
4. Tighten the bleeder screw to 18 inch lbs. (2 Nm).
5. Let up on the clutch pedal.
6. Repeat Steps 2 through 5 until all air is purged from the system.
7. Fill the reservoir to the top step with hydraulic clutch fluid.
8. Repeat this bleeding procedure if there is a grinding noise during the clutch spin down procedure.

AUTOMATIC TRANSAXLE

Understanding the Automatic Transaxle

The automatic transaxle allows engine torque and power to be transmitted to the front wheels within a narrow range of engine operating speeds. It will allow the engine to turn fast enough to produce plenty of power and torque at very low speeds, while keeping it at a sensible rpm at high vehicle speeds (and it does this job without driver assistance). The transaxle uses a light fluid as the medium for the transmission of power. This fluid also works in the operation of various hydraulic control circuits and as a lubricant. Because the transaxle fluid performs all of these functions, trouble within the unit can easily travel from one part to another. For this reason, and because of the complexity and unusual operating principles of the transaxle, a very sound understanding of the basic principles of operation will simplify troubleshooting.

Fluid Pan

Pan removal, fluid and filter changes are covered in Section 1 of this manual.

Park/Neutral Safety Switch (Transaxle Range Sensor)

REMOVAL & INSTALLATION

▶ **See Figures 43 and 44**

➡ **The park/neutral safety switch also functions as the back-up switch.**

1. Disconnect the negative battery cable.
2. Remove the shift linkage.
3. Detach the electrical connector from the switch.
4. Unfasten the switch-to-transaxle screws/bolts, then remove the switch.

To install:

5. If installing the old switch, proceed as follows:
   a. Place the shift shaft/control lever in **N**.
   b. Align the flats of the shift shaft with the switch, then loosely install the mounting bolts.

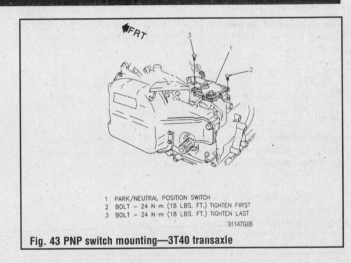

1 PARK/NEUTRAL POSITION SWITCH
2 BOLT – 24 N·m (18 LBS. FT.) TIGHTEN FIRST
3 BOLT – 24 N·m (18 LBS. FT.) TIGHTEN LAST

91147G06

Fig. 43 PNP switch mounting—3T40 transaxle

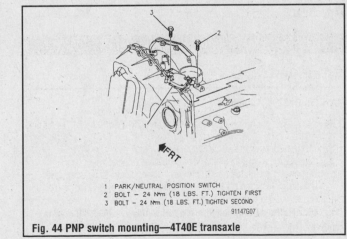

1 PARK/NEUTRAL POSITION SWITCH
2 BOLT – 24 Nm (18 LBS. FT.) TIGHTEN FIRST
3 BOLT – 24 Nm (18 LBS. FT.) TIGHTEN SECOND

91147G07

Fig. 44 PNP switch mounting—4T40E transaxle

c. Insert a gauge pin in the service adjustment hole and rotate the switch until the pin drops to a depth of 9/64 in. (9mm).

d. Tighten the bolts to 18 ft. lbs. (25 Nm), then remove the gauge pin.

6. If installing a new switch, proceed as follows:

a. Place the shift shaft/control lever in **N**.

b. Align the flats of the shift shaft to the flats in the switch, then install the switch assembly. Tighten the bolts to 18 ft. lbs. (25 Nm).

c. If the bolt holes do not align with the mounting boss on the transaxle, verify the transaxle is in the **N** position, do not rotate the switch.

d. If the shift has been rotated and the pin broken, the switch can be adjusted by following the procedure in Step 5.

7. Attach the electrical connector to the switch.

8. Install the shift linkage.

9. Connect the negative battery cable, then start the engine and check the switch operation.

❊❊ CAUTION

After switch engagement, make sure the engine will only start in P or N.

ADJUSTMENT

See removal and installation of the Park Neutral Safety Switch (Transaxle Range or TR sensor).

Automatic Transaxle Assembly

REMOVAL & INSTALLATION

3T40 Automatic Transaxle

▶ **See Figures 45, 46 and 47**

1. Disconnect the negative battery cable.
2. Properly drain the transaxle.
3. Remove the air intake duct.
4. Disconnect the TV cable. Remove the shift cable and bracket.
5. Tag and detach all necessary vacuum lines and electrical connections.
6. Remove the power steering pump and set aside.
7. Remove the transaxle filler tube.
8. Install engine support fixture J 28467-A or equivalent.
9. Remove the top engine-to-transaxle bolts.
10. Raise and safely support the vehicle.
11. Remove both front tire and wheel assemblies. Remove the left splash shield.
12. Remove both front ABS wheel speed sensors and the harness from the left suspension support.
13. As outlined in Section 8 of this manual, remove both lower ball joints.

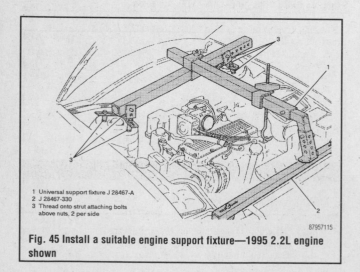

1 Universal support fixture J 28467-A
2 J 28467-330
3 Thread onto strut attaching bolts above nuts, 2 per side

87957115

Fig. 45 Install a suitable engine support fixture—1995 2.2L engine shown

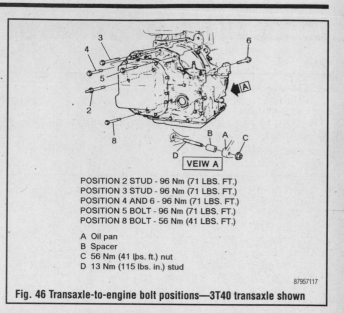

POSITION 2 STUD - 96 Nm (71 LBS. FT.)
POSITION 3 STUD - 96 Nm (71 LBS. FT.)
POSITION 4 AND 6 - 96 Nm (71 LBS. FT.)
POSITION 5 BOLT - 96 Nm (71 LBS. FT.)
POSITION 8 BOLT - 56 Nm (41 LBS. FT.)

A Oil pan
B Spacer
C 56 Nm (41 lbs. ft.) nut
D 13 Nm (115 lbs. in.) stud

87957117

Fig. 46 Transaxle-to-engine bolt positions—3T40 transaxle shown

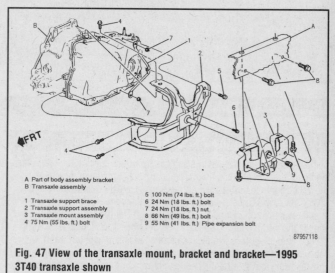

A Part of body assembly bracket
B Transaxle assembly

1 Transaxle support brace
2 Transaxle support assembly
3 Transaxle mount assembly
4 75 Nm (55 lbs. ft.) bolt
5 100 Nm (74 lbs. ft.) bolt
6 24 Nm (18 lbs. ft.) bolt
7 24 Nm (18 lbs. ft.) nut
8 66 Nm (49 lbs. ft.) bolt
9 55 Nm (41 lbs. ft.) Pipe expansion bolt

87957118

Fig. 47 View of the transaxle mount, bracket and bracket—1995 3T40 transaxle shown

14. Disconnect the stabilizer shaft links.
15. Remove the front air deflector.
16. Remove the left suspension support and both drive axles.
17. Disconnect the engine-to-transaxle brace, then remove the transaxle converter cover.
18. Remove the starter, as outlined in Section 2 of this manual.
19. Unfasten the flywheel-to-torque converter bolts.
20. Disconnect the transaxle cooler pipes.
21. Detach the ground wires from the engine-to-transaxle bolt.
22. Remove the cooler pipe brace and the exhaust brace.
23. Remove the bolts from the engine and transaxle mount.
24. Support the transaxle with a suitable jack.
25. Unfasten the transaxle mount-to-body bolts.
26. Remove the heater core hose pipe brace-to-transaxle nut and bolt.
27. Unfasten the remaining engine-to-transaxle bolts, then remove the transaxle assembly from the vehicle.

To install:

➡**Whenever the transaxle has been removed, the transaxle cooler lines should be flushed.**

28. Place a thin film of GM part no. 1051344 or equivalent grease on the torque converter pilot knob.

29. Move the transaxle assembly into position with the jack while installing the right drive axle. Make sure to properly seat the torque converter in the oil pump.

30. Install the lower transaxle retaining bolts in their proper positions, as shown in the accompanying figure.

31. Install the transaxle mount-to-body bolts as shown in the accompanying figure.

32. Install the engine and transaxle mount bolts.

33. Fasten the exhaust brace and the cooler pipe brace.

34. Connect the ground wires at the engine-to-transaxle bolt.

35. Attach the transaxle cooler pipes.

36. Apply adhesive/sealing compound GM part no. 12345493 or equivalent on the flywheel-to-torque converter bolts, then install the bolts. Install the converter cover/shield.

37. Install the starter.

38. Fasten the engine-to-transaxle brace.

39. Install the drive axles and the left suspension support.

40. Fasten the front air deflector.

41. Connect the stabilizer shaft links and the lower ball joints.

42. Install both ABS wheel speed sensors.

43. Fasten the left splash shield, then install the heater core pipe brace nut and bolt.

44. Install the front wheel and tire assemblies, then carefully lower the vehicle.

45. Install the top engine-to-transaxle bolts.

46. Remove the engine support fixture.

47. Install the filler tube.

48. Install the power steering pump assembly, then adjust the belt.

49. Attach the electrical connections and vacuum lines, as tagged during removal.

50. Install the shift cable and bracket. Connect the TV cable.

51. Fasten the air intake duct.

52. Connect the negative battery cable, then fill the transaxle to the proper level.

4T40E Transaxle

1. Disconnect the negative battery cable.

2. Remove the air cleaner assembly.

3. Disconnect the shift linkage from the transaxle.

4. Detach the wiring connections from the transaxle.

5. Install J 28467-A or equivalent engine support fixture.

6. Unfasten the upper engine-to-transaxle bolts.

7. Raise and safely support the vehicle.

8. Remove both front tire and wheel assemblies. Remove the left and right splash shields.

9. Remove both front ABS wheel speed sensors and the harness from the left suspension support.

10. Using tool J 24319-B or equivalent, remove both outer tie rods from the steering knuckle.

11. Separate both ball joints from the steering knuckle using tool J 38892 or equivalent.

12. Remove the front suspension support brace, then remove the engine mount strut from the strut mount bracket.

13. Support the suspension support assembly, then remove the bolts. Loosen the suspension support assembly enough to disconnect the steering coupling and both power steering fluid lines.

14. Remove both drive axles (halfshafts) from the transaxle, then support them.

15. Unfasten the engine-to-transaxle brace.

16. Remove the shift cable bracket.

17. As outlined in Section 2 of this manual, remove the starter.

18. Unfasten the retaining bolts, then remove the transaxle converter cover/shield.

19. Matchmark the flywheel-to-torque converter for reassembly, then unfasten the torque converter-to-flywheel bolts.

20. Disconnect the transaxle cooler pipes. Remove the brake hose bracket-to-body.

21. Unfasten the transaxle mount pipe expansion bolt.

22. Unfasten the transaxle mount-to-body bolts.

23. Carefully lower the vehicle.

24. Lower the transaxle with the engine support fixture enough to remove the transaxle.

25. Raise and safely support the vehicle.

26. Support the transaxle with a suitable jack.

27. Unfasten the remaining transaxle-to-engine bolts, then remove the transaxle from the vehicle.

To install:

➡**Whenever the transaxle has been removed, the transaxle cooler lines should be flushed.**

28. Place a thin film of GM part no. 1051344 or equivalent grease on the torque converter pilot knob. Make sure to properly seat the torque converter in the oil pump.

29. Position the transaxle in the vehicle, then secure with the lower transaxle-to-engine bolts. Tighten to the specifications shown in the accompanying figure.

30. Carefully lower the vehicle. Raise the transaxle with the engine support fixture.

31. Raise and safely support the vehicle.

32. Fasten the transaxle mount-to-body bolts.

33. Attach the brake hose bracket to body.

34. Connect the transaxle cooler pipes.

35. Fasten the torque converter-to-flywheel bolts. Hand start the bolts, then tighten them to 46 ft. lbs. (62 Nm). Install the converter cover/shield.

36. Install the starter.

37. Connect the shift cable bracket. Tighten the bolt to 18 ft. lbs. (25 Nm) and the nut to 37 ft. lbs. (50 Nm).

38. Install the engine-to-transaxle brace.

39. Install both drive axles (halfshafts).

40. Raise the suspension support assembly enough to connect the steering coupling and both power steering fluid lines.

41. Support the suspension support assembly, then install the retaining bolts.

42. Fasten the engine mount strut to the suspension support. Install the front suspension support brace. Tighten the retaining bolt to 49 ft. lbs. (66 Nm).

43. Attach both ball joints to the steering knuckle assembly, then connect both outer tie rods to the steering knuckle.

44. Attach both front ABS wheel speed sensors and fasten the harness to the left suspension support.

45. Install the right and left splash shields and the front tire and wheel assemblies.

46. Carefully lower the vehicle.

47. Install the upper transaxle-to-engine bolts, the remove the engine support fixture.

48. Attach the wiring connections to the transaxle, then connect the shift linkage to the transaxle.

49. Install the air cleaner assembly, then connect the negative battery cable.

50. Check the transaxle fluid lever, and fill with the proper type of oil, if necessary.

51. Apply the brakes, start the engine, then shift the transaxle from "Reverse" to "Drive". Fasten the transaxle mount pipe expansion bolt.

ADJUSTMENTS

Throttle Valve (TV) Cable

Setting of the TV cable must be done by rotating the throttle lever at the throttle body. Do not use the accelerator pedal to rotate the throttle lever.

1. With the engine OFF, depress and hold the reset tab at the engine end of the TV cable.

2. Move the slider until it stops against the fitting.

3. Release the rest tab.

4. Rotate the throttle lever to its full travel.

5. The slider must move (ratchet) toward the lever when the lever is rotated to its full travel position.

6. Recheck after the engine is hot and road test the vehicle.

Halfshafts

REMOVAL & INSTALLATION

The halfshaft removal and installation and overhaul are the same as a manual transaxle. Please refer to Manual Transaxle in this section.

TORQUE SPECIFICATIONS

Components	English	Metric
Automatic transaxle		
Shift cable bracket		
Retaining bolt	18 ft. lbs.	25 Nm
Retaining nut	37 ft. lbs.	50 Nm
Engine mount strut-to-suspension support	49 ft. lbs.	66 Nm
Axle hub nuts	185 ft. lbs.	260 Nm
Ball joint-to-steering knuckle	41 ft. lbs.	55 Nm
Clutch actuator bleeder screw	18 inch lbs.	2 Nm
Clutch master cylinder retaining nuts	18 ft. lbs.	25 Nm
Manual transaxle		
Back-up lamp switch (manual transaxle only)	24 ft. lbs.	33 Nm
Shift cable clamps	89 inch lbs.	10 Nm
Transaxle-to-engine bolts	55 ft. lbs.	75 Nm
Park/neutral safety switch	18 ft. lbs.	25 Nm
Pressure plate-to-flywheel bolts	①	

① Refer to procedure

91147C01

WHEELS 8-2
WHEEL ASSEMBLY 8-2
   REMOVAL & INSTALLATION 8-2
   INSPECTION 8-3
WHEEL LUG STUDS 8-3
   REMOVAL & INSTALLATION 8-3
FRONT SUSPENSION 8-4
MACPHERSON STRUT AND SPRING
  ASSEMBLY 8-4
   REMOVAL & INSTALLATION 8-4
   OVERHAUL 8-6
LOWER BALL JOINT 8-7
   INSPECTION 8-7
   REMOVAL & INSTALLATION 8-8
STABILIZER BAR 8-8
   REMOVAL & INSTALLATION 8-8
LOWER CONTROL ARM 8-9
   REMOVAL & INSTALLATION 8-9
   CONTROL ARM BUSHING
    REPLACEMENT 8-10
STEERING KNUCKLE AND SPINDLE 8-10
   REMOVAL & INSTALLATION 8-10
FRONT HUB AND BEARING 8-12
   REMOVAL & INSTALLATION 8-12
WHEEL ALIGNMENT 8-13
   CASTER 8-13
   CAMBER 8-13
   TOE 8-13
REAR SUSPENSION 8-13
COIL-OVER SHOCKS 8-13
   REMOVAL & INSTALLATION 8-13
REAR CONTROL ARM/AXLE 8-15
   REMOVAL & INSTALLATION 8-15
HUB AND BEARINGS 8-16
   REMOVAL & INSTALLATION 8-16
STEERING 8-17
STEERING WHEEL 8-17
   REMOVAL & INSTALLATION 8-17
HEADLIGHT/TURN SIGNAL/
  CRUISE/HAZARD (COMBINATION)
  SWITCH 8-18
   REMOVAL & INSTALLATION 8-18
WINDSHIELD WIPER SWITCH 8-19
   REMOVAL & INSTALLATION 8-19
IGNITION SWITCH 8-19
   REMOVAL & INSTALLATION 8-19
IGNITION LOCK CYLINDER 8-20
   REMOVAL & INSTALLATION 8-20
STEERING LINKAGE 8-21
   REMOVAL & INSTALLATION 8-21
POWER RACK AND PINION STEERING
  GEAR 8-22
   REMOVAL & INSTALLATION 8-22
POWER STEERING PUMP 8-24
   REMOVAL & INSTALLATION 8-24
   BLEEDING 8-24
COMPONENT LOCATIONS
  FRONT SUSPENSION COMPONENT
  LOCATIONS 8-5

REAR SUSPENSION COMPONENT
  LOCATIONS 8-14
STRUT ASSEMBLY EXPLODED
  VIEW 8-6
SPECIFICATIONS CHART
  TORQUE SPECIFICATIONS 8-26

8

SUSPENSION AND STEERING

WHEELS 8-2
FRONT SUSPENSION 8-4
REAR SUSPENSION 8-13
STEERING 8-17

WHEELS

Wheel Assembly

REMOVAL & INSTALLATION

➧ **See Figures 1 thru 8**

1. Park the vehicle on a level surface.
2. Remove the jack, tire iron and, if necessary, the spare tire from their storage compartments.
3. Check the owner's manual or refer to Section 1 of this manual for the jacking points on your vehicle. Then, place the jack in the proper position.
4. If equipped with lug nut trim caps, remove them by either unscrewing or pulling them off the lug nuts, as appropriate. Consult the owner's manual, if necessary.
5. If equipped with a wheel cover or hub cap, insert the tapered end of the tire iron in the groove and pry off the cover.
6. Apply the parking brake and block the diagonally opposite wheel with a wheel chock or two.

➡Wheel chocks may be purchased at your local auto parts store, or a block of wood cut into wedges may be used. If possible, keep one or two of the chocks in your tire storage compartment, in case any of the tires has to be removed on the side of the road.

7. If equipped with an automatic transaxle, place the selector lever in **P** or Park; with a manual transmission/transaxle, place the shifter in Reverse.
8. With the tires still on the ground, use the tire iron/wrench to break the lug nuts loose.

➡If a nut is stuck, never use heat to loosen it or damage to the wheel and bearings may occur. If the nuts are seized, one or two heavy hammer blows directly on the end of the bolt usually loosens the rust. Be careful, as continued pounding will likely damage the brake drum or rotor.

9. Using the jack, raise the vehicle until the tire is clear of the ground. Support the vehicle safely using jackstands.
10. Remove the lug nuts, then remove the tire and wheel assembly.

To install:

11. Make sure the wheel and hub mating surfaces, as well as the wheel lug studs, are clean and free of all foreign material. Always remove rust from the wheel mounting surface and the brake rotor or drum. Failure to do so may cause the lug nuts to loosen in service.
12. Install the tire and wheel assembly and hand-tighten the lug nuts.
13. Using the tire wrench, tighten all the lug nuts, in a crisscross pattern, until they are snug.
14. Raise the vehicle and withdraw the jackstand, then lower the vehicle.
15. Using a torque wrench, tighten the lug nuts in a crisscross pattern to 100 ft. lbs. (140 Nm). Check your owner's manual or refer to Section 1 of this manual for the proper tightening sequence.

✲✲ WARNING

Do not overtighten the lug nuts, as this may cause the wheel studs to stretch or the brake disc (rotor) to warp.

16. If so equipped, install the wheel cover or hub cap. Make sure the valve stem protrudes through the proper opening before tapping the wheel cover into position.
17. If equipped, install the lug nut trim caps by pushing them or screwing them on, as applicable.
18. Remove the jack from under the vehicle, and place the jack and tire iron/wrench in their storage compartments. Remove the wheel chock(s).

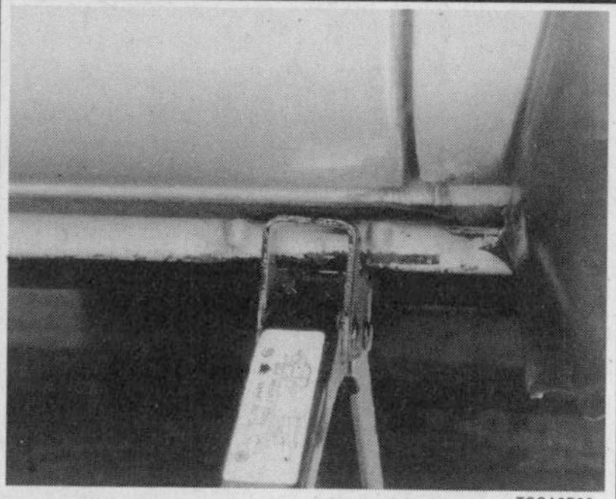

TCCA8P00

Fig. 1 Place the jack at the proper lifting point on your vehicle

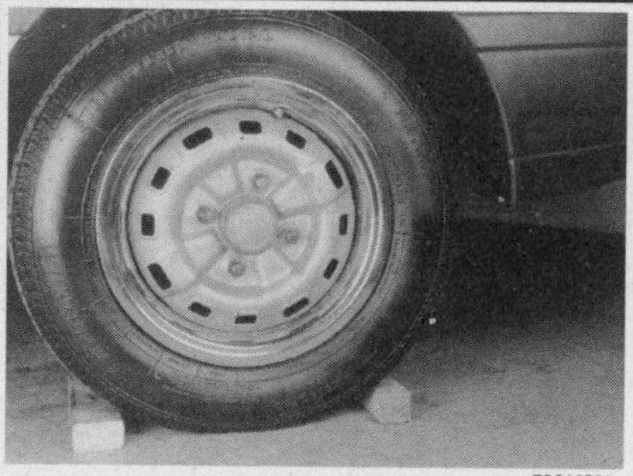

TCCA8P01

Fig. 2 Before jacking the vehicle, block the diagonally opposite wheel with one or, preferably, two chocks

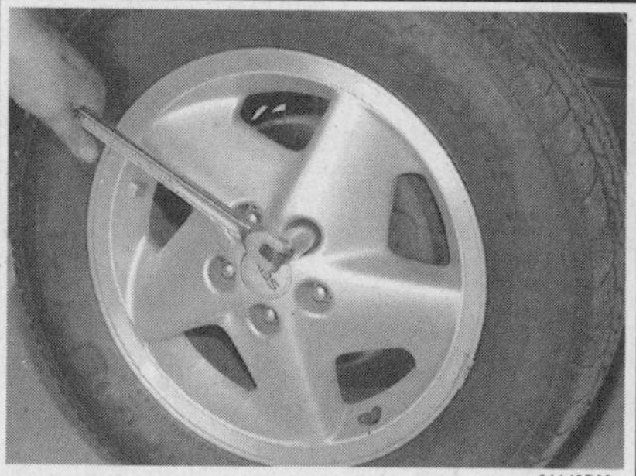

91148P03

Fig. 3 With the vehicle still on the ground, break the lug nuts loose using the wrench end of the tire iron

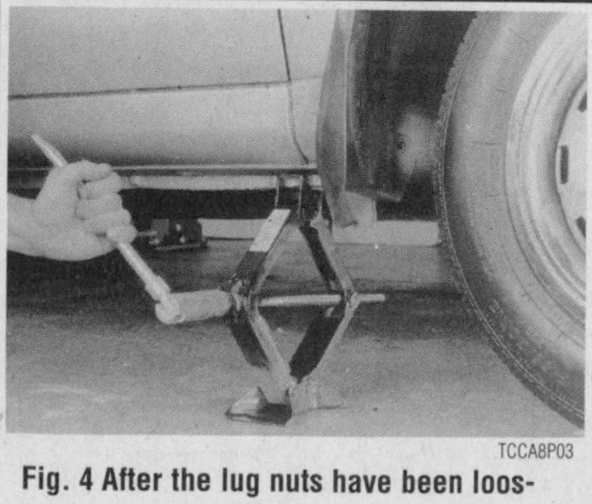

TCCA8P03

Fig. 4 After the lug nuts have been loosened, raise the vehicle using the jack until the tire is clear of the ground

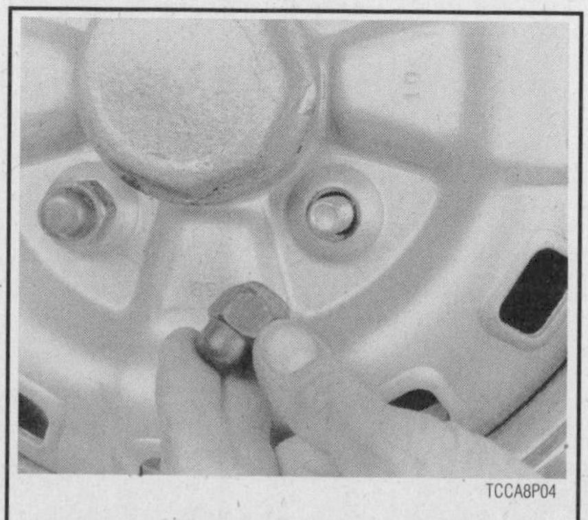

TCCA8P04

Fig. 5 Remove the lug nuts from the studs

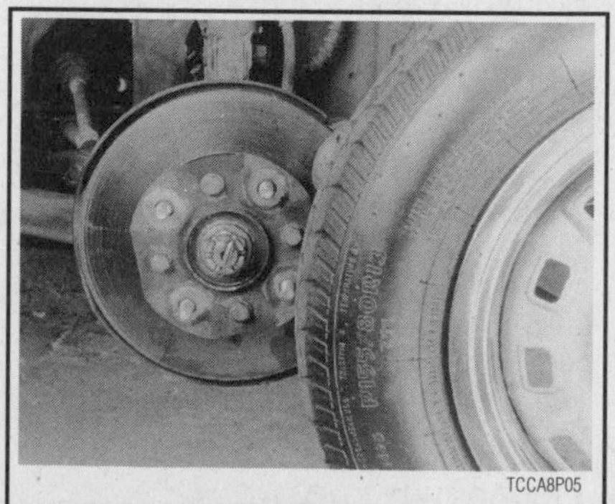

TCCA8P05

Fig. 6 Remove the wheel and tire assembly from the vehicle

19. If you have removed a flat or damaged tire, place it in the storage compartment of the vehicle and take it to your local repair station to have it fixed or replaced as soon as possible.

INSPECTION

Inspect the tires for lacerations, puncture marks, nails and other sharp objects. Repair or replace as necessary. Also check the tires for treadwear and air pressure as outlined in Check the wheel assemblies for dents, cracks, rust and metal fatigue. Repair or replace as necessary.

Wheel Lug Studs

REMOVAL & INSTALLATION

With Disc Brakes

♦ See Figures 9, 10 and 11

1. Raise and support the appropriate end of the vehicle safely using jackstands, then remove the wheel.
2. Remove the brake pads and caliper. Support the caliper aside using wire or a coat hanger. For details, please refer to Section 9 of this manual.
3. Remove the outer wheel bearing and lift off the rotor. For details on wheel bearing removal, installation and adjustment, please refer to Section 1 of this manual.
4. Properly support the rotor using press bars, then drive the stud out using an arbor press.

➡If a press is not available, CAREFULLY drive the old stud out using a blunt drift. MAKE SURE the rotor is properly and evenly supported or it may be damaged.

To install:

5. Clean the stud hole with a wire brush and start the new stud with a hammer and drift pin. Do not use any lubricant or thread sealer.
6. Finish installing the stud with the press.

➡If a press is not available, start the lug stud through the bore in the hub, then position about 4 flat washers over the stud and thread the lug nut. Hold the hub/rotor while tightening the lug nut, and the stud should be drawn into position. MAKE SURE THE STUD IS FULLY SEATED, then remove the lug nut and washers.

7. Install the rotor and adjust the wheel bearings.
8. Install the brake caliper and pads.
9. Install the wheel, then remove the jackstands and carefully lower the vehicle.
10. Tighten the lug nuts to the proper torque.

With Drum Brakes

♦ See Figures 12, 13 and 14

1. Raise the vehicle and safely support it with jackstands, then remove the wheel.
2. Remove the brake drum.
3. If necessary to provide clearance, remove the brake shoes, as outlined in Section 9 of this manual.
4. Using a large C-clamp and socket, press the stud from the axle flange.

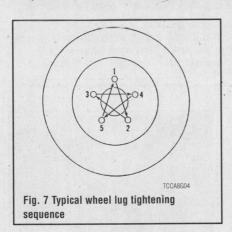

Fig. 7 Typical wheel lug tightening sequence

Fig. 8 Always tighten the lug nuts using a torque wrench

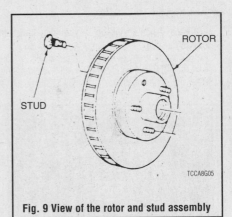

Fig. 9 View of the rotor and stud assembly

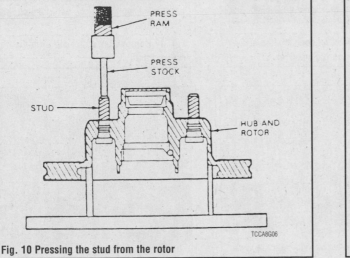

Fig. 10 Pressing the stud from the rotor

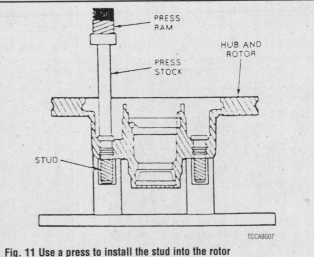

Fig. 11 Use a press to install the stud into the rotor

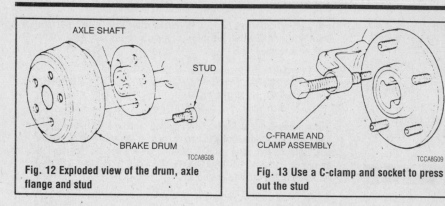

AXLE SHAFT

STUD

BRAKE DRUM

TCCA8G08

Fig. 12 Exploded view of the drum, axle flange and stud

C-FRAME AND
CLAMP ASSEMBLY

TCCA8G09

Fig. 13 Use a C-clamp and socket to press out the stud

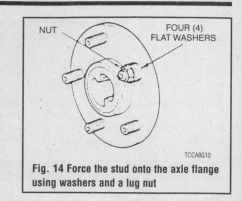

NUT

FOUR (4)
FLAT WASHERS

TCCA8G10

Fig. 14 Force the stud onto the axle flange using washers and a lug nut

5. Coat the serrated part of the stud with liquid soap and place it into the hole.

To install:

6. Position about 4 flat washers over the stud and thread the lug nut. Hold the flange while tightening the lug nut, and the stud should be drawn into position. MAKE SURE THE STUD IS FULLY SEATED, then remove the lug nut and washers.

7. If applicable, install the brake shoes.
8. Install the brake drum.
9. Install the wheel, then remove the jackstands and carefully lower the vehicle.
10. Tighten the lug nuts to the proper torque.

FRONT SUSPENSION

Macpherson Strut and Spring Assembly

REMOVAL & INSTALLATION

▶ **See Figures 15 thru 24**

1. From inside the engine compartment remove the upper strut-to-body nuts and/or bolts.
2. Loosen the wheel lug nuts, then raise and safely support the vehicle.
3. Place jackstands under the front subframe. Lower the vehicle slightly so the weight of the vehicle rests on the jackstands and NOT the control arms.

4. Remove the wheel and tire assembly.
5. Before removing front suspension components, their positions should be marked so they may assemble correctly.

✱✱ WARNING

Whenever working near the drive axles, use care to prevent damage from over extension of the drive shaft joints. When either end of the shaft is disconnected, over extension of the joint could result in separation of the internal components and possible joint failure.

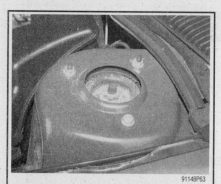

91148P63

Fig. 15 Remove the two strut-to-body nuts and the strut-to-body bolt

91148P37

Fig. 16 The tie rod end connects the steering gear to the steering knuckle

91148P04

Fig. 17 Remove the cotter pin from the tie rod end and . . .

91148P05

Fig. 18 . . . remove the retaining nut from the tie rod end

91148P06

Fig. 19 A special puller is recommended for removing the tie rod end from the steering knuckle without damaging the tie rod end

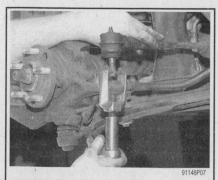

91148P07

Fig. 20 Remove the tie rod end from the steering knuckle

FRONT SUSPENSION COMPONENT LOCATIONS

1. Lower ball joint
2. Strut assembly
3. Sway bar link
4. Steering rack
5. Subframe
6. Lower control arm

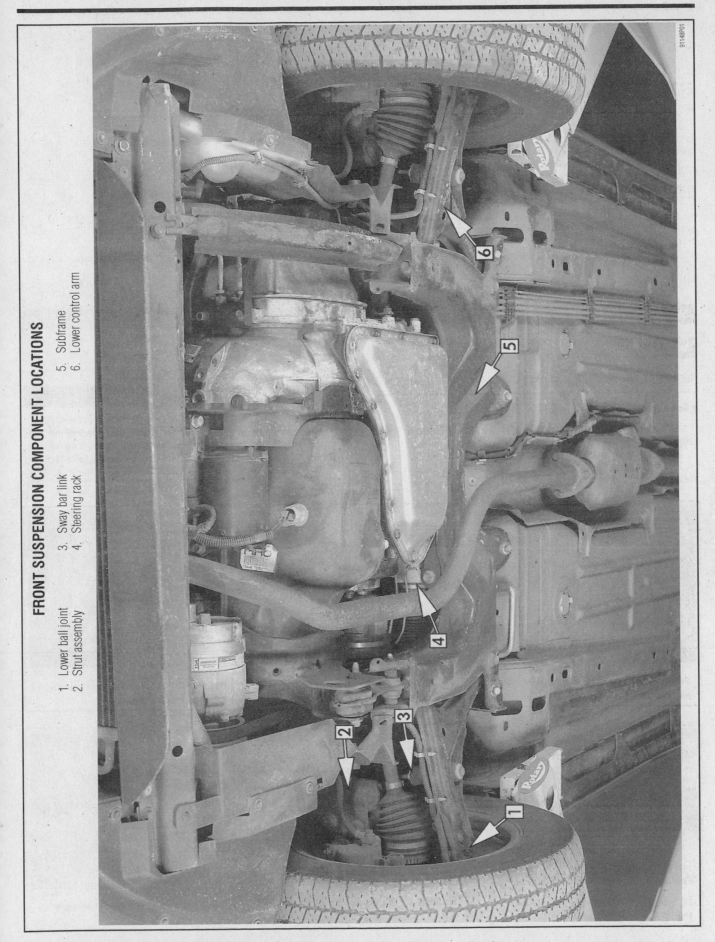

6. If necessary, remove the brake line bracket.

7. Remove the cotter pin and nut, then press the tie rod out of the strut bracket an appropriate puller. Discard the cotter pin.

8. Unfasten and remove the strut-to-steering knuckle bolts and carefully lift out the strut.

➡ The steering knuckle MUST be supported to prevent axle joint overextension.

9. Remove the strut assembly from the vehicle. Be careful to avoid chipping or cracking the spring coating when handling the front suspension coil spring assembly.

To install:

10. Move the strut into position, then install the nuts and/or bolts connecting the strut assembly to the body.

11. Align the steering knuckle with the strut flange scribe mark made during removal, then install the bolts and nuts. Tighten to 133 ft. lbs. (180 Nm).

12. Position the tie rod end into the strut assembly, then secure with the tie rod end bolt and new cotter pin. Tighten the tie rod end bolt to 44 ft. lbs. (60 Nm).

13. Tighten the nuts and/or bolts attaching the top of the strut to the body to 18–20 ft. lbs. (25–27 Nm).

14. Install the brake line bracket.

15. Slightly raise the vehicle, then remove the jackstands from under the suspension supports.

16. Install the tire and wheel assembly.

17. Carefully lower the vehicle, then final tighten the lug nuts to 100 ft. lbs. (140 Nm).

OVERHAUL

♦ **See Figures 25 thru 35**

1. Remove the strut assembly from the vehicle, as outlined earlier in this Section.

2. Mount the strut assembly into a suitable spring compressor.

3. Compress the strut approximately ½ its height after initial contact with the top cap.

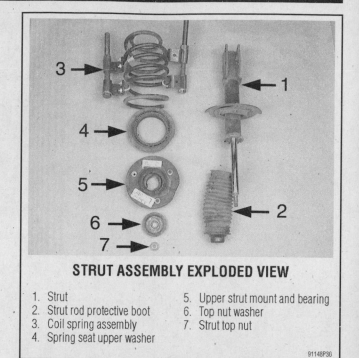

STRUT ASSEMBLY EXPLODED VIEW

1. Strut	5. Upper strut mount and bearing
2. Strut rod protective boot	6. Top nut washer
3. Coil spring assembly	7. Strut top nut
4. Spring seat upper washer	

91148P36

✳✳ WARNING

Never bottom the spring or dampener rod!

4. Remove the nut from the strut dampener shaft using an appropriate tool and place alignment/guiding rod J-34013–27 on top of the dampener shaft. Use the rod to guide the dampener shaft straight down through the spring cap while compressing the spring. Remove the components.

Fig. 21 Loosen the strut-to-steering knuckle mounting bolts

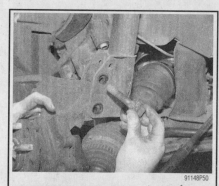

Fig. 22 Remove the strut-to-steering knuckle mounting bolts and . . .

Fig. 23 . . . separate the strut from the steering knuckle and . . .

Fig. 24 . . . remove the strut from the vehicle

Fig. 25 Install a suitable strut spring compressor onto the strut spring

Fig. 26 Tighten down the nuts on the top of the forcing screws on this type of spring compressor

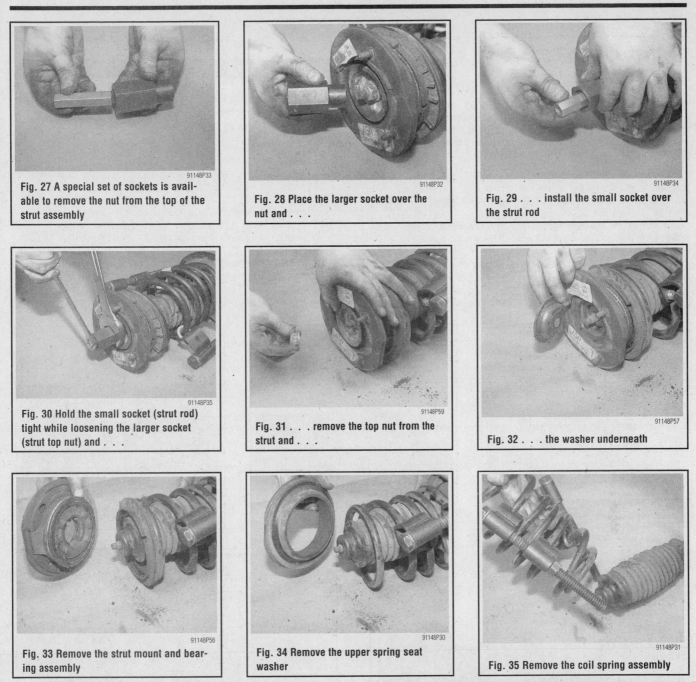

Fig. 27 A special set of sockets is available to remove the nut from the top of the strut assembly

91148P33

Fig. 28 Place the larger socket over the nut and . . .

91148P32

Fig. 29 . . . install the small socket over the strut rod

91148P34

Fig. 30 Hold the small socket (strut rod) tight while loosening the larger socket (strut top nut) and . . .

91148P35

Fig. 31 . . . remove the top nut from the strut and . . .

91148P59

Fig. 32 . . . the washer underneath

91148P57

Fig. 33 Remove the strut mount and bearing assembly

91148P56

Fig. 34 Remove the upper spring seat washer

91148P30

Fig. 35 Remove the coil spring assembly

91148P31

➡️Be careful to avoid chipping or cracking the spring coating when handling the front suspension coil spring assembly.

To install:

5. Extend the dampener shaft and install clamp J-34013–20 on the dampener shaft.

6. Install the spring over the strut.

7. Install all shields, bumpers and insulators on the spring seat. Install the spring seat on top of the spring. Be sure the flat on the upper spring seat is facing in the proper direction. The spring seat flat should be facing the same direction as the centerline of the strut assembly steering knuckle.

8. Install the guiding rod and turn the forcing screw on the spring compressor while the guiding rod centers the assembly. When the threads on the dampener shaft are visible, remove the guiding rod and install the nut.

9. Tighten the nut to 52 ft. lbs. (70 Nm).

10. Remove the clamp.

11. Install the strut into the vehicle.

Lower Ball Joint

INSPECTION

1. Raise and safely support the vehicles on jackstands. Allow the suspension to hang free.

2. Grasp the tire at the top and the bottom and move the top of the tire in and out.

3. Observe for any horizontal movement of the steering knuckle relative to the front lower control arm. If any movement is detected, replace the ball joint.

4. If the ball stud is disconnected from the steering knuckle and any looseness is detected, or if the ball stud can be twisted in its socket using finger pressure, replace the ball joint.

REMOVAL & INSTALLATION

▶ **See Figures 36, 37, 38, 39 and 40**

1. Raise and safely support the vehicle.
2. Remove the tire and wheel assembly.

➡**Care must be exercised to prevent the axle shaft joints from being over-extended. When either end of the shaft is disconnected, over-extension of the joint could result in separation of internal components and possible joint failure. Failure to observe this can result in interior joint or boot damage and possible joint failure.**

3. Disconnect the stabilizer link from the control arm.
4. Remove the cotter pin and nut from the ball joint.
5. Separate the ball joint from the steering knuckle using an appropriate tool.
6. Drill out the 3 rivets retaining ball joint to the lower control arm. Use an ⅛ in. (3mm) drill bit to make a pilot hole through the rivets. Finish drilling rivets with a ½ in. (13mm) drill bit.
7. Remove the ball joint from the control arm.

To install:

8. Install ball joint into the control arm.
9. Install 3 new bolts and nuts (supplied with new ball joint) and tighten.

13. Lower the vehicle.
14. Check front wheel alignment and adjust, if necessary.

Stabilizer Bar

REMOVAL & INSTALLATION

▶ **See Figures 41 and 42**

The stabilizer bar attaches to the front suspension support (subframe) and through a bolt and link, connects the lower control arms.

1. Raise and safely support vehicle and allow vehicle suspension to hang free.
2. Remove the front tire and wheel assemblies.
3. Remove the nuts attaching stabilizer bar to stabilizer links.
4. Remove the clamps attaching stabilizer bar to the subframe.
5. Support the rear of the subframe with adjustable safety stands.
6. Remove the rear and center bolts from subframe assembly and loosen the front bolts.
7. Lower the subframe 3 inches by adjusting the safety stands down.
8. Remove the stabilizer bar with insulators.

To install:

9. Place stabilizer bar with insulators into vehicle and hand-tighten.

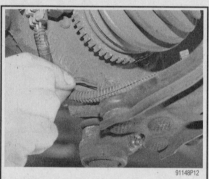

Fig. 36 Remove the cotter pin from the lower ball joint and . . .

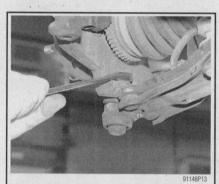

Fig. 37 . . . using a wrench, loosen and remove the ball joint retaining nut

Fig. 38 Use a suitable prytool to remove the lower ball joint/control arm from the steering knuckle

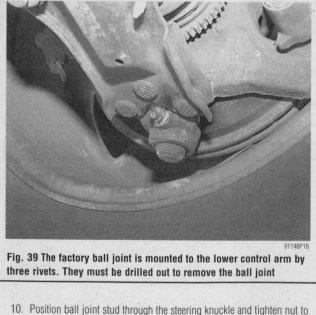

Fig. 39 The factory ball joint is mounted to the lower control arm by three rivets. They must be drilled out to remove the ball joint

10. Position ball joint stud through the steering knuckle and tighten nut to 41 ft. lbs. (55 Nm) and install a new cotter pin.
11. Connect the stabilizer link to stabilizer bar and tighten the nut to 13 ft. lbs. (17 Nm).
12. Install tire and wheel assembly.

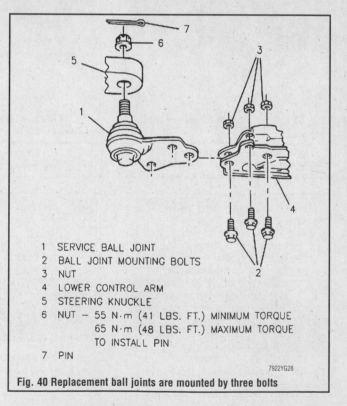

1	SERVICE BALL JOINT
2	BALL JOINT MOUNTING BOLTS
3	NUT
4	LOWER CONTROL ARM
5	STEERING KNUCKLE
6	NUT — 55 N·m (41 LBS. FT.) MINIMUM TORQUE
	65 N·m (48 LBS. FT.) MAXIMUM TORQUE TO INSTALL PIN
7	PIN

Fig. 40 Replacement ball joints are mounted by three bolts

10. Install the clamps attaching stabilizer bar to subframe assemblies and hand-tighten.

11. Install the subframe assemblies into position and install bolts (hand-tighten).

12. Tighten subframe bolts left rear outboard first, right rear outboard second, front upper third and rear inboard last.
   a. Tighten the left rear outboard to 96 ft. lbs. (130 Nm).
   b. Tighten the right rear outboard to 96 ft. lbs. (130 Nm).
   c. Tighten the front upper bolts to 96 ft. lbs. (130 Nm).
   d. Tighten the rear inboard bolts to 96 ft. lbs. (130 Nm).

13. Tighten the stabilizer-to-subframe clamp bolts to subframe to 49 ft. lbs. (66 Nm).

14. Tighten the stabilizer bar links to control arm nuts. Tighten the nuts to 13 ft. lbs. (17 Nm).

Fig. 41 The stabilizer bar link is mounted to the lower control arm

15. Install the tire and wheel assemblies.
16. Lower the vehicle.
17. Check wheel alignment and adjust as necessary.

Lower Control Arm

REMOVAL & INSTALLATION

▶ **See Figures 43, 44, 45, 46 and 47**

1. Raise and safely support vehicle.
2. Remove the tire and wheel assembly.
3. Remove the nut attaching the stabilizer link to stabilizer bar.
4. Remove the ball joint cotter pin and nut.

➡**Care must be exercised to prevent the axle shaft joints from being over-extended. When either end of the shaft is disconnected, over-extension of the joint could result in separation of internal components and possible joint failure. Failure to observe this can result in interior joint or boot damage and possible joint failure.**

5. Remove the ball joint from the steering knuckle using a suitable tool.
6. Remove the bolts attaching control arm to subframe.
7. Remove the control arm from the vehicle.

To install:

8. Install control arm into position and install bolts (leave loose to allow movement) attaching control arm to subframe.

9. Install the ball joint stud into the steering knuckle and install nut finger-tight.

10. Tighten the ball joint nut to 41 ft. lbs. (55 Nm) and install cotter pin.

11. Connect the stabilizer link to stabilizer bar and tighten the nut to 13 ft. lbs. (17 Nm).

12. Install tire and wheel assembly.

13. Lower the vehicle. Tighten the wheel lug nuts to 100 ft. lbs. (140 Nm).

14. With vehicle at curb height, tighten control arm bolts as follows:
   a. Tighten the front control arm to subframe bolt to 90 ft. lbs. (125 Nm).
   b. Tighten the rear control arm to subframe bolt to 125 ft. lbs. (170 Nm).

15. Check wheel alignment and adjust as necessary.

Fig. 42 The stabilizer bar-to-subframe mounting

Fig. 43 The stabilizer bar link is mounted to the lower control arm

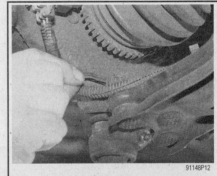
Fig. 44 Remove the cotter pin from the lower ball joint and . . .

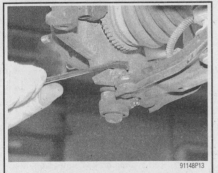
Fig. 45 . . . using a wrench, loosen and remove the ball joint retaining nut

Fig. 46 Use a suitable prytool to remove the lower ball joint/control arm from the steering knuckle

Fig. 47 The control arm-to-subframe mounting bolts

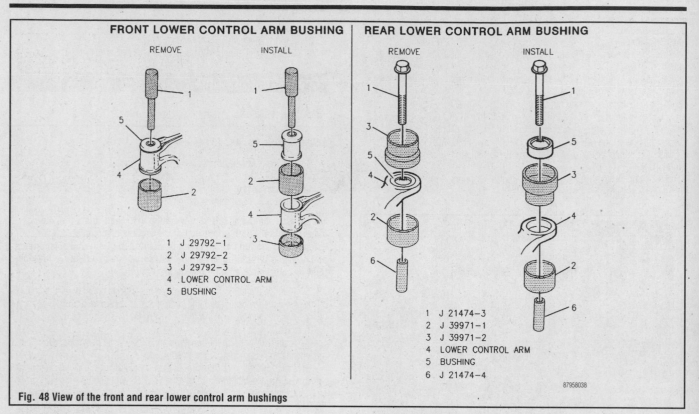

Fig. 48 View of the front and rear lower control arm bushings

CONTROL ARM BUSHING REPLACEMENT

▶ **See Figure 48**

1. Remove the lower control arm as outlined earlier in this section.
2. Install bushing removal tools J 29792 or equivalent.
3. Coat the threads of the tool with extreme pressure lubricant.
4. Remove the lower control arm bushings.

To install:

5. Install the bushing installation tools.
6. Coat the outer case of the bushing with a light coating of a suitable lubricant, then install the lower control arm bushings.
7. As outlined earlier, install the lower control arm.

Steering Knuckle and Spindle

REMOVAL & INSTALLATION

▶ **See Figures 49 thru 62**

1. Raise and safely support the vehicle.
2. Remove the tire and wheel assembly.

3. Remove the drive axle nut.
4. Remove the brake caliper bolts and support the brake caliper to the side.
5. Remove the brake rotor.
6. Detach the wheel speed sensor connector if equipped.
7. Remove the cotter pin and nut, then press the tie rod out of the strut bracket using an appropriate tie rod end puller. Discard the cotter pin.
8. Remove the cotter pin from the ball joint and remove the ball joint-to-steering knuckle nut. Separate the ball joint from the steering knuckle using an appropriate tool.
9. Support the steering knuckle and unfasten and remove the strut-to-steering knuckle bolts and carefully separate the knuckle from the strut.
10. Remove the steering knuckle from the vehicle.

To install:

11. If replacing the steering knuckle, transfer the hub and bearing assembly and the wheel speed sensor (if equipped) to the new steering knuckle.
12. Place the steering knuckle into position and install the knuckle-to-strut bolts finger-tight.
13. Position the ball joint into the knuckle and install the ball joint nut..
14. Tighten the knuckle-to-strut bolts to 133 ft. lbs. (180 Nm).
15. Tighten the ball joint nut to 41 ft. lbs. (55 Nm). Install a new cotter pin into the ball joint.
16. Install the brake rotor.

Fig. 49 Remove the hub nut from the axle shaft and . . .

Fig. 50 . . . the washer behind it

Fig. 51 Remove the brake caliper from the hub assembly and support it using mechanic's wire or another suitable device

Fig. 52 Remove the rotor from the hub assembly

Fig. 53 The tie rod end connects the steering gear to the steering knuckle

Fig. 54 Remove the cotter pin from the tie rod end and . . .

Fig. 55 . . . remove the retaining nut from the tie rod end

Fig. 56 A special puller is recommended for removing the tie rod end from the steering knuckle without damaging the tie rod end

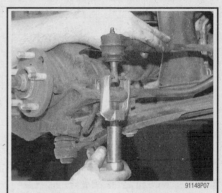

Fig. 57 Remove the tie rod end from the steering knuckle

Fig. 58 Remove the cotter pin from the lower ball joint and . . .

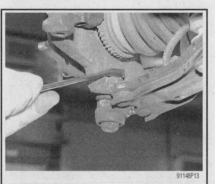

Fig. 59 . . . using a wrench, loosen and remove the ball joint retaining nut

Fig. 60 Use a suitable prytool to remove the lower ball joint/control arm from the steering knuckle

Fig. 61 Remove the strut-to-steering knuckle mounting bolts and . . .

Fig. 62 . . . separate the strut from the steering knuckle and remove the knuckle

Fig. 63 Remove the hub nut from the axle shaft and . . .

17. Install the brake caliper and bolts.
18. Attach the wheel speed sensor connector.
19. Install the axle nut and tighten it to 185 ft. lbs. (260 Nm).
20. Install the tire and wheel assembly.
21. Lower the vehicle.
22. Road test the vehicle and verify proper operation.

Front Hub and Bearing

REMOVAL & INSTALLATION

▸ **See Figures 63 thru 70**

1. Raise and safely support the vehicle.
2. Remove the tire and wheel assembly.
3. Remove the drive axle nut.

Fig. 64 . . . the washer behind it

Fig. 65 Remove the brake caliper from the hub assembly and support it using mechanic's wire or another suitable device

Fig. 66 Remove the rotor from the hub assembly

Fig. 67 The hub retaining bolts are accessible through the hole in the hub

Fig. 68 Remove the hub retaining bolts

Fig. 69 After removing the axle nut and the hub retaining bolts, pull the hub straight out to remove it

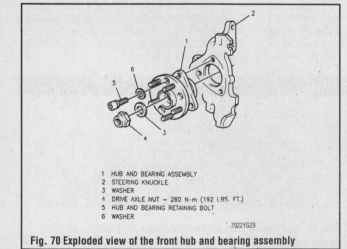

1 HUB AND BEARING ASSEMBLY
2 STEERING KNUCKLE
3 WASHER
4 DRIVE AXLE NUT — 260 N·m (192 LBS. FT.)
5 HUB AND BEARING RETAINING BOLT
6 WASHER

7922YG29

Fig. 70 Exploded view of the front hub and bearing assembly

4. Remove the brake caliper bolts and support the brake caliper to the side.
5. Remove the brake rotor.
6. Remove the 3 bolts that go through the steering knuckle from the back of the knuckle. Rust buildup may require a generous application of penetrating oil where the hub fits into the knuckle.
7. Remove the hub and bearing assembly from the steering knuckle.

To install:

8. Install hub and bearing assembly to steering knuckle while carefully inserting the drive axle through hub assembly.
9. Install hub and bearing bolts and tighten to 70 ft. lbs. (95 Nm).
10. Install the brake rotor.
11. Install the brake caliper and bolts.
12. Install the axle nut and tighten it to 185 ft. lbs. (260 Nm).
13. Install the tire and wheel assembly and tighten the lugnuts to 100 ft. lbs. (140 Nm).
14. Lower the vehicle.
15. Road test the vehicle and verify proper operation.

Wheel Alignment

If the tires are worn unevenly, if the vehicle is not stable on the highway or if the handling seems uneven in spirited driving, the wheel alignment should be checked. If an alignment problem is suspected, first check for improper tire inflation and other possible causes. These can be worn suspension or steering components, accident damage or even unmatched tires. If any worn or damaged components are found, they must be replaced before the wheels can be properly aligned. Wheel alignment requires very expensive equipment and involves minute adjustments which must be accurate; it should only be performed by a trained technician. Take your vehicle to a properly equipped shop.

Following is a description of the alignment angles which are adjustable on most vehicles and how they affect vehicle handling. Although these angles can apply to both the front and rear wheels, usually only the front suspension is adjustable.

CASTER

▶ See Figure 71

Looking at a vehicle from the side, caster angle describes the steering axis rather than a wheel angle. The steering knuckle is attached to a control arm or strut at the top and a control arm at the bottom. The wheel pivots around the line between these points to steer the vehicle. When the upper point is tilted back, this is described as positive caster. Having a positive caster tends to make the wheels self-centering, increasing directional stability. Excessive positive caster makes the wheels hard to steer, while an uneven caster will cause a pull to one side. Overloading the vehicle or sagging rear springs will affect caster, as will raising the rear of the vehicle. If the rear of the vehicle is lower than normal, the caster becomes more positive.

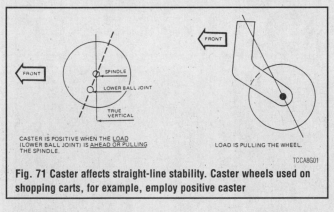

CASTER IS POSITIVE WHEN THE LOAD (LOWER BALL JOINT) IS AHEAD OR PULLING THE SPINDLE.

LOAD IS PULLING THE WHEEL.

TCCA8G01

Fig. 71 Caster affects straight-line stability. Caster wheels used on shopping carts, for example, employ positive caster

CAMBER

▶ See Figure 72

Looking from the front of the vehicle, camber is the inward or outward tilt of the top of wheels. When the tops of the wheels are tilted in, this is negative camber; if they are tilted out, it is positive. In a turn, a slight amount of negative camber helps maximize contact of the tire with the road. However, too much negative camber compromises straight-line stability, increases bump steer and torque steer.

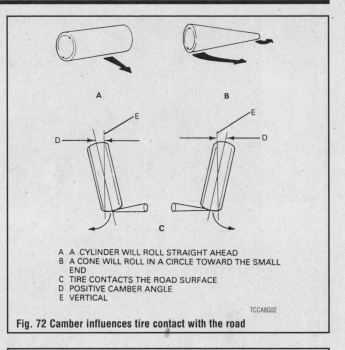

A A CYLINDER WILL ROLL STRAIGHT AHEAD
B A CONE WILL ROLL IN A CIRCLE TOWARD THE SMALL END
C TIRE CONTACTS THE ROAD SURFACE
D POSITIVE CAMBER ANGLE
E VERTICAL

TCCA8G02

Fig. 72 Camber influences tire contact with the road

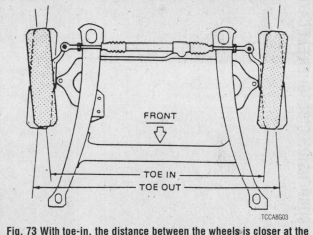

TCCA8G03

Fig. 73 With toe-in, the distance between the wheels is closer at the front than at the rear

TOE

▶ See Figure 73

Looking down at the wheels from above the vehicle, toe angle is the distance between the front of the wheels, relative to the distance between the back of the wheels. If the wheels are closer at the front, they are said to be toed-in or to have negative toe. A small amount of negative toe enhances directional stability and provides a smoother ride on the highway.

REAR SUSPENSION

Coil-Over Shocks

REMOVAL & INSTALLATION

▶ See Figures 74 thru 82

➡**Do not remove both shock absorbers at one time. Suspending the rear axle at full length could result in damage to brake lines and/or hoses.**

1. Open the trunk lid.
2. Remove the trim to access the coil-over shock retaining nut.
3. Remove the coil-over shock absorber retaining nut.
4. Raise and safely support the vehicle.
5. Support the rear axle with safety stands.
6. Remove the bolts from the coil-over shock upper mount.
7. Remove coil-over shock lower mount through bolt.
8. Remove the coil-over shock.

To install:

9. Install coil-over shock absorber at the lower attachment. Install bolt hand-tight.
10. Install bolts to the coil-over shock mount.
11. Lower the vehicle.

REAR SUSPENSION COMPONENT LOCATIONS

1. Hub and bearing assembly
2. Shock lower mount
3. Rear crossmember (axle)
4. Coil-over shock assembly

Fig. 74 Pull back the trim to access the . . .

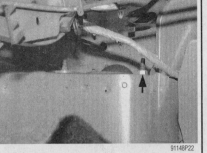

Fig. 75 . . . one retaining nut for the rear coil-over shocks. The other two bolts are accessible from underneath the vehicle

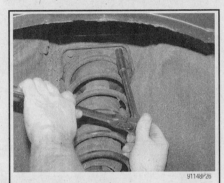

Fig. 76 Remove the retaining nut

Fig. 77 Support the rear suspension on the subframe under the lower shock mount

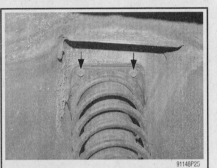

Fig. 78 The shock is retained by two bolts on the top mount accessible from underneath

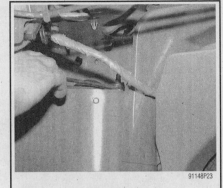

Fig. 79 Remove the two bolts on the upper mount

Fig. 80 Loosen the through bolt for the lower shock mount

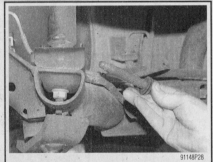

Fig. 81 Remove the bolt and carefully loosen the shock from the lower mount and . . .

Fig. 82 . . . remove the shock from the vehicle

12. Install the coil-over shock upper mount attaching nut.
13. Tighten the lower mount through bolt to 125 ft. lbs. (170 Nm).
14. Tighten the coil-over shock upper mount bolts to 21 ft. lbs. (28 Nm).
15. Remove the safety stands and lower the vehicle.
16. Tighten the upper coil-over shock retaining nut to 15 ft. lbs. (20 Nm).
17. Install the trim.
18. Road test the vehicle.

Rear Control Arm/Axle

REMOVAL & INSTALLATION

▶ **See Figures 83, 84 and 85**

1. Raise and safely support the vehicle. Support the rear axle with jackstands.
2. Remove the rear tire and wheel assembly.
3. Disconnect the brake line at the brackets from the axle assembly. This will ensure that the axle assembly is not suspended by the brake lines.

4. Unfasten the lower shock mount bolt.
5. Lower the rear axle.
6. Disconnect the parking brake cable at the equalizer unit right wheel assembly.
7. If equipped, detach the rear ABS wiring connector and mount clip located near the fuel tank.
8. Disconnect the right and left brake lines.
9. Unfasten the axle-to-body mount bolts and nuts, then remove the axle assembly.
To install:
10. Position the rear axle assembly and loosely install the axle-to-body mount bolts and nuts.
11. Connect the right and left brake lines.
12. Attach the ABS wiring connector and mount clip.
13. Fasten the parking brake cable at the right rear wheel cable connector and cable equalizer.
14. Install the lower mount bolt. Tighten the axle-to-body mount bolts and nuts to 52 ft. lbs. (70 Nm) plus a 120° rotation. Tighten the shock absorber lower attaching bolt and nut to 125 ft. lbs. (170 Nm).

15. Fasten the left and right side brake line bracket mount bolts to the body. Tighten the screws to 97 inch lbs. (11 Nm).

16. Install the tire and wheel assembly, then remove the jackstands from under the vehicle.

17. Carefully lower the vehicle, then bleed the brake system, as outlined in Section 9 of this manual.

Fig. 83 Loosen the through bolt for the lower shock mount

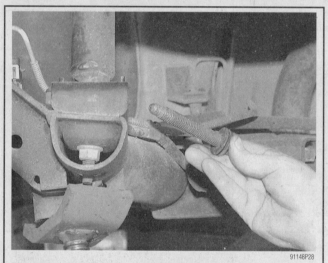

Fig. 84 Remove the bolt and carefully loosen the shock from the lower mount

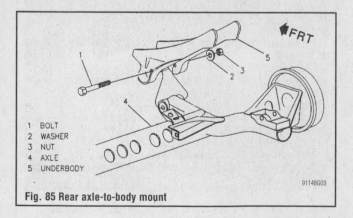

1 BOLT
2 WASHER
3 NUT
4 AXLE
5 UNDERBODY

Fig. 85 Rear axle-to-body mount

Hub and Bearings

REMOVAL & INSTALLATION

▶ **See Figures 86, 87, 88, 89 and 90**

A single-unit hub and bearing assembly is bolted to both ends of the rear axle assembly or rear knuckle assembly. This hub and bearing is a sealed unit which is supposed to eliminate the need for wheel bearing adjustments and does not require periodic maintenance.

1. Raise and safely support vehicle.
2. Remove the wheel and tire assembly.
3. Remove the brake drum.
4. Disconnect the ABS wheel speed sensor wire connector.
5. Remove the hub and bearing assembly mounting bolts. The top rear mounting bolt will not clear the brake shoe when removing the hub and bearing assembly. Partially remove the hub and bearing assembly prior to removing this bolt.
6. Remove the hub and bearing assembly from the axle.

Fig. 86 Detach the connector for the rear wheel speed sensor

Fig. 87 The hub retaining bolts are accessible through a hole in the hub flange

Fig. 88 The hub retaining bolt nuts are accessible from behind the wheel

Fig. 89 Insert a suitable tool through the hole in the hub flange and hold the retaining nut tight on the back of the hub, loosen the retaining bolts

Fig. 90 Remove the hub and bearing assembly from the vehicle

To install:

7. Install the hub and bearing assembly. Position the top rear mounting bolt in the hub and bearing assembly prior to installation to the axle housing.

8. Tighten the mounting bolts to 44 ft. lbs. (60 Nm).

9. Attach the rear ABS wheel speed sensor wire connector.

10. Install the brake drum.

11. Install the wheel and tire assembly. Tighten the lug nuts to 100 ft. lbs. (140 Nm).

12. Lower the vehicle.

13. Road test the vehicle.

STEERING

Steering Wheel

REMOVAL & INSTALLATION

▶ See Figures 91 thru 101

> ### ⁜ CAUTION
>
> The Supplemental Inflatable Restraint (SIR) system must be disarmed before removing the steering wheel. Failure to do so may cause accidental deployment of the air bag, resulting in unnecessary SIR system repairs and/or personal injury.

1. Properly disable the SIR (air bag) system. Refer to Section 6.

2. Remove the 2 screws from the back of the steering wheel that retain the air bag module. Disconnect the module CPA and electrical connection from the rear of the air bag module and remove the module. Set module aside.

> ### ⁜ CAUTION
>
> When carrying a live air bag, make sure the bag and trim cover are pointed away from the body. In the unlikely event of an accidental deployment, the air bag will then deploy with minimal chance of injury. When placing a live air bag on a bench or other surface,

always face the bag and trim cover up, away from the surface. This will reduce the motion of the module if it is accidentally deployed.

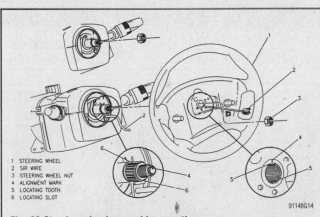

1 STEERING WHEEL
2 SIR WIRE
3 STEERING WHEEL NUT
4 ALIGNMENT MARK
5 LOCATING TOOTH
6 LOCATING SLOT

Fig. 92 Steering wheel assembly mounting

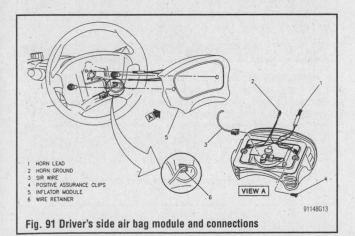

1 HORN LEAD
2 HORN GROUND
3 SIR WIRE
4 POSITIVE ASSURANCE CLIPS
5 INFLATOR MODULE
6 WIRE RETAINER

VIEW A

Fig. 91 Driver's side air bag module and connections

Fig. 93 The air bag is retained by two screws located in access holes on the back of the wheel

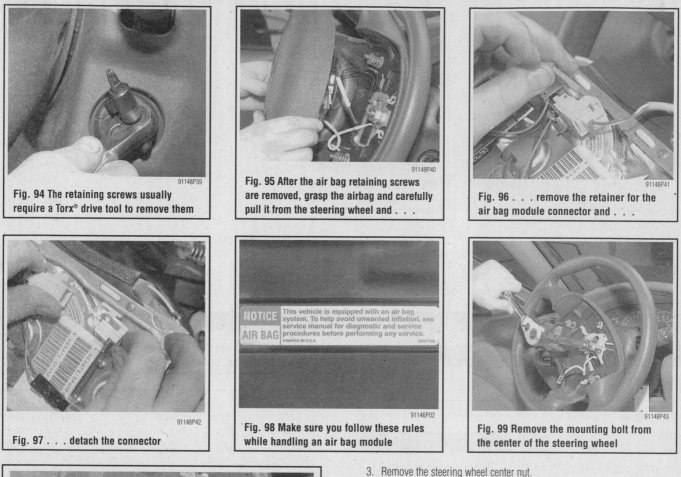

Fig. 94 The retaining screws usually require a Torx® drive tool to remove them

Fig. 95 After the air bag retaining screws are removed, grasp the airbag and carefully pull it from the steering wheel and . . .

Fig. 96 . . . remove the retainer for the air bag module connector and . . .

Fig. 97 . . . detach the connector

Fig. 98 Make sure you follow these rules while handling an air bag module

Fig. 99 Remove the mounting bolt from the center of the steering wheel

NOTICE AIR BAG This vehicle is equipped with an air bag system. To help avoid unwanted inflation, see service manual for diagnostic and service procedures before performing any service. PRINTED IN U.S.A.

Fig. 100 Install a suitable steering wheel puller and tighten down on the puller until . . .

Fig. 101 . . . the wheel separates from the steering column and then remove the steering wheel

3. Remove the steering wheel center nut.
4. Use a suitable steering wheel puller and remove the steering wheel from the steering column.
   To install:
5. Align the mark on the steering wheel with the mark on the shaft then install the steering wheel. Install the center nut and torque to 30 ft. lbs. (41 Nm).
6. Install the air bag module using care when making the horn and air bag connections. The air bag module retaining screws should be tightened to 89 inch lbs. (10 Nm).
7. Properly enable the air bag system.
8. Connect the negative battery cable.

Headlight/Turn Signal/Cruise/Hazard (Combination) Switch

REMOVAL & INSTALLATION

▶ See Figures 102 and 103

❈❈ CAUTION

The Supplemental Inflatable Restraint (SIR) system must be disarmed before working around the steering column. Failure to do so may cause accidental deployment of the air bag, resulting in unnecessary SIR system repairs and/or personal injury.

1. If equipped, disable the SIR system. Disconnect the negative battery cable.
2. Remove the upper steering column cover.
3. Remove the lower steering column cover screws and lower the steering column cover.
4. Remove the 2 switch mounting screws and remove the switch.
5. Detach all wire connectors from the combination switch. Push locking tabs to remove the wires.

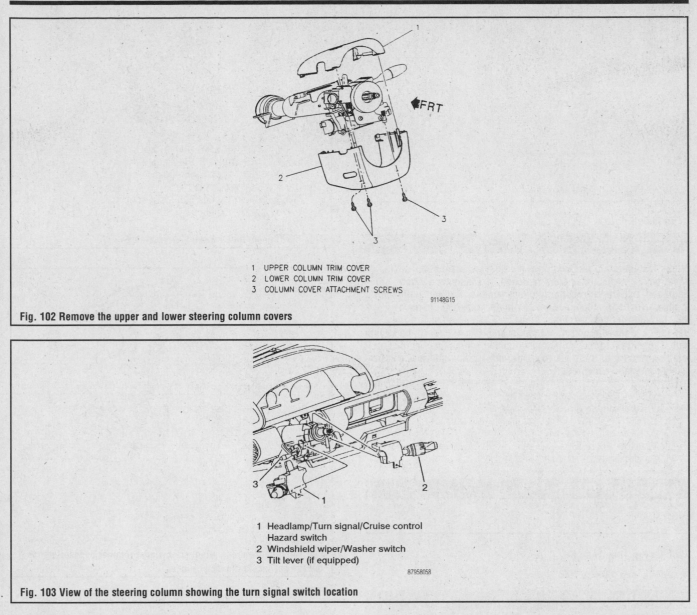

1 UPPER COLUMN TRIM COVER
2 LOWER COLUMN TRIM COVER
3 COLUMN COVER ATTACHMENT SCREWS

91148G15

Fig. 102 Remove the upper and lower steering column covers

1 Headlamp/Turn signal/Cruise control
   Hazard switch
2 Windshield wiper/Washer switch
3 Tilt lever (if equipped)

87958058

Fig. 103 View of the steering column showing the turn signal switch location

To install:
6. Attach all wire connectors to the combination switch.
7. Install the combination switch to the column with the 2 attaching screws.
8. Install the lower steering column cover screws and lower steering column cover.
9. Install the upper steering column cover and attaching screws.
10. Connect the negative battery cable.
11. Enable the SIR system, if equipped.

Windshield Wiper Switch

REMOVAL & INSTALLATION

▶ **See Figures 102 and 103**

1. If equipped, disable the SIR system. For details, please refer to the procedure located in Section 6 of this manual.
2. Disconnect the negative battery cable.
3. Remove the steering wheel from the column, as outlined in this Section.
4. If equipped, remove the tilt lever from the steering column.
5. Remove the upper and lower steering column covers.
6. Remove the dampener assembly.

7. Remove the headlight switch assembly, then remove the windshield wiper switch assembly.
8. Installation is the reverse of the removal procedure.

Ignition Switch

REMOVAL & INSTALLATION

▶ **See Figure 104**

❊❊ **CAUTION**

The Supplemental Inflatable Restraint (SIR) system must be disarmed before working around the steering column. Failure to do may cause accidental deployment of the air bag, resulting in unnecessary SIR system repairs and/or personal injury.

1. Disconnect the negative battery cable.
2. If equipped, disable the SIR system.
3. Remove the steering column.
4. The ignition switch is located at the base of the steering column. Disconnect the vehicle wire harness from the ignition switch.
5. Unfasten the mounting screws, then remove the ignition switch assembly.

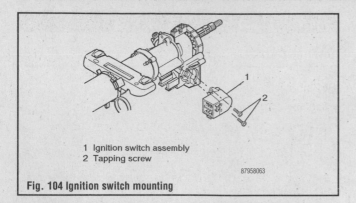

1 Ignition switch assembly
2 Tapping screw

87958063

Fig. 104 Ignition switch mounting

To install:

6. Position the ignition switch assembly.
7. Install and tighten the 2 mounting screws.
8. Connect the vehicle wire harness to the switch assembly.
9. Install the steering column.
10. Enable the SIR system.
11. Connect the negative battery cable.

Ignition Lock Cylinder

REMOVAL & INSTALLATION

Without Key (Key Lost)/Key Code

▶ See Figures 105 and 106

1. Disconnect the negative battery cable.

2. Remove the left side sound insulators from under the dash.
3. Remove the upper and lower steering column covers.
4. Remove the PASSLOCK® cylinder wire from the connector on Cavalier Z 24 and Sunfire GT models.
5. Remove the tilt lever from the steering column by twisting it counterclockwise.
6. Remove the defroster grille (Sunfire snaps out, Cavalier has 1 screw).

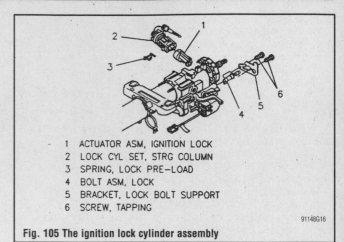

1 ACTUATOR ASM, IGNITION LOCK
2 LOCK CYL SET, STRG COLUMN
3 SPRING, LOCK PRE-LOAD
4 BOLT ASM, LOCK
5 BRACKET, LOCK BOLT SUPPORT
6 SCREW, TAPPING

91148G16

Fig. 105 The ignition lock cylinder assembly

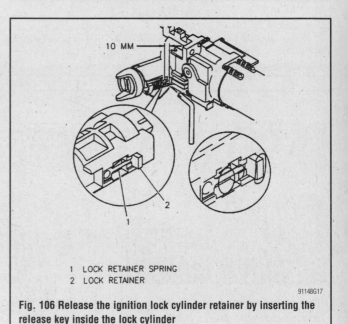

10 MM

1 LOCK RETAINER SPRING
2 LOCK RETAINER

91148G17

Fig. 106 Release the ignition lock cylinder retainer by inserting the release key inside the lock cylinder

7. Remove the instrument panel (IP) end trim covers (Cavalier snaps out, Sunfire has 1 screw).
8. On all Cavalier models:
   a. Remove the 8 retaining screws and the IP trim pad.
   b. Remove the IP trim plate.
9. On all Sunfire models:
   a. Remove the IP valance.
10. Remove the IP center trim panel.
    a. Remove the IP compartment panel and unplug the wiring harness.
    b. Remove the IP trim pad.
11. Remove the instrument cluster assembly.
12. Remove the steering column assembly.
13. Drill the back of the ignition lock cylinder housing using a 9/32 drill bit.
14. Insert tool J-41253 into the hole and engage retainer spring.
15. Twist tool J-41253 to remove the retainer spring.
16. Remove the ignition lock cylinder.
17. Hold the steering column vertical and tap on the housing to dislodge the retainer spring and remove any metal shavings.
To install:
18. Code new lock cylinder.
19. Place the new lock cylinder into the steering column (it will not go all the way in yet).
20. Install the key into the lock cylinder.
21. Ensure the key is in the **RUN** position.
22. Line up locking tab with the slot in the column and push the lock cylinder into the column

23. Install the steering column into the vehicle.
24. The balance of the installation is the reverse of removal.
25. Connect the negative battery cable.
26. Enable the SIR system.
27. Test the turn signals, high beams and wipers.
28. Install the lower sound insulator.

With Key

1. If equipped, disable the SIR system. For details, please refer to the procedure located in Section 6 of this manual.
2. Disconnect the negative battery cable.
3. If equipped, remove the tilt lever from the steering column by gripping the lever and twisting counterclockwise.
4. Remove the upper and lower steering column covers.
5. Turn the lock cylinder to the **RUN** position.
6. Push against the locking button on the back side of the bearing and housing assembly and remove the lock cylinder.

To install:
7. Rotate the lock cylinder to the **RUN** position.
8. Depress the lock cylinder button.
9. Carefully push the lock cylinder into place while rotating the key approximately 5° in the counterclockwise direction.
10. Install the upper and lower column covers.
11. If equipped, install the tilt lever by gently twisting the lever clockwise.
12. Connect the negative battery cable.
13. Enable the SIR system, if equipped.

Steering Linkage

REMOVAL & INSTALLATION

Tie Rod Ends

▶ See Figures 107 thru 115

1. Disconnect the negative battery cable.
2. Remove the wheel and tire assembly.
3. Remove the cotter pin and the castellated nut from the outer tie rod end. Discard the cotter pin.
4. Separate the outer tie rod end from the steering knuckle using an appropriate tie rod end remover.
5. Mark the outer tie rod jam nut on one side with a reference line for installation.
6. Hold the outer tie rod end with a wrench and loosen the tie rod end jam nut.
7. Back the tie rod end jam nut off ONE FULL TURN ONLY.
8. Remove the outer tie rod end from the inner tie rod spindle.

To install:
9. Clean the threads on the inner tie rod spindle (front wheel spindle connecting rod).
10. Thread the new outer tie rod end onto the inner tie rod until it bottoms on the jam nut.
11. Back the tie rod and jam nut out one full turn until the reference line is in the same position as before.

Fig. 107 The tie rod end connects the steering gear to the steering knuckle

Fig. 108 Remove the cotter pin from the tie rod end and . . .

Fig. 109 . . . remove the retaining nut from the tie rod end

Fig. 110 A special puller is recommended for removing the tie rod end from the steering knuckle without damaging the tie rod end

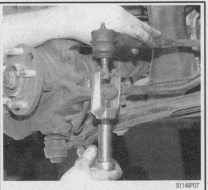

Fig. 111 Remove the tie rod end from the steering knuckle

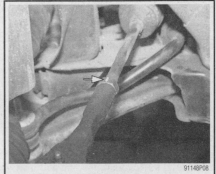

Fig. 112 Mark the outer tie rod jam nut on one side with a reference line for installation

Fig. 113 Use two wrenches, one to hold the inner tie rod, and one to loosen the jam nut

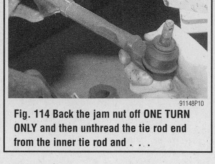

Fig. 114 Back the jam nut off ONE TURN ONLY and then unthread the tie rod end from the inner tie rod and . . .

Fig. 115 . . . remove the tie rod end from the inner tie rod

12. Place the outer tie rod end stud into the steering knuckle. Set the front wheels in a straight ahead position.

13. Install a new castellated nut onto the outer tie rod end stud.

14. Torque the nut to 44 ft. lbs. (60 Nm).

15. Continue to tighten the castellated nut until a new cotter pin can be inserted through the hole in the stud. Install a new cotter pin.

16. If required, repeat the procedure for the opposite side.

17. Reinstall the wheel and tire assembly. Torque the lug nuts to 100 ft. lbs. (140 Nm).

18. Reconnect the negative battery cable.

19. Check the alignment and set the toe adjustment to specification.

20. Torque the outer tie rod end jam nut to 50 ft. lbs. (68 Nm).

Inner Tie Rods

▶ **See Figures 116 thru 121**

1. Remove the rack and pinion (steering gear).

2. Working on one side, remove the outer tie rod end as outlined in this Section.

3. Remove the outer tie rod end jam nut.

4. Remove the outer clamp securing the inner tie rod boot to the rack and pinion.

5. Loosen the larger inner clamp using J-22610 boot clamp pliers or equivalent.

6. Slide back the dampener from the inner tie rod end (toward the rack assembly).

7. Hold the rack with a suitable wrench on the flat while loosening the inner tie rod nut (ball joint nut) with a suitable wrench.

8. Once the inner tie rod is loose, remove by hand.

9. Remove the inner tie rod from the vehicle and inspect the rack and pinion for seal leakage. Replace the rack and pinion if there is excessive leakage from the rack seals.

To install:

10. Install a new inner tie rod assembly.

11. While holding the rack with a suitable wrench nearest the rack end, tighten the inner tie rod nut (ball joint nut) using a suitable wrench to 74 ft. lbs. (100 Nm).

➡**Make sure the tie rod rocks freely in the rack before "staking" it.**

12. Support the rack and inner tie rod and "stake" both sides the inner tie rod, just behind the ball of the tie rod, to the rack assembly. Staking is accomplished by using a blunt instrument to crush a small "slot" in order to prevent the object from coming loose.

13. Inspect the "stakes" by trying to place a 0.010 inch (0.25 mm) feeler gauge between the stakes and the rack. The feeler gauge should not fit.

14. Apply a small amount of grease to the lip of the rack boot where it clamps to the inner tie rod spindle to allow the shaft to turn without twisting the bellows.

15. Install the boot with the larger inner clamp and tighten the clamp using J-22610 boot clamp pliers or equivalent.

16. Install a new outer clamp using needlenose pliers.

17. Install the jam nut onto the tie rod spindle.

18. Apply a small amount of grease to the outer tie rod threads and install the outer tie rod end using the same number of threads recorded during disassembly.

19. Repeat the procedure for the opposite side.

20. Reinstall the rack and pinion.

21. Reconnect the negative battery cable.

22. Check the alignment and set the toe adjustment to specification.

23. Torque the outer tie rod end jam nut to 50 ft. lbs. (68 Nm).

Power Rack and Pinion Steering Gear

REMOVAL & INSTALLATION

▶ **See Figures 122, 123 and 124**

1. Disconnect the negative battery cable.

2. Remove the left side sound insulator under the driver's side of the instrument panel.

3. Remove the upper pinch bolt on the intermediate-shaft assembly.

4. Remove the line retainer, if applicable.

5. Raise and safely support the vehicle.

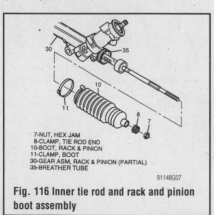

7-NUT, HEX JAM
8-CLAMP, TIE ROD END
10-BOOT, RACK & PINION
11-CLAMP, BOOT
30-GEAR ASM, RACK & PINION (PARTIAL)
35-BREATHER TUBE

Fig. 116 Inner tie rod and rack and pinion boot assembly

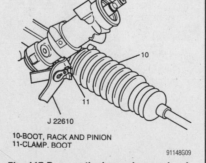

10-BOOT, RACK AND PINION
11-CLAMP, BOOT

Fig. 117 Remove the inner clamp using J-22610 boot clamp pliers or equivalent

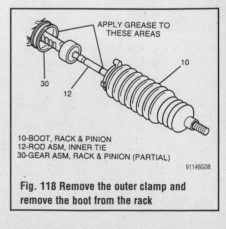

APPLY GREASE TO THESE AREAS

10-BOOT, RACK & PINION
12-ROD ASM, INNER TIE
30-GEAR ASM, RACK & PINION (PARTIAL)

Fig. 118 Remove the outer clamp and remove the boot from the rack

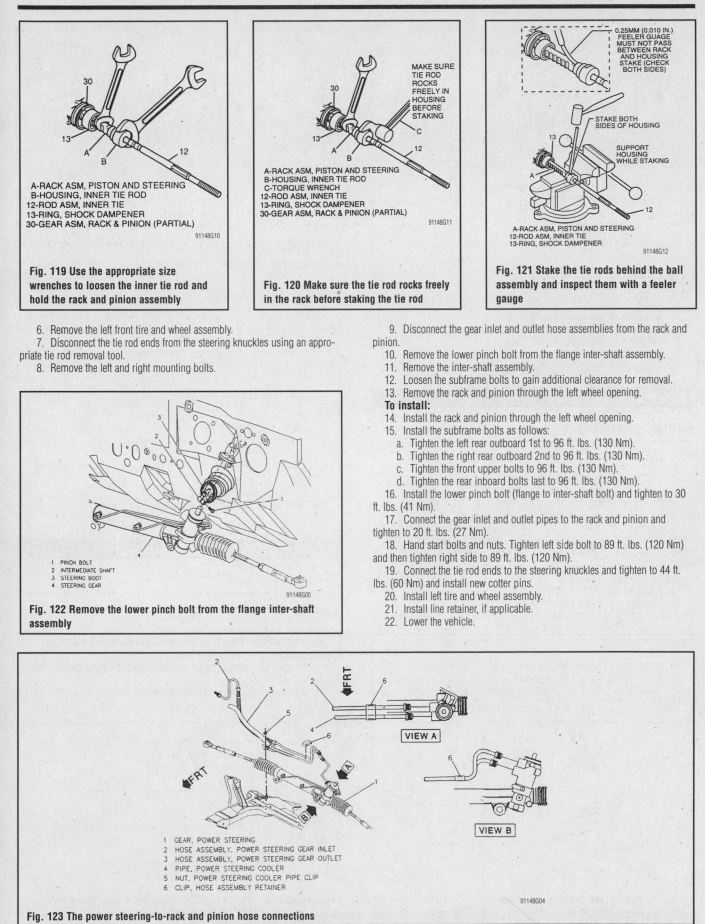

Fig. 119 Use the appropriate size wrenches to loosen the inner tie rod and hold the rack and pinion assembly

A-RACK ASM, PISTON AND STEERING
B-HOUSING, INNER TIE ROD
12-ROD ASM, INNER TIE
13-RING, SHOCK DAMPENER
30-GEAR ASM, RACK & PINION (PARTIAL)

91148G10

Fig. 120 Make sure the tie rod rocks freely in the rack before staking the tie rod

MAKE SURE TIE ROD ROCKS FREELY IN HOUSING BEFORE STAKING

A-RACK ASM, PISTON AND STEERING
B-HOUSING, INNER TIE ROD
C-TORQUE WRENCH
12-ROD ASM, INNER TIE
13-RING, SHOCK DAMPENER
30-GEAR ASM, RACK & PINION (PARTIAL)

91148G11

Fig. 121 Stake the tie rods behind the ball assembly and inspect them with a feeler gauge

0.25MM (0.010 IN.) FEELER GUAGE MUST NOT PASS BETWEEN RACK AND HOUSING STAKE (CHECK BOTH SIDES)

STAKE BOTH SIDES OF HOUSING

SUPPORT HOUSING WHILE STAKING

A-RACK ASM, PISTON AND STEERING
12-ROD ASM, INNER TIE
13-RING, SHOCK DAMPENER

91148G12

6. Remove the left front tire and wheel assembly.
7. Disconnect the tie rod ends from the steering knuckles using an appropriate tie rod removal tool.
8. Remove the left and right mounting bolts.

Fig. 122 Remove the lower pinch bolt from the flange inter-shaft assembly

1 PINCH BOLT
2 INTERMEDIATE SHAFT
3 STEERING BOOT
4 STEERING GEAR

91148G05

9. Disconnect the gear inlet and outlet hose assemblies from the rack and pinion.
10. Remove the lower pinch bolt from the flange inter-shaft assembly.
11. Remove the inter-shaft assembly.
12. Loosen the subframe bolts to gain additional clearance for removal.
13. Remove the rack and pinion through the left wheel opening.

To install:
14. Install the rack and pinion through the left wheel opening.
15. Install the subframe bolts as follows:
    a. Tighten the left rear outboard 1st to 96 ft. lbs. (130 Nm).
    b. Tighten the right rear outboard 2nd to 96 ft. lbs. (130 Nm).
    c. Tighten the front upper bolts to 96 ft. lbs. (130 Nm).
    d. Tighten the rear inboard bolts last to 96 ft. lbs. (130 Nm).
16. Install the lower pinch bolt (flange to inter-shaft bolt) and tighten to 30 ft. lbs. (41 Nm).
17. Connect the gear inlet and outlet pipes to the rack and pinion and tighten to 20 ft. lbs. (27 Nm).
18. Hand start bolts and nuts. Tighten left side bolt to 89 ft. lbs. (120 Nm) and then tighten right side to 89 ft. lbs. (120 Nm).
19. Connect the tie rod ends to the steering knuckles and tighten to 44 ft. lbs. (60 Nm) and install new cotter pins.
20. Install left tire and wheel assembly.
21. Install line retainer, if applicable.
22. Lower the vehicle.

1 GEAR, POWER STEERING
2 HOSE ASSEMBLY, POWER STEERING GEAR INLET
3 HOSE ASSEMBLY, POWER STEERING GEAR OUTLET
4 PIPE, POWER STEERING COOLER
5 NUT, POWER STEERING COOLER PIPE CLIP
6 CLIP, HOSE ASSEMBLY RETAINER

VIEW A

VIEW B

FRT

91148G04

Fig. 123 The power steering-to-rack and pinion hose connections

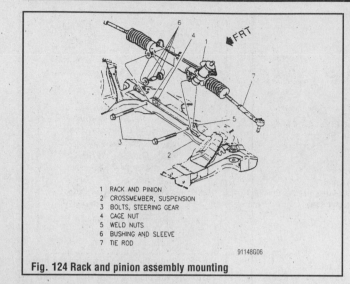

1 RACK AND PINION
2 CROSSMEMBER, SUSPENSION
3 BOLTS, STEERING GEAR
4 CAGE NUT
5 WELD NUTS
6 BUSHING AND SLEEVE
7 TIE ROD

91148G06

Fig. 124 Rack and pinion assembly mounting

23. Install the upper pinch bolt and tighten to 30 ft. lbs. (41 Nm).
24. Install the left side sound insulator.
25. Connect the negative battery cable.
26. Fill with fluid and bleed air from system.
27. Check toe setting and adjust as required.
28. Road test vehicle and verify no leaks.

Power Steering Pump

REMOVAL & INSTALLATION

▶ See Figures 125, 126 and 127

1. Disconnect the negative battery cable.
2. Remove the serpentine belt (2.2L engine only).
3. Disconnect and cap the lines at the pump.
4. Remove the mounting bolts, then remove the pump.
To install:
5. On the 2.2L engine, if the pump is being replaced, transfer the pulley to the new pump. Use J-25034-B or equivalent pulley remover with J-37609 or equivalent shaft adapter to remove the pulley. Use J-36015 or equivalent pulley installer to install the pulley.
6. Install the pump.
7. Tighten the mounting bolts to 22 ft. lbs. (30 Nm).

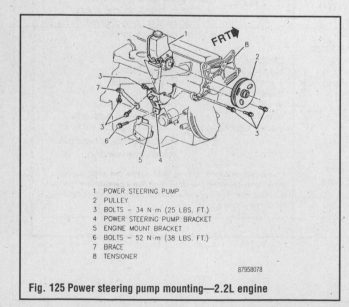

1 POWER STEERING PUMP
2 PULLEY
3 BOLTS — 34 N·m (25 LBS. FT.)
4 POWER STEERING PUMP BRACKET
5 ENGINE MOUNT BRACKET
6 BOLTS — 52 N·m (38 LBS. FT.)
7 BRACE
8 TENSIONER

87958078

Fig. 125 Power steering pump mounting—2.2L engine

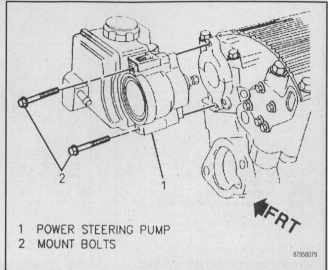

1 POWER STEERING PUMP
2 MOUNT BOLTS

87958079

Fig. 126 Location of the power steering pump—2.3L/2.4L engine

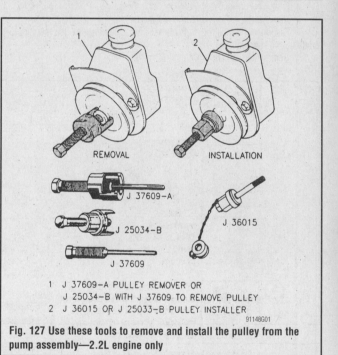

REMOVAL   INSTALLATION

J 37609-A

J 25034-B

J 36015

J 37609

1 J 37609-A PULLEY REMOVER OR
  J 25034-B WITH J 37609 TO REMOVE PULLEY
2 J 36015 OR J 25033-B PULLEY INSTALLER

91148G01

Fig. 127 Use these tools to remove and install the pulley from the pump assembly—2.2L engine only

8. Uncap and connect the lines to the power steering pump and tighten to 20 ft. lbs. (27 Nm).
9. Install the belt.
10. Connect the negative battery cable.
11. Fill the pump with fluid and bleed air from the power steering system.
12. Road test the vehicle and verify no leaks.

BLEEDING

▶ See Figure 128

1. Raise the front of the vehicle and support safely. This will minimize steering effort. Fill the power steering pump reservoir with the appropriate type of power steering fluid.
2. With the engine off, keep the reservoir full as an assistant turns the steering wheel from lock-to-lock several times. Stop with the steering system at one lock.
3. Start the engine and allow it to idle. Turn the wheel from lock-to-lock several times. Note the amount of air bubbles in the fluid. Repeat the procedure until no more air bubbles appear.

Bleeding Air from Power Steering Systems

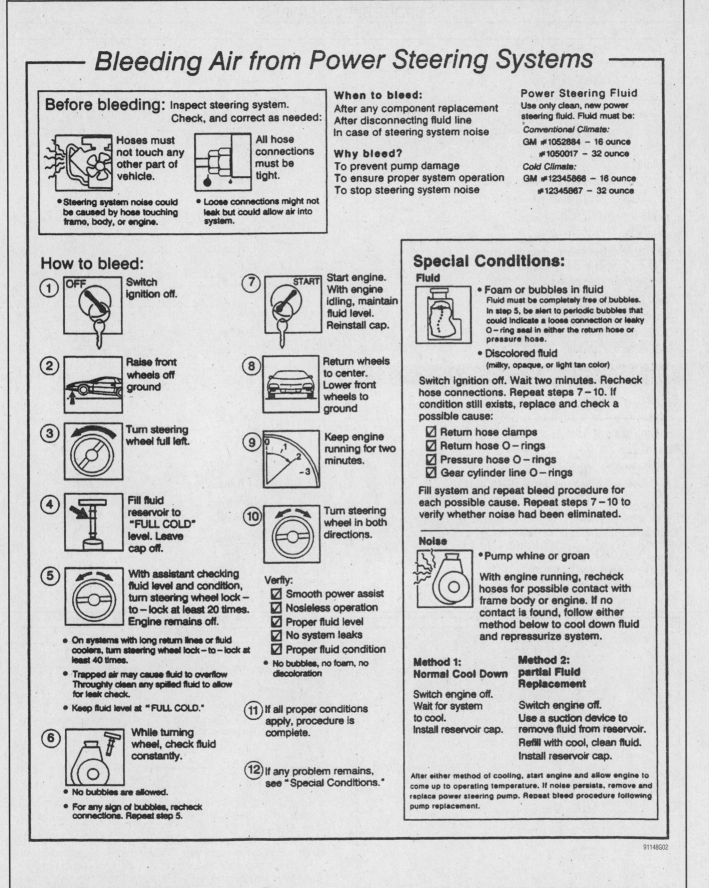

Before bleeding: Inspect steering system.
Check, and correct as needed:

Hoses must not touch any other part of vehicle.

- Steering system noise could be caused by hose touching frame, body, or engine.

All hose connections must be tight.

- Loose connections might not leak but could allow air into system.

When to bleed:
After any component replacement
After disconnecting fluid line
In case of steering system noise

Why bleed?
To prevent pump damage
To ensure proper system operation
To stop steering system noise

Power Steering Fluid
Use only clean, new power steering fluid. Fluid must be:
Conventional Climate:
GM #1052884 – 16 ounce
　 #1050017 – 32 ounce
Cold Climate:
GM #12345866 – 16 ounce
　 #12345867 – 32 ounce

How to bleed:

1. Switch ignition off.
2. Raise front wheels off ground
3. Turn steering wheel full left.
4. Fill fluid reservoir to "FULL COLD" level. Leave cap off.
5. With assistant checking fluid level and condition, turn steering wheel lock-to-lock at least 20 times. Engine remains off.

- On systems with long return lines or fluid coolers, turn steering wheel lock-to-lock at least 40 times.
- Trapped air may cause fluid to overflow. Thoroughly clean any spilled fluid to allow for leak check.
- Keep fluid level at "FULL COLD."

6. While turning wheel, check fluid constantly.

- No bubbles are allowed.
- For any sign of bubbles, recheck connections. Repeat step 5.

7. Start engine. With engine idling, maintain fluid level. Reinstall cap.
8. Return wheels to center. Lower front wheels to ground
9. Keep engine running for two minutes.
10. Turn steering wheel in both directions.

Verify:
- ☑ Smooth power assist
- ☑ Noiseless operation
- ☑ Proper fluid level
- ☑ No system leaks
- ☑ Proper fluid condition
- No bubbles, no foam, no discoloration

11. If all proper conditions apply, procedure is complete.

12. If any problem remains, see "Special Conditions."

Special Conditions:
Fluid

- **Foam or bubbles in fluid**
  Fluid must be completely free of bubbles. In step 5, be alert to periodic bubbles that could indicate a loose connection or leaky O-ring seal in either the return hose or pressure hose.

- **Discolored fluid**
  (milky, opaque, or light tan color)

Switch ignition off. Wait two minutes. Recheck hose connections. Repeat steps 7 – 10. If condition still exists, replace and check a possible cause:

- ☑ Return hose clamps
- ☑ Return hose O-rings
- ☑ Pressure hose O-rings
- ☑ Gear cylinder line O-rings

Fill system and repeat bleed procedure for each possible cause. Repeat steps 7 – 10 to verify whether noise had been eliminated.

Noise

- **Pump whine or groan**

With engine running, recheck hoses for possible contact with frame body or engine. If no contact is found, follow either method below to cool down fluid and repressurize system.

Method 1:
Normal Cool Down

Switch engine off.
Wait for system to cool.
Install reservoir cap.

Method 2:
partial Fluid Replacement

Switch engine off.
Use a suction device to remove fluid from reservoir.
Refill with cool, clean fluid.
Install reservoir cap.

After either method of cooling, start engine and allow engine to come up to operating temperature. If noise persists, remove and replace power steering pump. Repeat bleed procedure following pump replacement.

91148G02

Fig. 128 Power steering bleed procedure

TORQUE SPECIFICATIONS

Components	English	Metric
Air bag retaining screws	89 inch lbs.	10 Nm
Front Suspension		
Ball joint-to-steering knuckle	41 ft. lbs.	55 Nm
Control arm rear mounting bolt	125 ft. lbs.	170 Nm
Control arm front mounting bolt	90 ft. lbs.	125 Nm
Hub and bearing assembly-to-steering knickle bolts	70 ft. lbs.	95 Nm
Knuckle-to-strut bolts	133 ft. lbs.	180 Nm
Strut		
Strut dampener shaft retaining nut	52 ft. lbs.	70 Nm
Strut-to-body mounting bolts/nuts	18-20 ft. lbs.	25-27 Nm
Subframe mounting bolts	96 ft. lbs.	130 Nm
Sway bar-to-subframe bolts	49 ft. lbs.	66 Nm
Sway bar links-to-sway bar	13 ft. lbs.	17 Nm
Tie-rod end-to-steering knuckle nuts	44 ft. lbs.	60 Nm
Wheel hub retaining nut	185 ft. lbs.	260 Nm
Power rack and pinion		
Inner tie rod-to-rack and pinion	74 ft. lbs.	100 Nm
Intermediate steering shaft upper pinch bolt	30 ft. lbs.	41 Nm
Outer tie rod jam nut	50 ft. lbs.	68 Nm
Rack-to-subframe retaining bolts	89 ft. lbs.	120 Nm
Steering shaft-to-rack and pinion flange lower pinch bolt	30 ft. lbs.	41 Nm
Power steering pump		
Hose fittings	20 ft. lbs.	27 Nm
Pump retaining bolts	22 ft. lbs.	30 Nm
Rear suspension		
Coil-over shocks		
Coil-over shock-to-body mounting bolts	21 ft. lbs.	28 Nm
Coil-over shock-to-body mounting nut	15 ft. lbs.	20 Nm
Lower mount bolt	125 ft. lbs.	170 Nm
Control arm/axle		
Mounting bolts	52 ft. lbs. ①	72 Nm ①
Brake line bracket mounting bolts	97 inch lbs.	11 Nm
Wheel hub mounting bolts	44 ft. lbs.	60 Nm
Steering wheel center nut	30 ft. lbs.	41 Nm
Wheel lug nuts	100 ft. lbs.	140 Nm

① Rotate an additional 120°

91148C01

BRAKE OPERATING SYSTEM 9-2
BASIC OPERATING PRINCIPLES 9-2
   DISC BRAKES 9-2
   DRUM BRAKES 9-2
   POWER BOOSTERS 9-3
BRAKE LIGHT SWITCH 9-3
   REMOVAL & INSTALLATION 9-3
MASTER CYLINDER 9-3
   REMOVAL & INSTALLATION 9-3
   BENCH BLEEDING 9-4
POWER BRAKE BOOSTER 9-4
   REMOVAL & INSTALLATION 9-4
PROPORTIONER VALVES 9-5
   REMOVAL & INSTALLATION 9-5
BRAKE HOSES AND LINES 9-5
   REMOVAL & INSTALLATION 9-5
BLEEDING THE BRAKE SYSTEM 9-6
DISC BRAKES 9-7
BRAKE PADS 9-7
   REMOVAL & INSTALLATION 9-7
   INSPECTION 9-9
BRAKE CALIPER 9-9
   REMOVAL & INSTALLATION 9-9
   OVERHAUL 9-10
BRAKE DISC (ROTOR) 9-11
   REMOVAL & INSTALLATION 9-11
   INSPECTION 9-12
DRUM BRAKES 9-13
BRAKE DRUMS 9-14
   REMOVAL & INSTALLATION 9-14
   INSPECTION 9-14
BRAKE SHOES 9-14
   INSPECTION 9-14
   REMOVAL & INSTALLATION 9-14
   ADJUSTMENTS 9-16
WHEEL CYLINDERS 9-17
   REMOVAL & INSTALLATION 9-17
   OVERHAUL 9-17
BRAKE BACKING PLATE 9-19
   REMOVAL & INSTALLATION 9-19
PARKING BRAKE 9-19
CABLES 9-19
   REMOVAL & INSTALLATION 9-19
   ADJUSTMENT 9-20
PARKING BRAKE LEVER 9-20
   REMOVAL & INSTALLATION 9-20
ANTI-LOCK BRAKE SYSTEM 9-20
GENERAL INFORMATION 9-20
DIAGNOSIS 9-21
ABS HYDRAULIC MODULATOR/MASTER
  CYLINDER ASSEMBLY 9-21
   REMOVAL & INSTALLATION 9-21
BRAKE FLUID LEVEL SWITCH 9-23
   REMOVAL & INSTALLATION 9-23
ABS RELAY 9-23
   REMOVAL & INSTALLATION 9-23
ABS CONTROL MODULE 9-23
   REMOVAL & INSTALLATION 9-23

SPEED SENSORS 9-23
   REMOVAL & INSTALLATION 9-23
TONE (EXCITER) RING 9-24
   REMOVAL & INSTALLATION 9-24
BLEEDING THE ABS SYSTEM 9-24
   SYSTEM FILLING 9-25
   BLEEDING THE ABS HYDRAULIC
   SYSTEM 9-25
COMPONENT LOCATIONS
DISC BRAKE COMPONENTS 9-7
DRUM BRAKE COMPONENTS—
  INSTALLED (HUB REMOVED)—LEFT
  SIDE SHOWN 9-13
REAR DRUM BRAKE COMPONENTS—
  RIGHT SIDE SHOWN 9-13
SPECIFICATIONS CHART
BRAKE SPECIFICATION—GM J
  BODY 9-26

9

BRAKES

BRAKE OPERATING SYSTEM 9-2
DISC BRAKES 9-7
DRUM BRAKES 9-13
PARKING BRAKE 9-19
ANTI-LOCK BRAKE SYSTEM 9-20

BRAKE OPERATING SYSTEM

Basic Operating Principles

Hydraulic systems are used to actuate the brakes of all modern automobiles. The system transports the power required to force the frictional surfaces of the braking system together from the pedal to the individual brake units at each wheel. A hydraulic system is used for two reasons.

First, fluid under pressure can be carried to all parts of an automobile by small pipes and flexible hoses without taking up a significant amount of room or posing routing problems.

Second, a great mechanical advantage can be given to the brake pedal end of the system, and the foot pressure required to actuate the brakes can be reduced by making the surface area of the master cylinder pistons smaller than that of any of the pistons in the wheel cylinders or calipers.

The master cylinder consists of a fluid reservoir along with a double cylinder and piston assembly. Double type master cylinders are designed to separate the front and rear braking systems hydraulically in case of a leak. The master cylinder coverts mechanical motion from the pedal into hydraulic pressure within the lines. This pressure is translated back into mechanical motion at the wheels by either the wheel cylinder (drum brakes) or the caliper (disc brakes).

Steel lines carry the brake fluid to a point on the vehicle's frame near each of the vehicle's wheels. The fluid is then carried to the calipers and wheel cylinders by flexible tubes in order to allow for suspension and steering movements.

In drum brake systems, each wheel cylinder contains two pistons, one at either end, which push outward in opposite directions and force the brake shoe into contact with the drum.

In disc brake systems, the cylinders are part of the calipers. At least one cylinder in each caliper is used to force the brake pads against the disc.

All pistons employ some type of seal, usually made of rubber, to minimize fluid leakage. A rubber dust boot seals the outer end of the cylinder against dust and dirt. The boot fits around the outer end of the piston on disc brake calipers, and around the brake actuating rod on wheel cylinders.

The hydraulic system operates as follows: When at rest, the entire system, from the piston(s) in the master cylinder to those in the wheel cylinders or calipers, is full of brake fluid. Upon application of the brake pedal, fluid trapped in front of the master cylinder piston(s) is forced through the lines to the wheel cylinders. Here, it forces the pistons outward, in the case of drum brakes, and inward toward the disc, in the case of disc brakes. The motion of the pistons is opposed by return springs mounted outside the cylinders in drum brakes, and by spring seals, in disc brakes.

Upon release of the brake pedal, a spring located inside the master cylinder immediately returns the master cylinder pistons to the normal position. The pistons contain check valves and the master cylinder has compensating ports drilled in it. These are uncovered as the pistons reach their normal position. The piston check valves allow fluid to flow toward the wheel cylinders or calipers as the pistons withdraw. Then, as the return springs force the brake pads or shoes into the released position, the excess fluid reservoir through the compensating ports. It is during the time the pedal is in the released position that any fluid that has leaked out of the system will be replaced through the compensating ports.

Dual circuit master cylinders employ two pistons, located one behind the other, in the same cylinder. The primary piston is actuated directly by mechanical linkage from the brake pedal through the power booster. The secondary piston is actuated by fluid trapped between the two pistons. If a leak develops in front of the secondary piston, it moves forward until it bottoms against the front of the master cylinder, and the fluid trapped between the pistons will operate the rear brakes. If the rear brakes develop a leak, the primary piston will move forward until direct contact with the secondary piston takes place, and it will force the secondary piston to actuate the front brakes. In either case, the brake pedal moves farther when the brakes are applied, and less braking power is available.

All dual circuit systems use a switch to warn the driver when only half of the brake system is operational. This switch is usually located in a valve body which is mounted on the firewall or the frame below the master cylinder. A hydraulic piston receives pressure from both circuits, each circuit's pressure being applied to one end of the piston. When the pressures are in balance, the piston remains stationary. When one circuit has a leak, however, the greater pressure in that circuit during application of the brakes will push the piston to one side, closing the switch and activating the brake warning light.

In disc brake systems, this valve body also contains a metering valve and, in some cases, a proportioning valve. The metering valve keeps pressure from

traveling to the disc brakes on the front wheels until the brake shoes on the rear wheels have contacted the drums, ensuring that the front brakes will never be used alone. The proportioning valve controls the pressure to the rear brakes to lessen the chance of rear wheel lock-up during very hard braking.

Warning lights may be tested by depressing the brake pedal and holding it while opening one of the wheel cylinder bleeder screws. If this does not cause the light to go on, substitute a new lamp, make continuity checks, and, finally, replace the switch as necessary.

The hydraulic system may be checked for leaks by applying pressure to the pedal gradually and steadily. If the pedal sinks very slowly to the floor, the system has a leak. This is not to be confused with a springy or spongy feel due to the compression of air within the lines. If the system leaks, there will be a gradual change in the position of the pedal with a constant pressure.

Check for leaks along all lines and at wheel cylinders. If no external leaks are apparent, the problem is inside the master cylinder.

DISC BRAKES

Instead of the traditional expanding brakes that press outward against a circular drum, disc brake systems utilize a disc (rotor) with brake pads positioned on either side of it. An easily-seen analogy is the hand brake arrangement on a bicycle. The pads squeeze onto the rim of the bike wheel, slowing its motion. Automobile disc brakes use the identical principle but apply the braking effort to a separate disc instead of the wheel.

The disc (rotor) is a casting, usually equipped with cooling fins between the two braking surfaces. This enables air to circulate between the braking surfaces making them less sensitive to heat buildup and more resistant to fade. Dirt and water do not drastically affect braking action since contaminants are thrown off by the centrifugal action of the rotor or scraped off the by the pads. Also, the equal clamping action of the two brake pads tends to ensure uniform, straight line stops. Disc brakes are inherently self-adjusting. There are three general types of disc brake:

- A fixed caliper.
- A floating caliper.
- A sliding caliper.

The fixed caliper design uses two pistons mounted on either side of the rotor (in each side of the caliper). The caliper is mounted rigidly and does not move.

The sliding and floating designs are quite similar. In fact, these two types are often lumped together. In both designs, the pad on the inside of the rotor is moved into contact with the rotor by hydraulic force. The caliper, which is not held in a fixed position, moves slightly, bringing the outside pad into contact with the rotor. There are various methods of attaching floating calipers. Some pivot at the bottom or top, and some slide on mounting bolts. In any event, the end result is the same.

DRUM BRAKES

Drum brakes employ two brake shoes mounted on a stationary backing plate. These shoes are positioned inside a circular drum which rotates with the wheel assembly. The shoes are held in place by springs. This allows them to slide toward the drums (when they are applied) while keeping the linings and drums in alignment. The shoes are actuated by a wheel cylinder which is mounted at the top of the backing plate. When the brakes are applied, hydraulic pressure forces the wheel cylinder's actuating links outward. Since these links bear directly against the top of the brake shoes, the tops of the shoes are then forced against the inner side of the drum. This action forces the bottoms of the two shoes to contact the brake drum by rotating the entire assembly slightly (known as servo action). When pressure within the wheel cylinder is relaxed, return springs pull the shoes back away from the drum.

Most modern drum brakes are designed to self-adjust themselves during application when the vehicle is moving in reverse. This motion causes both shoes to rotate very slightly with the drum, rocking an adjusting lever, thereby causing rotation of the adjusting screw. Some drum brake systems are designed to self-adjust during application whenever the brakes are applied. This on-board adjustment system reduces the need for maintenance adjustments and keeps both the brake function and pedal feel satisfactory.

POWER BOOSTERS

Virtually all modern vehicles use a vacuum assisted power brake system to multiply the braking force and reduce pedal effort. Since vacuum is always available when the engine is operating, the system is simple and efficient. A vacuum diaphragm is located on the front of the master cylinder and assists the driver in applying the brakes, reducing both the effort and travel he must put into moving the brake pedal.

The vacuum diaphragm housing is normally connected to the intake manifold by a vacuum hose. A check valve is placed at the point where the hose enters the diaphragm housing, so that during periods of low manifold vacuum brakes assist will not be lost.

Depressing the brake pedal closes off the vacuum source and allows atmospheric pressure to enter on one side of the diaphragm. This causes the master cylinder pistons to move and apply the brakes. When the brake pedal is released, vacuum is applied to both sides of the diaphragm and springs return the diaphragm and master cylinder pistons to the released position.

If the vacuum supply fails, the brake pedal rod will contact the end of the master cylinder actuator rod and the system will apply the brakes without any power assistance. The driver will notice that much higher pedal effort is needed to stop the car and that the pedal feels harder than usual.

Vacuum Leak Test

1. Operate the engine at idle without touching the brake pedal for at least one minute.
2. Turn off the engine and wait one minute.
3. Test for the presence of assist vacuum by depressing the brake pedal and releasing it several times. If vacuum is present in the system, light application will produce less and less pedal travel. If there is no vacuum, air is leaking into the system.

System Operation Test

1. With the engine **OFF**, pump the brake pedal until the supply vacuum is entirely gone.
2. Put light, steady pressure on the brake pedal.
3. Start the engine and let it idle. If the system is operating correctly, the brake pedal should fall toward the floor if the constant pressure is maintained.

Power brake systems may be tested for hydraulic leaks just as ordinary systems are tested.

✳✳ WARNING

Clean, high quality brake fluid is essential to the safe and proper operation of the brake system. You should always buy the highest quality brake fluid that is available. If the brake fluid becomes contaminated, drain and flush the system, then refill the master cylinder with new fluid. Never reuse any brake fluid. Any brake fluid that is removed from the system should be discarded.

Brake Light Switch

REMOVAL & INSTALLATION

◗ See Figure 1

1. Disconnect the negative battery cable.
2. Remove the drivers side instrument panel trim panel/sound insulator.
3. Detach the switch electrical connector.
4. Remove the switch from the retainer by grasping it and pulling it toward the rear of the car.

To install:

5. Insert the brake light switch into the retainer until the switch body seats on the retainer.
6. Adjust the brake light switch, as follows:
   a. Pull the brake pedal upward against the internal pedal stop. The switch will be moved in the retainer providing proper adjustment.

➥**Proper switch adjustment is achieved when no clicks are heard as the pedal is pulled upward and when the brake lights do not stay on without brake application.**

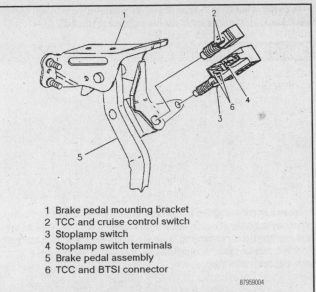

1 Brake pedal mounting bracket
2 TCC and cruise control switch
3 Stoplamp switch
4 Stoplamp switch terminals
5 Brake pedal assembly
6 TCC and BTSI connector

87959004

Fig. 1 The brake light switch is mounted on the brake pedal

7. Attach the switch electrical connector.
8. Install the hush panel/sound insulator.
9. Connect the negative battery cable.

Master Cylinder

REMOVAL & INSTALLATION

◗ See Figure 2

When the ABS modulator cylinder pistons are in their uppermost position, each motor has prevailing torque due to the force necessary to ensure each piston is held firmly at the top of its travel. This torque results in "gear tension," or force on each gear that makes motor pack separation difficult. To avoid injury, or damage to the gears, the "Gear Tension Relief Sequence" briefly reverses each motor to eliminate the prevailing torque. This procedure is one of the many functions of GM's Tech 1® scan tool. Use care when using a substitute. In general, make sure the ignition switch is in the **OFF** position. Install the Tech 1® or equivalent with the correct chassis cartridge. Turn the ignition switch to the **ON** position, leaving the engine OFF. Select the proper function. The "Gear Tension Relief Sequence" is F5 on the Tech 1® scan tool. Note that this same scan tool is needed to bleed the system after repairs to the hydraulic system.

91149P32

Fig. 2 The master cylinder and ABS hydraulic modulator assembly

➡To perform the Gear Tension Relief Sequence, a Tech 1® tool or equivalent scan tool must be used prior to removal of the ABS modulator/master cylinder assembly.

1. Perform gear tension release procedure using the Tech 1® scan tool or equivalent.
2. Remove the battery.
3. Remove the air cleaner assembly.
4. Detach the electrical connector from fluid level switch.
5. Detach the electrical connectors from the ABS solenoids.
6. Detach the 3-pin and 6-pin motor pack electrical connectors from the ABS hydraulic modulator.
7. Remove the 4 brake pipe tube nuts from master cylinder and modulator assembly. If necessary, tag for identification and placement. Place shop cloths on top of the motor pack to catch any dripping fluid. Take care not to allow brake fluid to enter the bottom of the motor pack or the electrical connectors.

➡When disconnecting the brake lines from the master cylinder and removing the unit, use care not to spill brake fluid on any painted surfaces or electrical connectors. Once the brake lines are disconnected from the master cylinder, plug the lines to prevent excess brake fluid loss and contamination.

8. Remove the master cylinder mounting nuts. It may be necessary to remove the vacuum check valve from the vacuum booster to access the nut closest to the check valve.
9. Remove the master cylinder and modulator as an assembly.
10. Separate the modulator assembly from the master cylinder assembly. Use the following procedure.
    a. Turn the assembly upside down so the flat gear cover is facing up.
    b. Remove the 6 gear cover attaching screws. This should allow access to the motor pack screws.
    c. Remove the 4 motor pack screws and separate the motor pack from the ABS modulator assembly.
    d. Remove the 2 Torx head through bolts that retain the master cylinder to the motor pack assembly. Use care not to loose or damage the 2 small transfer tubes that connect between the lower part of the master cylinder assembly and the hydraulic modulator assembly. Watch for O-rings seals at both the transfer tubes and the Torx head attaching bolt openings. The transfer tubes and all O-rings must be replaced with new parts whenever the master cylinder and modulator are separated.

To install:

11. Clean all parts well. Use new O-rings and transfer tubes to assemble the master cylinder to the modulator. If the hydraulic modulator is to be replaced, install the 3 gears in the same location on the replacement modulator. Note that no repair of the hydraulic modulator is authorized.
12. Make sure 2 O-rings are properly installed on each transfer tube. Lubricate the O-rings with clean brake fluid. Install the transfer tube assemblies in the ports in the hydraulic modulator and push in by hand until they bottom.
13. Lubricate with clean brake fluid, new O-rings for the 2 Torx head through bolts and install in both the master cylinder openings and the modulator. Assemble the modulator to the master cylinder. It may be helpful to clamp just the mounting flange of the master cylinder in a soft-jaw vise. Hold the modulator and rock it into position on the master cylinder, inserting the transfer tube assemblies into the master cylinder ports. Install the 2 Torx head through bolts and torque to 18 ft. lbs. (24 Nm).
14. With the hydraulic modulator upside down and the gears facing up, rotate each gear counterclockwise until movement stops. This procedure will position the piston very close to the top of the hydraulic modulator bore.
15. Assemble the motor pack to the hydraulic modulator. Install the gear cover.
16. Install the master cylinder and modulator assembly to the power booster assembly and tighten the mounting nuts to 20 ft. lbs. (27 Nm).
17. Connect the brake lines to the master cylinder and tighten them to 17 ft. lbs. (23 Nm).
18. Attach the electrical connector to the fluid level switch.
19. Connect the electrical connectors for both of the solenoids.
20. Attach the 3-pin and the 6-pin motor pack electrical connectors.
21. Fill the master cylinder to the proper level. The proper level is the MAX level indicator on the reservoir.
22. Bleed the hydraulic brake system.
23. Road test vehicle and verify proper operation.

BENCH BLEEDING

All new master cylinders should be bench bled prior to installation. Bleeding a new master cylinder on the vehicle is not a good idea. With air trapped inside, the master cylinder piston may bottom in the bore and possibly cause internal damage.

1. Secure the master cylinder in a bench vise using soft jaws.
2. Remove the master cylinder reservoir cap.
3. Manufacture or purchase bleeding tubes and install them on the master cylinder.
4. Fill the master cylinder reservoir with clean, fresh brake fluid until the level is within 0.25 in. of the reservoir top.

➡Ensure the bleeding tubes are below the level of the brake fluid, otherwise air may get into the system making your bleeding efforts ineffective.

5. Use a blunt tipped rod (a long socket extension works well) to slowly depress the master cylinder piston. Make sure the piston travels full its full stroke.
6. As the piston is depressed, bubbles will come out of the bleeding tubes. Continue depressing and releasing the piston until all bubbles cease.
7. Refill the master cylinder with fluid.
8. Remove the bleeding tubes.
9. Install the master cylinder reservoir cap.
10. Install the master cylinder on the vehicle.

Power Brake Booster

REMOVAL & INSTALLATION

▶ **See Figure 3**

➡It is not necessary to remove or disconnect the master cylinder from the vehicle in order to remove the vacuum booster. However, if both the vacuum booster and master cylinder are to be removed, remove the master cylinder first.

1. Disconnect the negative battery cable.
2. Remove the battery.
3. Remove the air cleaner assembly.
4. Unfasten the master cylinder-to-booster retaining nuts.
5. Separate the master cylinder from the booster. Move the master cylinder forward just enough to clear the studs on the vacuum booster. This will flex the brake pipes slightly; be careful not to bend or distort the pipes.
6. Disconnect the vacuum hose from the vacuum check valve.
7. Unfasten the booster retaining nuts.
8. Disconnect the vacuum booster pushrod from the brake pedal inside the car. Tilt the entire vacuum booster slightly to work the booster pushrod off the pedal clevis pin without putting undue side pressure on the pushrod.
9. Remove the booster from the vehicle.

To install:

10. Position the booster in the vehicle.

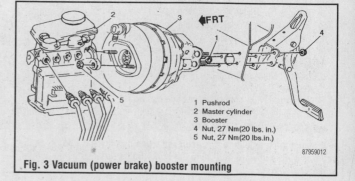

1 Pushrod
2 Master cylinder
3 Booster
4 Nut, 27 Nm(20 lbs. in.)
5 Nut, 27 Nm(20 lbs.in.)

87959012

Fig. 3 Vacuum (power brake) booster mounting

11. Connect the booster pushrod to the brake pedal. Tilt the entire booster slightly to work the booster pushrod onto the pedal clevis pin without putting undue pressure on the pushrod. Use your free hand to align the pushrod with the pedal and push together.

12. Install the booster attaching nuts, then tighten them to 20 ft. lbs. (27 Nm).

13. Connect the booster vacuum hose to the vacuum check valve.

14. Position the master cylinder to the booster and install the retaining nuts.

15. Install the air box and the battery.
16. Connect the positive battery cable
17. Connect the negative battery cable.

Proportioner Valves

REMOVAL & INSTALLATION

▶ **See Figure 4**

1. Remove the proportioner valve caps. It may be necessary to remove the master cylinder reservoir.

2. Remove and discard the valve cap O-rings.

3. Remove the proportioner valve piston springs, then remove the valve pistons using needle-nose pliers. Be careful not to scratch or damage the piston stems.

4. Remove the valve seals from the proportioner valve pistons.

5. Clean all parts in clean denatured alcohol, then dry with compressed air. Inspect the valve pistons for corrosion or deformation and replace if necessary.

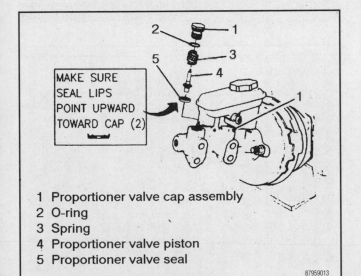

MAKE SURE SEAL LIPS POINT UPWARD TOWARD CAP (2)

1 Proportioner valve cap assembly
2 O-ring
3 Spring
4 Proportioner valve piston
5 Proportioner valve seal

87959013

Fig. 4 Removal of the proportioner valves

To install:

6. Lubricate new proportioner valve cap O-rings and valve seals with the silicone grease given in the repair kit. Also, lubricate the stem of the proportioner valve pistons.

7. Place new proportioner valve seals on the proportioner valve pistons with the seal lips facing upward toward the proportioner valve cap.

8. Position the proportioner valve pistons and seals into the master cylinder body.

9. Place new proportioner valve cap O-rings in the grooves in the proportioner valve caps.

10. Install the valve caps in the master cylinder body, then tighten the caps to 20 ft. lbs. (27 Nm).

11. If removed, install the master cylinder reservoir.

Brake Hoses and Lines

Metal lines and rubber brake hoses should be checked frequently for leaks and external damage. Metal lines are particularly prone to crushing and kinking under the vehicle. Any such deformation can restrict the proper flow of fluid and therefore impair braking at the wheels. Rubber hoses should be checked for cracking or scraping; such damage can create a weak spot in the hose and it could fail under pressure.

Any time the lines are removed or disconnected, extreme cleanliness must be observed. Clean all joints and connections before disassembly (use a stiff bristle brush and clean brake fluid); be sure to plug the lines and ports as soon as they are opened. New lines and hoses should be flushed clean with brake fluid before installation to remove any contamination.

REMOVAL & INSTALLATION

▶ **See Figures 5 thru 10**

1. Disconnect the negative battery cable.
2. Raise and safely support the vehicle on jackstands.
3. Remove any wheel and tire assemblies necessary for access to the particular line you are removing.
4. Thoroughly clean the surrounding area at the joints to be disconnected.
5. Place a suitable catch pan under the joint to be disconnected.
6. Using two wrenches (one to hold the joint and one to turn the fitting), disconnect the hose or line to be replaced.
7. Disconnect the other end of the line or hose, moving the drain pan if necessary. Always use a back-up wrench to avoid damaging the fitting.
8. Disconnect any retaining clips or brackets holding the line and remove the line from the vehicle.

➡**If the brake system is to remain open for more time than it takes to swap lines, tape or plug each remaining clip and port to keep contaminants out and fluid in.**

To install:
9. Install the new line or hose, starting with the end farthest from the master cylinder. Connect the other end, then confirm that both fittings are correctly threaded and turn smoothly using finger pressure. Make sure the new line will not rub against any other part. Brake lines must be at least 1/2 in. (13mm) from

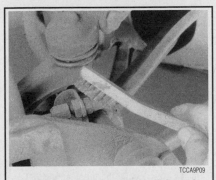

TCCA9P09

Fig. 5 Use a brush to clean the fittings of any debris

91149P14

Fig. 6 Use a suitable size flarenut or "line" wrench . . .

91149P15

Fig. 7 . . . to loosen the brake line fitting from the wheel cylinder

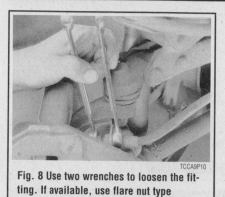

Fig. 8 Use two wrenches to loosen the fitting. If available, use flare nut type wrenches

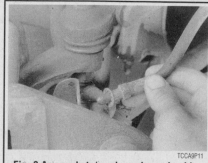

Fig. 9 Any gaskets/crush washers should be replaced with new ones during installation

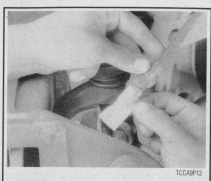

Fig. 10 Tape or plug the line to prevent contamination

the steering column and other moving parts. Any protective shielding or insulators must be reinstalled in the original location.

✳✳ WARNING

Make sure the hose is NOT kinked or touching any part of the frame or suspension after installation. These conditions may cause the hose to fail prematurely.

10. Using two wrenches as before, tighten each fitting.
11. Install any retaining clips or brackets on the lines.
12. If removed, install the wheel and tire assemblies, then carefully lower the vehicle to the ground.
13. Refill the brake master cylinder reservoir with clean, fresh brake fluid, meeting DOT 3 specifications. Properly bleed the brake system.
14. Connect the negative battery cable.

Bleeding The Brake System

▶ See Figures 11 thru 17

When any part of the hydraulic system has been disconnected for repair or replacement, air may get into the lines and cause spongy pedal action (because air can be compressed and brake fluid cannot). To correct this condition, it is necessary to bleed the hydraulic system so to be sure all air is purged.

When bleeding the brake system, bleed one brake cylinder at a time, beginning at the cylinder with the longest hydraulic line (farthest from the master cylinder) first. ALWAYS Keep the master cylinder reservoir filled with brake fluid during the bleeding operation. Never use brake fluid that has been drained from the hydraulic system, no matter how clean it is.

The primary and secondary hydraulic brake systems are separate and are bled independently. During the bleeding operation, do not allow the reservoir to run dry. Keep the master cylinder reservoir filled with brake fluid.

1. Clean all dirt from around the master cylinder fill cap, remove the cap and fill the master cylinder with brake fluid until the level is within ¼ in. (6mm) of the top edge of the reservoir.
2. Clean the bleeder screws at all 4 wheels. The bleeder screws are located on the back of the brake backing plate (drum brakes) and on the top of the brake calipers (disc brakes).

3. Attach a length of rubber hose over the bleeder screw and place the other end of the hose in a glass jar, submerged in brake fluid.
4. Open the bleeder screw ½–¾ turn. Have an assistant slowly depress the brake pedal.
5. Close the bleeder screw and tell your assistant to allow the brake pedal to return slowly. Continue this process to purge all air from the system.
6. When bubbles cease to appear at the end of the bleeder hose, close the bleeder screw and remove the hose. Tighten the bleeder screw to the proper torque:
7. Check the master cylinder fluid level and add fluid accordingly. Do this after bleeding each wheel.
8. Repeat the bleeding operation at the remaining 3 wheels, ending with the one closet to the master cylinder.
9. Fill the master cylinder reservoir to the proper level.

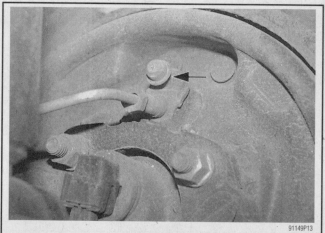

Fig. 11 The bleed screw for the rear brakes is located on the rear of the backing plate, just above the brake line

Fig. 12 Remove the protective rubber cap for the bleed screw

Fig. 13 Attach a hose connected to a bottle with a small amount of brake fluid in it to the bleed screw

Fig. 14 Slowly open the bleed screw and have an assistant depress the brake pedal while observing the hose for bubbles

Fig. 15 Remove the protective rubber cap for the bleed screw on the front brake caliper

Fig. 16 Attach a hose connected to a bottle with a small amount of brake fluid in it to the bleed screw on the brake caliper

Fig. 17 Slowly open the bleed screw on the brake caliper and have an assistant depress the brake pedal while observing the hose for bubbles

DISC BRAKES

DISC BRAKE COMPONENTS

1. Bleed valve
2. Steering knuckle
3. Caliper assembly
4. Outer brake pad
5. Inner brake pad
6. Brake line connection
7. Caliper piston

Brake Pads

REMOVAL & INSTALLATION

▶ **See Figures 18 thru 32**

❋❋ CAUTION

Older brake pads or shoes may contain asbestos, which has been determined to be cancer causing agent. Never clean the brake surfaces with compressed air! Avoid inhaling any dust from any brake surface! When cleaning brake surfaces, use a commercially available brake cleaning fluid.

1. Remove ½ of the brake fluid from the master cylinder reservoir.
2. Raise and safely support the vehicle.
3. Remove the wheel and tire assembly.
4. Remove the caliper-to-steering knuckle mounting bolts.
5. Lift the caliper off of the steering knuckle and support it using mechanics wire or another suitable device to prevent damage to the brake hose.

➡ **It may be necessary to compress the piston slightly to allow the removal of the caliper.**

6. Remove the outboard disc brake pad from the caliper.
7. Remove the inboard disc brake pad from the brake caliper.

To install:

8. Thoroughly clean the caliper and the steering knuckle where the pads contact.

Fig. 18 Remove the outer pad from the caliper by pressing the pad inward to release the mounting dowels from the center of the pad

Fig. 19 Compress the piston using a C-clamp or other suitable tool

Fig. 20 Remove the inboard pad by releasing the retaining clip from the piston

Fig. 21 Clean the pad guide mounts on the steering knuckle. Make sure there is no rust or build-up present

Fig. 22 Clean the caliper assembly of any build-up or rust before installing the new pads

Fig. 23 Apply a coat of anti-squeal lubricant to the pads before installing the new pads

ON SOME MODELS THE RETAINER SPRING IS ALREADY STAKED TO THE INBOARD SHOE.

Fig. 24 The inboard shoe and lining assembly has a retaining spring attached to the back

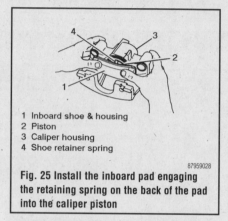

1 Inboard shoe & housing
2 Piston
3 Caliper housing
4 Shoe retainer spring

Fig. 25 Install the inboard pad engaging the retaining spring on the back of the pad into the caliper piston

Fig. 26 Insert the outboard pad and align the mounting dowels with the . . .

Fig. 27 . . . centering holes in the center of the piston

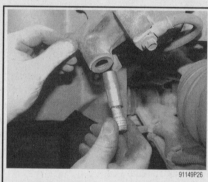

Fig. 28 Remove the mounting bolts and sleeve assembly from the caliper

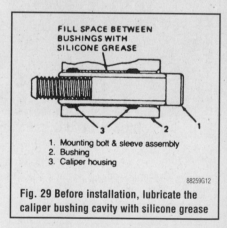

FILL SPACE BETWEEN BUSHINGS WITH SILICONE GREASE

1. Mounting bolt & sleeve assembly
2. Bushing
3. Caliper housing

Fig. 29 Before installation, lubricate the caliper bushing cavity with silicone grease

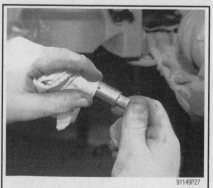

Fig. 30 Thoroughly clean the mounting bolt sleeves and . . .

Fig. 31 . . . apply a suitable disc brake slide grease to the sleeves

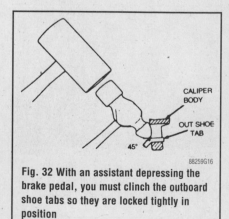

CALIPER BODY

OUT SHOE TAB

45°

Fig. 32 With an assistant depressing the brake pedal, you must clinch the outboard shoe tabs so they are locked tightly in position

9. If installing new disc brake pads, use a C-clamp or similar tool to push the caliper piston into the caliper bore. This will allow room for the new pads.

10. Coat the new pads with a suitable anti-squeal lubricant.

11. Place the outboard disc brake pad into position on the caliper ensuring that the mounting dowels are aligned with the holes in the caliper.

12. Place the inboard disc brake pad into the caliper piston and engaging the retaining clip.

13. Thoroughly clean the 2 mounting bolt sleeves and apply an appropriate coating of brake caliper slide grease, or another suitable lubricant.

14. Position the disc brake caliper onto the rotor.

15. Install the 2 mounting bolts and torque to 40 ft. lbs. (54 Nm).

16. Reinstall the wheel and tire assembly. Torque the lug nuts to 100 ft. lbs. (140 Nm).

17. Lower the vehicle.

18. Pump the brake pedal several times to achieve a good pedal before attempting to move the vehicle.

19. With an assistant depressing the brake pedal, you must clinch the outboard shoe tabs so they are locked tightly in position.

20. Check the brake fluid level in the master cylinder fluid reservoir and add fluid as necessary.

21. Road test the vehicle and check for proper brake system operation.

INSPECTION

▶ See Figure 33

1. Raise and support the vehicle.
2. Remove the tire and wheel.
3. Looking down through the inspection hole on the top of the caliper, inspect the brake pads. If the lining is worn down to within $\frac{1}{32}$ in. (0.8mm) of the shoe, the pads must be replaced.

➡**This figure may disagree with your state's automobile inspection laws.**

If the brake lining is soaked with brake fluid or grease, it must be replaced. If this is the case, the brake rotor should be sanded with crocus cloth to remove all traces of brake fluid, and the calipers and lines should be inspected for leaks.

If the lining is chipped, cracked, or otherwise damaged, it must be replaced with a new lining.

➡**Always replace the brake linings in sets of two on both ends of the axle. Never replace just one pad, or both on one side and not the other. When replacing the brakes, it is a good idea to replace one side at a time so that you always have an example to refer to if you get confused during reassembly.**

Brake Caliper

REMOVAL & INSTALLATION

▶ See Figures 34 thru 40

❉❉ CAUTION

Older brake pads or shoes may contain asbestos, which has been determined to be cancer causing agent. Never clean the brake surfaces with compressed air! Avoid inhaling any dust from any brake surface! When cleaning brake surfaces, use a commercially available brake cleaning fluid.

1. Siphon ⅔ of the brake fluid out of the master cylinder.
2. Raise and safely support the vehicle.
3. Remove the tire and wheel assembly.
4. If the caliper is to be completely removed from the vehicle for bench service, disconnect and cap the brake line from the caliper. Discard the old washers.

Fig. 33 Measuring the brake pad thickness to see if the pads need to be replaced

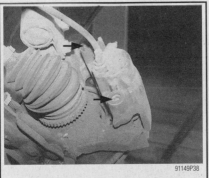
Fig. 34 The brake caliper is mounted to the steering knuckle with two bolts

Fig. 35 Remove the brake caliper-to-steering knuckle retaining bolts

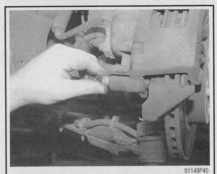
Fig. 36 In most cases, the mounting bolts will have to be slightly puled out further to allow clearance for the caliper to be removed

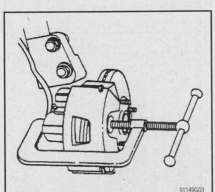
Fig. 37 If necessary for removal, the brake caliper piston can be compressed with the caliper mounted on the vehicle

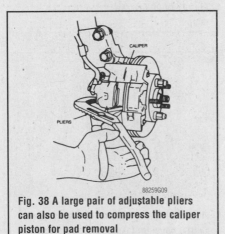
Fig. 38 A large pair of adjustable pliers can also be used to compress the caliper piston for pad removal

5. Remove the caliper mounting bolts and sleeves.
6. Remove the caliper from the knuckle.

➡If the caliper is tough to remove from the steering knuckle, compress the caliper piston back into the caliper bore using a large pair of pliers or a C-clamp.

7. Remove the brake pads from the caliper, if it is being replaced.

To install:

8. Install the brake pads in the caliper.
9. Install the caliper on the steering knuckle.
10. Install the mounting bolts and sleeves and tighten to 40 ft. lbs. (51 Nm).
11. If the caliper brake line was disconnected, uncap and connect the brake hose to the caliper using new washers. Tighten the mounting bolt to 35 ft. lbs. (44 Nm).
12. Refill the master cylinder and bleed the brake system.
13. Install the tire and wheel assembly and tighten to 100 ft. lbs. (140 Nm).
14. Lower the vehicle. Verify correct brake operation.

OVERHAUL

◆ See Figures 41 thru 48

➡Some vehicles may be equipped dual piston calipers. The procedure to overhaul the caliper is essentially the same with the exception of multiple pistons, O-rings and dust boots.

1. Remove the caliper from the vehicle and place on a clean workbench.

✳✳ CAUTION

NEVER place your fingers in front of the pistons in an attempt to catch or protect the pistons when applying compressed air. This could result in personal injury!

➡Depending upon the vehicle, there are two different ways to remove the piston from the caliper. Refer to the brake pad replace-

Fig. 39 Remove the brake caliper from the steering knuckle

Fig. 40 Remove the brake caliper from the hub assembly and support it using mechanic's wire or another suitable device

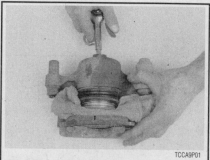
Fig. 41 For some types of calipers, use compressed air to drive the piston out of the caliper, but make sure to keep your fingers clear

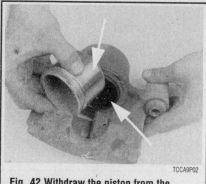
Fig. 42 Withdraw the piston from the caliper bore

Fig. 43 On some vehicles, you must remove the anti-rattle clip

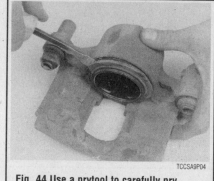
Fig. 44 Use a prytool to carefully pry around the edge of the boot . . .

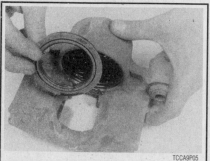
Fig. 45 . . . then remove the boot from the caliper housing, taking care not to score or damage the bore

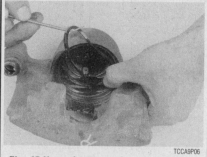
Fig. 46 Use extreme caution when removing the piston seal; DO NOT scratch the caliper bore

Fig. 47 Use the proper size driving tool and a mallet to properly seal the boots in the caliper housing

ment procedure to make sure you have the correct procedure for your vehicle.

2. The first method is as follows:

   a. Stuff a shop towel or a block of wood into the caliper to catch the piston.

   b. Remove the caliper piston using compressed air applied into the caliper inlet hole. Inspect the piston for scoring, nicks, corrosion and/or worn or damaged chrome plating. The piston must be replaced if any of these conditions are found.

3. For the second method, you must rotate the piston to retract it from the caliper.

4. If equipped, remove the anti-rattle clip.

5. Use a prytool to remove the caliper boot, being careful not to scratch the housing bore.

6. Remove the piston seals from the groove in the caliper bore.

7. Carefully loosen the brake bleeder valve cap and valve from the caliper housing.

8. Inspect the caliper bores, pistons and mounting threads for scoring or excessive wear.

9. Use crocus cloth to polish out light corrosion from the piston and bore.

10. Clean all parts with denatured alcohol and dry with compressed air.

To assemble:

11. Lubricate and install the bleeder valve and cap.

12. Install the new seals into the caliper bore grooves, making sure they are not twisted.

13. Lubricate the piston bore.

14. Install the pistons and boots into the bores of the calipers and push to the bottom of the bores.

15. Use a suitable driving tool to seat the boots in the housing.

16. Install the caliper in the vehicle.

17. Install the wheel and tire assembly, then carefully lower the vehicle.

18. Properly bleed the brake system.

Brake Disc (Rotor)

REMOVAL & INSTALLATION

▶ **See Figures 49 thru 54**

1. Raise and safely support the vehicle.
2. Remove the tire and wheel assembly.
3. Remove the caliper mounting bolts.
4. Using mechanic's wire or another suitable device, support the caliper out of the way. Do not disconnect the brake hose from the caliper or allow the caliper to hang from the brake hose.
5. Slide the rotor off the hub.

➡ **The rotor may have a rust build-up on it and will not slide off. If this happens a soft-faced or brass hammer should be used to aid in the removal of the rotor.**

To install:

6. Inspect the rotor for grooves, heat cracks or excessive run-out. A damaged rotor should be replaced.
7. If a new rotor is being installed the caliper piston will have to be pushed back into the caliper bore enough so the caliper will fit over the rotor. A large C-clamp or pair of pliers may be used to push the piston back into the caliper bore.
8. Slide the rotor onto the hub.
9. Install the caliper and caliper mounting bolts. Tighten the bolts to 40 ft. lbs. (54 Nm).
10. Install the tire and wheel assembly.
11. Lower the vehicle. Tighten the wheel lug nuts to 100 ft. lbs. (140 Nm).
12. Pump the brake pedal several times to seat the pads against the rotor before moving the vehicle.
13. Check and add brake fluid as necessary.

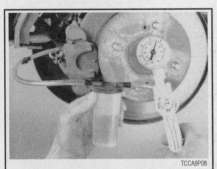

Fig. 48 There are tools, such as this Mighty-Vac, available to assist in proper brake system bleeding

Fig. 49 The brake caliper is mounted to the steering knuckle with two bolts

Fig. 50 Remove the brake caliper-to-steering knuckle retaining bolts

Fig. 51 Remove the brake caliper from the steering knuckle and . . .

Fig. 52 . . . support it using mechanic's wire or another suitable device

Fig. 53 Carefully slide the rotor from the hub and over the wheel lug nut studs . . .

Fig. 54 . . . and remove the rotor from the hub assembly

INSPECTION

Check the disc brake rotor for scoring, cracks or other damage. Rotor run-out should be measured while the rotor is installed, while rotor thickness/thickness variation may be checked with the rotor installed or removed. Use a dial gauge to check rotor run-out. Check the rotor thickness to make sure it is greater than minimum thickness and check for thickness variations using a caliper micrometer.

Thickness Variation

▶ See Figure 55

1. Measure the thickness at four or more points on the rotor. Make all measure measurements at the same distance in from the edge of the rotor. Use a micrometer calibrated in ten-thousandths of an inch.
2. A rotor that varies in thickness by more than 0.0005 in. (0.013mm) can cause pedal pulsation and/or front end vibration during brake applications. A rotor that does not meet these specifications should be resurfaced to specifications or replaced.

Lateral Run-out

▶ See Figure 56

1. Remove the wheel and tire assembly.
2. Fasten the lug nuts to retain the rotor.
3. Secure a dial indicator to the steering knuckle so the indicator button contacts the rotor at about 0.5 in. (13mm) from the outer edge of the rotor.
4. Set the dial indicator to zero.
5. Turn the wheel one complete revolution and observe the total indicated run-out.
6. If the run-out exceeds 0.003 in. (0.08mm), resurface or replace the rotor.

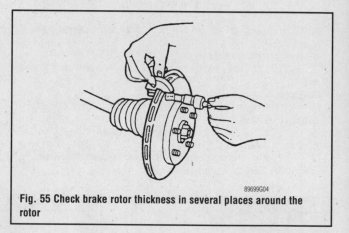

Fig. 55 Check brake rotor thickness in several places around the rotor

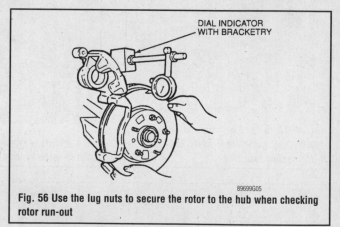

Fig. 56 Use the lug nuts to secure the rotor to the hub when checking rotor run-out

DRUM BRAKES

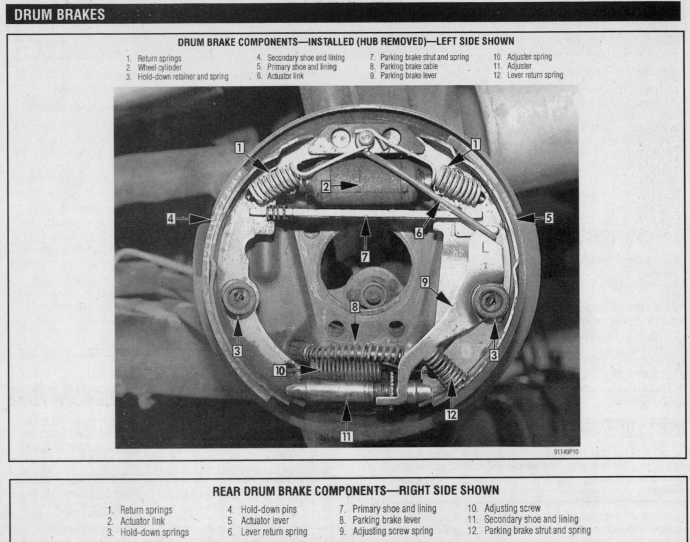

DRUM BRAKE COMPONENTS—INSTALLED (HUB REMOVED)—LEFT SIDE SHOWN

1. Return springs
2. Wheel cylinder
3. Hold-down retainer and spring
4. Secondary shoe and lining
5. Primary shoe and lining
6. Actuator link
7. Parking brake strut and spring
8. Parking brake cable
9. Parking brake lever
10. Adjuster spring
11. Adjuster
12. Lever return spring

91149P10

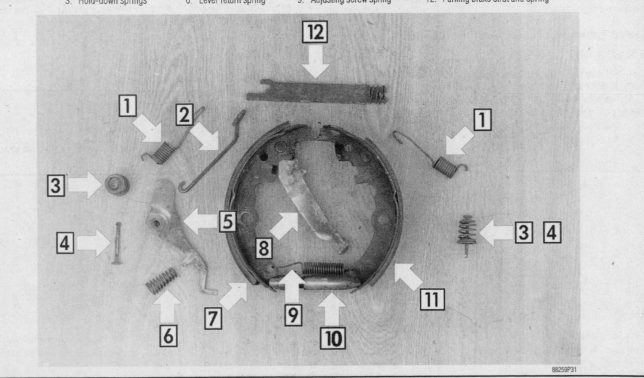

REAR DRUM BRAKE COMPONENTS—RIGHT SIDE SHOWN

1. Return springs
2. Actuator link
3. Hold-down springs
4. Hold-down pins
5. Actuator lever
6. Lever return spring
7. Primary shoe and lining
8. Parking brake lever
9. Adjusting screw spring
10. Adjusting screw
11. Secondary shoe and lining
12. Parking brake strut and spring

88259P31

Brake Drums

REMOVAL & INSTALLATION

▶ **See Figures 57 and 58**

1. Rasie and support the vehicle.
2. Remove the wheel and tire assembly.
3. Mark the relationship of the drum to the axle and remove the drum. If it cannot be slipped off easily, try the following:

    a. Check to see that the parking brake is fully released. If so, the brake shoes are probably locked against the drum. See the Adjustment procedure located under brake shoe removal for details on how to back off the adjuster.

    b. Remove the access hole plug from the backing plate and insert a suitable tool through the hole to push the parking brake lever off its stop. This will allow the shoe linings to retract slightly.

    c. Insert a punch tool through the hole at the bottom of the splash shield. Tap gently on the tool to loosen the drum.

    d. Use a rubber mallet to tap gently on the outer rim of the drum.

To install:

4. Reposition the drum making sure to align the matchmarks made during removal.
5. Install the wheel and tire assembly, then carefully lower the vehicle
6. The lug nut tightening specifications is 100 ft. lbs. (140 Nm).

INSPECTION

▶ **See Figure 59**

1. After removing the brake drum, wipe out the accumulated dust with a damp cloth.

> ✳✳ **CAUTION**
>
> **Do not blow the brake dust out of the drums with compressed air or lung power. Brake linings may contain asbestos, a known cancer causing substance. Dispose of the cloth used to clean the parts after use.**

2. Inspect the drums for cracks, deep grooves, roughness, or scoring. Replace any drum which is cracked; do not try to weld it up. Light scoring of the drum not exceeding 0.020 in. (0.51mm) in depth will not affect brake operation.

3. Smooth any slight scores by polishing the friction surface with fine emery cloth. Heavy or extensive scoring will cause excessive lining wear and should be removed from the drum through resurfacing, a job to be referred to your local machine shop or garage. The maximum finished diameter of the drums is stamped onto the outer surface of the brake drum.

4. Inspect the brake drum for excessive taper and out-of-round. When measuring a drum for out-of-round, taper and wear, take measurements at the open and closed edges of the machined surface and at right angles to each other.

Brake Shoes

INSPECTION

After removing the brake drum, inspect the brake shoes. If the lining is worn down to within ⅟₃₂ in. (0.8mm) of a rivet, the shoes must be replaced.

➡ **This figure may disagree with your state's automobile inspection laws.**

If the brake lining is soaked with brake fluid or grease, it must be replaced. If this is the case, the brake drum should be sanded with crocus cloth to remove all traces of brake fluid, and the wheel cylinders should be rebuilt. Clean all grit from the friction surface of the drum before replacing it.

If the lining is chipped, cracked, or otherwise damaged, it must be replaced with a new lining.

➡ **Always replace the brake linings in sets of two on both ends of the axle. Never replace just one shoe, or both shoes on one side and not the other. When replacing the brakes, it is a good idea to replace one side at a time so that you always have an example to refer to if you get confused during reassembly.**

Check the condition of the shoes, retracting springs, and hold-down springs for signs of overheating. If the shoes or springs have a slight blue color, this indicates overheating and replacement of the shoes and springs is recommended. The wheel cylinders should be rebuilt as a precaution against future problems.

REMOVAL & INSTALLATION

▶ **See Figures 60 thru 70**

> ✳✳ **CAUTION**
>
> **Older brake pads or shoes may contain asbestos, which has been determined to be cancer causing agent. Never clean the brake surfaces with compressed air! Avoid inhaling any dust from any brake surface! When cleaning brake surfaces, use a commercially available brake cleaning fluid.**

1. Loosen the lug nuts on the wheel to be serviced, raise and support the car, and remove the wheel and brake drum.

➡ **It is not really necessary to remove the hub and wheel bearing assembly from the axle, but it does make the job easier. If you can work with the hub and bearing assembly in place, skip down to Step 3.**

2. Remove the four hub and bearing assembly retaining bolts and remove the assembly from the axle.

3. Remove the return springs from the shoes with a pair of needle nose pliers. There are also special brake spring pliers for this job.

4. Remove the hold-down springs by gripping them with a pair of pliers, then pressing down and turning 90°. There are special tools to grab and turn these parts, but pliers work fairly well.

5. Remove the shoe hold-down pins from behind the brake backing plate. They will simply slide out once the hold-down spring tension is relieved.

Fig. 57 Some vehicles may have a retainer that must be removed before you can take off the drum

Fig. 58 Usually, the drum will slip off the hub and bearing with ease

Fig. 59 The drum maximum diameter is usually stamped onto the outside of the drum

6. Lift up the actuator lever for the self-adjusting mechanism and remove the actuating link. Remove the actuator lever, pivot, and the pivot return spring.

7. Spread the shoes apart to clear the wheel cylinder pistons and remove the parking brake strut and spring.

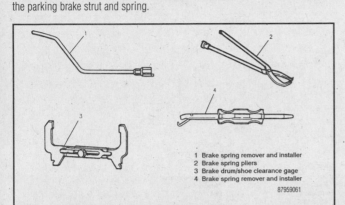

1 Brake spring remover and installer
2 Brake spring pliers
3 Brake drum/shoe clearance gage
4 Brake spring remover and installer

87959061

Fig. 60 Some special tools are required when servicing drum brakes

8. If the hub and bearing assembly is still in place, spread the shoes far enough apart to clear it.

9. Disconnect the parking brake cable from the lever. Remove the shoes, still connected by their adjusting screw spring, from the car.

10. With the shoes removed, note the position of the adjusting spring and remove the spring and adjusting screw.

11. Remove the C-clip from the parking brake lever and remove the lever from the secondary shoe.

12. Use a damp cloth to remove all dirt and dust from the backing plate and brake parts. See the warning about brake dust in the drum removal procedure.

13. Check the wheel cylinders by carefully pulling the lower edges of the wheel cylinder boots away from the cylinders. If there is excessive leakage, the inside of the cylinder will be moist with fluid. If leakage exists, a wheel cylinder overhaul or replacement is in order. Do not delay, because brake failure could result.

➡**A small amount of fluid will be present to act as a lubricant for the wheel cylinder pistons. Fluid spilling from the boot center hole, after the piston is removed, indicates cup leakage and the necessity for cylinder overhaul.**

88259P17

Fig. 61 Before beginning brake shoe removal, spray the components with a commercially available cleaner

88259P18

Fig. 62 Use a suitable tool to unhook the return springs

88259P19

Fig. 63 Unhook the right side return spring with a suitable brake spring removal tool . . .

88259P20

Fig. 64 . . . then remove the other return spring from the assembly

88259P21

Fig. 65 Use the brake tool to compress the hold-down spring and twist the plate to free the pin

88259P22

Fig. 66 After removing the actuating link, remove the actuator lever and pivot return spring

88259P23

Fig. 67 Remove the parking brake strut and spring

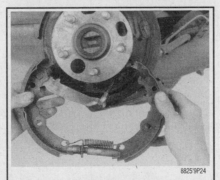

88259P24

Fig. 68 Spread the brake shoes enough to clear the hub and bearing . . .

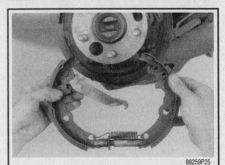

88259P25

Fig. 69 . . . then disconnect the parking brake cable and remove the shoe and spring assembly from the vehicle

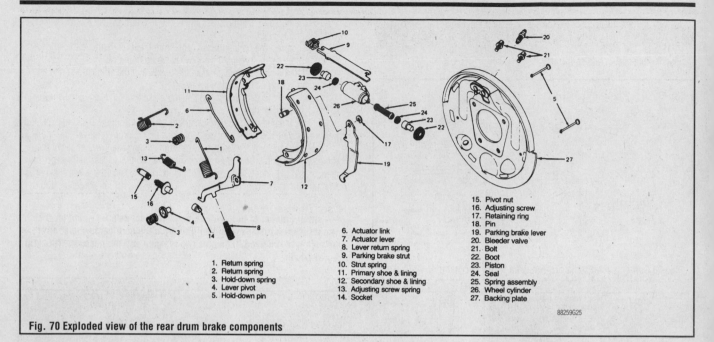

6. Actuator link
7. Actuator lever
8. Lever return spring
9. Parking brake strut
10. Strut spring
11. Primary shoe & lining
12. Secondary shoe & lining
13. Adjusting screw spring
14. Socket

1. Return spring
2. Return spring
3. Hold-down spring
4. Lever pivot
5. Hold-down pin

15. Pivot nut
16. Adjusting screw
17. Retaining ring
18. Pin
19. Parking brake lever
20. Bleeder valve
21. Bolt
22. Boot
23. Piston
24. Seal
25. Spring assembly
26. Wheel cylinder
27. Backing plate

Fig. 70 Exploded view of the rear drum brake components

To install

14. Check the backing plate attaching bolts to make sure that they are tight. Use fine emery cloth to clean all rust and dirt from the shoe contact surfaces on the plate.

15. Lubricate the fulcrum end of the parking brake lever with brake grease specially made for the purpose. Install the lever on the secondary shoe and secure with C-clip.

16. Install the adjusting screw and spring on the shoes, connecting them together. The coils of the spring must not be over the star wheel on the adjuster. The left and right hand springs are not interchangeable. Do not mix them up.

17. Lubricate the shoe contact surfaces on the backing plate with the brake grease. Be certain when you are using this stuff that none of it actually gets on the linings or drums. Apply the same grease to the point where the parking brake cable contacts the plate. Use the grease sparingly.

18. Spread the shoe assemblies apart and connect the parking brake cable. Install the shoes on the backing plate, engaging the shoes at the top temporarily with the wheel cylinder pistons. Make sure that the star wheel on the adjuster is lined up with the adjusting hole in the backing plate, if the hole is back there.

19. Spread the shoes apart slightly and install the parking brake strut and spring. Make sure that the end of the strut without the spring engages the parking brake lever. The end with the spring engages the primary shoe (the one with the shorter lining).

20. Install the actuator pivot, lever and return spring. Install the actuating link in the shoe retainer. Lift up the actuator lever and hook the link into the lever.

21. Install the hold-down pins through the back of the plate, install the lever pivots and hold-down springs. Install the shoe return springs with a pair of pliers. Be very careful not to stretch or otherwise distort these springs.

22. Take a look at everything. Make sure the linings are in the right place, the self-adjusting mechanism is correctly installed, and the parking brake parts are all hooked up. If in doubt, remove the other wheel and take a look at that one for comparison.

23. Measure the width of the linings, then measure the inside width of the drum. Adjust the linings by means of the adjuster so that the drum will fit onto the linings.

24. Install the hub and bearing assembly onto the axle if removed. Tighten the retaining bolts to 38 ft. lbs. (51 Nm).

25. Install the drum and wheel, tightening the lug nuts to 100 ft. lbs. (136 Nm). Adjust the brakes using the procedure given in this section. Be sure to install a rubber hole cover in the knock-out hole after the adjustment is complete. Adjust the parking brake.

26. Lower the car and check the pedal for any sponginess or lack of a hard feel. Check the braking action and the parking brake. The brakes must not be applied severely immediately after installation. They should be used moderately for the first 200 miles of city driving or 1000 miles of highway driving, to allow the linings to conform to the shape of the drum.

ADJUSTMENTS

◆ See Figure 71

1. Raise and support the vehicle safely.
2. Remove the tire and wheel assembly.
3. Matchmark the relationship of the drum to the axle flange, then remove the brake drum.
4. Measure the drum inside diameter using brake shoe gauge J 12177–A, or equivalent.
5. Turning the star wheel, adjust the shoe and lining diameter to be 0.030 in. (0.76mm) less than the inside drum diameter for each wheel.
6. Install the drums and wheels, aligning the previous marks.
7. Carefully lower the vehicle.
8. Tighten the wheel nuts to 100 ft. lbs. (140 Nm).

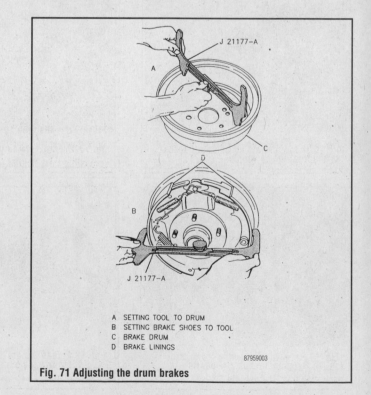

A SETTING TOOL TO DRUM
B SETTING BRAKE SHOES TO TOOL
C BRAKE DRUM
D BRAKE LININGS

Fig. 71 Adjusting the drum brakes

Wheel Cylinders

REMOVAL & INSTALLATION

▶ **See Figures 72 thru 78**

1. Raise and safely support the vehicle.
2. Remove the rear tire and wheel assembly.
3. Thoroughly clean the area around the brake line connection and the retainer bolts. A generous application of penetrating oil may make brake line removal easier.
4. Disconnect the brake line from the back of the wheel cylinder and plug the opening in the line to prevent fluid loss and contamination.
5. Remove the brake drum.
6. Remove the hub and bearing assembly.
7. Remove the 2 bolts from the back of the wheel cylinder using a No. 6 TORX® socket.
8. Remove the wheel cylinder.

To install:

9. Install wheel cylinder and tighten bolts to 15 ft. lbs. (20 Nm).
10. Install hub and bearing assembly and tighten nut to 43 ft. lbs. (58 Nm).
11. Connect the brake line to wheel cylinder and tighten to 17 ft. lbs. (23 Nm).
12. Install the brake drum.
13. Bleed the brakes.
14. Install the wheel and tire assembly.
15. Lower the vehicle.
16. Check brake fluid level and fill as necessary.
17. Road test the vehicle and verify proper operation.

OVERHAUL

▶ **See Figures 79 thru 88**

Wheel cylinder overhaul kits may be available, but often at little or no savings over a reconditioned wheel cylinder. It often makes sense with these components to substitute a new or reconditioned part instead of attempting an overhaul.

Fig. 72 Use a suitable size flarenut or "line" wrench . . .

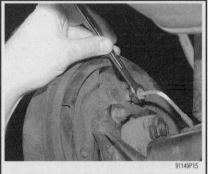
Fig. 73 . . . to loosen the brake line fitting from the wheel cylinder

Fig. 74 Detach the connector for the rear wheel speed sensor

Fig. 75 The hub retaining bolts are accessible through a hole in the hub flange

Fig. 76 The hub retaining bolt nuts are accessible from behind the wheel

Fig. 77 Insert a suitable tool through the hole in the hub flange and hold the retaining nut tight on the back of the hub, loosen the retaining bolts

Fig. 78 Remove the hub and bearing assembly from the vehicle

Fig. 79 Remove the outer boots from the wheel cylinder

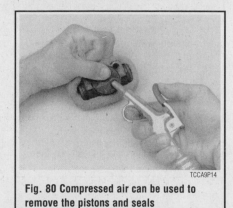
Fig. 80 Compressed air can be used to remove the pistons and seals

If no replacement is available, or you would prefer to overhaul your wheel cylinders, the following procedure may be used. When rebuilding and installing wheel cylinders, avoid getting any contaminants into the system. Always use clean, new, high quality brake fluid. If dirty or improper fluid has been used, it will be necessary to drain the entire system, flush the system with proper brake fluid, replace all rubber components, then refill and bleed the system.

1. Remove the wheel cylinder from the vehicle and place on a clean workbench.

2. First remove and discard the old rubber boots, then withdraw the pistons. Piston cylinders are equipped with seals and a spring assembly, all located behind the pistons in the cylinder bore.

3. Remove the remaining inner components, seals and spring assembly. Compressed air may be useful in removing these components. If no compressed air is available, be VERY careful not to score the wheel cylinder bore when removing parts from it. Discard all components for which replacements were supplied in the rebuild kit.

4. Wash the cylinder and metal parts in denatured alcohol or clean brake fluid.

❋❋ WARNING

Never use a mineral-based solvent such as gasoline, kerosene or paint thinner for cleaning purposes. These solvents will swell rubber components and quickly deteriorate them.

5. Allow the parts to air dry or use compressed air. Do not use rags for cleaning, since lint will remain in the cylinder bore.

6. Inspect the piston and replace it if it shows scratches.

7. Lubricate the cylinder bore and seals using clean brake fluid.

8. Position the spring assembly.

9. Install the inner seals, then the pistons.

10. Insert the new boots into the counterbores by hand. Do not lubricate the boots.

11. Install the wheel cylinder.

Fig. 81 Remove the pistons, cup seals and spring from the cylinder

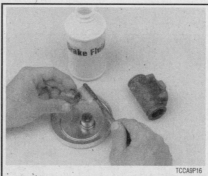

Fig. 82 Use brake fluid and a soft brush to clean the pistons . . .

Fig. 83 . . . and the bore of the wheel cylinder

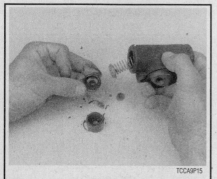

Fig. 84 Once cleaned and inspected, the wheel cylinder is ready for assembly

Fig. 85 Lubricate the cup seals with brake fluid

Fig. 86 Install the spring, then the cup seals in the bore

Fig. 87 Lightly lubricate the pistons, then install them

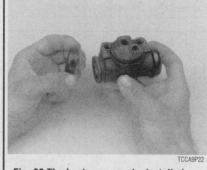

Fig. 88 The boots can now be installed over the wheel cylinder ends

Fig. 89 Use a box end wrench to release the parking brake cable from the backing plate

Brake Backing Plate

REMOVAL & INSTALLATION

◆ See Figure 89

1. Raise and safely support the vehicle. Remove the rear wheel(s).
2. Remove the drum, rear brake shoes and wheel cylinders as described earlier in this section.
3. Disconnect the parking brake cable from the backing plate.
4. If not removed already, unfasten the retaining bolts, then remove the hub and bearing assembly. For details, please refer to the procedure in Section 8 of this manual.

PARKING BRAKE

Cables

REMOVAL & INSTALLATION

Front Cable

◆ See Figures 90 and 91

1. Raise and safely support the vehicle.
2. Pull and hold the cable toward the rear of the car to create slack in the cable.
3. Bend the tang on the connector to allow cable removal.
4. Detach the cable from the connector.
5. Unfasten the fold over retaining clip, then remove the cable from the equalizer.
6. Carefully lower the vehicle.
7. Remove the console. For the Sunfire, remove the shifter boot.
8. Move the lever to the off position.

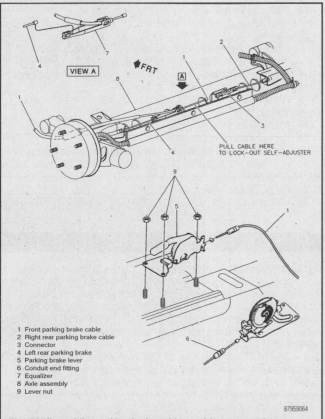

1 Front parking brake cable
2 Right rear parking brake cable
3 Connector
4 Left rear parking brake
5 Parking brake lever
6 Conduit end fitting
7 Equalizer
8 Axle assembly
9 Lever nut

PULL CABLE HERE
TO LOCK-OUT SELF-ADJUSTER

VIEW A

FRT

87959064

Fig. 90 View of the parking brake cables and lever mounting

5. Remove the backing plate from the vehicle.
To install:
6. Install the backing plate to the axle assembly.
7. Position the wheel cylinder to the backing plate and secure with the retainers.
8. Install the hub and bearing, then secure using the assembly bolts.
9. Connect the parking brake cable to the backing plate.
10. Uncap and attach the inlet tube and nut to the wheel cylinder. Tighten to 17 ft. lbs. (23 Nm).
11. Install the drum and rear brake shoes. Check the brake adjustment.
12. Bleed the brake system.
13. Install the rear wheel(s).
14. Carefully lower the vehicle, then tighten the lug nuts to 100 ft. lbs. (140 Nm).
15. Adjust the parking brake.

9. Remove the cable conduit end fitting from the handle assembly.
10. Pull the cable until the notch on the ratchet is visible through the cover plate opening.
11. Push the pawl spring downward toward the notch in the ratchet.
12. Release the cable slowly to allow the notch to catch the leg of the spring.
13. Remove the front parking brake cable button from the reel assembly.
14. Remove the left rocker panel/door sill plate.
15. Disconnect the grommet and retainer from the floor pan.
16. Detach the cable from the clip on the #2 bar, under the carpet.
17. Remove the front cable from the vehicle.
To install:
18. Route the cable through the floor pan, from the inside to the outside.
19. Attach the cable conduit fitting to the handle assembly.
20. Fasten the front cable bottom of the reel assembly.
21. Connect the cable to the #2 bar clip under the carpet.
22. Install the console. For the Sunfire, install the shifter boot.
23. Fasten the left rocker panel/door sill plate.
24. Raise and safely support the vehicle.
25. Fasten the fold over bracket to the body.
26. Attach the cable to the equalizer.
27. Fasten the cable to the connector. Bend the tang on the connector to hold the cable.

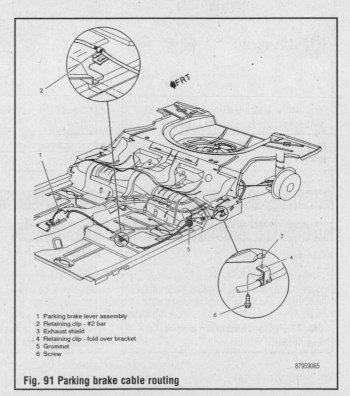

1 Parking brake lever assembly
2 Retaining clip - #2 bar
3 Exhaust shield
4 Retaining clip - fold over bracket
5 Grommet
6 Screw

FRT

87959065

Fig. 91 Parking brake cable routing

28. Carefully lower the vehicle.
29. Adjust the parking brake cable, as outlined in this section.

Right and Left Rear Cables

▶ See Figure 92

1. Remove the console. For the Sunfire, remove the shifter boot also.
2. Move the parking brake lever to the off position.
3. Disconnect the cable conduit fitting from the handle assembly.
4. Pull the cable until the notch on the ratchet is visible through the cover plate opening.
5. Push the pawl spring downward toward the notch in the ratchet, as shown in the accompanying figure.
6. Release the cable slowly to allow the notch to catch the leg of the spring.
7. Raise and safely support the vehicle.
8. Bend the tang on the connector to allow cable removal.
9. Pull and hold the cable towards the rear of the car to create slack in the cable.
10. Disconnect the cable from the equalizer.
11. Remove the tire and wheel assembly, then remove the brake drum.
12. Insert a suitable prytool between the brake shoe and the top part of the brake adjuster bracket, then remove the cable from the bracket.
13. While depressing the conduit fitting retaining tangs, remove the conduit fitting from the backing plate.

To install:
14. Position the conduit fitting into the backing plate.
15. Fasten the parking brake cable to the parking brake lever in the drum assembly.
16. Install the brake drum, then install the tire and wheel assembly.

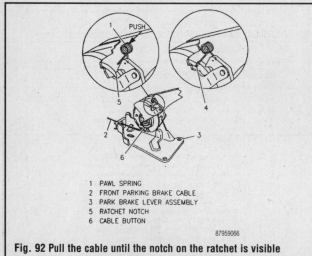

1 PAWL SPRING
2 FRONT PARKING BRAKE CABLE
3 PARK BRAKE LEVER ASSEMBLY
5 RATCHET NOTCH
6 CABLE BUTTON

87959066

Fig. 92 Pull the cable until the notch on the ratchet is visible through the cover plate opening, then push the pawl spring down toward the notch in the ratchet

17. Fasten the conduit fitting retaining tangs, and position the conduit fitting into the axle bracket.
18. Attach the cable to the equalizer.
19. Fasten the cable to the connector, then carefully lower the vehicle.
20. For the Sunfire install the shifter boot.
21. Install the console.
22. Adjust the parking brake. Check the brake tension. It may be necessary to adjust the rear brake to obtain proper tension.

ADJUSTMENT

The parking brake on these vehicles are basically self-adjusting. Fully apply and release the hand parking brake lever 4–6 times to self-adjust.

Parking Brake Lever

REMOVAL & INSTALLATION

1. Raise and safely support the vehicle.
2. Pull and hold the cable towards the rear of the car to create slack in the cable.
3. Bend the tank on the connector to allow cable removal, then detach the cable from the connector.
4. Carefully lower the vehicle.
5. Remove the console. For the Sunfire, remove the shifter boot also.
6. Move the lever to the off position.
7. Remove the cable conduit end fitting from the handle assembly.
8. Pull the cable until the notch on the ratchet is visible through the cover plate opening.
9. Push the pawl spring downward toward the notch in the ratchet.
10. Release the cable slowly to allow the notch to catch the leg of the spring.
11. Remove the front parking brake cable button from the reel assembly.
12. Detach the electrical connector.
13. Unfasten the retaining nuts, then remove the parking brake lever from the vehicle.

To install:
14. Make sure the pawl spring is engaged, as follows:
   a. Pull the cable until the notch on the ratchet is visible through the cover plate opening.
   b. Push the pawl spring downward toward the notch in the ratchet.
   c. Release the cable slowly to allow the notch to catch the leg of the spring.
15. Fasten the front parking brake cable to the handle assembly and secure the cable conduit fittings into the lever assembly.
16. Position the parking brake lever and secure with the retaining nuts. Tighten the nuts to 18 ft. lbs. (25 Nm).
17. Attach the electrical connector.
18. Raise and safely support the vehicle.
19. Attach the cable to the connector, then carefully lower the vehicle.
20. Fully apply and release the parking brake lever 4–6 times to activate the self-adjust system.
21. For the Sunfire, install the shifter boot.
22. Install the console.

ANTI-LOCK BRAKE SYSTEM

General Information

▶ See Figure 93

The Anti-lock Braking System (ABS) is standard equipment on all J-body cars covered by this manual. ABS provides the driver with 3 important benefits over standard braking systems: increased vehicle stability, improved vehicle steerability, and potentially reduced stopping distances during braking. It should be noted that although the ABS-VI system offers definite advantages, the system cannot increase brake pressure above master cylinder pressure applied by the driver and cannot apply the brakes itself.

The ABS-VI Anti-lock Braking System consists of a conventional braking system with vacuum power booster, compact master cylinder, front disc brakes, rear drum brakes and interconnecting hydraulic brake lines augmented with the ABS components. The ABS-VI system includes a hydraulic modulator assembly, Electronic Brake Control Module (EBCM) or Electronic Brake and Traction Control Module (EBTCM) (these are all different "Computer Control Modules" which differ depending upon vehicle year and application), a brake fluid level sensor, a system relay, 4 wheel speed sensors, interconnecting wiring and an amber ABS warning light.

The EBCM/EBTCM monitors inputs from the individual wheel speed sensors and determines when a wheel or wheels is/are about to lock up. The EBCM/EBTCM controls the motors on the hydraulic modulator assembly to reduce brake pressure to the wheel about to lock up. When the wheel regains traction, the brake pressure is increased until the wheel again approaches lock-up. The cycle repeats until either the vehicle comes to a stop, the brake pedal is

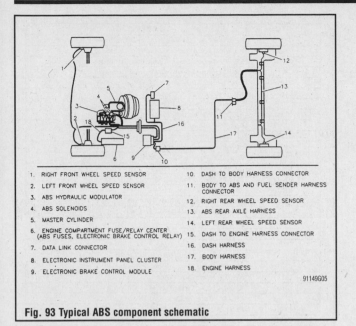

1. RIGHT FRONT WHEEL SPEED SENSOR
2. LEFT FRONT WHEEL SPEED SENSOR
3. ABS HYDRAULIC MODULATOR
4. ABS SOLENOIDS
5. MASTER CYLINDER
6. ENGINE COMPARTMENT FUSE/RELAY CENTER (ABS FUSES, ELECTRONIC BRAKE CONTROL RELAY)
7. DATA LINK CONNECTOR
8. ELECTRONIC INSTRUMENT PANEL CLUSTER
9. ELECTRONIC BRAKE CONTROL MODULE
10. DASH TO BODY HARNESS CONNECTOR
11. BODY TO ABS AND FUEL SENDER HARNESS CONNECTOR
12. RIGHT REAR WHEEL SPEED SENSOR
13. ABS REAR AXLE HARNESS
14. LEFT REAR WHEEL SPEED SENSOR
15. DASH TO ENGINE HARNESS CONNECTOR
16. DASH HARNESS
17. BODY HARNESS
18. ENGINE HARNESS

91149G05

Fig. 93 Typical ABS component schematic

released, or no wheels are about to lock up. The EBCM/EBTCM also has the ability to monitor itself and can store diagnostic codes in a non-volatile (will not be erased if the battery is disconnected) memory. The EBCM/EBTCM is serviced as an assembly.

The ABS-VI braking system employs 2 modes: base (conventional) braking and anti-lock braking. Under normal braking, the conventional part of the system stops the vehicle. When in the ABS mode, the Electromagnetic Brakes (EMB) action of the ABS system controls the two front wheels individually and the rear wheels together. If the one rear wheel is about to lock up, the hydraulic pressure to both wheels is reduced, controlling both wheels together.

Diagnosis

▶ **See Figures 94 thru 99**

The diagnosis of the ABS system is rather complex and requires quite a few special tools including scan tools, special test harnesses and other special and expensive tools. Alternative methods and common sense can be substituted, however, We at Chilton feel that it is beyond the scope of the average do-it-yourselfer. If you experience the amber ABS light on in the instrument cluster of your vehicle, check the fluid level in the master cylinder first. Low fluid level will usually illuminate the amber ABS light as well as, but not always, the red BRAKE lamp in the instrument cluster. The low fluid level could indicate a leak, but sometimes just indicates low, worn brake linings that have caused the caliper pistons and wheel cylinders to extend further, and thus using more fluid to exert force on them. Inspect the brake system for hydraulic fluid leaks and also inspect the brake linings for excessive wear.

Retrieving the Diagnostic Trouble Codes can be accomplished by the do-it-yourselfer with the proper scan tool. Attach the TECH 1-A scan tool or equivalent into the Diagnostic Link Connector (DLC) and follow the scan tool manufacturer's instructions to retrieve the DTCs from the ABS system.

ABS Hydraulic Modulator/Master Cylinder Assembly

REMOVAL & INSTALLATION

▶ **See Figure 100**

✳✳ CAUTION

To avoid personal injury, use the Tech 1® scan tool to relieve the gear tension in the hydraulic modulator. This procedure must be performed prior to removal of the brake control and motor assembly.

DIAGNOSTIC TROUBLE CODE	DESCRIPTION
14	Electronic Brake Control Relay Contacts Circuit Open
15	Electronic Brake Control Relay Contacts Circuit Shorted to Battery
16	Electronic Brake Control Relay Coil Circuit Open
17	Electronic Brake Control Relay Coil Circuit Shorted to Ground
18	Electronic Brake Control Relay Coil Circuit Shorted to Battery or Coil Shorted
21	Left Front Wheel Speed = 0
22	Right Front Wheel Speed = 0
23	Left Rear Wheel Speed = 0
24	Right Rear Wheel Speed = 0
25	Left Front Excessive Wheel Speed Variation
26	Right Front Excessive Wheel Speed Variation
27	Left Rear Excessive Wheel Speed Variation
28	Right Rear Excessive Wheel Speed Variation
32	Left Front Wheel Speed Sensor Circuit Open or Shorted to Battery/Ground
33	Right Front Wheel Speed Sensor Circuit Open or Shorted to Battery/Ground
34	Left Rear Wheel Speed Sensor Circuit Open or Shorted to Battery/Ground
35	Right Rear Wheel Speed Sensor Circuit Open or Shorted to Battery/Ground
36	Low System Voltage
37	High System Voltage
38	Left Front EMB Will Not Hold Motor
41	Right Front EMB Will Not Hold Motor
42	Rear ESB Will Not Hold Motor
44	Left Front Channel Will Not Move
45	Right Front Channel Will Not Move
46	Rear Axle Channel Will Not Move
47	Left Front Motor Free Spins
48	Right Front Motor Free Spins
51	Rear Motor Free Spins
52	Left Front Channel in Release Too Long
53	Right Front Channel in Release Too Long
54	Rear Channel in Release Too Long
55	EBTCM Malfunction
56	Left Front Motor Circuit Open
57	Left Front Motor Circuit Shorted to Ground
58	Left Front Motor Circuit Shorted to Battery or Motor Shorted
61	Right Front Motor Circuit Open
62	Right Front Motor Circuit Shorted to Ground
63	Right Front Motor Circuit Shorted to Battery or Motor Shorted
64	Rear Motor Circuit Open

87959079

Fig. 94 ABS Diagnostic Trouble Codes (DTCs)—1995 vehicles only

DIAGNOSTIC TROUBLE CODE AND SYMPTOM TABLE	
CHART	SYMPTOM
65	Rear Motor Circuit Shorted to Ground
66	Rear Motor Circuit Shorted to Battery or Motor Shorted
67	Left Front EMB Circuit Open or Shorted to Ground
68	Left Front EMB Circuit Shorted to Battery or Driver Open
71	Right Front EMB Circuit Open or Shorted to Ground
72	Right Front EMB Circuit Shorted to Battery or Driver Open
75	Serial Communication Malfunction
76	Left Front Solenoid Circuit Open or Shorted to Battery
77	Left Front Solenoid Circuit Shorted to Ground or Driver Open
78	Right Front Solenoid Circuit Open or Shorted to Battery
81	Right Front Solenoid Circuit Shorted to Ground or Driver Open
82	Calibration Malfunction
86	EBTCM Turned "ON" the Red "BRAKE" Warning Lamp
91	Open Brake Switch During Deceleration
92	Open Brake Switch When ABS Was Required
93	DTCs 91 or 92 Set in Current or Previous Ignition Cycle
94	Brake Switch Contacts Always Closed
95	Brake Switch Circuit Open
96	Rear Brake Lamp Circuit Open

87959080

Fig. 95 ABS Diagnostic Trouble Codes (DTCs)—1995 vehicles only, continued

1. Disconnect the negative battery cable.
2. Disengage the two solenoid electrical connectors and the fluid level sensor connector.
3. Detach the 6-pin and 3-pin motor pack electrical connectors.
4. Wrap a shop towel around the hydraulic brake lines, then disconnect the four brake lines from the modulator.

➡**Cap the disconnected lines to prevent the loss of fluid and the entry of moisture and contaminants.**

5. Unfasten the 2 nuts attaching the ABS hydraulic modulator/master cylinder assembly to the vacuum booster.
6. Remove the ABS hydraulic modulator assembly from the vehicle.
To install:
7. Install the ABS hydraulic modulator assembly to the vehicle. Secure using the two attaching nuts and tighten to 20 ft. lbs. (27 Nm).

DIAGNOSTIC TROUBLE CODE	DESCRIPTION
14	ABS Relay Contacts Circuit Open
15	ABS Relay Contacts Circuit Shorted to Battery or Always Closed
16	ABS Relay Coil Circuit Open
17	ABS Relay Coil Circuit Shorted to Ground
18	ABS Relay Coil Circuit Shorted to Battery or Coil Shorted
21	Left Front Wheel Speed = 0
22	Right Front Wheel Speed = 0
23	Left Rear Wheel Speed = 0
24	Right Rear Wheel Speed = 0
25	Left Front Excessive Wheel Speed Variation
26	Right Front Excessive Wheel Speed Variation
27	Left Rear Excessive Wheel Speed Variation
28	Right Rear Excessive Wheel Speed Variation
32	Left Front Wheel Speed Sensor Circuit Open or Shorted to Ground /Battery
33	Right Front Wheel Speed Sensor Circuit Open or Shorted to Ground /Battery
34	Left Rear Wheel Speed Sensor Circuit Open or Shorted to Ground /Battery
35	Right Rear Wheel Speed Sensor Circuit Open or Shorted to Ground /Battery
36	Low System Voltage
37	High System Voltage
38	Left Front ESB Will Not Hold Motor
41	Right Front ESB Will Not Hold Motor
42	Rear ESB Will Not Hold Motor
44	Left Front Channel Will Not Move
45	Right Front Channel Will Not Move
46	Rear Channel Will Not Move
47	Left Front Motor Free Spins
48	Right Front Motor Free Spins
51	Rear Motor Free Spins
52	Left Front Channel in Release Too Long
53	Right Front Channel in Release Too Long
54	Rear Channel in Release Too Long
55	EBCM/EBTCM Malfunction
56	Left Front Motor Circuit Open
57	Left Front Motor Circuit Shorted to Ground
58	Left Front Motor Circuit Shorted to Battery or Motor Shorted
61	Right Front Motor Circuit Open
62	Right Front Motor Circuit Shorted to Ground

87959081

Fig. 96 ABS Diagnostic Trouble Codes (DTCs)—1996 vehicles only

DIAGNOSTIC TROUBLE CODE	DESCRIPTION
63	Right Front Motor Circuit Shorted to Battery or Motor Shorted
64	Rear Motor Circuit Open
65	Rear Motor Circuit Shorted to Ground
66	Rear Motor Circuit Shorted to Battery or Motor Shorted
75	Serial Communication Failure
76	Left Front Solenoid Circuit Open or Shorted to Ground
77	Left Front Solenoid Circuit Shorted to Battery
78	Right Front Solenoid Circuit Open or Shorted to Ground
81	Right Front Solenoid Circuit Shorted to Battery
82	Calibration Malfunction
86	EBCM/EBTCM Turned "ON" the Red "BRAKE" Warning Lamp
91	Open Brake Switch Contacts During Deceleration
92	Open Brake Switch Contacts When ABS Was Required
93	DTCs 91 or 92 Set in Current or Previous Ignition Cycle
94	Brake Switch Contacts Always Closed
95	Brake Switch Circuit Open

87959082

Fig. 97 ABS Diagnostic Trouble Codes (DTCs)—1996 vehicles only, continued

DTC	DESCRIPTION
C1214	Electronic Brake Control Relay Contact Circuit Open
C1215	Electronic Brake Control Relay Contact Circuit Always Active
C1216	Electronic Brake Control Relay Coil Circuit Open
C1217	Electronic Brake Control Relay Coil Circuit Shorted To Ground
C1218	Electronic Brake Control Relay Coil Circuit Shorted To Voltage
C1221	LF Wheel Speed Sensor Input Signal = 0
C1222	RF Wheel Speed Sensor Input Signal = 0
C1223	LR Wheel Speed Sensor Input Signal = 0
C1224	RR Wheel Speed Sensor Input Signal = 0
C1225	LF Excessive Wheel Speed Sensor Variation
C1226	RF Excessive Wheel Speed Sensor Variation
C1227	LR Excessive Wheel Speed Sensor Variation
C1228	RR Excessive Wheel Speed Sensor Variation

91149G01

Fig. 98 ABS Diagnostic Trouble Codes (DTCs)—1997–00 vehicles only

DTC	DESCRIPTION
C1232	LF Wheel Speed Sensor Circuit Open Or Shorted
C1233	RF Wheel Speed Sensor Circuit Open Or Shorted
C1234	LR Wheel Speed Sensor Circuit Open Or Shorted
C1235	RR Wheel Speed Sensor Circuit Open Or Shorted
C1236	Low System Supply Voltage
C1237	High System Supply Voltage
C1238	LF ESB Will Not Hold Motor
C1241	RF ESB Will Not Hold Motor
C1242	Rear ESB Will Not Hold Motor
C1244	LF ABS Channel Will Not Move
C1245	RF ABS Channel Will Not Move
C1246	Rear ABS Channel Will Not Move
C1247	LF ABS Motor Free Spins
C1248	RF ABS Motor Free Spins
C1251	Rear ABS Motor Free Spins
C1252	LF ABS Channel in Release Too Long
C1253	RF ABS Channel in Release Too Long
C1254	Rear ABS Channel in Release Too Long
C1255	EBCM Internal Malfunction
C1256	LF ABS Motor Circuit Open
C1257	LF ABS Motor Circuit Shorted To Ground
C1258	LF ABS Motor Circuit Shorted To Voltage
C1261	RF ABS Motor Circuit Open
C1262	RF ABS Motor Circuit Shorted To Ground
C1263	RF ABS Motor Circuit Shorted To Voltage
C1264	Rear ABS Motor Circuit Open
C1265	Rear ABS Motor Circuit Shorted To Ground
C1266	Rear ABS Motor Circuit Shorted To Voltage
C1275	Serial Data Malfunction
C1276	LF Solenoid Circuit Open or Shorted to Ground
C1277	LF Solenoid Circuit Shorted to Voltage
C1278	RF Solenoid Circuit Open or Shorted to Ground
C1281	RF Solenoid Circuit Shorted to Voltage
C1282	Calibration Malfunction
C1286	EBCM Turned ON the Red BRAKE Warning Indicator
C1291	Open Brake Lamp Switch Circuit During Deceleration
C1292	Open Brake Lamp Switch Circuit When ABS Was Required
C1293	DTC C1291 or C1292 Set In Current Or Previous Ignition Cycle
C1294	Brake Lamp Switch Circuit Always Active
C1295	Brake Lamp Switch Circuit Open

91149G02

Fig. 99 ABS Diagnostic Trouble Codes (DTCs)—1997–00 vehicles only, continued

8. Uncap and connect the 4 brake pipes to the modulator assembly. Tighten to 13 ft. lbs. (17 Nm).

9. Attach the 6-pin and 3-pin electrical connectors.

10. Engage the fluid level sensor connector and the two solenoid electrical connections.

11. Properly bleed the ABS system, as outlined later in this section.

12. Connect the negative battery cable.

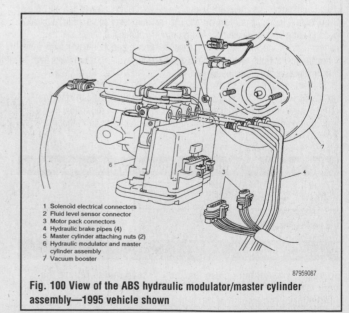

1 Solenoid electrical connectors
2 Fluid level sensor connector
3 Motor pack connectors
4 Hydraulic brake pipes (4)
5 Master cylinder attaching nuts (2)
6 Hydraulic modulator and master cylinder assembly
7 Vacuum booster

87959087

Fig. 100 View of the ABS hydraulic modulator/master cylinder assembly—1995 vehicle shown

Brake Fluid Level Switch

REMOVAL & INSTALLATION

▶ **See Figures 101 and 102**

1. Disconnect the negative battery cable.
2. Detach the electrical connector from the fluid level switch.
3. Using needle-nose pliers, compress the switch locking tabs at the inboard side of the master cylinder reservoir and remove the switch.

To install:

4. Press the fluid level switch into the master cylinder reservoir until it snaps into place.
5. Attach the switch electrical connector.
6. Connect the negative battery cable.

ABS Relay

REMOVAL & INSTALLATION

The ABS system relay is located in the fuse/relay box, also known as the power distribution box, located under the hood. Refer to Section 6 for location and removal procedures.

ABS Control Module

Depending upon vehicle year and application this control module is referred to as the Electronic Control Unit (ECU), Electronic Brake Control Module (EBCM) or Electronic Brake and Traction Control Module (EBTCM).

REMOVAL & INSTALLATION

▶ **See Figure 103**

1. Disconnect the negative battery cable.

2. Remove the driver's side kick panel.
3. Detach the control module (EBCM/EBTCM) electrical connectors.
4. Remove the screws attaching the EBCM/EBTCM to the bracket.
5. Remove the module from the bracket.

To install:

6. Position the EBCM/EBTCM to the bracket, aligning the screw holes.
7. Fasten the retaining hex head screws attaching the module.
8. Attach the electrical connectors.
9. Install the driver's side kick panel.
10. Connect the negative battery cable.

Speed Sensors

REMOVAL & INSTALLATION

Front

▶ **See Figures 104, 105, 106 and 107**

1. Disconnect the negative battery cable.
2. Raise and safely support the vehicle.
3. Disconnect the front wheel speed sensor electrical connector.
4. Remove the retaining bolt.
5. Remove the front wheel speed sensor. If the sensor will not slide out of the knuckle, remove the brake rotor and use a blunt punch or equivalent tool to push the sensor from the back side of the knuckle.

➡**If the sensor locating pin breaks off and remains in the knuckle during removal, remove the broken pin using a blunt punch. Clean the hole using sandpaper wrapped around a screwdriver or equivalent tool. Never attempt to enlarge the hole.**

To install:

6. Install the front wheel speed sensor on the mounting bracket.
7. Make sure the front wheel speed sensor is properly aligned and lays flat against the bosses on the knuckle.
8. Install the retaining bolt and tighten to 107 inch lbs. (12 Nm).

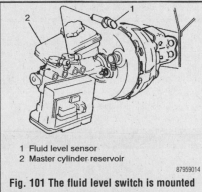

1 Fluid level sensor
2 Master cylinder reservoir

87959014

Fig. 101 The fluid level switch is mounted in the master cylinder reservoir

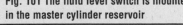

1 Fluid level sensor
2 Master cylinder reservoir
3 Master cylinder body

87959015

Fig. 102 Remove the switch by using needle-nose pliers to compress the switch locking tabs

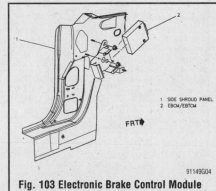

1 SIDE SHROUD PANEL
2 EBCM/EBTCM

FRT

91149G04

Fig. 103 Electronic Brake Control Module (EBCM) mounting

91149P04

Fig. 104 Detach the wheel speed sensor connector

91149P03

Fig. 105 The speed sensor is held by one retaining bolt that attaches to the steering knuckle

91149P05

Fig. 106 Remove the speed sensor retaining bolt and . . .

Fig. 107 . . . remove the speed sensor from the steering knuckle

Fig. 108 The rear wheel speed sensor is an integral part of the rear wheel hub and bearing assembly

Fig. 109 Detach the connector for the rear wheel speed sensor

Fig. 110 The hub retaining bolts are accessible through a hole in the hub flange

Fig. 111 The hub retaining bolt nuts are accessible from behind the wheel

Fig. 112 Insert a suitable tool through the hole in the hub flange and hold the retaining nut tight on the back of the hub, loosen the retaining bolts

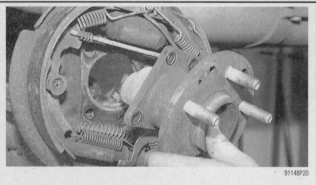

Fig. 113 Remove the hub and bearing assembly from the vehicle

9. Attach the electrical connector to the speed sensor.
10. Lower the vehicle.
11. Connect the negative battery cable.
12. Road test the vehicle and verify proper operation.

Rear

▶ **See Figures 108 thru 113**

1. Disconnect the negative battery cable.
2. Raise and safely support the vehicle.
3. Remove the rear tire and wheel assembly.
4. Remove the brake drum.
5. Disconnect the rear sensor electrical connector.
6. Remove the bolts and nuts attaching the rear wheel bearing and speed sensor assembly.

➡The drum brake assembly will be held in place only by the brake pipe connection after the bolts are removed. Use care not to bump or exert force on the drum brake assembly.

7. Remove the rear wheel bearing and speed sensor assembly.
To install:
8. Install the rear wheel bearing and speed sensor assembly.
9. Line up the bolt holes in bearing and sensor assembly and brake assembly and install mounting bolts.
10. Tighten the mounting bolts to 37 ft. lbs. (50 Nm).
11. Attach the electrical connector to the sensor.
12. Install the brake drum assembly.
13. Install the tire and wheel assembly.
14. Lower the vehicle.
15. Connect the negative battery cable.
16. Road test the vehicle and verify proper operation.

Tone (Exciter) Ring

REMOVAL & INSTALLATION

Front

The front exciter rings are located on the outer cv joints. Refer to Section 7 for halfshaft removal.

Rear

The rear exciter rings are located on the hubs. Refer to Section 8 for hub removal.

Bleeding the ABS System

✷✷ WARNING

Do **NOT** allow brake fluid to spill on or come in contact with the vehicle's finish as it will remove the paint. In case of a spill, immediately flush the area with water.

SYSTEM FILLING

The master cylinder reservoirs must be kept properly filled to prevent air from entering the system. No special filling procedures are required because of the anti-lock system.

When adding fluid, use only DOT 3 fluid; the use of DOT 5 or silicone fluids is specifically prohibited. Use of improper or contaminated fluid may cause the fluid to boil or cause the rubber components in the system to deteriorate. Never use any fluid with a petroleum base or any fluid which has been exposed to water or moisture.

BLEEDING THE ABS HYDRAULIC SYSTEM

Before bleeding the ABS brake system, the front and rear displacement cylinder pistons must be returned to the topmost position. The preferred method uses a Tech 1® or T-100® scan tool to perform the rehoming procedure. If a Tech 1® is not available, the second procedure may be used, but it must be followed EXACTLY.

Rehome Procedure

WITH TECH 1® OR T-100® (PREFERRED METHOD)

1. Using a Tech 1® or T-100® (CAMS), select "F5: Motor Rehome." The motor rehome function cannot be performed if current DTC's are present. If DTC's are present, the vehicle must be repaired and the codes cleared before performing the motor rehome function.
2. The entire brake system should now be bled using the pressure or manual bleeding procedures outlined later in this section.

WITHOUT TECH 1® OR T-100®

➡Do not place your foot on the brake pedal through this entire procedure unless specifically instructed to do so.

This method can only be used if the ABS warning lamp is not illuminated and not DTC's are present.
1. Remove your foot from the brake pedal.
2. Start the engine and allow it to run for at least 10 seconds while observing the ABS warning lamp.
3. If the ABS warning lamp turned "ON" and stayed "ON" after about 10 seconds, the bleeding procedure must be stopped and a Tech 1® must be used to diagnose the ABS function.
4. If the ABS warning lamp turned "ON" for about 3 seconds, then turned "OFF" and stayed "OFF," turn the ignition OFF.
5. Repeat Steps 1–4 one more time.
6. The entire brake system should now be bled by following the manual or pressure bleeding procedure.

Pressure Bleeding

▶ See Figures 114 and 115

➡The pressure bleeding equipment must be of the diaphragm type. It must have a rubber diaphragm between the air supply and the brake fluid to prevent air, moisture and other contaminants from entering the hydraulic system.

1. Clean the master cylinder fluid reservoir cover and surrounding area, then remove the cover.
2. Add fluid, if necessary to obtain a proper fluid level.
3. Connect bleeder adapter J 35589, or equivalent, to the brake fluid reservoir, then connect the bleeder adapter to the pressure bleeding equipment.
4. Adjust the pressure bleed equipment t o 5–10 psi (35–70 kPa) and wait about 30 seconds to be sure there is no leakage.
5. Adjust the pressure bleed equipment to 30–35 psi (205–240 kPa).

✳✳ WARNING

Use a shop rag to catch the escaping brake fluid. Be careful not to let any fluid run down the motor pack base or into the electrical connector.

6. With the pressure bleeding equipment connected and pressurized, proceed as follows:
   a. Attach a clear plastic bleeder hose to the rearward bleeder valve on the hydraulic modulator.
   b. Slowly open the bleeder valve and allow fluid to flow until no air is seen in the fluid.
   c. Close the valve when fluid flows out without any air bubbles.
   d. Repeat Steps 6b and 6c until no air bubbles are present.
   e. Relocate the bleeder hose on the forward hydraulic modulator bleed valve and repeat Steps 6a through 6d.
7. Tighten the bleeder valve to 80 inch lbs. (9 Nm).
8. Proceed to bleed the hydraulic modulator brake pipe connections as follows with the pressure bleeding equipment connected and pressurized:
   a. Slowly open the forward brake pipe tube nut on the hydraulic modulator and check for air in the escaping fluid.
   b. When the air flow ceases, immediately tighten the tube nut. Tighten the tube nut to 18 ft. lbs. (24 Nm).
9. Repeat Steps 8a and 8b for the remaining three brake pipe connections moving from the front to the rear.
10. Raise and safely support the vehicle.
11. Proceed, as outlined in the following steps, to bleed the wheel brakes in the following sequence: right rear, left rear, right front, then left front.
   a. Attach a clear plastic bleeder hose to the bleeder valve at the wheel, then submerge the opposite hose end in a clean container partially filled with clean brake fluid.
   b. Slowly open the bleeder valve and allow the fluid to flow.
   c. Close the valve when fluid begins to flow without any air bubbles. Tap lightly on the caliper or backing plate to dislodge any trapped air bubbles.
12. Repeat Step 11 on the other brakes using the earlier sequence.
13. Remove the pressure bleeding equipment, including bleeder adapter J 35589.
14. Carefully lower the vehicle, then check the brake fluid and add if necessary. Don't forget to put the reservoir cap back on.
15. With the ignition turned to the RUN position, apply the brake pedal with moderate force and hold it. Note the pedal travel and feel. If the pedal feels firm and constant and the pedal travel is not excessive, start the engine. With the engine running, recheck the pedal travel. If it's still firm and constant and pedal travel is not excessive, go to Step 17.
16. If the pedal feels soft or has excessive travel either initially or after the engine is started, the following procedure may be used:
   a. With the Tech 1® scan tool, "release" then "apply" each motor 2–3 times and cycle each solenoid 5–10 times. When finished, be sure to "apply" the front and rear motors to ensure the pistons are in the upmost position. DO NOT DRIVE THE VEHICLE.
   b. If a Tech 1® is not available, remove your foot from the brake pedal, start the engine and allow it run for at least 10 seconds to initialize the ABS. DO NOT DRIVE THE VEHICLE. After 10 seconds, turn the ignition OFF. The initialization procedure most be repeated 5 times to ensure any trapped air has been dislodged.
   c. Repeat the bleeding procedure, starting with Step 1.
17. Road test the vehicle, and make sure the brakes are operating properly.

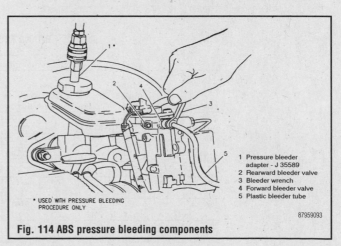

1 Pressure bleeder adapter - J 35589
2 Rearward bleeder valve
3 Bleeder wrench
4 Forward bleeder valve
5 Plastic bleeder tube

* USED WITH PRESSURE BLEEDING PROCEDURE ONLY

87959093

Fig. 114 ABS pressure bleeding components

Fig. 115 Position a shop rag to catch escaping brake fluid

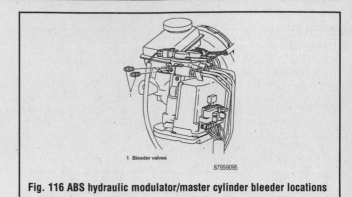

1 Bleeder valves

Fig. 116 ABS hydraulic modulator/master cylinder bleeder locations

Manual Bleeding

▶ See Figure 116

1. Clean the master cylinder fluid reservoir cover and surrounding area, then remove the cover.

2. Add fluid, if necessary to obtain a proper fluid level, then put the reservoir cover back on.

3. Prime the ABS hydraulic modulator/master cylinder assembly as follows:

a. Attach a bleeder hose to the rearward bleeder valve, then submerge the opposite hose end in a clean container partially filled with clean brake fluid.

b. Slowly open the rearward bleeder valve.

c. Depress and hold the brake pedal until the fluid begins to flow.

d. Close the valve, then release the brake pedal.

e. Repeat Steps 3b–3d until no air bubbles are present.

f. Relocate the bleeder hose to the forward hydraulic modulator bleeder valve, then repeat Steps 3a–3e.

4. Once the fluid is seen to flow from both modulator bleeder valves, the ABS modulator/master cylinder assembly is sufficiently full of fluid. However, it may not be completely purged of air. At this point, move to the wheel brakes and bleed them. This ensures that the lowest points in the system are completely free of air and then the assembly can purged of any remaining air.

5. Remove the fluid reservoir cover. Fill to the correct level, if necessary, then fasten the cover.

6. Raise and safely support the vehicle.

7. Proceed, as outlined in the following steps, to bleed the wheel brakes in the following sequence: right rear, left rear, right front, then left front.

a. Attach a clear plastic bleeder hose to the bleeder valve at the wheel, then submerge the opposite hose end in a clean container partially filled with clean brake fluid.

b. Open the bleeder valve.

c. Have an assistant slowly depress the brake pedal.

d. Close the valve and slowly release the release the brake pedal.

e. Wait 5 seconds.

f. Repeat Steps 7a–7e until the brake pedal feels firm at half travel and no air bubbles are observed in the bleeder hose. To assist in freeing the entrapped air, tap lightly on the caliper or braking plate to dislodge any trapped air bubbles.

8. Repeat Step 7 for the remaining brakes in the sequence given earlier.

9. Carefully lower the vehicle.

10. Remove the reservoir cover, then fill to the correct level with brake fluid and replace the cap.

11. Bleed the ABS hydraulic modulator/master cylinder assembly as follows:

a. Attach a clear plastic bleeder hose to the rearward bleeder valve on the modulator, then submerge the opposite hose end in a clean container partially filled with clean brake fluid.

b. Have an assistant depress the brake pedal with moderate force.

c. Slowly open the rearward bleeder valve and allow the fluid to flow.

d. Close the valve, then release the brake pedal.

e. Wait 5 seconds.

f. Repeat Steps 11a–11e until no air bubbles are present.

g. Relocate the bleeder hose to the forward hydraulic modulator bleeder valve, then repeat Steps 11a–11f.

12. Carefully lower the vehicle, then check the brake fluid and add if necessary. Don't forget to put the reservoir cap back on.

13. With the ignition turned to the **RUN** position, apply the brake pedal with moderate force and hold it. Note the pedal travel and feel. If the pedal feels firm and constant and the pedal travel is not excessive, start the engine. With the engine running, recheck the pedal travel. If it's still firm and constant and pedal travel is not excessive, road test the vehicle and make sure the brakes are operating properly.

14. If the pedal feels soft or has excessive travel either initially or after the engine is started, the following procedure may be used:

a. With the Tech 1® scan tool, "Release" then "Apply" each motor 2–3 times and cycle each solenoid 5–10 times. When finished, be sure to "Apply" the front and rear motors to ensure the pistons are in the upmost position. DO NOT DRIVE THE VEHICLE.

b. If a Tech 1® scan tool is not available, remove your foot from the brake pedal, start the engine and allow it run for at least 10 seconds to initialize the ABS. DO NOT DRIVE THE VEHICLE. After 10 seconds, turn the ignition **OFF**. The initialization procedure most be repeated 5 times to ensure any trapped air has been dislodged.

c. Repeat the bleeding procedure, starting with Step 1.

15. Road test the vehicle, and make sure the brakes are operating properly.

BRAKE SPECIFICATIONS
GM J BODY
All measurements in inches unless noted

Year	Model	Master Cylinder Bore	Brake Disc			Brake Drum Diameter			Minimum Lining Thickness		Brake Caliper	
			Original Thickness	Minimum Thickness	Maximum Runout	Original Inside Diameter	Max. Wear Limit	Maximum Machine Diameter	Front	Rear	Bracket Bolts (ft. lbs.)	Mounting Bolts (ft. lbs.)
1995	Cavalier	0.874	0.806	0.736	0.003	7.880	7.930	7.900	0.030	0.030	—	40
	Sunfire	0.874	0.786	0.736	0.003	7.870	7.930	7.900	0.030	0.030	—	40
1996	Cavalier	0.874	0.806	0.736	0.003	7.880	7.930	7.900	0.030	0.030	—	40
	Sunfire	0.874	0.786	0.736	0.003	7.870	7.930	7.900	0.030	0.030	—	40
1997	Cavalier	0.874	0.806	0.736	0.003	7.880	7.930	7.900	0.030	0.030	—	40
	Sunfire	0.874	0.786	0.736	0.003	7.870	7.930	7.900	0.030	0.030	—	40
1998	Cavalier	0.874	0.806	0.736	0.003	7.880	7.930	7.900	0.030	0.030	—	40
	Sunfire	0.874	0.786	0.736	0.003	7.870	7.930	7.900	0.030	0.030	—	40
1999	Cavalier	0.874	0.806	0.736	0.003	7.880	7.930	7.900	0.030	0.030	—	40
	Sunfire	0.874	0.786	0.736	0.003	7.870	7.930	7.900	0.030	0.030	—	40
2000	Cavalier	0.874	0.806	0.736	0.003	7.880	7.930	7.900	0.030	0.030	—	40
	Sunfire	0.874	0.786	0.736	0.003	7.870	7.930	7.900	0.030	0.030	—	40

91149C01

EXTERIOR 10-2
DOORS 10-2
  REMOVAL & INSTALLATION 10-2
  ADJUSTMENT 10-2
HOOD 10-2
  REMOVAL & INSTALLATION 10-2
  ALIGNMENT 10-3
TRUNK LID 10-3
  REMOVAL & INSTALLATION 10-3
  ALIGNMENT 10-3
FENDERS 10-4
  REMOVAL & INSTALLATION 10-4
FRONT BUMPER 10-4
  REMOVAL & INSTALLATION 10-4
REAR BUMPER 10-5
  REMOVAL & INSTALLATION 10-5
OUTSIDE MIRRORS 10-5
  REMOVAL & INSTALLATION 10-5
ANTENNA 10-6
  REPLACEMENT 10-6
CONVERTIBLE TOPS 10-6
  TOP REPLACEMENT 10-6
  MOTOR REPLACEMENT 10-7
SUNROOF 10-8
  REMOVAL & INSTALLATION 10-8
  GLASS ADJUSTMENT 10-9
INTERIOR 10-9
INSTRUMENT PANEL AND PAD 10-9
  REMOVAL & INSTALLATION 10-9
CENTER CONSOLE 10-10
  REMOVAL & INSTALLATION 10-10
DOOR PANELS 10-10
  REMOVAL & INSTALLATION 10-10
DOOR LOCKS 10-11
  REMOVAL & INSTALLATION 10-11
TRUNKLID LOCK 10-13
  REMOVAL & INSTALLATION 10-13
DOOR GLASS (WINDOW) 10-13
  REMOVAL & INSTALLATION 10-13
WINDOW REGULATOR AND MOTOR
 ASSEMBLY 10-14
  REMOVAL & INSTALLATION 10-14
WINDSHIELD AND FIXED GLASS 10-15
  REMOVAL & INSTALLATION 10-15
  WINDSHIELD CHIP REPAIR 10-15
INSIDE REAR VIEW MIRROR 10-17
  REPLACEMENT 10-17
  REMOVAL & INSTALLATION 10-17
SEATS 10-17
  REMOVAL & INSTALLATION 10-17
SPECIFICATIONS CHART
  TORQUE SPECIFICATIONS 10-18

10

BODY AND TRIM

EXTERIOR 10-2
INTERIOR 10-9

EXTERIOR

Doors

REMOVAL & INSTALLATION

1. If equipped with power door components, disconnect the negative battery cable.
2. Make sure the window is raised up to its fully closed position.
3. Remove the door trim panel, as outlined later in this section.
4. If equipped with power door components, move the water deflector enough to access the door wiring harness, then detach the electrical connectors and remove the harness.
5. Remove the rubber conduit from the door.
6. Unfasten the door hold-open bolt.
7. Have an assistant support the door.
8. Matchmark the position of the door hinge to the hinge pillar. Unfasten the lower and upper hinge bolts from the pillar.
9. With an assistant's help, detach the door from the body.
10. Matchmark the position of the door hinge to the door, then unfasten the upper and lower hinge retaining bolts. Carefully remove the door from the vehicle.

To install:

11. Snug the upper and lower hinge-to-door bolts so the door can be moved.
12. With the aid of an assistant, position the door to the body.
13. Snug the upper and lower hinge-to-pillar bolts and nuts so that the door can be moved.
14. Carefully close the door. Adjust the door for proper alignment.
15. Slowly open the door.
16. Tighten the upper and lower hinge-to-pillar bolts and nuts to 16 ft. lbs. (22 Nm).
17. Tighten the upper and lower hinge-to-door bolts to 16 ft. lbs. (22 Nm).
18. Check the door for proper alignment. If the door does not align properly, readjust.
19. Install the door detent-to-hinge pillar bolt, then tighten to 80 inch lbs. (9 Nm).
20. If so equipped, install the electrical harness through the conduit access hole and connect the electrical connectors to the power door components.
21. Fasten the rubber conduit to the door.
22. Reposition and secure the door water deflector.
23. Install the inner door trim panel, as outlined later in this section.
24. Connect the negative battery cable.

ADJUSTMENT

Door Height Adjustment

▶ See Figure 1

1. Open the door and carefully loosen the hinge bolts.
2. Carefully slide the door up or down accordingly until the height is correct.
3. Tighten the hinge bolts to 16 ft. lbs. (22 Nm).

Door Lock Striker Adjustment

▶ See Figure 2

1. Loosen the two striker bolts.
2. Snug the striker bolts down but still enough to allow the striker to be moved.
3. Open and close the door and adjust the striker so that the door-to-body and lock-to-striker align properly.
4. Tighten the striker bolts to 18 ft. lbs. (25 Nm).
5. The hinge-to-door bolts may need to be loosened to adjust the alignment properly.

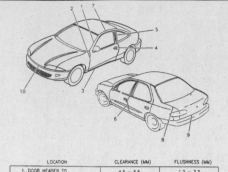

LOCATION	CLEARANCE (MM)	FLUSHNESS (MM)
1. DOOR HEADER TO WINDSHIELD	4.5 – 5.5	1.2 – 3.2
2. DOOR TO FENDER	3.5 – 5.5	0.0 – 1.5
3. DOOR TO ROCKER PANEL	4.0 – 6.0	0.0 – 4.0
4. DOOR TO QUARTER PANEL	3.5 – 5.5	0.0 – 1.5
5. DOOR TO QUARTER WINDOW (2 DOOR)	3.5 – 6.5	0.0 – 1.5
6. FRONT DOOR TO REAR DOOR (4 DOOR)	3.5 – 5.5	0.0 – 1.5
7. DOOR TO ROOF		2.3 – 3.3
8. DECK LID TO QUARTER PANEL	3.0 – 5.0	–1.0 – 1.0
9. DECK LID TO FASCIA	6.0 – 10.0	
10. HOOD TO FASCIA	2.5 – 7.5	

91140G10

Fig. 1 Body clearance specifications

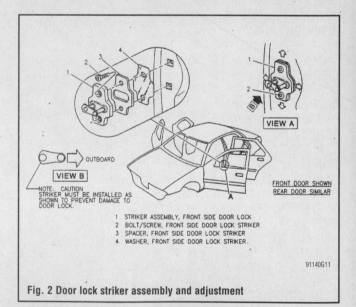

VIEW A

OUTBOARD

VIEW B

NOTE: CAUTION
STRIKER MUST BE INSTALLED AS
SHOWN TO PREVENT DAMAGE TO
DOOR LOCK.

FRONT DOOR SHOWN
REAR DOOR SIMILAR

1 STRIKER ASSEMBLY, FRONT SIDE DOOR LOCK
2 BOLT/SCREW, FRONT SIDE DOOR LOCK STRIKER
3 SPACER, FRONT SIDE DOOR LOCK STRIKER
4 WASHER, FRONT SIDE DOOR LOCK STRIKER

91140G11

Fig. 2 Door lock striker assembly and adjustment

Hood

REMOVAL & INSTALLATION

▶ See Figures 3 and 4

➡A helpful way of helping to avoid damaging the painted surfaces is to attach tape (BUT NOT DUCT TAPE) to the edges and corners of the panels and the hood assembly before removal.

1. Raise the hood and install protective coverings over the fender areas to prevent damage to the painted surfaces.
2. On the Sunfire only, remove the headlamp seal screw and remove the headlamp seal.

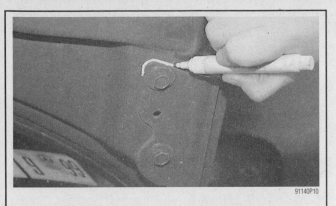

Fig. 3 Matchmark the position of the hood hinge to the hood

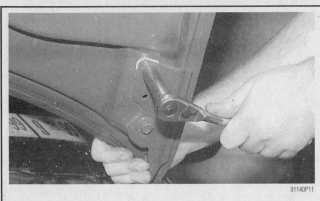

Fig. 4 Remove the hood hinge-to-hood bolts and remove the hood

3. Matchmark the position of the hinge on the hood to aid alignment during installation.

4. Have an assistant support the front of the hood, remove the hinge-to-hood screws/bolts on each side of the hood, then grasp the rear of the hood and remove it from the vehicle.

To install:

5. Position the hood, using the alignment marks made when removed.

6. Install the hood-to-hinge bolts snug, but do not fully tighten.

7. Inspect for proper hood alignment and adjust by moving the hood into position.

8. Tighten the hinge bolts to 20 ft. lbs. (27 Nm).

9. On the Sunfire only, install the headlamp seal and tighten the retaining screw.

10. Remove the protective covering from the fenders.

ALIGNMENT

▶ **See Figure 1**

To raise or lower the rear of the hood to achieve alignment with the rear of the fenders, proceed as follows:

1. Open and support the hood.

2. Adjust the front of the hood by:
   a. Remove the bolts for the hood latch.
   b. Adjust the front hood bumpers by:
   - Turning clockwise to lower the bumper
   - Turning counterclockwise to raise the bumper
   c. Tighten the hood latch bolts to 20 ft. lbs. (27 Nm).

3. Adjust the rear of the hood by:
   a. Measuring the difference in height between the hood and the fender.
   b. Remove the hood hinge bolts and place a shim of the measured distance under the hinge and around the bolt hole.
   c. Hand tighten the hinge bolts and verify the height is correct.
   d. Tighten the hinge bolts to 20 ft. lbs. (27 Nm).

4. Adjust the side-to-side clearance between the hood and the fenders/bumper (fascia) by:
   a. Loosening, but not removing the hinge bolts.
   b. Lower the hood assembly and adjust the hood until the clearances on either side is equal and correct.
   c. Raise the hood and tighten the hinge bolts to 20 ft. lbs. (27 Nm).

5. Close the hood.

Trunk Lid

REMOVAL & INSTALLATION

▶ **See Figure 5**

1. Disconnect the negative battery cable.

2. Open the trunk lid and cover the surrounding body panels with suitable protective covers.

3. Remove any trim from the underside of the trunk lid (if equipped).

4. Unplug the wire harness connectors and remove the harness from the trunk lid.

5. Remove the remote release cable from the trunk lid latch.

6. Matchmark the location of the hinges on the trunk lid.

7. Have an assistant hold the trunk lid on one side and remove the hinge bolts.

8. Remove the hinge bolts on the opposite side while holding the trunk lid.

9. Remove the trunk lid from the vehicle.

To install:

10. Using an assistant position the trunk lid into place.

11. Install the hinge bolts finger tight.

12. Line up the marks on the hinges and tighten the hinge bolts to 89 inch lbs. (10 Nm).

13. Install the release cable.

14. Install the wire harness into the trunk lid and attach the connectors.

15. Install the trim panel (if equipped).

16. Check alignment and correct as necessary.

17. Connect the negative battery cable.

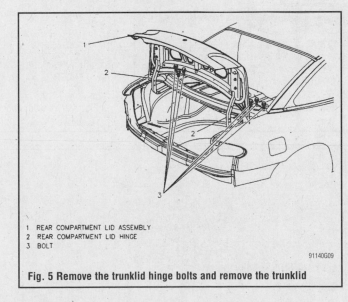

1 REAR COMPARTMENT LID ASSEMBLY
2 REAR COMPARTMENT LID HINGE
3 BOLT

91140G09

Fig. 5 Remove the trunklid hinge bolts and remove the trunklid

ALIGNMENT

▶ **See Figure 1**

The trunk lid should be inspected for fit along the trunk lid edges and the height in relation to the adjacent body panels. The trunk lid can be adjusted for height and side-to-side clearance. The height adjustment is made by installing a suitable shim under the hinge bolts in equal size to the difference in height. The side-to-side movement is made by loosening the hinge bolts and moving the trunk lid to the desired position.

Fenders

REMOVAL & INSTALLATION

▶ **See Figures 1, 6, 7, 8, 9 and 10**

1. Remove the hood from the vehicle.
2. Raise and safely support the vehicle, then remove the tire and wheel assembly.
3. Remove the splash shield and wheel housing.
4. Unfasten the fender lower bracket retaining bolts, then remove the bracket.
5. For the Cavalier, remove the front side marker lamp.
6. Detach the front fascia from the fender.
7. Unfasten the fender insulator retainers, then remove the insulator.
8. Remove the fender center bracket retaining bolts, then remove the bracket.
9. Unfasten the lower hood hinge bolts, then remove the hinge.
10. Remove the fender retaining bolts, then remove the fender from the vehicle.

To install:

11. Install the fender and the fender retaining bolts.
12. Tighten the fender retaining bolts to 62 inch lbs. (7 Nm).
13. Lower the hood hinge and install the hinge bolts.
14. Tighten the hinge bolts to 20 ft. lbs. (27 Nm).
15. Install the fender center bracket and the retaining bolts.
16. Tighten the bracket retaining bolts to 14 inch lbs. (1.6 Nm).

17. Install the fender center bracket-to-fender bolts and tighten to 27 inch lbs. (3 Nm).
18. Install the fender insulator and attach the retainers.
19. Attach the front fascia onto the fender.
20. For the Cavalier, install the front side marker lamp.
21. Install the fender lower bracket and tighten the retaining bolts to 27 inch lbs. (3 Nm).
22. Install the splash shield and wheel housing.
23. Install the wheel and tire assembly.
24. Lower the vehicle.
25. Install the hood.

Front Bumper

REMOVAL & INSTALLATION

Cavalier

▶ **See Figure 11**

1. Remove the front fascia, as follows:
   a. Remove the right and left splash shields.
   b. Unfasten the fender-to-fascia retaining bolts.
   c. Remove the retainers from the top of the fascia.
   d. Separate the fascia from the impact bar.
   e. Detach the connectors from the park and turn signal lamps.
2. Remove the energy absorber and the impact bar from the vehicle.
3. Installation is the reverse of the removal procedure.

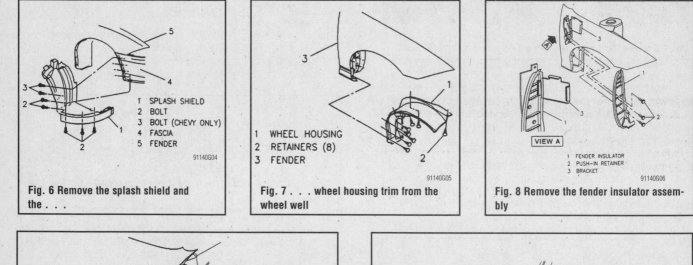

Fig. 6 Remove the splash shield and the . . .

```
1  SPLASH SHIELD
2  BOLT
3  BOLT (CHEVY ONLY)
4  FASCIA
5  FENDER
            91140G04
```

Fig. 7 . . . wheel housing trim from the wheel well

```
1  WHEEL HOUSING
2  RETAINERS (8)
3  FENDER
            91140G05
```

Fig. 8 Remove the fender insulator assembly

```
VIEW A
1  FENDER INSULATOR
2  PUSH-IN RETAINER
3  BRACKET
            91140G06
```

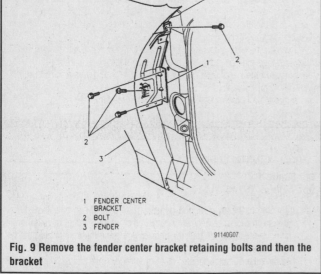

```
1  FENDER CENTER
   BRACKET
2  BOLT
3  FENDER
            91140G07
```

Fig. 9 Remove the fender center bracket retaining bolts and then the bracket

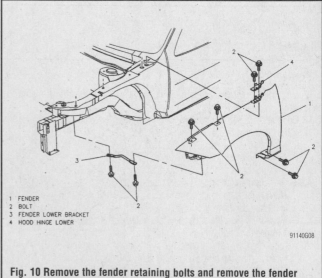

```
1  FENDER
2  BOLT
3  FENDER LOWER BRACKET
4  HOOD HINGE LOWER
            91140G08
```

Fig. 10 Remove the fender retaining bolts and remove the fender

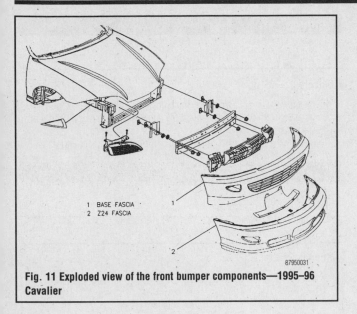

Fig. 11 Exploded view of the front bumper components—1995–96 Cavalier

1 BASE FASCIA
2 Z24 FASCIA

Sunfire

▶ See Figure 12

1. Remove the front fascia, as follows:
   a. Remove the right and left splash shields.
   b. Unfasten the tender-to-fascia retaining bolts.
   c. Remove the retainers from the top of the fascia.
   d. Separate the fascia from the impact bar.
   e. Detach the connectors from the park and turn signal lamps.
2. Unfasten the grille retaining screw, then remove the grille from the front fascia.
3. Remove the energy absorber and the impact bar from the vehicle.
4. Installation is the reverse of the removal procedure.

Rear Bumper

REMOVAL & INSTALLATION

▶ See Figures 13 and 14

1. Remove the rear fascia as follows:
   a. Remove the upper storage net retainers inside the trunk for access to the fascia retaining screws.

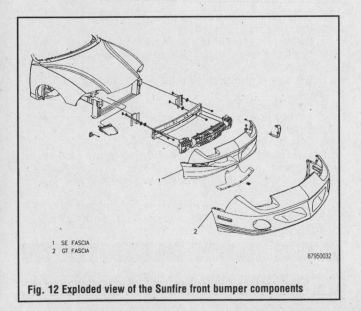

1 SE FASCIA
2 GT FASCIA

Fig. 12 Exploded view of the Sunfire front bumper components

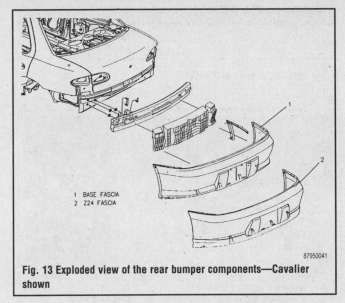

Fig. 13 Exploded view of the rear bumper components—Cavalier shown

1 BASE FASCIA
2 Z24 FASCIA

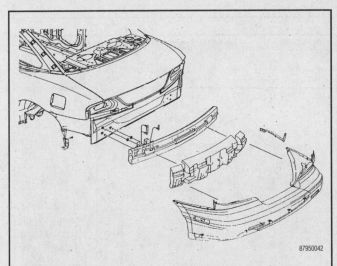

Fig. 14 Exploded view of the rear bumper components—Sunfire shown

   b. Unfasten the two retaining screws from inside the trunk.
   c. Unfasten the four fascia retaining screws located in the rear wheel housing.
   d. Remove the push-in retainers from the lower fascia, then remove the fascia from the impact bar.
2. Remove the energy absorber by removing the rivets. Depending upon application, they may be regular or push-in type rivets.
3. Unfasten the impact bar-to-rear end panel retaining nuts and remove the impact bar from the vehicle.
4. Installation is the reverse of the removal procedure.

Outside Mirrors

REMOVAL & INSTALLATION

▶ See Figures 15, 16 and 17

1. Disconnect the negative battery cable.
2. Remove the door upper trim panel.
3. Remove the absorber from the door covering the mirror retaining nuts.
4. If equipped with power mirrors, detach the electrical connector.
5. Remove the mirror retaining nuts from the door while supporting the mirror.
6. Remove the mirror assembly.

To install:

7. Position the mirror and hand tighten the retaining nuts.
8. Tighten the retaining nuts to 50 inch lbs. (6 Nm).
9. If equipped with power mirrors, attach the electrical connector.
10. Install the absorber onto the door.
11. Install the door upper trim panel.
12. Disconnect the negative battery cable.

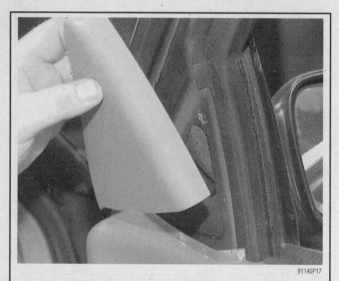

Fig. 15 Remove the retaining screw for the upper trim panel and . . .

Fig. 16 . . . remove the panel from the door

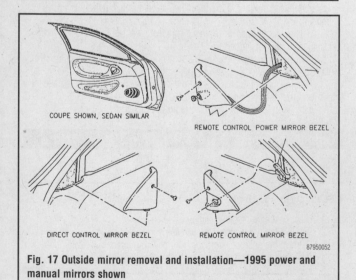

Fig. 17 Outside mirror removal and installation—1995 power and manual mirrors shown

REPLACEMENT

▶ **See Figure 18**

1. Unscrew the antenna mast, nut and bezel from on top of the quarter panel.
2. Open the trunk lid and disconnect the antenna cable from the bottom of the antenna base.
3. Remove the two antenna retaining screws from inside the trunk.
4. Remove the antenna from the vehicle.

To install:

5. Position the antenna into the vehicle and tighten the retaining screws to 18 inch lbs. (2 Nm).
6. Attach the antenna cable.
7. Install the antenna mast, bezel and nut. Tighten the nut to 53 inch lbs. (6 Nm).

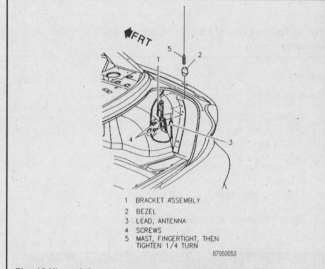

1 BRACKET ASSEMBLY
2 BEZEL
3 LEAD, ANTENNA
4 SCREWS
5 MAST, FINGERTIGHT, THEN TIGHTEN 1/4 TURN

Fig. 18 View of the antenna mounting—1995 vehicle shown

Convertible Tops

TOP REPLACEMENT

▶ **See Figures 19 and 20**

1. Disconnect the negative battery cable.
2. Unlatch the convertible (folding) top.
3. Remove the right and left side quarter trim panels.
4. Unfasten the screws retaining the headliner at the rear rail and quarter inner structure.
5. Remove the screws retaining the headliner to the closeout panel below the backlite.
6. Detach the heated backlite wire leads.
7. Remove the bolt, washer and bushing from the quarter window drive links and spur gears.
8. Carefully grasp and lower the quarter windows.
9. Make sure the note the wire routing, then detach the drive motor wire harness connectors.
10. Remove the retainers and fold the closeout trim panel forward.
11. Remove the back molding.
12. Remove the right and left side quarter panel belt outer moldings.
13. Unfasten the two staples retaining the convertible cover, backlite and stay pads to the quarter belt tackstrip.

✷✷ CAUTION

Protect eye goggles or safety glasses MUST be worn when drilling out the rivets to reduce the chance of personal injury.

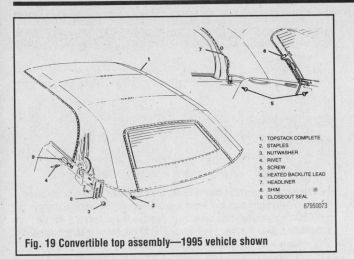

Fig. 19 Convertible top assembly—1995 vehicle shown

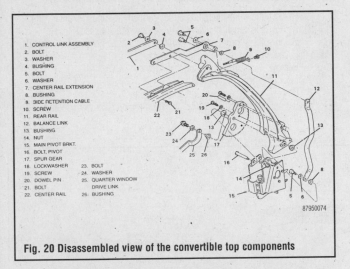

Fig. 20 Disassembled view of the convertible top components

14. Use a ⅛ in. (3mm) drill bit to drill out the four rivets retaining the convertible cover to the quarter belt flange.

15. Note the position of any shims used, then unfasten the three nutwashers retaining the main pivot bracket assembly to the mounting bracket.

16. With the help of an assistant, lift the convertible top assembly from the vehicle.

To install:

➡The convertible top assembly should be unfolded or in the UP position during installation to allow access to the main pivot bracket area.

17. As the convertible top is lowered into position, the quarter window drive links must be guided into the main pivot bracket to avoid trapping the links. With the help of an assistant, position the convertible top assembly to the vehicle, aligning the main pivot bracket doll pins with the holes in the mounting brackets.

18. If removed, install shims as noted between the mounting bracket and main pivot brackets.

19. Install the nutwashers retaining main pivot bracket assembly to the mounting bracket. Tighten the nutwashers to 17 ft. lbs. (24 Nm).

20. Attach the drive motor wire harness connectors to the body wire harness, routing the wires as noted during removal.

21. Connect the negative battery cable.

22. Attach the backlite assembly to the tackstrip. Fasten the heated backlite wire harness connectors.

23. Fasten the topcover and rear stay pads to the tackstrip and quarter panel structure flange.

24. Cycle and latch the convertible top to the windshield header and check the top's appearance and function.

25. Install the right and left side quarter panel belt outer moldings, then install the back belt molding.

26. Fasten the closeout trim panel and secure using the retainers.

27. Apply Loctite® 242, or equivalent, to the bolt threads. Carefully raise the quarter window glass and secure the drive links to the spur gears using the bushing, washer and bolt.

28. Install the screws securing the headliner to the closeout panel below the glass backlite.

29. Fasten the screws securing the headliner to the quarter inner structure and rear rail.

30. Install the right and left side quarter trim panels.

MOTOR REPLACEMENT

▶ **See Figure 21**

➡If any parts of the motor and pump assembly are found to be inoperable, it is recommended that the entire unit be replaced with a new motor and pump assembly.

Top Up

1. Disconnect the negative battery cable.
2. Unlatch the convertible top from the windshield header.
3. Remove the quarter trim panel.
4. Unfasten the headliner screws at the rear rail and quarter panel structure. Fold the headliner to access the drive motor assembly.
5. Note the wire routing, then detach the drive motor wire harness connector from the body harness.
6. Unfasten the bolts and lockwashers retaining the motor to the main pivot bracket assembly.
7. Remove the motor assembly by lowering the motor from the bottom of the main pivot bracket.

To install:

8. Position the motor assembly to the main pivot bracket.
9. Apply Loctite® 242, or equivalent, to the bolt threads. Install the bolts and lockwashers retaining the motor to the main pivot bracket. Tighten the bolts to 9 ft. lbs. (12 Nm).
10. Route the motor wire harness over the main pivot bracket and wire harness and attach the wire connector to the body harness.
11. Connect the negative battery cable.
12. Check the convertible top motor operation.
13. Fasten the headliner to the rear rail and structure using screws.
14. Install the quarter trim panel.
15. Raise and latch the convertible top.

Top Down

➡If the motor has seized and the convertible top is lowered, place the top bypass switch in the "Emergency Override" position and proceed as follows.

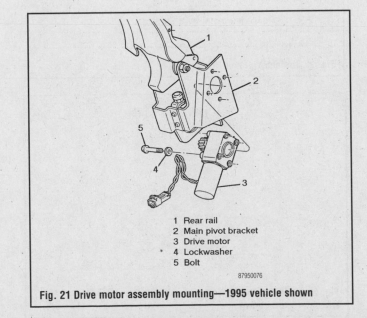

1 Rear rail
2 Main pivot bracket
3 Drive motor
4 Lockwasher
5 Bolt

Fig. 21 Drive motor assembly mounting—1995 vehicle shown

1. Disconnect the negative battery cable.
2. Remove the quarter trim panel.
3. Unfasten the headliner screw from the structure and position the headliner out of the way.
4. Unfasten the No. 4 bow slat-to-main pivot bracket bolt and spacer. Retain the bushing in the slat.
5. Remove the rear rail pivot bolt and nut at the main pivot bracket.
6. Apply Loctite® 242 or equivalent, to the bolt threads, then reinstall the No. 4 bow slat-to-main pivot bracket spacer and bolt.
7. Lift the rear rail and the spur gear off the motor gear and, with the help of an assistant, raise the convertible to the closed position. Do not latch the top.
8. Apply Loctite® 242 or equivalent, to the bolt threads, then fasten the bolt to the rear rail with the nut.
9. Remove and install the motor assembly, as outlined in the Top Up procedure beginning with Step 4.

Sunroof

REMOVAL & INSTALLATION

Glass Panel (Module)

▶ **See Figures 22 and 23**

1. Disconnect the negative battery cable.
2. Slide the sunroof shade open.
3. Position the sunroof glass panel in the fully closed position.

4. Remove the six screws (3 on each side) retaining the sunroof glass panel.
5. Remove the glass panel.
To install:
6. Position the glass panel into the opening.
7. Tighten the retaining screws until fully driven and seated, but take caution not to strip.

Motor (Power Only)

▶ **See Figures 22, 24 and 25**

1. Disconnect the negative battery cable.
2. Position the sunroof glass panel in the fully closed position.

➡**If the sunroof motor is inoperative, the glass can be closed by inserting the appropriate size hex head wrench into the drive gear. If there is a red retainer surrounding the screw, remove it and insert a flat tip screwdriver. Turn the hex head wrench until the glass is fully closed. It may require a significant amount of force to begin to move the motor. After the glass is fully seated, back the screw off approximately 15°.**

3. Remove the windshield side upper garnish moldings (A-pillar trim).
4. Remove the sunshade screws and remove the sunshade.
5. Remove the sunroof control switch assembly by gently prying it out from the headliner and detaching the connector.
6. Remove the sunroof opening trim lace.
7. Lower the headliner as required.
8. Detach the connector for the sunroof motor.
9. Remove the sunroof motor bracket bolts and remove the sunroof motor.

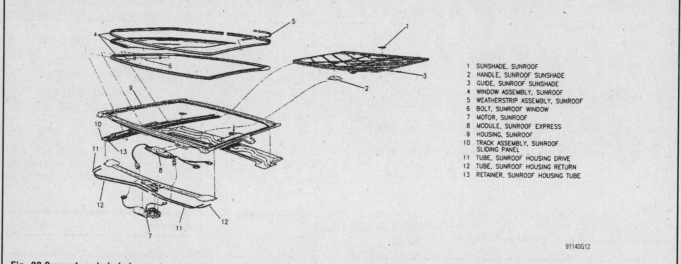

1 SUNSHADE, SUNROOF
2 HANDLE, SUNROOF SUNSHADE
3 GUIDE, SUNROOF SUNSHADE
4 WINDOW ASSEMBLY, SUNROOF
5 WEATHERSTRIP ASSEMBLY, SUNROOF
6 BOLT, SUNROOF WINDOW
7 MOTOR, SUNROOF
8 MODULE, SUNROOF EXPRESS
9 HOUSING, SUNROOF
10 TRACK ASSEMBLY, SUNROOF SLIDING PANEL
11 TUBE, SUNROOF HOUSING DRIVE
12 TUBE, SUNROOF HOUSING RETURN
13 RETAINER, SUNROOF HOUSING TUBE

91140G12

Fig. 22 Sunroof exploded view

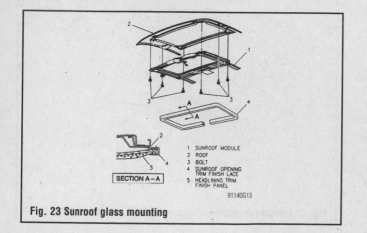

1 SUNROOF MODULE
2 ROOF
3 BOLT
4 SUNROOF OPENING TRIM FINISH LACE
5 HEADLINING TRIM FINISH PANEL

SECTION A—A

91140G13

Fig. 23 Sunroof glass mounting

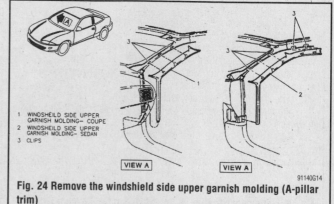

1 WINDSHEILD SIDE UPPER GARNISH MOLDING— COUPE
2 WINDSHIELD SIDE UPPER GARNISH MOLDING— SEDAN
3 CLIPS

VIEW A   VIEW A

91140G14

Fig. 24 Remove the windshield side upper garnish molding (A-pillar trim)

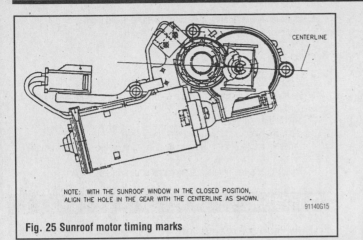

NOTE: WITH THE SUNROOF WINDOW IN THE CLOSED POSITION, ALIGN THE HOLE IN THE GEAR WITH THE CENTERLINE AS SHOWN.

91140G15

Fig. 25 Sunroof motor timing marks

To install:

➡ **Before installation, be sure that the motor is timed to the closed position, see graphic.**

10. Installation is the reverse of removal.

GLASS ADJUSTMENT

1. Slide the sunroof shade open.
2. Position the sunroof glass panel in the fully closed position.
3. Seperately loosen the six adjusting screws (3 on each side) and adjust the four corners of the glass panel.
4. Adjust the front of the glass panel to $\frac{1}{32}$ (1.0 mm) below the top surface of the roof, and the rear of the glass panel to $\frac{1}{32}$ (1.0 mm) above the top surface of the roof.
5. Tighten the adjusting screws until fully driven and seated, but take caution not to strip.

INTERIOR

Instrument Panel and Pad

REMOVAL & INSTALLATION

▶ **See Figures 26, 27, 28, 29 and 30**

1. If equipped, disable the SIR system, as outlined in Section 6 of this manual.
2. If not done already, disconnect the negative battery cable.

3. Unfasten the defroster grille retaining screw, then remove the grille.
4. To remove the instrument panel end-caps, for Cavalier, use a suitable prytool. Position the tool behind the cover and carefully pry outward. For the Sunfire, unfasten the end-cap retaining screws and remove the cap.
5. For the Cavalier, remove the instrument panel trim pad.
6. Remove the instrument cluster trim plate.
7. As outlined in Section 6 of this manual, remove the heater and A/C control panel.
8. Remove the radio assembly, as outlined in Section 6 of this manual.
9. Unfasten the air distribution ducts.

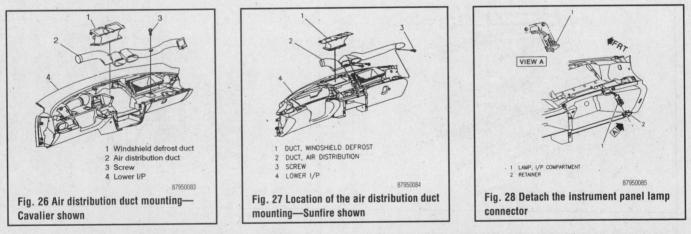

1 Windshield defrost duct
2 Air distribution duct
3 Screw
4 Lower I/P

87950083

Fig. 26 Air distribution duct mounting—Cavalier shown

1 DUCT, WINDSHIELD DEFROST
2 DUCT, AIR DISTRIBUTION
3 SCREW
4 LOWER I/P

87950084

Fig. 27 Location of the air distribution duct mounting—Sunfire shown

VIEW A

1 LAMP, I/P COMPARTMENT
2 RETAINER

87950085

Fig. 28 Detach the instrument panel lamp connector

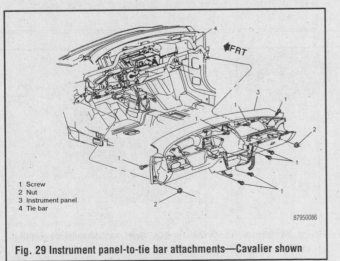

1 Screw
2 Nut
3 Instrument panel
4 Tie bar

87950086

Fig. 29 Instrument panel-to-tie bar attachments—Cavalier shown

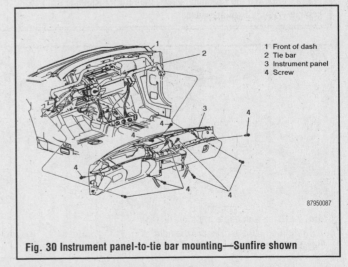

1 Front of dash
2 Tie bar
3 Instrument panel
4 Screw

87950087

Fig. 30 Instrument panel-to-tie bar mounting—Sunfire shown

10. Detach the instrument panel compartment lamp electrical connector.

11. Unfasten the screws to the tie bar, then remove the instrument panel from the tie bar.

To install:

12. Position the instrument panel to the tie bar, then secure with the retaining screws.

13. Attach the instrument panel compartment lamp connector.

14. Fasten the air distribution ducts.

15. Install the radio and the heater and A/C control.

16. Install the instrument cluster trim plate.

17. For the Cavalier, install the instrument panel trim pad.

18. Install the end caps.

19. Position the defroster grille, then secure with the retaining screw.

20. Enable the SIR system, if equipped. For details, please refer to the procedure located in Section 6 of this manual.

21. Connect the negative battery cable.

Center Console

REMOVAL & INSTALLATION

Cavalier

▶ **See Figure 31**

1. Open the console compartment.

2. Remove the console trim plate by gently prying it upward to disengage the retainers.

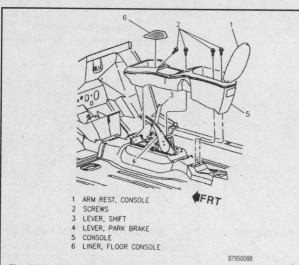
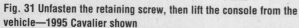

1 ARM REST, CONSOLE
2 SCREWS
3 LEVER, SHIFT
4 LEVER, PARK BRAKE
5 CONSOLE
6 LINER, FLOOR CONSOLE

87950088

Fig. 31 Unfasten the retaining screw, then lift the console from the vehicle—1995 Cavalier shown

3. Unfasten the retaining screws, then remove the console.

4. Installation is the reverse of the removal procedure.

Sunfire

▶ **See Figure 32**

1. Remove the shift control handle by unfastening the retaining clip and lifting the handle off.

2. Lift off the shift lever boot.

3. Remove the console compartment liner.

4. Unfasten the four retaining screws, then remove the console from the vehicle.

5. Installation is the reverse of the removal procedure.

Door Panels

REMOVAL & INSTALLATION

▶ **See Figures 33 thru 45**

1. Disconnect the negative battery cable.

2. On the Sunfire, remove the inside door handle trim bezel.

3. On the Cavalier, remove the power door lock switch.

4. If equipped, remove the power window switch.

5. If equipped, remove the manual window crank handle.

6. Remove the upper trim finish panel.

7. Remove the door panel lower retaining screws.

8. Remove the door armrest retaining screws.

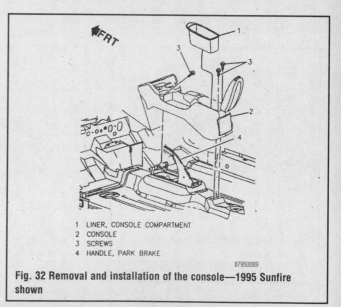

1 LINER, CONSOLE COMPARTMENT
2 CONSOLE
3 SCREWS
4 HANDLE, PARK BRAKE

87950089

Fig. 32 Removal and installation of the console—1995 Sunfire shown

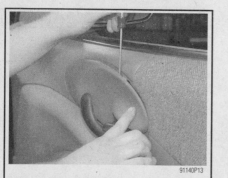

91140P13

Fig. 33 Using a suitable pry tool, release the retaining clips for the door handle bezel (Sunfire only) and . . .

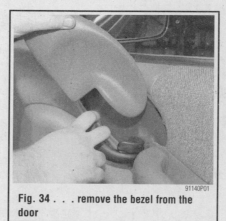

91140P01

Fig. 34 . . . remove the bezel from the door

91140P09

Fig. 35 The manual window crank handle is retained to the regulator by a retaining clip

Fig. 36 A special tool is available to release the retaining clip. Insert the tool behind the handle and release the clip to remove the handle

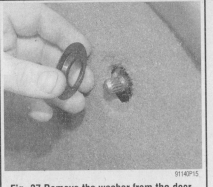

Fig. 37 Remove the washer from the door panel that sits behind the window crank

Fig. 38 Remove the retaining screw for the upper trim panel and . . .

Fig. 39 . . . remove the panel from the door

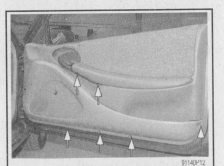

Fig. 40 The door panel is held by six retaining screws, two under the door handle and four along the bottom. Remove the four along the bottom and . . .

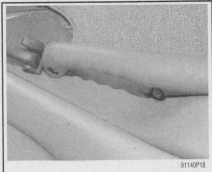

Fig. 41 . . . remove the two screws located under the door panel inside handle—front door

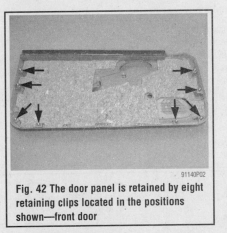

Fig. 42 The door panel is retained by eight retaining clips located in the positions shown—front door

Fig. 43 The retaining clips can be released by carefully pulling the door panel from the door assembly

Fig. 44 When all the retaining clips are disengaged, remove the door panel

9. On the Cavalier front door only, remove the door trim clips at the sealing strip.

10. Disengage the door panel retaining clips using tool J-24595 or equivalent.

➡The door panel retaining clips can also be removed by carefully and gently pulling on the door panel to disengage them from the door.

11. Remove the door panel from the door.

To install:

12. Ensure that the retaining clips are in place on the door panel.

13. Position the door panel on the door and gently push the panel into place to engage the retaining clips.

➡On the Cavalier front door only, push the panel outward and downward at the sealing strip to engage the trim clips at the sealing strip.

14. Install the all the door panel retaining screws.

15. The balance of the installation is the reverse of removal.

Door Locks

REMOVAL & INSTALLATION

Lock Assembly

♦ See Figures 46 and 47

1. Raise the window to the full up position.
2. Remove the inside door trim panel.
3. Detach the water deflector enough to access the lock actuator.
4. Disconnect the outside handle-to-lock assembly rod.
5. Disconnect the lock cylinder-to-lock assembly rod.
6. Disconnect the inside handle-to-lock assembly rod.
7. Unfasten the lock assembly screws/bolts and remove the lock from the door. If equipped, detach the electrical connectors.

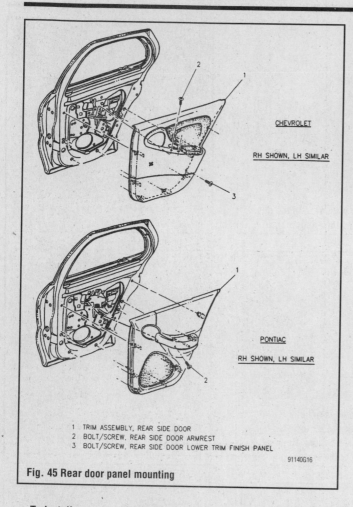

Fig. 45 Rear door panel mounting

1 TRIM ASSEMBLY, REAR SIDE DOOR
2 BOLT/SCREW, REAR SIDE DOOR ARMREST
3 BOLT/SCREW, REAR SIDE DOOR LOWER TRIM FINISH PANEL

91140G16

To install:

8. Attach the electrical connector (if equipped), position the lock assembly to the door and install the retaining screws/bolts. Tighten the screws/bolts to 62 inch lbs. (7 Nm). Do NOT overtighten.
9. Attach the outside handle to the lock assembly rod.
10. Connect the lock cylinder to the lock assembly rod.
11. Connect the inside handle to the lock rod and inside locking rod.
12. Fasten the water deflector.
13. Install the inside door trim panel.

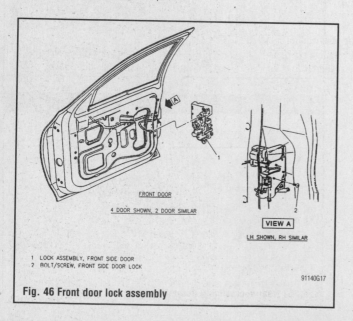

1 LOCK ASSEMBLY, FRONT SIDE DOOR
2 BOLT/SCREW, FRONT SIDE DOOR LOCK

91140G17

Fig. 46 Front door lock assembly

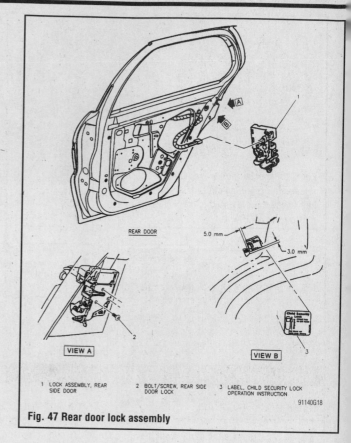

1 LOCK ASSEMBLY, REAR SIDE DOOR
2 BOLT/SCREW, REAR SIDE DOOR LOCK
3 LABEL, CHILD SECURITY LOCK OPERATION INSTRUCTION

91140G18

Fig. 47 Rear door lock assembly

Lock cylinder

▶ **See Figures 48 and 49**

1. Raise the window to the full up position.
2. Remove the inside door trim panel.
3. Detach the water deflector enough to access the lock actuator.
4. Remove the lower window channel retainer.
5. Remove the lock cylinder retaining clip.
6. Disengage the lock rod from the door lock cylinder and remove the lock cylinder.

To install:

7. Connect the door lock rod to the lock cylinder.
8. Position the door lock cylinder and engage the retaining clip.

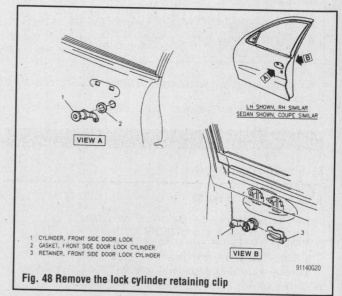

1 CYLINDER, FRONT SIDE DOOR LOCK
2 GASKET, FRONT SIDE DOOR LOCK CYLINDER
3 RETAINER, FRONT SIDE DOOR LOCK CYLINDER

91140G20

Fig. 48 Remove the lock cylinder retaining clip

4 DOOR SHOWN, 2 DOOR SIMILAR
RH SHOWN, LH SIMILAR

VIEW A
AFTER INSTALLATION

VIEW A
PRIOR TO INSTALLATION

VIEW B

1 ROD, FRONT SIDE DOOR LOCK CYLINDER TO LOCK

91140G19

Fig. 49 Disconnect the lock rod from the lock cylinder

9. Install the lower window channel retainer.
10. Fasten the water deflector.
11. Install the inside door trim panel.

Trunklid Lock

REMOVAL & INSTALLATION

Latch Assembly

1. Open the trunk lid and disconnect the latch release cable.
2. Unclip the cable door at the top of the rear compartment lock release box.
3. Disconnect the release cable from the lock release box.
4. Remove the trunk lid latch assembly bolts.
5. Remove the latch assembly.
To install:
6. Install the latch assembly.
7. Install the latch assembly bolts and tighten them to 53 inch lbs. (6 Nm).
8. Connect the release cable to the lock release box.
9. Install the cable door at the top of the rear compartment lock release box.
10. Connect the latch release cable.

Lock Cylinder

1. Open the trunk lid and disconnect the latch release cable.
2. On the Cavalier, remove the lock cylinder retainer.
3. On the Sunfire, remove the lock cylinder retaining rivets.
4. Remove the lock cylinder from the trunklid.
To install:
5. Position the lock cylinder and install the rivets or retainer as required by the model.
6. Connect the latch release cable.

Door Glass (Window)

REMOVAL & INSTALLATION

▶ **See Figures 50, 51 and 52**

This procedure applies to both the front and rear windows.
1. Lower door window to the full **DOWN** position.
2. Remove the door trim panel and water deflector.
3. Remove the glass-to-regulator attaching bolts.
4. Using care, raise the rear of the window then the front of the window assembly and remove the window from just inboard of the upper frame.

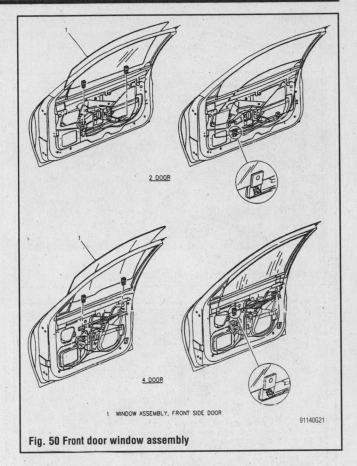

2 DOOR

4 DOOR

1 WINDOW ASSEMBLY, FRONT SIDE DOOR

91140G21

Fig. 50 Front door window assembly

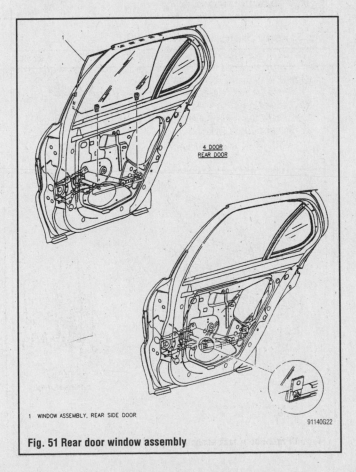

4 DOOR
REAR DOOR

1 WINDOW ASSEMBLY, REAR SIDE DOOR

91140G22

Fig. 51 Rear door window assembly

To install:

5. Tilt the front edge of the glass downward to position the glass in the door and carefully lower the rear of the window in.

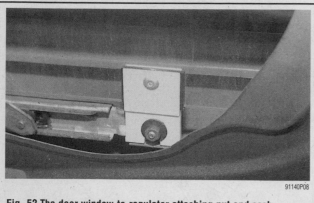

Fig. 52 The door window-to-regulator attaching nut and sash

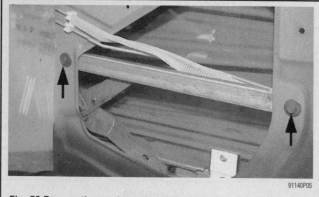

Fig. 53 Remove the regulator retaining bolts

6. Place the window into the sashes located on the regulator and install the nuts.
7. Tighten the nuts to 71 inch lbs. (8 Nm).
8. Check the window to make sure it operates correctly.
9. Reposition the water deflector and install the door panel.

Window Regulator And Motor Assembly

REMOVAL & INSTALLATION

▶ **See Figures 52, 53, 54, 55 and 56**

1. Remove the door panel and the water deflector.
2. Remove the door glass (window).
3. On front door regulators only, remove the regulator retaining bolts.
4. Using a ³⁄₁₆ in. (5mm) drill bit, drill out the regulator attaching rivets.
5. Move the regulator rearward and disconnect the wiring harness from the motor, if so equipped. Disengage the roller on the regulator lift arm from the glass sash channel.
6. Remove the regulator and motor through the rear access hole.

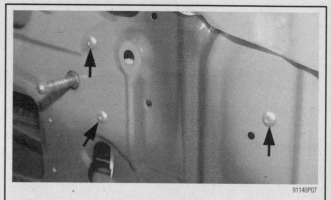

Fig. 54 Remove the regulator retaining rivets

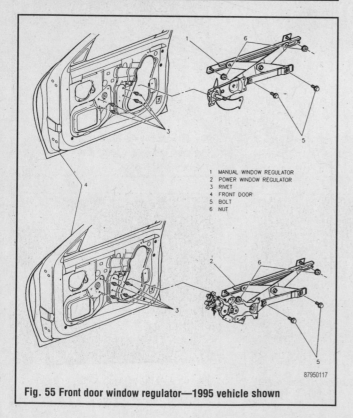

```
1  MANUAL WINDOW REGULATOR
2  POWER WINDOW REGULATOR
3  RIVET
4  FRONT DOOR
5  BOLT
6  NUT
```

Fig. 55 Front door window regulator—1995 vehicle shown

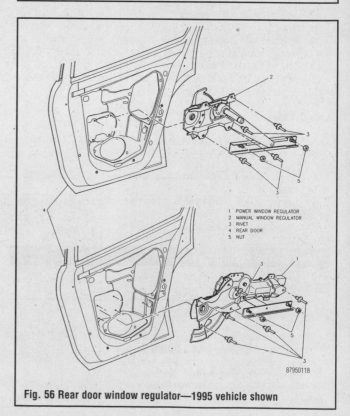

```
1  POWER WINDOW REGULATOR
2  MANUAL WINDOW REGULATOR
3  RIVET
4  REAR DOOR
5  NUT
```

Fig. 56 Rear door window regulator—1995 vehicle shown

To install:

7. If so equipped, attach the motor to the regulator using a rivet tool and ³⁄₁₆ in. (5mm) rivets or ³⁄₁₆ in. (5mm) nuts and bolts.

8. Place the regulator through the rear access hole into the door.

9. If an electric regulator is being installed, connect the wire connector to the motor prior to installing the regulator in the panel.

10. Locate the lift arm roller into the glass sash channel.

11. Using rivet tool J-29022 or equivalent, rivet the regulator to the door using ¼ in. x ½ in. (6mm x 13mm) aluminum peel type rivets (part No. 9436175 or equivalent).

12. On the front door only, install the regulator retaining bolts

13. Replace the door window assembly.

14. Install the water deflector and the door panel.

Windshield and Fixed Glass

REMOVAL & INSTALLATION

If your windshield, or other fixed window, is cracked or chipped, you may decide to replace it with a new one yourself. However, there are two main reasons why replacement windshields and other window glass should be installed only by a professional automotive glass technician: safety and cost.

The most important reason a professional should install automotive glass is for safety. The glass in the vehicle, especially the windshield, is designed with safety in mind in case of a collision. The windshield is specially manufactured from two panes of specially-tempered glass with a thin layer of transparent plastic between them. This construction allows the glass to "give" in the event that a part of your body hits the windshield during the collision, and prevents the glass from shattering, which could cause lacerations, blinding and other harm to passengers of the vehicle. The other fixed windows are designed to be tempered so that if they break during a collision, they shatter in such a way that there are no large pointed glass pieces. The professional automotive glass technician knows how to install the glass in a vehicle so that it will function opti-

mally during a collision. Without the proper experience, knowledge and tools, installing a piece of automotive glass yourself could lead to additional harm if an accident should ever occur.

Cost is also a factor when deciding to install automotive glass yourself. Performing this could cost you much more than a professional may charge for the same job. Since the windshield is designed to break under stress, an often life saving characteristic, windshields tend to break VERY easily when an inexperienced person attempts to install one. Do-it-yourselfers buying two, three or even four windshields from a salvage yard because they have broken them during installation are common stories. Also, since the automotive glass is designed to prevent the outside elements from entering your vehicle, improper installation can lead to water and air leaks. Annoying whining noises at highway speeds from air leaks or inside body panel rusting from water leaks can add to your stress level and subtract from your wallet. After buying two or three windshields, installing them and ending up with a leak that produces a noise while driving and water damage during rainstorms, the cost of having a professional do it correctly the first time may be much more alluring. We here at Chilton, therefore, advise that you have a professional automotive glass technician service any broken glass on your vehicle.

WINDSHIELD CHIP REPAIR

▶ See Figures 57 thru 71

➡ **Check with your state and local authorities on the laws for state safety inspection. Some states or municipalities may not allow chip repair as a viable option for correcting stone damage to your windshield.**

Although severely cracked or damaged windshields must be replaced, there is something that you can do to prolong or even prevent the need for replacement of a chipped windshield. There are many companies which offer windshield chip repair products, such as Loctite's® Bullseye™ windshield repair kit. These kits usually consist of a syringe, pedestal and a sealing adhesive. The syringe is mounted on the pedestal and is used to create a vacuum which pulls the plastic layer against the glass. This helps make the chip transparent. The

TCCA0P00

Fig. 57 Small chips on your windshield can be fixed with an aftermarket repair kit, such as the one from Loctite®

TCCA0P01

Fig. 58 To repair a chip, clean the windshield with glass cleaner and dry it completely

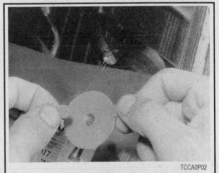
TCCA0P02

Fig. 59 Remove the center from the adhesive disc and peel off the backing from one side of the disc . . .

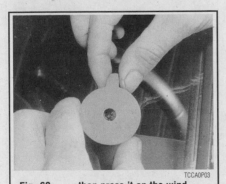
TCCA0P03

Fig. 60 . . . then press it on the windshield so that the chip is centered in the hole

TCCA0P04

Fig. 61 Be sure that the tab points upward on the windshield

TCCA0P05

Fig. 62 Peel the backing off the exposed side of the adhesive disc . . .

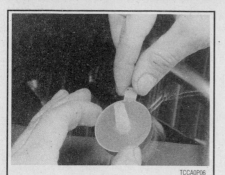

Fig. 63 . . . then position the plastic pedestal on the adhesive disc, ensuring that the tabs are aligned

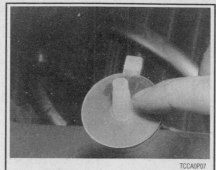

Fig. 64 Press the pedestal firmly on the adhesive disc to create an adequate seal . . .

Fig. 65 . . . then install the applicator syringe nipple in the pedestal's hole

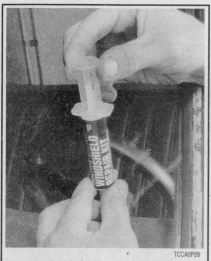

Fig. 66 Hold the syringe with one hand while pulling the plunger back with the other hand

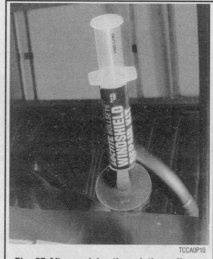

Fig. 67 After applying the solution, allow the entire assembly to sit until it has set completely

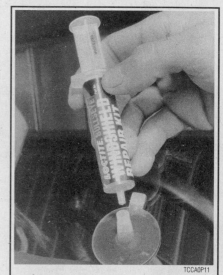

Fig. 68 After the solution has set, remove the syringe from the pedestal . . ,

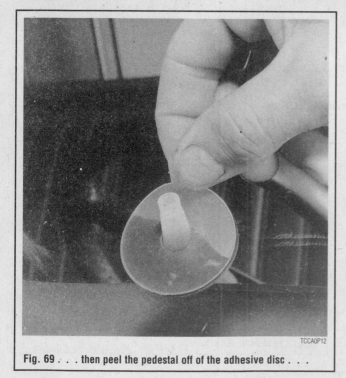

Fig. 69 . . . then peel the pedestal off of the adhesive disc . . .

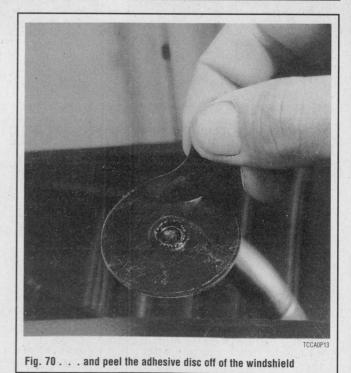

Fig. 70 . . . and peel the adhesive disc off of the windshield

Fig. 71 The chip will still be slightly visible, but it should be filled with the hardened solution

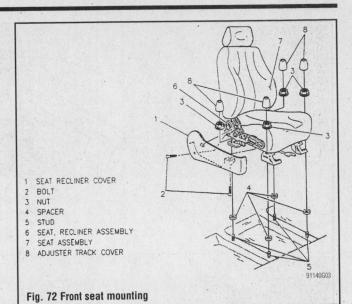

1 SEAT RECLINER COVER
2 BOLT
3 NUT
4 SPACER
5 STUD
6 SEAT, RECLINER ASSEMBLY
7 SEAT ASSEMBLY
8 ADJUSTER TRACK COVER

Fig. 72 Front seat mounting

adhesive is then injected which seals the chip and helps to prevent further stress cracks from developing. Refer to the sequence of photos to get a general idea of what windshield chip repair involves.

➡**Always follow the specific manufacturer's instructions.**

Inside Rear View Mirror

REPLACEMENT

The rearview mirror is attached to a support which is secured to the windshield glass. This support is installed by the glass supplier using a plastic-polyvinyl butyl adhesive. Service replacement windshield glass has the mirror support bonded to the glass assembly. Service kits are available to replace a detached mirror support or install a new part. Follow the manufacturer's instructions for replacement.

REMOVAL & INSTALLATION

1. Detach the mirror reading lamp connector if equipped.
2. Loosen the setscrew.
3. Slide the mirror off of the support.
To install:
4. Slide the mirror onto the support.
5. Tighten the setscrew.
6. Attach the mirror reading lamp connector if equipped.

Seats

REMOVAL & INSTALLATION

Front

▶ **See Figure 72**

1. Place the seat to the full-forward position.
2. Remove the adjuster rear foot covers or carpet retainers.
3. Remove the track covers where necessary, then remove the rear attaching nuts.
4. Remove the front foot covers, then remove the adjuster-to-floor pan front attaching nuts.
5. Remove the seat assembly from the car.
6. To install the seat assembly reverse the removal procedure.
7. Tighten the seat adjuster-to-floor pan attaching bolts or nuts to 21 ft. lbs. (28 Nm).

Rear

SEATBACK

▶ **See Figure 73**

1. Unlatch the rear seatback and tilt it forward 50°.
2. Unhook the rear seat outer seat belt from the rear seatback on both sides.
3. Remove the spacer on the passenger side at the right key pin.
4. Slide the seatback to the right and disengage the left key pin from the slot.
5. Slide the rear seatback to the left and disengage the right key pin from the slot.
6. Remove the seatback from the vehicle.
7. Installation is the reverse of removal.

SEAT CUSHION

▶ **See Figure 74**

1. Press the seat cushion retainer rearward with a flat bladed screwdriver.
2. Lift the seat cushion upward and remove it from the vehicle.
To install:
3. Place the seat cushion into place and push downward on the seat cushion to engage the retaining clips.

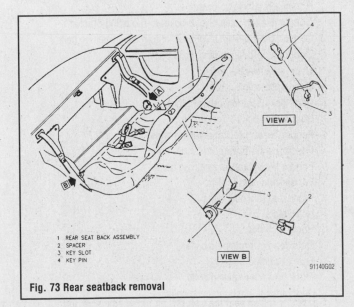

1 REAR SEAT BACK ASSEMBLY
2 SPACER
3 KEY SLOT
4 KEY PIN

VIEW A

VIEW B

Fig. 73 Rear seatback removal

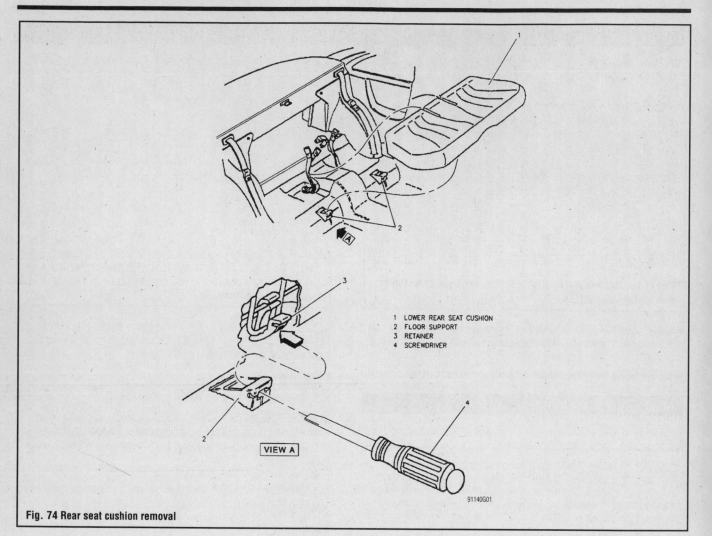

1 LOWER REAR SEAT CUSHION
2 FLOOR SUPPORT
3 RETAINER
4 SCREWDRIVER

VIEW A

91140G01

Fig. 74 Rear seat cushion removal

TORQUE SPECIFICATIONS

Components	English	Metric
Antenna nut	53 inch lbs.	6 Nm
Antenna retaining screws	18 inch lbs.	2 Nm
Convertible top main pivot bracket-to-mounting bracket	17 ft. lbs.	24 Nm
Convertible top main pivot bracket-to-motor retaining bolts	9 ft. lbs.	12 Nm
Door detent-to-hinge pillar bolts bolts	80 inch lbs.	9 Nm
Door hinge-to-door bolts	16 ft. lbs.	22 Nm
Door hinge-to-pillar bolts	16 ft. lbs.	22 Nm
Door lock assembly retaining bolts	62 inch lbs.	7 Nm
Door striker bolts	18 ft. lbs.	25 Nm
Fender center bracket retaining bolts	14 inch lbs.	1.6 Nm
Fender center bracket-to-fender bolts	27 inch lbs.	3 Nm
Fender lower bracket retaining bolts	27 inch lbs.	3 Nm
Fender retaining screws	62 inch lbs.	7 Nm
Front seat retaining bolts	21 ft. lbs.	28 Nm
Hood hinge bolts	20 ft. lbs.	27 Nm
Hood latch bolts	20 ft. lbs.	27 Nm
Outside mirror retaining bolts	50 inch lbs.	6 Nm
Trunk lid hinge bolts	89 inch lbs.	10 Nm
Trunk lid latch retaining bolts	53 inch lbs.	6 Nm
Door glass-to-sash retaining bolts	71 inch lbs.	8 Nm

91140C01

GLOSSARY

AIR/FUEL RATIO: The ratio of air-to-gasoline by weight in the fuel mixture drawn into the engine.

AIR INJECTION: One method of reducing harmful exhaust emissions by injecting air into each of the exhaust ports of an engine. The fresh air entering the hot exhaust manifold causes any remaining fuel to be burned before it can exit the tailpipe.

ALTERNATOR: A device used for converting mechanical energy into electrical energy.

AMMETER: An instrument, calibrated in amperes, used to measure the flow of an electrical current in a circuit. Ammeters are always connected in series with the circuit being tested.

AMPERE: The rate of flow of electrical current present when one volt of electrical pressure is applied against one ohm of electrical resistance.

ANALOG COMPUTER: Any microprocessor that uses similar (analogous) electrical signals to make its calculations.

ARMATURE: A laminated, soft iron core wrapped by a wire that converts electrical energy to mechanical energy as in a motor or relay. When rotated in a magnetic field, it changes mechanical energy into electrical energy as in a generator.

ATMOSPHERIC PRESSURE: The pressure on the Earth's surface caused by the weight of the air in the atmosphere. At sea level, this pressure is 14.7 psi at 32°F (101 kPa at 0°C).

ATOMIZATION: The breaking down of a liquid into a fine mist that can be suspended in air.

AXIAL PLAY: Movement parallel to a shaft or bearing bore.

BACKFIRE: The sudden combustion of gases in the intake or exhaust system that results in a loud explosion.

BACKLASH: The clearance or play between two parts, such as meshed gears.

BACKPRESSURE: Restrictions in the exhaust system that slow the exit of exhaust gases from the combustion chamber.

BAKELITE: A heat resistant, plastic insulator material commonly used in printed circuit boards and transistorized components.

BALL BEARING: A bearing made up of hardened inner and outer races between which hardened steel balls roll.

BALLAST RESISTOR: A resistor in the primary ignition circuit that lowers voltage after the engine is started to reduce wear on ignition components.

BEARING: A friction reducing, supportive device usually located between a stationary part and a moving part.

BIMETAL TEMPERATURE SENSOR: Any sensor or switch made of two dissimilar types of metal that bend when heated or cooled due to the different expansion rates of the alloys. These types of sensors usually function as an on/off switch.

BLOWBY: Combustion gases, composed of water vapor and unburned fuel, that leak past the piston rings into the crankcase during normal engine operation. These gases are removed by the PCV system to prevent the buildup of harmful acids in the crankcase.

BRAKE PAD: A brake shoe and lining assembly used with disc brakes.

BRAKE SHOE: The backing for the brake lining. The term is, however, usually applied to the assembly of the brake backing and lining.

BUSHING: A liner, usually removable, for a bearing; an anti-friction liner used in place of a bearing.

CALIPER: A hydraulically activated device in a disc brake system, which is mounted straddling the brake rotor (disc). The caliper contains at least one piston and two brake pads. Hydraulic pressure on the piston(s) forces the pads against the rotor.

CAMSHAFT: A shaft in the engine on which are the lobes (cams) which operate the valves. The camshaft is driven by the crankshaft, via a belt, chain or gears, at one half the crankshaft speed.

CAPACITOR: A device which stores an electrical charge.

CARBON MONOXIDE (CO): A colorless, odorless gas given off as a normal byproduct of combustion. It is poisonous and extremely dangerous in confined areas, building up slowly to toxic levels without warning if adequate ventilation is not available.

CARBURETOR: A device, usually mounted on the intake manifold of an engine, which mixes the air and fuel in the proper proportion to allow even combustion.

CATALYTIC CONVERTER: A device installed in the exhaust system, like a muffler, that converts harmful byproducts of combustion into carbon dioxide and water vapor by means of a heat-producing chemical reaction.

CENTRIFUGAL ADVANCE: A mechanical method of advancing the spark timing by using flyweights in the distributor that react to centrifugal force generated by the distributor shaft rotation.

CHECK VALVE: Any one-way valve installed to permit the flow of air, fuel or vacuum in one direction only.

CHOKE: A device, usually a moveable valve, placed in the intake path of a carburetor to restrict the flow of air.

CIRCUIT: Any unbroken path through which an electrical current can flow. Also used to describe fuel flow in some instances.

CIRCUIT BREAKER: A switch which protects an electrical circuit from overload by opening the circuit when the current flow exceeds a predetermined level. Some circuit breakers must be reset manually, while most reset automatically.

COIL (IGNITION): A transformer in the ignition circuit which steps up the voltage provided to the spark plugs.

COMBINATION MANIFOLD: An assembly which includes both the intake and exhaust manifolds in one casting.

COMBINATION VALVE: A device used in some fuel systems that routes fuel vapors to a charcoal storage canister instead of venting them into the atmosphere. The valve relieves fuel tank pressure and allows fresh air into the tank as the fuel level drops to prevent a vapor lock situation.

COMPRESSION RATIO: The comparison of the total volume of the cylinder and combustion chamber with the piston at BDC and the piston at TDC.

CONDENSER: 1. An electrical device which acts to store an electrical charge, preventing voltage surges. 2. A radiator-like device in the air conditioning system in which refrigerant gas condenses into a liquid, giving off heat.

CONDUCTOR: Any material through which an electrical current can be transmitted easily.

CONTINUITY: Continuous or complete circuit. Can be checked with an ohmmeter.

COUNTERSHAFT: An intermediate shaft which is rotated by a mainshaft and transmits, in turn, that rotation to a working part.

CRANKCASE: The lower part of an engine in which the crankshaft and related parts operate.

CRANKSHAFT: The main driving shaft of an engine which receives reciprocating motion from the pistons and converts it to rotary motion.

CYLINDER: In an engine, the round hole in the engine block in which the piston(s) ride.

CYLINDER BLOCK: The main structural member of an engine in which is found the cylinders, crankshaft and other principal parts.

CYLINDER HEAD: The detachable portion of the engine, usually fastened to the top of the cylinder block and containing all or most of the combustion chambers. On overhead valve engines, it contains the valves and their operating parts. On overhead cam engines, it contains the camshaft as well.

DEAD CENTER: The extreme top or bottom of the piston stroke.

DETONATION: An unwanted explosion of the air/fuel mixture in the combustion chamber caused by excess heat and compression, advanced timing, or an overly lean mixture. Also referred to as "ping".

DIAPHRAGM: A thin, flexible wall separating two cavities, such as in a vacuum advance unit.

DIESELING: A condition in which hot spots in the combustion chamber cause the engine to run on after the key is turned off.

DIFFERENTIAL: A geared assembly which allows the transmission of motion between drive axles, giving one axle the ability to turn faster than the other.

DIODE: An electrical device that will allow current to flow in one direction only.

DISC BRAKE: A hydraulic braking assembly consisting of a brake disc, or rotor, mounted on an axle, and a caliper assembly containing, usually two brake pads which are activated by hydraulic pressure. The pads are forced against the sides of the disc, creating friction which slows the vehicle.

DISTRIBUTOR: A mechanically driven device on an engine which is responsible for electrically firing the spark plug at a predetermined point of the piston stroke.

DOWEL PIN: A pin, inserted in mating holes in two different parts allowing those parts to maintain a fixed relationship.

DRUM BRAKE: A braking system which consists of two brake shoes and one or two wheel cylinders, mounted on a fixed backing plate, and a brake drum, mounted on an axle, which revolves around the assembly.

DWELL: The rate, measured in degrees of shaft rotation, at which an electrical circuit cycles on and off.

ELECTRONIC CONTROL UNIT (ECU): Ignition module, module, amplifier or igniter. See Module for definition.

ELECTRONIC IGNITION: A system in which the timing and firing of the spark plugs is controlled by an electronic control unit, usually called a module. These systems have no points or condenser.

END-PLAY: The measured amount of axial movement in a shaft.

ENGINE: A device that converts heat into mechanical energy.

EXHAUST MANIFOLD: A set of cast passages or pipes which conduct exhaust gases from the engine.

FEELER GAUGE: A blade, usually metal, or precisely predetermined thickness, used to measure the clearance between two parts.

FIRING ORDER: The order in which combustion occurs in the cylinders of an engine. Also the order in which spark is distributed to the plugs by the distributor.

FLOODING: The presence of too much fuel in the intake manifold and combustion chamber which prevents the air/fuel mixture from firing, thereby causing a no-start situation.

FLYWHEEL: A disc shaped part bolted to the rear end of the crankshaft. Around the outer perimeter is affixed the ring gear. The starter drive engages the ring gear, turning the flywheel, which rotates the crankshaft, imparting the initial starting motion to the engine.

FOOT POUND (ft. lbs. or sometimes, ft.lb.): The amount of energy or work needed to raise an item weighing one pound, a distance of one foot.

FUSE: A protective device in a circuit which prevents circuit overload by breaking the circuit when a specific amperage is present. The device is constructed around a strip or wire of a lower amperage rating than the circuit it is designed to protect. When an amperage higher than that stamped on the fuse is present in the circuit, the strip or wire melts, opening the circuit.

GEAR RATIO: The ratio between the number of teeth on meshing gears.

GENERATOR: A device which converts mechanical energy into electrical energy.

HEAT RANGE: The measure of a spark plug's ability to dissipate heat from its firing end. The higher the heat range, the hotter the plug fires.

HUB: The center part of a wheel or gear.

HYDROCARBON (HC): Any chemical compound made up of hydrogen and carbon. A major pollutant formed by the engine as a byproduct of combustion.

HYDROMETER: An instrument used to measure the specific gravity of a solution.

INCH POUND (inch lbs.; sometimes in.lb. or in. lbs.): One twelfth of a foot pound.

INDUCTION: A means of transferring electrical energy in the form of a magnetic field. Principle used in the ignition coil to increase voltage.

INJECTOR: A device which receives metered fuel under relatively low pressure and is activated to inject the fuel into the engine under relatively high pressure at a predetermined time.

INPUT SHAFT: The shaft to which torque is applied, usually carrying the driving gear or gears.

INTAKE MANIFOLD: A casting of passages or pipes used to conduct air or a fuel/air mixture to the cylinders.

JOURNAL: The bearing surface within which a shaft operates.

KEY: A small block usually fitted in a notch between a shaft and a hub to prevent slippage of the two parts.

MANIFOLD: A casting of passages or set of pipes which connect the cylinders to an inlet or outlet source.

MANIFOLD VACUUM: Low pressure in an engine intake manifold formed just below the throttle plates. Manifold vacuum is highest at idle and drops under acceleration.

MASTER CYLINDER: The primary fluid pressurizing device in a hydraulic system. In automotive use, it is found in brake and hydraulic clutch systems and is pedal activated, either directly or, in a power brake system, through the power booster.

MODULE: Electronic control unit, amplifier or igniter of solid state or integrated design which controls the current flow in the ignition primary circuit based on input from the pick-up coil. When the module opens the primary circuit, high secondary voltage is induced in the coil.

NEEDLE BEARING: A bearing which consists of a number (usually a large number) of long, thin rollers.

OHM: (Ω) The unit used to measure the resistance of conductor-to-electrical flow. One ohm is the amount of resistance that limits current flow to one ampere in a circuit with one volt of pressure.

OHMMETER: An instrument used for measuring the resistance, in ohms, in an electrical circuit.

OUTPUT SHAFT: The shaft which transmits torque from a device, such as a transmission.

OVERDRIVE: A gear assembly which produces more shaft revolutions than that transmitted to it.

OVERHEAD CAMSHAFT (OHC): An engine configuration in which the camshaft is mounted on top of the cylinder head and operates the valve either directly or by means of rocker arms.

OVERHEAD VALVE (OHV): An engine configuration in which all of the valves are located in the cylinder head and the camshaft is located in the cylinder block. The camshaft operates the valves via lifters and pushrods.

OXIDES OF NITROGEN (NOx): Chemical compounds of nitrogen produced as a byproduct of combustion. They combine with hydrocarbons to produce smog.

OXYGEN SENSOR: Use with the feedback system to sense the presence of oxygen in the exhaust gas and signal the computer which can reference the voltage signal to an air/fuel ratio.

PINION: The smaller of two meshing gears.

PISTON RING: An open-ended ring with fits into a groove on the outer diameter of the piston. Its chief function is to form a seal between the piston and cylinder wall. Most automotive pistons have three rings: two for compression sealing; one for oil sealing.

PRELOAD: A predetermined load placed on a bearing during assembly or by adjustment.

PRIMARY CIRCUIT: the low voltage side of the ignition system which consists of the ignition switch, ballast resistor or resistance wire, bypass, coil, electronic control unit and pick-up coil as well as the connecting wires and harnesses.

PRESS FIT: The mating of two parts under pressure, due to the inner diameter of one being smaller than the outer diameter of the other, or vice versa; an interference fit.

RACE: The surface on the inner or outer ring of a bearing on which the balls, needles or rollers move.

REGULATOR: A device which maintains the amperage and/or voltage levels of a circuit at predetermined values.

RELAY: A switch which automatically opens and/or closes a circuit.

RESISTANCE: The opposition to the flow of current through a circuit or electrical device, and is measured in ohms. Resistance is equal to the voltage divided by the amperage.

RESISTOR: A device, usually made of wire, which offers a preset amount of resistance in an electrical circuit.

RING GEAR: The name given to a ring-shaped gear attached to a differential case, or affixed to a flywheel or as part of a planetary gear set.

ROLLER BEARING: A bearing made up of hardened inner and outer races between which hardened steel rollers move.

ROTOR: 1. The disc-shaped part of a disc brake assembly, upon which the brake pads bear; also called, brake disc. 2. The device mounted atop the distributor shaft, which passes current to the distributor cap tower contacts.

SECONDARY CIRCUIT: The high voltage side of the ignition system, usually above 20,000 volts. The secondary includes the ignition coil, coil wire, distributor cap and rotor, spark plug wires and spark plugs.

SENDING UNIT: A mechanical, electrical, hydraulic or electro-magnetic device which transmits information to a gauge.

SENSOR: Any device designed to measure engine operating conditions or ambient pressures and temperatures. Usually electronic in nature and designed to send a voltage signal to an on-board computer, some sensors may operate as a simple on/off switch or they may provide a variable voltage signal (like a potentiometer) as conditions or measured parameters change.

SHIM: Spacers of precise, predetermined thickness used between parts to establish a proper working relationship.

SLAVE CYLINDER: In automotive use, a device in the hydraulic clutch system which is activated by hydraulic force, disengaging the clutch.

SOLENOID: A coil used to produce a magnetic field, the effect of which is to produce work.

SPARK PLUG: A device screwed into the combustion chamber of a spark ignition engine. The basic construction is a conductive core inside of a ceramic insulator, mounted in an outer conductive base. An electrical charge from the spark plug wire travels along the conductive core and jumps a preset air gap to a grounding point or points at the end of the conductive base. The resultant spark ignites the fuel/air mixture in the combustion chamber.

SPLINES: Ridges machined or cast onto the outer diameter of a shaft or inner diameter of a bore to enable parts to mate without rotation.

TACHOMETER: A device used to measure the rotary speed of an engine, shaft, gear, etc., usually in rotations per minute.

THERMOSTAT: A valve, located in the cooling system of an engine, which is closed when cold and opens gradually in response to engine heating, controlling the temperature of the coolant and rate of coolant flow.

TOP DEAD CENTER (TDC): The point at which the piston reaches the top of its travel on the compression stroke.

TORQUE: The twisting force applied to an object.

TORQUE CONVERTER: A turbine used to transmit power from a driving member to a driven member via hydraulic action, providing changes in drive ratio and torque. In automotive use, it links the driveplate at the rear of the engine to the automatic transmission.

TRANSDUCER: A device used to change a force into an electrical signal.

TRANSISTOR: A semi-conductor component which can be actuated by a small voltage to perform an electrical switching function.

TUNE-UP: A regular maintenance function, usually associated with the replacement and adjustment of parts and components in the electrical and fuel systems of a vehicle for the purpose of attaining optimum performance.

TURBOCHARGER: An exhaust driven pump which compresses intake air and forces it into the combustion chambers at higher than atmospheric pressures. The increased air pressure allows more fuel to be burned and results in increased horsepower being produced.

VACUUM ADVANCE: A device which advances the ignition timing in response to increased engine vacuum.

VACUUM GAUGE: An instrument used to measure the presence of vacuum in a chamber.

VALVE: A device which control the pressure, direction of flow or rate of flow of a liquid or gas.

VALVE CLEARANCE: The measured gap between the end of the valve stem and the rocker arm, cam lobe or follower that activates the valve.

VISCOSITY: The rating of a liquid's internal resistance to flow.

VOLTMETER: An instrument used for measuring electrical force in units called volts. Voltmeters are always connected parallel with the circuit being tested.

WHEEL CYLINDER: Found in the automotive drum brake assembly, it is a device, actuated by hydraulic pressure, which, through internal pistons, pushes the brake shoes outward against the drums.

ABS CONTROL MODULE 9-23
    REMOVAL & INSTALLATION 9-23
ABS HYDRAULIC MODULATOR/MASTER CYLINDER ASSEMBLY 9-21
    REMOVAL & INSTALLATION 9-21
ABS RELAY 9-23
    REMOVAL & INSTALLATION 9-23
ACTUATOR (SLAVE) CYLINDER 7-9
    HYDRAULIC SYSTEM BLEEDING 7-9
    REMOVAL & INSTALLATION 7-9
ADJUSTMENTS (DISTRIBUTORLESS IGNITION SYSTEM) 2-4
AIR BAG (SUPPLEMENTAL RESTRAINT SYSTEM) 6-7
AIR CLEANER (ELEMENT) 1-15
    REMOVAL & INSTALLATION 1-15
AIR CONDITIONING COMPONENTS 6-11
    REMOVAL & INSTALLATION 6-11
AIR CONDITIONING SYSTEM 1-27
    PREVENTIVE MAINTENANCE 1-27
    SYSTEM INSPECTION 1-27
    SYSTEM SERVICE & REPAIR 1-27
AIR POLLUTION 4-2
ALTERNATE TOWING METHOD—WHEEL LIFT 1-45
ALTERNATOR 2-7
    REMOVAL & INSTALLATION 2-7
    TESTING 2-7
ALTERNATOR PRECAUTIONS 2-7
ANTENNA 10-6
    REPLACEMENT 10-6
ANTI-LOCK BRAKE SYSTEM 9-20
AUTOMATIC TRANSAXLE 7-9
AUTOMATIC TRANSAXLE (FLUIDS AND LUBRICANTS) 1-35
    FLUID RECOMMENDATIONS 1-35
    LEVEL CHECK 1-35
    PAN & FILTER SERVICE 1-36
AUTOMATIC TRANSAXLE ASSEMBLY 7-10
    ADJUSTMENTS 7-11
    REMOVAL & INSTALLATION 7-10
AUTOMOTIVE EMISSIONS 4-3
AUTOMOTIVE POLLUTANTS 4-2
    HEAT TRANSFER 4-2
    TEMPERATURE INVERSION 4-2
AVOIDING THE MOST COMMON MISTAKES 1-2
AVOIDING TROUBLE 1-2
BACK-UP LIGHT SWITCH 7-2
    REMOVAL & INSTALLATION 7-2
BALANCE SHAFTS 3-33
    INSPECTION 3-35
    REMOVAL & INSTALLATION 3-33
BASIC ELECTRICAL THEORY 6-2
    HOW DOES ELECTRICITY WORK: THE WATER ANALOGY 6-2
    OHM'S LAW 6-2
BASIC FUEL SYSTEM DIAGNOSIS 5-2
BASIC OPERATING PRINCIPLES 9-2
    DISC BRAKES 9-2
    DRUM BRAKES 9-2
    POWER BOOSTERS 9-3
BATTERY 1-17
    BATTERY FLUID 1-18
    CABLES 1-18
    CHARGING 1-18
    GENERAL MAINTENANCE 1-17
    PRECAUTIONS 1-17
    REPLACEMENT 1-19
BATTERY CABLES 6-7
BELTS 1-19
    ADJUSTMENT 1-20
    INSPECTION 1-19
    REMOVAL & INSTALLATION 1-20
BLEEDING THE ABS SYSTEM 9-24
    BLEEDING THE ABS HYDRAULIC SYSTEM 9-25
    SYSTEM FILLING 9-25
BLEEDING THE BRAKE SYSTEM 9-6

MASTER

INDEX

BLOWER MOTOR 6-10
    REMOVAL & INSTALLATION 6-10
BODY 1-11
BODY LUBRICATION AND MAINTENANCE 1-43
    BODY LUBRICATION 1-43
    CAR WASHING 1-43
    INTERIOR CLEANING 1-44
    WAXING 1-44
BOLTS, NUTS AND OTHER THREADED RETAINERS 1-7
BOTTOM FEED PORT (BFP) INJECTION SYSTEM 5-3
BOTTOM FEED PORT FUEL INJECTORS 5-5
    REMOVAL & INSTALLATION 5-6
    TESTING 5-5
BRAKE BACKING PLATE 9-19
    REMOVAL & INSTALLATION 9-19
BRAKE CALIPER 9-9
    OVERHAUL 9-10
    REMOVAL & INSTALLATION 9-9
BRAKE DISC (ROTOR) 9-11
    INSPECTION 9-12
    REMOVAL & INSTALLATION 9-11
BRAKE DRUMS 9-14
    INSPECTION 9-14
    REMOVAL & INSTALLATION 9-14
BRAKE FLUID LEVEL SWITCH 9-23
    REMOVAL & INSTALLATION 9-23
BRAKE HOSES AND LINES 9-5
    REMOVAL & INSTALLATION 9-5
BRAKE LIGHT SWITCH 9-3
    REMOVAL & INSTALLATION 9-3
BRAKE MASTER CYLINDER 1-40
    FLUID RECOMMENDATIONS 1-40
    LEVEL CHECK 1-41
BRAKE OPERATING SYSTEM 9-2
BRAKE PADS 9-7
    INSPECTION 9-9
    REMOVAL & INSTALLATION 9-7
BRAKE SHOES 9-14
    ADJUSTMENTS 9-16
    INSPECTION 9-14
    REMOVAL & INSTALLATION 9-14
BRAKE SPECIFICATION—GM J BODY 9-26
BUY OR REBUILD? 3-40
CABLES 9-19
    ADJUSTMENT 9-20
    REMOVAL & INSTALLATION 9-19
CAMSHAFT AND BEARINGS 3-30
    INSPECTION 3-32
    REMOVAL & INSTALLATION 3-30
CAMSHAFT CARRIER COVER 3-5
    REMOVAL & INSTALLATION 3-5
CAMSHAFT POSITION (CMP) SENSOR 4-25
    OPERATION 4-25
    REMOVAL & INSTALLATION 4-26
    TESTING 4-25
CAPACITIES 1-49
CATALYTIC CONVERTER 4-13
    OPERATION 4-13
CENTER CONSOLE 10-10
    REMOVAL & INSTALLATION 10-10
CHARGING SYSTEM 2-6
CHASSIS GREASING 1-43
CIRCUIT BREAKERS 6-28
    RESETTING AND/OR REPLACEMENT 6-28
CIRCUIT PROTECTION 6-27
CLEARING CODES 4-29
CLUTCH 7-6
CLUTCH MASTER CYLINDER 1-42

FLUID RECOMMENDATIONS 1-42
    LEVEL CHECK 1-42
COIL-OVER SHOCKS 8-13
    REMOVAL & INSTALLATION 8-13
COMPONENT LOCATIONS
    DISC BRAKE COMPONENTS 9-7
    DRUM BRAKE COMPONENTS—INSTALLED (HUB REMOVED)—LEFT
        SIDE SHOWN 9-13
    ELECTRONIC ENGINE CONTROL COMPONENTS—2.2L ENGINE 4-5
    ELECTRONIC ENGINE CONTROL COMPONENTS—2.4L ENGINE 4-6
    FRONT SUSPENSION COMPONENT LOCATIONS 8-5
    REAR DRUM BRAKE COMPONENTS—RIGHT SIDE SHOWN 9-13
    REAR SUSPENSION COMPONENT LOCATIONS 8-14
    STRUT ASSEMBLY EXPLODED VIEW 8-6
CONTROL PANEL 6-11
    REMOVAL & INSTALLATION 6-11
CONVERTIBLE TOPS 10-6
    MOTOR REPLACEMENT 10-7
    TOP REPLACEMENT 10-6
COOLANT LEVEL SWITCH 2-11
    OPERATION 2-11
    REMOVAL & INSTALLATION 2-11
    TESTING 2-11
COOLANT TEMPERATURE SENDER 2-11
    OPERATION 2-11
    REMOVAL & INSTALLATION 2-11
    TESTING 2-11
COOLING SYSTEM 1-38
    DRAIN & REFILL 1-39
    FLUID RECOMMENDATIONS 1-38
    FLUSHING & CLEANING THE SYSTEM 1-40
    LEVEL CHECK 1-38
    TESTING FOR LEAKS 1-38
CRANKCASE EMISSIONS 4-4
CRANKCASE VENTILATION SYSTEM 4-7
    OPERATION 4-7
    REMOVAL & INSTALLATION 4-7
    TESTING 4-7
CRANKSHAFT AND CAMSHAFT POSITION SENSORS (DISTRIBUTORLESS
    IGNITION SYSTEM) 2-6
CRANKSHAFT POSITION (CKP) SENSOR (ELECTRONIC ENGINE
    CONTROLS) 4-24
    OPERATION 4-24
    REMOVAL & INSTALLATION 4-24
    TESTING 4-24
CRANKSHAFT PULLEY/DAMPER 3-25
    REMOVAL & INSTALLATION 3-25
CRUISE CONTROL 6-12
CRUISE CONTROL TROUBLESHOOTING 6-14
CV-BOOTS 1-22
    INSPECTION 1-22
CYLINDER HEAD (ENGINE MECHANICAL) 3-21
    REMOVAL & INSTALLATION 3-21
CYLINDER HEAD (ENGINE RECONDITIONING) 3-42
    ASSEMBLY 3-48
    DISASSEMBLY 3-42
    INSPECTION 3-45
    REFINISHING & REPAIRING 3-47
DETERMINING ENGINE CONDITION 3-39
    COMPRESSION TEST 3-39
    OIL PRESSURE TEST 3-40
DIAGNOSIS (ANTI-LOCK BRAKE SYSTEM) 9-21
DIAGNOSIS AND TESTING (DISTRIBUTORLESS IGNITION
    SYSTEM) 2-3
    CYLINDER DROP TEST 2-3
    SECONDARY SPARK TEST 2-3
DIAGNOSIS AND TESTING (TROUBLE CODES) 4-28
    CIRCUIT/COMPONENT REPAIR 4-28

INTERMITTENTS 4-28
VISUAL/PHYSICAL INSPECTION 4-28
DISC BRAKE COMPONENTS 9-7
DISC BRAKES 9-7
DISCONNECTING THE CABLES 6-7
DISTRIBUTORLESS IGNITION SYSTEM (DIS) 2-2
DO'S 1-6
DON'TS 1-6
DOOR GLASS (WINDOW) 10-13
REMOVAL & INSTALLATION 10-13
DOOR LOCKS 10-11
REMOVAL & INSTALLATION 10-11
DOOR PANELS 10-10
REMOVAL & INSTALLATION 10-10
DOORS 10-2
ADJUSTMENT 10-2
REMOVAL & INSTALLATION 10-2
DRIVEN DISC AND PRESSURE PLATE 7-6
ADJUSTMENTS 7-8
REMOVAL & INSTALLATION 7-6
DRUM BRAKE COMPONENTS—INSTALLED (HUB REMOVED)—LEFT
SIDE SHOWN 9-13
DRUM BRAKES 9-13
ELECTRICAL COMPONENTS 6-2
CONNECTORS 6-4
GROUND 6-3
LOAD 6-3
POWER SOURCE 6-2
PROTECTIVE DEVICES 6-3
SWITCHES & RELAYS 6-3
WIRING & HARNESSES 6-4
ELECTRONIC ENGINE CONTROL COMPONENTS—2.2L ENGINE 4-5
ELECTRONIC ENGINE CONTROL COMPONENTS—2.4L ENGINE 4-6
ELECTRONIC ENGINE CONTROLS 4-14
EMISSION CONTROLS 4-5
ENGINE (ENGINE MECHANICAL) 3-2
REMOVAL & INSTALLATION 3-2
ENGINE (FLUIDS AND LUBRICANTS) 1-33
OIL & FILTER CHANGE 1-33
OIL LEVEL CHECK 1-33
ENGINE (SERIAL NUMBER IDENTIFICATION) 1-11
ENGINE (TRAILER TOWING) 1-46
ENGINE BLOCK 3-49
ASSEMBLY 3-52
DISASSEMBLY 3-49
GENERAL INFORMATION 3-49
INSPECTION 3-50
REFINISHING 3-51
ENGINE COOLANT TEMPERATURE SENSOR 4-18
OPERATION 4-18
REMOVAL & INSTALLATION 4-19
TESTING 4-18
ENGINE FAN 3-19
REMOVAL & INSTALLATION 3-19
ENGINE IDENTIFICATION AND SPECIFICATIONS 1-12
ENGINE MECHANICAL 3-2
ENGINE MECHANICAL SPECIFICATIONS 3-55
ENGINE OVERHAUL TIPS 3-40
CLEANING 3-40
OVERHAUL TIPS 3-40
REPAIRING DAMAGED THREADS 3-41
TOOLS 3-40
ENGINE PREPARATION 3-42
ENGINE RECONDITIONING 3-39
ENGINE START-UP AND BREAK-IN 3-54
BREAKING IT IN 3-54
KEEP IT MAINTAINED 3-54
STARTING THE ENGINE 3-54

ENTERTAINMENT SYSTEMS **6-14**
EVAPORATIVE CANISTER 1-17
SERVICING 1-17
EVAPORATIVE EMISSION CONTROL SYSTEM 4-8
OPERATION 4-8
REMOVAL & INSTALLATION 4-9
TESTING 4-9
EVAPORATIVE EMISSIONS 4-4
EXHAUST GAS RECIRCULATION (EGR) SYSTEM 4-10
OPERATION 4-10
REMOVAL & INSTALLATION 4-13
TESTING 4-12
EXHAUST GASES 4-3
CARBON MONOXIDE 4-3
HYDROCARBONS 4-3
NITROGEN 4-3
OXIDES OF SULFUR 4-3
PARTICULATE MATTER 4-3
EXHAUST MANIFOLD 3-13
REMOVAL & INSTALLATION 3-13
EXHAUST SYSTEM 3-37
EXTERIOR 10-2
FASTENERS, MEASUREMENTS AND CONVERSIONS 1-7
FENDERS 10-4
REMOVAL & INSTALLATION 10-4
FIRING ORDERS 2-6
FLASHERS 6-29
REPLACEMENT 6-29
FLUID DISPOSAL 1-32
FLUID PAN 7-9
FLUIDS AND LUBRICANTS 1-32
FLYWHEEL/FLEXPLATE 3-37
REMOVAL & INSTALLATION 3-37
FOG/DRIVING LIGHTS (CHEVROLET CAVALIER Z-24 ONLY) 6-25
AIMING 6-27
INSTALLING AFTERMARKET AUXILIARY LIGHTS 6-26
REMOVAL & INSTALLATION 6-25
FRONT BUMPER 10-4
REMOVAL & INSTALLATION 10-4
FRONT HUB AND BEARING 8-12
REMOVAL & INSTALLATION 8-12
FRONT SUSPENSION 8-4
FRONT SUSPENSION COMPONENT LOCATIONS 8-5
FUEL AND ENGINE OIL RECOMMENDATIONS 1-32
ENGINE OIL 1-32
FUEL 1-33
OPERATION IN FOREIGN COUNTRIES 1-33
FUEL FILTER 1-15
REMOVAL & INSTALLATION 1-15
FUEL INJECTORS 5-15
REMOVAL & INSTALLATION 5-15
TESTING 5-15
FUEL LINE FITTINGS 5-2
FUEL PRESSURE REGULATOR (BOTTOM FEED PORT INJECTION
SYSTEM) 5-8
REMOVAL & INSTALLATION 5-8
FUEL PRESSURE REGULATOR (MULTI-PORT & SEQUENTIAL FUEL
INJECTION SYSTEMS) 5-18
REMOVAL & INSTALLATION 5-18
FUEL PUMP (BOTTOM FEED PORT INJECTION SYSTEM) 5-3
REMOVAL & INSTALLATION 5-4
TESTING 5-3
FUEL PUMP (MULTI-PORT & SEQUENTIAL FUEL INJECTION
SYSTEMS) 5-9
REMOVAL & INSTALLATION 5-13
TESTING 5-9
FUEL RAIL ASSEMBLY 5-16
REMOVAL & INSTALLATION 5-16

FUEL SYSTEM PRESSURE RELIEF 5-3
FUEL TANK 5-19
FUSES 6-27
   GENERAL INFORMATION 6-27
   REPLACEMENT 6-28
FUSIBLE LINKS 6-29
   REPLACEMENT 6-29
GASOLINE ENGINE TUNE-UP SPECIFICATIONS 1-26
GAUGES 6-20
   REMOVAL & INSTALLATION 6-20
GENERAL INFORMATION (AIR BAG) 6-7
   DISABLING THE SYSTEM 6-10
   ENABLING THE SYSTEM 6-10
   SERVICE PRECAUTIONS 6-9
   SYSTEM COMPONENTS 6-8
   SYSTEM OPERATION 6-7
GENERAL INFORMATION (ANTI-LOCK BRAKE SYSTEM) 9-20
GENERAL INFORMATION (CHARGING SYSTEM) 2-6
GENERAL INFORMATION (CRUISE CONTROL) 6-12
GENERAL INFORMATION (DISTRIBUTORLESS IGNITION SYSTEM) 2-2
   SYSTEM COMPONENTS 2-2
GENERAL INFORMATION (MULTI-PORT & SEQUENTIAL FUEL INJECTION
  SYSTEMS) 5-9
GENERAL INFORMATION (STARTING SYSTEM) 2-9
GENERAL INFORMATION (TROUBLE CODES) 4-28
   ELECTRICAL TOOLS 4-28
   SCAN TOOLS 4-28
GENERAL RECOMMENDATIONS 1-45
HALFSHAFTS (AUTOMATIC TRANSAXLE) 7-11
   REMOVAL & INSTALLATION 7-11
HALFSHAFTS (MANUAL TRANSAXLE) 7-3
   CV-JOINTS OVERHAUL 7-5
   REMOVAL & INSTALLATION 7-3
HANDLING A TRAILER 1-46
HEADLIGHT/TURN SIGNAL/CRUISE/HAZARD (COMBINATION)
  SWITCH 8-18
   REMOVAL & INSTALLATION 8-18
HEADLIGHTS 6-20
   AIMING THE HEADLIGHTS 6-20
   REMOVAL & INSTALLATION 6-20
HEATER CORE 6-10
   REMOVAL & INSTALLATION 6-10
HEATER WATER CONTROL VALVE 6-11
   REMOVAL & INSTALLATION 6-11
HEATING AND AIR CONDITIONING 6-10
HITCH (TONGUE) WEIGHT 1-46
HOOD 10-2
   ALIGNMENT 10-3
   REMOVAL & INSTALLATION 10-2
HOSES 1-21
   INSPECTION 1-21
   REMOVAL & INSTALLATION 1-21
HOW TO USE THIS BOOK 1-2
HUB AND BEARINGS 8-16
   REMOVAL & INSTALLATION 8-16
IDLE AIR CONTROL (IAC) VALVE 4-17
   OPERATION 4-17
   REMOVAL & INSTALLATION 4-18
   TESTING 4-17
IDLE SPEED ADJUSTMENT 1-26
IGNITION COIL PACK 2-4
   REMOVAL & INSTALLATION 2-4
   TESTING 2-4
IGNITION LOCK CYLINDER 8-20
   REMOVAL & INSTALLATION 8-20
IGNITION MODULE 2-5
   REMOVAL & INSTALLATION 2-5

IGNITION SWITCH 8-19
   REMOVAL & INSTALLATION 8-19
IGNITION TIMING 1-26
   GENERAL INFORMATION 1-26
INDUSTRIAL POLLUTANTS 4-2
INSIDE REAR VIEW MIRROR 10-17
   REMOVAL & INSTALLATION 10-17
   REPLACEMENT 10-17
INSPECTION 3-37
   REPLACEMENT 3-38
INSTRUMENT CLUSTER 6-20
   REMOVAL & INSTALLATION 6-20
INSTRUMENT PANEL AND PAD 10-9
   REMOVAL & INSTALLATION 10-9
INSTRUMENTS AND SWITCHES 6-20
INTAKE AIR TEMPERATURE SENSOR 4-20
   OPERATION 4-20
   REMOVAL & INSTALLATION 4-20
   TESTING 4-20
INTAKE MANIFOLD 3-9
   REMOVAL & INSTALLATION 3-9
INTERIOR 10-9
JACKING 1-47
JACKING PRECAUTIONS 1-48
JUMP STARTING A DEAD BATTERY 1-46
JUMP STARTING PRECAUTIONS 1-47
JUMP STARTING PROCEDURE 1-47
KNOCK SENSOR 4-26
   OPERATION 4-26
   REMOVAL & INSTALLATION 4-26
   TESTING 4-26
LAST CHANCE TOWING METHOD—DOLLY 1-45
LIGHTING 6-20
LOWER BALL JOINT 8-7
   INSPECTION 8-7
   REMOVAL & INSTALLATION 8-8
LOWER CONTROL ARM 8-9
   CONTROL ARM BUSHING REPLACEMENT 8-10
   REMOVAL & INSTALLATION 8-9
MACPHERSON STRUT AND SPRING
  ASSEMBLY 8-4
   OVERHAUL 8-6
   REMOVAL & INSTALLATION 8-4
MAINTENANCE INTERVALS 1-48
MAINTENANCE OR REPAIR? 1-2
MANIFOLD ABSOLUTE PRESSURE (MAP) SENSOR 4-21
   OPERATION 4-21
   REMOVAL & INSTALLATION 4-22
   TESTING 4-21
MANUAL TRANSAXLE 7-2
MANUAL TRANSAXLE (FLUIDS AND LUBRICANTS) 1-35
   DRAIN & REFILL 1-35
   FLUID RECOMMENDATIONS 1-35
   LEVEL CHECK 1-35
MANUAL TRANSAXLE ASSEMBLY 7-2
   REMOVAL & INSTALLATION 7-2
MANUFACTURER RECOMMENDED NORMAL MAINTENANCE
   INTERVALS 1-48
MASTER CYLINDER (BRAKE OPERATING SYSTEM) 9-3
   BENCH BLEEDING 9-4
   REMOVAL & INSTALLATION 9-3
MASTER CYLINDER (CLUTCH) 7-8
   REMOVAL & INSTALLATION 7-8
**MULTI-PORT (MFI) & SEQUENTIAL (SFI) FUEL INJECTION
  SYSTEMS 5-9**
NATURAL POLLUTANTS 4-2
OIL LEVEL SWITCH 2-11

OPERATION   2-11
   REMOVAL & INSTALLATION   2-11
OIL PAN   3-24
   REMOVAL & INSTALLATION   3-24
OIL PRESSURE SWITCH   2-12
   OPERATION   2-12
   REMOVAL & INSTALLATION   2-12
   TESTING   2-12
OIL PUMP   3-25
   REMOVAL & INSTALLATION   3-25
OUTSIDE MIRRORS   10-5
   REMOVAL & INSTALLATION   10-5
OXYGEN SENSOR   4-15
   OPERATION   4-15
   REMOVAL & INSTALLATION   4-16
   TESTING   4-15
PARK/NEUTRAL SAFETY SWITCH (TRANSAXLE RANGE SENSOR)   7-9
   ADJUSTMENT   7-10
   REMOVAL & INSTALLATION   7-9
PARKING BRAKE   9-19
PARKING BRAKE LEVER   9-20
   REMOVAL & INSTALLATION   9-20
PCV VALVE   1-16
   REMOVAL & INSTALLATION   1-16
POWER BRAKE BOOSTER   9-4
   REMOVAL & INSTALLATION   9-4
POWER RACK AND PINION STEERING GEAR   8-22
   REMOVAL & INSTALLATION   8-22
POWER STEERING PUMP (FLUIDS AND LUBRICANTS)   1-42
   FLUID RECOMMENDATIONS   1-42
   LEVEL CHECK   1-42
POWER STEERING PUMP (STEERING)   8-24
   BLEEDING   8-24
   REMOVAL & INSTALLATION   8-24
POWERTRAIN CONTROL MODULE (PCM)   4-14
   OPERATION   4-14
   REMOVAL & INSTALLATION   4-14
PREFERRED TOWING METHOD—FLATBED   1-45
PROPORTIONER VALVES   9-5
   REMOVAL & INSTALLATION   9-5
QUICK-CONNECT FITTINGS   5-2
   REMOVAL & INSTALLATION   5-2
RADIATOR   3-16
   REMOVAL & INSTALLATION   3-16
RADIO RECEIVER/TAPE PLAYER/CD PLAYER   6-14
   REMOVAL & INSTALLATION   6-14
READING CODES   4-29
   OBD-I SYSTEMS   4-29
   OBD-II SYSTEMS   4-29
REAR BUMPER   10-5
   REMOVAL & INSTALLATION   10-5
REAR CONTROL ARM/AXLE   8-15
   REMOVAL & INSTALLATION   8-15
REAR DRUM BRAKE COMPONENTS—RIGHT SIDE SHOWN   9-13
REAR MAIN SEAL   3-36
   REMOVAL & INSTALLATION   3-36
REAR SUSPENSION   8-13
REAR SUSPENSION COMPONENT LOCATIONS   8-14
REGULATOR   2-8
RELIEVING FUEL SYSTEM PRESSURE   5-9
ROCKER ARM (VALVE) COVER   3-4
   REMOVAL & INSTALLATION   3-4
ROCKER ARM/SHAFTS   3-7
   REMOVAL & INSTALLATION   3-7
ROUTINE MAINTENANCE AND TUNE-UP   1-13
SEATS   10-17
   REMOVAL & INSTALLATION   10-17

SENDING UNITS AND SENSORS   2-11
SERIAL NUMBER IDENTIFICATION   1-10
SERVICING YOUR VEHICLE SAFELY   1-6
SIGNAL AND MARKER LIGHTS   6-22
   REMOVAL & INSTALLATION   6-22
SPARK PLUG WIRES   1-25
   REMOVAL & INSTALLATION   1-25
   TESTING   1-25
SPARK PLUGS   1-22
   INSPECTION & GAPPING   1-24
   REMOVAL & INSTALLATION   1-22
   SPARK PLUG HEAT RANGE   1-22
SPEAKERS   6-14
   REMOVAL & INSTALLATION   6-14
SPECIAL TOOLS   1-4
SPECIFICATIONS CHARTS
   BRAKE SPECIFICATION—GM J BODY   9-26
   CAPACITIES   1-49
   ENGINE IDENTIFICATION AND SPECIFICATIONS   1-12
   ENGINE MECHANICAL SPECIFICATIONS   3-55
   GASOLINE ENGINE TUNE-UP SPECIFICATIONS   1-26
   MANUFACTURER RECOMMENDED NORMAL MAINTENANCE
      INTERVALS   1-48
   TORQUE SPECIFICATIONS (BODY AND TRIM)   10-18
   TORQUE SPECIFICATIONS (DRIVE TRAIN)   7-12
   TORQUE SPECIFICATIONS (ENGINE AND ENGINE
      OVERHAUL)   3-60
   TORQUE SPECIFICATIONS (SUSPENSION AND STEERING)   8-26
   VEHICLE IDENTIFICATION CHART   1-4
SPEED SENSORS   9-23
   REMOVAL & INSTALLATION   9-23
STABILIZER BAR   8-8
   REMOVAL & INSTALLATION   8-8
STANDARD AND METRIC MEASUREMENTS   1-10
STARTER   2-9
   REMOVAL & INSTALLATION   2-9
   SOLENOID REPLACEMENT   2-10
   TESTING   2-9
STARTING SYSTEM   2-9
STEERING   8-17
STEERING KNUCKLE AND SPINDLE   8-10
   REMOVAL & INSTALLATION   8-10
STEERING LINKAGE   8-21
   REMOVAL & INSTALLATION   8-21
STEERING WHEEL   8-17
   REMOVAL & INSTALLATION   8-17
STRUT ASSEMBLY EXPLODED VIEW   8-6
SUNROOF   10-8
   GLASS ADJUSTMENT   10-9
   REMOVAL & INSTALLATION   10-8
SYSTEM DESCRIPTION (BOTTOM FEED PORT INJECTION SYSTEM)   5-3
TANK ASSEMBLY   5-19
   REMOVAL & INSTALLATION   5-19
TEMPERATURE CONTROL CABLE   6-11
   ADJUSTMENT   6-11
   REMOVAL & INSTALLATION   6-11
TEST EQUIPMENT   6-4
   JUMPER WIRES   6-4
   MULTIMETERS   6-5
   TEST LIGHTS   6-4
TESTING (UNDERSTANDING AND TROUBLESHOOTING ELECTRICAL
   SYSTEMS)   6-6
   OPEN CIRCUITS   6-6
   RESISTANCE   6-6
   SHORT CIRCUITS   6-6
   VOLTAGE   6-6
   VOLTAGE DROP   6-6

THERMOSTAT   3-8
   REMOVAL & INSTALLATION   3-8
THROTTLE BODY (BOTTOM FEED PORT INJECTION SYSTEM)   5-5
   REMOVAL & INSTALLATION   5-5
THROTTLE BODY (MULTI-PORT & SEQUENTIAL FUEL INJECTION
  SYSTEMS)   5-13
   REMOVAL & INSTALLATION   5-13
THROTTLE POSITION SENSOR   4-23
   OPERATION   4-23
   REMOVAL & INSTALLATION   4-23
   TESTING   4-23
TIMING CHAIN AND GEARS   3-27
   REMOVAL & INSTALLATION   3-27
TIMING CHAIN COVER AND SEAL   3-26
   REMOVAL & INSTALLATION   3-26
TIRES AND WHEELS   1-29
   CARE OF SPECIAL WHEELS   1-31
   INFLATION & INSPECTION   1-30
   TIRE DESIGN   1-29
   TIRE ROTATION   1-29
   TIRE STORAGE   1-30
TONE (EXCITER) RING   9-24
   REMOVAL & INSTALLATION   9-24
TOOLS AND EQUIPMENT   1-2
TORQUE   1-7
   TORQUE ANGLE METERS   1-9
   TORQUE WRENCHES   1-8
TORQUE SPECIFICATIONS (BODY AND TRIM)   10-18
TORQUE SPECIFICATIONS (DRIVE TRAIN)   7-12
TORQUE SPECIFICATIONS (ENGINE AND ENGINE OVERHAUL)   3-60
TORQUE SPECIFICATIONS (SUSPENSION AND STEERING)   8-26
TOWING THE VEHICLE   1-45
TOWING YOUR VEHICLE BEHIND ANOTHER VEHICLE   1-45
TRAILER TOWING   1-45
TRAILER WEIGHT   1-45
TRAILER WIRING   6-27
TRANSAXLE (SERIAL NUMBER IDENTIFICATION)   1-12
TRANSAXLE (TRAILER TOWING)   1-46
TROUBLE CODES   4-28
TROUBLESHOOTING CHARTS
  CRUISE CONTROL TROUBLESHOOTING   6-14
TROUBLESHOOTING ELECTRICAL SYSTEMS   6-5
TRUNK LID   10-3
   ALIGNMENT   10-3
   REMOVAL & INSTALLATION   10-3
TRUNKLID LOCK   10-13
   REMOVAL & INSTALLATION   10-13
**UNDERSTANDING AND TROUBLESHOOTING ELECTRICAL
  SYSTEMS   6-2**
UNDERSTANDING THE AUTOMATIC TRANSAXLE   7-9
UNDERSTANDING THE CLUTCH   7-6

UNDERSTANDING THE MANUAL TRANSAXLE   7-2
VACUUM DIAGRAMS   4-31
VALVE LASH   1-26
VALVE LIFTERS   3-33
   REMOVAL, INSTALLATION & INSPECTION   3-33
VEHICLE   1-10
VEHICLE EMISSION CONTROL INFORMATION (VECI) LABEL   1-12
VEHICLE IDENTIFICATION CHART   1-4
VEHICLE SPEED SENSOR   4-26
   OPERATION   4-26
   REMOVAL & INSTALLATION   4-27
   TESTING   4-26
WATER PUMP   3-19
   REMOVAL & INSTALLATION   3-19
WHEEL ALIGNMENT   8-13
   CAMBER   8-13
   CASTER   8-13
   TOE   8-13
WHEEL ASSEMBLY   8-2
   INSPECTION   8-3
   REMOVAL & INSTALLATION   8-2
WHEEL BEARINGS   1-44
   REPACKING   1-44
WHEEL CYLINDERS   9-17
   OVERHAUL   9-17
   REMOVAL & INSTALLATION   9-17
WHEEL LUG STUDS   8-3
   REMOVAL & INSTALLATION   8-3
WHEELS   8-2
WHERE TO BEGIN   1-2
WINDOW REGULATOR AND MOTOR ASSEMBLY   10-14
   REMOVAL & INSTALLATION   10-14
WINDSHIELD AND FIXED GLASS   10-15
   REMOVAL & INSTALLATION   10-15
   WINDSHIELD CHIP REPAIR   10-15
WINDSHIELD WASHER FLUID RESERVOIR AND PUMP   6-19
   REMOVAL & INSTALLATION   6-19
WINDSHIELD WIPER BLADE AND ARM   6-16
   ADJUSTMENT   6-17
   REMOVAL & INSTALLATION   6-16
WINDSHIELD WIPER MOTOR   6-17
   REMOVAL & INSTALLATION   6-17
WINDSHIELD WIPER SWITCH   8-19
   REMOVAL & INSTALLATION   8-19
WINDSHIELD WIPERS (ROUTINE MAINTENANCE AND
  TUNE-UP)   1-28
   ELEMENT (REFILL) CARE & REPLACEMENT   1-28
**WINDSHIELD WIPERS AND WASHERS (CHASSIS
  ELECTRICAL)   6-16**
WIRE AND CONNECTOR REPAIR   6-7
WIRING DIAGRAMS   6-33